WOODROW WILSON

I: *American Prophet*

WOODROW WILSON
In Academic Robes

From the Wilson collection in the Library of Congress

WOODROW WILSON

I: American Prophet

by

ARTHUR WALWORTH

LONGMANS, GREEN AND CO.

NEW YORK · LONDON · TORONTO

1958

LONGMANS, GREEN AND CO., INC.
55 FIFTH AVENUE, NEW YORK 3

LONGMANS, GREEN AND CO., LTD.
6 & 7 CLIFFORD STREET, LONDON W 1

LONGMANS, GREEN AND CO.
20 CRANFIELD ROAD, TORONTO 16

WOODROW WILSON

I: AMERICAN PROPHET

COPYRIGHT © 1958

ARTHUR WALWORTH

PUBLISHED SIMULTANEOUSLY IN THE DOMINION OF CANADA BY
LONGMANS, GREEN AND CO., TORONTO

FIRST EDITION

LIBRARY OF CONGRESS CATALOG CARD NUMBER 56-12569

Printed in the United States of America

To

Betsy Ross

and

a little "Miss Ellie Lou"

ACKNOWLEDGMENT

SINCE THE DAY, some ten years ago, when Professor Arthur M. Schlesinger, Sr., spoke of the need for a biography of Woodrow Wilson suitable for his students, I have sought the aid of many men in the writing of one that would serve that purpose and interest other readers as well. The response has been generous and stimulating.

Professor Allan Nevins gave advice and encouragement at a time when the drawing together of the threads of research seemed a task almost insuperable. Stewart Mitchell, Director of the Massachusetts Historical Society, read the manuscript and offered constructive criticism. Certain chapters have been read and criticized by Helen Woodrow Bones, Louis Brownlow, Homer S. Cummings, Marjorie Brown King, Eleanor Wilson McAdoo, Bliss Perry, Sir William Wiseman, Professor Harvey Wish, and Robert W. Woolley.

My debt to President Emeritus Charles Seymour, who many years ago quickened my interest in history by his lectures, has been compounded by the patient and stimulating criticism that he has given freely.

The Woodrow Wilson Foundation has made it possible for me to extend my research and to have necessary secretarial assistance. Mrs. Julie d'Estournelles, Executive Director of the Foundation, has been most helpful in introducing me to the books and pamphlets collected by that organization.

My obligations to those who assisted me in the various libraries in which I have delved are too numerous to detail. The constant solicitude of Mrs. Zara Powers of the Yale University Library and of Laura E. Turnbull, Dr. Henry L. Savage, Alexander P. Clark, and Julie Hudson of the Princeton University Library was invaluable in exploring the large collections relating to Wilson in those institutions. As to Ray Stannard Baker and to many other writers, Katharine E. Brand has given help far beyond the call of duty. I am indeed fortunate to have had her guidance in approaching the vast collections in the Library of Congress, and particularly the Ray Stannard Baker Papers and the Wilson Collection itself, to which Mrs. Woodrow Wilson kindly granted access.

For sharing with me their recollections of Wilson and his family, in an interview or by letter, or both, I am indebted to the following: Margaret Calloway (Mrs. B. Palmer) Axson, B. Palmer Axson, Jr., Bernard M. Baruch, Julian B. Beaty, Helen Woodrow Bones, Edward W. Bradford, Thomas W. Brahany, Edward M. Brown, Louis Brownlow, Charles Bryant, Vincent Burns, William C. Bullitt, Robert C. Clothier, Edward Capps, Viscount Cecil of Chelwood, Gilbert F. Close, Edwin G. Conklin, Edward S. Corwin, Jack Randall Crawford, Homer Cummings, Jonathan Daniels, Joseph E. Davies, John W. Davis, Cleveland E. Dodge, George Dunlop, Will Durner, Luther P. Eisenhart, Captain Fred J. Elder, Margaret Axson Elliott, Virginia McMaster Foard, Raymond B. Fosdick, Arthur Hugh Frazier, Millard Gamble, Lawrence H. Gipson, Joseph C. Grew, Mrs. Charles S. Hamlin, Lord Hankey, Mrs. Will Harbin, Mrs. George McLean Harper, Mrs. J. Borden Harriman, Edith Benham Helm, Herbert C. Hoover, James Hoover, Stanley K. Hornbeck, Margaret Flinn Howe, Florence Hoyt, Wade C. Hoyt, Andrew C. Imbrie, Warren Johnson, Hugh McNair Kahler, Albert Galloway Keller, George Dwight Kellogg, Benjamin King, Marjorie Brown King, Katharine Woodrow Kirkland, V. K. Wellington Koo, Arthur Krock, David Lawrence, Margaret Lawton, Walter L. Lingle, Philena Fine Locke, Breckinridge Long, Eleanor Wilson McAdoo, Francis C. MacDonald, Alice Wilson McElroy, Charles H. McIlwain, Fitz Hugh McMaster, Colonel George McMaster, David Magie, Charles D. Mahaffie, A. Howard Meneely, John Moody, T. H. Vail Motter, Mr. and Mrs. Charles G. Osgood, Frederick Palmer, Bliss Perry, Lewis Perry, William Phillips, William E. Rappard, Edith Gittings Reid, Henrietta Ricketts, Ross Rollins, Hallie Alexander Rounseville, Henry L. Savage, Francis B. Sayre, Beth Hibben Scoon, Robert Scoon, Ellery Sedgwick, Lucy Marshall Smith, Charles Seymour, Charles Skillman, Frances Snell, Arthur Sweetser, Charles L. Swem, Herbert Bayard Swope, Huston Thompson, F. M. Tibbott, Mr. and Mrs. Randolph F. Tucker, Charles Warren, Thomas J. Wertenbaker, Fitz William McMaster Woodrow, James Woodrow, Thomas R. Woodrow, Mr. and Mrs. Thomas Woodward, Robert W. Woolley, Florence Young. Many of the above have generously permitted me to read pertinent manuscripts that are in their possession.

Mrs. Woodrow Wilson has granted permission to quote from certain unpublished letters of her husband, and Mrs. Eleanor Wilson McAdoo has allowed me to draw upon letters of her mother. I owe a debt, too, to Jonathan Daniels for unpublished passages from the diary of his father; to Charles Seymour, Curator of the House Collection at the Yale University Library, for unpublished quotations from the diary of Colonel House; to Henry Cabot Lodge for permission to quote from unpublished letters written by his grandfather to John T. Morse, Jr.; to Joseph C. Hostetter for a quotation from a letter of Newton D. Baker; to Martha Dodd Stern for permission to use the papers of her father, William E. Dodd, and to quote from them; and to Charles P. Taft for permission to quote from a letter of his father.

I appreciate, too, the patience of my publisher, Edward E. Mills, in awaiting the arrival of the manuscript and his faith that it would arrive eventually; and I have leaned heavily on my editor, John L. B. Williams, in the rigorous labor of cutting and condensing early drafts.

A. W.

Newton Centre, Massachusetts
December, 1957

CONTENTS

CHAPTER I

A Boy Finds God Amidst Civil Strife

DURING THE YEAR 1856 the political atmosphere of Europe was cleared, temporarily. The swords of national ambition that had let blood in the Crimea were returned to their scabbards at the Congress of Paris.

In the Hall of Clocks at Versailles a group of diplomats of the old school, dignified by high collars, black stocks, and side whiskers, faced one another around a velvet-topped table and invoked the principle of legitimacy—"*long live the* status quo." Undercover, the old game of power politics went on. Lobbyists, male and female, plied their trade. Intrigue was carried into the theater, the drawing room, even into the boudoir. Finally, after a month of plot and counterplot, one of the delegates at Versailles remarked: "Everybody is on edge. It is time to sign." And so a feather was plucked from a black eagle in the Jardin des Plantes, and a quill from it was used in signing a few of the twenty-eight documents of peace. A hundred and one guns boomed from the Hôtel des Invalides, and Europe was at peace!

It was a compact between haughty nations that held themselves above the moral standards that rule ethical individuals; and it brought to Europe a fragile truce that was destined to last but three years. To be sure, tenuous provision was made for containment of Russian expansionism and four "maxims" were set forth to strengthen the rights of neutrals on the high seas in time of war. These measures marked some progress toward the rule of national appetites by law, and within a year more than forty nations approved the Declaration of Paris. But the young United States stood out for complete freedom of the seas, contending that the maxims did not go far enough, that all innocent private property should be immune on the oceans of the world.

Europe's political resources had been running out. The years 1830 and 1848 had been darkened by barricades and bloodshed, and now the Continent was to sink into the morass of the hundred-year feud between France and Germany. In the mills, workers were ground fine on the wheels that were turning for the glory of Empire—or because of it. On the land, peasants bowed to the czar's manifesto: "Listen, ye heathen, and submit, for with us is God." Men lost faith in Europe and put their trust in the New World across the Atlantic. They saved and borrowed, sold some of their possessions, stowed some about their persons, and set their faces toward the west. Millions of them went, in the eighteen-fifties.

Among those who migrated in large numbers were the Scotch-Irish. Another wave of these restless folk had reached the American shore early in the eighteenth century and had broken into the Shenandoah Valley in the colony of Virginia. There they had laid off the town of Staunton as the seat of a territory that stretched from Pennsylvania to the Carolinas—a fertile, cloud-kissed region that George Washington called "the garden of America."

In 1856, Staunton was a town of some three thousand souls, most of whom had Scotch-Irish blood. It was a community always astir, a market for the farms of Augusta County. The inhabitants were vigorous folk, taking a lavish yield from the well-watered grasslands and fashioning articles from the coal and iron that the region provided. Public life in this county seat revolved about the courthouse, the schools, and the several churches: Catholic, Baptist, Lutheran, Methodist, and oldest and most aristocratic of all, Episcopalian, in which the legislature of Virginia had taken refuge during the darkest hours of the American Revolution. The intellectual tone of the town, however, was set by the Presbyterians, who worshiped on a hillside, in a brick church with a Grecian façade.

Next door was the Augusta Female Seminary, which was preparing to take in boarding pupils in dormitories then abuilding. A school of high repute in the Presbyterian denomination, the seminary had been directed for the past year by one of its trustees, a young Scotch-Irishman named Joseph Ruggles Wilson. He was a hearty man whom his girls thought "not very strict—you could go walking without a teacher"; but he clung to the traditions of the school, training the young ladies to be homebodies rather than social butterflies, to cook well and lead charitable enterprises rather than to dance cotillions.

Dr. Joseph Wilson served also as pastor of the Presbyterian church and lived in its manse. This residence, built only ten years earlier, stood on a spacious corner lot, on a slope facing the kirk and the school. There, behind a shielding fence, the preacher's wife and two daughters dwelt in sanctuary, removed from the bustle of trade and traffic. The square brick house was painted white and had wide, pillared porches and large chimneys. Writing his sermons on a veranda at the back of the manse,

Joseph Wilson could look out over his wife's garden, over the roofs and chimneys of the town.

In the ground-floor chamber of the Wilson manse, near midnight on the third day after the Christmas of 1856, Jeanie Wilson gave to her Joseph his first son. They named him Thomas Woodrow,[1] after his maternal grandfather.

The baby was put into a well-fashioned crib and was cared for and fed by free Negroes who cooked in the cellar over an open fire, baked in a brick oven, and drew water from a well. Before the child was a month old, arctic winds swept down upon Staunton and drove snow through the cracks of less substantial houses. The town was cut off from the world for ten days. But in his snug home the infant was safe and warm, and grew larger and fatter than his sisters had been. In four months Jeanie Wilson was writing to her father that she had a baby whom everyone called "beautiful," and that he was "just as good as he can be," that Joseph's congregation was growing and there was "no desirable thing" that God had not done for her.

Her husband and children were life itself to Jeanie Wilson. From under wide brows her eyes looked out luminously, understanding and sympathizing with all that was good. Pursuing the ways of her Scottish ancestors and respecting Southern traditions of gentility, she kept her distance from worldly folk. She was not a "joiner" of church societies, was not content to let the Lord provide, but insisted on looking out for even the smallest needs of her dear ones. Her resentment against defamers of her clan was as fierce as a storm in the Highlands, and her self-respect as strong as her fealty. She was content to leave the foreign relations of the family in the hands of her aggressive husband.

Dr. Joseph Wilson liked to cut a figure in his little world. Squarely built, and not so tall as his son grew to be, he transfixed his hearers with fiery brown eyes and a long, straight nose that flexed at the tip. Side and chin whiskers and a heavy shock of hair framed his commanding face. He talked rather too much, and punned habitually. Once a parishioner, noticing dust or dandruff on his coat collar, remarked that his horse was better cared for than its owner, and the preacher retorted: "Yes. The reason is that I keep my horse and I am kept by my congregation." Occasionally his wit lashed unkindly at men whose intentions were better than their performances. As a young teacher he had once

---

[1] Through boyhood and college days, Woodrow Wilson signed his name "Thomas W. Wilson" and was called "Tommie." His mother was born "Janet" but came to be called "Jessie," and by her family "Jeanie."

felled an impertinent student with his fist. He was never a man to be ignored. Compelling in the pulpit and courtly in the parlor, he constrained men of the world to heed him; and his yielding little wife, too refined to laugh heartily at his boisterous jokes, listened well and managed a smile when courtesy required it.

Growing up under the eyes of this masterful man and dutiful lady, Tommie absorbed so much of domestic virtue that when he himself became a parent he was moved to bless God for his "noble, strong, and saintly mother" and for his "incomparable father."

The marriage of Joseph Wilson and Jeanie Woodrow had grown out of love at first sight and had been confirmed by the bonds of Scotch-Presbyterian faith. They were well fortified by inheritance to bear the chafe of life. For generations both Woodrows and Wilsons had made their own way among men, fighting not with money or swords but with words and the Word. Though quick to move about, they had clung tenaciously to moralities from which their words and acts sprang. Joseph's parents had come to America in 1807 from County Down in the North of Ireland, whither their ancestors had migrated from Scotland. They were a high-spirited couple—James Wilson a handsome, rollicking lad of twenty, and Anne Adams a homely, determined, humorless lass of sixteen; and they came to the New World not in pursuit of any cause or faith but simply to get on in the world.

Always restless, Grandfather James Wilson moved repeatedly westward: first across the Atlantic to Philadelphia—where he became a printer and an associate of William Duane, publisher of the rabidly Jeffersonian *Aurora*—then to Pittsburgh, into Ohio at Lisbon, and finally to Steubenville, where in 1815 he took charge of the *Western Herald and Gazette*. Under the masthead was printed: "Principles, not men." He was consistently antislavery and protariff.

Elected to the Ohio legislature, James Wilson held himself duty bound to vote as his constituents wished; but when proposed as a candidate for governor he was unacceptable because, it was said, his bold words marked him as "a conspicuous politician, one heretofore marked for assault and vilification." An opponent referred to him, in a private letter, as "Paddy Wilson." The editor spent his fervor in castigating his adversaries rather than in praise of the Lord: the non-Jefferson newspapers were scorned as "anything or nothing, some singing lullabies and others up for sale." He feared no power on heaven or earth except perhaps his wife, who induced him merely to attend the church to which she gave zealous allegiance.

Though not a lawyer, the editor was made an associate judge of the

Court of Common Pleas. Judge Wilson pioneered in many a local enterprise, becoming president of a turnpike company, taking part in promoting the building of the first bridge over the Ohio River, serving as a director of a bank, dabbling in real estate, and finally undertaking the building of a great house for his family of ten children. In the midst of this operation, however, he was seized by a fatal attack of cholera. His grandson Tommie never saw him; nor is there evidence that he ever knew churchgoing Grandmother Wilson, who capably managed her husband's business in his absences and had an intense moral pride that made her shut her heart implacably against a daughter who eloped.

From his mothers's clan, the Wodrows, Tommie Wilson received a faith no less compelling, though more gently manifested. The Wodrows had been distinguished for scholarship for three centuries. In Scotland many of the family were theologians or elders of the Presbyterian Church. For six generations at least one of them had been a minister. Some were writers, one was a famous editor, and almost all were jealous of their thoughts. The men were eloquent and gentlemanly; the women, soft-spoken and very feminine. Yet all had a sinewy moral rectitude, were afire with passion for Absolute Truth, and were zealous in propagating it as they conceived it. They were a stock hard as blackthorn, and sometimes as prickly.

Thomas Woodrow,[2] Tommie Wilson's grandfather, was disciplined rigidly in the classics and the theology of the kirk and went forth to proclaim the gospel in the Orkney Islands. Later he accepted a call to the pulpit of the Independent Church at Carlisle, England, and in doing so became the first of his line to move out of Scotland for four hundred years. With him he took a bride, Marion Williamson, whose ancestors were Highlanders; and she bore him eight children, Jeanie arriving in 1826.

In November of 1835, after a long pastorate at Carlisle, all the Thomas Woodrows sailed for America. Two months after setting out from Liverpool they landed at New York; but the mother was so shaken by the stormy voyage and by the severity of the American winter that she died five weeks later. Fortunately, however, her sister Isabella had accompanied the family and assumed the duties of a mother.[3]

[2] When Thomas Wodrow left Scotland, he changed the spelling of his name to "Woodrow" to conform with English pronunciation.

[3] Later Thomas Woodrow married her and had four more children. Jeanie lived in Chillicothe with her brother Thomas and her sister Marion at the time of her betrothal to Joseph Wilson; and these three formed strong bonds of fraternal devotion.

After a short term of missionary work in Canada, Dr. Woodrow went to Ohio and served as pastor of several churches, striving to maintain Glasgow standards of learning among Philistines. This short, dynamic preacher spoke with a burr that broadened with rising enthusiasm. He was a rock of conservatism, scholarly, most fervent in prayer. He went straight to the pith of the gospel; and his action, like his speech, was direct and vigorous. He instructed his children and grandchildren and encouraged them to converse well at table. He found recreation in solving mathematical puzzles; and the harder they were the more fun he had.

Woodrow Wilson was often to acknowledge the two strains that ran in his veins: that of the Woodrows—pure Scottish, scholarly, tenacious, gentle, modest; and that of the Wilsons—Scotch-Irish, boisterous and mercurial, loving drama, applause, and exaggeration. From both he inherited a capacity for ferocious devotion to his kin and to a Scotch-Presbyterian God.

It was of the pure Scottish blood of the Woodrows that Tommie was to become most proud. But feeling that there was a streak of Irish in his Wilson ancestry, he gave it free play when he wished to escape from his strait-jacket conscience. In his forty-fourth year, speaking with Hibernian extravagance, he was to prophesy before a gathering of proud Yankees that Scotch-Irish memorialists one day would record "how every line of strength in the history of the world is a line coloured by Scotch-Irish blood."

In the year of Woodrow Wilson's birth, while European statesmen were meeting at Versailles to patch the flimsy fabric of international law, Americans were agitating the causes of peace and justice. In the vestry of Dr. Wilson's church at Staunton one could hear excited whisperings about John Brown and "bleeding Kansas." Men lingered on the church steps to ask one another whether the issue of slavery could be settled without more bloodshed. Peace-loving folk were citing Charles Sumner's declaration of war against war: "Can there be any peace that is not honorable, any war that is not dishonorable?" And possibly some brother, deep in dissenting thought, was quoting a political essay of that year written by Parke Godwin: ". . . there can be no finality in politics, except in the establishment of justice and truth."

When the Civil War began, Tommie Wilson's father was preaching in the First Presbyterian Church of Augusta. Though born and bred in the North and the son of an abolitionist, Dr. Wilson accepted the political views of his parishioners; and when in 1861 the Presbyterian Church divided on the issues of the war and split into two factions, the Southern branch held its first General Assembly in the church at Augusta. Joseph Wilson became clerk of his sect—a position that he was to hold for thirty-seven years. Moreover, he served as a chaplain in the Confederate Army, and one Sabbath morning when a battle was impending, he sent his flock scurrying to the local ammunition factories to roll cartridges. Dr. Wilson kept slaves and had created a Sunday school for Negroes, but he did not venture to defend or to indict the institution of slavery. However, the North's denial of the right to secede grated on his independent spirit.

During the hostilities the Woodrows and the Wilsons were each a clan divided. Children of the frontier and the kirk rather than of North or South, their roots not fixed in any region, they went along with the political sympathies of their neighbors. But during the strife Joseph Wilson and his wife grew lonely for their clans, and in 1866 the tide of blood affection that had been dammed up for four years flowed freely once more. The pastor in Georgia wrote to his father-in-law in Ohio: ". . . my people will be greatly pleased to have you occupy my pulpit, even if you have voted the radical ticket! . . . I feel sure that you are mistaken with reference to some important points of existing differences between the two sections. But you, at least, are thoroughly honest in your convictions, and I honor you none the less for your expression of them. We can, as Christians, talk over these matters when we shall meet . . ."

With his own brothers and sisters in the North, however, Dr. Wilson found reconciliation more difficult. When he traveled to Ohio in 1866 for a gathering of the clan, the brothers, some of whom had fought for the North, fell to bickering about political principles. Though Tommie Wilson had some fifty first cousins, he became intimate with only a chosen few of his relatives, almost all on the Woodrow side.

Only a few of the war's events took root in the boy's memory. At the age of three, standing at the door of the manse in Augusta, he heard a strident voice yell: "Mr. Lincoln's elected. There'll be *war!*" Toddling into his father's study, he asked: "What is war?" That was the first occurrence in his life that he could remember; and another experience of the war years—that of standing beside General Lee and looking up into his face—was one that Tommie Wilson was to treasure all his life.

Dr. Wilson's church was used as a hospital for Confederate soldiers and, standing on the sidewalk, Tommie peered anxiously toward prisoners who were fenced within the churchyard. But the manse was a sheltered home, though the Wilsons ate unsalted cow-pea soup and plug tobacco was hoarded in the attic, and a little gold. The suffering of the family was not so great that they could not remember those whose needs were more dire: one Sunday during the war the doctor took up a collection to support missions in China.

The years of Reconstruction left their mark on Tommie. Jefferson Davis marched past the lad under guard of federal troops. The enemy occupied Dr. Wilson's church and the town was overrun with human derelicts. Glum prisoners, groaning casuals, Negroes on the loose, and marauding Yankees haunted Tommie up to the beginning of adolescence. What he observed at Augusta and in summers spent in Staunton —the efforts of his family and other good folk to preserve whatever was left of the virtues of their life—ground into the boy's marrow a sympathy that was never to leave him. He was able to say later that the only place in the country, the only place in the world where nothing had to be explained to him was the South.

In the manse at Augusta the Wilsons [4] had time and means for the good life. The children learned neither to crave nor to scorn money, but to ignore the pursuit of it. The minister of the First Presbyterian —the most active if not the most aristocratic of Augusta's churches— was a man of mark and substance. Yet, in spite of the duties of his office, time was reserved for occasions that were sacred to the family alone: daily prayers, with everyone kneeling; hymn singing, at dusk on Sundays and at other times; and long readings of fiction, especially of Dickens and Scott. The doctor would recline on the floor, his back against an upturned chair, while his wife sat erect and knitted and Tommie, lying flat on his back, was carried away by his father's voice and infectious laughter.

To his son, Joseph Wilson was preceptor, confessor, playmate. Dr. Wilson's mind worked with precision and to his son his expression seemed Godlike. In conversation he did not hesitate to pause in the middle of a sentence to conjure up *le mot juste*; and the boy marveled

---

[4] In 1856, the year of Thomas Woodrow Wilson's birth in Staunton, his sister Marion was six years of age and Annie Josephine Wilson was two. Another boy was born in 1866. He was called Joseph R. Wilson—not Joseph Ruggles Wilson, a name that the father reserved for himself alone. Marion married the Rev. Ross Kennedy, a Presbyterian minister in Arkansas. Annie married George Howe, M.D., of Columbia, S.C. Joseph R. became a political writer in Tennessee and editor of the Nashville *Banner*.

at his skill in producing it. Often during meals the table was piled high with intellectual fare—books that had been fetched to elucidate topics that were under discussion, reference works such as *Inquire Within, or Over Thirty-Seven Hundred Facts Worth Knowing*. From his father Tommie took many a drubbing at chess and a few at billiards. They did not play cards, however. In the manse a rigid line was drawn between tests of skill and games of chance.

Neither Tommie's father nor his mother, who resented having been forced to study Latin in her sixth year, hurried the formal schooling of their boy. Though he early learned many of the secrets of good talk and could join in the family's singing, he could not read with ease until he was eleven. He confessed to being lazy, intellectually. When finally he went to Professor Derry's "select classical school" to study Latin, history, writing, and bookkeeping, his work was below average, his attitude indifferent.

Yet the preacher thought his son's brain a gem worth polishing. Tommie learned more from him than most boys learn at school in their earliest years. Dr. Wilson devoted Sunday afternoon, in particular, to the cultivation of Tommie's mind; and at that time they talked like master and scholar of classical times, the father giving the boy, in digestible doses, what he had learned of the world, of literature, the sciences, and theology—imparting it all with humor and fancy. Then, on Mondays, the two usually went on an excursion into the shops of the city or into the neighboring country. Often these forays took in a cotton gin, or a mill, or the factories that made ammunition for the Confederacy. Tommie was told how corn was grown and ground, learned how power was generated and how it worked, and saw sooty-faced men who labored beside furnaces and darting sheets of flame.

After returning home the boy was quizzed about what he had seen and what he had been told. "Do you thoroughly understand?" he was asked; and when he replied "Oh, yes," he was told to put his ideas in writing. Then the father would pounce upon the paper that was handed to him: "What did you mean by that; did you mean such and such a thing?" And when Tommie said "Yes," his preceptor went on: "Well, you did not say it, so suppose you try again and see if you can say exactly what you mean, and if not we'll have another go at it." The boy was sent to the dictionary to get precise definitions, and he was coached in oral expression. "Learn to think on your feet," his father ordered. "Make your mind like a needle, of one eye and a single point. Shoot your words straight at the target. Don't mumble and fumble."

The boy was quizzed mercilessly on the books that he read, and father and son together tried to improve upon the writings of Charles Lamb and Daniel Webster. They played with words, and scored by speaking in a novel or striking way.

There were readings, too, in the big leather-bound Bible. The doctor penciled notes in the margins that interpreted the text in the language of the day. His religion had no cant and was suffused with a love of mankind that often overflowed sectarian bounds.

Young Tommie was exposed to the best that Augusta offered in religious education. In the Sunday school, of which Uncle James Bones was superintendent, the boy memorized the Shorter Catechism. To his roving mind this was as painful as formal schooling, and he did not remember the words permanently.

Yet Tommie was a child of the kirk and it was always with him. Often he rode in his father's buggy when the preacher made parish calls. His favorite playground was the shady churchyard, inside a picket fence that had been made by the hands of slaves. From the window of his bedroom he could see the solitary white spire, pointing confidently above the dark hackberry grove to the one true way. Even as he lay in bed on summer evenings the strains of the organ soothed him. Music affected his emotions: he would sometimes weep at the communion service when moving hymns were sung.

While taking part in the daily events about him the lad sometimes gave the impression that he was absorbed in something beyond the ken of his fellows. Particularly at Sunday services he seemed to indulge in the long, long thoughts of youth. Sitting in the family pew, four from the front, his little legs dangling, his earnest face elevated toward the pulpit so that the sharpness of his nose and chin impressed those who sat near, Tommie's pride of kin swelled as his father mastered adult minds, summoned doubters to acknowledge Christ as their Savior, or charged the elders to take heed unto themselves and to all the flock. If his father hesitated for a word, Tommie would silently supply one; and if his word came forth from the pulpit, a thrill ran along his spine. He noted the doctor's rare mistakes and brought them up for discussion in the privacy of the manse, where father and son could laugh together over each other's errors.

It was inevitable that a young lad who was spoken of as "Dr. Wilson's son" should feel that he was predestined to lead others. But how could a slip of a lad who was always minimized by the diminutive "Tommie" and never called "Tom," who was freckle-faced, wore glasses, had a head that was awkwardly large at the back, and a finger that had been jammed out of shape—how could such a boy be a leader of playmates whose families were as distinguished as his own?

Before he was ten years old Tommie played much with girls. His mother would tell stories to the children, often from *The Talisman,* and with quiet determination Tommie would manage dramatizations. During the war years there were no toys or properties except those made at home. Broomsticks became Arab steeds, banners were made from scraps of yellow homespun daubed with charcoal, and coats of mail were fashioned out of skeletons of carpets that had been raveled of their wool for soldiers' mufflers. A euonymus bush was a medieval castle from which Christian maidens were boldly rescued. The boy's motive was usually succor, never revenge or ambition.

Sometimes Mrs. Wilson traveled north in the summer. Then the lad, seated firmly on his father's big horse, would ride out to the country to visit his aunt Marion Woodrow Bones. Her daughter Jessie was a tomboy and had an imagination equal to that of her cousin Tommie. Together they read Cooper's Indian tales and conspired in crime. Staining their skins with pokeberry juice, feathering their heads, and arming themselves with bows and arrows, they went deep into the pine woods and stalked pickaninnies, terrifying them with war whoops and whirling tomahawks. Jessie offered herself for scalping and burning by the big-chief cousin whom she idolized. Once she impersonated a squirrel up a tree, and that time Tommie made the mistake of hitting her with an arrow. She fell in a limp heap, unconscious but not seriously hurt; and he carried her to the house, remorsefully bawling, "I killed her! It's no accident. I'm a murderer!" The Woodrow conscience already had fastened itself upon him.

When he outgrew the company of girls Tommie took part in the normal pursuits of boyhood; and everything that he did, except studying, he did with intensity. There were ball games, bull-in-the-pen at recess, rides on bobtail streetcars, rooster fights, and games of hide-and-seek among the bales of cotton in a warehouse near school. One day he ran away to the circus, and on the way back he took the precaution of padding himself with cotton against the wrath of his teacher.

In these pursuits Tommie was just one of a gang, and his frustrations showed themselves in occasional moods and fits of temper that kept him from running constantly with his playmates. When the talk and play became too rough, he would withdraw shyly into the protection of his father and mother. But the instinct for leadership would not be downed; and finally the boy hit upon his *metier*. Though he could not excel physically, he found that, thanks to his father's coaching, he could talk better than the other boys.

In the Wilson back yard, only a few rods from the slave quarters, stood a little stable that had a hay loft. Up there, instead of tumbling and frolicking, Tommie organized a gang of boys into the "Lightfoot Club." Under a red picture of His Satanic Majesty torn from an advertisement, the minister's son prepared the constitution of the body, presided over the meetings, and insisted on the niceties of parliamentary procedure. His chums noted that he was deliberate in his speech and measured in his movements, and they listened to him even though he belonged only to the second baseball team. Thus he came to feel the thrill of mastering men with words.

Finally, in the autumn of 1870, the boyhood days in Augusta came to an end. Dr. Wilson resigned his pastorate and became a professor in the theological seminary at Columbia, the capital of South Carolina; and the Wilsons moved to a city that, only five years before, had been reduced to ruin by Sherman's troops. Indeed, the government of South Carolina was still in the hands of carpetbaggers and scalawags.

During the years in Columbia the boy found his God and learned to hate war and all its works. There he fell under the tradition of Henry Timrod, the poet and prophet who throughout the war had tried to keep alive a vision of universal peace but, dying in ravaged Columbia in 1867, had seen only "beggary, starvation, death, bitter grief, utter want of hope." Two-thirds of the buildings had been burned, leaving a wilderness of crumbling walls, naked chimneys, and unroofed pillars. The luxurious shade trees of what had been called the most beautiful of state capitals were reduced to charred trunks. In desolated gardens the fountains were dry, the basins cracked. Banks and insurance companies were insolvent. The most respected citizens were barred from public office; in the college, the professors were unpaid and the student body had shrunk from two hundred fifty to thirteen; the theological seminary was holding chapel services in a made-over stable, its faculty barely able to meet the needs of life. Freed Negroes had trailed Sherman's soldiers into the city, and many of them thought that "freedom" gave license to loaf, to thieve, and to rape. Even by 1870, Main Street had been only half rebuilt with shacks of frontier style.

In ravaged Columbia, where Uncle James Woodrow was a neighbor and joined with Dr. Wilson and other pillars of the church in efforts to restore political order, Master Tommie found inspiration for an ambition to serve his fellow men. He absorbed much of the theology of his elders from lectures by his father that he chose to attend, from visits to the house of his favorite Uncle James, and from his white-bearded, rosy-cheeked Grandfather Woodrow, who read the Bible in Greek and in Hebrew on his way to breakfast, sang old Scottish ballads in a treble voice, pipe in his mouth and a toddy at his fingertips, and until his death in 1877 never let his grandson forget the answer to the question in the catechism: "What is the chief end of man?"

In such an environment, with the outer world of the unsaved in chaos, the boy inclined toward a relationship with God that would build the confidence and purpose that his elders showed. When he was sixteen his religious awakening was quickened by the leadership of a young zealot named Francis J. Brooke, who held prayer meetings in the little stable-chapel where the faithful sat on wooden benches and faced pictures of the saints. Finally, on July 5, 1873, the boy who had once led the Lightfoot Club under the picture of His Satanic Majesty made his confession and applied for membership in the church. And so the native Scottish fiber of the boy was encased within the steel of Calvinist faith. From this day hence he prayed on his knees at his bedside every night.

The Shorter Catechism taught that every man was a distinct moral agent, responsible not to other men but through his own conscience to his Lord and Maker. The compulsion of others, a Presbyterian Scot might escape; but the dictates of his own conscience, never! Man was a lonely soul confronted by the Source of all souls, and he must study deeply so that he might surely know the truth.

The immediate effect of the boy's allegiance to a divine power was improvement in his studies. At his "select school" he struck the son of the master as extremely dignified, not like the other boys, and yet popular and helpful to his younger mates. He showed little interest in natural science. Now that his strong will was reinforced by belief in divine sanction, the lad more than ever let his creative impulses work in their own channels. In the gropings of adolescence he strained the understanding of even his loving family, as his mind sprouted in directions of his own choosing. He had a queer way of going off by himself, sometimes down to see the railroad trains come and go early in the morning. In the lovely building of the theological seminary that housed the library, he tucked himself away in an alcove with favorite books. Especially he steeped himself in the romances of Marryat and Cooper. In his imagination he roved the seas, pursued pirates into uncharted lairs, and delivered their captives. These campaigns were not the whim of an hour or a day, but lasted for weeks and months. The young commander knew every type of sailing ship, its sails, spars, sheets, and shrouds; and he sketched vessels by the hundreds. He filled a scrapbook with news clippings about yacht races, with pictures of famous steam frigates and hydraulic docks, with news of college rowing regattas. Save for his attachment to kirk and kin, he was very much alone—a leader without a "gang." There were, to be sure, tentative gropings that later were magnified in his memory into "scrapes" and "love adventures." But in the main his kin absorbed his affections. In the summers, during his teens, the Wilsons joined the families of Uncle Thomas Woodrow and Aunt Marion Woodrow Bones; and the cousins played together in the intimacy of clan affection.

The boy was finding a goal more practical than the capture of imaginary pirates in dream ships. In his copy of one of Cooper's novels he left a slip of paper on which he had practiced signing first his father's name and then his own in a script distinguished by boldness and flourish—such signatures as might be attached to documents of state by great men. One day Cousin Jessie Bones came upon him studying under an unfamiliar portrait and asked who the old man in the picture was; and the lad's face lighted up as he replied: "That is the greatest statesman who ever lived, Gladstone, and when I grow to be a man I mean to be a great statesman too." Thomas Woodrow Wilson was finding his models and his heroes in Britain—the land from which his grandparents had migrated, the nation that had befriended the Confederacy and to which the old aristocracy still looked for their culture and their styles.

Materially, his family fared better than others of their station in the South. In addition to his post in the theological seminary, Dr. Wilson filled the pulpit of the First Presbyterian Church; and his wife had received a legacy. They bought a lot and Mrs. Wilson drew up plans for a new house and planted magnolia trees in the front yard. In 1872 the family moved in, and they were established in comfort when Tommie left Columbia with Brooke, in the autumn of 1873, for the rigorous life that then prevailed at Davidson College. It was understood that he, like his friend, would prepare himself for the ministry.

The wrench of the boy's first separation from his home was painful. "I remember how I clung to her," he wrote of his mother many years later, "(a laughed-at 'mamma's boy') till I was a great big fellow." [5] In his teens, as in later years, he exchanged the most affectionate of let-

[5] W.W. to Ellen Axson Wilson, April 19, 1888. With the exceptions noted, this and all subsequent quotations from the correspondence between Woodrow Wilson and Ellen Axson Wilson are taken from Ray Stannard Baker, *Woodrow Wilson: Life and Letters* (hereinafter referred to as Baker). He alone among the biographers of Wilson has had access to all this correspondence.

ters with his parents, worded with precision and penned impeccably. And when father and son met after a separation, they always kissed. In the unremitting battle that the clan felt they were waging with chilling grievance and sin, the warmth of family affection was all the more cherished.

Davidson College, a struggling Presbyterian institution of which Dr. Wilson was a trustee, stood on the plank road north of Charlotte. Its sponsors aimed to bring the benefits of education within reach of impecunious students and to prepare them for the ministry. Life on that campus challenged a boy's body as well as his mind; and Tommie Wilson, entering very young and ill-prepared in mathematics, required all his new-found resolution to stick it out. He subsisted on a boarding-house diet in a region that had not recovered from the war. He made his bed, filled his own oil lamp, hauled water from the well, served on a Stove Committee that fetched wood and pine knots to heat the hall, and learned to dress in the cold in record time so that he might dart into the chapel before the door was closed.

The lad stood high in his classes and took part in outside activities. As corresponding secretary of the Eumenean Literary Society he copied the constitution of the organization in a new record book. Though once fined for "improper conduct in the hall," he led the society in prayer and delivered a "select speech" and an original oration. The lad wrestled with a chum on the floor of his room, but threw his energy more into mental than physical activity: as outfielder for the freshman baseball team he was thought lazy, though once he saved a game by a leaping catch of a hard-hit ball. The months at Davidson gave solid food to his quickening power to understand and to reason, and he saw men cheerfully endure physical hardship in order to get intellectual light.

The high emotional intensity that had gone into the lad's religious experience in Columbia made his mind vibrate too fast, and poor diet and lack of exercise began to tell on him. Moreover, he was given to morbid introspection, to self-reproach for having spent so few years "in the fear of God" and so many "in the service of the Devil." He resolved, in writing, to try to serve the Lord thenceforth, to seek perfection in character. In the spring of 1874 illness caused several absences from class; and in May the boy withdrew and returned to his kin, his body exhausted by nervous indigestion. For a year and a half he remained at home. Asked why he left college, he said that he liked it but wanted "to get closer to where they are doing things."

During the year 1874, Tommie accompanied Dr. Wilson to a new pastorate at Wilmington, North Carolina.[6] There the intimacy of father and son was renewed. The lad was tutored in Greek and in other studies and read much in books and magazines, especially the *Edinburgh Review* and the *Nation,* and from these journals he derived a philosophy of Manchester liberalism. He read proof for the preacher; and the doctor set him to editing and auditing the reports that came to him, as stated clerk of the denomination, from county presbyteries. When the boy raised philosophical doubts, the doctor dispelled them by saying: "My son, don't you worry about these doctrinal problems. Ask yourself this question: Do I love and want to serve the Lord Jesus Christ? If you can answer that in the affirmative, you need not worry."

At Wilmington, Tommie was as restless as ever; but now, in his maturing young manhood, he did not seek escape at the circus or in daydreams in a library, but instead thought of running off to sea. He talked much about it and puttered around the docks, once hurting himself by falling into the hold of a vessel. During the Civil War many a blockade runner had nested in the Cape Fear River, and tales of derring-do gripped the lad's imagination. Even in his play he was thinking of his British heroes, of foreign ships that had aided the cause of the Confederacy.

Overgrown and gangling, more than ever drawing apart from the life around him, the lad seemed to the Negro butler to be "an old young man who tried to explain the reason of things." He did his best to cultivate manners worthy of a great preacher's son, took his mother on his arm to church, cared for her devotedly during an illness, and

---

[6] During Wilson's year at Davidson a controversy developed among the religious leaders at Columbia that became bitter and drew out some of his father's worst qualities. Dr. Wilson had never been one to overrate the intelligence of his parishioners or to undervalue his own worth. He liked to tell of boyhood days when, as he practiced oratory in a barn, an old cow looked at him over her shoulder, goggle-eyed, heaved a sigh, and went on chewing her cud. "She was about as intelligent as my subsequent congregations proved to be," the preacher would add. He preached sometimes as if he had had a revelation of ideas that he presented as divine but that, a reporter of the local *Daily Union* wrote, might strike some folks as "novel and speculative."

At Columbia his congregation decided to employ a pastor, in addition to their preacher, to perform the pastoral duties in which Dr. Wilson had not given the comfort and satisfaction that his flock craved. This action so infuriated the doctor and his friends that they tried to retaliate by requiring their students to attend chapel services in the seminary instead of going to the First Presbyterian Church. Thirteen students asserted that this was an interference with their religious liberty, carried their case to the Presbyterian General Assembly, and were sustained. As a result, Dr. Wilson and an associate resigned, attendance at the seminary was cut in half, and the institution barely kept alive until, in the next decade, another bitter controversy, of which Tommie's Uncle James Woodrow was the center, compelled it to close. (*See* p. 59.)

Dr. Wilson, still highly esteemed as a preacher, was called to Wilmington in 1874, and there enjoyed the longest pastorate that the church had had up to that time. *See* S. L. Morris, *An Autobiography,* p. 5; and George Osborn, "The Influence of Joseph Ruggles Wilson on His Son, Woodrow Wilson," *North Carolina Historical Review,* October, 1955.

conscientiously took as much notice of the young ladies as fine breeding demanded.

There were few people in Wilmington with whom Tommie enjoyed discussing the long, deep thoughts over which he brooded as he sat in his room with elbows on knees or nose in a book. Other fellows would think him queer, he feared; and as for girls, he found none with whom he could converse with satisfaction. He had no young friend to share good talk save one, John D. Bellamy, who later became a member of Congress. These two went on "reading raids," walking together to an abandoned Confederate camp and speculating on the powers that elevated the world's eminent men—Cromwell and Gladstone, Stonewall Jackson and Robert E. Lee.

The lad was already well launched upon the course that he was to follow all his life and to which he was to devote the intense mental energy that he had inherited, the understanding that had come to him as he watched economics and politics operate in their most elementary forms during Reconstruction, and the driving passion for truth and for service that his religion instilled. The restless blood of pioneers, the agony and the gentility of the South, the yeast of Scottish Calvinism—all these forces were churning within him when he started north in the fall of 1875 to the College of New Jersey at Princeton.

CHAPTER II

A STUDENT COMMANDS HIS OWN DEVELOPMENT

IN THE EIGHTEEN-SEVENTIES the college at Princeton was gradually regaining the reputation that it had held before the Civil War as an ideal school for young gentlemen of the South. Moreover, it was still known as an institution where upcountry youth learned "to preach, to reform, and to lead." Into this tradition young Wilson, a son of the South and a grandson of the middle frontier, fitted well, and as the son of a Presbyterian pastor he was entitled to free tuition. His father had studied at the theological seminary in Princeton; but when Tommie arrived on the college campus he was too shy to present a letter that Dr. Wilson had written to President McCosh.

James McCosh was an educator of whom the Wilsons could approve heartily. Born on the banks of the River Doon, he boasted that he had *talked* with men who "dr-runk whiskey with Bur-rns." In his mature years he had won renown as a religious reformer, and when he had arrived at Princeton in 1868 he had dared to attack the brutalities of hazing and the societies that had operated in secret, had encouraged sport for sport's sake, and had gone himself to the college games. The boys loved him as much as they feared his righteous wrath and laughed at his burr and his extravagances. He insisted that college students should be treated as growing mortals and not as disembodied intellects and that teachers were, properly, *in loco parentis* and responsible for developing men of character. Every Sunday afternoon he lectured on religious subjects, and once a week he heard students recite on his lectures and on the Bible.

To make up for inadequate preparation, Tommie's energy at first went mainly into his studies; but in June he was not among the twenty honor students of his class. In sophomore year, however, his mind came into its own, and at the end of his college course he stood among those who for the four years had maintained an average of 90 per cent. The boy gained confidence, and wrote to his father that he had discovered he had a mind. He took notes in the neat shorthand that he had mastered, by correspondence course, as a means of saving time; but he did not rely greatly on his teachers, who were not men of marked genius. His grades in the humanities were consistently higher than those in

18

science and mathematics. He did not work for credit alone, though after junior year he lamented that he had dropped to thirty-seventh place in the class and had fallen into the seventies in physics because of "the injustice of old ———." He was using the college library freely and made the most of Dr. McCosh's elective system, driving himself to develop a persuasive style of expression and to learn all that he could about the history and theory of government and the lives of statesmen. It was in the realm of government rather than in that of theology that this Wilson was finding causes to love and for which to fight.

"Principles, not men," had been the motto of Grandfather Wilson; and yet Tommie even in his teens seemed aware that in order to advocate causes effectively he would do well to study the lives of great men of principle. He saw that progress depended on leadership; he began to note the ways in which political leaders had used levers of power; and he cultivated the spontaneous style of oratory that was in vogue in the House of Commons rather than the set form in which American declamation of the day was strait-jacketed.[1] He was delighted to find that at Princeton there were some who took him seriously.

Not content to mouth the great truths of democratic government, he took the lead in putting them into action. He did not compete on the college debating team; and, though he joined the old Whig Society that James Madison had founded and took part in discussions of business and constitutional matters, he was fined more than once for nonperformance when it was his turn to write an essay. He was more interested in organizing a Liberal Debating Club that experimented with the British parliamentary system under a constitution drafted by "Secretary of State" Wilson. Subjects of vast scope were attacked: such as "Resolved, that morality does not keep pace with civilization." Questions were raised from the floor and if the prime minister could not defend his policies successfully his "party" was turned out. Though this club was Tommie's first love at Princeton and gave him experience in leadership, he did not scorn the disciplines that could be found in other activities.[2]

---

[1] Wilson talked much of Edmund Burke and spoke of "our kinship with England"; and in a "private" diary he noted particularly two phrases in Morley's life of Burke: "In studying the problems which confront us in matters of government we must have regard 'not merely to forms of government and law' but more especially to 'whole groups of social facts which give to law and government the spirit that makes them workable.' "

[2] Wilson served as managing editor of the *Princetonian*—a position that required him to keep well posted on the affairs of the college and to guide and stimulate the reporters and the other editors. Moreover, he wrote editorials on many phases of college life: sportsmanship, discipline, the instrumental club, and the need of funds for adequate buildings. Though not an

In commanding his own development, Wilson refused to be diverted from ultimate goals by the lure of immediate gain. "We wish the training," he wrote in the *Princetonian*, ". . . and the prizes are of secondary importance." Urged to submit a literary essay in competition for a prize that many thought he could win easily, Tommie refused to do the necessary studying because the subject did not fit into his chosen path. Again, when the luck of the draw ordained that he debate in favor of a protective tariff, Wilson refused, for he did not believe in a tariff for protection. Already he was focusing his oratorical powers on causes that his conscience could approve. To him debate was not an opportunity to show off, but a means of arriving at truth and educating men who were less discerning.

In the presence of boys with whom he was not intimate, Tommie carried himself with the easy, affable air of a Southern gentleman, refusing smokes and drinks without offensiveness, telling clean jokes without prudery and without making a clown of himself. He could jest about his personal ambitions without weakening them. Sometimes he told his intimates that he would argue out a point when he met them "in the Senate"; and he left in one of his books a card on which he had scrawled "Thomas Woodrow Wilson, Senator from Virginia." He could not be baited into emotional outbursts about the miseries of the South, though he stood ready to debate rationally with those who were keen to get at the truth about the Civil War and Reconstruction.

Formal, perfunctory expressions of religion did not appeal to Tommie. One evening when a professorial knock on the door surprised him in a forbidden game of euchre, his opponent swept the cards under the table, went to the door, and, glancing back before opening it, saw Tommie roguishly reading the Bible with a mien of mock innocence. It was as if he were saying, in derision of Puritan cant: "See, what a good boy am I! I read the Bible, and so wouldn't *think* of playing cards."

At social functions he was self-conscious. Once, entering a long, elegant drawing room, he slipped on a small rug, skated over a glossy floor, arms thrown out for balance, and stopped just short of an imposing hostess. The memory of his misery plagued him for years.

Living in stylish Witherspoon Hall, where the boys decorated their rooms with bits of lace, bonbons, locks of hair, and tintypes, Tommie

---

athlete of varsity caliber (as a senior he weighed only a hundred and fifty-six pounds and stood 5 feet 11 inches), Wilson commanded the respect of his heavier-muscled friends and was chosen president of the baseball association and secretary of the college football organization.

fell in with Princeton traditions. Yet he kept his distance, and went with
a crowd only when it was going his way. Those who knew the lad best
could perceive at times that dissenting blood was skirling beneath his
pleasing manners. Sometimes he had difficulty in controlling his
temper; and for all his gentleness and gaiety he could turn stubborn
quickly on a matter of principle. He was happiest in a small circle in
which he was the leader in good-fellowship, using his voice to sing with
the "gang" in his dormitory rather than in the formal concerts of the
Glee Club. With a few intimates he forged friendships that were
founded as much on mutual delight in eating, singing, storytelling, and
theatergoing as on a sharing of deeper interests. His intimates looked to
him to take the initiative in correspondence. "I suppose," he wrote to
one of them, "that they think my writing powers—my gift of gab—
unlimited."

The parting from his classmates after graduation, he told one, "most
emphatically and literally struck in." Perhaps he sensed the fact that
never again would he find the essence of human friendship so purely
distilled. The Princeton friends became even dearer in later years, as
Wilson placed less and less confidence in his associates. He never forgot
a solemn covenant that he had made with his classmate Charles Talcott, to acquire knowledge so that they might have power, to drill themselves in the art of persuasion so that they could enlist others in their
purposes.

At Princeton the gangling lad had become a man. He might have
been as well taught at other colleges: but what he himself had created
on the New Jersey campus—the Liberal Debating Club, political essays,
and the spirit of comradeship—he could later recollect in no other setting. He was to look back on his undergraduate years as the most satisfying of his life.

As Tommie Wilson was setting his future course by stars that were
both high and permanent, the way that he was to travel was magnified
by a foreign glass. At Princeton he happened to read bound volumes of
the *Gentleman's Magazine* of London, which was at that time publishing reports of proceedings in the British Parliament. To less receptive
eyes the articles were not epoch-making. But they thrilled the lad who
already had been worshiping the great parliamentarians, the leaders of
the nation that had befriended and trusted the South. The young man's
own powers were challenged and brought into play. With the reports
from London to inspire him, he could suck the last drop of meaning
in his readings in Bagehot and Macaulay, Burke and Bright, and

Green's *Short History of England*. From the last, particularly, he gained a deep reverence for Anglo-Saxon institutions, and he was stirred to envision the writing of the story of the continuance and modification of those institutions in America. Books that he used were annotated to the very edges of the pages.

At Princeton, the writings of Tommie Wilson brought him greater fame than his speeches. He contributed two significant essays to the *Nassau Literary Magazine*. One, on Bismarck, was written in his sophomore year; the other, on Pitt, won a prize in his senior year, though Wilson confessed to his bosom friend, "Bobby" Bridges [3] that he thought it a "rather lame affair." He was swept along in the Iron Chancellor's ambition and carried away by the intense earnestness of the English statesman. Though in his essays he showed mature judgment in anlyzing the talents of his heroes and in describing the national atmospheres in which they worked, and though he recognized their failings, his youthful generosity condoned them. He insisted that his readers keep in view the long-range purposes of the statesmen, the devotion with which they pursued them, and the successes that they achieved. Like these heroes, ideal political leaders should be "men of independent conviction, full of self-trust, and themselves the spirit of their country's institutions." Such were the qualities that young Wilson worshiped. In contrast, congressmen of his own country seemed petty and weak. The legislative body that had inflicted the horrors of Reconstruction on the South found no indulgence in the mind of this Southerner.

It was a London critic, Walter Bagehot, who gave the young Anglophile a model for his criticism of American political institutions. A banker, member of Lloyd's, and editor of the *Economist,* Bagehot delighted in paradox and surprise, in re-examining old concepts of political economy in the light of new ideas and the actual conditions of his day. Years later Wilson looked up to him as "my master, Bagehot—the most vivacious, the most racily real, of writers on life—whether the life be political, social, or separately intellectual." Bagehot's essays on the English Constitution set Wilson to analyzing his own nation's Congress in similar terms, and the Englishman's frankness gave the young American courage to speak his mind.

In his senior year at Princeton, Wilson developed his ideas in a maga-

---

3 Of Bridges, Wilson wrote that this "dear, genuine old Scot" was his *"best* friend in the world," if he had any. "None of Bob is on the surface, but the deeper you dig the finer the ore." W.W. to Ellen Axson, Nov. 20, 1884. After a journalistic career, Bridges became editor of *Scribner's Magazine.*

zine article on "Cabinet Government in the United States." To the young critic the cardinal fact was that frank and open debate is the essential function of a popular representative body. "Congress," he asserted, "is a deliberative body in which there is little real deliberation; a legislature which legislates with no real discussion of its business. Our Government is practically carried on by irresponsible committees. . . . There could be no more despotic authority wielded under the forms of free government than our national Congress now exercises."

Wilson wished Cabinet members to have seats in Congress, the right to initiate legislation, and some part of the privileges of the standing committees. By such a move, the writer argued, the President's power would be enlarged and the balance intended by the framers of the Constitution would be restored.

The article was accepted by the *International Review,* of which one Henry Cabot Lodge was a junior editor. This was by far the greatest triumph of Wilson's university days. He had stepped out beyond his classmates and had become a man among men. The independence and sureness of his thought were acclaimed as rare in an undergraduate. To the ideals that he set forth in this paper—insistence on open and candid transaction of public affairs and upon responsible executive leadership —he was to cling with all the tenacity of his Scotch-Presbyterian blood.

It was the dream of Tommie's family that he would add one more devoted life to the line of Woodrows and Wilsons who had served the church; but in spite of the young man's reverence of God and his love for his kin, his course already was set in a different direction when he was graduated from college. Educated young gentlemen of the South were expected to enter a profession; but the higher statesmanship to which Wilson aspired and to which he hoped to give professional dignity was a calling wtihout a well-defined course of training, a vocation toward which boys born in log cabins and bred in camp meetings and in frontier rough-and-tumble started with some advantage over sons of the manse. And so, instead of taking the easy way that led through theological school into an assured but circumscribed career, Wilson chose to study for the law—a profession that he heartily disliked in its commercial applications but that, as "a branch of political science," might contribute to his preparation for what he conceived to be his larger work. He would filter his enthusiasm for his profession, he said, "through the dry dust of law."

There was only one law school suitable for a Southern gentleman who

aspired to statesmanship, and that was at Thomas Jefferson's University
of Virginia. There Wilson fell under the charm of the tradition and the
beauty of the campus of Charlottesville. But actually Woodrow Wilson
was not cast of Virginia clay. Fundamentally he was of harder substance—the moral granite of Scotland and the rough-hewn timber of
frontier press and pulpit. Not moved even to walk out to Monticello,
Tommie considered himself "somewhat of a federalist" who was intensely concerned for national unity. Though he would gladly learn
from his elders *how* to think and to talk, no one, not even his dearest
relatives, could dictate *what* the young man thought.

In Virginia's Department of Law young Wilson worked under Dr.
John B. Minor, whom he regarded as, next to his father, his greatest
teacher—"I can say with perfect sincerity that I cannot conceive of a
better," he wrote to Bridges. An aristocrat of impressive presence, a stern
Socrates in the classroom, Minor disciplined the minds of his pupils
unmercifully. To Wilson the knowledge that he was forced to digest
was "as monotonous as . . . Hash." However, he prided himself upon
"swallowing the vast mass of its technicalities with as good a grace and
as straight a face as an offended palate will allow." Actually, he did
succeed in mastering the trifling points of procedure, the precedents,
and the language of the law; and he acquitted himself so well that in
the second year he was honored by being chosen judge of the university's
"moot court."

At the same time this law student managed to read many volumes of
orations, history, biography, and poetry. In one month he drew out
Wirt's *Henry,* Jebb's *Attic Orators,* and Stubbs' *Constitutional History
of England.* The next month he held out Shelley's poems so long that
he was fined 50 cents. "Passion is the pith of eloquence," he had written
in his essay on Pitt, but "imagination must be present to give it wings
and a graceful flight."

Because of the distinction of his family and the quality of his published article on Cabinet government, Wilson was a marked man when
he came to Charlottesville. At Virginia there were two competing debating societies, the Washingtonian and the Jeffersonian. Wilson joined
the "Old Jeff," four days later was chosen its secretary, and eventually
became president. Here he could indulge freely in debate. Immediately
he attracted his fellows by suggesting lively subjects for argument, fresh
themes that were of current concern to the man in the street, issues that
were being aired in the press, topics on which he had thought much
himself. According to the *Magazine,* a new constitution adopted by the

Old Jeff reflected "great credit in every respect on its framers, Messrs. T. W. Wilson, etc."

In March of 1880, Wilson delivered an oration on John Bright that commanded more than local attention. So famous had the orator become that both outsiders and ladies of the university asked to be admitted and people were standing in the aisles before the challenging opening sentence came forth. The *Magazine,* which later published the speech in full, reported that "he was listened to with much attention; even the ladies who find it so difficult to restrain their natural and charming propensity to chin-music were unusually quiet." Their enthusiasm was not wasted on the speaker; one of the professors felt that he never knew a man who more keenly relished applause.

The oration on Bright revealed a growth of perception into the realities of politics: "Tolerance is an admirable intellectual gift; but it is of little worth in politics. Politics is a war of causes; a joust of principles." This young man who had heard his elders stake their positions on theological principles could understand political conflict. Taking his hero's message to heart, before his audience of Southerners, Wilson justified John Bright's opposition to recognition of the Confederacy. "I yield to no one precedence in love for the South," he said. "But *because* I love the South, I rejoice in the failure of the Confederacy. Suppose that secession had been accomplished? Conceive of this Union as divided into two separate and independent sovereignties! . . . Even the damnable cruelty and folly of reconstruction was to be preferred to helpless independence."

These words were a challenge to the intellects of this Southern audience. Perhaps their minds would not have been able to triumph over their emotions had the argument been presented less persuasively. The speaker had learned to conquer the nervous tension that oppressed him when he rose to speak. He was thin, his complexion was not clear, and his searching blue eyes looked out from under heavy, dark hair. He loved the Anglo-Saxon tongue and rarely used a word of other derivation.

The spring of 1880 was a busy time for Wilson. The very next month after his speech on Bright he was represented in the university magazine by a powerful article on Gladstone. In this essay there appeared the concept, so strong in Scots, that required in great men a moral or romantic quality that elevates them above worldly standards of success. The mainspring of the statesman's mental processes was seen in his intuitive concept of Right and Wrong. Wilson found in his hero "a keen poetical sensibility, such a sympathy as makes a knowledge of men an intuition instead of an experience," a sort of power that enables statesmen to put themselves in the place of the nation over which they are set. He made it clear that, once Gladstone was given responsibility, his abstract theories broke down at once and completely.

In a university debate Wilson was one of two men chosen to support the negative of the question: "Is the Roman Catholic element in the United States a menace to American institutions?" To accommodate those who wished to hear the debate, it was transferred to a larger hall. The contest was an annual event for which two medals were awarded by the judges: one, considered the first prize, to the best debater; the other, in effect the second prize, to the best orator. Many of the audience disagreed with the decision, and Wilson was disappointed in failing to win what was commonly regarded as the first prize. He felt that he had made no pretense of oratory and was the best debater or nothing. Moreover, salt was rubbed into the wound when an essay by William Cabell Bruce won a medal, and Wilson's efforts on Bright and Gladstone received only honorable mention. Showing some of the pettiness of spirit that his father had displayed when his parishioners had appointed an assistant pastor without his consent, the young man set his own prejudiced opinion against that of the judges and was disinclined to accept the orator's medal that was offered as second prize. Finally, however, he overcame his grievance and allowed himself to be persuaded by friends to take the proffered prize at Commencement, which was to him a time "of dancing and monotony." His speech of acceptance was praised by the university magazine as "one of the clearest, soundest, most logical, and thoroughly sensible addresses ever pronounced here at the University by a man so young."

Thus Wilson turned defeat into a triumph: and, more important, he curbed the tendency to feud that ran so strongly in his blood. In August he wrote humbly to Bridges, declaring himself "fortunate" to have won the orator's medal and "not a good speaker yet by any means," though more competent than he had been at Princeton. And in a subsequent letter he wrote: "I know you will not mistake candid confidence for brag." [4] To Bridges, of whose "intellectual sympathy" he felt sure, he

[4] W.W. to Bridges, Feb. 25 and Aug. 22, 1880, and Jan. 1, 1881. Conscious of his progress toward his goal of statesmanship, Wilson gladly accepted a suggestion from his mother that he write his name "T. Woodrow Wilson" so that all his inheritance would be displayed; and later he dropped the "T" as superfluous. W.W. to Bridges, Aug. 22, 1881. "You see I am gradually cutting my name down to portable size," he jested in a postscript to Bridges. W.W. to Bridges, April 1, 1882.

could confess shortcomings that his pride would not allow him to discuss with strangers.

In song as in debate, his voice was smooth and strong and contributed much to the choir and to Sunday evening singing at Dr. Minor's home. Sometimes rambles of the Glee Club led at night to the windows of ladies whence, amidst tittering, flowers and cards of thanks were thrown to the troubadours.

Wilson was courteous and affable to all, though sometimes his wit, to raise a laugh, spared neither himself nor others. Within a month of his arrival in Charlottesville he was initiated into a secret society that had no "house" in which to meet. He had a few intimates who were honored and charmed by his company. He would dramatize by ludicrous twists of his face and preferred the slapstick of vaudeville to the delicate humor of comedy. The bleakness of the dormitory often was relieved by elaborate pranks, and no one could put mock pomp into a college parade so well as Tommie Wilson; but he missed his Witherspoon gang and wrote nostalgic letters to them. As in earlier years, Wilson took one friend more closely to his heart than all others at Charlottesville. His new chum was Heath Dabney. These comrades vied in expressing the mock contempt that young men often use to veil strong fraternal feeling. Wilson's choice epithet for Dabney was "thou very ass"; Dabney's for Wilson, "illimitable idiot." They corresponded almost up to Wilson's death.

In the early winter of his second year in Charlottesville, Wilson overreached the limit of his energy. In addition to the prescribed work he had been riding his own hobby hard.

A spirit so ambitious chafed bitterly under frailties that afflicted the flesh. "How can a man with a weak body ever arrive anywhere?" he asked gloomily, apparently not realizing that he had been putting out energy at a suicidal rate. For heat he had only a fireplace that burned soft coal. Though he had tried to diet strictly and had exercised regularly, he complained that he was "exceedingly ill fed" and troubled with indigestion. He suffered from catarrh and his complexion gave evidence of dyspepsia. He was stricken with a cold that left him unfit for study at examination time, and in January his father advised him to come home. He was paying again, as at Davidson College, for the boyhood hours spent in the library instead of on the playing field.

The break with the campus was made hurriedly, but with honor. The *Magazine* broke precedent to print a laudatory paragraph about the departing genius. To Wilson, studying law at home in Wilmington, the associations of Princeton and Charlottesville were cheering rays in his solitude. He corresponded with Dabney and begged for news of the campus and the fellows of the Old Jeff. Some of his memories, however, were not kindly. He had only scorn for classmates who were slovenly in appearance or affected in manner, though he himself was cultivating side whiskers that he had described to Bridges as "quite *distingué* compared with which yours—much bragged of, of you— were but as a fleeting shadow!"

Again, as after his withdrawal from Davidson College on account of illness, Wilson lingered for a year and a half at the family hearth. Dutifully he went on church picnics, though he thought them too promiscuous. He confided to his favorite cousin, Harriet Woodrow, that one was never sure of having a nice time "because one could never be sure of being able to pick one's company for the day." He shrank from religious orgies, and thought of camp meetings as "flirting made easy." Young men and women could hardly be blamed, he thought, for yielding to a temptation that everything conspired to make irresistible. He knew well enough, he once confessed to Bridges, that he could pretty safely predict his own course under such circumstances.

With only church and family duties, musicales at which he played a violin and his mother strummed a guitar, swimming parties, and rides on a little mare, life would have seemed empty for one who aspired to so much had Wilson not read constantly and persisted daily in grinding at the law and in exercises in elocution. Finally he made his delivery so eloquent that he could imagine that the empty pews in his father's church smiled when he addressed them. Reading omnivorously in Cicero, Trollope, Trevelyan's *Fox,* and the English Men of Letters series, he reacted with strong emotion, favorably to the classics and scathingly to stupid writing.

There seemed to be no question in any mind that the young man would be capable of completing his studies under his own direction. In June of 1882 he received the degree of LL.B. *in absentia*; and that autumn he was ready to be tested for the bar. It surprised no one that he made one of the best records ever to come under the eyes of the examining judge.

CHAPTER III

AMATEUR IN LIFE

AT THE UNIVERSITY OF VIRGINIA Wilson's yearning for a mate became violent. From his room in West Range, in the fall of 1880, he could look through the portico to the Blue Ridge and dream of fair maids in an idyllic valley beyond the setting sun; and sometimes the stirrings of his blood moved him to journey over those hills to Staunton to visit the Augusta Female Seminary, of which his father had once acted as principal. At one time five of his cousins were at school there. He seemed interested mostly in his own kin, perhaps fearing to look outside the clan for the warm genius in homebuilding that his relatives had shown. Thinking himself in love with Cousin Harriet Woodrow, a handsome girl of many talents, he applauded her loudly when she played the piano in a concert; but when he went to a party with her he stood awkwardly with his back to a wall, looking wistfully at fun in which he was too shy to mingle, until the embarrassed Harriet had to beg her friends to be kind to him. The ardor of his attention provoked idle gossip that annoyed the girl; and when he heard of this it pained him and he apologized to her.

However, Tommie made opportunities to see Harriet at the home of their cousins, gave her a volume of Longfellow's poems that appealed to him because it was handsomely bound, and inscribed it "with the warmest love of Cousin Tommie." He took long walks with her over mountain roads, reciting from the lawbook that Blackstone had written for the gentlemen of England, and vowing that he was going to settle down in the practice of law and make money to support a wife. He wrote often to Harriet, addressing her as "My Sweet Rosalind." Remarking that his notes were a "labor of love," he asserted that ladies are the only natural writers of letters; but after they had exchanged a few notes filled with amiable gossip and nonsense, he confessed that thoughts slipped more easily from his pen than from his tongue. Warning the girl against insincere suitors, he commiserated with her on having a music teacher who did not respect the Sabbath and, a little jealous, suggested that such a man was not worthy of her respect. As for himself, he feared that the girls of Wilmington, who had heretofore thought him very sedate, might be surprised to find that he was a real "ladies' man"!

In the summer of 1881 he went to Chillicothe to make his proposal at the home of Thomas Woodrow, the girl's father and the uncle who had cared for his mother before her marriage. There was much picnicking and whist, and the cousins sang duets. Even in reproving his younger relatives, Cousin Woodrow endeared himself to them, and to one he seemed "the cleanest man ever known." But he did not enjoy the parties, and in the middle of a dance he took Harriet aside and said that he could not live without her and they must be married right away.

While courting in Chillicothe, Wilson tried to get on with his legal career by reading law in the office of a half uncle. But he was obviously a misfit. He had brilliant talents, worked hard, and could state the terms of a contract precisely; but the clients were not drawn to him, and so his uncle advised him to give up the law and go into college teaching.[1]

Wilson quit the office in a huff and told Harriet that if she rejected him he would renounce the law and "do teaching." One night he wrote a final appeal to her, begging her to reconsider the dismissal that she had given him that evening, complaining that he could not sleep, grasping for one faint hope to save him from the terror of despair. But, though Harriet was fond of him, she did not love him. To spare his feelings she told him that it would not be right for them to marry because they were first cousins; but when he insisted that their parents approved, she had to tell him that she did not love him as he wished. At that, he left the house abruptly and went to a hotel. There he wrote a last desperate plea, on a torn bit of yellow paper, explaining that the strain had been so intense that he could no longer trust himself to leave the subject alone in the girl's presence and so had gone away to spare her feelings. The next morning she received him and assured him that she loved him as dearly as ever, as a cousin. But he refused the invitation of the Woodrows to continue the visit and retired to Wilmington, whence he wrote to implore his love to send a photograph posed just as he liked to remember her. Though she assented to this, and broke off their correspondence in order to help him forget, the burning of his heart was unappeased and his confidence in his legal career was shaken.

---

[1] Letter and statement from Henry T. Bannon of Portsmouth, Ohio, in the Alderman Library, University of Virginia. The half uncle was Henry Woodrow, son of the elder Thomas Woodrow by his second wife, Isabella.

Not until the next spring was he able to write of the affair to so close a friend as Bridges and to assert that he had refused to be "unmanned even by a disappointment such as this"; and even then he could not confess that Harriet had not desired him, and preferred to hide his wound under the excuse that she had given.

Finally the young man's spirits rose and impelled him to face the world alone. To a young attorney who hoped to swim in the main current, Atlanta seemed the best place to make the plunge. There the wheels of industry were beginning to turn more rapidly and a thriving commerce promised work for the legal profession. Moreover—perhaps more important, in Wilson's view—the city was the capital of a "thrifty" state, the center of Georgia's cultural life, and the home of such progressive leaders as Henry W. Grady of the Atlanta *Constitution*. He wished to begin work in a large city where there was at least opportunity for great things to be accomplished, whether he was equal to their accomplishment or not.

The move to Atlanta was discussed throughly in family councils; for Dr. Wilson, justly estimating his son's quality, was concerned that each step should lead toward a great career. Once the decision was made, the young lawyer's parents supported him with both love and money. His mother made shirts for him; and when she learned that her boy had found a partner of good Virginia stock and irreproachable character, she wrote that that was the thing she was "most glad of."

Wilson thought his associate, Edward Renick, a lovely being, and found in him a mind kindred in scholarly pursuits. As a business partner, however, he was as ineffectual as charming. In Atlanta there was a lawyer for every two hundred seventy of the population, and newcomers could hope to attract customers only by aggressive tactics. Unfortunately, Renick and Wilson were more interested in discussing ways and means of reconstructing the world, in reading together in the *Aeneid,* and in going to the theater. Wilson watched the Georgia legislators in action and thought them crude and bumbling. He sputtered when they refused to vote adequate support to the schools of the state and, taking the easiest course politically, shirked their responsibility and begged aid from Washington. But the partners built no law practice, and Wilson's only important client was his mother. Nevertheless, his political education was advanced in Atlanta when Dr. Wilson made his son an aide and gave him a seat on the platform at the General Assembly of the Southern Presbyterian Church, of which the doctor was then moderator. There young Wilson could learn to catch the sense of a meeting of free souls, could witness the calling together of a congregation of elders for discussion of church polity.

While more aggressive attorneys slapped backs and pumped hands in courthouse corridors, joined clubs, and celebrated Christmas Day by going on what Wilson called a "universal drunk," the son of the manse practiced elocution in his office and lived quietly at a boardinghouse where he was known as "the professor" and where, he said, his landlady's pretty niece helped him "nobly to while away" the time. Actually, Wilson was gradually swinging into his lifework—the thing that he wanted to do above everything else. Through Robert Bridges, who acted as his literary agent in New York, he sold an article on convict labor to the *Evening Post*. He was less anxious than he had been to get his work published, more content with his own view of it, and ready to wait until no one would be responsible for what he wrote but himself. He wanted reputation, not quick money, he informed Bridges. "I want a *start*, and am willing to make it on any terms within my reach." He so loved to write, he said, that he sometimes imagined that he would be "happy and useful" on the staff of some such paper as the *Nation*. Though he could easily bear rejection of articles that he wrote for his own pleasure, he considered it a "dismal failure" when Bridges failed to place a piece [2] in which he rehashed the arguments for parliamentary reform that he had presented in "Cabinet Government."

However, Wilson did not allow himself to grieve long over the rebuff of the editors. Actually, as his business became a liability, his avocation was opening paths to a career. In the fields of letters and government he was making valuable friends and a reputation that carried beyond Georgia. He kept up his study of elocution, for it was by oratory that governments had been made and unmade in Parliament and he must keep his weapon sharp for his day of opportunity.

In September of 1882 he had his first chance to influence national legislation. One day an energetic young reporter came into the little law office on the second floor back. Renick introduced him as an old friend, Walter Hines Page of the New York *World*. A Democrat and fellow Southerner, Page had come to town with federal commissioners who were to hold a hearing at Atlanta on the tariff. Convinced that the public good was not served by protection, he had been traveling about with the officials; and in Wilson's view he had been destroying

---

[2] This article finally appeared in January, 1884, in the *Overland Monthly*, under the title, "Committee or Cabinet Government." See *The Public Papers of Woodrow Wilson*, edited by Ray Stannard Baker and William E. Dodd, Vol. I, 95. This is a work designated hereafter as *P.P.*

their reputation and overthrowing their adventitious dignity by smart ridicule.

Page was impressed quickly by the earnestness with which Wilson set forth his views on the tariff, and he persuaded the young lawyer to address the commission, promising that, though Wilson could not expect to impress the commissioners, his speech would be printed in the *World* and included in the report to Congress. And so, when other young attorneys were serving commercial interests that would pay them spot cash, Wilson appeared at the hearing to speak gratuitously for the common welfare. To him, the six commissioners who sat smugly around the table in the breakfast room of a hotel, surrounded by local dignitaries and the press, were incompetents.

Though he was annoyed by the sneers of prejudiced partisans and tripped on a point of fact by the commissioners, he pleaded the cause of peace and international trade so eloquently that the local congressmen remarked that he knew "what to say and how to say it."

The protectionist "advocates a system which prepares for war," he argued, "while it has not any consideration for the requirements of the country in time of peace. I ask, is it worth while during fifty years of peace to provide by taxation for one year of war?" Quoting Gladstone and referring to Mill, he maintained that "manufacturers are made better manufacturers whenever they are thrown upon their own resources and left to the natural competition of trade rather than when they are told, 'You shall be held in the lap of the government, and you need not stand upon your feet.'" Asked whether he advocated the repeal of all tariff laws, he replied: "Of all protective tariff laws."

That very night, with Page still present, Wilson called a few disciples together in the humble little law office to discuss the issue of the day, and in a few months this group had become a branch of the Free Trade Club of New York. They became a miniature House of Commons, in which almost all the talking was done by Wilson. Quite serious and very self-conscious, the youth was casting himself in a traditional role —half Southern rebel, half English Parliamentarian—as he set forth the standard arguments of the cotton-planting aristocracy.

When Wilson qualified for the federal courts, in March of 1883, he could pay only half the fee of ten dollars. For a year his father staked him, with no more complaint than the casual remark that Tom "didn't seem to be earning his salt." The young man who had told manufacturers that they should stand on their own feet, and who had sometimes been critical of indolent Southern gentlemen, was himself dependent still upon his family. This shamed him to the marrow; and yet he was not willing to sell himself to the prosecution of causes that to his Presbyterian conscience were immoral and, to his highly trained and richly stored mind, insignificant. He still drew back from any wooing of Mammon. His intellect would not permit him to join in the spectacular corporation baiting of Hoke Smith, who was later to become senator from Georgia. To him the philosophical *study* of the law—a pleasure to any thoughtful man—was a very different matter from its "scheming and haggling practice."

At the University of Virginia, beaten in an oratorical bout, Wilson had learned to accept defeat without letting it blight his aspirations. It was comparatively easy, now, to endure failure in an enterprise into which he had never put his heart. At the university, however, there had been coolness toward his antagonist; and even now, in leaving Atlanta, he threw bitter words over his shoulder. Describing himself as "buried in humdrum life down here in slow, ignorant, uninteresting Georgia," he complained to Dabney that "hereabouts culture is very little esteemed."

Leaving Atlanta and shaking himself free of the dust of trade, Woodrow Wilson still carried in his mind's eye the prospect that since boyhood had been most precious to him. The goal of political leadership still lured him; but he realized that without an independent income he could be at best an "outside" power in politics, "a speaker and writer of the highest authority on political subjects." What he needed, he wrote Dabney, was a profession that offered moderate support, favorable conditions for study, and considerable leisure. "What better can I be, therefore, than a professor, a lecturer upon subjects whose study delights me?"

Though Woodrow Wilson had no natural bent toward science or mathematics, he could not ignore the value of the scientific disciplines that were currently being applied to graduate studies in his chosen field of politics. Before the 1870's this subject had been scarcely at all taught in American colleges. At Princeton most of Wilson's study in economics and politics had been carried on in an atmosphere dominated by reverence for the *status quo*; but in an oasis that had opened in 1876 at The Johns Hopkins University he might expect to drink deeply of strong elixirs. Content to house the new graduate school in modest old residences, President Gilman was spending funds generously to attract teaching genius to Baltimore; and Walter Page commended the Hopkins as a path to a career in public affairs.

To this burgeoning source of academic life the frustrated lawyer in Atlanta resolved to go. He hoped to enter as an endowed fellow; but realizing that he had little evidence of his qualifications to submit, he resolved in any event to attend the university lectures and pursue his own work in the library, with the purpose of winning a subsidy. Fortunately, at the time when Wilson was turning his back once and for all on the legal market place, he fell in love with a woman of fine understanding.

In June of 1883, flaunting a newly grown mustache and plagued no more by the catarrh that had weighed on him for two years, the young man set out for the town of Rome, to consult his Uncle James Bones about his mother's affairs. It was an escape to make the heart beat faster, from the confinement of Atlanta, past Kennesaw Mountain, along the uplands and through the crisp air of northwest Georgia.

Once at Rome, Wilson's thoughts were brought back to his boyhood by the Cousin Jessie with whom he had once played Indian and who was now a young matron. It happened, too, that there was another old friend in town of whose presence the visitor was unaware. In Augusta, at the age of seven, "Tommie" Wilson had once insisted on holding in his arms a dimpled baby daughter of a friend of his father's. As Woodrow walked along a street in Rome, that very girl, now in the bloom of youthful beauty, looked down on him from the porch of a friend's house, marked the confident bearing, the clean, sharp features, the wide, sensitive mouth, and asked:

"Who is that fine-looking man?"

He did not see her then; but when he went with his cousins to the Presbyterian church, of which the girl's father was minister, he saw, under a black crape veil, what he later was to remember as "a bright, pretty face" with "splendid, mischievous, laughing eyes." Her hair shone like a ripe chestnut. For the hot summer months she had made herself a long straight frock of white muslin, with a fichu knotted at her breast.

After the service Woodrow looked more closely and concluded that it would be very clever to seek an introduction. "When I learned that this was Miss 'Ellie Lou' Axson, of whom I had heard so often," he confessed, "quite a flood of light was let in on my understanding and I was conscious of having formed a small resolution. I took an early opportunity of calling on the Rev. Mr. Axson." [3]

---

[3] W.W. to Ellen Axson, Oct. 11, 1883. Helen Welles Thackwell, daughter of Harriet Woodrow Welles, has reported that, while her mother and Woodrow Wilson were at Rome to attend

When Wilson made his call at the parsonage, the minister was mourning for his deceased wife and leaned heavily on his eldest child. She helped him to carry on the flower garden that her mother had loved; and often she called on sick parishioners in her father's stead, her arms filled with flowers. Intent on carrying out her dead mother's charge to care for her delicate father, she also undertook to rear two young brothers and a baby sister.

Mr. Axson received young Wilson's visit without suspicion of its motives. However, when the caller asked pointedly about his daughter's health, Ellen was summoned to the parlor and the young man was given an opportunity to exhibit his conversational charm on the question: "Why have night congregations grown so small?"

That very evening Woodrow escorted Ellen home from a party and was so entranced that he resolved to court the girl and make himself worthy of her. He was working against odds; for she had rebuffed her local admirers and, feeling responsible for her motherless brothers and baby sister, had vowed never to marry. The young man's family were helpful. Cousin Jessie planned a picnic; and when Woodrow asked whether he should bring lunch, Miss Ellie Lou replied that she had enough for two. The young folks rode the six miles to the head of Silver Creek in a wagon padded with straw, Woodrow and Ellie Lou turning their backs to the others. By the time the party came from wading in the creek and prepared to eat, the couple had disappeared.

Gradually, on long walks and rides, these two children of the manse found a deep communion of ideas, and the girl's formality relaxed a little. Her "noticeable man with large grey eyes" was making progress. They dated by letter. Ellen's first begins "Mr. Wilson" and is signed "Sincerely your friend." The second is signed "Very sincerely," and simply informs her beau that she will be ready "at the appointed hour." But in the third she opens her heart most charmingly to "Mr. Woodrow":

Very unwillingly, and with the firm conviction that I am the most unfortunate of mortals, I write to tell Jessie with my best thanks, that I won't be able to go on this picnic either—I last evening made an ill-timed engagement

---

the funeral of Aunt Marion Bones (who died Sept. 24, 1882), Harriet Woodrow took her rejected suitor to call on Ellen Louise Axson. *Princeton University Library Chronicle*, XII, No. 1 (Autumn, 1950), 16. It is difficult to reconcile this statement with Wilson's letter to Ellen Axson, quoted above, or with accounts of the first meeting of the lovers at Rome as recorded in Baker, I, p. 161. Helen Woodrow Bones, daughter of Marion Bones, rejected the Thackwell account. *See* letters, Helen Woodrow Bones to the writer, Feb. 15 and Mar. 28, 1951.

to take a boat-ride on that afternoon, and like Sterne's starling "I can't get out" of it.

There is no reason nor even—strange to say—*disinclination*, to prevent my saying most truthfully that I will be happy to walk with you this afternoon.

They saw each other only a few times at Rome. Slowly and gravely Ellen's sweet nature unfolded itself and she revealed an appreciation of art and literature that widened the horizon of Woodrow's intense and self-disciplining mind. He could see, too, that, though unambitious for herself in a worldly sense, she regarded life's responsibilities as seriously as did he. It was a severe strain on the patience of the suitor to make love slowly, and at a distance.

Finally, in September of 1883, he wrote from home that he could stand the suspense no longer, that since he could not win her consent by correspondence, he would come to the resort in North Carolina where she was visiting friends and woo her directly. Thrown into a panic, knowing that she could not resist him, yet feeling that her first duty was to her own dependent family, Miss Ellie Lou packed and prepared to hasten home in response to news that her father's incurable melancholia had taken a turn for the worse. On the way to the railroad she stopped at a hotel in Asheville and sat down before a window from which she could see the road. Her beau, driving up from the train by hack, happened to pass the hotel. Looking up from the street, he caught sight of the back of a shapely head as it receded from a window. The hair was coiled in a way curiously familiar. Bounding up the steps, he hurried to his Ellen and, pacing up and down on the veranda, confessed his need of her, explaining that a bachelor was actually what Bagehot had called him—"an amateur in life." He would help her to take care of her father and brothers, he pleaded.

It was too much for even the defenses of a conscience nurtured in Presbyterianism. She had done her utmost to flee temptation and the fate of coincidence had pursued her. She capitulated then and there. When they went the separate ways to which duty called them they were engaged.

Returning to Georgia and finding her father near death, Ellen told her brother that she was betrothed to "the greatest man in the world and the best." Going on to Baltimore to enter the Johns Hopkins Graduate School, Woodrow proclaimed to a friend that his Ellen was "the most beautiful woman in the world." He said a cavalier farewell to bachelorhood in a letter to Dabney: "I've fallen in love and *become engaged.* Yes, it's so. I'm bagged! . . . Of course it goes without saying that I am the most complacently happy man in the 'Yewnighted States.'" His Ellen, he said, "grew up in the best of all schools—for manners, purity, and cultivation—a country parsonage." He was proud to tell his old chum that Ellen's drawing and painting of portraits had won a reputation and had contributed to her support. Yet he did not fall in love with her, he confessed, because of any intellectual conviction that she would be the perfect helpmate. "I fell in love with her," he wrote, "for the same reasons that had made the same thing easy to several other fellows who were *not* students: because of her beauty and gentleness and intelligence: because she was irresistibly lovable. Why *she* fell in love with *me* must always remain an impenetrable mystery."

The love of these two souls was well fortified, at its very start, to survive the gales of life. To Ellen, it was instinctive understanding of a great and struggling soul that obviously needed her; to Woodrow, love was something to be analyzed and rationalized. His letters ran into dozens of pages, as he poured out everything that was in his heart and in his mind. Sure of her love, he made her the keeper of his secrets, the sharer of all his hopes.

At Princeton, Wilson had reveled in the discovery that he had a mind. Now he was learning, with infinite joy, that a woman could have a mind that he could respect and on which he could depend to complement his own. His understanding with Ellen seemed constantly to be widening and growing deeper. In contrast, his affection for Harriet had been puppyish.

As soon as he had Miss Ellie Lou's consent, in the autumn of 1883, he wanted to forego the work that he was undertaking at the Johns Hopkins and marry immediately. Though convinced that he had chosen the best place in America to study, Wilson chafed against the yoke of research and scoffed at the quality of the teaching in the Historical Seminary. Around a long, dull-red table, under the beetling busts of great statesmen, Wilson talked in this sanctum with young men who were to set the pace of American scholarship. Herbert B. Adams, cloaked in the authority of a Ph.D. from Heidelberg, sat as umpire at the head of the table and deftly led his scholars closer to the vital facts of what he called "institutional history": the evolution of town meetings and land systems, the organization of the Spanish settlements in Florida, and the structure of socialistic communities such as Brook Farm. Adams was reminded of a race horse as he watched Wilson's strong, powerful face, saw a nostril quiver or the head toss back in revolt against academic bridles. "Facts, facts, facts!" the youth protested to his Baltimore friends. "What do I care about his facts? What I want to know is what he does with them." [4]

He had gone to Adams and asked to be relieved of historical research so that he might devote all his energy to studying the working of government in his own day. Though he criticized his teacher for too great tolerance in managing the Historical Seminary, he saw no inconsistency in asking for special consideration for himself. His mind was afire with truth that had been revealed to him, his soul so imbued with a sense of mission that he seemed to be pleading for preferment not for himself but for great purposes that were at work through him.

Dr. Adams gave the colt his head, and Wilson plunged furiously into the writing of a book. Other students had been composing sterile monographs for a scholarly series to which Wilson did not contribute; and when he read his virile work to them it was acclaimed as better than anything of the sort ever done at the Hopkins. It was so good that he dared to send a sample to Houghton, Mifflin & Company. Encouraged to submit the completed work, he went home to Wilmington with his books and worked there during the summer of 1884, writing in shorthand and transcribing on a typewriter that he had purchased. He took regular walks and gymnastic exercises, and exacted the last throb of mental energy from a body that was no more than normal, maintaining, as he said, "that free spirit of courageous, light-hearted work in which I pride myself."

In the fall the completed manuscript for *Congressional Government* went to the publisher and the author held his breath. Finally he reported to Miss Ellie Lou: "They have actually offered me as good terms as if I were already a well-known writer! The success is of such proportions as almost to take my breath away—it has distanced my biggest hopes." Of all the pronouncements of Woodrow Wilson on government, none was more privy to the author's heart than this first volume.[5]

[4] Edith Gittings Reid, *Woodrow Wilson*, p. 37. Pursuing his favorite political studies at the Hopkins, Wilson took in his first year the usual formal courses: International Law, Advanced Political Economy, English, Constitutional History, and Sources of American Colonial History. In his second year he studied Modern Constitutions, Public Finance, Commerce, Administration, and History of Politics.

[5] Though the first edition sold out within a few weeks, *Congressional Government* was not a book of the moment or of the month or of the year. Gamaliel Bradford, whose earlier articles in the *Nation* (see Arthur S. Link, *Wilson: The Road to the White House*, pp. 15–19) set forth many of the ideas developed by Wilson, praised the book, made a pilgrimage to Baltimore to see the author, and asserted that "in a resolute advocacy of such a proposition lies the broadest and most open road to the Presidency." *Nation*, No. 1024 (Feb. 12, 1885), pp. 142, 143. How-

Congressional Government won the attention of the nation's reviewers and was acceptable to Dr. Adams as a thesis for a doctor's degree. It was the first scholarly analysis of what happens in the United States when the Presidency grows weak and the standing committees of Congress hold sway.

At the end of the first year at the Hopkins, wanting Ellen and enough money to live with her in comfort, Wilson complained to her that he had never been of any practical use to anyone, that he had yet to become a "breadwinner." He was inclined to sell himself to the most generous of the institutions that were bidding for him, degree or no degree. He wrote sixteen pages to his father in analysis of his dilemma, and the old preacher supported his inclination. But when he consulted his Ellen, she did not agree.

He had made himself a man of mark; and the Johns Hopkins, which the year before had denied him the fellowship of which he thought himself worthy, now recognized his merit and voluntarily offered one for his second year. At this juncture Woodrow Wilson was held steady in the long course by his Ellen. She insisted that no thought of her should stand in the way of his career. She was ready even to release him so that he might not have to wait to marry until she fulfilled her duty to her own family. But when he received a letter to this effect, Wilson took the first train, ran all the way from the station to her, swore that he would die if she did not remain his. When she insisted that he return to Baltimore to complete the studies that he had undertaken and work for a degree, he accepted her judgment. His better self was drawn out and he vowed to her: "I *must* be true to myself . . . and no chance of getting my name before the public shall tempt me to do what I should some day regard as beneath my reputation, as weakly done." And so he went back for a second year of academic digging, explaining to friends in Baltimore that Ellen put humility first among the virtues

ever, the true importance of both the work and the author was to dawn slowly upon the nation. In 1892 the book was awarded the John Marshall Prize at the Johns Hopkins. James Bryce was influenced by it and quoted from it in *The American Commonwealth*. It has been translated into several foreign languages and printed thirty times in the United States—the last time in 1956, with an introduction by Walter Lippmann.

The first review to reach Wilson came from Walter Hines Page, who, buggy-riding in North Carolina with Josephus Daniels, prophesied greatness for the author. But the response that most touched his heart came from his father, to whom the book was dedicated. "The 'dedication' took me by surprise," the old man wrote, "and never have I felt such a blow of love. Shall I confess it?—I wept and sobbed in the stir of the glad pain." Joseph Ruggles Wilson to W.W., Jan. 30, 1885. For the dissenting minority of reviewers Wilson had only scorn. He referred disapprovingly to "a sneering review in a small local sheet of no circulation." He was ready to fight all comers in defense of the truth as it was revealed to him.

and that he "took all this pother" to please her. To his studies he added the responsibility of acting as correspondent for the New York *Evening Post*; and to earn money he lectured in outlying towns, characterizing socialistic reformers as "long-haired and wild-eyed," and then explaining to Professor Ely, who challenged him, that by saying such things one could make people believe that one was a conservative, and then go ahead and do progressive things.[6]

In April, 1886, Wilson wrote from Bryn Mawr to Adams that he had "all along coveted such recognition as a Ph.D. from the Hopkins would give." Explaining that he needed the degree *now*, that he always cut "a sorry figure" in exams, "from sheer perversity of natural disposition," that he was a nervous fellow who could not for the life of him "pull in ordinary harness," Wilson persuaded Adams and Ely to make his "a case of special arrangement." An interview took the place of a formal oral examination and he was granted a Ph.D. degree. On May 29 he wrote to his Ellen: "Hurrah—a thousand times hurrah—*I'm through, I'm through*—the degree is actually secured! Oh, the relief of it! I won the degree *for you*."

At Baltimore, Wilson had a select circle of friends, and to them he gave his heart. But he ignored men whom he found dull or pompous, overzealous in backslapping, or too ready with a belly laugh. He liked to dodge crowds and sit aside with friends for quiet chats. In a tête-à-tête he said: "No man would, on account of my Scotch physiognomy, ever familiarly slap me on the back in a hail-fellow-well-met way . . . I should just hate it; I should be most uncomfortable; I could not conceivably slap him back, and what a prig I should feel because I couldn't."

Strangers who tried to be too familiar were rebuffed by shy distrust. To anyone suspected of sycophancy Wilson presented a hard and insulating shell. At formal Baltimore parties he protected his oversensitive feelings with a mask of diffidence. Even that, however, was distinguished. "How does he manage that bed-side manner and make his dress clothes look like a preacher's?" people asked. "He's terribly clever but he is provincial." Jokingly they warned him not to become a "Hopkins genius"—a grind who could not mix in the society of the city. They valued the traditions of Southern gentility and culture far above efficiency in scholarship. Some of Wilson's friends felt sorry because a gentleman of his background was forced to yield to eccentric men of no social standing who had been given places on the Hopkins faculty. They tried to draw him out, asking, "How do you like the Hopkins?"

[6] Ely, *Ground Under Our Feet*, p. 109.

Hesitating, he answered that it lacked the cultural atmosphere of the University of Virginia, but that it was sponsoring splendid research and was a wonderful place in its way. "Unfortunately," he added, "I like my own way too much for my own and other people's comfort."

Draw him out on the theme of his deepest intellectual loves, and to his intimates he would expose his soul. When national politics came under discussion, he threw back his head as if to get the highest perspective possible. Then he would talk very precisely, every trace of diffidence gone, appraising the presidents from Washington to Cleveland ("Washington gave America her liberty; Lincoln's gift was the heart"). Answering those who told him that he was cut out to be an English rather than an American statesman, he would argue: "Would you pigeon-hole a man as an alien because he imports some of his fuel from outside? . . . I think there are few things so poor and cheap as prejudice—and so pernicious." He loved to voice his deep faith in democracy, and proclaimed that the old order of Baltimore society was giving way to an age of vigorous individualism. Then he would drop from his eagle's view and his far-ranging judgments and fall into the rut of the general talk with a little whimsical turn of phrase.

The young scholar at the Hopkins warbled with the Glee Club regularly. Once they went to a suburb to give a benefit concert for factory workers and came home hilariously roaring and rattling through the sleepy city in a four-horse bus. The affairs of the club were not always serene, however. Wilson was smitten with a "conviction," even in this pagan activity. He felt that the organization should stand on its own feet, financially, and to this end should be permitted to charge admission to its concerts. President Gilman offered to subsidize the club with university funds; but the young man insisted, and had his way. To overcome the conviction of this Presbyterian on a matter of right and wrong required a more rugged soul than that of either Gilman or Adams. Only Miss Ellie Lou could bend the will to which no man but old Joseph Wilson could dictate. When his Baltimore friends spoke of her, Woodrow would drop his humors and his poses and reveal the depth of his love for his Ellen.

Once, en route to New York after a visit to his parents, the lovers stopped in Washington long enough to board a trolley car and go uptown so that Miss Ellie Lou might see the White House. They joined two girls from Rome for the journey to New York, where they were met by a wealthy friend who was so well dressed that the girls were ashamed of the old linen duster that Wilson wore. But clothes could neither make nor mar the man in the eyes of Miss Ellie Lou. When he went away to his boardinghouse at Baltimore, leaving her to study at the Art Students League, she threw herself on her bed and wept.

In his love Wilson found power to overcome what he called "discursive habits." More important, perhaps, he had a confidante to whom he could say: "You are the only person in the world—without any exception—to whom I can tell *all* that my heart contains." Reminding her that the intellectual life was "a fearfully solitary one," he wrote: "I have the uncomfortable feeling that I am carrying a volcano about with me. My salvation is in being loved . . . There surely never lived a man with whom love was a more critical matter than it is with me!"

He shared his joys of literary discovery with his Ellen, often reading aloud to her. Such occasions he considered "both tonic and food," and he felt that his "literary partner" furnished "more of the capital" than he. He had read little in philosophy or in current poetry or prose, no books in foreign languages (though he could read in French), and scarcely any scientific works. His fancy was caught by certain poems, not by famous names. He might read and enjoy one poem of an author and yet feel no inclination to read further in his works. He delighted at times in books not widely known. Wilson's taste in literature and art, nourished and enriched by Miss Ellie Lou, became catholic.

The young lover's enjoyment of the theater was intense, for he had developed a histrionic sense in his practice of oratory. In a long letter to his fiancée, filled with keen appraisal of details, he described the *Hamlet* of Henry Irving and Ellen Terry. "Miss Terry," he concluded, "quite won my heart—but only my *audience,* my dramatic heart, not the one that belongs to you!"

When her husband's "dramatic heart" was captured, Miss Ellie Lou always understood. If she had not been sure that she was enshrined in his inmost heart she might have succumbed to jealousy when he wrote of flirtatious sallies at Baltimore. Since Ellen thought him a "noticeable man," in spite of his awkward exterior, he began to fancy himself as a gallant and boasted teasingly of "numerous frolics" with a young lady at a candymaking party. At dinners he could bandy toasts with piercing wit, and he loved to play the *enfant terrible.* Cavalierly, he wrote to Ellen: "It may shock you—it ought to—but I'm afraid it will not, to learn that I have a reputation (?) amongst most of my kin and certain of my friends . . . for being irrepressible, in select circles, as a maker of grotesque addresses from the precarious elevation of chair seats, as a wearer of all varieties of comic grimaces, as a simulator of sundry

unnatural, burlesque styles of voice and speech, as a lover of farces—
even as a dancer of the 'can-can.'"

Always understanding, always giving her man the benefit of any
doubts that arose, Ellen shared Woodrow's deepest allegiance only with
his God. He joked often about "orthodoxy," for nothing so much irked
this spirited practitioner of religion as the cant of fundamentalists. He
laughed uproariously when a little girl confessed to him that at a
Methodist revival meeting she had allowed herself to be swept along in
the tide of "salvation." A decision of the Presbyterian Synod against
the damnation of infants made him laugh and say: "Think of all those
dear little babies that have been burning in hell so long; now they will
all be released!" To him and to Ellen, hell was only a state of mind.

Religion was more than a matter of creeds, taboos, hallelujahs, and
amens. Wilson believed that "all things work together for good—
through the careful performance of duty," that the only faith worth
cultivating is one that shines through a man's daily acts. His belief in
the God of his fathers inspired his actions and gave him strength and
comfort. When Ellen, who read deeply in philosophy, was beset with
doubts, Woodrow would bring his more rugged faith to her support.
When Samuel Axson died, he could reassure his fiancée: "Your dear
father, however sad or tragic his death may have been, is happy now."

She waited two years while he completed his studies at the university.
They were married on June 24, 1885, at Savannah, in the manse in
which Ellen was born and which she treasured as her home after her
father's death. Grandfather Axson and Dr. Wilson performed the simple ceremony in the presence of a few relatives and friends. Of the bride,
sublime in tulle and orange blossoms, a grand dame of the city was
heard to say: "What a pity for such a beautiful girl to throw herself
away on an unknown!" [7]

After a week with Wilson's sister in Columbia, the honeymooners
spent the summer in a place in the hills of North Carolina that bore
the name of Arden. There he sang and they walked and read much
together, and Woodrow Wilson's confidence in his destiny was given
an impulse that his Presbyterian God had not been able to supply.

[7] Margaret Godley, "Savannah's Most Famous June Wedding," *Savannah Life Magazine*,
June, 1947; also Mrs. B. Palmer Axson to the writer.

CHAPTER IV

Noticeable Man

Late in 1884, Wilson had been introduced to the dean of a new Quaker college for women that was to open the next fall at Bryn Mawr, Pennsylvania. Martha Carey Thomas had returned from graduate study in Europe converted to worship of facts and reason and in full revolt against the Victorian sentimentality of her elders. With an inflexibility of purpose that to Southern gentlefolk seemed brazen, she resolved to exalt American girls to the level of masculine scholarship at a "Miss Johns Hopkins."

Wilson was interested in the new venture in spite of himself. He could pay only lip service to German scholasticism, and neither he nor Ellen was devoted to the ideal of education for women. He preferred not to teach girls; and it irked him to think that, although he might hope to be his own master and there would be other men on the faculty, his chief would be a woman no older than himself, and positive in her opinions.

On the other hand, here was a new frontier, with some of the glamour that pioneering always held for Woodrow and Wilson blood. "The higher education of women is certain to come in America whatever I think on the subject," he said to a Baltimore friend. Moreover, he wanted to "get a chair somewhere and get into permanent harness," and Bryn Mawr offered certain advantages: leisure for private study; proximity to the Johns Hopkins, where he hoped to give a course of lectures; and an opportunity to get experience before seeking a more conspicuous and more demanding place. And so at Bryn Mawr, as at the Hopkins, he plunged into a spawning pool of ideas that were to rule American education for a generation or more.

He expected to be offered a salary of $2,000 and was so shocked at an offer of $1,200 that he refused point-blank. Finally he informed Ellen that he had been elected "associate" in history for two years at $1,500 a year, and he asked: "Would you be altogether satisfied to have me accept? . . . Tell me without reserve *exactly* what you think . . ."

Ellen told him. She was not happy over the prospect. But Dean Thomas granted Wilson's request that he be allowed to add to his income by giving outside lectures, and soon he was writing to persuade Miss Ellie Lou, not to ask advice. "You talk," he wrote, "as if a salary of $1,500 must plunge us into positive discomfort . . . But the salary promised will be enough for us *to live on* for two years—and it will be enough to preclude all necessity for your turning your talents again to money-making . . . your companionship is more essential to my *ambitions* than the books I cannot yet own or the journeys I cannot take. My first need is *you*—these things come *far* behind!"

Two days later, before he could hear again from Miss Ellie Lou, he sent his acceptance of the offer to President Rhoads. He had made up his own mind and he had his father's approval.

She came along, protesting that they did not appreciate the quality of her man. From their honeymoon the couple went to live, in the autumn of 1885, in the little rural village ten miles northwest of Philadelphia. There were only forty-two students and two buildings that first year. The tiny community offered little to do but study and teach, and on Sundays go to the Quaker chapel service. While his wife sewed, Wilson got up courses in ancient and modern history as well as in constitutional law, his favorite subject.

The young teacher composed his lectures during afternoon walks over the rolling countryside. After half an hour of such exercise, he said, he was "warm as toast." Typing what he had created, he tried paragraphs on Ellen to make sure that they were clear. His wife was giving him companionship that kept him out of moods of morbid introspection. But twice she had to leave him to visit an aunt in Georgia—and each time she returned with a baby girl. "Woodrow's little annuals," old Joseph Wilson chuckled.

Even in the company of Ellen Wilson the young instructor found no enjoyment in the "society" of nearby Philadelphia. He was always to think of the "Main Line" as the narrowest stratum of American society. Moreover, the light dramatics that the girls put on at Bryn Mawr cloyed and sickened him. They seemed mere frothy cleverness, enjoyable perhaps to some but to him far less satisfying than the mastery that an orator exerts over his hearers. And he found the "social" chatter of the audience utterly boring. He preferred to stay at home and protect his little castle. Once, when a maniac was thought to be prowling in the woods outside the house, the laird went out and fired his pistol.

As the months passed, Wilson's domestic bliss was not matched by an equal satisfaction in his work. Only by "very constant and stringent schooling," he said, could he endure academic methods. The business of teaching women threw him into an inescapable dilemma. The girls, their most ladylike instincts evoked by their courteous, gallant professor, wrote down even his jokes in their notebooks, and in the examinations they faithfully handed back what he had given. Though he allowed time for the asking of questions, he did not succeed in drawing out intelligent discussion. The thinking, and most of the talking, was done by the professor. In permitting this he showed himself an inexpert teacher, according to the tenets of Dean Thomas; but had he encouraged his girls to raise their voices in masculine argument he would have been no gentleman, according to the tradition of his family.

As he began his third year at Bryn Mawr his perplexity flamed into rebellion and he protested to his wife: "I'm *tired* carrying female Fellows on my shoulders! . . . When I think of you, my little wife, I love this 'College for Women,' because *you* are a woman; but when I think only of myself, I hate the place very cordially . . ." He brooded over his lot, worried about his health, and wondered how he could earn a living by teaching undergraduates and at the same time keep his literary fancy free.

He felt again the urge to strike out for himself in a statesman's career. This, he had written to his Ellen before their marriage, was his "heart's primary ambition" and his "mind's deepest secret." Doubting that he had ability enough to indulge this desire, and still allured by what he called "the stir of the world," he hoped in 1887 that he might find "a seat on the inside of the government—a seat high enough to command views of the system." The offer of a federal position, whether he accepted it or not, seemed a good asset in getting ahead in his profession. Going to Washington to call on Renick, formerly his partner at Atlanta and now an official in the Treasury, he paid his first visit to Congress and interviewed chiefs of bureaus. But it was suggested to him that, much as a government post might benefit Woodrow Wilson, the country could be better served by men drilled in the service; and he quickly saw the justice of that argument.

But his aspiration toward political leadership kept surging up. He wrote to Talcott of "special work in administration"[1] that he wanted to do eventually, and suggested to this Princeton classmate that they renew their covenant of college days and form a "committee of correspondence" composed of a half dozen vigilantes. He wanted, he said,

---

[1] While at Bryn Mawr Wilson wrote "The Study of Administration," an essay that was published in the *Political Science Quarterly* in June of 1887.

to meet "men who have direct touch with the world," so that he might study *affairs* rather than doctrine. "What I go in for," he wrote to Professor Adams, "is the *life,* not the texts, of constitutions, the practice not the laws of administration."

He reviewed Bryce's *American Commonwealth,* criticizing the author's reliance on description, his scanting of the historical experience that testifies that "for a body of English people *the fundamental principles of the law are at any given time substantially what they are then thought to be."* He himself undertook to supply what he found lacking in Bryce, showing in an essay how America's government had changed under the spur of a world-wide "drift toward democracy" and under the pressures that resulted from immigration and the industrial revolution. American democracy is "a stage of development," he wrote. "Its process is experience, its basis old wont, its meaning national organic unity and effectual life. It came, like manhood, as the fruit of youth. Immature peoples cannot have it, and the maturity to which it is vouchsafed is the maturity of freedom and self-control . . ."[2]

Though he still paid tribute to Bagehot and to Burke, who, combined with Montesquieu, represented for him all that had force in political thought, the ardor of Wilson's worship of parliamentary heroes had cooled somewhat since his undergraduate days. The boyish feeling that he had long cherished, he confided to his Ellen in 1889, was giving way to another feeling—"that I need no longer hesitate (as I have so long and sensitively done) to assert myself and my opinions in the presence of and against the . . . opinions of old men, 'my elders.' " An admirer at Baltimore had interrupted him once to ask: "Do you never think yourself wrong?" And he had answered: "Not in matters where I have qualified myself to speak."

On his thirty-third birthday, in 1889, he wrote in his journal: "I have great confidence in progress; I feel the movement that is in affairs and am conscious of a persistent push behind the present order." Why, he asked himself, might not his age write through him its political autobiography?

Wilson's passion for leadership expressed itself in 1890 in a Commencement address entitled "Leaders of Men," delivered at the University of Tennessee. Denied satisfaction of his impulse to lead men in political action, he tried to resolve "the perennial misunderstanding between the men who write and the men who act." He explained "the

---

[2] *P.P.,* I, 176–77. For illustration of the way in which Wilson refined his writing when he repeated, cf. *Woodrow Wilson, An Old Master and Other Political Essays,* pp. 116–17.

well-nigh universal repugnance felt by literary men towards democracy." The leader that he aspired to be—and must wait decades to become—would be a thinking man in action.[3]

All the while, as he wrote in this vein, the instructor stayed close to his home and his college girls, conceiving a gargantuan feat of scholarship. He proposed, he wrote to editor Horace Scudder, to apply the inductive method to the study of democratic government, and especially to its genesis and development in the United States. "The true philosophy of government," he asserted, "can be extracted only from the true history of government." Aristotle, he pointed out, had studied politics in that manner but did not go beyond the outward differences of institutions; Wilson would "press on beyond logical distinctions to discover the spiritual oneness of government, the life that lives within it." For years this grandiose dream haunted him. Allusions to it appear in his jottings, and his family spoke longingly of the day "when father comes to the writing of the p.o.p."—The Philosophy of Politics.

Instead of plunging into such a soul-satisfying work, however, the professor had to be content with a commission to write a college textbook to be called *The State*—"a fact book," he called it, "a plebeian among books . . . vulgar-looking." For this work he had to consult sources in German. He could not read that language at sight and hesitated to speak foreign tongues for fear that the purity of his English might be tainted; but now he wanted to take his family to Berlin. It was too costly, though; and so, when Ellen was not sewing clothes or caring for her infant or made ill by a baby that was expected, and when Woodrow was not studying or teaching or writing, they attacked German texts together, one using the dictionary, the other writing down translations. Putting notes and references on cards and filing them meticulously, outlining each chapter in a page of shorthand, the author worked for three years on *The State*. But when the book came out old Joseph Wilson read it and asked: "Woodrow, couldn't you have put more juice into it?" [4]

The author himself was not proud of this textbook. Yet in it the seed germs of a league of nations were sprouting. International law, Wilson wrote, "*ought* to govern nations in their dealings with each

---

[3] *See* T. H. Vail Motter (ed.), *Leaders of Men*. Wilson delivered his address on this theme four times in the nineties, but did not publish it. Motter has suggested that his diary, under date of Jan. 17, 1897, explains his desire for privacy. Though "a living and effectual utterance of himself might validate him," Wilson wrote, it was "an unnecessary risk—a hazardous exposure of his workship and materials." *Leaders of Men*, p. 11.

[4] Stockton Axson, "Woodrow Wilson as Man of Letters," Rice Institute Pamphlet, XXII, No. 4, 251.

other," but lacked "forceful sanction." And it was while he was working on *The State* that he wrote in a magazine article: "There is a
tendency—is there not?—a tendency as yet dim, but already steadily
impulsive and clearly destined to prevail, towards, first the confedera-
tion of parts of empires like the British, and finally of great states themselves. Instead of centralization of power, there is to be wide union with
tolerated divisions of prerogative. This is a tendency towards the American type—of governments joined with governments for the pursuit
of common purposes, in honorary equality and honorable subordina-
tion."

Old Joseph Wilson had proclaimed an ecumenical gospel; and,
nourished on it, Woodrow Wilson's mind easily envisioned the political
union of mankind under the ideal of peace and justice. He did not,
however, expect to reach Utopia overnight. "In government, as in virtue," he explained, "the hardest of hard things is to make progress."
But his faith in the future was boundless.

At the same time, in his early political writing, Wilson warned against
revolution as a means of political progress, explaining that violence was
always followed by reaction. In the last chapter of *The State* he came
to grips with the problem of reconciling a liberal philosophy of politics
with contemporary social conditions. The state must perform certain
functions that were obviously "necessary," he wrote; but "optional"
functions might well be left to private agencies. Just what powers
should be exercised by government, and how far, must be determined
by experience and the demands of the times.

While the Bryn Mawr professor was pursuing these literary paths, in
the eighties, little Wesleyan College asked him to join its faculty at a
salary higher than that paid at Bryn Mawr. He got a legal opinion as
to whether the three-year agreement under which the girls' college had
reappointed him in 1887 was still binding. Advised that it was not, he
accepted the post at Middletown, Connecticut, realizing that he had
"for a long time been hungry for a class of *men*." [5]

[5] W.W. to Bridges, Aug. 26, 1888, in Baker, I, 295. Wilson's negotiations with the trustees
of Bryn Mawr left wounded feelings. In June of 1888, Wilson proposed to resign, saying to Dr.
Rhoads, courteously but firmly, that he regarded his agreement with Bryn Mawr as terminable
at any date that would allow time for the appointment of a successor. He held that there was
still time, before the following September. The trustees felt that Wilson had committed a serious
breach of faith and were inclined to try to hold him; but Dr. Rhoads, seeing that he would
never be contented at Bryn Mawr, advised that they release him and wish him well. *See* Edith
Finch, *Carey Thomas of Bryn Mawr*, pp. 174–78, 330–32. *Also see* Cornelia Meigs, *A History
of Bryn Mawr College*, pp. 48–49, and folder, "Resignation of Woodrow Wilson," in the
Bryn Mawr archives.

For two years, at Wesleyan, Wilson instructed all seniors and juniors in political economy
and the Constitution of the United States. He gave optional courses at Wesleyan in the history
of England, of France, of the United States, and of "institutions."

In observing the machinations of student cliques and secret societies, he received an education in the ways of boss politics; and a fight that he waged to place the ablest men on the athletic teams, without consideration of social status, presaged larger battles to come. He made a lifelong friend of his pastor, nicknamed his colleagues and called them "a faculty with less dead wood" than any similar body of his acquaintance. They laughed at his endless repertoire of stories, thought him a good fellow who put on no airs.

Absences from home brought tears at parting. On his "sprees," the professor kept a careful account of his expenses and wrote loving letters to his wife, assuring her that without her he could not have discovered his "whole self," that she made him the man that he was, and at the same time detailing his many and catholic activities: a trip on a coastwise steamer; a visit to Robert Bridges in his office at Scribner's; nights at the theater, once to hear Sothern, later to see *Bootle's Baby*; a boat ride and concert at Coney Island; a day at Seabright, and another at a professional baseball game. Freed from the work in which his conscience drove him, he could have been a famous sybarite. He liked to see his fellow Americans diverted by innocent amusement as much as he delighted in seeing them energized by a positive faith. Although four years previously he had criticized an eloquent, demagogic harangue by Henry Ward Beecher as "shallow" and "noisy," it did not offend his religion or his intelligence to see Dwight L. Moody practice personal evangelism in a barbershop in Middletown.

Another man might have settled into lifelong enjoyment of academic serenity and the easy and companionable society of Middletown; and a humorless man might have reveled in the adulation that his lectures evoked. But the life of a "lion" could not satisfy the urges of his blood. Woodrow Wilson was still looking toward the intellectual horizon, toward new fields to be cultivated by his mind. He could hardly hope that his passion for good government among free men could be requited in teaching history in a small college. What he craved was a chair in public law at his own College of New Jersey. From such a pulpit he would be able to advise and criticize the nation's statesmen.

Fortunately he had in Robert Bridges a loyal and ardent campaign manager. This chum and classmate had introduced him to Francis L. Patton, who succeeded Dr. McCosh in the presidency of the College of New Jersey. Impressed by a reading of *Congressional Government*, Patton suggested that Wilson fill a vacant chair in political economy for a year, until a professorship of public law could be created for him.

Bridges urged him to acceptance, saying that Professor Sloane had been overburdened by carrying the teaching in political economy and was anxious to be relieved of it, that his influence with the trustees was very great. "Speaking confidentially, and with some guile," Bridges wrote, "I believe that he is a good man to conciliate . . . you could sail along beautifully together, notwithstanding radical differences in your historical points of view."

For the sake of his loved ones, Wilson had sometimes swallowed his pride and played the worldly game of getting ahead from which he had revolted as a bachelor at Atlanta. In 1886 he had at first refused to go to a dinner of Princeton alumni in New York because his conscience would not let him spend time or money for pleasure; but when they had asked him to speak he had accepted, hoping to identify himself with Princeton. Wilson's speech had been far too long and too serious for the taste of banqueting alumni, and he feared that it had hurt his chances for a Princeton professorship. He caused the idea of endowing a chair at the College of New Jersey to be insinuated into the mind of a philanthropist, hoping that he might occupy it himself. And now he wrote to Professor Sloane and was informed, very cordially, that there was no immediate prospect of a division of labor in his department.

Declining to consider a call to Williams College, Wilson decided to wait for a chair of public law. Meanwhile, Bridges warned that "the Philistines" at Princeton were "whispering behind their hands." This faithful friend campaigned for Wilson among the trustees of the college, bringing pressure on one opponent who disliked Wilson's position on the tariff, on another who complained that he was a Southerner and would "make trouble," and on several who feared that his learning was too deep to permit him to interest the boys! [6]

Finally, in February, 1890, word came of his election to a professorship of jurisprudence and political economy. Thereupon the authorities at Wesleyan let it be known that they would grant almost any request to induce the brilliant lecturer not to move. Old loyalties as well as the needs of the family pulled toward Princeton, however; and after doing everything in his power to get a strong man to take over at Wesleyan, the professor packed up his household and moved. "I find," he wrote

[6] Wilson had feared rather that the authorities at Princeton would not think him learned enough. The *Nation*, in reviewing one of his books, had classed him with those who "impose only on the vulgar." And in submitting a light essay to *Scribner's Magazine*, Wilson had signed it with a *nom de plume*, explaining that it was whimsical and contained half-playful opinions that university trustees might think *infra dig*.

to his father, "that everybody regards my election to Princeton as a sort of crowning success." [7]

In his new post, in the nineties, Wilson still found time to write. He evaluated the heroes of American history in an essay called "A Calendar of Great Americans." In this work he showed that he had so developed his critical faculties that he could no longer give himself wholly to emulation of any hero. "I can find no man in history I should care to be like. I want to be myself," he said to his Ellen.[8]

Fresh and far-ranging as were Wilson's writings on politics during the eighties and nineties, they were criticized by scholars who found his thought hazy and out of focus, his sentences overrhetorical. By exercising the love of words that his father had instilled in him as a boy, Wilson built a vocabulary of some 62,000 words. But he had no smugness about his style. Though he confessed to his Ellen that he was immensely pleased that his writing should have been considered good, he was forever reaching out for the moon, complaining that his sentences were "stiff, dry, mechanical, monotonous," that the effect was altogether "too staccato."

It occurred to him that by writing on lighter, more literary themes he might loosen and vary his style. Though he had been unsuccessful in selling short stories, he had not given up his ambition to write literature; and in his view the poets of the race came nearer than the scholars to the eternal verities of politics and economics. He was quite aware,

[7] W.W. to Joseph Ruggles Wilson, March 20, 1890. Writing to Bridges, Wilson explained that there was but one argument for Princeton: "namely, that it is Princeton—a big institution of the first class, with superior facilities for work, with the best class of students, and affording a member of its faculty a certain academic standing." Patton hesitated to agree that Wilson should go on with his lectures at the Johns Hopkins, and Wilson thought him "afraid of the Trustees and the faculty—of jealousy on their part—for Princeton, for themselves." The young professor was inclined to make an ultimatum either of the continuation of the Hopkins lectures or of a greater salary, and preferably the former, for he felt that he derived much more than money from his continuing association with the Hopkins. He asked the advice of Bridges, on whom he depended, he said, in closest friendship and completest trust. W.W. to Bridges, Feb. 13, 1890.

[8] As his confidence in his own powers grew he ventured to criticize a book by John W. Burgess of the Columbia Law School, the teacher of Theodore Roosevelt and probably at that time America's most influential student of government. Burgess seemed to write in the language of natural science, not in that of literature and political fact, to apply the theory of the survival of the fittest too patly to politics, and to believe that the Teuton dominated the world by his superior political genius.

The true nature of government, Wilson had insisted in *The State*, is "hidden in the nature of Society," which is "compounded of the common habit, an evolution of experience, an interlaced growth of tenuous relationships, a compact, living, organic whole . . ."

Referring to "social organisms" and characterizing the evolution of political institutions as "scarcely less orderly and coherent than that of the physical world," Wilson occasionally fell into the phrasing of popular interpretations of social Darwinism, but he felt that the social Darwinists attached too little importance to the human will. Such understanding as he had of Spencer probably came indirectly, through Bagehot.

he had written to Miss Ellie Lou, that at his birth "no poet was born" and had asked her whether it was not a legitimate ambition "to wish to write something (!) that will freshen the energies of tired people and make the sad laugh and take heart again: some comedy full of pure humor and peopled with characters whose lives are in order, who live up to the moral that life, even with the pleasures of vice left out, is worth living; lay sermons full of laughter and a loving God: a fiction that may be suffered to live, if only because it has real people in it and no sham enthusiasm?" He could wish, he said, to be "the favoured correspondent of children, as well as a counsellor of the powers of the earth." [9]

He composed essays [10] that were designed not to please editors or scholars, but only himself and the bosom friends to whom he dedicated them. With one of these, brother-in-law Stockton Axson, he bicycled from Princeton out into the country; and sitting on an old stone bridge he threw out a challenge: "We who know literature by sight have the responsibility of carrying on a war with those to whom the so-called 'scholarship' is everything." Even in the writing that he had undertaken for relaxation and diversion problems of style began to haunt him. If only he might equal the "quick stroke, intermittent sparkle, and jet-like play" that he so admired in Walter Bagehot! Fond of epigram, he shuddered at the cheap, the smart-aleck, the sentimental. He would not admit to his writing the offhand gleams of farce that shone in his intimate talk. He fretted, corresponded with friends, picked to pieces some of his books.

It was clear, in the mid-nineties, that Woodrow Wilson would not make an indelible mark on the world by impressing scholars with political treatises or his intimates with belles-lettres. As an essayist and textbook writer he was competent; but his editor had complained that he wrote as if there were "an audience before some of his sentences." When the audience came alive, however, and the prophet could address it directly, he showed himself to be superb.

Ever since he had sat as a boy in his father's churches and been thrilled by what came from the preacher's lips, Woodrow Wilson had been excited by the spoken word. His command of it had given him his

[9] W.W. to Ellen Axson, Oct. 30, 1883, unpublished letter printed by permission of Eleanor W. McAdoo and Edith Bolling Wilson.

[10] Among the random literary essays were such autobiographical papers as "The Author Himself," "On an Author's Choice of Company," and "When a Man Comes to Himself." After publication in magazines, some of the pieces were collected and bound in volumes that were given such titles as *Mere Literature* and *On Being Human*.

greatest triumphs at college and law school, and at the Hopkins he said of oratory: "It sets my mind—all my faculties—aglow . . . I *feel* a sort of transformation—and it's hard to go to sleep afterward." Like his ancestors who had expounded the Word, he felt "absolute joy in facing and conquering a hostile audience . . . or thawing out a cold one." And when his chosen medium—the spoken word—was applied to his favorite of all subjects—politics—Woodrow Wilson reached his greatest heights.[11]

Haunted by the memory of mediocre teaching to which he himself had been exposed, Wilson resolved never to be dull. Good oratory, he once explained to Ellen, "does not generally come into the lectures of college professors; but it should. Oratory is not declamation, not swelling tones and excited delivery, but the art of persuasion, the art of putting things so as to appeal irresistibly to an audience . . . Perfunctory lecturing is of no service in the world. It's a nuisance."

And so Wilson lectured at Princeton with a persuasiveness that he had labored for years to perfect. In the chapel—the largest classroom on the campus—he spoke on public law: "its historical derivation, its practical sanctions, its typical outward forms, its evidence as to the state and as to the character and scope of political sovereignty." This was his heart's blood, the subject on which he felt that he had qualified himself to speak as an oracle. So completely did he master both subject and pupils that he drew classes that increased from about 150 in 1890 to 305 in 1902.

Looking down on his students, he stood squarely on his long legs, his short body slanting forward a bit and his fingertips barely touching the top of the desk before him. Above a turnover collar and black string tie, his features stood forth in all their Scotch-Irish bluntness: jutting jaw, big upper lip over a strong mouth, large ears that fitted close below a long and narrow cranium. Black straight hair thatched his head and eaved down in short side whiskers. His Adam's apple and the tip of his

---

[11] At the Johns Hopkins, Wilson had taken it upon himself to reform the constitution of the Literary Society as well as to improve its oratory. "It is characteristic of my whole self," he had confessed to Miss Ellie Lou, "that I take so much pleasure in these proceedings . . . I have a sense of power in dealing with men collectively which I do not feel always in dealing with them singly . . . One feels no sacrifice of pride necessary in courting the favour of an assembly of men such as he would have to make in seeking to please one man."

At Wesleyan, Wilson had encouraged the boys to transform the old college debating society into a new "Wesleyan House of Commons," where causes were argued from conviction rather than by assignment. He felt, however, that the House was "kept moribund by the vitality of fraternities," and the tendency toward too rapid changes of ministry was as pronounced as in France. At Princeton, the professor urged students to join one of the debating societies even if they must slight the work of his course.

nose flexed vertically, and he moved his arm first up, with palm pressing upward, then down, with fingers drooping. Now his full, mobile lips would flash out a smile, baring teeth that were patched; and later his jutting jaw would snap with finality on the end of a period of graceful phrases.

On the stroke of the classroom bell this imposing figure said "Good morning, gentlemen," and the boys came under the spell of his luminous eyes. From his lecture notes, typed out and underlined in red for emphasis, he would read a series of statements, sometimes emphasizing their sequence by curling his fingers in his palm and then gracefully opening them one at a time, the forefinger first. The most important points were stated twice, and after the repetition the lecturer stopped while pencils flew. Telling the boys to put their notebooks aside, he would compel their attention by a barrage of wit, characterization, and word pictures. He used current news stories to illustrate points of law, and when he dramatized a town meeting, boys felt that they were seeing the real thing. He was at his best in depicting scenes in the age-long battle for free government. Valuing the moral lessons of history above scholarly analysis of the facts, Wilson once said to an instructor in the classics: "I should be quite content if the students entered Princeton knowing only those parts of Roman history that are not *so!*" [12] His class did not forget their professor's account of the signing of the Covenant on a Sunday in 1638, by rugged Scots, on a flat tombstone in Greyfriars' Churchyard. Sometimes they interrupted him with cheers, and many were moved to pursue into the library those paths of which he gave alluring glimpses. His language, the light in his eyes, the pleasing clarity and fullness of his voice—these made converts. Like his preaching father, he engendered courage, hope, faith—along with knowledge and understanding.

Wilson suffered torture from the strict standards of expression that his conscience forced upon him. In talking with students he sometimes used vivid slang phrases, but it was done with a wrinkling of his nose; and the crudeness of the language of his boys made him writhe. After helping to coach the debating team he feared to go to the debates, flinching at the thought of the pain that would strike him if his boys spoke ineffectively.

To many students Wilson was unique among professors as a personification of the majesty and power of ideas. To save time he rode a bicycle to class, in tall hat and striped trousers. His coattails flew out

12 George Dwight Kellogg to the writer.

and he pedaled at a precise pace, neither too fast nor too slow. Once a student, trying out one of the first motorcycles to burst upon the quiet village, came on Wilson bicycling outside the town and offered him a tow. The professor caught the rope that was thrown to him and put it over his handlebars; but, after being pulled to the edge of the village, he signaled the boy to stop, suggesting that it would not be appropriate for him to be seen crossing the campus at a breakneck pace behind a machine that conservatives then regarded as an invention of the devil.

When his boys came to him seeking a good subject for debate or suggestions for independent reading, or help in tutoring obtuse football players, or merely aid in getting out of a scrape, "Tommie" Wilson was their man. He was secretary of the board of football directors, and a delegate to the Intercollegiate Football Association; one autumn he drove the eleven through practice, giving more of inspiration than of useful instruction; and as long as he was at Princeton he kept an eye on the team and spoke in sympathy to boys who were injured. He served as class officer for the seniors and for five years as a member of one of the strictest discipline committees in the history of Princeton. In his course in public law, the first year, he gave few A's and one boy in thirteen flunked. Students thought his standards severe but knew him to be everlastingly fair. Year after year they voted him the most popular of professors. Almost everyone wanted to "take Wilson," and promising students came to Princeton just for that purpose. Very soon he became an institution.

In everything that the young professor did, he had an eye for morale and lifted the spirits of those about him. Breathing fresh air into the college's little parliament—its faculty meeting—he soon skirmished with President Patton. In 1893 the undergraduates petitioned that they be put on their honor as gentlemen and not patrolled as presumptive cheaters. Wilson, who had seen the honor system operate with success at the University of Virginia, supported the plea. President Patton, however, foreign born and less sympathetic than the Southern-bred professor with the code of honor of American lads of good breeding, took the floor and opposed the proposal with ridicule that hurt. White-hot with anger, Wilson kept his poise and pressed his arguments so eloquently that he carried the faculty with him. The honor system went into effect, to the joy of the undergraduates. From that time on, whenever "Tommie" Wilson spoke in faculty meeting there was a quickening of interest.

In the eighteen-nineties Wilson was much sought after as a lecturer and did his best to satisfy the popular craving for culture. He developed powers that could lead to greatness, though his talks seemed to some critics a bit too facile, too formally set in the lyceum style of the day. A fellow professor, turning away from a speech in which Grover Cleveland had banged home a truth with a trip-hammer sentence, remarked that that was "just the weapon for a President," and then went on to say: "You know, you don't want to have a President of the United States write with as fine a style as Woodrow Wilson." To reach prophetic stature the professor needed to be fired by the challenge of large issues and great occasions. He himself knew this, and wrote: "Style is an instrument, and is made imperishable only by embodiment in some great use."

Editors were commenting on the speeches of Woodrow Wilson and academic honors began to come to him. Old Joseph Wilson wrote from his theological school in Tennessee: "I am beginning to be known as the father of my son . . . You are preaching a gospel of order, and thus of safety, in the department of political morals and conduct, such as has not heretofore been heralded . . ."

It was in the field of education, however, rather than in politics that the first occasion arose to bring Wilson the orator into national prominence. When he began to apply his forensic power to the exaltation of American education, the colleges were growing fast and their presidents had great influence over national affairs. Students were coming in larger numbers from the homes of traders and manufacturers, and these boys and their parents often rebelled against clerical scholasticism. Graduate schools, professional schools—even technical schools—were springing up. Philosophy was being freed from theological bonds, and rhetoric and belles-lettres began to lose devotees. It was becoming clear that colleges that would remain in business would have to give their boys more freedom in choosing their work and more courses from which to select. Wilson was aware, too, as he returned to the campus in 1890, that the alumni were becoming the most important patrons, and thus the university was coming more and more to transmit its essential qualities.

Wilson found many changes at Princeton. McCosh had reformed the curriculum and had raised funds for several buildings, cannily making the most of the paradox that no university can be prosperous that is not on the verge of bankruptcy. Princeton was still under the spell of his personality, and buildings continued to sprout from seed that he had planted. The emphasis on science that marked the age was facilitated by improved laboratories and a new observatory. McCosh had boldly accepted the teaching of emancipated science, declaring that "when a scientific theory is brought before us, our first inquiry is not whether it is consistent with religion, but whether it is true." A course was offered on Harmony of Science and Religion.

In his championing of a rational view of science McCosh was a man after the heart of James Woodrow. A few years before Wilson came to teach at Princeton, this revered uncle had shaken Southern Presbyterianism to its foundations in an Olympian controversy. Unlike McCosh, whose magnetism could allay the resentment of even the stuffiest theologians, James Woodrow was not personally popular among all his Presbyterian brethren. A careful and calm thinker, he had exercised his brilliant mind in many fields, having taken a degree in science at Heidelberg, *summa cum laude,* superintended a Confederate laboratory for the making of medicines, promoted businesses, and printed religious journals and state papers. Delegating nothing, unlocking his own office, and keeping his own books, he was too busy to cultivate friendships.

James Woodrow respected nothing so much as truth, and finally insisted on telling his students in the Columbia Theological Seminary that the Darwinian hypothesis was "probably true." Some of his colleagues protested, and a schism developed in the faculty. Without giving Woodrow a chance to answer his inquisitors, the trustees elected another man to fill his chair. Though he cared nothing for his position —he had many other interests—James Woodrow saw and seized the opportunity to educate the brethren. He engaged in a battle that dragged on for three years, was threshed out in state synods, in the Augusta Presbytery, and finally, in 1888, in the General Assembly of the Southern Presbyterian Church.[13]

Woodrow Wilson was there at the trial before the General Assembly at Baltimore, sitting on the edge of his chair and all but cheering as James Woodrow's stilettos of dialectic, aimed without regard for tact or expediency, made his defamers writhe and his friendly advisers mutter: "*Why* did he have to say *that?* We told him *not* to say *that.*"[14] People who were acquainted with both nephew and uncle saw simi-

13 In most of the trials and hearings, Woodrow was not upheld. He was separated from the seminary and, as in the case of Joseph Wilson's controversy in 1873, the institution was shaken to its foundations. (Cf. p. 16 n.) In this case it had to close temporarily. Professor Woodrow held the respect of his denomination, however, and later served as president of South Carolina College and moderator of the Synod of South Carolina.

14 Edith Gittings Reid, who was present at the hearing with Dr. Thornton Whaling, to the writer. Also an article quoting Whaling, Louisville *Journal-Courier,* July 19, 1925.

larities in their characters—mental vigor, purposefulness, complete devotion to kith and kin, and capacity for protecting their inmost thought from both irrelevance and irreverence. To the idealistic nephew his dissenting uncle was a martyr.

Unlike McCosh and the Woodrows, President Patton found it hard to reconcile his Calvinist theology with the worldly impulses that were pressing the colleges; and he was particularly fearful of economic theories that might be regarded by some of the brethren as heresies. Nevertheless Professor Wilson, who thought utilitarian economics arid and too much complicated by mathematical calculation,[15], gave a course in political economy during his first year at Princeton in which he managed to explain current theories of socialism and Henry George's single-tax proposal. At first, boys from conservative families thought their professor a "radical"; but soon they realized that he was doing his duty as a competent teacher. He compiled notes for an elective course in socialism in 1890, but it was not given. When he suggested that his assistant teach sociology, Patton's religious scruples were touched and he ruled that, if work in a new field must be provided, public finance would be a safer subject. Much as Patton's brilliant preaching was admired by Wilson, he thought the president suffering from "paralysis of the will."

Wilson was given an opportunity in 1893 to present his own convictions regarding education when he was asked to speak at the World's Fair at Chicago, before the International Congress of Education. His subject was specific and limiting. However, he injected life into his talk by taking the point of view of the average citizen rather than that of the expert. Speaking for "the self-interest of the community," this scholar who had himself rebelled against a formal doctoral examination now criticized the selfishness of students who wished to get professional degrees quickly so that they might turn them into cash. He struck out at overspecialization—"that partial knowledge which is the most dangerous form of ignorance"—and argued that professional men should get a liberal education along with their technical training. Many of his ideas came forth again the next year in other addresses, and he was recognized far and wide as a spokesman for the adjustment of education to the needs of the age.

[15] In "Of the Study of Politics," which appeared in the *New Princeton Review* of March, 1887, Wilson showed a distrust of economic generalizations that reflected his devotion to Bagehot, the "literary politician" of London. Wilson set down the new-school economists as "doctrinaire" and called their so-called picture of life a mere "theorem of trade." He objected that they deliberately stripped man of all motives save self-interest.

In the autumn of 1896 came an occasion that brought the "noticeable man" to the platform at Princeton before august scholars and statesmen. His "primary" ambition was stirred, and his deep affection for Princeton called forth every volt of oratorical power that he could generate. The Old College of New Jersey had awakened to the new voices, and on the hundred fiftieth anniversary of its founding was to become Princeton University. Woodrow Wilson, the favorite lecturer of the undergraduates, was invited to be the orator of the day. This was the great opportunity for which he had been preparing since boyhood. He must not fail.

After a summer of travel in Europe, his ideas finally took shape. On Nassau Street, one day, his bicycle overtook a colleague's buggy and he shouted: "I've decided on my opening sentence. That means the battle is won." The first magic words had sprouted, the phrases were in blossom, the whole had been pruned into noble prose: "Princeton pauses to look back upon her past, not as an old man grown reminiscent, but as a prudent man still in his youth and lusty prime and at the threshold of new tasks, who would remind himself of his origin and lineage, recall the pledges of his youth, and assess as at a turning in his life the duties of his station."

The title of Wilson's address—"Princeton in the Nation's Service"—made it apparent that he was resolved to strike at issues that were fundamental and general in American colleges. "It has never been natural, it has seldom been possible," he said, "in this country for learning to seek a place apart and hold aloof from affairs." The Presbyterian ministers who founded Princeton, he pointed out, acted as if under obligation to society rather than to the church. Religion, conceive it but liberally enough, is the true salt wherewith to keep both duty and learning sweet against the taint of time and change; and it is a noble thing to have conceived it thus liberally, as Princeton's founders did . . . Duty with them was a practical thing, concerned with righteousness in this world, as well as with salvation in the next."

Having looked to the past to see what gave the place its spirit and its air of duty, Wilson talked of "progress": "There is nothing so conservative of life as growth; when that stops, decay sets in and the end comes on apace. Progress is life, for the body politic as for the body natural. To stand still is to court death."

With this assertion, however, went a warning: "Not all change is progress, not all growth is the manifestation of life." He was much mistaken, he went on, if the scientific spirit of the age was not doing a great disservice. For the achievements of science Wilson had only praise, but he objected to the projection of the scientific spirit into other fields of thought: "It has made the legislator confident that he can create, and the philosopher sure that God cannot. Past experience is discredited and the laws of matter are supposed to apply to spirit and the make-up of society." He suspected science of having enhanced passions by making wealth "so quick to come, so fickle to stay."

"Can anyone wonder, then," he went on, "that I ask for the old drill, the old memory of times gone by, the old schooling in precedent and tradition, the old keeping of faith with the past, as a preparation for leadership in days of social change? . . . Of course, when all is said, it is not learning but the spirit of service that will give a college place in the public annals of the nation. . . . We dare not keep aloof and closet ourselves while a nation comes to its maturity. The days of glad expansion are gone, our life grows tense and difficult; our resource for the future lies in careful thought, providence, and a wise economy; and the school must be the nation." He had read a draft of his speech to Ellen Wilson and she had asked for a Miltonian touch, and so he had conjured up an exalted dream of a scholar's paradise. And then, at the very end, he asked a question: "Who shall show us the way to this place?"

The applause left little doubt about the answer. Princeton, in the person of Woodrow Wilson, had an hour of triumph before the nation and the world. At last the full power of the whole man had come forth in dazzling brilliance. There was a blissful truce in the intermittent war between his conscience and his impulses. It healed his strained nerves to hear the cheering that interrupted the oration time and again and to have his hand wrung by Princetonians who were in a frenzy of pride because one of their number, a homebred, had so moved a gathering so distinguished. Editors quoted and commented, and a magazine published the address in full. Commanding the respect of both scholar and Philistine, the prophet had won eminence in his own land.

But still his striving for style did not slacken. "After forty years," a friend said, "your style is yourself—as much as the shape of your hands. You couldn't, you shouldn't try to change it." His laugh was a little wistful as he said: "You are thinking of a man who has arrived; I, of one imprisoned in a task." [16]

16 Reid, op. cit., 81–82.

Wilson's triumph at Princeton's Sesquicentennial gave his name luster in the eyes of the trustees. One of them wrote to him that there was no honor too high for him in the future so far as Princeton was concerned; and several alumni, to hold him for five years, volunteered to pay him $2,400 annually in addition to his salary.

The new age was demanding strong men who would apply business efficiency to matters that could not be allowed to drift at the mercy of sentiment and theological conviction; but at the same time the new type of leader must be a man whose academic record would command the respect of teachers. For the next few years, when an important university post became vacant, eyes usually turned toward the professor at Princeton. The University of Virginia, feeling that an administrator was needed to preside over its faculty, wooed its prominent alumnus; but Wilson feared that by accepting he would end his literary career and hurt beloved Princeton.

If a call came from his own institution, his answer might be different. However, he gave no evidence that such a possibility was prominent in his thoughts at the turn of the century and seemed rather to withdraw from administrative affairs and to wrap himself in literary work and to retire into a world of historical truth. Writing was the escape most accessible to him, and it gave opportunity to commune with his permanent gods, think in terms of "the chief end of man," political principles, the common good; and he could continue to go his own way without giving offense to others. His wife, seeing that both his soul's longings and practical necessity would be served, cheered him on and criticized his work. "I shall write for you," he told her. "We must be partners in this . . . else I shall grow cold to the marrow, and write without blood or life."

During the years near the turn of the century, Wilson was still exercising his style in literary essays; but his major effort in this period went into two works in history that were written for the general reader. He had already made his mark as a historian in a small book entitled *Division and Reunion,* which treated the political history of the United States between 1828 and 1893. In it he had shown himself able to write objectively about Civil War and Reconstruction. This was the more remarkable because he was in Georgia, body and soul, during the summers when he was composing the book. He still loved the old South of tradition. "Bless the old section," he wrote to Dabney, "as it was before the 'money Devil' entered into it!" But he did his scholarly duty and judged the South to have been legally right, but historically wrong. Northern critics marveled that this Southern historian had stood so apart from his background, and *Division and Reunion*, ably edited by Professor Albert Bushnell Hart of Harvard, was accepted as his best work in history.

The author was pleased when a note came from Professor Frederick J. Turner of Wisconsin, proclaiming that the book had "vitality—a flesh and blood form." [17] Wilson had lectured to Turner at the Johns Hopkins and they had boarded at the same house. They talked and corresponded much, and Turner had thrilled his friend by reading aloud to him his revolutionary paper on "The Significance of the Frontier in American History." Wilson already had revolted against the concept that viewed American development as a projection of New England across the continent. "The typical Americans," he asserted, "have all been Western men, with the exception of Washington."

Unfortunately for Wilson's reputation as a historian, this "exception" diverted him from his deeper purposes. He wrote, for book and serial publication in 1897, what passed as a biography of George Washington. Actually it was a long essay on American history of the eighteenth century, with the hero strutting on and off the scene, on stilts. Old Joseph Wilson perceived that his son's love of the picturesque and the dramatic had got out of hand. "Woodrow," he remarked, "I'm glad you let Washington do his own dying." Unlike the boyish author who had flared up at those who had scoffed at his first book, the professional writer of *George Washington* not only accepted criticism meekly but added some of his own.

Wilson wished to undertake profitable historical writing that would be more significant. In 1894 he had tried without avail to interest Scribner's in a popular history of the United States and had assured their editor, his friend Bridges, that he would be "quite as slow as may be decent" in coming to terms with a publisher. He had never been one to bargain, having once instructed an agent to sell a piece of his Princeton real estate to a friend on terms as advantageous as possible to the buyer. At the turn of the century, however, he felt that he had been too

---

[17] F. J. Turner to W.W., Dec. 24, 1894, Wilson Papers. Wilson did his best to lure Professor Frederick J. Turner from Wisconsin to Princeton; but a financial impasse that President Patton did not break finally forced Wilson to write to his friend on Dec. 12, 1896: "A plague on boards of trustees! . . . Our president daunts us by having no will or policy at all." *See* W. R. Jacobs, "Wilson's First Battle at Princeton," *Harvard Library Bulletin*, Winter, 1954, pp. 74–87. Wilson continued, however, to correspond warmly with the great historian, who wrote a few years later: "You can make your letters bring you more nearly in person than anyone else I know." Turner to W.W., Mar. 12, 1900. As early as 1889, Turner saw in Wilson a future President of the United States. Letter, Fulton Mood to the writer, July 11, 1951.

sentimental in his literary business; and when George Harvey of Harper's offered $12,000 for a history of the United States in twelve installments, author and publisher came to terms for the most extensive of Wilson's published works—*A History of the American People.*[18]

Actually, the feverish wooing of style served only to water the historical sense of the work to a thinness that, to the taste of professional historians, approached insipidity. "A *tour de force* of fine writing," one of his colleagues called it. The author himself was not fond of his longest work. To a friend who asked about the reception of the book he wrote: "I have reason to believe that it is growing in popularity and will prove a useful work. Walking along the street last week I saw a faker at the corner selling patent medicine. He was standing on a box marked 'Wilson's *History of the American People.'* If all the fakers in the country buy this book I ought to be satisfied. Don't you think so?" Realizing that John Fiske was using a surer and a lighter touch in making literature of history, the professor said with a rueful smile: "I wish he would keep out of my bailiwick."

Yet there were in his historical writings certain political themes that were sacred. Still mindful of James Bryce's slighting of history in his description of the American commonwealth, Wilson had an eye for the forces that had given vitality to America's exercise of democracy. In his view the life of the frontier was such a force. He could see here a connecting link between the stirrings of democracy in the Old World that he had studied and written about and the moving, vital spirit of political adjustment that was to him the hope and salvation of America.

Complaining that scholars were parching their story in a desert of footnotes, Wilson conceived of the history of nations as spiritual, not material, a thing not of institutions but of the heart and the imagination. "I love history" he wrote to Turner, "and think that there are few things so directly rewarding and worthwhile for their own sakes as to

18 "I am corrupted," Wilson wrote to his Hopkins classmate, Franklin Jameson. ". . . it is a piece of work I meant to do anyway,—and I alter the quality not a bit,—nor dilute the stuff, neither,—to suit the medium." Writing to Turner about the difficulty of weaving the story of the American colonies into historical narrative, Wilson said: "I pray it may grow easier or it will kill me. And yet it would be a most pleasant death. The ardour of the struggle is inspiriting. There is a pleasure in the very pain,—as when one bites on an aching tooth." W.W. to Turner, Dec. 27, 1894, in Jacobs, *op. cit.,* pp. 74–87.

Lay readers bought Wilson's *History* by the thousands, from agents who came into their homes and offices. Published in *Harper's Magazine* in 1901 and in five volumes in 1902, the work went through many editions and was translated into several foreign languages. Within two years of publication, the author was rewarded by royalties larger than any theretofore received in the same time for any work of nonfiction of a similar number of words. In 1900, Wilson's "extra earnings" from writings and lecturing amounted to more than $7,000. It was still a source of regret, however, that he lacked means to give his little Nellie a pony.

scan the history of one's own country with a careful eye, and write of it with the all absorbing desire to get its cream and spirit out." These were not the concerns of a historian's historian; and yet Wilson was accepted into the brotherhood of the American Historical Society. At a meeting of that organization he fell into an acrimonious discussion with Henry Cabot Lodge,[19] a Harvard-trained scholar who saw history from a New England bias and had written a biography of George Washington that was scarcely more scholarly than Wilson's.

Meanwhile, as Professor Wilson devoted himself to profitable writing in history, the drums of revolt were beating more insistently on the Princeton campus. Dissatisfaction with Patton's administration mounted. He was criticized, during the summer of 1899, by malcontents who gathered on the porch of Professor Andrew West. The alumni, now more numerous and better organized than ever, doubted that the president shared their sentimental devotion to the college. They grew impatient with his inertia. Patton went to football games only from a sense of duty, while Wilson went as a "rooter" for Princeton, swinging along in step with the band, sitting in the stands with his cane between his knees, thumping it and cheering in a loud staccato when his "Tigers" scored. Men like Wilson and Professor Henry B. Fine took up the intellectual leadership that Patton shirked.

Finally, in 1902, one of the trustees wrote to the president to ask for his resignation "in order to make way for urgent needs in the matter of university reform." Patton, weary and content to withdraw into his own studies, gave in. He resented criticism of his administration by trustees who had made Professor Andrew West dean of graduate students. And now, to prevent the choice of West as his successor, he suddenly recommended the university's greatest orator, the idol of the undergraduates, the favorite of the younger alumni and the Western men, but a man with little executive experience—Woodrow Wilson.

Twenty-four of the twenty-eight trustees of the university—ex-President Grover Cleveland was among them for the first time—met with Patton on June 9, 1902, accepted the president's resignation, and appointed a committee on the choice of a successor. That very afternoon the committee reported that they had agreed with the president on the name of Wilson. Suspending a section of the bylaws that would have delayed the final balloting, a unanimous vote was cast for the popular

[19] Edward Channing to Stewart Mitchell to the writer. For criticism of Lodge's *George Washington, see* John A. Garraty, *Henry Cabot Lodge,* pp. 57–59. Writing to Howard Pyle, illustrator of his own *George Washington,* Wilson referred to Lodge's life of Washington as the "latest authoritative biography," but a "secondary authority." W.W. to Pyle, Jan. 12, 1896.

professor, and three trustees of the Class of '79 went immediately to notify their classmate.

Though not surprised, the house of Wilson was overwhelmed by the speed and unanimity of the action. Ellen Wilson had noted that her husband had "a great taste for administration" and had been successful as chairman of important committees, but she wrote now to a friend: "It is enough to frighten a man to be so loved and believed in." Sheafs of congratulatory messages came in. Old Joseph Wilson, lying in his son's home on his deathbed, sent for his three granddaughters and, peering from deep-set eyes that had softened almost to tears, said solemnly: "Never forget what I tell you. Your father is the greatest man I have ever known . . . This is just the beginning of a very great career." [20]

In facing up to his responsibility Wilson was both humble and confident. "Definite, tangible tasks," he thought, would take "the flutter and restlessness" from his spirits. He might have doubted whether he was the man for the job had he not been for a long time intimately acquainted with the life of the university. If he had needed chastening he would have found it in a message from his old chum Dabney: "Who could have guessed that an Illimitable Idiot would ever be selected as the President of a great university?"

There was criticism of the haste with which the new leader had been chosen, and it was noted that Wilson was the first president of Princeton without formal theological training. But the tradition of his family guaranteed that he would not depart from the spirit of the old religion, and there was no doubt that he belonged to the campus in mind and body and soul. He was thrilled when the applause of reunioning alumni assured him that the Princeton family loved him. But with his exaltation he felt a twinge of renunciation. "No doubt I shall have to give up writing for the next three or four years," he wrote, "and that is a heartbreaking thing for a fellow who has not yet written the particular thing for which he has been training all his life."

Near the end of October, crowds poured into the little village for the inauguration. Orange-and-black banners floated against red and yellow leaves and the slanting sun struck everything into gold. Scores of educational dignitaries of America and Europe fell into line. The great of the nation were there—Grover Cleveland and Theodore Roosevelt,

[20] Eleanor Wilson McAdoo, *The Woodrow Wilsons*, pp. 59–60. The year before, at Wilmington, the preacher had told his Negro servant, David Bryant, that someday "Mr. Tommie" would be a candidate for the Presidency of the United States and made the Negro promise to cast a vote as his proxy.

J. P. Morgan and Mark Twain, George Harvey and Walter Hines Page. Lawrence Lowell of Harvard was a house guest of the Wilsons'. Booker T. Washington came, and at the dinner following the ceremonies made what Wilson thought was the best speech of the occasion.

To Woodrow Wilson the inaugural address was as vital as the first speech of a prime minister to a parliament. In "Princeton in the Nation's Service," at the Sesquicentennial, he had talked of the institution's great past and had set a spiritual tone for its future. Now, however, he must come to grips with immediate issues.

In meeting the rising demand for technical and professional education, he explained, universities had so spread and diversified the scheme of knowledge that it had lost coherence. Of the two supreme tasks of a great university—"the production of a great body of informed and thoughtful men and the production of a small body of trained scholars and investigators"—Wilson was concerned chiefly with the former. The new president could not be satisfied with anything less than "a full liberation of the faculties" of the undergraduates; and yet he felt that in the organization of a university, as in a political democracy, there must be discipline and system before there could be effective freedom. He would pick up the "threads of system" that had been dropped, would knit them together in a comprehensive course of study that the undergraduates and his preceptors would plan together.

The prophet reminded his audience that he had charge "not of men's fortunes, but of their spirits." The final synthesis of learning is in philosophy, he said, and he held the philosophy of conduct dear. He advocated the "energy of a positive faith," insisting that "we are not put into this world to sit and know; we are put into it to act." The new generation "must be supplied with men who care more for principles than for money, for the right adjustments of life than for the gross accumulations of profit . . . We are here not merely to release the faculties of men for their own use, but also to quicken their social understanding, instruct their consciences, and give them the catholic vision of those who know their just relations to their fellow men."

If the Sesquicentennial address had been a Gospel, this was The Acts. Those who heeded it knew that the days of drift were over. Afterward the orator's friends crowded around him, cheering incessantly. He appealed to them for understanding and confidence: "I ask that you will look upon me not as a man to do something apart, but as a man who asks the privilege of leading you and being believed in by you while he tries to do the things in which he knows you believe." The still-youthful executive yearned to be loved and trusted as passionately as he insisted on crusading for what he thought right; and in the two passions—the bonhomie and the Covenanter's devotion to Truth—was potential enough to tear the man asunder when the currents crossed.

Some among the alumni may not have been converted, some may not even have understood, but they could not fail to note that "people said" that their man Wilson was a great leader. They were convinced that he would keep school faithfully and that the boys would like him, and surely this Scot would use money thriftily. As for his "principles," they were, to some of the Princeton family, just good talk. "Very beautiful speech of Wilson's, very noble," remarked a visiting journalist, "but over the heads of two trustees who sat in front of me."

It was over the head, also, of William J. Thompson, "Duke" of the Gloucester race track, a little Democratic politician who sat in the audience and was overwhelmed by the power of the speaker. Perceiving only that this orator would make a "great candidate," he boasted: "Why, I could twiddle that man right around my fingers. . . . I know the boys who can reach him."

CHAPTER V

FAMILY MAN

THE NOTICEABLE MAN was now president of a great university. The independent critic, the rollicking chum, the heady lover, the wooer of the Muses—all these fell now under the pressure of pastoral responsibility. The eloquent prophecy that had stirred the Princeton constituency would have to be tempered by tact and patience; for as the servant-leader of an academic community he must concern himself not only with principles but with men of many kinds—those whom he had to love as well as those whom he liked to love.

Soon after coming to Princeton to teach, Wilson had written to his father: "My mind cannot give me gratification. I know it too well and it is a poor thing. I have to rely on my heart as the sole source of contentment and happiness, and that craves, oh, so fiercely, the companionship of those I love." In the early nineties, in a house that the Wilsons rented on Library Place, there had been time to revel in the love of kin and the comradeship of friends. In the absence of shows, automobiles, and country clubs, the college faculty found their recreation in good conversation. And they talked brilliantly: Harry Fine, blunt and hearty, an unwavering disciple of Wilson's educational principles; Jack Hibben, whom the students toasted as "the whitest man in all the fac"; George Harper, authority on beloved Wordsworth; charming Bliss Perry; quizzical Winthrop Daniels; witty President Patton. There were guests, too, from the outside world; Humphry Ward, Walter Hines Page, and Mark Twain. Ellen Wilson arranged that brilliant men and women should come into their drawing room.

When there was occasion to meet strangers, however, Wilson often turned shy and made excuses. Ellen would have to coax him; but, once introduced, he enjoyed himself and dominated the talk. After telling a story he did not chuckle, but fixed a challenging eye on his hearers until they laughed. People who saw Wilson in repose often thought him homely; but once his countenance burst into conversation, they watched his mouth in awe at the precision of the words that came from it. In familiar conversation he was not didactic, and he was utterly candid.

In one breath he could be witty, ridiculous, profound. He could listen well, too, to talk worthy of his mettle. Emotional reactions showed in his face, and usually he could respond with an anecdote or comment that was pat. When his mind worked at its highest pitch, he dazzled even those who knew him best.

His powers of talk ran riot in the presence of ladies whom he thought "charming and conversable"; and it often happened that he thought the more charming the more conversable. He liked to air his literary fancies before what he regarded as the "deeper sensibilities" and "finer understanding" of intelligent women. He particularly enjoyed the "lightly turned laughter" of ladies of the South. When he discovered feminine charm he would write to his Ellen about it with the ardor of a prospector striking gold. Like his father, he enjoyed playing the lion with women who could crack the whip of conversation sharply and deftly. But at a hint of sensuality, heaviness, or petty jealousies he revolted. There were only a few women quick enough in word and understanding to hold his friendship through the years.

Feeling that she was not by nature "gamesome," Ellen Wilson encouraged and shared her husband's friendships with brilliant ladies. And his gallant adventures served only to raise the pedestal on which he kept his Ellen enthroned. ("I am not a fellow to be imposed upon, Madam, by superficial charms or a first impression. Very few people, alas! wear well with me; but your charm deepens with every year . . .") They kept their covenant, made before their marriage, to be quite open with each other in everything. All their treasures were held in common—books, money, pleasures, and friends, both men and women. Their opinions often differed, but even their closest relatives never heard them quarrel. His letters courted her constantly. Sometimes she would read them to her daughters, occasionally skipping a page or two, saying with a smile, "This part is sacred."

As the strain of Wilson's duties became heavier and began to tell on his health, his wife watched over him, realizing, as she said to a friend, that "a woman's place is to keep one little spot in the world quiet."

In her home she created an atmosphere in which a man could transmute his love into literary achievement. Beaming warmly on the family teasing that eddied around her, she did not allow her husband's impatience with stupidity to get out of hand. When Wilson, in the privacy of the family, blurted out an opinion that was hasty or unkind, his wife would say: "Oh, Woodrow, you don't mean that." And the professor would reply: "Madam, I ventured to think that I meant that until I was corrected." Ellen Wilson could be intense in argument, but never showed bad temper except when she thought her husband unfairly attacked or imposed upon.

She had books before her as she dressed in the morning, and she read aloud at night. One moment she would soar with the poets into a realm in which she could best release her husband from his implacable conscience. Or, alone, she would burrow into a deep work in history or philosophy and lose herself in it until some of her family came in and made a game of catching her attention with signs, whispers, clearings of the throat, and finally, voices. Then she would be all sympathetic eagerness, keen to listen and advise.

Under masses of coppery hair and bangs that hid a forehead that she thought too high, her brown eyes shone with varied lights, now tender in sympathy, now bright with laughter. Before going out to parties she sometimes crushed rose leaves and applied them to her cheeks with a rabbit's foot that she kept hidden in a drawer for shame at such stooping to artifice.

Life in the household moved with a smooth rhythm. Fresh flowers were kept in their bedroom. Nothing was out of place: not so much as one stocking was allowed to lie on the floor. Ellen Wilson made dresses for herself and her girls and one year took pride in spending less for clothes than her husband spent for books. She trained two white servants, who stood loyally by her for decades. Drawling softly, she imparted to the cook the secrets of the Southern dishes that her husband relished. Sitting at lunch with him after a morning of proofreading, they would make a game of their labors. "I dare not have the blues!" she wrote to a girlhood friend. "If I am just a little sky blue he immediately becomes blue-black!"

In this serene home Wilson achieved an output that would have been creditable even for a man who did nothing but write. Though at first without secretarial help, he responded to appeals from dozens of relatives and personal friends, whether they wanted advice, criticism, money, or sympathy. He initiated projects in correspondence, too— sometimes more than he could carry through. Even with the aid of shorthand, the mechanical labor of writing became so great at one time that he suffered severely from neuritis, or "writer's cramp," and lost the use of his right hand for months. For a while he depended on his wife to write letters for him; but soon he had driven himself to learn to write clearly with his left hand. And by massage, rest, and regular exercises his ailing right hand was restored to usefulness.

His driving conscience worked his mind as hard as his muscles. When his train of expression came to an unbridged chasm he did not boggle. Keeping his thoughts straight on the course, he sat rigid over his typewriter, conjuring up a trestle of words. When the *mot juste* eluded him, he forced himself to sit with his fingers on the keys and make the right word come. He had no doubt that the word that came was the right one. "A Yankee always thinks that he is right, a Scotch-Irishman *knows* that he is right," he liked to quote. His discipline and concentration increased with the years and permitted him to plow through work with a smoothness that concealed the worry that it cost him. But as he neared the end of his longest book his mind became so jaded that one afternoon, going upstairs to dress for dinner, he absent-mindedly undressed and climbed into bed. Ellen Wilson made a joke of it, and yet worried about him and persuaded him to bicycle in England the next summer.

In the early nineties he had traveled far in America, making lecture trips to Chicago, to Massachusetts, and to Colorado. But it was not until cramps attacked his arm, in 1896, that he made his first trip abroad. He went alone, seeing the things that appealed to him most, writing frankly and freshly to his Ellen of his enthusiasms and impressions. To her he sent grass from the grave of Adam Smith, a leaf from the burial place of Walter Bagehot, to be pressed and kept for him. The colleges of Cambridge struck him as "beyond measure attractive," and a mere glance at Oxford was "enough to take one's heart by storm." From his visits to the universities he drew inspiration for his later work at Princeton. ". . . and yet," he asserted, "I have not seen a prettier dwelling than ours in England!"

Mostly he occupied his time with pilgrimages to literary shrines—the cottage in which Burns was born, the Shakespeare country, the plain church and simple tablet beside which Burke lay, and most exhilarating of all, the Lake Country and Wordsworthian shrines. Of all landscapes that he saw, the River Wye won his heart most completely; and sitting on a grassy bank near Tintern Abbey he was filled with exalted emotion as he quoted from Wordsworth.

At London he looked up James Bryce, invited him to lecture at Princeton. Big cities were distasteful to him, and he stayed in the capital only long enough to see as few specific objects as possible, besides the Abbey, the Museum, the National Gallery, and the House of Commons.

Again, in 1899, Wilson went off to the British Isles at his wife's insistence, this time with Stockton Axson, Ellen's brother. His conscience hurt him because he feared that he was not tired enough to justify the expense and pain of separation. "Here I am simply spending money and pining for you!" he wrote to his Ellen.

He went over much of the same ground as in 1896 but passed more time in the Burns country. Bicycling from Scotland to England, traveling sometimes thirty miles in a day, he was impressed by the privacy of walled gardens, the English tradition that a man's home is his castle. Stopping at modest inns, he would slake his thirst with a mild whisky-and-soda. He made a second visit to Bagehot's grave, and to Wells, which seemed "to retain her antiquity alive," and where, he wrote, "take it all in all, I should rather be than anywhere else in England." The travelers lounged on the sward near Ely Cathedral, then by the smooth River Cam and in the close at New College, Oxford, sitting out the long summer evenings. After a trip to Dublin, where he wandered through the greens of Trinity College with his thoughts full of Burke, he sailed for home from Glasgow. In a fog the ship struck an iceberg and careened badly. Most of the passengers feared that she would go down, but when Axson went up on deck he found his comrade chatting and laughing casually with a friend. Afterward Wilson said that he considered this a test of his nerve in an emergency.

From each of his foreign tours he came home revived; and it sustained his lifted spirits to feel once more the love of his "three little thoroughbreds" and their incomparable mother. It was good to sit again at his own hearth in the evening, with his Ellen beside him, embroidering and mending while she helped her daughters with their lessons. And in the daytime he would come upon her making paper dolls and teaching the girls how to color them, or tucked away in her own room painting a portrait of a daughter.

The Wilsons tried to give their children serenity of soul, as well as knowledge and grace. On the Sabbath their household was slowed down. No games were permitted, and only readings that built character. The Wilsons did not send their daughters along the easy and conventional path to Sunday school. Feeling that most teachers in church schools were not trained to give a true view of religion, Ellen Wilson gave Bible lessons to her daughters in her own room. Mostly, the parents taught by example, making virtue attractive and good manners and morals habitual. "I feel daily more and more bent," Wilson once wrote to his father, "toward creating in my own children that combined respect and tender devotion for their father that you gave your children for you. Oh, how happy I should be, if I could make them think of me as I think of you!" Though sobered by paternity, Wilson felt "a great deal of the boy revived" in him by the companionship of his little ones.

In the few instances in which moral suasion was not enough, Ellen Wilson spanked. Her face grew pink, and she was as likely as the child to shed tears; but she did not bother her husband with accounts of this unpleasantness. To the girls their father was all tenderness, gaiety, and play. He had a way with children. First he would listen solemnly to whatever childish concept they might express, then he would use his mobile face and dramatic talent to amuse them, perhaps blowing his cheeks into balloons to be patted by childish fingers, or pulling out loose flesh on his face and snapping it, or letting his chin sag lower, notch by notch. His hands seemed to his children to have life of their own. He could make his fingers creep like animals on the arm of his chair, or slapping his knees he could do the galloping horse—slappety-slap, slappety-slap, growing louder and then fading gradually as if in the distance. A little playmate of his sister-in-law called him "a regular guy."

Insisting that the girls be punctual at meals, he came to breakfast at eight o'clock sharp. Before eating he said a formal blessing, slowly and reverently; but grace was not offered at the end of meals, as in the homes of some church folk of that day. Instead, after breakfast and lunch, the children were dismissed by delicious nonsense, jingled in singsong: "Now, chickens, run upstairs, wash your face and hands, brush your teeth and put your bibs away before I count three—or I'll tickle, pinch, and spank-doodle you."

In the evening, after the "now-I-lay-mes" were said, the father read Uncle Remus or sat by the nursery fire and sang "Sweet and Low," "Watchman, Tell Us of the Night," and lilting rhymes of nonsense. Once, when Nellie had scarlet fever, Wilson relieved his wife in keeping vigil, building with the child's blocks in favorite Norman designs. He fed the little one and slept beside her, wrote letters for her and sent them to her sisters in a basket that traveled on a pulley that he had rigged. Visiting the sickroom of his little sister-in-law when she was shaken by malarial fever, he cheered her by telling of a victim of chills who shivered so hard that when he drank milk it turned to butter. And as he told the story his supple body shuddered, acting it out.

For economy, the furnace was kept low. Wilson himself stoked it, taking aim as carefully as when he tried to play golf on a rough course that colleagues had laid out back of his house. He enjoyed working in the garden, sometimes mowed the lawn, and polished his shoes; and one night when a guest left his boots outside the door, Wilson polished those too. Each year he and his Ellen budgeted his salary.

As the children grew and relatives joined the household, more space was needed. And so the Wilsons decided to build a new house, to stand on a lot next to the one in which they were living. There were trees ready grown for the family to worship: pines and oaks, a large sycamore, and in the rear a radiant copper beech, with huge limbs spaced just right for climbing, and beneath them a sun-speckled fairyland for children's play. The beech was the chief reason, Ellen Wilson told her friends, for building on this lot.

Wishing to temper dignity with grace, the Wilsons chose the half-stone, half-stucco style of the English Norman country home, with trimmings of stained wood. They spent hours in discussing the line of the roof. Woodrow drew the plans and Ellen made a clay model; and when the architects' bids ran $2,000 above their resources, he resolved to lecture for the University Extension Society to make up the difference. For a hedge they decided on privet, for quick growth. Their children were offered a nickel for every basket of weeds that they pulled from the lawn. Flowers and shrubs were planted copiously, and ivy to creep on the walls. After a year of building, Ellen Wilson supervised the moving in; and her husband came home one night to find everything installed in the new house: furniture, pictures, maids, children, canary, and Puffins the cat.

On the first floor back was a spot sacred to Wilson alone—his study. Here were hung likenesses of the professor's favorite gods: over the mantel his father; and elesewhere crayon enlargements that Ellen Wilson had made of Washington, Webster, Gladstone, Bagehot, and Burke. These were the only ornaments of the room. It had the air of a place of business. The drawers of the desk were labeled in neat script, and there were metal filing cases and a revolving bookcase. Two of the walls were lined to the ceiling with books. They were accumulating rapidly. Ponderous tomes were arriving for a study of the German legal system. When students came to his office he put them at ease with courtesy and good humor, and insisted that they call him not *Dr.* or *Professor*, but *Mr.* Wilson. Once convinced of the good faith of those who came to him, he would talk to them like a father. When a boy whom he tried to help failed to confide in him, he was distressed; but he could be brusque with those bent merely on ingratiating themselves.

In his composition, as in his professional appointments, the professor was a clock of regularity. He never left his desk in disorder, but wiped his pen, put it in place, closed the inkwell, tidied his papers, covered his typewriter, and returned the books that he had been using to their places on the shelves. From a window seat he could look out into the garden and watch his children at play under the glorious copper beech. When they came to the window or to his door, he was not too preoccupied to give a quick, loving glance. He never demanded absolute quiet in the house while he worked; but when quarreling broke out he would call the girls into his study, ask them what the trouble was, and explain gently the rights and wrongs of the case. Once, when the little Wilsons and Clevelands fought with neighbors of Republican heritage, he said: "You must never quarrel about religion or politics. Both are very private, and you will never change anyone's mind." [1] When the children tried to divide the world among themselves, he arranged straws for them to draw.

When the roll top of their father's desk slammed, the lock clicked and the youngsters heard a soft whistle and a jingling of keys. They knew then that their choicest playfellow might join them for merrymaking. They voted their father "the world's greatest orator" and thought him capable of being president of the United State or of anything else. But sometimes, when the problems of composition seemed insuperable, Woodrow Wilson threatened to give himself to the writing of stories for children. Once, attacking hypocrisy in education, he said: "We must believe the things we tell the children."

Growing older, the Wilson girls sat up evenings with the family in the central living room, where their father would prance and jig with them. Or he might take off a drunk, or a stuffy, monocled Englishman. He could tell stories in dialect—Scottish, Irish, and Negro. Dressing up for a charade, he would put on a lady's hat and a feather boa, wrap himself in a long velvet curtain, hold one hand high for a "social" handshake, and gush in high falsetto in burlesque of a grand dame. Sometimes it would be the "heavy villain" of melodrama, or a Fourth of July orator who gestured with his legs instead of his arms. Or he would take up the Ouija board, ask it the name of the latest beau of one of the girls, and regard her dismay with a chuckle as the name of the most outlandish campus character was spelled out.[2] Often his clear tenor would pour out "The Kerry Dance" or "The Duke of Plaza-Toro," a

---

[1] Eleanor Wilson McAdoo to the writer, March 10, 1952.
[2] F. C. MacDonald and Eleanor Wilson McAdoo to the writer.

Scottish ballad or an old hymn of the kirk. He liked quaint sayings such as "Good Lord deliver us from witches and warlords and from things that say woo-oo in the night."

On New Year's Eve, in Scottish fashion, the clan gathered in the dining room, drank a toast, sang "Auld Lang Syne," standing each with one foot on a chair and the other on the table, and then ran to open the front door so that the old year might go and the new year enter. On one of these occasions the president of Princeton threw his family into fits of laughter by mimicking the classic figures that stood in the hall—a proud Roman emperor and Apollo with finger coyly poised. Sometimes he feared the very momentum of his own spirits, once confessing that he "dared not let himself go because he did not know where to stop." [3]

He was as clever in conjuring up rhymes to fit occasions as was his wife in quoting serious verse that was apropos. Often he called his memory the "silliest" in the world, for he never forgot a nonsense rhyme and didn't know one piece of fine poetry by heart. Yet he loved to read and to hear his Ellen read the English poets. Wordsworth was his favorite: he himself aspired to be "the happy warrior"; his Ellen was to him "a phantom of delight." When *A Shropshire Lad* was read to him, Wilson was repelled, asked whether it was *all* about wanting to die, and turned to Henry V—"something with good red blood in it."

Often relatives joined in the fellowship of the home on Library Place. They came to make visits in the Southern tradition—to stay for weeks, months, sometimes years—and the Wilsons were not hurried or flurried. Ever since their marriage they had planned for the education of kinfolk who had less of the world's goods. Wilson threw gentle, fatherly protection over all the clan. He would draw out confidences from each one and he taught them that selfishness was very nearly the deadliest of sins and the root of most crime. It was assumed in the household that one tested one's conduct by asking whether it would be possible to "sleep happily with one's self." But Wilson would not allow holier-than-thou criticism of even the black sheep of the clan. "After all," he would say, "he is your own flesh and blood." [4]

To her orphaned brothers and little sister, Ellen Wilson was a mother. Stockton Axson had lived in her home as an undergraduate at Wesleyan; and joining the family at Princeton, he became Wilson's dearest

---

[3] Helen Woodrow Bones to Baker, R. S. Baker Papers. Also Miss Bones to the writer, at the Biltmore Hotel, Asheville, N.C., April 5, 1948.
[4] Helen W. Bones to the writer, April 5, 1948.

comrade. Together they would bandy wit and bookish fun for hours on end. Axson was pure-bred Southerner, of a nature milder than that of Wilson; and in the nineties he fitted easily into the gaiety of the Wilson household, helped to keep its spirits and ideals high.[5]

In the attic of the home on Library Place young Edward Axson, an undergraduate specializing in science, carried on experiments in a world of instruments and odors far removed from the child play and literary talk that went on below. Wilson helped the lad to overcome a habit of stuttering; and Edward fixed the household gadgets when they broke. This brother-in-law and his classmate George Howe, Wilson's nephew, stood in Wilson's eyes in the place of sons.

At the turn of the century the household was primarily one of men. Dominating them all with his masculine vigor was Joseph Wilson, who was made to feel at home in the house on Library Place. The doctor was still a doughty contender. When his theological school was in danger of losing the support of the synod, the old warrior informed his son that he "met the Kentucky men throughout a four hours' debate. The upshot was that we routed them, horse, foot and dragoon . . . I made a good speech—the papers saying that Tennessee ought to be proud of me, etc., etc.,—you know the sort of nonsense . . . We have to become men of the world sometimes in order to keep from being men of the monastery. The stilts of study are not good for *constant* use." Dr. Wilson's dislike for narrow theology grew with advancing age.

Often during the nineties the father wrote letters of extravagant affection, speaking frankly of his parental pride and of his concern for Woodrow Wilson's brother and sisters. The oldest, Marion Wilson Kennedy, died in Arkansas in 1890, and the Wilsons took thought for the care of her four orphaned children. But the blow that touched the Wilsons most was the death of their brother-in-law and old friend, Dr. George Howe. "Oh, for some great heart-word to tell you what we suffer . . ." Wilson wrote to his sister Annie in sympathy. For years the Woodrow Wilsons had depended on Dr. Howe for medical advice, by correspondence. It was a close-knit family, the members sometimes lending money to one another without interest, and after Dr. Howe's death the care of his wife and children fell to some extent on the already strained treasury of the Wilsons. "We are one," the old doctor used to write, quoting Scripture. But when the preacher learned of

[5] In one of the two books that Woodrow Wilson did not dedicate to his wife is this tribute: "To Stockton Axson; By every gift of mind a critic and lover of letters, by every gift of heart a friend: This little volume is affectionately dedicated." Dedication of *Mere Literature*.

brother-in-law James Woodrow's controversy with the fundamentalists, he wrote to his son: "I regret this exceedingly. . . . What asses Presbyterians are capable of becoming—whose ears extend to all the earth."

Joseph Wilson's vanity was puffed by the fact that he was the only man who could dictate to his prominent son. To young lady relatives from the South, the old man was sometimes an irascible bear. The fiancée of one of his grandsons baited him with: "Now that I have met you at last, I see where your grandson got his good looks." And the old man trumpeted, "He did not! I still have my good looks!"[6] In his seventies he took a fancy to a widow to whose religious journal he contributed, and wrote more than a hundred letters filled with religious admonition and mawkishness.

Woodrow Wilson would endure teasing from his father with filial patience. But he did not like to have the preacher at his lectures. Once, when the old man crouched in a rear seat as if to escape detection, his son felt like a boy who would have to answer to him afterward for everything said.

Often, after lunch, the men of the family would sit on the porch and talk. Stockton Axson noticed a resemblance to Emerson but found no sympathy for transcendentalism in the mind of Woodrow Wilson. The old doctor's leonine head was fuller of knowledge than Woodrow's, but less subtle in interpretation, less energetic in concentration, less skillful in application. Once, reading one of his son's manuscripts, he was moved to kiss him tearfully and lament: "Oh, Woodrow, I wish, with that genius of yours, you had become a preacher." Though a better debater than the doctor, the son would not push points home in conversation. Sure that his father was by far the abler man, he used to scold him for not publishing anything.

In 1901 the old preacher had an attack of "rigor" at Wilmington. His son gave up a projected trip to Europe and brought him to Princeton, where he lingered for almost two years. As his arteries hardened, he grew childish and querulous, was put out when his boy went on lecture trips without saying goodbye to him, felt better when favorable reports of a Wilson speech came in. Finally, at the end of 1902, Ellen Wilson was writing to a friend: ". . . he had to be attended to exactly like a baby . . . He seems to suffer constantly and when coming out of his stupors moans and cries—even screams—for hours . . . I am very glad that Woodrow is out of the house and out of town so much about his business that he sees very little of it . . ." When his son could be at

[6] Mrs. Margaret Flinn Howe to the writer, at Columbia, S.C.

his bedside he comforted the old man by singing to him—"Crown Him with Many Crowns" and other favorites.

Finally the end came, in January of 1903. Jack Hibben was at the bedside, and seeing the bed start to give way beneath the weight of the agonized figure, he quickly crawled under and held it up, remaining there until there was no life to support.[7]

Woodrow Wilson, stony-faced and inconsolable, picked Princeton ivy from the vine of the Class of '79 and put it on the old man's casket, went down to Columbia for the funeral, and begged his sister to make the slip grow over their father's grave in the churchyard.[8] For a few hours he could feel that he had fallen again into the slow-paced Southern life that seemed to him the most natural of all. He himself composed a long epitaph for his father's stone, and in a pocket notebook treasured these lines:

> Enough to know
> What e'er he feared, he never feared a foe.[9]

Bereft of his most devoted friend and teacher, Wilson returned to Princeton feeling that he was now on the firing line, with no older generation ahead of him. He gave thanks that he still had all that was best of long association with the departed saint, as "spiritual capital" to live upon.

On the first day of 1904 he was attacked by neuralgia, and sat with his wife before the study fire and discussed ways of getting rest. He was solicitous, too, for her health under the burdens that she assumed as Princeton's first lady. Sometimes he restored his own powers by giving himself the pleasure of strengthening hers. In the summer of 1903 they traveled together in France and Italy; and in 1904 he sent her abroad with a daughter while he took responsibility for the household.

Soon after her return she was thrown into the deepest sorrow of her life. Brother Edward Axson was drowned, with his wife and baby, while ferrying across a swollen river in the South. Ellen Wilson was inconsolable for weeks, and was sent by her husband to recuperate in the quiet town of Lyme, Connecticut. Woodrow Wilson went himself to the bedside of ailing Stockton Axson, remarking as he related the tragedy that dear Jack Hibben was standing by and watching over the family in its grief.

[7] Professor and Mrs. Robert Scoon to the writer, letter of June 15, 1950, and enclosure.
[8] Mrs. Margaret Flinn Howe to the writer.
[9] Clipping from a poem by Hugh MacNaughten, found in W.W.'s pocket notebook for 1902-3.

Margaret Axson was stunned by the blow. But Woodrow Wilson took her into his study, spoke of Edward as they had known him in his sweet, mischievous boyhood, of the growth of his finely disciplined mind and high character. "He had all the virtues I could have wished for a son of my own," he said, "even the virtue of not being too good." And the impressionable girl forgot the horror of the drowning. Suddenly she had him back again, her brother, as she would always remember him. "Thank you," she said, looking up into the clear eyes of a brother-in-law who always understood.

The household revolved around Woodrow Wilson, and especially around his voice, which played chords on the keyboard of human emotion. Given a family of daughters, he strove to make himself agreeable to girls. If he would have preferred boys, he never allowed those nearest him to suspect it. Of the peccadilloes of his young kinsfolk he could disapprove sternly, but he could tease them out of their bad habits without, like his father, inflicting pain. His regard for the feelings of others was immense. Even when his quick, precise mind was irritated by dullness or repetition, he tried to conceal his impatience, though to his immediate family he would often complain: "I can't understand why people tell me the same thing over and over—I'm really not a fool." He did not lose his temper over petty personal hurts. But let one of his sacred causes be attacked unfairly or untruthfully, and his face would turn white and his quiet, sharp words would fairly bite. In one of their family evenings together, someone asked for the one word that would describe the most admirable human quality, and Woodrow Wilson said: "Loyalty." Within the circle of intimates there was fealty fierce and stout. They would cut their bones for each other and for their mutual causes.

They needed all their morale, now that the master of the house had become president of Princeton. As a concession to college tradition, they had to move to a campus residence from the sweet home in which they had lived so blithely on Library Place. They were now public personages immured in an architectural monstrosity called Prospect. Ellen Wilson, however, was equal to the challenge. Removing affectations that were *fin de siècle*, she restored the main rooms to good taste. In place of the old Victorian garden that had been heavy with coleus and canna, she planned a wistaria-draped pergola at the end of a walk lined with rhododendrons and cedars and, beyond, a garden like one that she had seen in Italy, with marble seats and sundial. In the presence of the family, Woodrow and Ellen Wilson did not flinch under their new responsibilities. But one night the girls overheard their mother crying and her husband saying, very tenderly: "I should never have brought you here, darling. We were so happy in our own home."

The atmosphere of Prospect, however, was not uncongenial to Woodrow Wilson. Sitting at the long flat desk in the same study that McCosh had occupied, he enjoyed conjuring up recollections of old "Jimmy" opposite him. But his holy of holies was the room high in Prospect's square tower. There, with windows on all sides, he got perspective and did most of his vital writing. When he retired to that eyrie he was "out" to visitors.

In their own home the Wilsons had been able to choose their guests; but at Prospect much of their entertaining was in the name of the college. Though the president tried to select Sunday preachers of wit and eloquence, irrespective of creed, he sometimes felt like saying from his seat behind the pulpit: "Oh, let's quit and sing a hymn!" [10] But on Saturday nights the dull ministers had to be cared for at Prospect with the same warmth that was lavished on the inspired. The Wilsons hated to say polite nothings to guests to whom they could not give their hearts. Ellen Wilson feared to profane the spirit of true hospitality by entertaining the wealthy friends of the university. She did her duty, however, and in one winter had sixty-five dinner parties. Wine was served, cigars were passed, and the men were expected to smoke as they wished. Once, when the women retired to take coffee before a log fire in the living room, Beatrice Webb remained with the men to smoke, and even Ellen Wilson lost her composure.

Thus the cloud of responsibility descended to brood over the idyllic home, and along with it thunderbolts of illness and death. Joseph Wilson and Edward Axson had been snatched away, and Stockton Axson had an attack of melancholia that lasted for six months. In the two years after the inauguration, Prospect became a household of women. A man surrounded by adoring ladies had to make a success of his life, he told them; for they wouldn't let him fail.

[10] Benjamin Chambers, typescript, in the possession of Cleveland E. Dodge, p. 42.

CHAPTER VI

University Pastor

WHEN WOODROW WILSON entered the presidency of Princeton, in the autumn of 1902, he could feel sure of his pre-eminence in the service of the university. One of the professors who had opposed Patton wrote to the new leader to assure him that he was the one under whom they wished to serve, that they would stand by him until things were "right." But in his hour of ascendancy Wilson turned to Bliss Perry with a grim and knowing smile and said: "If West begins to intrigue against me as he did against Patton, we must see who is master!"

Andrew Fleming West, a graduate of the Class of '74, had not been content to remain merely an able professor of the classics at Princeton. He had larger ambitions and had worked hard for their realization. But in the nineties it had been plain that his ideals and Wilson's were not compatible. In a soft, mellow voice West lulled his boys with the verse of Horace. Somewhat casual about attendance at classes, he had come to depend more on wit and social charm than on intellectual effort to maintain his place in the Princeton community. His home saddened by the chronic illness of his wife, he found pleasure in the company of cultivated men; and as a charming diner-out, and a greeter adept at making returning alumni feel at home, he appeared to be striking up friendships with men from whom he might hope to get financial support for his educational ambitions. While Woodrow Wilson, who rarely praised and never jollied anyone designingly, was wearing himself thin over his typewriter and in public speaking, ruddy-cheeked Andrew West was expanding his huge frame and genial spirit in good living and in deeds of personal kindness to his friends and colleagues.[1] He was in his element in New York's Gin Mill Club,

---

[1] West took an active part, too, in Princeton's administration and publicity. As secretary of the Committee on the Schedule, he had labored to make the old College of New Jersey into a university. He it was who had organized and promoted the Susquicentennial celebration; and under his aegis was published a lavish and pompous memorial tome. West had observed the fine points of academic protocol at English universities and was restless to import them to Princeton. He had taught Latin in a high school and in 1883 had received a Ph.D. degree at Princeton and had become a professor of the classics there. He had produced no considerable scholarly work of depth.

84

which Professor Sloane frequented and to which Trustee Moses Taylor Pyne once undertook, unsuccessfully, to introduce Woodrow Wilson.[2]

Having been made dean of graduate students, responsible to a committee of trustees, West continued to hold that position in Wilson's presidency, and in university councils he championed the causes of the graduate school and the classics.[3] He argued that Greek must remain compulsory, even though as a result Princeton might lose boys of great promise in other fields. Wilson, thinking his spirit too close, noted in his diary one day: "Interview with West, in wh. he showed the most stubborn prejudice about introducing a Unitarian into the Faculty."

In the absence of endowment, Dean West found that if he was to house his graduate students well he must find patrons; and among those from whom he hoped for support was President Grover Cleveland. In November of 1896, looking forward to escape from the responsibilities of the White House, Cleveland had written to West "a little bit confidentially" that he wanted a house at Princeton with some ground about it, and a pleasant social life. The mansion that West found for him was named "Westland," and as the years went by West did his best to make the Clevelands feel at home in Princeton society. He hunted and fished with the ex-President, was invited in for "potluck" and to play billiards, and wrote of the joy that he derived from their friendship. Cleveland amused himself with the nominal duties of a Princeton trustee, cherishing a patriotic hope that a graduate school might be established at the university that would make it unnecessary for American boys to go to Europe for advanced study. The prestige of his name was great, his knowledge of the business that education was becoming, dangerously sketchy.

If West felt disappointment when another was elected to lead the university for which he had labored so long, he concealed it well. He was sent abroad by the trustees to study graduate education. His attitude toward the new president was punctiliously correct; and Wilson reciprocated by acknowledging that the Tudor Gothic style of archi-

---

[2] President Nicholas Murray Butler of Columbia University explained, in an understatement, that Wilson "was not the sort of person to adjust himself to the atmosphere which this group had created." After Pyne took him to the annual Christmas luncheon of the Gin Mill Club, he was not asked again. Butler, *Across the Busy Years*, II, 418.

[3] West not only was responsible to the trustees' committee on graduate work, but was expected to report to the faculty annually. Moreover, he was as much responsible to the president as any other professor.

Wilson himself valued the study of Greek highly, but thought it impractical to insist on it. "The man who talks Greek," he wrote, "puts himself—is not driven—through the process that produced the modern mind." See Charles Osgood, "Woodrow Wilson," in *The Lives of Eighteen from Princeton*, p. 288.

tecture that had been advocated by West had added a thousand years to the history of the university.

In the autumn of 1902, with his God-given assurance reinforced by a mandate from a united constituency and conscious that the educators of the nation were looking toward Princeton for portents of the future, Woodrow Wilson was ready to move forward rapidly on lines that he and some of his colleagues already had projected and to try to sweep West along with the rest in devotion to the larger interests of the university. Declining an invitation to address an association of historians, he explained that he had ceased to be a historian and had become involved in a business so absorbing that he must devote himself wholly to the learning of it. He conceived that he was preparing history for future generations. He seemed to be straining ferociously at the bonds of health, impetuous to make Princeton "the perfect place of learning." Stockton Axson had sensed the change in the late nineties, had heard his brother-in-law cry out: "I am so tired of a merely talking profession! I want to *do* something!"

The new president conducted faculty meetings with courtly dignity, spoke briefly, kept discussion pointed toward constructive ends. He liked to get quickly to the pith of every matter that he took up. His diary records: "Day of routine. Kept in my office till quarter of 5 on business that might have been finished before 3 if academic men were only prompt in movement and brief in statements!" When discussion strayed, he would drop a tactful hint by apologizing politely for having a one-track mind. Very soon he reconstituted the faculty committees, except that on the graduate school, which was headed by Dean West.

Determined to be gentle as well as just, he schooled himself in patience. When deadwood had to be pruned from the faculty or the student body—or, for that matter, from the board of trustees—he talked frankly, man to man, with as much regard for humane feeling as for the dictates of duty. A face-to-face talk was better than a letter, he believed. To a mother who was to be operated on and feared that she would die of shock if her boy, a cheater, was expelled from college, Wilson said: "Madam, you force me to say a hard thing, but if I had to choose between your life or my life or anybody's life and the good of this college, I should choose the good of the college." And then he went to luncheon, white and unable to eat.

Students were expected to be gentlemen. They could drink, but drunkenness was taboo; and dishonesty was cause for dismissal. The president did not allow smoking in classes and insisted on a careful record of attendance. Daily chapel was retained, he said, because it was one of the oldest customs and had been productive of good. And yet he knew that religion could not be "handled" like learning. "It is a matter of individual conviction," he wrote in the Introduction of a *Handbook of Princeton*, "and its source is the heart. Its life and vigour must lie, not in official recognition or fosterage, but in the temper and character of the undergraduates themselves."

He frowned upon hazing: once, coming suddenly upon a group of sophomores who were forcing a freshman to grovel and pick up twigs with his teeth, he said icily: "Isn't that a fine occupation for a gentleman?" [4] Yet sometimes, looking back on the rough-housing of his own college days, he wondered whether the boys were not now too docile, whether their spirits were high enough to lift them to great lives. The lads were quick to sense the new vigor of the place. "Square and loyal, firm and true," they sang of their "Tommie" Wilson, "a man we honor through and through."

As the standards of scholarship rose, boys dropped out by the scores and fewer candidates for admission were accepted. The class admitted in 1902 under the lax standards of the old regime, lost one-fourth of its members in a year; and by 1904 the entering class was smaller by one-eighth. The boys jested grimly about the high rate of mortality. Though Wilson well understood that the undergraduate's love was "for sport and good comradeship and the things that give zest to the common life of the campus," yet he insisted that "the ordinary undergraduate" was being educated, knew it, and had a certain strong, even if unconscious, respect for the thing that was happening to him. He refused petitions for the introduction of "cinch" courses and encouraged boys to develop their minds by study in fields unfamiliar and difficult. Taking the longer view, Wilson knew that Princeton was acquiring prestige that would be priceless in the educational market place. But alumni who set more store by quantity than by quality were disturbed by the decline in enrollment.

Conceiving progress to be something "to be compounded out of common counsel," Wilson thought it his duty to canvass the best minds that he could call on, listen carefully, arrive at the most valid policy that he could conceive, and then act accordingly. This procedure was as sacred to him as his religion. He would follow it honestly, let emotions and sentiments suffer as they might. He could battle with strong men on this ground and come out of his differences without hurt

[4] Edward W. Bradford to the writer, Sept. 2, 1956.

feelings. Henry B. Fine, who seemed to Ellen Wilson like "Aaron upholding the arm of Moses," and who, whether traveling abroad or working at Princeton, appeared never to let up in his drive to strengthen his chief's efforts for a renaissance of intellect, argued and disputed often with Wilson, gave advice more often than he received it, and yet remained a friend. In his writings on political science Wilson had stressed the importance of viability; and now as a responsible executive he showed himself ready to meet the minds of others and arrive at compromises that did not profane his basic principles.

Swiftly and surely, Wilson guided the sentiment of the faculty in revising the course of study and setting up a departmental organization that the trustees authorized. The demands of the age had brought in many new and uncoordinated courses, and both faculty and students had regretted Patton's failure to reorganize the curriculum. The problem was intricate, raveled as it was with men's ambitions and jealousies.[5]

It was necessary to redefine jurisdictions, do away with duplication and overlapping, weigh the time allotted to the various subjects. Building on a plan for curriculum revision that had been formulated by a faculty committee under Dean West's chairmanship and submitted unsuccessfully to Patton, Wilson met weekly with a group of his colleagues. Minor questions were referred to subcommittees. During the negotiations he once showed irascibility toward a weak, unoffending professor and thereby provoked a flare-up of feeling; but on the whole, the task was done to the satisfaction of the campus family. ". . . we began," he told Ellen Wilson, "a group of individuals and ended a *body* agreed in common counsel,—except for a final, purely temperamental 'kick' by ——— who will quietly get over it."

When the committee's report was presented to the entire faculty— Wilson's "House of Commons"—the president took the floor, with Dean Fine temporarily in the chair, and debated the new measure; and in a few days he was able to report to his wife: "It took only four meetings to put it through all its stages . . . Everyone seemed to accept the *principle* of the report and all the main features of the scheme at once and without cavil; and the final adoption was characterized by real cordiality. All of which makes me very happy. It is not, as it stands now, exactly the scheme I at the outset proposed, but it is much better."

[5] Harvard, under Eliot, had given boys almost unlimited choice of studies, with the faculty absolving themselves of responsibility. Yale, after Hadley became president in 1899, had broken away from an overrigid regimen: all absolute requirements were abolished, Greek was no longer essential for entrance, and the course was revised in such a way as to give some freedom of choice within limits that guaranteed reasonable breadth, continuity, and concentration.

It was one of Woodrow Wilson's major parliamentary achievements, conceived in the spirit of the times and prosecuted with a balance of persistence and tact that promised much for his future as an administrator.[6]

Having settled what was to be taught in the university, Wilson turned next to put vigor into the teaching and to prevent the stuffing of knowledge into heads that were made receptive only by fear of examinations. Wilson's own tests often called on boys for more than categorical answers. Some of his colleagues thought his examinations too lax; but one of his students once protested, much to his professor's delight: "This question is unfair. It requires thought." Wilson aspired, as he told alumni, "to transform thoughtless boys performing tasks into thinking men."

To achieve his ideal, the new president of Princeton had a plan ready —a concept that he had been turning over in his mind for twelve years or more and that grew out of observation of tutorial work at Oxford and Cambridge and out of discussions of tutorial teaching that had arisen among his colleagues.[7] It seemed clear that, if Princeton was to fill men with enthusiasm for study, inspire them to independent reading and investigation, and wean them from the pap of textbooks and formal lectures, it would be necessary to infuse new blood into the faculty— young instructors on fire with love of scholarship, men who were gentlemen and good comrades. Such tutors, Wilson felt, could live in the dormitories, meet the boys in their own studies or in small classrooms,

[6] On Feb. 3, 1915, addressing the United States Chamber of Commerce on "Cooperation in the Business of Government," Wilson referred to the reorganization of the Princeton course of study as one of his "happiest experiences" in "common counsel."

The new course of study retained the classics as the basis of work in the humanities, but allowed candidates for the degree of B.S. to substitute a modern language for Greek. The number of courses was reduced and, in general, the time given to each was extended. The work of the first year was prescribed for all boys; in the second year some freedom of choice was allowed among studies that were fundamental to the work to be taken later; and in the upper years there was to be wide choice within a scheme of related subjects, and at the same time an insistence that the student should round out his understanding by electing at least some work outside his particular field of concentration. Formal departments of study, with responsible chairmen, were set up; and the faculties of the college and the Green School of Science were combined and the separate budgets were abandoned.

The president was able to say to the trustees, in the fall of 1904, that the system was "cordially received even by that arch-conservative, the undergraduate himself."

[7] Wilson's ideal of preceptorial work doubtless was inspired in part, at least, by the concept of university education presented in an article by Walter Bagehot. "In youth," Wilson's hero wrote, "the real plastic energy is not in tutors or lectures or in books 'got up' but . . . in books that all read because all like; in what all talk of because all are interested; in the argumentative walk or disputatious lounge; in the impact of young thought upon young thought, of fresh thought on fresh thought, of hot thought on hot thought; in mirth and refutation, in ridicule and laughter . . . Quoted by Wilson in "A Wit and a Seer," *Atlantic Monthly,* October, 1898, pp. 527–40.

and walk and talk informally with groups of lads. Keep these preceptors not more than five years, Wilson cautioned, and avoid the error of English universities that allowed dons to go to seed in tutorial service.

More than the reform of the course of study, Wilson considered this project his own; and he did not discuss it with his colleagues in faculty meeting. But his eloquence and enthusiasm won alumni, faculty, and trustees to the scheme; and he pressed on even though the students seemed apathetic and some professors wondered whether the fifty recruits that Wilson desired could be absorbed quickly and peacefully into the teaching ranks and given the promotions that they would want.

The most serious question was that of funds. Even before his inauguration Wilson had asked his trustees for more than six million dollars [8] to finance several projects. He was eager to handle affairs in a manner that would be thought businesslike. The institution was "insufficiently capitalized for its business," he had told the trustees in his first report. ". . . our staff is overworked and underpaid, the University lacks necessary equipment in almost every department . . . We are not doing honestly what we advertise in our catalogue." He threatened, if millions were not forthcoming, to "earnestly advocate a sufficient curtailment of . . . present work to put it on a business-like basis of efficiency." In presenting his program to a gathering of New York alumni in December, 1902, he mentioned the cost of a preceptorial system and the audience whistled. Undaunted, he struck back: "I hope you will get your whistling over, because you will have to get used to this, and you may thank your stars I did not say four millions and a quarter, because we are *going* to get it. I suspect there are gentlemen in this room who are going to give me two millions and a quarter to get rid of me." There was not another university in the world, he boasted, that "could transmute twelve millions and a half into so much red blood."

---

[8] Two and one-quarter millions for a preceptorial system of teaching, one million for a school of science, and two and three-quarter millions for buildings and increases for teachers. Also, as future objectives, Wilson requested three millions for a graduate school and almost two and one-half millions for a school of jurisprudence, a school of electrical engineering, and a museum of natural history. For an institution that in 1902 had productive resources totaling less than four millions, this was a tremendous sum. When Wilson became president, it had already become traditional for the university to roll up annual deficits that were met by emergency gifts from alumni. These deficits grew from about $30,000 in 1901 to about $145,000 in 1906, as the faculty increased from 112 to 174 men; but the special gifts increased even more, so that each year between 1905 and 1910 the deficit was overcome. Actually, by constantly pressing for new developments, Wilson was increasing the annual income of the university, as well as its endowment.

In his crabbed shorthand the president drafted letters asking gifts from wealthy philanthropists. He could deliver bold and eloquent appeals to masses of men; but confronting a prospective donor, the thin skin of his conscience would be pierced and he would lose assurance, feeling himself something of a beggar. There was not enough brass in his make-up to enforce his threats to the New York alumni. He was not facile, as McCosh had been, in showing "the menagerie" to anyone who had money to give. He and Mrs. Wilson could not bring themselves easily to entertain philanthropists in the hope of extracting gifts. A committee of the trustees, however, worked with the president to secure contributions of moderate size so that the perceptorial plan, though not endowed, was assured of support for a few years at least; and in June of 1905 it was formally approved by the board.

When it came to recruiting the preceptors, Wilson's genius shone at its brightest. As a professor he had attracted talented teachers, and by 1902 the one-man department of jurisprudence had grown to a six-man department of history, economics, and politics. Now, faced with the task of finding fifty exceptional teachers within a few months, he put the problem before his department heads, helped them to sift the records of hundreds of applicants, sought opinions on the worth of the candidates, talked with each of them, touched them with his fervor for the new work at Princeton. The importance of the whole system lay in the characters of the men obtained, he explained. Like McCosh, he asked first about each candidate: "Is he alive?"

Vigorous young teachers flocked to him, convinced that here was a leader who knew his business and sympathized with their impatience with conditions that they had found restrictive elsewhere. Wilson in turn took the preceptors to his heart, gave generously of counsel and inspiration to those who needed it, often concluding his advice with a friendly "Don't you think so?" To the youngest, most inexperienced, he would say a fatherly word of reassurance, invite them to come to him at any time for aid. In his study they found their god to be a very human man. He urged his young protégés to informality, breadth of view, and at the same time, accuracy. Conscious of the power of nomenclature, Wilson insisted that meetings of preceptors with students should be called "conferences," not "classes." Preceptors were to find out not what the boys knew but what they did not know, so that they might be guided to sources of enlightenment. Excoriating the use of syllabi, he insisted that students were not to be spoon-fed, but urged to independent investigation; and the boys were to be examined on what they read rather than on what they were told in the classroom. He himself met with a small preceptorial group.

In his zeal for perfection the president let it be known that he thought competition the life of teaching, as of trade. Catching a bored student in the act of skipping class by way of a window and fire escape, he merely asked: "Who is the lecturer? He must be very nearsighted. Was it very dull?" He would have liked to make attendance at some lectures optional, so that each professor would have to hold his boys by sheer ability. Preceptors who married wealthy wives and seemed to lose enthusiasm for their teaching sometimes became the object of cutting remarks at the Wilson dinner table, where personal likes and dislikes were aired frankly.

There were features of the preceptorial plan that in practice had to be changed or dropped. Scarcity of funds made it impossible, sometimes, to attract competent men to replace those who were not content to delay their advancement by remaining in preceptorial service. However, in introducing the conference method of teaching and a corps of able young instructors Wilson contributed new vitality to Princeton and to American education. The drawing force of his personality called forth such a flowering of teaching genius as neither money nor pure reason could duplicate. In the spring of 1906 he could say to alumni with confidence that his words were substantiated by good works, that he was "covetous for Princeton of all the glory that there is, and the chief glory of a university is always intellectural glory."

In groups of five or six that met once a week, sometimes in a preceptor's room or home, boys learned to talk naturally and wittily about books, plays, public questions, personalities, and the Jersey countryside through which they often walked. Bonds of intellectual comradeship were formed that lasted for decades. Students began to make more use of the library, mischief decreased, scholarship improved, and soon graduates of Princeton were carrying off high honors in professional schools elsewhere. Many of the older professors responded to the challenge, shared in the new spirit of fellowship, rewrote their lectures, gave more attention to individual boys. "We are all preceptors," the president was able to say when his experiment was scarcely a year old. There was an air of renaissance on the campus, and pride in a rising aristocracy of brains. The seniors caught the spirit of informality, sang:

> Here's to those preceptor guys,
> Fifty stiffs to make us wise.

In the first three years of his presidency, in addition to outside addresses, efforts to raise funds, the working out of the new course of study and the preceptorial plan, and a guiding interest in his own department, Wilson found time to strengthen the university in other respects. His attitude toward science, which in earlier years had been based largely on his experience in an elementary course that was taught by lectures and table demonstrations, had been broadened by talks with Fine and other colleagues. In his inaugural address he had not repeated the misgivings about the influence of scientific method on education that he had expressed in 1896. In fact, he had proclaimed that science opened a new world of learning, as great as the old.

The trustees' committee on buildings and grounds, which was created to put the administration of the university's property on a businesslike basis, had the active assistance of the president. Determined that there should be coherence in the physical development of the university, that donors should not prescribe diverse and conflicting styles of architecture nor place their buildings in helter-skelter pattern nor construct laboratories that looked like factories, Wilson laid down the law. He insisted on the appointment of Ralph Adams Cram to coordinate Princeton's landscape, architecture, and building material, explaining that he had not the next decade merely but the next fifty years in view.

When it was made clear that it would be economical to concentrate the business of all departments under one manager, he quickly brought to the trustees a resolution providing for a "financial secretary." The president himself found time to attend to irritating little flaws in the operation of buildings. In a notebook he recorded the presence of rats in a cellar. He had a little time even for pastoral care of the university community: when Grover Cleveland's daughter died, he carried a note of sympathy to the house, where the butler took it through a crack in the door. He remembered to write, each year, an affectionate letter to the Hibbens on the anniversary of their marriage; and one night, when Jennie Hibben telephoned that her husband was away and there was a burglar in the house, Wilson rushed out to the rescue while his family called after him: "*Must* you go?"

He was the only man at Prospect now. In the spacious dining room, where sun flooded a long window filled with greenery, at a table decorated with flowers in season, the president presided over a court of ladies. "I am submerged in petticoats," he would say in jest. The girls would joke with him, but none of their soft voices rose strenuously against his will; and the more paternal he became the more he bristled toward the outside world in defense of the family's snug and blissful security.

To protect his wife's garden and the privacy of his girls, the president had an iron fence built. It offended students, who now had to walk around instead of across a corner of the lot. Alumni thought it marred the beauty of the campus. Students paraded in indignation, carrying derisive placards; and one night the structure was toppled into a trench dug for it, and buried so that only its spiked top protruded. The next morning Wilson was on the scene early, and his eyes were a steely blue-gray as he struck at the spikes with his cane. The fence was rebuilt, and the next June it was guarded by college proctors.

Gone now were the days when Edward Axson's practical mind balanced the Wilson household, the hours of philosophical contemplation with Stockton Axson and old Joseph Wilson, the afternoons passed at the Faculty Club at billiards or in chat with fellow professors. Instead of going to the barbershop and catching the drift of village gossip, he now stropped his razor and shaved himself, to save time. Then, too, to conserve his energy he felt that he must post afternoon office hours— an innovation that discouraged casual and informal calls from friends. Even the two-mile walks that had taken the place of bicycling were usually made alone, exactly at five o'clock. He was drawing apart from the actual conditions of life that he had commended so warmly to the attention of men who would lead a people. And in drawing apart from individuals he was depending more and more on intuitive insight to tell him what motives and ideas ruled the minds of Princeton men.

One Christmas, Ellen Wilson had a billiard table installed in the east wing of Prospect, hoping that men would come in to play; but when they did, usually they leaned on their cues and talked, and soon the seamstress was using the table for the cutting of dance frocks for the girls. And so, gradually, as the duties of office exacted more and more of the president's energy and the transcendence of his mission for Princeton possessed him, there developed a legend that he was cold and inaccessible.

Immediately after his inauguration in 1902, Wilson had expressed the hope that he might not lose direct contact with undergraduates in the classroom. He continued to lecture regularly all through his presidency. He expected his audience to take him seriously, even on the morning of the football game with Yale. His humor was often gay. He jested about his pince-nez, remarking that he thought of wearing them on the end of his nose so that he could see his words before they came out. He was still calculating the effect of every word, disgressing now and then from his subject to try out bits of homely wisdom that he later used in public speeches. Sometimes, before the bell gave the signal for the lecture to begin, he sat at his desk concealed behind the morning newspapers. When he had said all that he planned to say, he did not extemporize until the bell announced the end of the period. He would leave the room quickly by a side door, unless boys came to his desk with worth-while questions. But on the days when he continued to talk after the last bell, and students rushed pell-mell from neighboring classrooms, Wilson's boys would sit quiet and hear him out.

There were occasions when the lowliest of undergraduates could draw close to their godlike master. Sometimes a winning debating team was invited to dine at Prospect; and he spoke informally in the halls of the debating societies and attended dress rehearsals of college shows. Occasionally Ellen Wilson would entertain and invite girls to help her, but the president proved a greater attraction and the students would drift into the library to hear him tell stories. The boys found out their "Tommie," too, after athletic victories. They would snake-dance up to his porch and call him out. He had only to speak quietly to still the uproar. Then, raising his voice in boyish glee at the triumph, he would send them off howling like a jungle pack.

One spring it was announced that the president was to speak informally to the campus religious society and the traditional singing on the steps was postponed to give everyone a chance to hear him. Standing halfway up the aisle, he confided in the earnest young disciples, told them how his own father had helped him, in his youth, to understand things that his mind could not then grasp. Speaking of the Bible as "the book that best sums up the human spirit," he proclaimed the way of Christ the hardest of paths, and as proof of the vitality of Christianity he cited "the great amount of modern preaching it survives." [9] Good character was to him a by-product that came not from seeking, but from doing right at every turn, from sticking to a job, day in and day out.

Invitations to speak outside Princeton were received at the rate of three a day. Many came from former students, in behalf of alumni clubs. It gave the president joy to drop his cares and renew old associations. With the old grads he could revel in the spirit of comradeship from which health and conscience separated him on the campus. Often he would surprise them by calling them by name and asking about

9 Chambers MS.

their Princeton relatives. After he had dined and addressed them he would jump down from the platform and join vigorously in their lockstep "pee-rades."

His moral sense was often offended as he saw alumni lounging and drinking in their clubs and airing irresponsible views on the nation's institutions. But when he was impelled to suggest reproof he spoke with sly wit. Chatting once with two of his old boys in a Washington club, he saw youngsters take a nearby table and drink excessively. One of his companions asked the other: "Are those habitués of your club?" And Wilson cut in quickly with: "No. They must be sons-of-habitués." [10]

Though Wilson had set aside both literary and political ambitions, his health was strained by the intensity of his efforts in the classroom and on public platforms. Even during his first year in the presidency he had felt so pressed by responsibility that sometimes when he went home at night he seemed to meet himself coming back in the morning. He could afford only part-time secretarial help from students, and handled his own mail and did much of his own typing.

With his Ellen's help he had disciplined himself in diet, in work, and in relaxation; and when opportunity to sleep came, he could drop his cares and doze off quickly. The family spent much of the long summer vacations out of doors, on the Maine coast in 1902 and later at Muskoka Lake in Canada, where Wilson taught his children how to paddle a canoe and cooked their food over open fires, and during a squall on the lake felt intimations of mortality so keenly that he made a will soon afterward. Early in 1905 he was operated on for a rupture that had resulted from portaging a canoe; and during his recovery he was stricken with phlebitis. After five weeks in the hospital, he was taken to Florida by his anxious wife. When they returned she was thinner and paler than he.

The next year was critical for Wilson's health and fortunes. He could have rested on his record, secure in the knowledge that by reforms already accomplished he had raised the standing of Princeton among American universities. He could have safeguarded his health, relaxed into tweedy geniality, and let his able and loyal lieutenants carry on. But he conceived that he was a responsible minister, elected on a reform platform and given authority to execute the wishes of his constituency. He had been reminded by illness that life was short, and there was much to be done. Princeton must rise to the top, and serve the nation.

[10] George Dunlop, Princeton '92, and one of Wilson's companions on this occasion, to the writer.

Determined that the good fight should go on, he stepped up the tempo of his speechmaking. In 1905-6 he made a dozen powerful addresses. Speaking to the Western alumni at Cleveland, he began in a light, facile vein, saying: "About this table I recognize the faces of some who were ingenious in resisting the processes of learning—and if they have applied as much ingenuity to their business as they did then to their pleasure, I congratulate them upon their success." And then gradually and artfully he warmed to his subject: the new teaching at Princeton.

The ideals that we talk about, the ideals that we try to translate into definite programmes of study, are not things which we can take or leave as we please, unless you believe that we can take or leave life itself as we please . . . If there remain any little band of men keeping the true university spirit alive, that band will, after a while, seem to be all that there is of a great nation, so far as the historian is concerned . . . And so, our ambitions for a university which retains this spirit are not hopes so much as a definite confidence that certain things must come to pass. The best thing, to my thought, about what we call the Princeton spirit is the manliness and the unselfishness and the truthfulness that there is in it . . .

Eleven times the short speech was interrupted by cheering, and at the end the applause was thunderous and prolonged. The Western alumni loved, respected, trusted their "Tommie" Wilson.

CHAPTER VII

Voice in the Wilderness

On a may morning in 1906, Woodrow Wilson awoke and found that he could not see out of his left eye. For some time his left shoulder and leg had been racked by neuritic pains, and his right hand had been affected again. Apprehensive, his wife took him to two specialists. Having watched Joseph Wilson die only four years before, she was terrified by the verdict. "It is hardening of the arteries," she wrote to a friend, "due to prolonged high pressure on brain and nerves. He has lived too tensely . . . Of course, it is an awful thing—dying by inches, —and incurable. But Woodrow's condition has been discovered in the very early stages and they think it has already been 'arrested.' " He would have to meet not only the physical danger of the hardening of his arteries,[1] but also the psychic ravages of fear—dread that he might not live long enough to make Princeton "the perfect place of learning," that he might suffer the excruciating agonies of his father.

The prospect of physical suffering seems not to have shaken Wilson's confidence. "I have never *felt* as if there were anything the matter with me, except the eye," he wrote to his sister. He accepted the doctor's diagnosis calmly and prepared to carry out the prescription of three months of rest. Dean Fine was made acting president of Princeton, and Hibben acting dean.

For refreshment after mental strain, Wilson always had leaned heavily on friends. Now, when forced to leave the campus in search of health, he was reminded how much his friends loved him. Messages of good-will came from trustees, alumni, associates. "Dear love and good-bye," Jennie Hibben wrote, "and try to be careful of yourself through this trying week. How lovely and good you are to us! Ever devotedly yours." Andrew West wrote to wish the president a summer "in every way delightful" and closed his letter with "ever sincerely yours."

Wilson's family took him to the English Lake Country, the pastoral

---

[1] Fifty-year arteries do not go back to an earlier condition. Modern doctors realize, better than did those of 1906, that vascular occlusions may be followed by sleeplessness, moods of emotional uplift and depression, nervous breakdown, spastic indigestion, even moral relaxations. Dr. Robert Monroe to the writer. See Dr. Walter C. Alvarez, "Cerebral Arteriosclerosis," in *Geriatrics*, I (May–June, 1946) 189–216.

realm in which his mind often had sought release. At Rydal he communed not only with natural beauty but with a friendly artist who was seeking to interpret it. Stopping once on a bridge and looking down into the Rothay River, he heard an unfamiliar voice ask: "Is this President Wilson?" The words came from a sensitive face that was topped by tousled gray hair. "My name is Yates." the stranger went on. "We live near here. We are poor but, thank God, not respectable." Wilson needed to look at such a man but once, to love him. An idyllic friendship began there, between Fred Yates the artist and his wife and daughter and the Wilsons. The two families talked, read, and sang together. The sillier the songs the more relaxation Wilson found in them.

As sight came back in his eye he became restless to go on with his mission at Princeton. He consulted a wise old doctor in Edinburgh and was advised that, if everyone stopped work because of such a condition as his, a good many of the world's tasks would remain unfinished. It seemed a mistake for a man of his temperament to be kept away from his duties while the university was in session; and so he was allowed to return to the campus in the autumn and to work moderately. His left eye never recovered fully, in spite of his assurance to his wife that he would train it to behave. His hand still bothered him, but a pen with a large handle was made to relieve the pain of writing. After meals a bottle of whisky was set beside him and he measured out a medicinal dose, then apologized roguishly to his family for not sharing his liquor with them. By pruning his engagement calendar, systematizing his work, and insisting on ample sleep, he was able to take up his task again.

The accumulation of business was so great that he wrote in November: "I did not take a long breath for two weeks." After three months of overwork, however, he kept a promise that he had given the doctors and made the first of several trips to Bermuda. "I love my work too much," he said, "to be willing to run the risk of rendering myself unfit for it!" He begged his Ellen to go with him, but she said that she must stay in her home "like the fixtures."

In Bermuda, Wilson wrote lectures and preached in a local church on the text: "The letter killeth, the spirit giveth life." But to restore his own spirits he craved human comradeship. Fortunately, he found escape in a blithe friendship with Mary Allen Hulbert Peck. The first husband of this lady had been killed in an accident and she was estranged from her second, Thomas D. Peck, a manufacturer of Pittsfield, Massachusetts. She dwelt unconventionally in an Eden of sunlight and fancy, without stripping the boughs that hung well laden all around her. She was at home in cosmopolitan society, could fence nimbly with both swords and words, and knew how to listen to men who talked well.

He met Mary Allen Peck at a dinner party, and she diverted him, rallied his spirit of gallantry. In her the frustrated poet found the mind that he most desired to see in woman—a wit that stirred him without irritating, amused and yet subtly instructed. In him she at once saw a Christlike quality, a serene radiance that reminded her of Phillips Brooks. He rang true, and promised intellectual stimulation. She arranged a party for him at her home; and he held the men spellbound with good after-dinner talk, so that the ladies were left long alone. Then there was music and general chat, and the guests went home under a deep violet sky.

He loved to walk on the shore road with Mary Peck and read to her from the *Oxford Book of Verse*. But being a man who did not smoke, drink, or dance, he was inevitably a looker-on, and held her scarf when she joined the dancers in the ballroom of the Hamilton Hotel. Gossip linked Mary Peck and the governor in matrimony; and Woodrow Wilson protested in jest that he resented such talk, though she brushed it aside as "the inevitable tattle." Other women, protesting the best of intentions and showing the worst of motives, asked Wilson about her with a particularity and persistence that made him boil. But he could laugh uproariously when his fondness for Mary Peck led him into situations that set malicious tongues awagging. One Sunday morning, as they returned from a walk to the South Shore, the congregation was coming out of the church in which Wilson had preached.

"This is terrible!" he said in mock horror, as he doffed his cap to the worshipers. "Last week, dressed in solemn black, I stood up before that congregation and admonished them about their Christian duty—and here I am today standing, just like an undergrad, under a tree with a pretty girl."

And when she laughed he went on: "Worse, distinctly worse. Caught laughing with a pretty girl on the holy Sabbath-day. Here goes my last shred of reputation."

In Bermuda, Wilson loved the company of Mark Twain, too, and would spend mornings with him over croquet, or a game of miniature golf of their own invention. Though the humorist and his friend H. H. Rogers cut capers and clowned together, they put on party manners when the president of Princeton approached. This made it hard for him to

lose his dignity in the carefree, boyish play of which he seemed never
to have had enough. He could not cut loose from his position. Even
when he visited the aquarium he was driven up on his professional
stilts by an attendant who insisted on exhibiting his scientific knowledge.

He liked to watch people in Bermuda, especially the sleepy drivers
of the leisurely carriages, and he contemplated with horror the coming
of automobiles. To prevent such a desecration of paradise, he drafted
a petition to the island legislature.[2] He never bought an automobile
for himself. They were to some men, he thought, a symbol of the
"arrogance of wealth."

The simplicity of life in the Lake Country and in Bermuda accentuated, by contrast, new ways of life at Princeton that seemed to Wilson
to divert his undergraduates from "the chief end of man." Returning
from vacations, he felt that he was moving from idyllic reality to
masquerade.

Once there had been a social line drawn down the middle of Princeton's main street. In the early years the teachers of the college had been
consigned by the estate owners to the side that was inhabited by
shopkeepers and workmen; but gradually the aristocracy of wealth had
merged with that of intellect to form a "gown" society with interests
remote from the town of Princeton. The rift widened with the coming
of wealth from the cities. A very few local patrons of the college, including trustees, lived on a scale that seemed to poor professors to be
palatial; and yet some of the academic men tried to keep pace with
their affluent neighbors. In a few country places millionaires extolled
the virtues of the simple life. Only one thing was lacking in these
twentieth-century affectations of the Sabine Farm. Where was Horace?
The patrons found him in the person of "Andy" West—a comrade
hearty, jovial, kindly, able to deliver Latin inscriptions to order.

The Wilsons themselves were astraddle the social line. Ellen Wilson
was a descendant of Nathaniel Fitz-Randolph, who had given acres
of land to the infant College of New Jersey; but by joining the lesser of
the village's two Presbyterian churches[3] she and her husband had put
themselves on friendly terms with the villagers. Once Wilson stopped

----

    [2] Hudson Strode, *The Story of Bermuda*, p. 147. The petition said in part: "It would, in our
opinion, be a fatal error to attract to Bermuda the extravagant and sporting set who have made
so many other places entirely intolerable to persons of taste and cultivation."
    [3] The family had joined the smaller church because they thought it in need of help and
Wilson served as an elder. He encouraged the merging of the two churches, but when his congregation refused to do this, the Wilsons thought them shortsighted and went over to the
larger First Church. Eleanor Wilson McAdoo to the writer, March 10, 1952.

on a street corner, hat in hand, to answer a random question from an old Negress. To watch the annual sleigh race he would stand on the curb, and after the sleighs had swished by he would linger to chat with other spectators. Moreover, he encouraged worthy young men of the village who were entering politics; and once he took a hand in ridding the town of a "bucket shop."

Black sweaters and corduroy pants, once worn proudly as emblems of democracy, were giving way to tweeds. President Wilson complained, in his first statement to the trustees, that Princeton was in danger of being regarded, "to her great detriment and discredit," as one of the most expensive places for students to live. He felt that too many boys came to college to get social sophistication, and frittered away time in dilettantism and campus politics. Dean West pleaded that boys be admitted by certificate from a favored private school, while valedictorians from public schools had to prove themselves. Moreover, and probably most distressing of all to an old Princetonian like "Tommie" Wilson, the debating societies that had been so dear to him had lost their glamour and were no longer self-supporting. The students now threw their social energies into "heeling" for election to one of the eating clubs where talk was more informal and far less exalted, and members were tempted to spend their evenings playing billiards or sprawled before an open fire reading popular journals.

After the abolition of secret societies at Princeton in the presidency of McCosh, clubs had grown up to satisfy the natural desire of students to eat with a congenial crowd. Wilson himself, as an undergraduate, had belonged to "The Alligators." Twenty-five years later, however, these simple organizations were so rooted in tradition and so heavily endowed that Wilson spoke publicly, in 1906, of their dangers. The influence of the clubs on the extracurricular life of the university was in many ways admirable; unlike the abolished fraternities, they were not secret and they countenanced no dangerous hazing. Moreover, their members continued to reside in the college dormitories. They were rallying grounds of alumni loyalty to the college, and the president of the university appreciated their virtues as much as he deplored their tendency to separate undergraduates one from another and from intellectual pursuits.

As early as 1897, Wilson had told Stockton Axson that if he were president of Princeton he would reorganize the social life so that clubs would not cut off freshmen from contact with older students. And in 1905 he had developed this last thought further. "The most influential

Seniors," he wrote, "govern their own class and the University in all matters of opinion and of undergraduate action . . . They lead because they have been found to be the men who can do things best . . . 'Leading citizens' are everywhere selected in the same way . . . The university authorities consult the leading Seniors as a matter of course upon every new or critical matter in which opinion plays a part and in which undergraduate life is involved . . . Such comradeship in affairs . . . breeds democracy inevitably. Democracy, the absence of social distinctions, the treatment of every man according to his merits, his most serviceable qualities and most likeable traits, is of the essence of such a place, its most cherished characteristic." [4]

For ten years there had been talk of reform in the club system at Princeton, and other colleges were facing the same problem; but nothing was being done. In Wilson's view the situation had grown critical since his inauguration, as new and more palatial clubhouses had appeared on Prospect Avenue. Another two years of such growth and, he feared, the university might be only an antiquarian and artistic background for club life. But not until the preceptorial system was in action was he ready to crusade for the social regeneration of Princeton. Surely if any university president in America could force action, Woodrow Wilson—a great orator, a magnetic leader, a man with the credential of uninterrupted success—might hope to prevail. And if his morale needed any spur, it was perhaps found in a reminder from a relative that the crest of the Woodrows bore a bull's head with the motto: *Audaci favit fortuna.*

In December of 1906 he gave to the trustees a clear outline of a constructive plan—"heretical in character," he told them quite frankly. but "the fruit of very mature consideration." He alluded to the elaboration of club life and "the decline of the old democratic spirit of the place." Describing unhealthful trends, complaining that, under the current system of electioneering, comrades were chosen in social groups rather than as individuals, he expressed willingness to preserve the better values of the clubs. Cautioning that it would be unwise as yet to discuss the matter publicly, he nevertheless set forth his conviction that it was time for action.

Wilson wished to make the undergraduates live together, not in clubs but in colleges. "I propose," he said, "that we divide the University into

---

[4] John Rogers Williams, *The Handbook of Princeton*, p. xvi. In Wilson's notebook for 1907 is this line: "Plans: A conference of Seniors at the beginning of each academic year, to talk of the self-government of the university."

colleges and that the strong upperclass clubs themselves become colleges under the guidance of the University. By a college I mean not merely a group of dormitories, but an eating hall as well with all its necessary appointments where all the residents of the college shall take their meals together. I would have over each college a master and two or three resident preceptors, and I would have these resident members of the faculty take their meals in hall with the undergraduates. But I would suggest that the undergraduates of each college be given a large share of the self-government . . . Each college would thus form a unit in itself, and largely a self-governing unit." [5] The question of expense was, Wilson then thought, a minor one. "The changes necessary to effect the transition," he said, "would be, in form at any rate, very slight."

The reaction of the board was sympathetic, though some thought the proposal "just one of Woodrow's pipe dreams." A seven-man Committee on Social Coordination was appointed, with Wilson as chairman, to study the matter and report six months later, in June.

Less than a week after the presentation of the plan to the trustees, the first whisper of opposition came to Wilson's ears; and it did not come, strangely enough, from the student or alumni members of the clubs. Grover Cleveland, who in 1904 had become chairman of the trustees' committee on the graduate school, complained to a colleague that the realization of Wilson's plan might postpone the day when Dean Andrew West would have new buildings for his graduate college.

Only a few months earlier, West reported that he had been called to the presidency of the Massachusetts Institute of Technology, at an increase in salary. As his terms for remaining at Princeton he had asked "the cordial and unanimous assurances of the President and Trustees that a renewed and determined effort will be made to secure the Graduate College." He had felt that his work for Princeton was unappreciated and accused Wilson of personal unfriendliness. "The trouble . . ." he had complained to the president, "is that I have not hit it off with you." He did not wish to leave Princeton, however, and could be sent away only if the president denounced him before the trustees. Some of Wilson's warmest supporters on the board thought that the

[5] Some of the concepts presented by Wilson had been set forth by Charles Francis Adams in June of 1906 in an address delivered before the Phi Beta Kappa Society at Columbia University on "Some Modern College Tendencies." And, more specifically, in a footnote added by Adams when his paper was printed in a book, *Three Phi Beta Kappa Addresses,* in 1907. In the footnote Adams quoted from Wilson's "Annual Report for 1906" on Princeton's experience with the preceptorial system. In a faculty meeting Wilson alluded to Adams's view.

time had come to make it clear to West what his responsibilties were to the whole university and its president. By a nod of his head Wilson could have separated the dean from Princeton or put him firmly under the president's control. But Wilson leaned back. Distrusting the dean's capacity for putting Princeton's best interests before his own and yet recognizing West's value to the university, disliking to feud, putting his emphasis on constructive principles, and rising above the temptation to petty recriminations that West's reproaches had put before him, Wilson wrote a resolution urging the dean to remain. "The board," it said, "has particularly counted upon him to put into operation the Graduate College which he conceived and for which it has planned . . . It begs to assure him that he cannot be spared." West took this as a promise that he was to have virtually a free hand in directing graduate affairs.

However, sympathetic as he was to the development of graduate work, Wilson persisted in giving priority to the plan that would affect the larger number and thought it "small-minded" of West to let his desire for a residential college for a few graduate scholars stand in the way of the building of quadrangles that would benefit hundreds of undergraduates. It seemed to the president that the two projects might well go along side by side. Grover Cleveland, however, with whom West had become ever more intimate, could not be convinced of this; and West, who four years earlier had acquiesced in the placing of major emphasis on undergraduate work, had been so emboldened by the offer from Massachusetts that from now on he was to press implacably for the realization of his own vision.

In the early months of 1907 the president's proposal of residential quadrangles for undergraduates—familiarly called the "quad plan"— was the talk of the campus. There was general agreement on the need for reform, and some of the trustees went further than their leader in condemnation of the *status quo*. From many Princetonians, however, the reaction was not wholly positive.[6]

<hr>

[6] President Emeritus Patton, who had become president of the Princeton Theological Seminary and to whom Wilson had shown scant courtesy, spoke in general terms about arrogant assumption of omniscience by university administrators. Senior members of the faculty were not pleased by their president's failure to take them into his confidence. Dean Fine, loyal to his chief and believing in his purposes, expressed himself in favor, yet was heard to remark: "We dearly love Woodrow, but he does drive too fast!" Hibben, too kind to dampen the ardor of his friend's virtuous intent, admitted the evils but was noncommittal about the remedy. Professor Henry Van Dyke, whom some had considered a candidate for the presidency of the university in 1902, differed with Wilson on principle, felt that through the natural foregathering of boys of similar interests, the proposed quandrangles would become stereotypes, like English "colleges." This opponent expressed gentlemanly regret at the president's haste and complained to alumni that proposals for greater deliberation "were rejected by authority." Van Dyke offered to resign; but Wilson and the faculty, respecting his opposition as sincere, persuaded him not to leave.

Wilson rethought and revised his purposes and drafted a new statement. His committee of trustees discussed it and gave it general approval; and on June 10 he read it to the entire board in a solemn session. To that company of able men who both loved and trusted him,
he said: "I have never had occasion, I probably never shall have occasion,
to lay a more important matter before you than the proposals contained
in this report." He pleaded for his plan, not primarily as a means of
reforming the club system but rather as an indispensable part of his
effort "to give the University a vital, spontaneous intellectual life." Reviewing what had been accomplished already—an achievement in
which Princeton men took pride—he went on to explain in what ways
the social clubs were, in all innocence, stifling the intellectual life of the
boys. Without entering into controversial detail, he elaborated somewhat on the bare description of the proposed residential colleges that
he had given six months before. The report ended with a recommendation that "the President of the University be authorized to take such
steps as may seem wisest for maturing this general plan, and for seeking the cooperation and counsel of the upper-class clubs in its elaboration . . ."

Wilson had contemplated asking the trustees for authorization "to
take such steps as may seem wisest for maturing *and executing*" the
quad plan; but he omitted the last two words when one of his close
friends on the board advised him to do so in order to give the trustees
the privilege of further consideration.

The confidence that he placed in his board proved, at the June, 1907,
meeting, to be justified. Only one trustee, wishing more time for deliberation, voted against the adoption of the report. The president was
authorized to "mature" his ideas.

Allowing his ardor to outrun the letter of the law, Wilson jumped
to the conclusion that future debate would turn "not upon the facts,
but only upon the means and methods of organization." He said: "We
have a body of Alumni for whom the interests of the University as a
whole, as they may be made to see those interests at any moment of
action, take precedence of every other consideration, give free and
wholesome vigour to the life of the University . . ."

The idealism of college youth responded to this. But Wilson had also
to deal with businessmen who loved their clubs and honored tradition
and property as well as scholarship. His report to the trustees was
printed during Commencement Week, and reinforced by spirited addresses from the president. But Wilson had not taken pains to talk with

the editor of the *Alumni Weekly* and other leaders of the younger graduates, to win them man by man to support his grand design. Instead, he caused an explanation of his plans to be read at the annual banquets of the clubs. Thus many of the alumni in reunion, having heard only rumors, first drew the full import of the new plan from the cold phrases of a formal article at the very time when they were reveling in the pleasures that their clubs afforded. Would they follow their president in devotion to Princeton's intellectual glory?

There were some indications that some men would not, and sensing this, Wilson showed the determination with which men of his clan had been accustomed to meet opposition: ". . . now there is a great deal of wild talk," he wrote to one of the most steadfast trustees, "and amidst the wild talk scores of particulars come to life which show that the situation is even worse than I had supposed, and that the remedy is absolutely imperative."

Soon the discussion had become a dispute, the dispute a bitter feud that ramified through all the Princeton community. Students, professors, families of professors, resident alumni—all took sides; and waves of gossip and recrimination slapped about in that little social sea. As argument fell from educational principles to personalities, the president was cursed as a confiscator of property, a spoilsport, a prig, a tyrant, a fool; defenders of the clubs were called tories, plutocrats, dissolutes.

Wilson felt that without residential colleges of some sort his preceptorial system could not come to full bloom. "The fight is on," he wrote on the first of July, "and I regard it, not as a fight for the development, but as a fight for the restoration of Princeton. My heart is in it more than it has been in anything else, because it is a scheme of salvation." He would fight, as his ancestors had fought, for the truth. He felt that he was engaged in nothing less than the most critical work of his whole administration, the work upon which its whole vitality and success depended. Wilson's will, like his arteries, was hardening, and was driving full speed ahead, with little regard for obstacles.[7] The president considered that he had convenanted with the trustees, and they with him, to go forward. There seemed to be no valid reason for hesitation.

Dean West burst into righteous indignation and addressed to the

---

[7] Wilson's purpose was strengthened by moral support from educators in other universities. To a new trustee who was a leader among the younger alumni he wrote: "As for myself, I feel that we are here debating, not only a plan, but an opportunity to solve a question common to all the colleges and obtain a leadership which it will not be within our choice to get again within our lifetime." W.W. to Andrew C. Imbrie, July 29, 1907.

president an accusation of disregard for the interests of the graduate work. But, patiently reproving the dean for lack of faith in his character and without retreating from his understanding that the board had approved his plan in essence, Wilson bade the doubters among his colleagues to wait until autumn, when opportunity would come to debate the plan. So certain had he been of his hold upon the confidence of his faculty that he had never discussed his quad plan with them; and now he had to explain that he had gone to the trustees first because the matter involved many elements that lay within the province of the board alone.

Unconvinced, West continued to encourage opposition among his friends; and he and the Clevelands brought their arguments to bear even upon trusted Jack and Jennie Hibben.

During the summer the trustees were bombarded with protests from alumni. They were responsible for the financial accountability of the university, and the deficits that had to be made up by emergency gifts had grown annually larger. How, they wondered, were they to get support for expensive new quadrangles? On this question there was a division of opinion. Some were convinced that patrons would not give willingly to a university that was overshadowed by private clubs. On the other hand, among the protesting club men were many large givers who seemed determined to donate neither buildings nor money to the proposed quandrangles. Wilson himself persisted in hoping that the clubs might be absorbed rather than abolished. If only the jumpy economic nerve of his trustees could be soothed, the protests of the opposition would subside, he felt sure.

During the summer he sought sanctuary in the Adirondacks. His imagination had been caught often by hill-rimmed security; though he seldom perused novels, he had read *Lorna Doone* over and over. Now, while the prophet guarded his vision behind Doone Gate, within a valley in his mind, disaffected alumni agitated the plains and clouds of dust arose. The quadrangles would end "class spirit," they were saying: on the contrary, said their leader, "nothing is more damaging to the homogeneity and spirit of the classes than what is going on." To the cry that "no one should make a gentleman associate with a 'mucker,'" Wilson repeated that the primary object of his reform was not social but intellectual. More than once he wrote: "I should be very much distressed to have the plan regarded as an attack on the clubs." The president gave much of his vacation to answering, as fully and persuasively as only he could do it, many letters of query that came to him. Meanwhile Hibben was yielding to the counsel of West and the protest of clubmen. "Woodrow does not know the trustees as I do," he warned. "Some will not stay hitched. He is going to split the college."

If anyone could influence Wilson in the name of friendship, Hibben was the man. Partly from shyness, partly from fastidiousness in choosing friends, Wilson had seldom indulged his passion for genuine friendship. But the Hibbens had made themselves utterly agreeable and the president had dared to admit them to the bosom intimacy that a Scot reserves for a very few. "What I really wanted to say to you today stuck in my throat through dryness," he had written one day to Hibben. In his own mind, and without Hibben's consent, he had bound this dear friend by a clannish covenant of allegiance. Now he felt that this disciple must be held loyal. And so Wilson wrote to assure him that not the least shadow had darkened their perfect understanding, that he still valued Hibben's advice on the quad plan, and that it had disposed him to look for opportunities of concession. But never could he yield his dearest principle, he explained: the club system must give way to an organization absolutely controlled, not negatively but constructively and administratively, by the authorities of the university. Not to insist on that, the president thought, would be to temporize with evil.

Hibben was summering in Greensboro, Vermont, where he was in correspondence with members of the opposition. He knew the strength and determination of West and the Van Dykes, of Cleveland and the Morgans. And so he went up to the prophet's retreat in the mountains to plead expediency, to try, as he put it, "to save Woodrow from himself."

No approach could have insulted Wilson more. It pained him that his bosom friend understood him so poorly as to imagine that he could surrender educational principles so essential. He had prepared his soul for martyrdom, if need be. Though there was no irreparable break then and there, the family saw their man's face turn white with anger at what he regarded as the defection of a weak disciple. "Jack keeps driving into my ears—delay," he said, "but the one thing to do is to go ahead and fight. The trustees have spoken . . . There are men on that board who will stand pat till the skies fall."

Determined to go on through what he called, optimistically, a "dust cloud," Wilson came down from the Adirondacks in the fall of 1907 with will unshaken. He was now ready to do battle at close grips. During the summer his undergraduates had been influenced by the talk of clubmen among the alumni. He must bring them back to "things of the mind" and "discipline of the spirit." At the annual dinner of the college newspaper he rose with eyes steely and jaws jutting. The applause was light and chilling, and he began low and clear: "It is my lonely privilege, in gatherings of educated men, to be the only person who speaks of education." Opposition had sharpened all his latent pride and put it on the tip of his tongue. His family had never heard him speak in this tone before. To his opponents the effect was one of arrogance, while his friends saw the "independent conviction" and "self-trust" that "Tommie" Wilson in his student days had thought essential to a political leader. Ten minutes later, after he had scorched his defamers and condemned their unresponsiveness to the intellectual glory that might be Princeton's, his boys were on their feet, climbing tables, cheering. When asked why they applauded a speech with which many of them did not agree, a student replied: "They know a man when they see one." Even Dean West's son was moved to remark: "Sometimes I wish that I were on the other side." [8]

The speaker sat down, grim and silent. Walking home across the campus, he muttered, "Damn their eyes! Damn their eyes!" It seemed to him that they were growing to resemble their fathers, praising him when he talked about democracy but refusing to follow him in democratic action when their "interests" were touched.

In September the faculty threw itself into the fray in earnest. The young preceptors supported their president almost to a man. Factions formed among the older professors, however, and met to discuss plans of action. The opposition met at West's house, which once had been the center of opposition to President Patton; the loyalists, at Dean Fine's.

Finally the time came for the faculty to debate the quad plan in Princeton's House of Commons. Tense and worried, Wilson's colleagues filed in to the vaulted room in historic Nassau Hall, where in three formal meetings the issue was joined and the arguments aired. In the first session Henry Van Dyke made a motion that was designed to sidetrack Wilson's proposal for further study of the quad plan. When Hibben seconded the motion, Wilson turned pale. Controlling his voice with difficulty, the president asked: "Do I understand Professor Hibben seconds the motion?"

"I do, Mr. President."

The silence was sepulchral. Woodrow Wilson, who could be easily hurt by a close friend, suffered a martyr's agony.

[8] Francis C. MacDonald, who sat next to Randolph West, to the writer.

Then West led a sniping attack, suggesting that Wilson's quads would resemble the "quod" (jail) at Princetown, England, and would curtail liberty by making students come in early of evenings. And Wilson in an extravagance of enthusiasm retorted: "Certainly not. We'll have ladders at every window!" [9] The debate took on a tone more common to political bodies than to convocations of scholars.

In the second meeting of the faculty a vote on the Van Dyke resolution gave Wilson a majority of twenty-nine to twenty-two of the old faculty and the support of all but one of the preceptors.

In the third meeting, in a speech that friend and enemy alike hailed as superb, the president again set forth his educational principles. Quoting statistics, he said that the records showed that the clubmen were not taking their share of academic honors. No vote was taken, but at the end of the discussion that followed it was evident that the "prime minister" had held his House of Commons in line and would go with their support to the House of Lords—the board of trustees.[10]

When the trustees met on October 17 their interest in the quad plan had been dampened by the waves of criticism that had come from students and from alumni, more than half of whom opposed the president's project. The influence of the secular alumni had now grown to such strength that it dared to challenge the administration on a point of educational policy. In the face of threats of withdrawal of financial support and in the absence of funds for new buildings, the trustees felt themselves powerless. Convinced that the day was lost, Wilson yielded to the advice of his supporters and announced that his Committee on Social Coordination had no report. A resolution offered by Chairman Pyne proposed that the action taken in June be reconsidered, that the president be requested to withdraw the plan, and that the committee be discharged; but to recognize the rectitude of Wilson's conscience and his right to free speech, the trustees stated that they had "no wish to hinder him in any way in his purpose to endeavor to convince the members of the Board and Princeton men that this plan is the true solution." Moreover, Grover Cleveland proposed that the trustees resolve that *something* be done about the problem of the clubs.

The man who had forced the plan into the consciousness of the

---

[9] F. C. MacDonald to the writer.

[10] V. L. Collins recorded that West told him, on April 14, 1930, that Wilson arranged to have his quad plan tabled without approval at the third faculty meeting (Oct. 17) because Pyne had warned him that the trustees would request his resignation if a faculty vote were taken. *See* Collins's notes in a copy of Baker's *Woodrow Wilson: Life and Letters,* Vol. II, in the Princeton University Library. Collins attended the meetings as secretary of the faculty.

nation felt that he got nothing out of the transaction except complete defeat and mortification. For the first time his family saw his high spirits yield to the discouragement of disillusion. The Hibbens called at Prospect to cheer him, as they had done so many times before; but Wilson treated them so discourteously that he was moved the next day to write in repentance, begging to be forgiven for what he called boorish behavior. When a "black mood" settled on him, he explained, he seemed to forget that he was bred a gentleman. Despite the apology, however, the old familiar relationship was never resumed.

The president told his faculty that the trustees plainly could not support him further in the only matters in which he felt that he could lead and be of service. He thought of resigning, but refrained, he said, because he saw that he did not have the right to place the university in danger of going to pieces.[11]

Wilson was not willing to offer up Princeton on the altar of Absolute Truth. He loved his own *alma mater* too much. He must have marked the similarity of his fight to that of Uncle James Woodrow, whom the trustees of the Columbia Theological Seminary had supported until the financial secretary had expressed fear of the effect of the new ideas on unenlightened contributors. Dear, gentle, crusading uncle, who had just entered eternal peace—the last of the great saints of the older generation—"a man made to love (in the quiet, self-contained Scottish fashion, but very, very deeply, none the less)"! In a wilderness of secularity the prophet at Princeton was now very much alone.

The faith that was bred in Woodrow Wilson and that had survived Civil War and Reconstruction was not shaken. Within a week of the fateful meeting of the trustees, pitching his voice above the whispers of expediency, he preached to his boys on "the importance of single-mindedness," on "principles held with steadfastness," using as his text: "He that observeth the wind shall not sow; he that regardeth the clouds shall not reap."

The press was dramatizing the controversy at Princeton as a battle for social democracy that had national import. Loyal trustees were goading their leader with fighting letters, suggesting that from now on the battle must be frankly one of democracy against special privilege. A theologian trustee assured Wilson that the controversy was "being taken most seriously by the great public who are interested in the matter far more deeply than the smart set of the Clubs or the scared set of

---

11 A year later Pyne assured Wilson that he was still "Princeton's best asset," that he was needed "more than ever" to help to "clean up the finances."

the Board at present realize." Later the president was urged to make clear "the money spirit of the opposition."

Wilson caught his breath quickly and took the warpath. In November he wrote to a loyal trustee: "If we can bring our Princeton constituency to see the necessity of the reform, it is clearly our duty to do so, no matter how long it takes or how hard the task may prove.'

Soon he was showing that he had the stuff of which political campaigners were made. His pluck in fighting on alone when hope seemed dim was endearing him to millions of Americans. In Tennessee, in Maryland, in Indiana, he spoke hotly in rebellion against educational ineffectiveness, keeping his argument on professional grounds. When an honest opponent of the quad plan was proposed as a candidate for the board of trustees, he called the suggestion "excellent."

In January he escaped for a few weeks to Bermuda, spraining his knee on the rough voyage and, once ashore, allowing Mary Allen Peck and her mother to coddle and humor him into gayer spirits. The vitality and ingenuity of his words claimed Mrs. Peck's affection; but he was no Lothario, and he knew it. "The trouble with my face," he used to tell her, "is that there's too much skin . . . I feel at home in Glasgow for it's the only place where my long, lean face goes unremarked." And again, "Women would not look at me twice, dear lady, if they did not think I was something in particular and did not find I had a store of amusing stories."

In Bermuda, Wilson was able to jest about the defeat that had cut so deep. "I didn't get the quads," he said, "but I got the wrangles." [12] He always came back from the island, he wrote, "more sane about everything." [13] Returning in the winter of 1908 with nerves rested, he was determined "to make the issue clear without making it exasperating." He appealed to the alumni and, lifting the issue to a national level, warned: "The particular threat that seems to me most alarming to our life at the present moment is that we are beginning to think in classes." He continued to make it clear to his audiences that, as he said in a speech at Chicago, he was "a good fighter," that "on the whole" he "would rather fight than not . . ." And he was finding that the more belligerent were his words the more hearty was the applause of the Western alumni. [14]

[12] To Mrs. Borden Harriman. Mrs. Harriman to the writer, Feb. 22, 1951.
[13] W.W. to O. G. Villard, Jan. 26, 1908, Villard Papers (Houghton Library, Harvard University, Cambridge, Mass.).
[14] Wilson got a sympathetic response, too, from the undergraduate club members, when he could talk to them in their houses. Invited in the spring of 1909 to the Cottage Club, he listened

A committee of friendly trustees investigated the clubs and in April presented their findings to the board. The report recognized evils in the system but at the same time undermined Wilson's position by remarking that club life did not seem to discourage study in itself or to lower academic standards. Choking with frustration, Wilson confessed to Stockton Axson what he had been too diplomatic to say in his public utterances. At last he was accepting the issue that had been drawn first by one of the clubmen and later by the press of the nation and by friendly trustees. "I'll never win," he admittted grimly. "What I am opposing is privilege. They would let me do anything in educational reform, but here I am attacking their social privileges."

To be sure, there had been formal honors aplenty from those who had ears to hear a prophet. He had been elected to the American Academy of Arts and Letters, had been made a member of the board of the Carnegie Foundation, had been awarded his ninth honorary degree, and had received more invitations than ever to speak to distinguished audiences. Moreover, Lawrence Lowell, soon to assume the presidency of Harvard, had come to his support in a speech at the Princeton Commencement. "Your President," he said, "is one of the men who have grappled with the problem as it exists today, the problem of the college, of the undergraduate department. He has begun solutions which are an example and encouragement to every college in the United States."

But the gentle Scottish soul beneath the crusading armor longed for peace and friendship, and his ideal comradeship with Hibben had been broken. His beloved undergraduates had disappointed him. He had lost his adored Uncle James Woodrow. However, there were resources in his religion that fortified him in his personal grief. He spoke of them in his Baccalaureate to the class of 1907: "To one deep fountain of revelation and renewal few of you, I take it for granted, have had access yet,—I mean the fountain of sorrow, a fountain sweet or bitter according as it is drunk in submission or in rebellion, in love or in resentment and deep dismay. I will not tell you of those waters; if you have not tasted them it would be futile,—and some of you will understand without word of mine. I can only beg that when they are put to your lips,

---

to a brilliant attack on his quad plan, delivered in Biblical parable by President Emeritus Patton and responded extemporaneously in the same style, carried the boys with him, and sat around and entertained them until midnight.

Walking by the Cottage Club one day, Wilson said to Julian Beaty, his student secretary: "I think they ought to change its name to Castle." Then he added: "Perhaps I shouldn't say that, as I think I am an honorary member." J. Beaty to R. S. Baker, July 2, 1926. Confirmed by Beaty to the writer.

as they must be, you will drink of them as those who seek renewal and know how to make of sadness a mood of enlightenment and of hope."

The prophet could face up to his personal losses and accept them if only his cause prospered. But it was not easy to reconcile himself to the fact that he had failed to give effect to what he regarded as the will of God for Princeton. He had not provided the tactful planning and the liaison with men of wealth and influence that were required for the realization of a sound but revolutionary educational ideal. One of his careless remarks—trenchant and indiscreet—had leaked into circulation: "After all, what does Grover Cleveland know about a university?" [15] And Cleveland had retaliated by writing to a friend [16] that the president of Princeton was without a vestige of professional honesty.

[15] Bliss Perry to the writer.
[16] Prentiss Bailey, editor of the Utica *Observer*. See O. G. Villard, *Fighting Years*, p. 228 n.

CHAPTER VIII

Principles, Not Men

With wilson's plan for undergraduate quadrangles decently buried, the trustees could give closer attention to constructing the graduate college for which Dean West had been pressing.[1]

In 1902, after studying graduate work at European universities, West drew up a formal plan for a graduate college that would be so placed that the undergraduates would pass by in their daily walks. This was a scheme close to the heart of Wilson. In his first report to the board, on October 21, 1902, he asked for three million dollars for endowment of a graduate establishment. He told the trustees what he later wrote in a preface for a pamphlet in which West's plan was printed: that the project was one by which "a group of graduate students are most apt to stimulate and set the pace for the whole university." And in his inaugural address Wilson had been even more explicit. The graduate college would be built, he said, "not apart, but as nearly as may be at the very heart, the geographical heart, of the university; and its comradeship shall be for young men and old, for the novice as well as for the graduate." During his years at the Johns Hopkins Graduate School, as student and as lecturer, Wilson had seen the advantage that came to both undergraduates and graduate students from close association outside the classroom. The younger men caught something of the serious intent of the professional scholar, and the graduates were saved from scornful misunderstanding of the men whom they were preparing to teach.

The board of trustees had not formally adopted the proposals made in West's pamphlet and approved by Wilson. The president's drive for funds for the preceptorial system, which West supported heartily, had made it impossible for the dean to make rapid headway until, in 1905—the year after Grover Cleveland became chairman of the trustees' committee on the graduate school—West finally accumulated resources

---

[1] The trustees, acting upon a faculty report signed by Wilson in 1896, recognized a graduate residence as "of the first importance for the organization and development of the graduate work." Memorial to the trustees, Dec. 10, 1896, from a faculty committee appointed by Patton and including Wilson but not West.

116

enough to take over an old estate that he named "Merwick." There, about a half mile from the campus, he installed a few of his scholars. But when he asked that the drive for funds for the tutorial program be supplemented by "a determined and unremitting effort in behalf of the graduate college," the trustees merely encouraged him to campaign on his own. The dean did as suggested; and early in 1906 a wealthy Princeton lady, Mrs. Swann, left a bequest to the university to further the dean's purpose. Wilson expressed delight over the gift, and on December 13 expressed his pleasure over the work at Merwick and the fact that the college to be built would enlarge the community life of the graduate students.

In the spring of 1908, at the very session of the trustees at which Wilson's quad plan was dealt its death blow, it was voted to accept Ralph Adams Cram's recommendation that the Swann bequest should be used for the construction of a graduate college at the heart of the campus. This was an endorsement of Wilson's views, contrary to the desire of West and Cleveland that the new unit be placed off campus, preferably at Merwick.

There the issue rested in the summer of 1908, when Wilson sought relaxation by traveling in England. When trustees offered to pay the expenses of the trip, he declined, saying to his wife: "I may have to oppose some of these men upon the vital educational policies of Princeton, and I should be trussed up if I accepted such favours from them."

On the byways of Scotland and at Carlyle's birthplace, Wilson found his appetite for life reviving, though his afflicted eye and his pen hand still bothered him. From abroad he could look with magnanimity on Grover Cleveland, who died late in June. "I do not think," he commented in a letter to his wife, "that my knowledge of how he failed and disappointed us during the past few years . . . will long obscure my admiration for his great qualities and his singularly fine career."

When he reached the Lake Country, his old friend Mrs. Yates threw a hospitable arm about him and he looked up to a Wordsworthian hill that rose before him "like some great nourishing breast." At Carnegie's Skibo Castle he met a fascinating assortment of fellow guests and enjoyed talk with Burke's biographer, John Morley, whom he thought an "old goose" for accepting removal to the House of Lords from the House of Commons. He found his hostess "*very* sweet and true," but in writing to Ellen he reserved "for the modulations of the voice" many things "not suitable to be written down"—his opinion of his host in particular. And yet, for dear Princeton's sake, he had to be civil to the philanthropist.

Returning to the campus in the autumn of 1908, his vigor completely restored, Wilson found that the problems of social life were becoming more acute. He revealed his discomfiture and restlessness to Frank A. Vanderlip, a banker who, he hoped, might secure a large gift from Carnegie that would make the quad plan practicable. "I must get the money . . ." he wrote. "If I cannot do this, I must turn to something else than mere college administration—forced not by my colleagues but by my mind and convictions, to the impossibility of continuing at things I do not believe in . . ."

Several of the trustees had come to see what a few had commented on in 1906—the folly of allowing Dean West to remain at Princeton and carry on graduate work without an exact understanding of his accountability to the president and the faculty. In the spring of 1909, at the urging of new professors whom Wilson had attracted to Princeton, the trustees decided to correct this situation by lodging control of graduate studies in a six-man faculty committee of which Dean West was made a member. To his associates on this body, West seemed stubborn in his prejudices—a man who ruled by exceptions.[2] Fireplaces and private baths, they said, could not be afforded by many of the scholars who were qualified for admittance. In fact, they felt that graduate students of serious purpose would be repelled by any scheme that laid emphasis on considerations other than scholarship.

Wilson doubted that this committee would bring lasting peace. Appreciative of the refinements of culture and realizing that they were "too hard to find in America," he had warned that "culture is a word it is easy to drawl and make too mawkish distinctions about." He feared that Andrew West was making a fool of himself. In the ideal graduate college, Wilson said, "a certain simplicity of life still of necessity prevails. The studious pursuits of such schools are of necessity so important, so engrossing, so directly related to the practical success of the men who have sought the place out for preparation that little else is heeded." Such luxuries as West recommended might make of the graduate college merely another club where the minds of the scholars

[2] The newcomers, like Dean Fine who became the leader of the majority group of the new committee, had had more experience than West in the ways of graduate study both abroad and in America. One of them, for example, Edward Capps, had taken the degree of Ph.D. at the Yale Graduate School, had done graduate work in Germany and at Athens, and had taught graduate students at the University of Chicago and at Yale. A majority of the new committee did not take kindly to certain luxuries in the elaborate plans that West presented.

would become as soft as the cushions on which they would sit, and Princeton would fall far short of the standard of graduate study that Wilson had himself known. Moreover, the undergraduate work needed funds so badly that it seemed wasteful, from the point of view of the entire university, to supply unnecessary luxuries to graduate scholars. West, who understood that his leadership had been endorsed in 1906 when he had been urged not to go to M.I.T., asked Wilson why control of graduate education had been given to the new faculty committee; and Wilson replied: "I wish to say to the Dean somewhat grimly that he must be digested in the processes of the university."

When an opportunity came to fight back, West seized it and chose his weapon shrewdly. William Cooper Procter, a former student and a wealthy manufacturer of soap, offered a half-million dollars toward the fulfillment of West's dreams, provided that his gift was matched by others totaling the same amount. Examining the site near Prospect that Cram had recommended for use of the Swann bequest, Procter pronounced it unsuitable and said that his offer was made on the understanding that some location be chosen that would be satisfactory to him. This meant, everyone knew, that the site must be acceptable to Andrew West.

Promoters of Princeton were thrilled by the prospect of a further addition to what the college newspaper had headlined as the "unprecedented material growth of the university." But there were hard, cold reasons why Woodrow Wilson felt that he could not accept the Procter offer.[3] Moreover, he had been emotionally prejudiced against it by disturbing gossip, rumors that gifts were being solicited for Princeton behind the president's back. Wilson had protested that "all of this movement of groups in entire independence of each other" made him very uneasy and rendered "proper government of the University impossible." He was not reassured when Procter addressed his proposal not to the trustees or the president, but to Dean West, who had been authorized to negotiate with the donor as a representative of the trustees' committee on graduate work.

The balance of power at that juncture lay in the hands of Moses Taylor Pyne, who had succeeded Cleveland as chairman of the trustees' committee on the graduate school. A kindly, disinterested man who hated discord, he could be depended on to base his opinions on an hon-

---

[3] Wilson believed that the legal terms of the earlier bequest of Mrs. Swann would prevent its use with the Procter gift for a plant off-campus; and he accepted the condition attached to the Swann contribution the more readily because it coincided with his educational plan.

est devotion to the interests of Princeton University as he conceived them.

This genial philanthropist was at first neutral in the controversy over the location of the graduate college; but when Procter, who preferred to build at Merwick, agreed to compromise on the golf links as a site, Pyne supported that proposal and with West [4] campaigned actively for a vote of the board that would satisfy the desire of the alumni for acceptance of the proffered money on any terms that would seem reasonable to laymen.

Wilson told a friendly trustee that he felt the pressure and embarrassment of his position keenly; but he reined his temper well. He resented the presumption of a benefactor in dictating the use of a gift. And yet, realizing that his accountability to trustees and alumni forbade the refusal of a half-million dollars without a determined effort to find a way to use it effectively, aware that any strong stand on his part would merely add power to the cry of "dictator" that his enemies had been raising, Wilson pleaded with Procter. But the West faction would not consider the campus as a site for the new college, though they could give no convincing educational argument for their dissent; and the clamor of the alumni was becoming more insistent.

That summer Wilson tucked himself away in the quiet town of old Lyme, Connecticut, and tried to fortify his spiritual resources. Free from the whirl of university politics, covenanting only to obey the law of inertia, he meditated on the philosophy that always had guided him. He felt young again, his thoughts reverted to his childhood, and he consoled himself in the knowledge that in his own mind he was as independent as when he was a dreaming boy. He was beginning to remind his daughters, now, that there were some people who could not be trusted.

After two summer months spent in comparative idleness and in small and chivalrous attentions to his loved ones, he was chafing again for contact with affairs that were hard and essential. Work appealed to him as an end in itself, and the most wholesome and satisfactory thing in an uncertain world. It was never straightforward, independent work that harassed him at Princeton, but rather the tiresomeness of sophomoric young fools, the long-windedness of professorial old ones, the pathetic delusions of doting parents, the empty and injudicious

---

[4] As in the case of his relations with Cleveland, West had not been backward about cultivating a friendship with Pyne. On Pyne's birthday in 1907, West had presented an original poem, luxuriously printed and bound, and inscribed with a Greek phrase meaning "Keep young, dear soul."

minds of young alumni, the officious pomp of certain trustees, the importunities of vain patrons. And these crosses were never so hard to bear as when they interfered with constructive work designed to quicken the intellectual life of the university.

In the fall of 1909, when he had an opportunity to speak to young ministers at Chicago, Wilson seized upon the occasion to put backbone into individuals, including himself. In directing his sermons at his own needs, he said, he hoped also to help others who were like him. "The great danger of our day," he warned, ". . . is that men will compound their conscientious scruples on the ground that they are not free to move independently . . . For they say, 'The penalty will be that we shall be absolutely crushed.' The organization must dictate to us, if we be members of a corporation; if we be members of a union, the union; if we be members of a society of whatever kind, the programme of the society must dominate us . . . Every turning point in the history of mankind has been pivoted upon the choice of an individual, when some spirit that would not be dominated stood stiff in its independence and said: 'I go this way. Let any man go another way who pleases' . . ."

In a magazine article he tried to answer the question: "What is a College for?" It is "for the use of the nation," he reiterated, "not for the satisfaction of those who administer it or for the carrying out of their private views." He remarked upon the increasing number of rich students, feared that their wealth would remove all incentive to work and they would be "foredoomed to obscurity." In the colleges of the day, he complained, "the side shows are so numerous, so diverting—so important, if you will—that they have swallowed up the circus, and those who perform in the main tent must often whistle for their audiences, discouraged and humiliated." Do not cast out the side shows, he advised, but they must be subordinated.

In October the majority of the faculty committee on the graduate school presented a report to the trustees—not published until February, 1910—in which they argued that the separation of the graduate residence from the campus would impair efficiency both in administration and in student work. Further, they pointed out that "the untoward effect of the isolation of particular schools has been witnessed at Columbia, at Pennsylvania, at the Johns Hopkins, and elsewhere; and early mistakes in location have been remedied, where possible, at great expense." However, Hibben joined with West in signing a minority report that recommended an off-campus site, justifying this position by the success of the graduate residence at Merwick.

When finally the Hibbens stood openly with West on graduate policy, the Wilsons believed that their friends were not only disloyal but ambitious, as well, for the presidency of Princeton. Ellen Wilson, who had observed Jennie Hibben's preference for the company of Mrs. Cleveland, now let it be known that there would be no forgiveness. The door was closed.

As for West, Wilson had concluded that it was impossible to deal directly with him. To a proposal that the dean sent through Professor Daniels, the president replied: ". . . the method he is using is entirely illegal . . . The letter . . . fills me with amazement." Wilson asked Daniels to report this reaction to West, in order to avoid the delivery of a reprimand in faculty meeting. Personal recrimination made him ill; moreover, it would merely strengthen West's feeling that he was persecuted. It was better, he felt, to preach general principles and to encourage the faculty committee to argue the case on its merits.

In the eyes of many lay alumni, however, the refinements of educational policy were blurred. They could see only folly in rejecting a half-million dollars in deference to ideals that were to them both nebulous and pious; and some businessmen took the attitude that if West made the sale to Procter he should have the credit. So, in October of 1909, the board of trustees, faced with a large deficit for the preceding year, noting that Wilson had made no successful effort to secure funds for the graduate college, sensitive to alumni opinion, and confident that another half million could be raised to match Procter's offer, voted to overrule the majority report of the faculty committee, to accept the gift, and to build the new unit on the golf links almost a mile from the university library, provided that the earlier Swann bequest could be used legally on that site.

Wilson's close friends, now a minority of the trustees, ridiculed the decision. They laughed at the haste with which certain educators and clergymen on the board clutched at the half-million dollars, regardless of the merits of the proposition. Wilson himself was stunned. He was now losing a battle that, before the appearance of Procter's money, had been won. He could only conclude that the trustees had acted as they did, not because they trusted West—whom he now considered an archintriguer—but because money had talked more convincingly than their president. Wrath rioted in his veins and muddled his thinking. Disheartened and disgusted, he feared that his sharp tongue would betray his scorn and that a careless word might irreparably damage the institution that he loved and for which he was responsible. His impulse was to resign and let his antagonists explain their case to the country as best they could. But he told himself that it would not be sporting to quit while there was any chance of winning.

A few weeks later, driven by concern for Princeton's harmony, he forced himself to suggest a compromise, to carry out a precept that he had given his students: "There can be no compromise in individual morality; but there *has* to be a compromise, an average, in social morality. There is indeed an element of morality in the very fact of compromise on *social* undertakings." [5] On December 31, Wilson suggested to Pyne, unofficially and tentatively, that the Swann bequest be used to build a residential college for graduate students on the campus and the Procter gift be used for graduate instruction on the golf links site. This personal suggestion, a makeshift, seemed to Pyne "a ridiculous solution of the question" and "not worth considering."

And so, at the end of 1909, Wilson was in deepest gloom. In October the University of Minnesota had tried to lure him to its presidency and he still had that offer under consideration when he made a last effort, on December 22, to convert Procter to the compromise proposal that Pyne had rejected. He was desperately worried, he said, for he felt that as prime minister of Princeton he was assuming all the responsibility that Procter suggested should belong to the trustees. When the philanthropist said, "You had better change your board of trustees," Wilson replied, "No, I think they had better change their president." Failing in his effort to compromise, learning that Procter and West were determined to dictate the disposal not only of the Procter gift but of the matching half million and—illegally, he thought—of the Swann bequest as well, Wilson saw no further hope of serving Princeton. Sitting down in the railroad station at Jersey City, he penciled this sentence to Pyne: "The acceptance of this gift has taken the guidance of the University out of my hands entirely—and I seem to have come to the end." He had failed to command the confidence of the constituency on the quad plan, and now on his policy for the graduate college.

When Pyne, alarmed at the loss of educational prestige that the university would suffer, replied that he hoped that the president's note from Jersey City did not "represent . . . well considered conclusions" and that it would be withdrawn, Wilson sat down at his desk on Christmas Day and unburdened himself. The board's acceptance of the Procter offer, Wilson wrote to Pyne, reversed the policy of the faculty and

[5] Raymond Fosdick's address, "Personal Recollections of W.W.," given at the University of Chicago, Jan. 30, 1956.

the leading concept of his whole administration in an educational matter of fundamental importance. "I am not willing to be drawn further into the toils. I cannot accede to the acceptance of gifts upon terms which take the educational policy of the University out of the hands of the Trustees and Faculty and permit it to be determined by those who give money . . . I cannot consent, if the gift is deliberately accepted on such terms, to remain responsible for the direction of the affairs of the University or for the development of her educational policy."

Reviewing the history of the controversy, Wilson reminded Pyne that "West's first idea" contemplated a graduate college that lay in every sense at the heart of things, and that modification of his purpose [6] had played no small part in depriving him of the confidence of his academic colleagues. "He has now lost their confidence completely," Wilson wrote, "and nothing administered by him in accordance with his present ideas can succeed."

His passionate concern for academic freedom led Wilson to add to his denunciation of Dean West a fateful sentence: "Indeed, nothing administered by him can now succeed." Wilson all but accused his ambitious colleague of trying to buy position and preferment. A few days later he wrote to a friendly trustee: "We now know, indeed, that Mr. Procter's gift is made to put West in the saddle, but we cannot make that a matter of public discussion." To do so, he said, would "make it appear a personal matter, which the friends of the University would certainly misinterpret greatly to our discredit." When he was asked, later, what sort of fellow West was, he said merely: "A little difficult. I suspect he thinks I am too." Discussing the dean's educational policies, however, he flared into incandescence.

The absolute necessity of the moment, Wilson thought, was that his friends should find money with which to buy freedom.[7] Pyne confessed that he was "torn almost in two." Finally, in a last-minute effort at reconciliation, Procter was persuaded to accept the compromise that

[6] It was indeed true that West had modified his views and purposes, chiefly in the direction of luxury and concentration of executive power in his own hands. For Wilson's considered opinion of West's policies, see the statement that Wilson drew up in 1912 and that is printed in Baker, II, 358–60. In this statement Wilson asserted that he had opposed West's plan "in the essential particular of its site and consequent spirit and character, and sought by every possible suggestion to bring it back to what it had been originally intended to be."

[7] Professor Harper thought that the issue before the board was boiling down to this: "which can Princeton least afford to lose, Professor West and $500,000, or Woodrow Wilson and an honorable rank among American universities?" The faculty, Harper thought, would decide in favor of President Wilson by a vote of four to one. George McLean Harper to Wilson Farrand, Feb. 3, 1910, Farrand Papers (Princeton University Library).

had been proposed on December 22 by Wilson, personally and unofficially and with no confidence that it was a proper solution—a compromise that Pyne had thought not worthy of consideration.

This about-face was reported in meetings of the graduate-school committee and the full board of trustees in January. Thrown into confusion by the sudden blurring of the issue that he had drawn so clearly, surrendering to the temptation of friends who had advised him to denounce West publicly, Wilson made an extravagant statement that later was to be regretted. Dean West's ideas and ideals, he said, were not those of Princeton. Upsetting with a short, careless phrase all the professional argument on the question of site that had been built up over a period of years, the president contended that *his* faculty could make the graduate school a success "anywhere in Mercer County." He had been startled into letting down the shield of conviction and opening himself to attack as a feuding dictator.

His friends understood and applauded.[8] The opposition, however, had embarrassing questions to ask. Why, they queried, had the president for so long made the site the main issue? Unable or unwilling to comprehend the forbearance that executive responsibility had forced on him, they thought that he had been insincere in insisting on location as the basic issue, that in reality he had been acting all along out of spite against West.[9] And their wavering confidence was further shaken by a characteristic lapse of memory on the part of the president. Attempting to dramatize the issue, Wilson held up before the trustees a copy of West's original printed report, *Proposed Graduate College of Princeton University*, and exclaimed: "The fundamental difficulty with Mr. Procter's offer is that it is specifically intended to carry out the ideals of that book. A graduate school based on these ideals cannot succeed." In impulsively seizing on this publication as an objectification of all that West stood for, Wilson forgot, in his flurry of emotion, that when it was printed, in 1903, West had not expressed either his present views on the site of the graduate college or the desire for dictation of policy and personnel that now seemed so outrageous. Actually, except

[8] A majority of the faculty committee on the graduate school gave the trustees a statement buttressing the president's disapproval of the dean's plans, asserting: ". . . we cannot attract strong men by adherence to dilettante ideals." Baker, II, 324.

[9] The truth is that Wilson liked neither West nor his ideas and thoroughly distrusted his motives. As a responsible executive, however, his only effective course of action was to argue on an ideological plane. There is no evidence to show why the president at first chose to stress the question of site above the educational considerations that were raised by the majority of the faculty committee on the graduate school: perhaps because, being a more concrete matter, it could be grasped more easily by the minds of laymen; but more likely, because it was Procter's attempt to dictate the site that raised the essential question of academic freedom.

for a tendency toward unproductive luxury, most of what West had written in 1902 could still be approved by Wilson in 1910. In fact, *he himself had written a preface commending the very work that he was now damning!* [10]

West's supporters saw the inconsistency and exploited it. One of them asked why Wilson had praised West's report in his preface if it was so unacceptable. Completely confounded, the president could only mumble an unconvincing and very damaging remark to the effect that he had not really seen West's pamphlet when he wrote the preface.

Wilson had assured his students that a man of simple truthfulness had no need to worry about petty details, that only liars had to remember everything carefully to avoid incriminating themselves by inconsistencies.[11] His own memory, so notoriously defective that he had been known to repeat an anecdote to the very man who had told it to him the day before, did not come to his rescue and remind him, in this atmosphere of cross-examination, that most of the anathema had crept into West's doctrine during the eight years since his pamphlet was printed. As a trial lawyer Wilson was not, had never been, convincing. He had not yet learned that an executive must keep up his guard even when among those whom he counted as friends. Before he could be a great parliamentarian he would have to learn to put less trust in the confidence of his associates in his good intentions.[12]

As a result of the give-and-take of the January meeting, and in spite of a conciliatory note from the president, Pyne lost all confidence in Wilson's integrity and in his executive ability, and from that time on opposed him at every turn. He could explain the president's contradictory statements only on the ground either that he was mentally unbalanced or that he was suffering from extreme jealousy. He tried to conspire with Procter to force the resignation of Wilson, and a trustee warned the president that things would be done purposely to goad him into a position where he would want to resign. Pyne haunted Wilson's

10 *See* p. 116 above.
11 Chambers MS, p. 28.
12 Wilson's confusion was further confounded in a bristling skirmish over the reasons for his change of opinion regarding the compromise plan that Procter had first refused but later accepted. It came out that Wilson had presented the makeshift plan to Pyne with assurance that it had the "hearty concurrence" of his faculty colleagues, and that actually the proposal had so offended them that some of them had since persuaded the president that it was unwise. (The phrase "hearty concurrence" was but another instance of the prophet's tendency to project his own ideas into other men's minds without their leave.)

Wilson was utterly unable to defend himself against the sudden and unforeseen attack on his integrity. "I was so . . . angered at the evident trick that had been played upon us," he wrote afterward, "that I did not feel at all sure that I had acted with self-control and propriety . . ." W.W. to Henry B. Thompson, Jan. 17, 1910, in Baker, II, 322.

dreams as a man incalculable, almost irresponsible, prowling deviously in the underbrush while the president, like a treed cat, held himself poised to jump in any direction.

Despite the crosscurrents in the January session of the board, the tide of opinion was still flowing toward the president. He was empowered to appoint a special committee of five trustees which was to report at the next meeting. While this body was at work, Procter, seeing that his offer was about to be declined, withdrew it.[13] In February the special committee gave to the full board a unanimous report opposing an off-campus site for the graduate college.

All the meetings, reports, and letters had been hedged about by secrecy and an air of high tension. Trustees had conferred excitedly in twos and threes. Little groups of rumormongers had whispered and agitated in Eastern cities; but there were no public blasts until, in January, distorted and sensational stories began to appear in New York newspapers. On February 3 the lid blew off completely. H. B. Brougham, editor of the *New York Times*, had learned about the controversy, had composed an editorial supporting Wilson, and, just before publishing it, asked him for confirmation; and he, pressed for time, again lowered the guard of executive responsibility for a moment and sent to the editor what he considered to be a "perfectly candid and confidential statement of the whole matter." Procter, Wilson wrote, had insisted on certain ideas that a majority of the faculty thought demoralizing. Following his wishes would result in fastening on graduate students "the same artificial and unsound social standards" that already dominated the life of undergraduates. There was no obscuring the fact, he asserted, that the issue was now joined between a college life into which all the bad elements of social ambition and unrest intrude themselves and a life ordered upon a simpler plan under the domination of real university influences and on a basis of genuine democracy.

The editor of the *Times* fell hungrily upon Wilson's words, disregarding their "confidential" nature. Appropriating a few and paraphrasing others, he prefaced the whole with nation-shaking rhetoric: "At Princeton, the scene of a battle fought a century and a third ago

---

[13] Replying to a letter from the Committee of Five asking him to define the conditions of his gift, Procter withdrew his offer and explained that he had acted under the belief that Dean West's pamphlet of 1902 "bore the authority of the university." He had perhaps been misled by West's statement therein to the effect that "the proposal" had been "adopted by the Board of Trustees, after full consideration." Actually, the trustees had not formally adopted West's proposal of 1902 but had merely approved, in 1896, a proposal made by the faculty "to establish a graduate school at Princeton." *See* the Minutes of the Princeton Trustees' Meeting, Feb. 10, 1910, Report of the Special Committee of Five.

for the establishment of the American democracy, is in progress today a struggle not less significant for the future of American youth and of Government in the United States . . . The Nation is roused against special privilege. Sheltered by a great political party, it has obtained control of our commerce and our industries. Now its exclusive and benumbing touch is upon those institutions which should stand pre-eminently for life, earnest endeavor, and broad enlightenment."

The question to be settled, the *Times* editorial asserted on February 3, was whether Princeton and other endowed universities were to "bend and degrade" their energies "into fostering mutually exclusive social cliques, stolid groups of wealth and fashion, devoted to non-essentials and the smatterings of culture . . . All the college Presidents have cried out against this stultifying influence, and none more earnestly than President Woodrow Wilson of Princeton."

The prestige that came to Wilson's name from this editorial and from subsequent discussions in the press was a valuable asset to a man who had always aspired to serve the nation; but the words of the *Times* fell into the camp of the enemy like sparks of dry powder. Pyne and his friends sent a refutation of the charges to the *Times* for publication and tried to smoke out Wilson's attitude toward the editorial, calling on him to reject it as "unquestionably false." Paul Van Dyke called on the president and denounced it as a slander on Grover Cleveland.

Wilson replied that Cleveland, lacking experience in education, had been misled by West, as he himself had been for a time. The president maintained that, though the color of the editorial was much exaggerated, it was founded in truth. Though the men supporting West were not consciously trying to foster "stolid groups of wealth," that would be the effect of their plans, Wilson said. Actually, as he wrote Brougham a few days later, he believed "every word" of the editorial to be true. Pyne, his "life-long friend," had been misled, he asserted.

Further publicity was given to the controversy in February when two key reports were published in the *Princeton Alumni Weekly* on February 16.[14] The arguments were now in the open, to be bandied about by anyone who might care to strike.

Two days before the committee reports became public, Wilson broke away for a short trip to Bermuda. It gave him "an unspeakable sense of

14 The reports published were that of the special Committee of Five of the trustees and that of the majority of the faculty committee on the graduate school, which had been presented to the trustees in the preceding autumn.

relief," he wrote to Dodge before he sailed, to have been made free, by the withdrawal of Procter's offer, "to govern the University as our judgments and consciences dictate! . . . I know what is coming; but nothing can put me from the presidency now except some adverse *action* of the Board itself. The heavier the storm, the tighter I will sit."

His spirits rose at the arrival of messages of support from alumni, especially from the Western men. Soon his jangling nerves were quieted and he could write to his Ellen: "We have no compromises to look back on, the record of our conscience is clear in this whole trying business. We can be happy, therefore, no matter what may come of it all. It would be rather jolly, after all, to start out on life anew together, to make a new career, would it not? Experience deepens with us . . . and with experience love, and I thank God with all my heart!"

Returning from Bermuda, the president found Mrs. Wilson uneasy, and feeling as if the whole air about her was poisoned. He was reassured, however, by letters of encouragement from A. Lawrence Lowell and from President David Starr Jordan of Stanford University. To his old friend Hiram Woods he outlined his policy for meeting personal attacks: "The other side is not in a temper to receive any statement from me. Their attack is personal and not on its merits . . . To state the interior of this business would be to discredit a number of men of whom the alumni at present have a high opinion. I think it would do the University more harm than good to do such a thing, because it would add bitterness untold to the controversy. It is much better that I should take the brunt of it than to do that."

What Wilson called the "little Princeton party" was most vociferous in the Eastern cities. There alumni were proposing as a new trustee a man who would strengthen their cause. To hold his majority in Princeton's "House of Lords" the president felt that he must make an appeal to the country, and so he took the stump at five Princeton alumni meetings. His argument was rational, conciliatory, soothing.

In New York at the Princeton Club he confronted the Philistines face to face, coming down off the "stilts of study" as his father had taught him that a real man must do. To a suggestion that he might wish to dine in private before his address, he replied that he would not like to appear to avoid his antagonists. Because there had been occasions on which reporters had attributed to Wilson certain words that he disavowed, responsible stenographers were brought to this dinner to record every word spoken. The speaker was received by cold and formal applause for the "president of Princeton," instead of the usual "tiger" for Wilson.

Talking to these businessmen about the "business of a university," he reminded them that "just when all the academic world was waiting for somebody to take the initiative . . . Princeton had the audacity to step forward and take it." Undergraduate work had made great strides but the graduate studies had lagged, he said: while the graduate enrollment at Yale had more than quintupled, Princeton's had increased very slowly up until 1909. And why? "The graduate school of Princeton University was, by the bylaws of the Board of Trustees, kept during most of those years in the hands of a single officer . . . The energy and enthusiasm of the faculty was not behind the enterprise." Now that a committee of the faculty had been given control of the graduate school, he pointed out, the number of students had doubled within a year. In one of the oversimplifications to which Wilson's oratory was prone, he said that Princeton must decide whether to take Procter's money "at the risk of having no graduate students, or get the graduate students at the risk of having no money."

He went on with mounting fervor: "Divorce the universities of this country from their teaching enthusiasm, divorce them from their undergraduate energies, and you will have a thing which is not only un-American but utterly unserviceable to the country." And in a final grand hyperbole: "There is nothing private in America. Everything is public; everything belongs to the united energy of the nation . . . We must not be afraid of publicity."

To his sophisticated audience this sounded like the "political talk" of William Jennings Bryan and his cohorts. Not since Wilson made his first immature speech to New York alumni, more than twenty years before, had an audience received him so coldly. He talked more than an hour and made few converts; but this time, at least, they heard him through.

At St. Louis, Western graduates rallied to cheer him as he reviewed and defended his policy. Suggesting that the faculty be trusted to settle the difficulties, he asserted: "If they should vote against my judgment, I should yield my own judgment, not because they outvoted me but because I should feel that I was wrong if they did not agree with me."

But the faculty were not permitted to vote. As Wilson feared, at their April meeting the trustees postponed reference of graduate school issues to the faculty and favored a new plan for persuading Procter to renew his offer. When one vote on which he had counted swung the decision against him, as a trustee argued that to consult the faculty at so late a date would be merely to add to the confusion, Wilson plainly showed his resentment.

The prophet's cup of bitterness was full. Worried about his health, he went to his physician for his annual checkup and was reassured. "Wilson, there is just one thing," the doctor said to him. "Keep your enemies fighting you." He thrived on a fight, once the issue was clearly drawn and the battle fairly joined. But now he was caught in a tragic conflict of responsibilities. He must provide for his precious family; yet without the approval of his own conscience and the respect of his colleagues, his spirit would starve. "Members of Congress and ministers of the Gospel should not marry," he once remarked, "so that they would be free always to fight for what is right." [15]

Twenty-five years earlier he had said of one of the antagonists of his Uncle James Woodrow: "I hope that the Seminary *will* die, and die soon, if such pestiferous fellows as he are to be put into its hitherto honored chairs." And now Woodrow Wilson was tempted to let Princeton go with Dean West to perdition. Yet he loved the college that he had known in the seventies and in the nineties, still treasured the loyalty of his "little band of university men" in whom he saw the spirit of truth persisting and who would go through hell-fire with him, still looked with fatherly affection on the boys whom he was leading. If he were to follow his impulse to apply his talents to the service of state or nation, what *would* become of the university that was so dear to him?

Torn by these conflicting emotions, Woodrow Wilson went in mid-April to Pittsburgh to address a gathering of alumni. The speech that he made there proved to be the crossing of the Rubicon in a march to the nation's capital.

In speaking to alumni at Pittsburgh, the president of Princeton was returning to the battleground of the grandfather he had never seen, the Jeffersonian editor who set up the first mechanized printing press in the city and who never sidestepped a verbal fight. In what he said to his twentieth-century constituency there were echoes of the spirit of the Scotch-Irish "movers" of frontier days.

There was still wilderness left in America, to be sure, in the year 1910. Men with wandering feet could roam at will. But the best land had been

<hr/>

[15] Chambers MS, pp. 21, 53.

taken, and the rainbow of vast opportunity was ceasing to shine in men's imaginations. Turner had relegated the frontier to history, and Woodrow Wilson said in 1895: "The westward march has stopped, upon the final slopes of the Pacific, and now the plot thickens . . . The stage of America grows crowded like the stage of Europe. The life of the new world grows as complex as the life of the old."

As a young man Wilson had sensed the great challenge of the industrial age to human intelligence. "Civilization," he had written to Bobby Bridges in 1881, " has taken to itself steel wings which never tire and steam lungs which are never exhausted and voices electric and telephonic which disregard distance, and man must be smart indeed to escape her influence. "Writing a decade later as a historian surveying the state of the nation, he had observed in *Division and Reunion*: "Individual fortunes came almost suddenly into existence such as . . . the world had seldom seen since the ancient days of Eastern luxury or Roman plunder. Self-indulgence and fashion displayed and disported themselves as never before in the sober republic." But at the same time the Princeton professor sensed that "the nation felt itself big and healthy enough to tolerate even folly for the sake of freedom . . . the new troubles bred new thinkers, and the intellectual life of the nation was but the more deeply stirred."

In the new age of machinery, financial powers had grown up that were beyond the experience of the Woodrows and the Wilsons. The capitalists of the day led a precarious life, subject alike to the strain on moral fiber that comes with great riches and to the threat of bankruptcy in periods of panic. Some became sensitive, even supersensitive, to actions and words that might upset the very delicate balance in which the new machine economy hung. They were, they thought, America's indispensable men. They were making the nation's economy viable, just as Wilson was aspiring to give viability to education. They fed the goose that laid the golden eggs that fed the government. They maintained churches, schools, charities. The material blessings of the new Princeton that Wilson had created were made possible by their wisdom and beneficence. Who would finance and direct industrial growth so that it would be efficient and productive if they did not? Certainly not the government, they thought, with its councils responsive to inexpert and unstable opinions.

As the machines became more complicated and the financing of them more complex, the directors of industry were drawn into deeper and more absorbing study. They seemed willing to leave political matters to agents of slight intellect and weak conscience. Soon they were far beyond the boundary of Wilson's economic background; and he, in turn, had a perspective on American society and government that far outspanned that of financial managers.

To anyone except a man blinded by self-interest, the depredations of the financial leviathans were as obvious as the blessings that they conferred. Some trustees and managers had proved themselves faithless: some had brazenly bought the favor of public officials. Corporation lawyers of a type that had sickened Wilson at Atlanta were in evidence. Any alert layman could not help but be aware of lobbies that were trying to divert the minds of legislators from the common welfare to biased interest; any Presbyterian elder who took responsibility for his fellow man must lament the amassing of squalor that came with the sequestering of wealth. What would be the end of it all? Would the sons of the free men who had come over in the nineteenth century, along with the Latins and Slavs of later migrations, be caught now in a twentieth-century treadmill?

The "children of Israel"—the God-fearing, hard-working marrow of America—were crying out for a prophet, a responsible leader, someone who could tell them what it all meant, who could either justify or curb the vast power that sheer money had gained. Their hope for a revival of the old, rosy spirit of the frontier lay in the appearance of a political messiah—a prophet who would utter wisdom and give justice.

Curiously enough, their leader arrived quite by accident.

When he went to Pittsburgh in April of 1910 to speak to some of his Princeton family, Woodrow Wilson was moody. His nerves were on edge and he was wearied by lavish entertaining—a sightseeing tour of the city and dinner at a fashionable club. The Princeton trustees had just refused to refer the question of the graduate college to the faculty of the university. A bitterness was writhing in the president, such an acridity as he had felt toward Atlanta when he left that city after failing in the practice of law. With his personal resentment was mingled another sentiment—a deep sympathy for able, honest men to whom fate had been unkind. He had no sympathy for idlers, whether rich or poor. He was interested in the preserving of opportunity—such opportunity as the old frontier had presented—for a man to make good on his own.

As a teacher, Wilson had been an employee of what the Western democracy was calling "the money power." He had borne himself in public as a patrician, a charming and witty littérateur, a respectable son of an honored clergyman. To workmen on the Princeton campus he had seemed an archaristocrat striding about in formal dress, wearing a silk hat. They did not know that at home he danced jigs wearing the hat cocked on the side of his head. They did not know that when he watched them work on a new dormitory he wished that he could handle ideas as precisely as they laid stones. Nor were they aware that he had often ridden through a slum area of the village, his head so bowed in meditation over the manifestations of poverty that he had to be reminded that he was breaking an ordinance by riding on the sidewalk. The accumulation of money had never obsessed him. He had angered a colleague by arguing that men had no natural right to store up the world's goods without limit and without regard to the rights of other men. He expected only to be made comfortable in return for services gladly given. His old father had taught him what was written in the family Bible: "No station or wealth can buy heaven."

In the Johns Hopkins Graduate School, under the teaching of Richard T. Ely, Wilson had begun to question conventional theories of economics and during the following decade he had watched the clouds of social pressures massing on the political horizon. He could not escape from Bagehot's maxim: "The public good is not to be achieved by following the rules of private good." [16] Either Wilson's political conviction or his economic beliefs had to yield; and since he thought himself "born a politician," his preference for laissez-faire economics inevitably had to give ground. The yielding, however, was slow and uncertain, and took the form of "exceptions" rather than of any basic change of philosophy.

Wilson had come to regard the partisan drives of economic groups as forces not to be ignored, and as challenges to the flexibility of the national polity. He had insisted that it was within the province of the

[16] Walter Bagehot, *Physics and Politics*, 1948 edition, Introduction by Jacques Barzun, p. xiv. Wilson's sense of moral responsibility prevented him from asserting cynically, as had Bagehot, that men in the mass were ruled by "the weakness of their imaginations," that governments needed symbols "to impose on their quiescent imaginations what would otherwise not be there." *Ibid.*, Introduction, p. xvi. He came to think of Bagehot as a writer whose youthful, athletic exuberance had settled in an old man grown "fat, gross, and ruddy." Professor Wilson had preferred to stress the glory of the shepherd rather than the abjectness of the herd. He sometimes sighed "for a generation of 'leading people' and of good people who shall see things steadily . . . and whole." Chambers MS, pp. 60–61.

In *Congressional Government* (p. 296) he had quoted from William Graham Sumner's *Andrew Jackson*: "The modern industrial organization . . . is largely regulated by legislation. Capital is the breath of life to this organization, and every day, as the organization becomes more complex and delicate, the folly of assailing capital or credit becomes greater. At the same time it is evident that the task of the legislator to embrace in his view the whole system, to adjust his rules so that the play of civil institutions shall not alter the play of economic forces, requires more training and more acumen."

social scientist "to study wealth from the social, as well as the political point of view." Yet he feared that socialism would hasten the centralized and corruptible kind of government that good men were seeking to escape.

In the spring of 1908, frustrated by the opposition of financial supporters of Princeton, he allowed himself to make intemperate generalizations. Addressing the National Democratic Club at New York, he inveighed against wealth made through speculation.

"Predatory wealth," he said, was to be found "in stock markets, not in the administrative offices of great corporations where real business is conducted, real commodities made or exchanged." During the presidential campaign in the autumn he declared to the American Bankers' Association that legitimate undertakings had been "pushed to illegitimate lengths," that men feared their new, impersonal ruler and were "jealous of its domination." And again, in January of 1910, he told bankers assembled in the Waldorf-Astoria Hotel that they had allowed their minds to narrow and took no interest in the small businessman. "You don't know the country or what is going on in it and the country doesn't trust you," he charged. "You are not interested in the development of the country, but in what has been developed." At the head table J. P. Morgan puffed at his cigar and looked glum. Could this, he must have wondered, be the same man whom he had heard speak so conservatively at the inauguration at Princeton in 1902? When the banker told Wilson that the aspersions hurt him personally, the speaker replied that he was talking of principles, not of individuals, and expressed surprise that Mr. Morgan should think of himself as the nation's banking system.

It had been thirteen years now since Wilson had said to the Virginia Bar Association: "This is not a day of revolution, but it is a day of change, and of such change as may breed revolution, should we fail to guide and moderate it." In those years the tocsin had grown louder —it was always ringing distantly in the ears of the president of Princeton. Unfamiliarity with the workings of finance combined with disgust at its abuses to breed mistrust in the mind of the prophet. His Scottish imagination saw bogies in the mist, witches on Wall Street. He had his revelation.

When he thought that he saw financiers fail to encourage healthy business activity, Wilson could assuage his conscience with the belief that such things were of no direct concern to a professor of political science. He had even been able to bear political abuses with only intellectual distress and protest. But when he conceived that the power of money was dominating and corrupting churches, courts, and even universities, that was too much for a good Presbyterian and a good American to abide. The money-changers were invading the temple, and the prophet's temper came to the boiling point in April, 1910, at Pittsburgh.

Surfeited with entertainment and sightseeing, and suffering from one of his black moods of dejection and world-weariness, Wilson was taken by his hosts to the big reunion tent that had been erected in the dining room of the Hotel Schenley and decorated with fluttering orange-and-black banners. An orchestra played, a quartet sang "Going Back to Nassau Hall," favorite alumni were called on for their stock stories; and as a grand climax, the waiters trotted in bearing ices decorated by a papier-mâché tiger, recumbent under a paper coconut tree, its eyes illuminated. The prophet took it all in, listened while an ardent purveyor of homely epigrams, cigar atilt and jaws snapping, said: "I am not going to refer to *that little matter*. But I am satisfied that we will get that five hundred thousand back—some way." And then the toastmaster introduced the guest of honor—"the true type of American statesman" who "has loved truth for truth's sake, and for truth's sake alone."

The prophet could no longer contain himself. Over the gaudy scene he vented his feelings in clouds of fire, relaxing the strict discipline under which he usually ruled his emotions. He had taught many of those to whom he spoke, and so felt that he was talking within a family that would chant a filial "Amen!"

Andrew Jackson, when his Scotch-Irish dander was up, had so choked on his rage that he could not articulate. When he had wanted to speak up for his immigrants and backwoodsmen—whom Wilson once described as a "roughened race . . . delicate in nothing but the touch of the trigger"—he could only stand in the Senate and froth and splutter. But now they had an eloquent champion, those descendants of the old frontier, of the James Wilsons and the Thomas Woodrows. The ire of this leader burned like dry ice. He would not just splutter. He might be weary, he might be despondent, he might be furious; but so well had his weapon been forged and tempered that he could wield it eloquently. When his prophetic fire was unloosed, it burned quickly through the artifices by which he had decorated his talk in the academic world—courtesy, tact, humor, literary polish—all these fine furbelows were consumed in the oxygen of frontier air.

Gusts often had blown through great spaces in this prophet's soaring imagination. Sometimes they were steady tradewinds, driving away mist and cloud and leaving the purest of airs. But not now. His own nature, as he had said of Henry Clay's, "was of the West, blown through with quick winds of ardor and aggression, a bit reckless and defiant; but his art was of the East, ready with soft and placating phrases, reminiscent of old and reverenced ideals, thoughtful of compromise and accommodation." The manners of the Old South could make a polished man of letters; they were not enough to make a great political leader of all the United States. The "ardor and aggression" must be there.

Though Wilson was not consciously trying to make political capital out of his position at Princeton, any doubts about the sureness of the political appeal of the man's ideas could hardly have survived his speech at Pittsburgh. Blurting out convictions that had been pent within him for months because of the confidential nature of the proceedings at the university, he addressed himself to the nation over the heads of the alumni and trustees. "The people are tired of pretense," he declared, "and I ask you, as Princeton men, to heed what is going on." In the private universities, he asserted, "we look for the support of the wealthy and neglect our opportunities to serve the people." State universities, however, were honestly striving to serve "the people," were "sensitive to the movements of general opinion, to the opinion of the unknown men who can vote." From "the great mass of the unknown," he reminded his hearers, came the strength of America. "Most of the masters of endeavor in this country have not come through the channels of universities, but from the great rough-and-ready workers of the world." With a vast metaphor he reached out to embrace the virile manhood of the nation:

The great voice of America . . . comes in a murmur from the hills and woods and the farms and factories and the mills, rolling on and gaining volume until it comes to us from the homes of common men. Do these murmurs echo in the corridors of the universities? I have not heard them.

Lincoln's value to his country would have been impaired by education in a private university, Wilson said.

Finally he worked himself up to a spasm of zeal. "I have dedicated every power that there is in me," he said, "to bring the colleges that I have anything to do with to an absolutely democratic regeneration in spirit." He vowed to follow this ambition until the colleges were imbued with "the same thought, the same sympathy that pulses through the whole great body politic . . . Will America tolerate the idea of having graduate students set apart? America will tolerate nothing except unpatronized endeavor. Seclude a man, separate him from the rough-and-tumble of college life, from all the contacts of every sort and condition of men, and you have done a thing which America will brand with contemptuous disapproval."

And then he pressed his attack into the fields of religion and government. "I trust that I may be thought among the last to blame the churches, yet I feel it my duty to say that they—at least the Protestant churches—are serving the classes and not the masses of the people. They have more regard for pew rents than for men's souls. They are depressing the level of Christian endeavor . . . The American people will tolerate nothing that savours of exclusiveness. Their political parties are going to pieces." He had at last let himself go and, as he had feared, he did not know where to stop. "What we cry out against," he charged, "is that a handful of conspicuous men have thrust cruel hands among the heartstrings of the masses of men upon whose blood and energy they are subsisting." His long-suffering patience was gone. Fearing that the day of opportunity for peaceful change was slipping away, he ended his speech by predicting that "if she loses her self-possession, America will stagger like France through fields of blood before she again finds peace and prosperity under the leadership of men who know her needs."

"Disaster Forecast by Wilson—Denounces Churches—Talks about Blood!" So screamed a headline the next morning, and the explosion at Pittsburgh reverberated through the press of the nation. The opposition at Princeton was furious and had "that Pittsburgh speech" printed for all who would read it. Impartial editors thought that Wilson had been rash and intemperate, and the speaker himself, when he read snatches of the address in cold print, felt that he had blundered. He had failed to heed the counsel of Bagehot, who had noted that Anglo-Saxons fear nothing so much as bloody revolution and have therefore an inexhaustible capacity for tolerating mediocrity in the name of moderation. After the event Wilson realized that, as a responsible administrator whose duty it was to make men of diverse opinions work constructively and in harmony, he should not have aired his personal feelings so freely. In his "deep excitement" over an adverse vote of the Princeton trustees just two day before, he explained, he "did not stop to think how it would sound in the newspapers." He should have done so, he said. In a manuscript of his Pittsburgh talk that he corrected for publication, the incendiary final sentence was omitted. To the New York *Evening Post* he complained that reports of his speech had, by piecemeal quotation, conveyed an entirely false impression. And a few days later he refused to write an article on college fraternities, "in order not to complicate an already complicated situation."

In the next important address before Princeton graduates, Wilson's instinct for responsible leadership reasserted itself. In preparing a talk for Chicago alumni, he again assumed the yokes of charity and humility; and the message that he gave was less menacing, more challenging to constructive action, more closely confined to Princeton affairs.

It was too late, however, to retract what had been said at Pittsburgh or to rub out the mark that the news reports had made on the public consciousness. In unmasking deep personal feelings the speaker had touched sensitive chords in millions of his fellows who identified themselves with the "masses of men upon whose blood and energy" a "handful of conspicuous men" were "subsisting." Woodrow Wilson had played—by ear—the music that lures votes. The destiny that he had wooed was claiming the boy who had worshiped Gladstone's picture and prepared himself to lead a people.

In the black mood into which he had fallen at Pittsburgh, Wilson had despaired of spiritual regeneration either in education or in politics. He had complained to his host that his life had been a failure, that in taking the moral position to which his conscience drove him he was throwing away all opportunity of realizing his educational ideals. Moreover, he was not blind to economic consequences: outside of his salary, he said, he had little means for the support of his large family. "But what can I do?" he asked Woods. "I must follow what I think is right." He had long since committed his life into the hands of the God of truth and service. Like his uncle under the attack of theologians, like the Scottish prophets who came before him, he could only speak out. Had he kept silent his career might have ended, and with it the spiritual force that he personified.

As an academic executive, Wilson had failed. But in failure he had learned lessons invaluable to an administrator. He had held the confidence of precious friends and of most of the Princeton faculty. He had retained his youthful vision of political leadership and his faith in the American people and in the great principles that he loved to proclaim. He had reason to believe that the people of New Jersey wanted his leadership. But anyone who might try to purchase Woodrow Wilson's assets for advantage to person or party would do so at his own risk. Let the buyer beware!

CHAPTER IX

From Campus to Political Arena

Negotiations at princeton dragged on into the month of May. Trustees arranged a compromise that was acceptable to the moderate men of both factions; but neither of the principals would yield. The proposal was nothing new, Wilson thought, and to accept it was to forgo his fundamental judgment in the whole matter of education. When one of the friendly trustees tempted the president to resign in June, arguing that in this way he could at once confound his enemies and enhance his political position before the country, Wilson was unmoved. He would not be vindictive, and he would not make capital for himself at Princeton's expense. He would not resign in petulance, nor would he recant.

Andrew West, meanwhile, had been busily seeking financial support for his concept of a graduate college. A millionaire alumnus named Wyman had signed a will that left his fortune in the hands of two executors, one of whom was West. Wilson, reluctant fund-raiser that he was, had written a polite letter to the prospective donor, but West had taken pains to entertain Wyman's agent and to give him a flattering invitation to ride at the head of an alumni parade.

Suddenly death took old Mr. Wyman, and in taking him solved the problem of the graduate college.

On May 22, near midnight, the president of Princeton was awakened by a phone call. It was a telegram from West, reporting the filing of the Wyman will and a bequest amounting to "at least two million and maybe more." Mrs. Wilson heard enough to catch the import of the message and leaned back in her chair, close to tears. As her husband put down the receiver, he was grim. He could "lick a half-million," but this was too much. The bequest was to finance a graduate college at Princeton that was to be controlled by the board of trustees. Using the free hand that had been given to him to solicit funds, West had tied himself into the will with such firm legal bonds that Princeton would have to accept him as trustee of the Wyman millions.

Wilson could take some satisfaction in the thought that the new gift was large enough so that a separate faculty of outstanding ability could be attracted to the graduate college. He was now ready, he said, to entertain a renewal of Procter's offer for a building on the site chosen by the donor, provided there was no restriction on the policies and management of graduate work. As he saw it, he must either yield in the matter of the site and remain in control of the administration and stand by his friends on the faculty and the board, or else retire. To quit immediately would be to risk the demoralization of Princeton, he felt. What the future would bring was still an open question. West's prestige was now tremendous. President Butler of Columbia sent him "hearty congratulations"; and Moses Taylor Pyne, to whom West wrote gleefully of his triumph in a letter signed "Little Willie," assured the dean that he had "made good in every sense of the word." Recognizing West's great power under Wyman's will, Wilson realized that the dean must be handled most wisely and diplomatically, and he was not at all sure that he had a strong enough stomach for it.

Early in June, encouraged by the acceptance of the Wyman bequest, Procter renewed his offer of a half-million dollars and it was accepted by the board. At Commencement it was apparent that, though the alumni elected a trustee favorable to Wilson, a majority of the board had lost confidence in their president's usefulness to Princeton. Some thought that in his public speeches he had maligned the university and ruthlessly stepped upon it in a climb to high political office.

Commencement Week, 1910, was one of Woodrow Wilson's finest hours. He played out the game, making no public show of pique or petulance when the alumni celebrated the Wyman gift and toasted its procurer. Though his wife suffered a social snub, Wilson made a felicitous speech of presentation when Pyne was given a silver cup in recognition of twenty-five years of service to Princeton. West gave a dinner to celebrate the bequest, inviting none of Wilson's supporters; and the president, attending, tried to ignore the pall of conspiracy that he felt in the very air.

Addressing the Class of 1910, at the close of his Baccalaureate Sermon the president warmed their hearts at the altar of loyal sentiment.

The atmosphere was one of "farewell" rather than of "au revoir." His boys were loath to let him leave, and revised their old faculty song to let "Tommie" knew how they felt about his going into politics:

> Here's to Wilson, king of men,
> He rules this place with 1910.
> We have no fear he'll leave this town
> To try for anybody's crown!

And then they told off West and his millions:

> Here's to Andy eight-million West,
> Sixty-three inches around the vest,
> To get him Boston tried her best,
> He winked his eye—you know the rest.

After the valedictory they cheered their president again and again and again, until tears streamed down his face. The alumni, too, warmly applauded his speech at their luncheon; and his supporters on the board told him that he was free to go or stay, as he pleased, though he was reminded that he was "the soul of the fight." Thinking his friends the finest in the world, he resolved not to disappoint them in character even if he should disappoint them in ability. He preferred to fall fighting, rather than seem to run away from the university. One Saturday afternoon, when politicians were coming to Prospect to press him to become a candidate for the governorship, he packed his bag for a trip to New York and said: "Ellen, I don't want to be away over the weekend. But I don't want to meet those men." [1]

However, certain politicians were becoming persistent in efforts to "reach" the patrician-Democrat at Princeton and use him to restore the fortunes of a party that had been out of power so long that its leaders found it difficult to raise campaign funds. A tide of public protest was rising in New Jersey; and the bosses of the old regime, lacking a will to meet demands for reform, saw in Wilson a man who might appease insurgents by his prestige and his words.

Muckraking journalists had given New Jersey a reputation as a sanctuary for corporations. Citizens had begun to understand how public service companies, by financing a few bosses in each party, were buying influence over the legislature, and how the bosses in turn were controlling elections by nominating the candidates and buying votes in return for jobs and other benefits. With perfect understanding of each other's method's, politicians of both parties had been playing exciting games with the public trust. Already many voices had been raised in protest. Everett Colby had risen in a one-man revolt and had whipped the candidate of the Republican machine to win a seat in the state Senate, where he rallied a group of insurgents who were devoted to what they called the "New Idea." In Jersey City, Mayor Mark M. Fagan had employed a progressive adviser named George L. Record to help him reform the municipal government. A persuasive speaker, Record

---

[1] James Woodrow, who was present, to the writer.

had swung from the Democratic to the Republican party in protest against Byran's silver policy, had accepted Henry George's condemnation of monopolies based on special privileges, read Emerson, covered his walls with pictures of Lincoln, and let it be known that he "didn't give a damn about being personally popular." It was "these ideas" that were important, he insisted. Record and other progressives had achieved the enactment of a state civil service reform law and tentative measures for direct primaries and control of corporations.

To compete with the leadership that had been given to Republicans by progressives and liberal thinkers, Democratic bosses had been angling for Wilson for several years. Impressed by his inaugural address at Princeton, "Planked-Shad" Thompson had commended him to James Smith, Jr., boss of Essex County. A wealthy banker and publisher, Smith had served in the United States Senate and had made himself obnoxious to Wilson by opposing Cleveland's efforts at tariff reform for reasons that seemed to reflect an undue concern for sugar interests. He was known as "Sugar Jim." Portly and well dressed, a man of magnetism, he was an utter realist, so sardonic that he could say to a fly-fisherman, with the irony of mock innocence: "You not only *kill* your fish. You deceive them as well." [2] Smith's "fish" voted as he told them to vote, with not too close scrutiny of the reasons. And when he delivered his catch, he held that he was delivering marketable goods.

This cynic, observing that his party had been out of power so long that corporations no longer "came across" with campaign funds,[3] saw at once that Wilson could be useful in ending the famine. But he doubted that the time was ripe. After all, the educator was not a native son and his religion was not congenial to the rank and file of the party. Moreover, no one knew Wilson's exact feelings toward corporations, unions, and the liquor interests. Nevertheless, Smith insisted that, if the Democrats were ever to elect another governor of the state, it would have to be a man like the president of Princeton; and he had passed the word along to George Brinton McClellan Harvey, president of the reorganized firm of Harper's and publisher of Wilson's successful *History of the American People.*

Harvey had been conspicuous at the inauguration at Princeton—"fascinatingly ugly," one observer had thought him, a man arrogant, with defiant inferiority, carrying upon a scrawny neck a death's-head whose eye sockets were dark as inkwells and whose thin tight lips smiled

2 John Pursel, who heard Smith say this, to the writer.
3 John Moody, *The Long Road Home,* pp. 106–7.

superciliously.[4] Reading everything that Wilson had written, Harvey
became convinced that this man was of sufficent stature to take the
leadership of the Democratic party away from William Jennings Byran
and to rehabilitate it on sound principles. In the winter of 1905–6,
when the popular president of Princeton was stepping out of academic
bounds often to exhort the public to serve the nation, Harvey gave a
dinner in honor of his hero at the Lotos Club in New York and spoke
with a sense "almost of rapture" of the possibility of voting for Woodrow Wilson for the Presidency of the United States; and the next month
the publisher set forth in *Harper's Weekly* thirteen qualifications of his
candidate. Though Wilson was not convinced, and spoke modestly of
"other wires taller than mine which will attract the lightning," the
response in the press and through the mails showed isolated ripples of
interest that might one day merge in a booming wave. From that
time Wilson's name was bandied about freely by men who aspired to
manage Democratic policy.

In 1906, Wilson was appointed to his first public office—membership
on the New Jersey Commission on Uniform State Laws; and in the
autumn it was rumored that he might be the Democratic candidate
when the New Jersey legislature chose a United States senator in 1907.
It was not expected that a Democrat could win a Senate seat; but Harvey
calculated that the publicity of the campaign would redound to the
credit of his man on the national scene.

Wilson was at first cold to the idea, telling reporters that his first duty
was to Princeton. Yet when it became sure that the Republicans would
win the election, Wilson fell in with Harvey's suggestion. The honor,
even though an empty one, beguiled the educator.

Meanwhile, young Democrats in New Jersey were rebelling against
Smith and the other bosses whom Harvey had enlisted in support of
his candidate for the Senate. The reformers proposed the name of
Edwin A. Stevens, of the Princeton class of 1879. Wilson told this

---

[4] *See* George Watt, *Is the Liar In?*, pp. 285–91. A Vermonter who had made good as a
political reporter in New Jersey, Harvey had become banking commissioner in that state and
an honorary "colonel" on the staff of the governor. As editor of the New Jersey edition of the
New York *World*, he had aided Smith to reach the Senate in 1892.

In undertaking to promote Wilson for the Presidency of the United States and thus enhance
his value as an author to the house of Harper's, Harvey was perhaps encouraged by a letter
from "An Old-fashioned Democrat," printed in the Indianapolis *News* on May 5, 1902, endors-
ing Wilson for the Presidency. Moreover, in June of 1902, Dwight L. Moody introduced Wilson
at a student conference at Northfield as a man who might someday be president of the
United States. Allan Lightner, who heard Moody, to the writer, Sept. 30, 1955. Even as early
as 1901 and 1902, Princeton students saw in Professor Wilson a future candidate for the
Presidency of the nation.

classmate that he would not run in opposition, but refused to state this publicly for fear of intervening in what seemed to be mere "factional differences." [5] The president of Princeton was not yet sure of himself in the political arena, not quite ready to joust with professional campaigners.

Wilson was thrilled to feel that he would not be forever a mere "outside force" in government. He had never entirely given up his "primary ambition" to be a statesman; and in 1902, the year in which he assumed the Princeton presidency, he confided to his friend Turner that he had been "born a politician" and asked a classmate what his duty to Princeton would be if he were called to lead a political constituency.[6] But now that his opportunity was at hand, his first glow of delight was followed by reaction in his spirits. Realizing his ignorance of the ways of practical politics, he became worried and suspicious. He had welcomed the intercession of Robert Bridges in behalf of his appointment to the Princeton faculty, for he had felt that his classmate acted out of pure friendship. But Harvey might have other motives in promoting his name. Whether this publisher believed in Wilson's power to serve the nation or was gambling on large future returns, the "literary politician" could not be sure. Though inexperienced, he was naturally canny enough to have misgivings. He feared that the trial balloon might burst in his face and make him ridiculous. "This linking of my name with political office," he told Stockton Axson, "is doing no good to either Princeton or me." When Harvey began to sound out the conservative leaders of the Democratic party,[7] Wilson became so embarrassed that he asked his sponsor to desist.

[5] Finally Stevens peeled the eyes of the novice, made him see that the bosses were using the name of the president of Princeton to delude earnest reformers. Wilson, believing in the honesty of Stevens and still conscious of his own inexperience in such matters, wrote to Harvey, thanked him politely for his support, said that it was not possible in good faith to oppose Stevens, and asked advice on the "most courteous and convenient way" to withdraw. And Harvey told his protégé how to extricate himself from the muddle without giving offense to anyone and without strengthening the cause of the reformers. Wilson fell in with the prescribed formula and failed to support Stevens.

[6] Stephen Wise, *Challenging Years,* p. 161. There had never been a time, Wilson said to Rabbi Stephen Wise years later, when he was not preparing himself for the White House. Eleanor Wilson McAdoo feels that this statement was made in jest, and states that her father's intimate letters to her mother indicate that when he took the presidency of Princeton it was with the expectation of devoting the rest of his life to that charge. E. W. McAdoo to the writer, March 10, 1952. It is clear that in 1899 Wilson's interest in an active political life was keen. In that year he kept a book of "Notes on Statesmanship" and spoke to Grover Cleveland of his desire to find practical ways in which men of conscience could influence the machinery of political parties. And it was at about this time that he complained to Stockton Axson of popular superstitions about the incompetence of academic men as public officials.

[7] Harvey's trial balloons were kept aloft by support from conservative idealists, particularly those from the South. Wilson "would not stir up discontent; he has no fortune; he does not

Eloquent as Professor Wilson had been in virtuous generalities, his public utterances on political issues of the day, like those on economic problems, had become cautious; and when he had lectured to classes on current politics, he had the doors closed and had asked that he be not quoted outside the campus. He had been content for the most part to teach the energizing principles of jurisprudence and the origin of law in public opinion. He thought that education could be only "minor statesmanship," and yet continued to preach to his university constituency about their patriotic responsibilities. He accepted the political party as an American institution, but took a lofty view and distrusted both Democrats and Republicans.

When a friend asked him why he didn't "get out and tell the world," he replied: "Simply because I cannot afford to. Sometimes I feel strongly tempted to do so, and perhaps the time will come when I can take a hand in political business." [8] On a Bermuda beach, in 1908, he discussed his future with Mary Allen Peck. "My friends tell me," he said, "that if I will enter the contest and can be nominated and elected Governor of New Jersey, I stand a very good chance of being the next President of the United States. Shall I, or shall I not, accept the opportunity they offer? . . . The life of the next Democratic President will be hell and it would probably kill me." When the lady encouraged him, he stood with hat off and said: "Very well, so be it!"

To beat Bryan, he confided, a man must personify a cause and not be content to offer himself as a candidate ready to listen to anything expedient.[9] But in giving himself unreservedly to a principle, a man opened himself to attack as an ambitious dictator. There was the rub. Let some other fellow run the risk, Wilson was thinking. He would be glad to help, but not to take the chief onus. Perhaps, though, if the

---

speak the language of Utopia or riot," wrote Walter Hines Page in 1907. ". . . he is a Democrat of the best traditions. What if a political miracle should happen and the long-lost old party should find itself by nominating such a man?" Three reactionary Democrats invited Wilson to dine with them at Delmonico's in New York; and afterward, when one of them tried to draw out his thoughts on politics, he responded with a draft of a "Credo" in which he denounced labor unions as threats to individual liberty and expressed faith in the Constitution and the provisions of civil and criminal law as adequate safeguards of morality in the operation of those corporations that had become necessary to the efficient conduct of business. It seemed to Harvey and his friends that Wilson was an innocuous moralist who might appeal to voters sated with Bryan and alarmed by Roosevelt.

8 Patterson, op. cit., p. 38.

9 In the revealing talk that he delivered four times during the eighteen-nineties—"Leaders of Men"—Wilson had asserted that "the dynamics of leadership lie in persuasion." Great leaders must have insight of the heart rather than of the intellect. "By methods which would infallibly alienate individuals they master multitudes, and that is their indisputable title to be named 'leaders of men.'"

Princeton trustees did not awaken to their responsibilities toward the university's intellectual life, he might retire from the presidency in two years and become free to be a martyr to the rehabilitation of the Democratic party. It occurred to him that he might lead in a movement of reform and that, after the fire of the opponents had been irrevocably centered upon his own head, he could withdraw in favor of another man. He was fancying himself as a campaigner born and bred, and saw in the rough and manly cudgeling of political warfare a welcome relief to bouts fought with innuendo-tipped swords on a confining university floor. First, however, he must find a worthy cause that could overwhelm his fear of showing personal egotism. His old father had jotted on the margin of his Bible, beside a verse in *John*: "No preacher has any light of his own to show—but he is a witness only to the *heavenly light* —a light-bearer." Woodrow Wilson had been carrying a torch too bright for the eyes of Princeton alumni; but he was groping, at the end of 1908, for a torch that a political following would heed and steer by. He had not forgotten what he had written in one of his essays: "Politics is a war of causes, a joust of principles."

During the next two years Wilson remained the figure that he had described in *Mere Literature*—"a man with an imagination which, though it stands aloof, is yet quick to conceive the very things in the thick of which the politician struggles." Refusing to let his name be considered at the Democratic convention in the summer of 1908, he nevertheless continued to proclaim a political gospel.[10]

Observation of President Theodore Roosevelt's strong grasp on national affairs was confirming Wilson's faith in the opportunity of the chief executive as a leader in reform; and Roosevelt's sympathy for progressive causes helped to convince him that statesmen must heed the new voices of the times. Nevertheless, when Roosevelt succeeded

[10] In a series of lectures at Columbia University, published in 1908 under the title *Constitutional Government in the United States,* Wilson coldly analyzed American politics and showed a deeper understanding of the machinery of Congress than he had possessed when he wrote *Congressional Government.* He now referred to the iniquities of "special interests," lobbies and newspapers, declared that "our very constitutional principle has fallen into dangerous disrepair" because of the advantage in prolonged litigation that was given to certain men by the very fact of their wealth; but he conceived of the Senate as relatively free from corrupting influences and in truth "the choice of the people." His lectures at Columbia set forth two concepts that were to guide him when he came to take a responsible part in government: first, a faith in state governments as potentially "real organs of popular opinion"; second, emphasis on presidential, rather than Cabinet, leadership in the federal government. His lectures, moreover, held out the American system as a faith for other peoples to embrace. The relation of the states with the federal union, he thought, might yet give the entire world a model of federation and constitutional liberty.

As president of Princeton Wilson wrote comparatively little and sometimes spoke disparagingly of his earlier output, calling it a symptom of "literary afflatus."

McKinley, the Princeton professor had remarked privately: "What will happen to the country—with that mountebank as president?" Wilson had not been greatly impressed when Roosevelt praised a speech of his and invited him to spend a night at the White House. In 1905 he considered the President of the nation "not quite a statesman," incapable of analyzing fundamental social problems or leading Congress in solving them; and at a meeting of the Princeton faculty he raked TR's record fore and aft.

When Roosevelt came to Princeton for a football game he was entertained by the Wilsons in the charming tradition of the South. But his manners were those of the jungle. His voice boomed above all other sounds. At dinner he had eyes only for colorful Margaret Axson, slambanged the table, and shouted teasing remarks about "the gray-haired old grandfather" on her left and "the rich bachelor" on her right until she was moved to wish that, if that was the way presidents behaved, she might never meet another. Afterward she asked her brother-in-law: "Woodrow, who on earth would ever want to be president?" And he replied, half in jest: "I should; I know a whale of a lot about the Constitution of this country and I'd rather like to watch the wheels go round."

Though Wilson's mind accepted the strengthening of the Presidency as a historical fact, his conscience was troubled by the threat posed to constitutional processes. He protested against efforts being made in Congress to carry the implications of federal powers "beyond the utmost boundaries of reasonable and honest inference." Moreover, he inveighed against the "passion for regulative legislation" that the Roosevelt administration had shown. He predicted that, even should regulation by government come, it would "sooner or later be completely discredited by experience." He distrusted rule by the discretion of individual officeholders as a substitute for a rule of law. The shifting of responsibility from corporations to government bureaus, from courts to commissions, he looked on with suspicion. Appealing to "the old Jeffersonian principle: as little government as possible," he recalled that the United States was built on a belief that free men had a much more trustworthy capacity for taking care of themselves than any government had ever shown or was ever likely to show in taking care of them. "What we need," he said in the spring of 1907, "is not a square deal, but no deal at all—an old-fashioned equality and harmony of conditions—a purged business and a purged law." He called not for more law but rather for honest enforcement of existing laws.

Being suspicious of the ultimate effects of measures that were being proposed by hotheaded and shortsighted reformers, it was natural for the prophet to fall back on Scripture and Thomas Jefferson, and preach a "new morality." He talked on such themes as "True Patriotism," "Ideals of Public Life," and "Law or Personal Power." Corporations could not be attacked effectively, he pointed out, but their directors could.

By speaking for the common good and recommending a morality that would serve it, Wilson identified himself more and more with the interests of government. Government, he explained, had had to step in to restrain those who were abusive of the very privileges that the government itself had guaranteed. It seemed unfair to one concerned for the vitality of democracy that those who had thrived in democratic air should suffocate others who were striving to breathe as freely.

As Wilson perceived in the opposition at Princeton the same repressive spirit that he saw in the nation at large, his impatience grew. What was needed, he thought, was an intellect to champion social justice, a leader to show the people where their own best interests lay. He said in February of 1909: "We have heat enough; what we want is light. Anybody can stir up emotions, but who is master of men enough to take the saddle and guide those awakened emotions?" Woodrow Wilson was still exuding sweetness and light, in 1909, but a fire was smoldering. His soul was as unsatisfied by the moralizings of a college president as by the theorizing proper to a professor.

Thus, in the years 1908 and 1909, the prophet's utterances on social and economic problems gained in boldness, in frankness, in power of expression.[11] Gradually he had been setting up ideals of political administration that only Woodrow Wilson himself could be trusted to execute. His impulses had not crystallized in consistent specifications of policy, but he stood by the generalizations set forth in 1888 in *The State,* believing still that the sovereign people should allow their government to assume only "necessary" powers. In this and in his philosophy of slow, reasoned change, in his preaching of a "new morality," in his

[11] In 1909, Wilson carried his championing of individual freedom and efficiency into discussion of labor problems. He avowed himself "a fierce partisan of the open shop and of everything that makes for individual liberty," and warned his graduating class at Princeton that the labor of America was "rapidly becoming unprofitable under its present regulation by those who have determined to reduce it to a minimum." Yet he could sympathize with workmen in their struggle with industrial monopolies. He was nostalgic still for the sort of employer that Heath Dabney's grandfather had been—the "chivalrous gentleman" of humane and noble outlook. Both corporations and unions were thought beneficial to society only in so far as their managers respected the welfare of their whole industries and of the nation. Wilson's generalizations regarding the labor movement drew strong protests from labor leaders.

pleading for the common good against the pressures of special interests —in these large and general thoughts he offered a program of definite and enduring principle.

Wilson's doctrine appealed to the bedrock Americanism of free men who were as doubtful of the benefits of revolution as they were suspicious of large organizations that promoted selfish economic causes. The nation's middle class, then growing rapidly, was skeptical of "rackets"—whether of capital, of labor, or of government bureaucracy. The president of Princeton, as his educational views diverged more and more from those of alumni and trustees, was falling into sympathy with the instinctive sense of fair play and the almost superstitious fears and prejudices of citizens who were being hurt by large corporations that used competition to kill rather than to stimulate and took advantage of tariff rates and a monopoly position to lift prices outrageously. Small businessmen, church folk, and professional people sensed the man's passion for service of the right, his utter sincerity of purpose; and they were not greatly disturbed by his exaggerations and inaccuracies.

In January of 1910, Wilson addressed a gathering of reformers. Like the ideal orator whom he had envisioned, he himself showed power to "make men drunk with this spirit of self-sacrifice." The liberals thought him "a great leader of progressive impulse and thought," but "politically impossible." Ray Stannard Baker, who had exposed railroad malpractice and had written frankly of the plight of labor, was so captivated by what he recognized as "the finest mind in American life" that he went to Princeton to interview the prophet; and his questions were met squarely by practical, well-reasoned explanations and without regard to the concentration of political power and the winning of sectional votes.

In 1910, moreover, the prophet was speaking out boldly in party councils. Early in March, when Villard of the New York *Evening Post* quizzed him about his political aspirations, Wilson said that, though nothing was decided, his mind was leaning toward the governorship of New Jersey. Democratic leaders who felt that Princeton's president should "make the sacrifice" and accept the nomination for governor organized a dinner at Elizabeth; and though their hero refused to have his candidacy proclaimed, he could not keep the audience from shouting "Our next governor!" In his speech he aligned the Republican party with the vested interests, described the Democrats as the party of profound and abiding confidence in the people. In this he spoke like the young Wilson whose blood had danced when the Irish cause was advanced in Parliament or when Gladstone won an election. Once during his early academic years he had written to his wife: "It is singular, considering the judicial frame of mind I *try* to cultivate, what a partisan I am in politics." Yet now, on the threshold of his own political career, he did not plead merely for the selfish interest of the party, but for "a glory which it will itself be glad to see merged and identified with the glory of the nation."

George Harvey heard Wilson's speech at Elizabeth and was carried away by its eloquence. In January of 1910, surveying the politics of the nation from his New York office, the publisher had sensed that the Republican party and its conservative Congress were riding toward disaster; and he thought the time auspicious for launching Wilson on a political career. He conferred twice with his old friend James Smith, Jr.

Enchanted at the prospect of promoting a promising candidate for the presidency in 1912, Smith agreed to swing the party regulars of New Jersey into line behind Wilson, provided Harvey could give assurance that his candidate would accept nomination for the governorship. But when the publisher spent a night with Wilson at Princeton and sounded out his man, he found him preoccupied by university affairs and determined not to seek the honor. However, when Harvey asked whether the nomination would be accepted if it came "on a silver platter" and without any pledge, Wilson said he would regard it his duty "to give the matter very serious consideration." Temporarily, this response satisfied Smith.

On April 16, Wilson delivered the speech at Pittsburgh that so clearly displayed his potentiality as a political campaigner. Three days afterward he wrote to his old friend Dabney: "I find myself very much disinclined to go into politics, but I must say that it is getting a little difficult to keep out of them in the present situation of affairs—not so much the present situation in the university as the present movement of opinion among my friends in this part of the country." A year earlier Wilson had felt that the forming of a third party in 1912 was inevitable, and he thought that he might be its presidential candidate. But now he did not "despair of seeing the Democratic party drawn back to the definite and conservative principles which it once represented."

By the middle of June, Smith found that a majority of his men demanded assurance that Wilson would play the game. Would he, if elected, act like a "Presbyterian priest"? Smith wanted a positive statement to aid him in lining up his forces for the election. And so a former student of Wilson's was persuaded to write a letter saying that Smith had no desire that the candidate commit himself in any way as to principles, measures, or men, but did wish to be satisfied that, if Wilson was elected, he "would not set about fighting and breaking down the existing Democratic organization" and replacing it with one of his own. To this letter Wilson replied on June 23 that he would not do so, that in fact he would not antagonize the Smith organization so long as it worked "with thorough heartiness for such policies as would re-establish the reputation of the state" and so long as he was left "absolutely free in the matter of measures and men."

Though Smith himself was satisfied with this, he found some of the party men leaning away from Wilson and inclined to look for a more "regular" candidate. Finally convinced that he must secure a guarantee that his man would accept nomination for the governorship if it was offered to him, Smith telephoned to Harvey for help.

With the pay-off of his efforts to build up Wilson now in sight, the publisher went into action. He tried to arrange a powwow on the evening of Sunday, June 26. Smith would be there, and Colonel Watterson —"Marse Henry," editor-politician of Louisville. But Wilson did not find it convenient to come, for there was no Sunday train from Lyme, Connecticut, where he was summering again at the Old Griswold Place.

In the summer of 1910, the talk *en famille* at Old Lyme became more serious. The family spoke often of political prospects, as they chatted privately in the big square bedrooms of the boardinghouse, and Wilson and his wife talked for hours about duty and service and about the hardships of a public career. She was fearful. "Politics" was a word that grated on sensitive academic ears: smoke-filled rooms, deals, front-page publicity seemed to threaten the idyllic domesticity of the family. She quoted Mr. Dooley to her husband: "If anny Dimmicrat has a stiddy job he'd better shtick to it." And yet good government was a cause dear to Ellen Wilson, and she knew that her man had never lost his youthful ardor to lead men in righteous political action.

It was during this time of vacillation that an agent of Harvey's presented himself at the door of the Griswold house. He had been commissioned to bring the reluctant candidate to the conference that had been arranged with Smith and Watterson.

Wilson showed no surprise and offered no resistance. He packed his bag, and by taxi and train was whisked to the publisher's home at Deal Beach, New Jersey, arriving just in time for dinner. In the evening the three promoters revealed their ambition to make him president of the United States. If he would accept nomination for the governorship, the party leaders of New Jersey would give that to him by acclamation. They had been urged to do so by representative politicians of the Middle West with whom Smith had talked and who already looked with favor on Wilson as a presidential candidate. They gave him a week in which to make a final decision.

Returning to Old Lyme the next day, June 27, he found the family agog for news. Teasingly, he walked calmly across the room, sat down on a trunk, took a rubber tee from his pocket, deliberately placed it on the floor, found a golf ball and demonstrated the use of the new gadget, and then put it back in his pocket.

Finally he told them. He had been offered the nomination in New Jersey, without pledges; and Smith, whose motives he mistrusted much, would not be a candidate when it came time for the next legislature to choose a United States senator.[12] A little wistfully, the paterfamilias added: "Colonel Watterson says it will inevitably lead to the Presidency."

Before committing himself finally, Wilson consulted his strongest supporters among the Princeton trustees, confessing to them that he felt like a man in a maze, that acceptance of the New Jersey nomination might look like a mere case of personal ambition. He was not, he insisted, allowing the prospect of the presidency of the nation to form his opinion as to his duty in the matter of the governorship. His friends absolved him of further responsibility to Princeton, urged him to follow his own inclination, and promised support if he chose to enter politics.

Early in July, therefore, he gave his consent to Harvey and Smith. His keen boyish zest for political eminence had been dulled by the wear and tear of executive experience, and yet the old longings still ran in his blood. Moreover, after preaching to Princeton students on the duty of the educated man to undertake just such service as this, Wilson did not see how he could stand aside. Yet he confessed to "a sneaking hope that the thing may not, after all, come off." [13]

The boom began early in July. One of Harvey's staff went to Old Lyme to write a news story that would "humanize" the candidate.

---

[12] E. W. McAdoo, 109. Smith later said that no statement was made that justified this conclusion by Wilson. (See pp. 171 n., 176.)

[13] W.W. to Huston Thompson, July 14, 1910. Wilson wrote to Villard on Aug. 23, 1910: "I consented to let my name be considered for the nomination in New Jersey with many misgivings, and only because I felt that I had no choice in the matter, if I would practice what I have preached all my life." Villard Papers (Houghton Library, Harvard College).

Smith's newpapers, and also leading "New Idea" journals in New Jersey, began to promote Wilson's candidacy; and a Hearst paper was screaming, much to the distress of the candidate: "Wall St. to put up W. Wilson for President." [14]

On July 12, Harvey invited influential politicians and a corporation attorney to meet Wilson at luncheon at the Lawyers' Club in New York; but he had to beg his guest of honor to come, and to assure him that notorious bosses would not be present. The politicians listened impassively when Wilson declared that he would not accept the nomination unless it came unanimously, that he was definitely not seeking office. When Smith, thinking it essential that he have the support of the liquor interest, bade a lieutenant to sound out the candidate on this issue, Wilson did not mince words. "I am not a prohibitionist," he declared. "I believe that the question is outside of politics. I believe in home rule, and that the issue should be settled by local option in each community." When reminded that Smith and the party had been fighting against local option for years, he said: "Well, that is my attitude and my conviction. I cannot change it." Later he gave the same reply to the Anti-Saloon League, and it coincided with what he had written some twenty years before: "The state ought not to supervise private morals."

Three days after the conference at the Lawyers' Club, in a letter to New Jersey newspapers, Wilson announced publicly that, though he would not campaign for the nomination, he would deem it his duty to accept it should it prove to be true that he was the choice of "a decided majority of the thoughtful Democrats of the State." Most of the local press welcomed this statement as an omen for better government for New Jersey.

Thinking that he had "reached" Wilson, Smith went into action in earnest. Forming an alliance with Boss Robert Davis of Jersey City and Hudson County, he lined up about two-thirds of the votes that would be needed to nominate his man in the party convention in September; and then, one by one, he induced the leaders of other local organizations to board the "band wagon."

The progressives in the party protested. Otto Wittpenn, who as mayor of Jersey City had been fighting Davis's machine, carried his case directly to Wilson at Old Lyme. Did the professor not know, he asked, what was notorious—that the Smith-Davis organization stopped at

---

[14] New York *Journal*, July 8, 1910. This was not the first time the Wilsons had been embarrassed by the Hearst press. The divorced wife of Cousin Wilson Woodrow had written trashy stories for a Hearst magazine under the name of "Mrs. Wilson Woodrow."

nothing, that their men stuffed ballot boxes, hired "repeaters" at the
polls, levied blackmail, and took orders from the corporations? The
delegates of Wilson's own county turned against him and pledged
support to another man. Progressive newspapers proclaimed that the
president of Princeton was allowing himself "to be used as a cat's paw,
to serve the purposes of the bosses," that he was the tool of corporation financiers, "window-dressing" for a discredited machine.

Soon Wilson was under a barrage of embarrassing questions. Would
he have courage to practice the principles that he had been preaching
so glibly? the insurgents were asking. Face to face, now, with political
realities and still lacking in *savoir-faire*, Wilson turned to Harvey for
advice and received sound professional counsel. Every two or three
days—sometimes oftener—he was in communication with his mentor,
who wrote him little undated notes of reassurance, reporting that he and
Smith had made "a fairly satisfactory understanding with Wittpenn,"
that all reports were good, that "the situation is well in hand; there
are no breaches in the walls." The candidate must put on a bold front
and say nothing definite about current issues, and must realize that it
was necessary to have opposition in order to forestall allegations that
the campaign was being railroaded through by bosses.

For a while Wilson avoided commitments, while suspicion grew that
progressive newspapers were right in charging that he was "afloat on
a bad hull." He fumed over a cartoon that depicted him as a weary
horse dragging a cart in which a tiny Harvey was conducting a huge
Smith to a United States senatorship. Charges of hypocrisy were fired
at him, and his silence was held to be proof of his opposition to progressive ideas. But Harvey, warning the candidate that inevitably he
would be "berated somewhat on account of the friends made" and that
the liberal New York *World* doubtless would be "after" him, wrote
seductively: "The talk about the Interests is wholly ignorable up to
date . . . I should duck. Your position now is perfect." They had only
to stand pat, the impresario insisted, and no one would dare asperse the
president of Princeton.

For weeks Wilson followed Harvey's advice and refused to let his
ideas be drawn out. To grant interviews to journalists, he informed
James Kerney of Trenton, would be to give an impression that he was
seeking nomination. However, when academic utterances made previously by Wilson against certain activities of labor unions were circulated out of context—particularly a speech on "Unprofitable Servants"
in which he had excoriated abuses of labor's power along with the

moral failings of businessmen—even Smith and his henchmen could not check the growing antagonism among workmen. A letter written on August 18 by Edgar R. Williamson, editor of the *American Labor Standard*, informed Wilson that the state federation had just condemned him as a foe of organized labor. Asked for his views, the candidate composed a two-page statement on his typewriter. Declaring that he had always been "the warm friend of organized labor" and that his criticisms had been made in a friendly spirit, he asserted that it was absolutely necessary that laborers form unions in order to secure justice from organized capital. Harvey told Wilson that the labor letter was "precisely timed and wholly effective."

In August and September the tide ran toward the amateur campaigner. Conviction grew that he was the ablest among the candidates. In the primaries of September 13, Smith and Davis easily carried their key counties for Wilson; and it seemed clear that when the nominating convention met on the 15th it would choose the president of Princeton. Wilson himself was so confident that he had already drafted a speech of acceptance that Harvey had outlined.

On the morning of convention day the candidate played golf at Princeton, ignorant of the rough-and-tumble in Trenton, where Harvey and Smith were toiling mightily to hold the lines against ferocious but disorganized attacks by independent leaders. The two archpromoters had been working all night, from their stale-aired rooms in the Trenton House, to cast their nets around wobbling delegates; but despite all their persuasiveness and the confident blarney of the men who heeled for them—Planked-Shad Thompson, Jim Nugent, and the rest—sharp words cut at the name of the candidate when it was put in nomination on the floor of the convention.

Judge John W. Wescott of Camden County, elder statesman of the progressives, shouted against "bargain and sale and double cross," against dictation by a "financial machine"; but Thompson merely reminded the convention that two-thirds of the delegates from Wescott's own county were already committed to Wilson. Antagonistic delegates from Wilson's Mercer County objected to the listing of the candidate as a resident of Princeton; but forty Princeton men, seated on the stage under the leadership of Smith's son, broke into a football cheer. Progressives howled and stamped and shook their fists; but the men of the machine sat tight and kept their eyes on their leaders. The bosses, the marching clubs, the bands had done their work well. If there was not an answer for every question, there was at least a long drink and a confident handshake. It was Wilson on the first ballot, with a few more votes than necessary. "Tommie" Wilson had been set on the road to high office by the very sort of convention that he had damned thirty years earlier as "his country's curse."

Judge Wescott bolted from the hall in disgust. As the other delegates were about to leave—the progressives among them morose and resentful—the secretary of the convention announced: "We have just received word that Mr. Wilson, the candidate for the governorship, *and the next President of the United States*, has received word of his nomination, has left Princeton, and is now on his way to the Convention."

Actually, Harvey had commissioned an agent to have Wilson in Trenton even before the nomination was made. The candidate was brought by automobile from Princeton and was kept in a hotel room in ignorance of the moil and barter that were giving him his opportunity. He was summoned to the hall for a well-timed entrance on the stage so expertly set. In contrast with the bosses, who wore frock coats and silk hats, he was dressed in the clothes in which he had been playing golf—a soft felt hat and a gray sack suit, a knitted golf jacket showing under his coat.

He was escorted by police through a mob that milled and cheered outside the stage door of the opera house. "God! Look at that jaw!" a ward heeler was heard to exclaim. There was nothing of the pallid academician in this man as he strode onto the platform. His weathered skin was flushed from the excitement of the occasion and the summer of outdoor living.

Joseph Patrick Tumulty of Jersey City, a sincere progressive who had worked for reform in the state legislature,[15] moved sullenly forward

[15] Like Woodrow Wilson, Tumulty had a grandfather who had immigrated from Ireland; and like Wilson, Tumulty loved parades, orations, and fights in a righteous cause. He had cut his teeth in the gerrymandered slum area of Jersey City that was called the Horseshoe, where in boyhood he had heard the affairs of the nation discussed in his father's grocery store. At the age of seventeen he made his debut as a political orator; and when Bryan paraded at Jersey City in 1896 he shot off firecrackers and orated on what he thought the great moral issue of the campaign—"the attempt of eastern financial interests to dominate the government of the United States."

Tumulty thought that the most effective way to work for reform was through the Democratic organization. In order to be elected to the Assembly, he had accepted the support of Davis and his minions and as an assemblyman had voted for many a "boodle" bill, knowing that in return the county boss would leave him free to work with the New Idea men for progressive laws for the state. His legislative leadership was so marked that in 1910, at the age of thirty-one, he was endorsed by his party to be speaker of the Assembly; but he felt that he must return to the practice of law to provide for his growing family. Tumulty and his progressive friends hoped that a Democrat true to their ideals might be nominated for governor. *See* John M. Blum, "Tumulty and the Wilson Era," a dissertation submitted to Harvard University, and the book based on this study, *Joe Tumulty and the Wilson Era* (hereinafter referred to as Blum, *Tumulty*).

to get a "close-up" of the man whom he thought the bosses had foisted on the party. But now he was astounded by the words and the manner of the candidate. Ignoring the bosses, proclaiming that the nomination had come to him "absolutely unsolicited," Wilson pledged himself to serve the people of the state with singleness of purpose if he was elected. Did you ever desire, he asked the delegates, to do right because it is right and without thought of doing it for your own interest? "At that period your hopes are unselfish. This in particular is a day of unselfish purpose for Democracy . . ."

The little men in that crowded hall were swept up above their petty interests and given a vision. Now it was not Princeton, but the Democratic party, that was committed to serve the state and the nation in righteousness. Their candidate was sharing his dearest ideals, openly and intimately, with winning smiles and with such phrasing as they had never heard before on a political platform. "Government is not a warfare of interest," he warned. "We shall not gain our ends by heat and bitterness." In tones that almost sang, he came to an overwhelming climax:

The future is not for parties "playing politics" but for measures conceived in the largest spirit, pushed by parties whose leaders are statesmen not demagogues, who love, not their offices but their duty and their opportunity for service. We are witnessing a renaissance of public spirit, a reawakening of sober public opinion, a revival of the power of the people, the beginning of an age of thoughful reconstruction that makes our thought hark back to the great age in which democracy was set up in America. With the new age we shall show a new spirit . . .

"Go on, go on," they yelled, thanking God that a leader had come among them. A peroration to the flag brought tears, and it was over. The crowd stood in their seats and cheered madly. Joe Tumulty's allegiance was won: throwing his arms around a friend, he predicted that Jim Smith might find that in Wilson he had a political "lemon." Delegates swarmed forward and tried to lift the candidate to their shoulders. Finally, protecting policemen took him to an automobile. Even then ebullient Democrats mobbed the running-board to shake hands with their new-found messiah.

The prophet was getting through to the people without intervention of trustees or bosses. Wilson told Stockton Axson that the people accepted him because he could find moving words to express the feelings that were in their hearts, groping for release. The secret of his power was the secret that had made his forebears great preachers.

With her husband plunged into a political campaign, Ellen Wilson foresaw new and ominous intrusions into the privacy of the family. "Sugar Jim" Smith, bringing his warriors to Prospect for a powwow, was so charmed by the house and garden that he asked why anyone could be "damn fool enough to give up this for the heartaches of politics." President Lowell of Harvard wrote: "Are not the seas of university management boisterous enough that you must seek the storms of politics?" And in reply Wilson confessed that he was still uncertain whether he had done the right thing or not. "I shall start out upon the new career as bravely as possible," he promised; and, characteristically, he took courage from preaching boldness to boys of the student Christian association who packed a college hall. "Don't go about seeking to associate only with good people," he advised them. "Endure hardness . . . The man who is working is the man who goes out and joins battle." From a current magazine he clipped a new poem, "If," by Rudyard Kipling: "If you can dream—and not make dreams your master . . . If you can talk with crowds and keep your virtue." Later he had a copy of "If" framed; and it remained with him until the day of his death.

What the candidate dreaded most, perhaps, was news reporters. Some he came to trust; but all his life he suspected the press of a lack of veracity and good taste. He had particularly resented sensational reporting of his speeches that represented them as attacks on wealth. Thinking now that he would avoid misquotation by releasing only written statements, he drafted an imaginary "interview"; but when one of Hearst's men bluntly asked him why he had allowed himself "to be nominated by the interests," the candidate forgot his academic preparations and blurted out, hotly: "It is a humiliating and absurd thing to say that I am the Wall Street candidate for governor of New Jersey." Not a fast reader, Wilson himself kept up with only one daily newspaper, the New York *Evening Post*; but his wife read the important journals of New Jersey and New York and gave him hundreds of clippings. After scanning them, he recorded ideas in a vest-pocket notebook.

Once Wilson began to campaign actively for election, a majority of the board of trustees decided that he could no longer serve as president of Princeton. There had been rumors that his enemies had been trying to get rid of him by promoting his political candidacy, and Wilson had been apprised of this possibility.[16] Relying on the carte blanche that his

[16] On July 18, 1910, Z. C. Felt, a Princeton classmate, wrote to Wilson thus: "Last spring one of your bitterest opponents unfolded to me quite at length the plans they hoped to carry into effect to get you out of Princeton. And one of these was to convince you that it was *your* *duty* to accept the nomination."

friends among the trustees had given to him, Wilson wished to devote three days a week to lecturing and to remain president at least until the election in November. However, a delegation was sent to tell him that he must withdraw from the presidency, and a resolution was prepared formally calling on him to resign, to be passed in case the informal suggestion was refused. He reluctantly accepted the inevitable, and on October 20 he read a letter of resignation to the trustees and left the room while they stood in silence.[17]

When Wilson discovered the actual feeling toward him on the part of what he called "the Pyne party," mortification would have broken him had it not been for the continuing confidence of certain friends. Deep within him as life itself were the bonds that had been forged with individuals whom he had come to love and respect—the "Witherspoon gang," Cleveland Dodge and the other loyal trustees, his preceptors and protégés, Henry B. Fine and the little band of university men. Princeton was the promised land to which in his last years he was to yearn to return. Lying at the gate of death he said to one of his old boys: "If they cut me open afterward, they'll find engraved on my heart—PRINCETON!" [18]

The rejected prophet lacked courage to admit to strangers that he had failed as the chief executive of a privately endowed corporation.[19] Yet the truth is that he had slipped from his platform of principle and been drawn into a feud with a powerful antagonist. He had weakened

[17] See Link, op. cit., p. 90. In wishing to retain his office until the election, Wilson probably was influenced by the plea sent by Henry B. Fine in a letter of July 10: "The only request which we, your Princeton friends, can in fairness make is that you do not retire from the presidency of Princeton until *actually elected Governor of New Jersey.*" His election would be "very probable" but not "certain," Fine went on, and "Princeton should have the benefit of the difference between the certainty and the probability."

Accepting Wilson's forced resignation on Oct. 20, 1910, the trustees requested him to continue in his professorship of jurisprudence and politics as long as possible, and conferred on him the degree of Doctor of Laws. John A. Stewart, the senior trustee, was made president pro tem. Both the trustees and his students presented elaborate testimonials upon Wilson's departure. He refused to continue his teaching, however, and declined persistent offers by the university to continue his salary for a few months, taking nothing after Oct. 20, the effective date of his resignation, and moving from Prospect to the Princeton Inn within a few weeks.

Left without income, except for about $2,000 a year from investments and royalties from his books, Wilson applied to the Carnegie Foundation for a pension. Cf. pp. 212–13 below.

Wilson paid the personal expenses of the New Jersey campaign out of his own small funds. Later, when he discovered how expensive campaigning could be, he was forced to accept financial donations from friends who he thought could be depended on not to press him for political favors.

[18] Roland Morris to Francis C. MacDonald to the writer.

[19] For example, replying to a request of Oct. 31, 1912, from a Princeton admirer, Henry D. Pierce of the Class of 1868, for information about the Princeton controversy, Wilson wrote that there was at no time "the least likelihood" of his being forced out of the Princeton presidency. Such a statement as this gave support to the contention of West and his friends that Wilson was an unconscionable liar.

his position by suggesting an irrational but well-intentioned compromise on the location of the graduate college. His rectitude had kept him from wooing men as friends when his conscience told him that he wanted them only as patrons. His scorn of pettifogging had made him less than careful of the letter of truth. His conviction of the rightness of his cause had made him contemptuous, rather than sympathetic, toward contrary opinions and had chilled the feelings of both trustees and alumni who did not understand their president.

Nevertheless, in spite of his failure to hold the support of the entire constituency, Princeton had flourished under his leadership. New impulses had taken root that were to flower gloriously for decades afterward. Undergraduate scholarship had improved; and under the impetus of the new faculty committee on the graduate school, the number and intellectual quality of graduate students had grown. Moreover, the university had become richer in equipment, in annual gifts, and in endowment.

Woodrow Wilson would engage in shindies aplenty in future years; he would have to contend with men who, unlike Cleveland and Pyne, were ruled by self-interest; and he would have to bear malicious personal attacks that even Andrew West was to brand as false. But for the most part the hostility and its animus would be as obvious as gross. Never in subsequent struggles in the political arena, he said later, did he meet an antagonist as crafty as Andrew Fleming West.

CHAPTER X

FALL OF AN OLD REGIME

THE NOMINATION at Trenton put Woodrow Wilson on the front page. It was unprecedented for a man so renowned as a scholar to venture to give active political leadership. To what extent would he be able to make his ideals effective? everyone wondered. Did he understand them, the plain people, and their wants and needs in the autumn of 1910? Was he indeed the messiah to lead them through the economic wilderness without bloodshed?

Wilson himself, leaving the work to which he had given the best twenty years of his life and staking his family's livelihood on his ability to serve the people of New Jersey, wondered. "Am I equal to this big work when I failed in a much smaller one?" he asked an old friend a little wistfully. Then, reassuring himself, he said: "Yes, I believe I am, for now I shall be speaking to the American people, not to an academic group rooted in tradition and fearful of progress."

For several weeks he and the people sounded each other out, and reached only tentative conclusions. Folks were quick to see that they were being offered leadership of a caliber that was strange to them. They caught the awe that Smith had reflected from the floor of the nominating convention when he said: "It is not to be assumed that such as I should be acquainted with such as he, but it is clear from all I have heard that he will make a superlative governor."

The candidate, for his part, stepped lightly and uncertainly through the first weeks of the campaign. Meeting the Democratic leaders with great warmth and charm, he dodged state issues by taking refuge in discussion of national policies and academic generalities. He was keeping up his guard, not trusting all men to accept his virtuous intent as guarantee of his wisdom.

In council with party men it was decided that the candidate should woo the hearts of his new constituents by the eloquence of set speeches rather than the give-and-take of interviews. Twenty-seven addresses were scheduled. He was nervous about these public appearances, at first, begging his wife to stay away for fear that he would disgrace her by some deviation from perfection; and when his daughters went to hear him, they hid behind the curtains of a box so that he would not see them and become embarrassed. He had had little experience in addressing political audiences, and feared that he might not give the satisfaction that they demanded; and he did not write texts in advance, "in cold blood."

In his first speech to the electorate, at Jersey City, he was obviously ill at ease, lugged in irrelevant anecdotes, rambled a bit. Then he made a frank confession: "I never before appeared before an audience and asked for anything, and now I find myself in the novel position of asking you to vote for me for governor of New Jersey." That broke down the barriers; and at the end of his talk he drew prolonged cheers by stepping to the front of the platform and saying ingenuously: "And so, gentlemen, I have made my first political plea. I feel that I am before a great jury. I don't want the judge to butt in. I am content to leave the decision in your hands." They stopped him there, with applause that came from their hearts. They saw no haughty intellectual in this candid, friendly Scotch-Irishman. The crowds were bigger than expected; and even the newsmen were so affected that they sometimes neglected their work.

He did not harangue, though he occasionally indulged in a peroration —"those boys are strong for perorations," he sensed. For the most part he used simple words and short sentences. But one night, after a New York editor had taken exception to his diction, he began to speak waggishly in ornate and stilted phrases. Then suddenly he laughed, thrust his hands in his pockets, walked forward, and lifted the frowns from the faces in front of him by saying, "Confidentially, ladies and gentlemen, that's the way the New York —— thinks I should talk to you, but I prefer a more informal way of speaking."

His powers of mimicry and repartee were brought into play. The Republican party, he told one audience, was like the mule on a Mississippi River steamboat that ate the destination tag that was tied to its collar. "Cap'n," shouted a Negro deckhand. "Dat mule done et up whar he gwine to!"

Yet his humor was not displayed at the expense of sincerity. Listeners were convinced that he was that very rare specimen: a completely frank candidate for office. He seemed to be thinking out loud in their presence, to be sharing himself with them most intimately. In the audiences that to prissy academic folk seemed "roughneck" Wilson saw genuine individuals who were moved by normal human impulses. He idealized men who knew their business and worked hard. In talking face to face with the people of New Jersey, Wilson felt the thrill that had come to him at the Cooper Union in New York six years before. He had testified then that the most penetrating questions ever addressed to him "came from some of the men who were the least well-dressed in the audience, came from the plain fellows, came from the fellows whose muscle was daily up against the whole struggle of life. They asked questions which went to the heart of the business and put me on my mettle."

Wilson's first campaign speeches were lectures in political science, each growing logically out of the preceding. Advocating the specific and immediate reforms—such as administrative reorganization, fairer taxation and regulation of corporations, and an effective corrupt practices act—he carefully held himself within the limits that were set by the party platform that he had helped George Harvey to draft. He was observing and evaluating the program being put forward by the progressives of both parties, remembering that a cautious regard for popular feeling made the difference between the parliamentary statesman and the wild-eyed reformer.

He took the campaign rather casually in the early days. In order to hold him to his speaking schedule, James Nugent, the party chairman and a man for whom Wilson had little respect, had to threaten to take the candidate's place in any meeting that Wilson missed. In late September, Democratic headquarters sent Joseph Tumulty to West Hoboken to hold an audience until the candidate could get there; and the young progressive performed his mission so brilliantly that Wilson made him his comrade and understudy on speaking trips and began to call him "my dear boy." Tumulty found the man unaffected and affable, able to restore his energy between speeches by taking catnaps in their automobile, willing to drive long distances in order to get home at night. But Tumulty still suspected his chief of being a wolf in sheep's clothing, playing "the old game of thimblerig" at the bidding of the bosses. Asked for his honest opinion of the first campaign speech, he told Wilson that it was most disappointing.

Other progressives begged the Democratic candidate to declare that he would not allow any corporations or bosses or machines to rule the state; and Wilson took this advice, feeling himself not yet expert in electioneering strategy. In his first speech in Smith's home city of Newark he urged that the state intervene to prevent men from "taking joy rides in corporations." Explaining the party platform in terms that all could understand, he stirred thunderous applause.

Before the address, Smith had sent an agent to Wilson to ask him to speak out against local liquor option in order to please the majority of the Newark audience. The candidate had refused, and escaped heckling on the issue by riveting the attention of his hearers on more vital topics. The persistence of Smith in trying to change what he knew to be Wilson's convictions on local option reawakened the suspicions of the prophet. He asked one of Sugar Jim's agents what the bosses really were up to; and when he was reminded that these men had nominated him and could elect or defeat him, Wilson replied: "I went in without pledges, asked or given, and it is the people, not the bosses, who will elect me if I am elected, and to whom I shall be responsible."

"If you are elected," the agent predicted, "you are going to hear a lot from Jim Smith."

In the treacherous footing at Princeton he had slipped from the code of his grandfather—"principles, not men"—but now it was commanding every move. He won converts from the progressive wing of the Republican party by asserting that he was being attacked personally, as a "professor," rather than on grounds of principle. Tumulty would have him slug it out with the Republicans and ridicule the political record of their candidate, but Wilson insisted on dealing mainly with the principles that were to prevail in the future.

A few days later, however, at Trenton, using a phrase that had been put in his mouth by an editor of that city, Wilson bluntly told the people that he would not, like his Republican opponent, be merely a "constitutional governor," but would truly represent all-of-them. He threatened that, if the legislators did not pass the laws that the people demanded, he would "take every important subject of debate in the legislature out on the stump and discuss it with the people." Then his lips compressed and his eyes seemed to narrow, as his deeper feelings surged up and he challenged: "If you don't want that kind of governor, don't elect me." He went on: "If you give me your votes, I will be under bonds to you— not to the gentlemen who were generous enough to nominate me."

It was no ordinary political campaign, he told them. There was more sincerity; people had come out to the meetings in unprecedented numbers, as if something was to be accomplished. Bearing down on the importance of close contact between government and public opinion, the candidate challenged his hearers to play out their role. "You have got into the game," he told them, "but are you going to stay there?"

In his October speeches, his blood started by the spur of competition, Wilson was projecting himself headlong into liberal thinking. He spoke of "the splendid program of the progressives—to put things forward— by justice, by fairness, by a concern for all interests, until men shall think in terms of the common weal and not in the terms of special interests or partisan advantage." Moreover, he got down to cases, argued that the price of gas could be cut in half by efficient regulation of the Public Service Corporation, explained just why New Jersey's election laws were "so loose and evil." He came to think of himself as representing "the reorganized Democratic party." Finally, he made the extravagant claim that he was and always had been an insurgent. "I am accused of being a radical," he said. "If to seek to go to the root is to be a radical, a radical I am."

He would not pander to labor unions any more than to corporations or to the liquor interests, in spite of their great voting strength. Warning laborers that the Republicans would not carry out their glib promises to the workingmen, he urged them to think of the best interests of "the people." And who were "the people"?

Do capitalists constitute the people? Certainly not. Do the merchants constitute the people? Certainly not. When you speak of the people are you thinking of levels? Are you thinking of those who are poor, are you thinking of those who are well-to-do . . . are you thinking of those who are very rich? The interesting thing is that the people consist of all these classes put together; it does not consist of any one, it does not consist of any two of them, or of any combination, except the combination that constitutes the whole.

As he warmed to the battle, the candidate tended more and more to stand apart. He became cockily assertive as he carried the political thought of the state, including that of the Republican candidate, far to the left. As a Trenton newspaper pointed out, he was "uniting the insurgent forces of New Jersey." The contest became one of personalities and character, with both candidates appealing to the fervor of the people for reform. The questions became: Which candidate would the people believe to be more sincere? Which would be strong enough to rule the reactionaries in his party? Which would lead the legislature and not merely follow it?

A chance to bind the confidence of the independent voters was provided by George L. Record, who publicly accepted a challenge to public debate that Wilson had flung out impulsively to "any politician in the state." However, the Democratic leaders saw only danger in such an event, fearing that Record might ask questions about the party machine that could not be dodged gracefully. After a conference with Wilson, Chairman Nugent wrote a public letter offering to arrange "joint meetings" if Record would appear as the accredited Republican spokesman. Actually, everyone knew that this could never be; and so Record met Nugent's parry with scorn. "The great Dr. Wilson," he taunted, "who is to lift the politics of New Jersey to a new and higher plane, at the first test has gone down to the Jim Nugent plane and commences to dodge and pettifog."

This, and the urging of progressive friends, goaded Wilson to direct action. Ignoring his party organization, he wrote a letter to Record saying that they would have to deal with each other as individuals rather than as party men. His speaking program, he explained, kept him from arrranging a debate. Yet he realized that he must not seem to try to dodge Record's challenge if he was to win the votes of the "New Idea Republicans." And so he suggested that Record's questions be propounded in a public letter to which a reply could be made for publication. In this way he ran no risk of being confounded by sharp cross-examination; moreover, intermediaries were working to prevent any trickery in Record's queries.

Wilson's suggestion was taken, and the nineteen questions that were drafted and published in the newspapers covered every important issue in detail. The problems raised were those that had been turning over in Wilson's mind for weeks. Intuition told him that they were in the minds of the voters, too; and both pastoral responsibility and political expediency required that he reply. By meeting the challenge both fearlessly and intelligently, he proved not only that he had been "born a politician," but that he was developing the stature of statesmanship. After days of stumbling and groping in a strange political wilderness—a land in which he had previously roamed only as a critic, never as a responsible leader—the intensely moral mind slowly settled on what it could regard as God's business in government. At last Woodrow Wilson felt "qualified to speak." When he sat down on October 24 to write his reply to Record, his words were exclusively and intimately his own.

Asked whether he favored election reforms, a corrupt practices act, and certain measures that would regulate public utilities more effectively, Wilson answered affirmatively; but on one issue—that of the nomination of candidates for office by direct primary elections—he no longer expressed doubts that he had held a few weeks before. Inconsistencies in his views on an issue from time to time never embarrassed him, so long as he was true to his basic principle of reasoned change. In a campaign speech he reminded the people: "We are not in the same America we were ten years ago. The standpat program is always wrong." And on another occasion he said: "I'll agree not to change my mind if someone with power to do so will guarantee that if I go to bed at night I will get up in the morning and see the world in the same way."

It was in replying to the last five questions that Wilson wrote an important page in American political history. Record condemned the government of the state as a conspiracy among bosses of the two parties and the public service corporations—"an evil that has destroyed representative government . . . and in its place set up a government of privilege." In return for certain privileges, he alleged, the party leaders were awarded favors by the corporation managers in "the form of either direct money payments, or heavy contributions for campaign expenses, or opportunity for safe and profitable business ventures, according to the standard of morality of the particular boss or leader." Did Wilson agree with this statement? the Progressive leader asked.

"Of course," the candidate replied, the existence of the evil was "notorious."

How would Wilson abolish it, if elected?

By the reforms agreed upon, and "by the election to office of men who will refuse to submit to it and bend all their energies to break it up, and by pitiless publicity."

Tapping what he thought would be the most sensitive nerve of all, the inquisitor named names. Wherein, he asked, did the relation of the corporation interests to the Republican bosses differ from the relation of the same interests to "such Democratic leaders as Smith, Nugent, and Davis?"

The answer came straight to the mark: The Republican bosses "differ from the others in this, that they are in control of the government of the State, while the others are not and cannot be if the present Democratic ticket is elected." Wilson went even further in order to drive misgivings from the minds of progressive voters. Attacking a doubt that was implied in several of Record's questions, he wrote:

If elected I shall not, either in the matter of appointments to office or assent to legislation, or in shaping any part of the policy of my administration, submit to the dictation of any person or persons, special interest or organization. I will always welcome advice and suggestions from any citizen, whether boss, leader, organization man or plain citizen, and I shall constantly seek the advice of influential and disinterested men, representative of their communities and disconnected from political "organizations" entirely; but all suggestions and all advice will be considered on their merits, and no additional weight will be given to any man's advice or suggestion because of his exercising, or supposing that he exercises, some sort of political influence or control. I should deem myself forever disgraced should I in even the slightest degree cooperate in any such system or any such transactions as you describe in your characterization of the "boss" system. I regard myself as pledged to the regeneration of the Democratic party which I have forecast above.

To Record's last query, asking whether Wilson would require candidates for the legislature "to pledge themselves in writing prior to the election in favor of such of the foregoing reforms" as he personally favored, Wilson replied: "I will not. Because I think it would be most unbecoming in me to do so. That is the function of the voters in the several counties."

Wilson's reply was published in a flyer and circulated. Record was dumfounded. Independent progressives and restless Republicans came into the Democratic camp in thousands. Joseph Tumulty told the candidate that the New Jersey democracy—meaning the progressive wing of it—gladly accepted his "virile leadership." Smith, with the election only weeks away, could only swallow the sword that had been aimed at him and hoped that it was made of rubber. "A great campaign play," the bosses told each other, whistling to keep up courage.

Actually, however, the sword became stiffer and sharper as the candidate made a final whirlwind tour of northern Jersey in a week of slush and snow. Perhaps, he said, the bosses had picked out the wrong man after all. And with mordant threats he mixed discussion of specific reforms.

In a final speech, at Newark, Wilson served notice that if elected he would consider himself chosen to lead his party, to conduct the government of the state in the interest of the people only, using party and party coherents for that service. "What I seriously object to," he said, "is any government conducted upon the basis of private understanding with anybody." There was nothing self-conscious or stylistic about his expression now. He no longer strained for effect, but showed the confidence and competence of one who had learned how. After this address an admirer climbed the platform, slapped the back of the speaker, and shouted: "Doc, you're a winner!" Smith, emotionally stirred by the man from whom he both hoped and feared much, turned to Tumulty with tears welling, and said hoarsely: "a great man . . . destined for great things."

Victory on election day was an anticlimax, but the plurality surpassed expectations. It was almost fifty thousand, in a state that the Republican presidential candidate had carried by some eighty thousand votes two years before. The counties of Smith and Davis gave Wilson large majorities, and even his own recalcitrant Mercer County finally supported the ex-president of Princeton.[1]

At ten o'clock on election night it became clear to Wilson that the people of New Jersey had chosen him to lead them. Soon the blare of bands rose above the hubbub inside Prospect, and fireworks and waving torches could be seen from the windows. He stepped out and looked upon the largest parade ever seen in Princeton. For hours the family sat up, talking it over, wondering how they would keep the air of their home breathable. Students and townspeople swarmed over the lawn to pay tribute with yells and cheering. Deeply moved, their hero said very simply: "It is my ambition to be the governor of all the people of the state, and render to them the best services I am capable of rendering."

New Jersey editors did not let the Governor-elect forget that his victory was but the culmination of the surge of protest that had started with the New Idea revolt; and realizing his debt to progressive pioneers, Wilson took pains to respond appreciatively to a letter of congratulation from Record. He made light of his triumph by explaining to his intimates that he had been "kicked upstairs" into public service; but his friends exulted in the new honor as evidence of the sure grinding of the mills of the gods. Fred Yates, the English painter, who had been visiting at Prospect during the campaign and had found the atmosphere of the Wilson home remarkably unrestrained and "breathable," remarked: "Yes, it's the same old story—the biggest are always the simplest. Dear W.W. is in a fight . . . There is only one danger . . . whether he can stand against the intriguers—whether he is not by nature an autocrat . . . He is a fighter—and I believe he loves the fight —I believe he has only one eye for anything and that is Truth. Jesus died for that—and Socrates—single-eyed— How few men . . ."

Very soon, however, the rosy afterglow of the election was overcast by the cloud of another battle. James Smith, Jr., unctuous and ready to be rewarded for services rendered, paid a visit to Prospect. He said that his health, to which rumor had attributed his apparent lack of interest in the forthcoming election of a United States senator by the state Assembly, was remarkably better. Now that a Democratic majority had come unexpectedly into control of the legislature, senatorial elec-

---

[1] John Blum has pointed out that a raise of 20 per cent in commuters' fares shortly before the election played a part in Wilson's capture of a larger share of the suburban vote than ever went to him again. *See* Blum, *Tumulty*, p. 24.

tion was no longer so unessential a matter to Smith as Wilson had been led to believe in July.[2]

There had been rumors, already, that Smith had been lining up support among the incoming legislators by the use of promises of patronage that he had no right to dispense. And when the plausible boss sat down in Prospect, where hundreds of lectures on political morality had been composed, and indicated his desire to go to the Senate, Wilson's composure was severely taxed. His sense of professional honesty was outraged. He had received letters from reliable witnesses that confirmed his suspicion that Smith had betrayed a political trust.[3] If he supported Smith's aspirations to the Senate, Wilson would become an accomplice in deceiving the voters; for Smith's name had not been entered in the primary election by which, under a new law sponsored by the progressives, the people had indicated whom they would like to have their legislature choose for the Senate.

The candidate who had won the preference of the few people who had bothered to vote in the primary was one James E. Martine, a Bryan Democrat whose progressive ideas were more enthusiastic than rational but who had the support of journals in Newark and Jersey City.

Wilson was in a dilemma as difficult as any that had faced him in the university. He could pay a personal debt and lose the confidence of progressive voters by supporting Smith, whom he thought able but dishonest. He could uphold a primary law that he thought good in principle, and accept Martine, the well-intentioned but incompetent candi-

2 Smith had never publicly renounced his ambition to return to the Senate. He had told Harvey that he would be willing to make a public disavowal if ever that should become necessary in order to relieve Wilson of the disrepute that might result from accusations that his campaign for the governorship was in reality only a means of furthering Smith's personal ambition. That was a gesture of magnanimity that Smith could well afford to make, so slight was the chance that there would be a Democratic legislature at Trenton to elect him. Harvey had informed Wilson of Smith's offer, yet had refused to accept it immediately for fear of alienating Smith's henchmen, whose support had been needed to nominate Wilson at Trenton. While allowing their ingenuous candidate for the governorship to think that Smith had no plan to run for the Senate, the master tacticians calculatingly had built up the power of Sugar Jim by letting the minions think that he might become a senator and a source of federal patronage that would be worth following. And at the same time, from the other side of his mouth, Smith was time and again reassuring the progressive, editor James Kerney, that he would not run for the Senate. The assurances given to Kerney must have reached Wilson, sooner or later, and must have affirmed the impression of Smith's disinterestedness that Wilson had reported to his family after returning from the July conference at Deal. (*See* pp. 153 and 176.)

3 Wilson was warned against Smith by John Moody in a letter of Nov. 29, 1910, telling of Moody's experience in soliciting campaign funds from Smith in 1903: "He apparently assumed that as I was a Wall Street man, I was naturally interested in politics 'for revenue only' and he was very frank . . . He told me in so many words that for many years he had been the dispenser of money received from the Pennsylvania Railroad and other corporations to influence legislation in the State of New Jersey. He explained that any men we might send to the legislature should surely 'behave themselves.' " John Moody to the writer, confirmed by a letter, Nov. 19, 1955.

date whom the Democratic voters had endorsed. He could urge the party to find a compromise candidate. He could stand aside and point out that he was under no legal obligation in the matter.

As usual, he made no immediate decision. Striving desperately to veil the moral indignation that Smith had aroused, Wilson suggested to him, when he called at Prospect, that by entering the senatorial race at this point Smith "would confirm all the ugliest suspicions of the campaign." Even if one assumed that the vote for Martine had been so small that it was inconclusive, he argued, the only way to give dignity to the new primary law was to take the outcome of it seriously. He did not flay this infidel, as he had Andrew West, by telling him grimly that it was necessary that he "be digested in the processes" of good government. Rather he pleaded with Smith, and told him that if he was not satisfied to have Martine represent the party he could suggest a compromise candidate who would represent no special interests, but the opinion of the entire state.

Smith, however, saw through the Governor's tactful subterfuge. Choosing a "compromise" candidate, after all, would invalidate the primary election just as thoroughly as if Smith himself were chosen. For all of his valiant efforts at diplomacy, Wilson's personal revulsion was obvious to his caller. There was academic reprobation in the air; and Smith went away feeling, as he told Harvey later, that back of the polite words "there seemed to be something arbitrary and autocratic." The boss's pride was hurt. ". . . by God," he told Harvey, "I guess I'll let him beat me!" Finally, in mid-November, he declared publicly that if his friends thought he should make the fight he would enter the race and would win it.

Another shindy was brewing. First Wilson listened to cautious counselors who advised him not to take sides. Then with his wife he sought guidance in prayer. Mindful of his pledge to the people to give leadership to the legislature, Wilson asked himself the question attributed to an Irishman whom he liked to tell about—a man who, entering a saloon and seeing a tangle of writhing, bleeding bodies on the floor, said: "Tell me now, is this a private fight or can I get into it?" Independent editors and other citizens had been importuning him to enter the fray. Judge Wescott warned that, if Smith ran and was elected, Dr. Wilson's "usefulness in American regeneration" would end.

Wilson had no stomach for governing a boss-ridden state, any more than he had for presiding over a university that could be directed by absentee wealth. If the party bosses were not going to leave him "absolutely free in the matter of measures and men," if they would not "work with thorough heartiness for such policies as would re-establish the reputation of the State," he felt no obligation to honor his part of the pre-election covenant—his promise not to replace the Smith organization.

Wilson sent influential go-betweens to try to dissuade Smith. Colonel Watterson of the Louisville *Courier-Journal* tried his hand at it, and failed. Cleveland Dodge brought pressure to bear indirectly and reported: "It is evident that Smith proposes to go to the Senate. I hear from a reliable source that all the Democratic Assemblymen but six are under such financial obligations to him that he owns them absolutely."

Wilson made use, also, of the good offices of his canny publisher in New York. To George Harvey he sent a letter that was composed obviously for the eyes of Smith. Again his distrust was masked by the promptings of gratitude and diplomacy. He wrote to Harvey on November 15:

I am very anxious about the question of the senatorship. If not handled right it will destroy every fortunate impression of the campaign and open my administration with a split party. I have learned to have a very high opinion of Senator Smith. I have very little doubt, that if he were sent to the Senate he would acquit himself with honour and do a great deal to correct the impressions of his former term. But his election would be intolerable to the very people who elected me and gave us a majority in the legislature . . . It was no Democratic victory. It was a victory of the "progressives" of both parties, who are determined to leave no one under either of the political organizations that have controlled the two parties of the State . . . It is grossly unjust that they should regard Senator Smith as the impersonation of all that they hate and fear; but they do, and there is an end of the matter. If he should become a candidate, I would have to fight him; and there is nothing I would more sincerely deplore. It would offend every instinct in me, except the instinct as to what was right and necessary from the point of view of public service. I have had to do similar things in the University. By the same token, ridiculous though it undoubtedly is, I think we shall have to stand by Mr. Martine . . .

Woodrow Wilson had closed the door: he had decided in favor of honesty and incompetence, against ability and what he knew, in spite of the conciliatory phrases written to Harvey, to be deceit. The letter went on:

I have stripped my whole thought and my whole resolution naked for you to see just as it is. Senator Smith can make himself the biggest man in the

State by a dignified refusal to let his name be considered. I hope, as I hope for the rejuvenation of our party, that he may see it and proceed to do so.

It is a national as well as a State question. If the independent Republicans who in this state voted for me are not to be attracted to us they will surely turn again in desperation to Mr. Roosevelt, and the chance of a generation will be lost to the Democracy: the chance to draw all the liberal elements of the country to it, through new leaders, the chance that Mr. Roosevelt missed in his folly, and to constitute the ruling party of the country for the next generation.

Gently and tactfully as the letter frustrated his ambition, Smith, nevertheless, was infuriated. By the end of November his forces had united with those of Robert Davis, and Wilson paid a surprise visit to the law office of Joseph Tumulty, Davis's friend, to ask practical advice. That astute young politician saw the intellect of the Governor-elect at work, weighing all the arguments that had come already from conservative friends, asking for the ideas of the progressives, listening avidly, with the conviction growing that in the longer, larger view both right and destiny compelled acceptance of progressive counsel.

Tumulty took Wilson to Davis's home. The plump, merry little man was dying of cancer in the house from which he had ruled Hudson County for decades. With a dramatic gesture that appealed to Irish hearts, Wilson went to the bedside of the boss and warned of the effect on the fortunes of the Democratic party if it went back on the principle of direct election that it had been advocating. Seeing a larger vision than the little men of New Jersey, Wilson was convinced that, unless there was a "new deal," the party would be put out of credit for the rest of their lives. But Davis, a man who boasted that he had never broken a promise, could only reply that he had given his pledge to Smith and that the Pope himself could not make him retract it. Suggesting a deal, Davis said that, if Wilson would keep his hands off, the bosses would support his whole legislative program. But Wilson did not trust this proposal, knowing that the prestige that would accrue to Smith from election to the Senate would undermine the Governor's influence over the legislature. In the end Davis took no strong measure to bind his men to Smith. To drive the wedge more deeply, however, Tumulty suggested that Wilson talk personally with the wavering Hudson County assemblymen. And so the delegates were invited to Prospect, and Wilson argued with them for Martine and for the popular election of senators. Only in this way, he said, could the party keep faith with the voters.

The Governor-elect was confident enough, now, to force the issue;

and Villard of the New York *Evening Post* was advising him that "from a personal point of view" he could do nothing better than to make a public declaration against Smith's candidacy. Before going to this extreme, however, Wilson called on the boss at Newark and begged him to preserve party unity by living up to the precampaign intentions that Wilson understood he had avowed. At the same time he served notice that, unless Smith withdrew by the evening of the second day, he would feel compelled to make a public announcement in favor of Martine and to oppose Smith "with every honourable means" at his command. When the boss asked whether the patronage would be used against him, Wilson replied: "No, I should not regard that as an honourable means. Besides, that will not be necessary."

Smith, who had sacrificed much for the cause of the party through the lean years and in the recent campaign, felt that he deserved better. Furthermore, Sugar Jim said, he wanted to redeem his name as a senator, for the sake of his children. It was a moving human appeal, and Wilson had genuine sympathy for the motive. But two days after the conference, having heard nothing further from the boss, Wilson wrote: "Ex-Senator Smith proves to be the tough customer he is reputed to be, and there is nothing for it but to fight him openly and to a finish. It is a hard necessity . . ." Refraining from any attack on the vulnerable political morality of his opponent, Wilson explained publicly that he felt morally bound, as elected "spokesman and adviser of the people," to tell the legislature what he deemed their duty to be in electing a senator. The preference that the people had expressed for Martine was to him conclusive, he said; and it was his opinion that it should guide the legislators.

Half an hour after releasing this public endorsement of Martine, Wilson received a letter from Smith asking for a delay of a few days. But the words could not be recalled.

Smith was surprised, hurt, then hotly indignant. He hammered upon Wilson's statement with all the arguments that his shrewd political sense could adduce. The assault on him, he said, was dictatorial, heartless, unfair. It was an "unwarranted attempt" to coerce the legislature on a matter that both state and federal constitutions had placed outside the province of the Governor, "a gratuitous attack upon one who had befriended him," and a grab at party leadership by a man who knew nothing of the toilsome grubbing for votes that built up a party and who had done nothing for the Democratic organization until he himself stood to benefit personally from its operations.

It was to be a duel on a frontier scale, fought out in Wilson's favorite medium, the free air of open publicity. One contestant inevitably would be killed, politically; the other would be supreme in New Jersey politics. And if Wilson won, the victory would take him far along the road to the Presidency.

Smith's Irish was up and he resolved to go down fighting. On December 14 he publicly announced his candidacy and his platform, in what was very nearly a vacuum of articulate sentiment.

In a powwow of progressive leaders, it was decided that the Governor-elect should stump for Martine as many times as seemed necessary. But more effective were Wilson's personal appeals to the individual assemblymen. In letters and in interviews, he revealed the full strength of his mind and heart. Even the delegates from Smith's own county came to listen to the prophet and went away impressed. "He is a great man," one of the them acknowledged, "and he talked to us as a father would."

They were veteran politicians, these men, of the sort whom Lincoln had described as "a set of men . . . who, to say the most of them, are, taken as a mass, at least one long step removed from honest men." Wilson could not meet them as a fellow frontiersman on the flat land of politics, could not add, as Lincoln had: "I say this with the greater freedom because, being a politician myself, none can regard it as personal." The Governor-elect of New Jersey never had been on the level of the ground, and below, with "the boys." He had to depend rather on the grace of his Presbyterian God to keep him humble, to make his heart beat in rhythm with the hearts of the little men from the Jersey counties. He talked as a preacher giving pastoral advice, offering no *quid pro quo,* asking the delegates merely to seek the truth and follow the dictates of conscience.

He gave these men a forthright account of his understanding of the senatorial controversy. In this, and in a statement that he released for publication, he was careless about the letter of fact. Once again, in the excitement of controversy, preoccupation with the larger issues blurred his view of the laws of evidence. When he alleged publicly that Smith had promised him, personally, not to run for the Senate, Smith challenged his truthfulness; and neither contestant wished to bring George Harvey into the dispute as a witness to what had actually been said in the conference at Deal in July of 1910.

In the heat of battle Wilson came to realize his need for an adviser who was instinctively expert in political tactics. In his safari into the political jungle Wilson wanted a guide who had grown up in its savagery. Moreover, if Smith, a Roman Catholic, should appeal to religious prejudices, it would be well for the Governor-elect to have politically enlightened men of that faith around him. And so Joseph Tumulty, who for some time had been urging Wilson to overcome his reluctance to attack Smith personally, was invited to serve as private secretary. The smart, sentimental young Irishman accepted the invitation from the man whom he had already begun to revere, and thus began a long stewardship that was to be filled to overflowing with both laughter and tears. Tumulty's bright blue eyes, yellow curls, and cherubic cheeks cheered Wilson, and his practical jokes served often to lift "the Governor" out of somber moods.

Tumulty managed the campaign of Martine; and at the beginning of 1911 it appeared almost certain that they would win. But the pace of the attack did not slacken. Smith was to be thoroughly drenched in what Wilson called "the cold bath of public opinion."

On January 5 the Governor-elect faced the first of a series of uproarious crowds. Introduced by Tumulty at Jersey City as "a great man with a great soul," he gave free rein to his caustic tongue as he damned the Smith-Nugent machine as "a wart" on the body politic and part of a domineering alliance of rascals of both parties who worked for corporate interests. The bosses had been "thrashed" at the recent election, he said, and they were "going to stay thrashed." Turning theatrically to Martine, who was sitting on the stage, Wilson begged him never, under any circumstances, to withdraw. Accepting a tactical suggestion from editor James Kerney, he spiked whispered rumors that he was anti-Catholic by citing Tumulty and others as "a group of men who illustrate in their lives and conduct not only public morality but the teachings of the great church of which they are members." Men sometimes forget, he said, "that religious principle is the one solid and remaining foundation. Find a man whose conscience is buttressed by that intimate principle and you will find a man into whose hands you can safely trust your affairs." His own heart went into the passage, he declared afterward.

In the speech at Jersey City the prophet called down the curse of war on the Philistines, and wavering minds were scorned as cowardly. It was camp-meeting evangelism, complete with everything but trumpet and choir of angels. Who was to be on the Lord's side, and therefore on the side of his true prophet? Such a harangue would have made the Princeton man of letters shudder ten years before. No college president could have put on such a performance and retained the intellectual respect of his associates. Free rein was given, now, to the spirit of extravagance that had made "Tommie" Wilson love a Pee-rade. The speech was egotistical, blatant, harsh, inaccurate—and effective!

Smith struck back immediately. Tripping up Wilson on a point of fact, he protested that his opponent talked of principle to some and of his powers to others. Referring to the diplomatic overture that Wilson had made to him privately—that a compromise candidate be named for the Senate in spite of the primary vote for Martine—Smith complained: "In private he laughs at the primary law and scowls at its 'preference.' In public he treats both as holy."[4] But this politician, who usually had been able to find human weakness through which he could work his will, was helpless before the fervor of the stampeding prophet. The people saw before them two men with contrasting records, essentially different philosophies.They already knew which man they could trust to act for the welfare of all-of-them. And great was their joy when they found that their prophet could talk their language as well as think their thoughts about such things as justice, responsibility, liberty, God.

In his last speech against Smith, Wilson let himself go as he had before the Princeton alumni at Pittsburgh. Elevating the immediate issue, he illuminated it with the fire of exalted prophecy, tracing great figures in the sky just above the horizon of his audience:

Gentlemen, what is it that we are fighting for? Does not your blood jump quicker in your veins when you think that this is part of the age-long struggle for human liberty? What do men feel curtails and destroys their liberty? Matters in which they have no voice . . . Whenever things go to cover, then men stand up and know and say that liberty is in jeopardy, and so every time a fight of this sort occurs, we are simply setting up the standard again. One can almost see the field of battle. On the one hand a fort that looks strong but that is made of pasteboard. Behind it stand men apparently armed with deadly weapons, but having only play-things in their hands. And off cowering in the distance for a little while is the great mass of fearful, free men. Presently they take heart: they look up; they begin to move slowly. You can see the dust of the plain gather. . . . And they go on, and, as in the Bible stories, the first shout of victorious and irresistible free men causes the stronghold to collapse.

In mid-January the legislature convened, and Wilson and Tumulty kept up pressure on the members until the final vote was taken. Davis had died, and Tumulty, wielding the state patronage, had little trouble

---

4 Trenton, *True American*, Jan. 7, 1911, in Link, *op. cit.*, p. 231. Again, as in the irrational proposal to William Cooper Procter (*see* pp. 124–25 and 126 n.), a generous effort to compromise boomeranged to damage Wilson's case.

in making the party bosses in his native county see that Smith's cause was lost. Wilson was learning from his campaign-hardened secretary how to fight the devil with fire. Working all night, they put backbone into wobbly assemblymen. With Tumulty at his elbow, Wilson could now play the game of electioneering with the shrewdest. On January 25, in spite of a noisy Smith demonstration of the sort that had helped to nominate Wilson for the governorship, the legislature elected Martine by a large majority.

The victor recapitulated the battle in simple terms: "They did not believe that I meant what I said, and I did believe that they meant what they said." To the journalists, however, the controversy was a sensational drama. "Cloistered Professor Vanquishes the Big Boss!" one of them wrote: "this long-haired bookworm of a professor who had just laid his spectacles on his dictionary, came down to the Trenton State House and 'licked the gang to a frazzle.'" Only a part of the people could appreciate the message of the prophet, but all of them could love and respect a good fighter. The legislators of New Jersey now looked to the Governor as the source of patronage and an oracle of political wisdom. He was succeeding in his new milieu as extravagantly as he had triumphed in his first years as president of Princeton.

On January 17, 1911, eight days before Smith's defeat in the legislature, Wilson was inaugurated at Trenton. The ceremonies were pompous. Four prancing horses drew the landau of the Governor-elect and his predecessor from the State House to the Opera House. State troops in fancy dress marched to the beat of three bass drums. In a hall decorated with flags, evergreens, and Southern smilax, Wilson took the oath of office with his hand on the Bible, received the official seal, and, after the crowd had wildly cheered the playing of "Hail to the Chief" and seventeen guns had saluted, he was presented by the president of the Senate to the members of the legislature.

The Governor stood forth from those behind him as a man from another world. By the poise of his figure, the richness of his voice, the rugged force of his countenance, he commanded the hall to its farthest corners, more than ever a "noticeable man." For him the occasion had all the seriousness of a communion service. Under the awe of a new responsibility he departed from his custom of speaking from notes and suiting his words to the temper of the audience. This address was written out in advance, on the basis of advice from public men whom he trusted, and after long deliberation. He wished to confine himself to matters that had been prominent in the campaign and to enter office with as simple a manifesto as possible. "We have never seen a day," he said, "when duty was more plain, the task to be performed more obvious, the way in which to accomplish it more easy to determine . . ." Asserting the need for the specific reforms that had been set forth in the platform and in his open letter to Record, he developed, parenthetically but at some length, a vote-catching argument that Harvey had suggested.[5] Taking facts and figures from his adviser, Wilson accused food dealers of northern New Jersey of holding large supplies of meat and eggs in cold storage in order to keep prices high and urged the legislature to push through "some effective law of inspection and limitation."

Toward the end of his address he dwelt briefly and bluntly on economy, and committed himself to "familiar business principles so thoroughly understood and so intelligently practiced by Americans, but so seldom applied to their governments." He spoke, too, of his duty to conserve the natural resources of the state. In conclusion, he charged the legislators to serve the people, the whole people, to make their interest a constant study, and he held out to them "the satisfaction of furthering large ends, large purposes, of being an intimate part of that slow but constant and ever hopeful force of liberty and of enlightenment that is lifting mankind from age to age to new levels of progress and achievement . . ."

The speech was brief, businesslike, utterly serious. Those who knew the consistency of Woodrow Wilson's character could predict with certainty that he would press on for action, confident that the welfare of both self and party was secure only as long as the larger interests of the people were served. The scion of the preaching Woodrows and Wilsons at last had a congregation almost large enough to satisfy his zeal. He could shout joyfully, with St. Paul: "For a great door and effectual is opened unto me, *and* there are many adversaries."

[5] To keep Wilson before the nation as a progressive who must be reckoned with in the next presidential election, Harvey proposed the attack on the cold-storage interests as one that would not be too distasteful to his conservative friends in New York and yet would give evidence of Wilson's determination to put his state in such good order that the intervention of federal reformers would not be necessary. Such a proposal would be "a master-stroke at the psychological moment," Harvey assured Wilson in a letter written on Dec. 21, 1911.

CHAPTER XI

"Prime Minister" of New Jersey

As he settled into the routine of office at Trenton, Woodrow Wilson was deeply moved, he said, by his "new responsibilities as representative and champion of the common people against those who have been preying upon them." He took delight in his congregation of all sorts and conditions of men, and he felt very close to them. He was finding politics "the very stuff of life, its motives . . . interlaced with the whole fibre of experience, private and public, its relations . . . intensely human, and generally intimately personal." In a speech in November he had remarked that "a man's fortune is interesting only when it is lifted upon a great tide." Discovering that the current of popular feeling was running strongly with him, Woodrow Wilson thrived in body and spirit.

To his family the Governor-elect was still the knight in glistening armor, and for his sake they put up with danger and discomfort. Their hearts fluttered when at the inaugural ball two officers forbade guests to carry muffs or handbags, for fear of concealed weapons. Moving into a small suite in the Princeton Inn, eating in a public dining room, the Wilsons felt cramped financially as well as materially. In the absence of housekeeping duties, however, Ellen Wilson could concentrate her talents on her husband's business. She learned the tactics of politics quickly. Tumulty loved her as he had loved the mother whom he had lost. "She's a better politician than you are, Governor," he said to his chief.

One day, pestered by a fanatical idealist, Wilson remarked: "There should be a sign on the desk of every reformer: 'DON'T BE A DAMN FOOL!' " He must call a tune that his people could be persuaded to follow. And so, in aiming his program for reform legislation, the Governor restrained impulse with cold reason and concentrated on the measures most needed to give the people a healthful sense of control over their government and with it a feeling of responsibility. Realizing that the Democrats who sat in the legislature [1] would press for the passage of

[1] In the new Assembly the Democrats had a majority of 42 to 18, but at least ten of the party's assemblymen were henchmen of the fallen bosses. In the Senate the Republicans held a majority of 12 to 9, though in the Democratic minority Wilson was able to find four able spokesmen.

a certain number of petty laws, the Governor decided to throw all his own energy into the enacting of four bills that would redeem the pre-election pledges of the party by assuring (1) the expression of the will of the people through direct nomination of candidates for office, (2) the honest conduct of elections, (3) the just compensation of injured workmen, and (4) the fair regulation of public utility corporations. The day before his inauguration he invited New Jersey politicians and newspapermen to lunch with Record in New York; and he and the Republican progressive tried to imbue the men with zeal for the four measures.

Wilson had not been in office three weeks before he acted to give effect to concepts of direct democracy that appealed to the progressives of the nation.[2] He moved first for legislation that would compel respect for preferences expressed by the people in primary elections.

Soon after taking office the Governor arranged to have Record's primary and election bill introduced in the legislature, so that Smith's deceit could not be repeated and slates could no longer be rigged in secret and put over on the people. The sponsor of the proposed measure was a former student at Princeton named Geran; but behind him, campaigning among the legislators with every legitimate wile that Tumulty could devise, was Woodrow Wilson. To the Governor the battle for the Geran Bill was the senatorial contest all over again—the same forces arrayed against him and the same sort of fight needed for victory. He explained the measure in public meetings and issued this challenge: "Let no man oppose this thing unless he is willing to oppose it in public and for reasons." Sweeping aside the charges of dictatorship that Smith's newspaper leveled against him, he said: "I am not trying to run the Legislature . . . I know a majority of the members of that Legislature pretty well and I respect them thoroughly, and let me tell you that those men are going to act upon their consciences and cannot be run by anybody."

[2] In his inaugural speech, Wilson recommended that New Jersey's preferential primaries should be extended to every elective office, and he commended progressive laws of the state of Oregon as models.

Wilson had recently had a stimulating talk with William S. U'Ren, a progressive leader in Oregon, about the use of the initiative and referendum to force the will of the people on their representatives. In *The State*, many years before, Wilson had described these devices historically and had felt that, theoretically, they were unsound. But, though he continued to oppose the recall of judges, he had become convinced that in Oregon the initiative and referendum had proved their worth, in practice, as useful tools for an emergency. Moreover, his growing faith in direct primaries had been strengthened by testimony given to him by U'Ren. Oregon might also be a guide, he said in his inaugural, in framing new laws for the control of corrupt practices at the polls.

Having started a popular backfire, the Governor went to work on the legislators. He talked with the assemblymen individually and in groups. In a full Democratic caucus, on March 6, in which opponents hoped to kill the Geran Bill in secret, the Governor again showed that he could mix with the rank and file and talk their language. For more than half of a four-hour meeting he held the floor, answering questions, bringing to bear his academic knowledge of electoral practices in other times and other lands. When one of the party men complained that the Geran Bill would wreck the organization that had elected the Governor, Wilson insisted that the reform would strengthen the party by aligning it more exactly with the wishes of the people. The Governor had gone to the caucus without sanction of precedent, and a man of the Old Guard challenged his right to be present. There were hints, even, of impeachment. Did the Governor not respect the old American shibboleth of separation of powers? What constitutional rights had the executive to interfere in the drafting of legislation?

In the first place, Wilson replied, he conceived that the voters had made him leader of his party: they had elected him on that specific issue. Secondly, he read a passage from the constitution of the state: "The governor shall communicate by message to the legislature at the opening of each session, and at such other times as he may deem necessary, the condition of the state, and recommend such measures as he may deem expedient." He explained that he would have preferred to introduce the electoral reform bill to the legislature personally, but had used the good offices of Assemblyman Geran out of deference to regular legislative procedure. In the third place, it was in keeping with parliamentary tradition that the leader of a party should openly and personally direct the making of policy. How else could he be responsible?

"You can turn aside from the measure if you choose," he said solemnly; "you can decline to follow me; you can deprive me of office and turn away from me, but you cannot deprive me of power so long as I steadfastly stand for what I believe to be the interests and legitimate demands of the people themselves. I beg you to remember, in this which promises to be an historic conference, you are settling the question of the power or impotence, the distinction or the ignominy, of the party to which the people with singular generosity have offered the conduct of their affairs."

Woodrow Wilson was now practicing ideals of citizenship that he had been preaching for decades. He was now trying to make "free men" of politicians who had never fully sensed the glory of Greek and Anglo-

Saxon democracy. In the legislative caucus even the most hardened of the party hacks felt that they were listening to a major prophet whose appeal was to conscience rather than to self-interest. They came out of the room awed and chastened. The fight for the Geran Bill was as good as won, and it had been won by the power of the Word.

But James Nugent, who was still state chairman of the party, did not give up without trying all the stock tricks of legislative manipulation. Lurking in the offices and lobbies of the State House, he used threats and sarcasm to combat the zeal of the prophet. When the Governor politely asked the boss to keep off the floor of the legislature, of which he was not a member, Nugent went away in a huff. But Wilson took care to do nothing to give gratuitous offense; and to a reporter who rashly wrote that the Governor had "threatened to use fisticuffs" against Nugent, Wilson administered what the young newsman described as "the worst ten minutes a reporter ever had."

When assemblymen pressed for amendments to the Geran Bill, Wilson was not entirely unyielding. However, efforts by the opposition to kill the measure by shunting it to an inappropriate committee and by introducing a substitute bill were scotched. Finally, when Nugent came sullenly to the Governor's office and hinted that Wilson had used the state patronage to buy the votes of legislators, the Governor buttoned up his coat in the way that he had when ready for action, rose to his full height, swept his arm toward the door, and delivered a scorching "Good afternoon, Mr. Nugent!" Cartoonists made the most of the incident, depicting Nugent licking his wounds with Smith. "It was a most unpleasant incident, which I did not at all enjoy," Wilson confided to Mary Allen Peck; "but apparently it did a lot of good . . . I cannot help feeling a bit vulgar . . . I feel debased to the level of the men whom I feel obliged to snub. But it all comes in the day's work."

On March 21, after Record had swung vital Republican votes in favor of the Geran Bill, the Assembly passed the amended measure by a narrow margin; but difficulty was foreseen in securing its approval by the Republican-controlled Senate. Tumulty sensed that the situation called for more than logical and spiritual persuasion. His scouts among the legislators had reported that, though the lawmakers found their governor open and frank in conference, they felt that they did not really know him intimately. Wilson had made a formal talk at a dinner given to him by the senators and thought of them as "good and honest men, for the most part," though he did not then know how he would get the necessary votes from them. There were so many "personal equations" to solve that it seemed to him "a fascinating, as well as nerve-racking business."

Tumulty knew that some of the equations could be solved better by conviviality than by logic, and so he arranged an opportunity for Wilson to turn the warmth of his personality on the senators at a supper in the Trenton Country Club. Over fried chicken and waffles Wilson found the lawmakers "as jolly as boys." After exchanges of repartee a Republican senator, Walter Edge, persuaded the Governor to prance with him in a turkey trot. "This at least seems gained," Wilson wrote afterward. "I am on easy and delightful terms with all the senators. They know me for something else than 'an ambitious dictator.'" The Governor was neither a "Presbyterian priest" nor a doctrinaire professor, the legislators saw, but only a fellow who had never had chance enough to play. After the romp at the country club, Wilson felt that Republicans resorted to his office for counsel almost as freely as Democrats, and that he had "established relations almost of affection" with several.

In the Senate's deliberations on the Geran Bill, Record again entered the battle, revising the politically inspired amendments of the Assembly in order to give the measure consistency. Defending the bill in committee, he warned his fellow Republicans that they would oppose the measure at the risk of giving the Governor good ammunition to use against them when they stood for re-election in the fall. That was no empty threat; every legislator knew what Wilson might do to him in an election campaign, in full view of the people. There was such a thing as the fear of God.

The Senate adopted the Geran Bill unanimously, and the Assembly accepted the act with Record's revisions.[3] On the day of passage, the Governor was speaking in Indiana as the guest of Governor Thomas Riley Marshall, a man whom Wilson found likable. When a telegram announcing the Senate's vote came to the auditorium at Indianapolis, the toastmaster read it and the crowd cheered. Woodrow Wilson had taken another long step toward national leadership.

Once the channel of reform had been dredged and the Geran Bill launched, the floating of other measures of good government was easier. The need for electoral reform had been highlighted in the election of

[3] The Geran Law required that all elected officials and delegates to national conventions be nominated in direct party primaries. District election officials were to be chosen after examination by the Civil Service Commission and the courts were to supervise the choice of local election officials. In large cities, voters in general elections had to register in person; and provisions were made for the mailing of sample ballots and the use of an official ballot in place of a party ballot. See Laws of New Jersey, 1911, Chapter 183, pp. 276–325.

1910, when dummy voters, repeaters, and bought votes had been detected and officeholders had been lubricating the party machine with the oil of corruption. Even before the Geran Bill had become law, Record was lobbying in the Senate for a corrupt practices measure that he had drafted and that Wilson thought drastic enough to be effective. In April his bill passed both houses by unanimous votes. By its provisions, candidates for office in New Jersey had to file statements of expenditures and of personal contributions. It became illegal to hire "watchers" at the polls, to accept campaign gifts from corporations or majority stockholders, to register falsely, to stuff ballot boxes, to bet on election results. A violator of the law must forfeit his office as well as suffer other penalties.

By the time the bill providing for the regulation of public utilities came to a vote,[4] Assembly and Senate were vying with each other to have the honor of sponsoring the measure. The bill that the legislature passed—the Osborne-Egan Act—was one of the most thorough of its kind in regulating "public utilities," among which it included purveyors of transportation, communications, and domestic conveniences. A commission of three, to be appointed by the Governor with the consent of the Senate, was empowered to appraise corporation property, fix and enforce rates, and set standards of service; and the orders of the commission were to be subject to review by the Supreme Court of the state.

In achieving the enactment of his fourth bill—a measure for the compensation of disabled workmen—the Governor's powers of persuasion were taxed. The state law in this field was of the sort that Wilson described as a coat outgrown ("If you button it over the belly," he said, "it will split up the back!"). A laborer could secure recompense for injury only by bringing suit and establishing negligence on the part of his employer. The preceding governor had appointed a commission to

---

[4] In his inaugural Wilson had tried to clear the murky view of those who were frightened by the rapid concentration of economic power in corporate bodies. "Corporations," he said, "are no longer hobgoblins which have sprung at us out of some mysterious ambush, . . . but merely organizations . . . which have proved very useful but which for the time being slipped out of the control of the very law that gave them leave to be and that can make or unmake them at pleasure. We have now set ourselves to control them, soberly but effectively, and to bring them thoroughly within the regulation of the law." The abuse of the privilege of incorporation must be prevented, he declared. "In order to do this it will be necessary to regulate and restrict the issue of securities, to enforce regulations with regard to bona fide capital, examining very rigorously the basis of capitalization, and to prescribe methods by which the public shall be safeguarded against fraud, deception, extortion, and every abuse of its confidence . . . The matter is most obvious when we turn to what we have come to designate public service, or public utility, corporations." The Public Utilities Commission, which thus far had hardly more than powers of inquiry and advice, must be given complete regulative powers.

investigate this matter, and Republican Walter E. Edge, chairman of this body, reported to Wilson that a bill was ready for introduction into the Senate. Explaining that compulsory compensation would not be approved by the courts, Edge told the Governor that the commission had thought it best to make the plan one for optional adoption by agreement of workmen and employers. Doubtless thinking the statement as insincere as it was plausible, Wilson's impatience with legalism cropped out and he said petulantly: "I have no patience with either the Constitution or the Supreme Court." He urged Edge to accept a bill for *compulsory* benefits that a labor leader was trying to push through the Assembly. But Edge refused; and fearing a stalemate between the two houses, Wilson persuaded the assemblymen to accept the bill as it was rather than risk adjournment without action. Thus, by leading legislators to compromise, Wilson made it possible for a new compensation law [5] to take effect and completed his four-bill program for the legislature substantially as he had envisioned it.

Other reforms rode through the legislature: advances in school legislation, in the inspection of food storage and of factories, and in regulation of hours and conditions of labor for women and children. The Governor gave moral support to these measures, and nothing more was needed to assure their enactment.

Wilson was more active, however, in supporting a bill that would authorize a commission form of government for cities in which the henchmen of Smith and Nugent had taken cover.[6] His interest in this bill became keener when he was advised that this type of government was appealing to voters on his political horizon, in the Western states. In championing this measure the Governor again met resistance from entrenched interests in the municipalities, for local reform threatened the last defenses of the bosses. Nugent conspired with the Republican leader in the Assembly to secure the adoption of a crippling amendment;

[5] The Edge Act defined a schedule of benefit payments that was to take effect when employer and employee accepted them, abolished provisions of the common law behind which employers had sought immunity, and defined "willful negligence." *See* Walter E. Edge, *A Jerseyman's Journal*, pp. 73–75.

[6] Municipal reform was a cause that had long been close to Wilson's heart. True to form, and doubtless influenced by James Bryce's censure of the politics of American cities, Wilson had lectured at the Johns Hopkins on the superiority of the government of English cities. He had advocated making a few men responsible for municipal functions in America, integrating municipal agencies, and divorcing the judicial from other functions. Moreover, he called for universal suffrage in the election of city councils. Asserting that a city was "not an economic corporation but a humane economic society," Wilson thought it unsafe to "look to the selfish interest of leading classes alone to advance the interests of the city." *See* Henry W. Bragdon, "Woodrow Wilson Addresses the Citizens of Baltimore, 1896," *The Maryland Historical Magazine*, XXXVII, No. 2 (June, 1942).

and after the Democratic leader of the Senate also had capitulated to undercover influences, the progressives had to accept the Walsh-Leavitt Bill, with the emasculating provision only slightly revised. Less than half the cities of the state voted to adopt commission government.

During the session of 1911 the Governor vetoed only a few bills—usually to prevent wasteful expenditures of public money or effort or to protect the right of localities to rule themselves. In all cases his vetoes were sustained. His appointments met with the approval of the legislators; and the progressives were particularly pleased when he insisted that corporation lawyers should not be made prosecuting attorneys and when he appointed the first Jew ever to sit in the Supreme Court of the state—a man who had helped young Joe Tumulty to plead charity cases in the Jersey City criminal court, who had served individual clients against corporations, and who soon justified his appointment by finding a legal formula that made it possible to break the grip of racketeers who held the people of Atlantic City in fief. Men who were known to the Governor personally as exceptionally able and honest were brought by him into the service of the state.[7] He often asked questions about the character of men who were recommended to him; but he was too busy with larger affairs and too little interested in building a personal machine to give attention to the filling of minor offices. "The question of appointments drives me nearly distracted," he confessed, "it is so nearly impossible to get true information or disinterested advice about persons—and so many persons are trying to impose upon me. I shall get used to it, but am not yet, and it goes hard." Usually he solved the problem by telling Tumulty and other advisers to "make out a list"; and the aide used the prerogative of patronage so shrewdly that he gave substance to the charge with which Nugent had angered Wilson. When faced by demands that his appointees be removed, Wilson would endure much criticism before consenting. His Covenanting sense of loyalty could not be shaken easily; and once he had worked with a man and found him satisfactory he hated to break the relationship.

At the end of the legislative session of 1911, Wilson could justly rejoice in his debut as a responsible prime minister. He had made expert use of the prestige that had come to him from the battle with Smith.

---

[7] Notably Professor Winthrop M. Daniels, as a member of the Public Utilities Commission, and Calvin N. Kendall, an "outsider" to the local politicians, as head of the state's schools. Record, the Republican progressive who for years had given much time to public service without compensation, was at last recognized by appointment to the State Board of Railroad Assessors, though for a time Wilson hesitated to take this action. He had been attacked by Smith newspapers for surrendering his leadership to Record, and perhaps feared that the appointment of one who had so greatly aided his election might be regarded as a *quid pro quo*.

His zeal for civic virtue and pure democracy had cut across both party and sectarian lines. To be sure, he had not been able to realize a dream of revising the state constitution along parliamentary lines, and he had failed to persuade the Republican Senate to approve an amendment of the federal Contitution authorizing income taxes, though the Assembly ratified the measure unanimously. Nevertheless, conceding that there were still reforms to be achieved, he could point to the fulfillment by the legislature of every campaign pledge. Elated, he wrote boastfully to Mary Allen Peck: "The result was as complete a victory as has ever been won, I venture to say, in the history of the country . . . I came to the office . . . when opinion was ripe on all these matters, . . . and by merely standing fast, and by never losing sight of the business for an hour, but keeping up all sorts of (legitimate) pressure *all the time*, kept the mighty forces from being diverted or blocked at any point. The strain has been immense, but the reward is great . . . I am quietly and deeply happy that I should have been of just the kind of service I wished to be to those who elected and trusted me."

Wilson's faith in the inarticulate power of the plain people had been justified. It had become an article of religion, an understanding delicate and mystic. Yet his ardor for the good fight was not satisfied. He conceived that he was keeping himself "in training" for another bout with "the forces of greed" and prayed God for strength enough "to tip the balance in the unequal and tremendous struggle."

There were clear indications now that the prophet's voice was penetrating to ears outside New Jersey. Editors measured his achievement, the *New York Times* found it "really very great" and the Washington *Post* saw in him "a national rather than a purely local figure." However, before he won the right to serve the nation, more shots were fired in a running feud with the bosses of New Jersey's discredited Democratic machine.

James Nugent had clung to his chairmanship of the Democratic State Committee. But by the middle of 1911 his control of that body had weakened; and at a party at which liquor flowed, he shocked fellow Democrats by proposing a toast to the Governor, "an ingrate and a liar." Seeing his hold slipping, he brought strong-arm supporters into a meeting of his committee. Nevertheless, the committeemen, urged on by Tumulty, voted him out of office and replaced him with a chairman who cooperated with the Wilson forces.

Nugent's fall was only one result of the reorganization that Wilson and Tumulty effected during the summer and autumn of 1911. Actually, Grover Cleveland's prediction was coming true: the Democratic party was being made over in the image of its strongest man, the Governor of New Jersey.

Wilson was speaking now more like an avenging prophet than a servant of the people. In September, when the first primary election under the new Geran Law was to be held, he cracked the party whip repeatedly. He made a scorching attack on fraudulent voting in Essex County, but this bailiwick of Smith was the only one in which Wilson Democrats were not victorious. In Hudson County, Tumulty made enough concessions to carry the vote, and when the elected delegates met in convention they approved the Governor's policies; but when they tried to endorse Wilson for the Presidency of the nation, he opposed such a motion as inconsistent with the spirit of the new election laws of the people of New Jersey.

The next test came in the legislative election in November, and it drove him to work as hard as he had labored in the primary. His strategy was to widen the rift already made between the progressives and the regulars of the opposing party. Ridiculing the Republican machine, he called its platform "one of these old-fashioned, smooth-bore, brass-mounted affairs, that goes off like a blunderbuss . . . it has the same promises put in such phrases that they can be read backward or forward and mean the same thing; just the kind of thing you have been familiar with and never did know the meaning of." Pouring volley of sarcasm after fusillade of censure, he shamed the voters. At Atlantic City, in particular, he tried to inject the stuff of manhood into a citizenry that had been cowed by a boss who was under indictment for election frauds. "As I have stood here tonight and looked into your faces I have wondered how it feels to live under a reign of terror. How does it feel? How does your self-respect fare in the circumstance? You are my fellow-countrymen; you are men like myself . . . I have come to challenge you to self-consciousness. Have you been asleep?" He could not enforce the law, he admitted, but he could speak the truth in public. "Any gentleman who is a candidate to have his name gibbeted knows how to apply."

By and large, Wilson's speeches in this campaign lacked positive challenge to definite, constructive action. Perhaps from carelessness and overconfidence, perhaps from preoccupation with national politics, he failed to grip the imagination of the voters as securely as before. In Essex County the weak Smith-Nugent delegates, with little support from either their bosses or Wilson, were defeated by Republicans; and though in the rest of New Jersey the Democrats ran slightly ahead of their majorities of the preceding year and captured a plurality of the state vote, control of both houses of the legislature went to the Republicans.

Canny George Harvey, from his New York office, had foreseen the setback; and before the election he had sent his man Inglis to arrange a council of war. The publisher had hoped that the Governor might be persuaded to put up an umbrella against defeat by asserting before the election that the bosses of Essex County were about to try to undermine him.

Inglis caught up with the campaigning Governor in a New Jersey town and found him no longer the uncertain aspirant who had gone meekly from his summer boardinghouse to dine with the politicians at Deal in 1910. On that occasion, more than a year before, Inglis had seen a homely smile on the broad and powerful mouth, the eyes gleaming in kindness, a man "neither lacking dignity nor over-loaded with it, most companionable—in short, neighbor Wilson," lean and stringy-muscled, a Western rather than a Southern man. Now in New Jersey, however, Harvey's aide found a hardened campaigner on the warpath, a leader who walked with "stateliness" at the head of an entourage, a man with only seven hours for sleep between an evening speech and an early-morning departure for another engagement. Distantly cordial, Wilson offered his hand with a downward thrust[8] and said that he was too busy that week to give even ten minutes to his original sponsor. If Harvey would telephone his secretary, Wilson said, he might make an appointment for a few weeks later. Inglis returned to his chief with this report; and Harvey put the best face possible on the situation by analyzing the New Jersey election returns in such a way as to show that, outside of Essex County, Wilson had gained.

The legislative skies that had been so rosy were now overcast, and the Governor entered upon a six-month period that Tumulty called the "dark days." Wilson could no longer expect to dictate to the legislature. In his first message to the body in 1912 he sought not to drive but to help, to cooperate in every program that was for the common benefit. He proposed a thoroughgoing reorganization of the state's administrative agencies and the tax structure, and additional legislation in the fields of labor and public health. The Republican majorities, however,

---

[8] To protect his sensitive right hand from overzealous pumping, Wilson made it a practice to seize the other man's hand first, gingerly and from above. The effect, to William Allen White, was that of seizing "a ten-cent mackerel" and contributed to that journalist's impression of Wilson as "a cold fish." Wm. A. White, *Autobiography,* p. 479.

had no desire to pass laws that might pave Wilson's path to the Presidency of the nation; and the Governor in early 1912 was showing more interest in future prospects than in present problems. Even in his appointments he was tending more and more to favor his political allies, to strengthen the bonds of the Wilson Democrats in the state against the knives that were still wielded by Smith and Nugent. It was obvious that, if he was to win nomination to the Presidency at the Democratic National Convention, he must command the vote of New Jersey's delegation.

However, he provoked bitter enmity by vetoing fifty-seven measures—about one-tenth of those adopted by the legislature of 1912. Many of the bills were trivial and wasteful; some were attempts to emasculate the reform laws passed in 1911. Many of the veto messages were attacked by Republicans, who asserted that the measures did not get proper study because of Wilson's absence, campaigning for the Presidency. The Governor, however, brushed aside this accusation, which had some grounding in truth, as a "partisan attack" that did not take into account the physical impossibility of studying scores of bills within a few days.[9] By the end of the session the implacable streak in his nature was asserting itself and he was attributing personal maliciousness to politicians who differed with him because of loyalty to the opposing party. Woodrow Wilson found it hard to make sport of political principle: when his ideal won out, he was frankly elated, as by the great hymns of the church; and when one of his causes was buried by partisan opposition, he stood at the grave and mourned moodily.

"I am a person, I am afraid, who observes no sort of moderation in anything," Wilson once wrote of himself. It was true of his loves and his hates, of his work and his play, and especially of his dreams. After his election as governor he had been warned against self-intoxication by H. S. Pritchett, his colleague on the board of the Carnegie Foundation. "You are enough of an orator to be carried along by the sweep of your own speech," Pritchett had written. "It is a fine quality and the source of great power. It has however the danger that it betrays its

---

[9] Though Wilson left New Jersey many times in order to further his professional candidacy, his absences were so well timed that he was able to say, after the legislative session of 1912: ". . . the statement that I have by my frequent absences from the State in any degree neglected my duties as Governor, is absolutely false. No important matter of business has been allowed to fall in arrears in my office . . . I have been absent from the State only two of the session days of the legislature." See Link, *Wilson: The Road to the White House,* p. 305. He was resentful when the Senate of the state, giving the Governor the traditional dinner near the end of the session, arranged a menu in the form of a railroad timetable that poked fun at Wilson's travels.

possessor into saying things on his feet which go further than his cool judgment would permit. If you can keep a sharp eye on this it will save you from difficult situations."

By his very intemperateness, in Princeton and the state, Wilson had swept his constituency into immediate and constructive reforms. Then the momentum had been lost, mean-spirited men had undermined him, and the prophet, envisioning new mountains to climb, out on the horizon, had turned away in scorn from souls of little faith.

The spirit of the Governor rose above his stifling surroundings in Trenton, as he performed the routine duties of his office day after day. In a heavily paneled room with a tiny fireplace, a bronze Washington, rows of lawbooks, and portraits of past governors gazing solemnly from the walls, Wilson sat down each morning first to care for his correspondence and then to consider the problems of state in the order of their importance. Never a pen or a paper was out of order on his desk; and pressure of time did not fluster him. He tried a dictaphone, but his voice sounded so uncanny that he reverted to his old custom of typing many notes for himself. Sometimes he dictated more than a hundred letters in a morning, many of them at the behest of Tumulty or others well versed in political protocol. When his work permitted, he would tell jokes to whoever was at hand or stroll into the waiting room through the door that always stood open and chat with the citizens whom he found there. The Governor was trying conscientiously to be the practicing Democrat, though it went sorely against his instincts. His spirit flung itself about within him, he said, like a "wild bird in a cage." To relieve his restlessness he would turn in his swivel chair and look through the window on the muddy Delaware and the tides of traffic moving up and down State Street. Afternoons were consumed by tedious conferences and public hearings, and it was not until evening that he could be alone to concentrate on putting his ideas meticulously in order.

Even in the summer there was little privacy for a public man. At the stuffy executive cottage at Sea Girt on the Jersey coast, where as a concession to popular prudery a naked Narcissus had to be removed from the front hall, the Governor spent part of his Sundays perched on a horse—wearing a high hat and frock coat—while troops marched by on the adjoining parade ground. Or he would sit on the piazza confronting the breech of a gun, a row of military officers, and an official chaplain.

Here and there people began to trade on his name. Clubs and fraternal orders competed for his presence at their functions; photographers delighted to catch him with a hot dog in his mouth; and when he failed to attend the field day of the Woodrow Wilson Club of Trenton, the gate receipts slumped and in petulance the club changed its name. Sometimes, when his emotions were worn by inescapable appearances at state institutions, his wit stiffened his nerve: he said that, in the home for epileptics, three were driven to fits by his speech.

Wilson's daughters were now away from home much of the time, pursuing their interests in music, painting, and social work; and in the autumn of 1911, moving from the cramped quarters in the Princeton Inn, the family shared a house in Cleveland Lane with Lucy and Mary Smith. A half-timbered dwelling, with bay windows and fireplaces, and a studio and a garden that enchanted Ellen Wilson, it evoked memories of the old, carefree days in the beloved home on Library Place. But when he looked at the Hibben house next door or walked about the town, Wilson thought he detected hostility from those whom he had loved and sought to serve. He felt a lump in his throat and could have wept from disappointment and pity. Nevertheless, in his new home he hoped to find contentment. Commuting to this haven from his office at Trenton, the Governor delighted in the comradeship of relatives and guests. Vivacious Lucy Smith and her sister chatted and read with Ellen Wilson and conspired with the girls to relieve their father and mother of anxieties. Mary Allen Peck paid a visit and smoked cigarettes so charmingly that the Wilsons could not take offense, but she seemed to the Wilson girls overfastidious about clothes and too boastful of her gentlemen friends.

The face of Woodrow Wilson, which had flexed in comic grimaces in earlier years, had now set in a rigid "official" mask; yet smile lines suggested the old jesting spirit that was still alive, and it often shone out. Once when a Negro butler announced pompously, "Dinner is now being served in the dining room," Wilson caught the arm of his daughter Nell and swayed through the hall in imitation of a passenger on a railroad train. On occasion his eyes could still twinkle. Introduced at a meeting as "a plain man and learned statesman," he repeated a favorite limerick:

> "For beauty, I am not a star;
> There are others handsomer, far;
> But my face—I don't mind it,
> For I am behind it;
> 'Tis the people in front that I jar."

Often he conjured up "the night and sweet radiant spaces, the familiar houses and scenes of dear Bermuda." He wrote almost every Sunday to Mary Allen Peck, who personified that idyllic spot and whom he idealized as a paragon of misunderstood virtue. "Sometimes," he confided to her, ". . . my whole life seems to me rooted in dreams—and I do not want the roots of it to dry up. I lived a dream life (almost too exclusively, perhaps) when I was a lad and even now my thought goes back for refreshment to those days when all the world seemed to me a place of heroic adventure, in which one's heart must keep its own counsel while one's hands worked at big things."

The Governor of New Jersey found escape both near and far, in nature human and inanimate. He invited witty people to joke with him at luncheon in a Trenton restaurant, where he took a side table and was embarrassed by special attention from the waiters. With Tumulty and favorite journalists he walked for miles in the park and along the river. Sometimes he sought relief in losing his identity in a crowd, on the street, or at an athletic contest.

Of all the pleasures to which Wilson's passionate dreaming led him, none was greater than that of turning to "the friend with whom you never have to consider a phrase or a thought—with whom you can *let yourself go!*" The ideal of perfect friendship—a relationship that was "all largess," with nothing given from a sense of duty—was not one that he could give up, even after the disillusionment that he had suffered at Princeton.

The wound of that experience was still sore and open.

Wilson and his friends tried to bring about the election of Fine to the presidency of the university. The choice of Hibben, he thought, ought to be prevented at all hazards because no one else would so lay the dear university at the mercy of the "reactionary forces." To the ex-president the campus was now a blighted spot, inhabited by depressed scholars. The legality of the golf links as a site for the graduate college was approved by the chancellor of the state, Pyne and Procter made additional gifts, and ground was broken for Andrew West's enterprise. Early in 1912, Hibben was chosen as the administrator most likely to draw together the West and Fine factions. "The worst has happened at the University," Wilson lamented. West remained dean of the grandiose new graduate college, and Wilson felt that Hibben never would be strong enough to achieve greatness for Princeton.

As governor of the state, Wilson was also president ex officio of the board of trustees of the university, and protocol demanded that he attend the inauguration of Hibben in May of 1912. But the prophet could not so prostitute his intellect. "If I say what is in my heart and mind the dinner would end in a riot," he told a friend. "If I get up and indulge in the usual platitudes, the words would stick in my throat." He felt like a "runaway," he said, and "ungenerous," and staying away was hard for a man who took pride in the grim performance of duty. Not trusting his emotions, he arranged to be out of the state on the day of the inauguration. Reasoning it out, he concluded: "Perhaps it is better to love men in the mass than to love them individually!"

During the governorship, Wilson's intimates were women of wit and fine understanding. In repartee and persiflage with these ladies he found emotional release without fear of tragic conflict between friendship and public duty, without risk that what he called the "sensitive chain" of complete understanding might snap under the tension that a Covenanter's conscience placed on it. Had Woodrow Wilson always lavished his unreasoning passion for friendship on none but women, he might have been spared much suffering.

It seemed that his love would never be given again to any man as it had been poured out to Hibben. His associates in the business of government were not men whom he could take to his heart. Tumulty he liked, Record he respected for his clear intellect and devotion to the cause of good government. But these men lacked the grace of soul and the mellowness of philosophy in which a harried executive could find sanctuary.

And then, in the autumn of 1911, Woodrow Wilson met Edward Mandell House.

From the beginning the men were drawn toward each other. Like Wilson himself, House had been possessed in his youth by a passion to take part in great affairs. He had entered Cornell University but had not been graduated, for he had slighted his studies and had spent much time with friends at Washington just to be near the center of things. Like Wilson, he could recollect the horror of Civil War and Reconstruction in the South. Young Edward had thrived on mischief and on boyish games that were played with firearms, and twice he had almost killed playmates. When only twelve years old, he had fallen on his head from a swing and his health had been impaired permanently. Never strong enough himself to carry the ball in the political game, and lacking powers of oratory, he had shown genius in managing other players from the bench; and in applying New England capital to the development of a railroad in Texas, he had held the confidence of financiers and had become an expert in public relations. In a society in which a single discordant word might provoke a volley of bullets, the gentle-spoken, trouble-scenting little man had kept on friendly terms with hot-blooded frontiersmen without using the six-shooter that he sometimes carried. Governor Hogg, whose campaign for political reform had been furthered by House in 1892, had made his adviser a "colonel" on his staff; and, much to the distress of its recipient, the title had stuck.

For almost twenty years, from his hospitable porch on the hill at Austin, Colonel House had manipulated political candidacies without making enemies and had gained a reputation for sagacity. He read widely and observed keenly. His touch upon the affairs of the state was sensitive, devious, deft, and at times bold.

In 1910 the Colonel sensed the political opportunity of the hour for his party and was seeking a national leader to whom he might render the same service that he had given freely to governors of Texas. He was seeking, specifically, an Eastern man who would be acceptable to William Jennings Bryan of Nebraska, without whose approval, House felt, no Democrat could hope to be nominated for the Presidency. Like Wilson, he had given up Bryan on the currency question as "not sus-ceptible to argument"; yet in a practical, reasonable way, the Colonel's own convictions on many matters of public policy were as progressive as those of Nebraska's "Great Commoner." He took pride in asserting that in municipal reform Texas led the way; and he was proud of pro-gressive measures that Governor Hogg had advocated, such as laws regulating securities and the railroads. He had worked for reforms, not for Texas alone but in the hope that they might be taken up by the country at large.

By the summer of 1911, even before he met Wilson, Colonel House had fixed his mind on the Governor of New Jersey, not as the man "best fitted" to be president but as "the best man who can be nominated and elected." In the fall there were exchanges of letters between the men; and House, through Thomas W. Gregory, urged the Governor to accept an invitation to speak in Texas.[10] Moreover, ascertaining that

---

[10] Cf. 211 below. Thomas W. Gregory was a lawyer at Austin who had served the state of Texas as special counsel in prosecuting corporations for violating antitrust laws. Thomas B. Love, commissioner of insurance and banking in Texas, already had been working for Wilson and had promised that an invitation would be given to visit that state in the fall of 1911. Love to W.W., Dec. 1, 1910. Love told Ray Stannard Baker that Texas would have supported Wilson even if House had never existed and claimed that he had given more money to the cause than had House.

House's support of Wilson in Texas was less obvious than Love's for a reason that is ex-

Wilson had voted for the Democratic candidate in the last three presidential elections, he assured Texans, through Senator Culberson, of the party regularity of the Governor. The effectiveness of Wilson's address in Texas strengthened the colonel's interest in him as a presidential candidate. Then, on November 24, House's judgment was put to the test of a personal interview.

When Wilson went alone to New York to meet the Texan, who had been commended to him by George Harvey, he found a short, slight gentleman dressed in good taste, a man who walked with a firm, easy step and whose words seemed as unobtrusive and as well groomed as his gray mustache. Only a few months before, Wilson had written to Mary Allen Peck that, now that he was in politics, he was careful of *everybody*. But in an hour's talk, and in subsequent visits, House's friendliness broke down the monitoring caution. The Texan's soft speech and eager listening drew out the Scotch-Irish heart from under its shield of formality. Here was a counselor more soothing and respectful than Harvey—the high-strung, calculating Yankee. Moreover, the Texas colonel had an instinctive understanding of the Old South and at the same time shared the aspirations of the West. And the man's record of friendly service showed that he wanted nothing for himself but the delight of serving.

For his part House, physically handicapped but still ambitious to be in the thick of affairs, saw in Wilson a man with power to put wise counsel into action, a voice through which an adviser could speak effectively to the nation and to history. The colonel was captivated by a warmth of heart and strength of intellect such as he had never seen in the politicians of his own state. The day after the meeting he wrote to his wife's brother-in-law, President Sidney Mezes of the University of Texas: "We had a perfectly bully time. He came alone, so that we had an opportunity to try one another out. He is not the biggest man I have ever met, but he is one of the pleasantest and I would rather play with him than any prospective candidate I have seen. From what I had heard, I was afraid that he had to have his hats made to order;

---

plained in an entry in House's diary, Oct. 6, 1921. "Texas headquarters would have closed," the Colonel wrote, "if I had not sent Gregory to Cato Sells, who was the nominal manager, to tell him that he, Gregory, would guarantee Sells the expenses. My name was not mentioned because I feared they would be extravagant if they knew I was the real sponsor." Diary of Edward M. House, House Collection, Yale University Library, hereafter referred to as House Diary. Regarding House's work in Texas, Gregory said to Ray Stannard Baker on May 29, 1928: "I have never seen such a revolt against the duly constituted officials and machinery of a political party."

but I saw not the slightest evidence of it . . . Never before have I found both the man and the opportunity."

Within the next week they dined together alone, and they were soon exchanging confidences. Wilson felt the stimulus that always came to him from what he called "the laying of minds alongside each other." Encouraging each other to talk frankly, they found that, while their natures were complementary, their thoughts ran in agreement on most of the issues of the day.

Although ill that winter, House worked intensely in Texas while at the same time exerting his influence—always quiet, persistent, unofficial —upon national leaders of the party. He had a way of insinuating ideas into the minds of dull men so that they took pride in them as their own. He was wise enough never bluntly to oppose Wilson on a matter of principle or policy: when he differed he kept silent or else argued so subtly that Wilson could not take offense. When, for example, he presumed to advise his friend on tariff policy—a subject on which the Governor spoke with the pride of competence—he used as his mouthpiece a man whom Wilson might respect as a professional.[11]

The Wilsons quickly perceived House's peculiar gifts for confidential service—his capacity for objective and analytical thought, his discretion and disinterestedness, his tact and persuasiveness in contacts with politicians with whom a presidential candidate had to deal.

11 David F. Houston, formerly president of the University of Texas, was placed next to Wilson at a dinner party, after House had reviewed Houston's academic theories on the tariff with the purpose of making them more comprehensible to the general public. Wilson's views on the tariff probably were little changed, though the occasion may have influenced him to give an important speech on the subject to the National Democratic Club a month later. But, at House's dinner, Houston was completely won by Wilson. The next day he wrote: "Wilson is the straightest-thinking man in public life, and can say what he thinks better than any other man . . . I am for him. Wilson is clean, courageous, and disinterested." And of House he wrote: "He has a vision. I should like to make him Dictator for a while . . ." Dr. D. F. Houston to Dr. S. E. Mezes, Dec. 11, 1911, in Charles Seymour, *The Intimate Papers of Colonel House*, I, 48. Hereinafter this four-volume work is referred to as *House Papers*.

CHAPTER XII

CANDIDATE FOR THE PRESIDENCY

BY THE SPRING of 1911 the Governor, through the brilliance of his campaign against Smith and his leadership of the New Jersey legislature, had made himself a popular American hero. On the national scene, in 1910, the Democrats won the House of Representatives for the first time since 1892 and secured the governorships in several states that were normally Republican. But in all the country no effort was more vital than Wilson's. He had done more than anyone, the New York *World* asserted, "to raise the political, moral, and intellectual level of the campaign"; and Theodore Roosevelt's *Outlook* acknowledged that Wilson, as the leader of the progressive movement in New Jersey, deserved to be elected. Wilson-for-President clubs had sprung up spontaneously. Encouragement and pledges of support had come in innumerable letters and telegrams from personal friends, educators, journalists, former students at Princeton, idealistic strangers. Colonel Harvey, perceiving the set of the journalistic tide, had written to his candidate late in 1910: "The pebble chucked into the pool has produced, not ripples, but waves."

As in the case of the New Jersey governorship, Wilson was a reluctant candidate for the Presidency. He protested that he was incorrigibly simple in his tastes, that while he would love to have a hand upon the affairs of the world, he shrank from the harness and trappings of high office. Tactically, it was still too early for a "boom"; moreover, a series of diplomatic crises around the Mediterranean had inflated his doubt of his adequacy. Wilson thought he would know better where he stood in the estimation of the people after a few public appearances in various states. Feeling a bit like a race horse, he allowed the National Democratic Club to size him up at Philadelphia and gave them a speech that led Judge Wescott, now fully converted, to write to Tumulty: "I pronounce it greater than the immortal efforts of Demosthenes . . . this personalized force has a great destiny."

In March of 1911, Wilson invaded Georgia to address the Southern Commercial Congress on "The Citizen and the State." Dejectedly, almost shamefacedly, he told himself that his only reason for going to Atlanta was because it was "politic." His conscience was in revolt. He feared even that he would not speak well, so self-interested was his motive. Old Judge Hillyer, who had licensed him to practice law back in 1882, introduced him as "a man who is going to be President of the United States," and the orator appealed to the South to "take its place in the councils of the nation." The audience of eight thousand responded with an ovation that Wilson thought better than those given to the other speakers—Theodore Roosevelt and President Taft. He was enheartened, and before leaving Atlanta he made tentative plans for a campaign in his behalf in Georgia.

A few weeks later he spoke at Norfolk with the feeling that the South was still essentially conservative. His conscience told him that, now conceiving himself a "radical" who would go to the roots of good government, he should speak out to prevent his boyhood neighbors from voting for him under the misapprehension that he was a standpat favorite son. Pleading for free speech and for exposure of corruption in government and in business, he pleased the agrarian progressives of the South as much as he alarmed the reactionaries who were hoping to deliver the delegates of the region to Governor Harmon of Ohio. And yet conservatives saw that, if they could not make Western Democrats accept Harmon, Wilson offered an alternative more safe and sane than Bryan.

It was apparent, in 1911, that to receive the presidential nomination a candidate must win the approval, if not the active support, of Bryan. Three times, in lean years, that peerless orator had carried the party's standard unsuccessfully in the presidential race; but of the 1912 campaign he said to his wife when she urged him to run again: "This may be the year for a Democrat to win. The other boys have been making their plans. I would not step in now."

Like Wilson, the Great Commoner was the son of both the frontier and the South, a zealous Presbyterian who led his family in morning prayers and could orate in Biblical figures. He was Scotch-Irish, too, with more of the Irish than ran in Wilson's blood. He thought untidily, his letters were scrawled to the very edges of the paper, and his oratory appealed chiefly to the emotions. From the age of twenty he had been a political campaigner, but never a responsible administrator. He could rouse a Western audience and hold its devotion to a cause as no American had done since Patrick Henry; but in the science of government he was, by Princeton standards, ignorant. He terrified responsible men in the large cities—"the enemy's country." They thought him a fanatic, bent on denuding every man who wore a clean shirt. In his presidential campaigns he had shaken confidence in New York by threatening to avenge from the White House what he considered to be wrongs committed by "the money power."

In Wilson, Bryan saw a new power in the East to be reckoned with. He rejoiced in the fight to democratize Princeton and sent a congratulatory telegram after the New Jersey elections. He could not quite forgive the Princeton professor for opposing the crusade for free silver in 1896, but approved his attitude toward legislation in 1911. The Nebraskan had sounded the depth of the progressivism of the new aspirant by sending him a copy of the Democratic platform of 1908 and asking for comments on its planks. Receiving a general endorsement, he went further, and asked the Governor to urge New Jersey's legislature to approve the adoption of the income tax amendment to the federal Constitution. When Wilson acted promptly on this suggestion, Bryan was more fully persuaded that the Governor's progressivism was no superficial gloss.[1]

Two years before this, Wilson had thought of Bryan—"The Great Inevitable"—as "the most charming and lovable of men personally, but foolish and dangerous in his theoretical beliefs"; and he had refused to speak from the same platform with the Nebraskan, explaining that what he would be obliged to say would introduce "a most inharmonious note." Yet, though thinking of Bryan's remedies for the country's economic maladies as mere nostrums, he could not, he said, quarrel with a large part of his diagnosis.

In the spring of 1911 the two great prophets of the party were preaching each his own gospel, but developing all the while a deeper respect for the voice and spirit of the other. It was Ellen Wilson who set the stage for the harmonizing of their tongues. Hearing that Bryan was to speak at the Princeton Theological Seminary on March 12, she telegraphed her husband to hurry home from Atlanta and arranged an intimate dinner at the Princeton Inn. There the two giants—the veteran campaigner and the aspirant—sat down for the first time together and capped each other's stories and confirmed each other in pastoral faith

---

[1] There were indications, as early as 1910, that Bryan might approve Wilson as a presidential candidate. Thomas B. Love, who had been trying to ascertain the attitude of Bryan, reported to Wilson that a mutual friend had told him that Bryan felt that Wilson was "covering himself with glory" in the fight against Smith. Love to W.W., Dec. 19, 1910. Another correspondent called Wilson's attention to a statement by Bryan in the current number of his journal, the *Commoner*, to the effect that Wilson was one of the four Democrats qualified as presidential timber. R. W. Jennings to W.W., Dec. 30, 1910.

in the great American congregation. Bryan's concept of Wilson as a cold scholar was challenged, though not eradicated, by the Governor's wit and spirits. Discussion of controversial issues was avoided, and the pleasantness of the occasion stirred Tumulty to tell Mrs. Wilson that she had as good as nominated her husband for the Presidency. And when Bryan spoke that evening at Alexander Hall, Wilson found him "a truly captivating man."

Three weeks later Bryan shared a platform with the Governor at a local Democratic rally and for the first time heard Wilson talk. Each spoke of the other as a preacher welcoming a visiting brother to a pulpit. Wilson testified: "Mr. Bryan has borne the heat and burden of a long day . . . it is because he has cried America awake that some other men have been able to translate into action the doctrines that he has so diligently preached." And the Great Commoner responded with what Wilson's promoters most wanted to hear: "Our hopes in the West are raised by Governor Wilson's record." [2]

If Wilson wanted the nomination he would have to convince Bryan's people of the sincerity of his concern for their welfare and, moreover, he would have to do this without alienating all the conservatives of the East and the South. The force of this necessity already had impressed three promoters—Walter Hines Page; [3] Walter McCorkle, who had just been chosen president of the Southern Society in New York; and William F. McCombs, a New York lawyer who had studied under Wilson at Princeton and idolized his former teacher as "a red-blooded man . . . a fighting man . . . the young man's man."

These three Southerners convinced Wilson that, in order to get the necessary support of Western delegates to the Democratic convention in 1912, he would have to talk to the people of the West. Among them,

---

[2] Trenton *True American*, April 6, 1911. Several weeks later Bryan gave further evidence of his deepening respect for the younger prophet, writing to Speaker Champ Clark: "Wilson is making friends because he *fights*. His fight against Smith was heroic . . . The people like a fighter . . . The right wins in the end . . ." Bryan to Champ Clark, May 30, 1911, in *The Memoirs of William Jennings Bryan*, p. 336. Bryan was disappointed by Clark's lack of aggressiveness and, later, by his inability to control his managers.

Bryan had doubts about Wilson's fitness as an executive. Visiting George Harvey, the Nebraskan warned against too exclusive commitment to Wilson, whom he still thought "an autocrat by training." The Great Commoner predicted: "If he should be elected president, everybody else would have to be a servant. Neither you nor I nor anybody else having self-respect could serve a full term in his cabinet. And when he got through there wouldn't be any Democratic party left. There might be a Wilson party, but the old Democracy would be gone." Bryan, however, gave Harvey the impression that either Clark or Wilson would be an acceptable candidate.

[3] In February of 1911, Wilson had sent McCorkle and other inexperienced impressarios to Page for "hard headed advice." Page, then editing *World's Work*, sent one of his journalists to "write up" the Governor of New Jersey. Wilson himself had no flair or enthusiasm for writing promotional articles.

they raised $3,000 and hired a publicity agent to arrange a speaking trip to the Pacific coast.

At the beginning of May, Wilson set out with his agent to meet the people of the Western states and to speak to representative organizations of businessmen. With them went a journalist representing the Baltimore *Sun*. While other candidates, such as Congressman Underwood and Speaker Champ Clark, worked down from Congress through party leaders, the prophet set forth with his two comrades into the grass roots, lugging a huge suitcase with his own hand. Never before had he been west of Denver; and he was intensely curious about what he saw and heard along the way. He rode in an open section so that he could meet his fellow travelers, and he shaved and rubbed elbows in the washroom. He would get off at stations and walk and take breathing exercises; and on a cold morning he delighted his comrades by dancing a hornpipe. Something in his blood was thrilled by the enterprise of the Westerners. These were the men of whom Turner had written and from whose stock Wilson's American heroes had sprung. He felt at home in their country, spoke of the West as the most genuinely American part of the nation.

To get good space in the newspapers, his agent wanted to give out advance copies of speeches. Wilson protested, however, that it was not his custom to write out his addresses in full and that the whole game of publicity repelled him. Finally, he was induced to prepare tentative drafts a week in advance, but usually he departed from them when he faced audiences and took their pulse and temperature. Only when his manager insistently reminded him that he was a national figure did he consent to talk with reporters who were not satisfied with the mere text of his speeches.

In his first address, delivered at Kansas City, Missouri, to a gathering in which Republicans predominated, Wilson set the keynote for his tour. He described his mission as the awakening of his congregation to the welfare of the whole nation, the conditioning of their spirits to the weather of progressive adjustment. Things do not stand still, he said, they go forward or backward. Sound politics demanded reasoned change in everything except the very principle of change. His remarks so frightened party leaders in the East that they later omitted the text of this speech from their campaign publicity. For example, the popular initiative and referendum and the recall of administrative officials, which Bryan and Theodore Roosevelt already had endorsed, were boldly recommended now by Wilson, not as a substitute for legislative action but rather as a means of taking government out of the hands of machines and restoring it to the people. Americans of both parties, he asserted at Kansas City, had been cheated by their own political machinery in the field of industrial action, and the liberty of individuals was being hampered and impaired. Though speaking in nonpartisan terms, he did not fail to assert that "the Democratic party is more in sympathy with the new tendencies." A demagogue without conscience, he warned, "could put this whole country into a flame"; as for himself, he was advocating "fundamentally conservative processes." What was needed, he declared, was an "alignment of all men free and willing to think, and to act without fear upon their thought."

Wilson's straight talk was refreshing to his Western audiences. Here was a man of learning who understood their problems and spoke their language. His prescriptions for reform fell as "cooling good sense," one editorial writer said, on the demagogue-ridden people of the West. And the candidate, for his part, rejoiced in the feeling that they liked him and accepted him as genuine.

On May 7, by lucky chance, the prophet had an opportunity to touch a chord in the Westerner on which Bryan knew so well how to play. Expecting to speak to a small Presbyterian congregation at Denver in celebration of the tercentenary of the King James version of the Bible, Wilson found that the meeting had been moved to the municipal auditorium, where the governor of Colorado would introduce him. Having only an hour in which to prepare an address worthy of the occasion, he felt utterly abashed when he confronted an audience of twelve thousand, with only a few notes in hand.

In the emergency he fell back on what was bred most deeply within him—the Presbyterian concept of man's relation to God. He wished to talk of the Bible, he declared, as "the people's book of revelation . . . a book which reveals men unto themselves, not as creatures in bondage, not as men under human authority, not as those bidden to take counsel and command of any human source. It reveals every man to himself as a distinct moral agent, responsible not to men, not even to those men whom he has put over him in authority, but responsible through his own conscience to his Lord and Maker. Whenever a man sees this vision he stands up a free man, whatever may be the government under which he lives, if he sees beyond the circumstances of his own life."

Calling the Bible the " 'Magna Carta' of the human soul," he went on: "Nothing makes America great except her thoughts, except her ideals, except her acceptance of those standards of judgment which are written large upon these pages of revelation . . . Parties are reformed and governments are corrected by the impulses coming out of the hearts of those who never exercised authority and never organized parties." Those impulses were the sources of strength, he said, in "that untiring and unending process of reform from which no man can refrain and get peace." He challenged every man and woman in the audience to baptize his soul in daily perusal of Holy Scripture.

The Christian soldiers of progressivism, their thoughts marching onward in step with the prophet's, saw in his leadership the coming of the Lord. One of the great forensic triumphs of his life and the culmination of the wooing of the Word by generations of Woodrows, the Denver speech was taken down by a stenographer and circulated during the next year to more than a million readers. Better perhaps than any other utterance, it revealed to the people the moral mainsprings of the candidate's character.

After two more speeches, Wilson was the hero of the city. On the day on which telephone communication was opened with New York, Denver reported: "The town is wild over Woodrow Wilson and is booming him for President."

The prophet had arrived on a local train and walked to his hotel carrying his own bag. Leaving on a day coach, he had a frugal lunch of fruit at the railroad station. But thenceforth the trip was a Roman triumph. At San Francisco, alumni of Princeton, Yale, and Harvard sponsored a dinner for which invitations went out on the stationery of a street railway company that had a finger on the city's politics. Hiram Johnson, the progressive governor, stayed away; and Wilson was advised not to identify himself with "the interests" by attending. Characteristically, he was made only the more eager to attend. He pricked the consciences of the businessmen and made them like it.

Visiting Portland next, Wilson won Oregon for good and all. At a dinner at the University Club he let loose a diatribe on clubmen, and then challenged his hosts to invest their "capital of heart and mind" in the service of the world. They thought him a great man because he dared to criticize the social obtuseness of those who posed as the elect and all-powerful of their state. "Wilsonism is today one of the largest facts in American life," a local journal proclaimed. "It is popular leadership with a safety valve. It is popular government with a balance wheel. It is statesmanship without demagogy . . ." Talking with U'Ren, the reformer who had convinced the theorizing Princeton professor of the value of the initiative and referendum, Wilson studied the "Oregon system" of direct government and heartily congratulated the citizens for "breaking the machine." At the same time he pleased his more conservative adherents in the East by remarking, to a New York reporter, that the system was not necessarily applicable to states where different conditions prevailed.

Wilson carried his scholarly point of view into Minnesota, where he spoke in the twin cities and received the state's military salute. Here the approval of leading Bryan Democrats came to the candidate; and he further identified himself with the cause of the Great Commoner by praising that leader at Lincoln, Nebraska—Bryan's home town. The orator himself was away on a speaking trip in New Jersey, but he sent a cordial telegram. His wife entertained Wilson, his brother contributed to the campaign fund, and the candidate responded with a gorgeous flight of eloquence that brought the audience to its feet and marked the speaker as a fellow crusader of their hero. But visiting the home of the Great Commoner, where a hodgepodge of political trophies was strewn about the room, Wilson thought the place resembled "a cross-section of Mr. Bryan's mind."

Wilson sensed at first hand the spirit of revolt that was agitating the West. The Socialist mayor of a town in Nebraska—a railroad laborer clad in jumpers—boarded the train and explained that he had been elected by a vote that was 20 per cent Socialist and 80 per cent protest. This seemed to sum up the feeling of the country. "Taft will be renominated by the Republicans," Wilson said. "Unless the Democrats nominate someone whom the people can accept as expressing this protest, there will be a radical third party formed and the result may be little short of a revolution."

Was the prophet now ready to consider himself a candidate for the Presidency? He asked himself the question many times. Away from his dear ones, traveling in a man's world, his conscience was gradually possessed by his own words. His sense of commitment to the congregations that he had addressed had grown until, on the long train ride across the Northwest, he said to his associates: "I do want to be president and I will tell you why: I want this country to have a president who will do certain things. There are men who could do these things better than I can. Of that I am sure; but the question is, *would they do them?* . . . I am sure that I will at least try to the utmost to do them."

But there were moments, too, when his thoughts withdrew into the inner temple of the scholar, into the Valley of the Doones. As a man—

a husband and father—he did not want to be president. "It means giving up nearly everything that one holds dear," he said. "The Presidency becomes a barrier between a man and his wife, between a man and his children. He is no longer his own master—he is a slave on the job. He may indulge no longer in the luxury of free action or even free speech."

En route to Washington he visited old Columbia, where as a boy he had watched his elders wage a brave battle for political order. Talking with the widow of his adored Uncle James Woodrow, he was overcome again by the foreboding that had once struck him on a beach in Bermuda.

"Now, Tommie," said his aunt, to whom "politics" was a career unworthy of a Woodrow, "what's all this talk about your running for the Presidency?"

"Aunt Felie," he replied, "I can only tell you this. If I am nominated, I'll be elected; and if I'm elected, I won't come out of the White House alive." [4]

Though at that time Wilson made no public statement of his intentions, it was generally understood when he returned to the East that he was a candidate in the fullest sense. He had identified himself, in the minds of millions of Western voters, with the cause of popular government; and he had shown himself a sincere "progressive" rather than a "radical." He had stimulated a gestation of opinion at the grass roots. Some of the political leaders, even, had come to think that the Wilson band wagon now had enough momentum to assure them of a good ride. There was a movement in Indiana toward the Governor of New Jersey; a senator from Oklahoma announced his support; and an informal poll of a group of Democrats in the House of Representatives showed four-fifths for Wilson. And so the pioneering solo flight into the West had cultivated ground from which in good time wonderful fruit was to sprout.

Turning north from Columbia, Wilson conferred with Josephus Daniels at Raleigh.[5] He reached Washington on June 4, 1911, having made thirty-three speeches in nine states. He was welcomed by Page and McCombs and Tumulty, who were enheartened by the response

[4] James Woodrow, who heard the conversation, to the writer, June,' 1949; also Woodrow to Lewis, Sept. 9, 1950, Lewis Papers (Princeton University Library).

[5] Daniels had been for years a loyal Bryan Democrat, but shortly before Wilson's visit to Raleigh in 1911 he had met George Harvey at a shooting party. Harvey had taken the opportunity to plead for Wilson and, sizing up Daniels as a man who could be influenced by flattery, he had directed that a page of *Harper's Weekly* be given to celebration of an anniversary of Daniels's editorship of the Raleigh *News and Observer*.

of the people in the West and were now impatient to organize a national campaign.

But still Wilson hung back. First he wanted to talk with other potential candidates, especially with Congressmen Champ Clark of Missouri and Oscar Underwood of Alabama. The latter's handling of tariff legislation had led Wilson to hope that he might retire from the race in favor of the Alabaman; but after a conference he felt forced to conclude that Underwood was not emotionally committed to the fundamentals of democracy. And when Clark called on him, Wilson did not change his opinion that the Missourian was "a sort of elephantine smart Aleck." There seemed to be no escape from the conclusion that, if the American people were to be led along paths of reason and justice, Wilson could not indulge his desire to direct the drama off stage. He would have to face the music himself. Finally, he yielded to his promoters to the extent of allowing them to answer the heavy mail that now was coming to him. Fearing to create an impression of having "descended into the arena," he consented merely to the opening of a "bureau of information." [6]

During the summer the little group of managers was joined by another Southerner—a descendant of men of the Tennessee hills who believed in Judgment Day and of dueling planter-generals who had fought Indians with Andrew Jackson. One of seven children of a university professor, William Gibbs McAdoo had made his own way as a lawyer at Chattanooga until a street railway that he was promoting fell into bankruptcy. Taking his family to New York in 1892, in debt and without influence, he had learned the ways of corporate finance. It became clear to him that the center of gravity in the field of statecraft had shifted from the political to the economic plane. Hoping both to make money and to serve society, he undertook to promote the building of tunnels under the Hudson River. On the one hand, he held the confidence of financiers; at the same time, he developed and man-

[6] W.W. to Page, June 7, 1911. Wilson gave these instructions to Stockbridge: "I am not to be put forward as a candidate for the Presidency. No man is big enough to seek that high office. I should not refuse it if it were offered to me, but only if the offer came from the people themselves; no man is big enough to refuse that. You must not ask anyone to say a word or print a line in my behalf. Confine your activities to answering requests for information." Frank P. Stockbridge, "How W.W. Won his Nomination," *Current History*, July, 1924.

Rooms were rented at 42 Broadway and Stockbridge's name was put on the door. The bureau collected news clippings, which by August came in at the rate of 20,000 a week, and printed and distributed cuttings from the best of them. Meanwhile McCombs devoted himself to soliciting funds. By December he had collected about $35,000, half of which was contributed by Cleveland Dodge; but at the same time he was dispensing money rapidly, and at the end of 1911 the balance on hand was less than a hundred dollars.

aged property under the motto: "The public be pleased." His tunnel building had caught the imagination of the nation and brought congratulations from President Taft.

Going down to Princeton to see a sick son, McAdoo had been introduced to the president of the university. Wilson had liked the cut of the man's jib, his sincere concept of practical public service, his capacity for getting things done. When McAdoo asked, in the fall of 1910, whether his position as president of a traction company would prevent him from giving entirely disinterested aid to the crusade for good government, Wilson had congratulated him on his achievements and assured him that his help would be welcome. Wilson commended him to Page as "very sagacious and wide-awake." McAdoo lunched weekly with McCombs; and occasionally they were joined by Page and by Villard of the New York *Evening Post*, leaders of pro-Wilson sentiment among intellectuals.

As Wilson came to depend more and more on McAdoo's judgment, McCombs grew insanely jealous. Cynical suspicions worked upon his nerves. Lamed in boyhood, he was incapacitated by illness for days at a time. He flew into rages and was secretive about his plans. But the Governor was showing himself large enough to keep both "Macs" working for the cause. Already he had told Page that he did not need a man of "large calibre" to run his campaign.

With McCombs and others attending to the business of political promotion, Wilson continued to seek out the hearts of the voters. While enemies in the East began to whisper that Woodrow Wilson was a "dangerous" man and McCombs was urging him not to encourage such talk by advocating anything "new," Bryan was demanding answers to questions that were designed to commit him to the progressive cause. Letters from the West were urging Wilson to respond unequivocally.

The line of the candidate's strategy took direction gradually in addresses made in the summer and autumn of 1911. Addressing the Pennsylvania Federation of Democratic Clubs, he identified his party —"the party of the present and the future, the party of young men"— with his whole program of progressive reform: the return of the machinery of political control to the voters; serving the people through such agencies as postal savings banks and parcel post, revision of the tariff, conservation of national resources, and regulation of corporations. Finally, he made a general assault on "the money monopoly."

The leaders of the Pennsylvania Democracy recognized this as the best sort of electioneering talk, and the honor of recognition as the genuine Wilson organization was sought by both factions of the party in the state—the conservatives, dominated by national committeeman Guffey; and the progressives, led by such young men as Vance McCormick, A. Mitchell Palmer, and Roland S. Morris. Wilson immediately recognized the progressives as the party leaders in Pennsylvania.

In October the candidate visited two other states in which there were strong progressive sympathies in the Democratic party. Speaking at Madison, Wisconsin, he fell in with the reform movement that had already started under LaFollette's leadership. Then, going to Texas to make three addresses in one day, Wilson was introduced at the state fair grounds at Dallas by Senator Culberson, one of the ex-governors of Texas whom Colonel House had served. Speaking of the states as "the political laboratories of a free people"—a concept dear to House— Wilson pleaded for "a just, well-considered, moderately executed readjustment of our present economic difficulties." A Wilson-for-President movement already had gathered some momentum in Texas; and the candidate's appearance in October facilitated the work of organization that House was later to carry through so brilliantly.[7]

Support from Pennsylvania, Wisconsin, and Texas was to prove vital to Wilson's nomination. Moreover, the candidate made friends among the governors of other states who convened in September at Sea Girt. By the end of 1911, as the campaign for the Presidency was to swing from an informal movement into an avowed candidacy, Wilson's strength had become so conspicuous that he was marked by his enemies as a man to be beaten at all costs.[8]

Wilson's extravagant attacks on "the money monopoly" did not pass unnoticed by New York financiers. To responsible men who had less faith than he in the wisdom and restraint of the people, many of his remarks had seemed incendiary and demagogic. Personally, he had cut himself free of a fiduciary obligation by resigning in July from the board of the Mutual Life Insurance Company of New York, on which he had served since 1909. Moreover, he had impulsively denounced a

---

[7] When House began his work in the winter, Joseph W. Bailey, the conservative junior senator who opposed Wilson, controlled most of the votes of the Texas State Executive Committee. Asked how he achieved the miracle of the election of a solid Wilson delegation to the Democratic Convention in 1912 was achieved, the Colonel said: "We just picked the right people. That was all. We didn't use any brass bands." See A. D. Howden Smith, *Mr. House of Texas*, p. 48.

[8] Franklin K. Lane, a political observer who at that time never had met Wilson, pointed out that "on the Democratic side all of the forces have united to destroy Wilson, who is the strongest man in the West. The bosses are all against him." Lane to John Crawford Burns, Dec. 13, 1911, in *The Letters of Franklin K. Lane*, pp. 84–85.

plan for a centralized banking system simply because it had been proposed by Nelson Aldrich, a New York financier and senator who had recently sponsored a Republican tariff bill that Wilson thought iniquitous.

Wilson was forgetting Pritchett's warning against the effect of intemperate political talk upon his own judgment. Challenged by the *New York Times* and others, he was compelled to admit that he had erred in attacking the Aldrich plan; and an apologetic letter that he wrote was circulated widely among financial men by Colonel House, who had expressed the opinion that the Aldrich proposal seemed "a long way in advance of the money trust" that dominated the credit of the nation. He wished that Wilson, instead of shilly-shallying over ground that had been made very slippery by memories of Bryan's unsound monetary policies, would concentrate on one safe cause, such as reform of the tariff. Clark and Underwood already had taken the initiative in advocating this. Finally, in January of 1912, several weeks after House had used David F. Houston as a mouthpiece to insinuate relevant suggestions in Wilson's ear, the candidate spoke out against Republican tariff making. The theory of protection, he asserted in New York, had been thrust on the government by business interests who went to Washington and said: "If you don't give us these things, who is going to pay the campaign expenses next year?" He proposed to take tariffs out of politics by imposing them for revenue only.

This change in the direction of his attack, however, hardly relieved the nervous spasms into which Wilson's association with Bryan and his criticisms of "the money power" had thrown certain financiers. Friends and patrons of Harvey were pressing him to turn against the Governor, and the publisher expressed himself as ready to do so if he became convinced that Wilson was "a dangerous man." Men whom the prophet had damned in New Jersey found willing allies among New York journalists—notably Edward P. Mitchell, editor of the New York *Sun*, and William Randolph Hearst.

The *Sun* got wind of the fact that the candidate had applied for a pension from the Carnegie Foundation, on the executive committee of which he had himself served. Wilson's case was first discussed by the Carnegie trustees at a time when he had refused to take salary from Princeton and had not been elected governor.[9] He was therefore

[9] On Nov. 1, 1910, Wilson addressed a letter of resignation to the board of trustees of the Carnegie Foundation. On the 16th, Secretary Thwing wrote to notify him that the foundation accepted the resignation with assurance of the "great respect and regard of its members." H. S. Pritchett to W.W., Nov. 3, 1910, C. F. Thwing to W.W., Nov. 16, 1910. Wilson's claim for a pension was discussed informally by trustees early in November; but Pritchett, president of the board, wrote to Wilson on Nov. 3: "I will not bring up the matter of the pension until I

without income, except from his writings and from small investments. His formal application was encouraged by President Pritchett of the foundation, he resigned from the board before making it, and after he went on the payroll of the state he acquiesced in the board's refusal, which was based upon a change of policy.

Disregarding these considerations, biased editors and newsmen slanted the story for political effect. The great champion of the poor was himself a two-timing moneygrubber, they insinuated. The New York *American* went so far as to accuse him of willingness to accept largess "steeped in the human blood of Carnegie's workers." Induced to issue a rebuttal, Wilson did not take pains, in his rage of scorn, to make it either complete or entirely accurate.

And then there were assaults on his personality: the old cry of "autocrat" and "schoolmaster," accusations of political disloyalty and ingratitude. It was crafty George Harvey who fixed these arrows in the back of his quondam puppet. Colonel House inadvertently suggested the trap; and Wilson was betrayed into it by his natural candor. When *Harper's Weekly* displayed a Wilson-for-President slogan, Western Democrats suspected that New York money was supporting Wilson. To allay this suspicion, House tried to arrange through Martin (an associate of Harvey) to have *Harper's Weekly* "mildly criticize Wilson."

This advice reached Harvey at the very time when the editor was being pressed by New York friends to renounce Wilson as a second Bryan and when it was obvious that young amateurs had taken over the promotion of Wilson's candidacy without consultation with Harvey, who called himself "the original Wilson man." Yet the publisher could not, without himself losing prestige, suddenly desert the man whom he had long sponsored. If there was to be a break, the responsibility for it must be thrown upon Wilson.

Harvey's opportunity came at a political conference with the Governor at the Manhattan Club in New York, on December 7. They met

get your letter in regard to it, which, I take it, might better wait until after the election and after our annual meeting. In sending it give me the details of your twenty-five years of service . . . It is not necessary for me to tell you that the executive committee will consider any such suggestion in the most friendly spirit."

On Dec. 29 [1910?], Pritchett wrote: "A Mr. D. G. Slattery who claimed to be a newspaperman called at my office today and asked the details concerning the matter of a retiring allowance for you. I declined any talk with him and merely send you this line because I suspect he was trying to work up a story in the interest of those who are fighting you. Where he got such information as he seemed to have I do not know. I think he is a Trenton man. Yrs. faithfully." As Slattery was leaving, Pritchett reported, he asked whether Pritchett was "friendly" to Wilson, and got an unequivocal reply.

Wilson himself later felt that he had fully earned the pension and was "arbitrarily and unjustly refused it." W. W. to Tumulty, June 23, 1914, Swem transcription. *See also* E A. W. to Dabney, Feb. 9, 1911.

before a log fire in the room of "Marse Henry" Watterson, the Louis-ville editor who alone among Harvey's original group of Wilson sup-porters had remained loyal. The night before, Colonel Watterson had arranged for Wilson to meet Frederick Penfield, who gave generously to the campaign fund; but the candidate had vetoed a suggestion by Watterson that money be accepted from the reactionary Thomas F. Ryan. Though unconvinced, Watterson had acquiesced. As the three men were leaving the room at the Manhattan Club after an hour or two of cordial conversation, Harvey urged Wilson to say frankly whether there was "anything left of that cheap talk . . . about my advocating you on behalf of 'the interests'?" The Governor, hurriedly putting on his coat and intent on keeping an appointment with his wife, said that he was sorry this question was raised, that actually some of his advisers had told him that such talk was indeed "having a serious effect in the West."

Declaring that he feared Wilson might feel that way, Harvey re-marked: "Then I will simply sing low." Watterson agreed that this would be wise, and the men discussed ways of convincing the public of *Harper's* independence of Wall Street.

Wilson sensed no undercurrent. He did not imagine that Harvey could be piqued at a frank statement on a matter of political business, particularly when the remark was solicited by the publisher himself. Soon after the conference at the Manhattan Club, however, the Wilson-for-President slogan disappeared from *Harper's Weekly*. Stockton Axson scented trouble; and though astounded by his brother-in-law's reaction, Wilson nevertheless took the precaution of writing this pro-testing note to Harvey:

Personal

My Dear Colonel   21 Dec. 1911

Every day I am confirmed in the judgment that my mind is a one-track road, and can run only one train of thought at a time! A long time after that interview with you and Marse Henry at the Manhattan Club it came over me that when (at the close of the interview) you asked me that question about the *Weekly*, I answered it simply as a matter of fact, and of business, and said never a word of my sincere gratitude to you for all your generous support, or of my hope that it might be continued. Forgive me, and forget my manners!

Faithfully yours,

WOODROW WILSON

Two weeks later Harvey answered in a long letter, signed "Very truly yours," in which Wilson thought he saw evidence of a wound still open. So he wrote again in apology. And this time Harvey replied in six lines, saying that he had uttered no word of criticism and concluding with the statement: "I *have* to print a word of explanation to the *Weekly's* readers, but it will be the briefest possible."

Harvey saw that, coming from Marse Henry—an elder statesman of the party—the story of the Manhattan Club conference would strike the public far more forcefully than if it were told by the injured party himself. Therefore, keeping Wilson's apology to himself, the publisher importuned Watterson to take the initiative in revealing all that he knew. Marse Henry confided his story to at least two Democratic editors in the South. Soon rumors were circulating.

Through a letter written to her cousin in Louisville on January 12, Ellen Wilson succeeded in getting the whole story of the Manhattan Club affair before Watterson. Marse Henry's cocksureness was jolted by this evidence of the duplicity of his New York confederate. Knowing that Harvey already had drafted a statement for publication, in explanation of the removal of Wilson's name from *Harper's Weekly,* the Kentuckian telegraphed to ask that the release be held. But it was too late. Harvey had thrown his stiletto on January 16, giving to the press the statement that he had prepared.

Telling only a part of the true story, neglecting to explain that Harvey had himself raised the question that led to the break, the release announced that at Wilson's suggestion *Harper's Weekly* would cease to advocate his nomination. The implication was that Wilson was a shameless ingrate. The Hearst press, and others who were ready to believe anything evil about the Governor of New Jersey, had a day of unrestrained joy. "He who abandons a friend will abandon a principle," warned one Hearst editor, "and what a man does to an individual he will do to a people."

The truth came out the next day in a statement from Watterson. Marse Henry revealed that the Governor had not been discourteous to Harvey, but merely had given a frank answer to a direct question. However, reflecting his own pique at the rebuff that had been given to his offer to get money from Ryan, Watterson complained that the candidate's manner was "autocratic, if not tyrannous," that he did not make common cause with his political associates.

The air was cleared, but not in the way that Harvey anticipated. House could now recommend Wilson to Bryan as a candidate unembarrassed by support from "Wall Street," and spokesmen for the Governor had the ammunition they needed for a counterattack. "Ingratitude is one of the rarest virtues of public life," the New York *World* proclaimed. " 'Gratitude' is responsible for many of our worst political abuses. Upon 'gratitude' . . . is founded the power of every ignorant and unscrupulous boss; in 'gratitude' is rooted the system of spoils, of logrolling, of lobbying."

Bryan rejoiced with the fervor of a preacher welcoming a lost sheep and a week later he was sanctifying the break with Harvey as a "shining illustration that Mr. Wilson is the best modern example of Saul of Tarsus." The affair ended with Watterson's [10] railing at both Wilson and Harvey in a forlorn effort to smooth his own ruffled plumage, and with both principals keeping a grim silence. "I feel as though I had been walking through mud," Wilson said to his old friend Hiram Woods. "I just do not understand Harvey." His feelings were hurt by the break with this man for whom he had enough affection to write, a little more than a year before: "I have admired very deeply your disinterested part and your true friendship . . ." Once again Woodrow Wilson had been grievously disappointed by a friend to whom he had mistakenly ascribed blind loyalty.

And so George Harvey went over into the camp of Champ Clark, a candidate nominally progressive but more amenable to the traditions of political barter. As a result Wilson was without the shrewd advice that had been so vital to his election in New Jersey. House was busy in Texas, organizing a prenomination campaign; and McCombs and McAdoo were proving to be more valuable as executives than as policy makers. The Governor now had only his wife and Tumulty to advise him in meeting day-by-day problems. Neither was experienced in national politics, though both were learning rapidly.

Wilson was a target for just the sort of mudthrowing that had made the prospect of holding high office so distasteful to him. He was in mortal conflict with skillful manipulators of public opinion. Indeed, the Carnegie pension "exposure" was still being talked about and Harvey's implied aspersions were unrefuted when a third attempt was

[10] As Joseph F. Wall has observed in his *Henry Watterson, Reconstructed Rebel*, pp. 269–81, Watterson was offended when the New York *Sun* quoted Wilson as saying: "The statement that Colonel Watterson was requested to assist in raising money in my behalf is absolutely without foundation." This seemed poor thanks for the zeal that Watterson had shown in helping to get a contribution from Penfield and in suggesting an appeal to Ryan. According to Arthur Krock, Watterson's influence was decisive in giving Champ Clark the endorsement of Kentucky for the Democratic nomination for the Presidency.

made by hostile journalists to put an end to the presidential candidacy of Woodrow Wilson.

This effort was aimed at bringing about an irreparable break between Wilson and Bryan. On January 7, 1912, a day before the Governor was to join the Great Commoner in Washington to address the Jackson Day dinner of the Democratic party, the conservative editor of the New York *Sun* published a five-year-old letter in which the president of Princeton had written: "Would that we could do something, at once dignified and effective, to knock Mr. Bryan, once for all, into a cocked hat!"

The recipient of that letter, a railroad president named Adrian H. Joline, later had opposed Wilson's plans at Princeton; [11] and then Wilson's feelings toward both Bryan and Joline had changed. The *Sun's* stroke of malevolence threatened to undo all the wooing of the Great Commoner that had been arranged by Ellen Wilson and House.[12] How would Bryan react?

The question was answered on January 8, 1912, when Democrats gathered for the Jackson Day dinner that marked the beginning of the drive for votes in the June nominating convention. En route to Washington, Bryan stopped to visit Josephus Daniels, who did his utmost to assuage the irritation that was caused by the publication of the Joline letter, and by the time he reached the capital the *Sun*, rather than Wilson, was the main target of the Nebraskan's anger.

As for Wilson, he was content to stand on the truth and make no apologies that might seem to put him on the defensive. He was not ashamed, he said, of what had been an honest statement when it was written, although he was now of another opinion. "Don't be nervous about this," he advised his family before he left for Washington. "It is

[11] Wilson's "cocked-hat" letter of April 29, 1907, applauded a speech that Joline had delivered before his board of directors on April 4, 1907, bitterly attacking Bryan's proposal for government ownership of railroads as "the cry of the envious against the well-to-do—the old story." Within two or three years Wilson had turned against this reactionary, and after his election to the Presidency he said to a colleague who mentioned Joline: "If I wrote what I think of that man, it would have to be on asbestos." Luther P. Eisenhart, "The Far-Seeing Wilson," in William S. Myers (ed.), *Woodrow Wilson: Some Princeton Memories*, p. 67.

[12] The Bryans had lived next door to the Colonel one winter in the nineties, and House had found Mrs. Bryan very amenable to advice and suggestion, but Bryan himself wildly impracticable. During 1911, using his intimate insight into the mental processes of the Bryan family, House had begun to "nurse Bryan" in order to bring him around to his own way of thinking. He had faithfully informed the Nebraskan of threats by Underwood and Clark to his leadership of the party, and had played on Bryan's prejudices by sending all evidence that he could collect of the antipathy of "Wall Street" to Wilson and of its preference for Clark. On Nov. 11 the Colonel wrote to the Governor: "I have been with Mr. Bryan a good part of the morning and I am pleased to tell you that I think you will have his support . . . My main effort was in alienating him from Champ Clark and I believe I was successful."

only small men who allow such things to affect them and Mr. Bryan is not a small man."

When he came home from the Jackson Day dinner he told his loved ones all about it. Sitting before an open fire in the studio of the house on Cleveland Lane, deliberately taking off his glasses and balancing them on his thumb while he rubbed his eyes, he made them see the love feast with Bryan into which the Washington dinner had developed. They saw the Great Commoner enter, late, walk to the table where the presidential candidates and the entire Democratic National Committee were seated, turn first to greet Clark and then to put his arm around Wilson's shoulder. They could hear the rowdy friends of James Nugent who, when Wilson started to speak, hissed and heckled but were shouted down with cries of "Shame!" They could imagine the two great prophets rising to embrace each other in warm phrases.

Of the man whom he had once damned as a demagogic office seeker, Wilson said in all sincerity: "I for my part, never want to forget this: That while we have differed with Mr. Bryan upon this occasion and upon that in regard to the specific things to be done, he has gone serenely on pointing out to a more and more convinced people what it was that was the matter . . ." And then, with a burst of healing eloquence: "Let us apologize to each other that we ever suspected or antagonized one another; let us join hands once more all around the great circle of community of counsel and of interest which will show us at the last to have been indeed the friends of our country and the friends of mankind."

After Wilson's peroration, the ovation was tremendous. Bryan put a hand on the speaker's shoulder, murmuring "Splendid! Splendid!" Rising to respond, he declared himself ready to give more valiant service to the man who would bear the standard of the party than he could ever render to himself. Was the Nebraskan at last ready to abdicate leadership of the Democracy? his people wondered.

Wilson had now, at the beginning of the critical year 1912, been under heavy fire on a national battleground. He was learning to control his righteous ire and to fight back with the weapons magnanimity, tact, and silence. "All these things," he said of the malicious attacks upon him, "in the long run, discredit only those who do them, but for a while they are very trying."

There were still other machinations that Wilson's Celtic imagination ascribed to persecutors on "Wall Street": the threat of publication of a letter alleged to have been written by Grover Cleveland to Henry Van

Dyke of Princeton, impugning Wilson's self-control and intellectual integrity; [13] the financing of a great "trust" designed to divide political spoils among Harmon, Underwood, and Clark "with a division of territory quite after the manner of the industrial combinations."

Far more embarrassing than the canards of the conservatives were the efforts of pseudo progressives to prove Wilson an archreactionary. Hearst and other publicists for Champ Clark and Underwood were prominent in this campaign. Their evidence, taken largely from Wilson's *History of the American People*, was actually in print and in circulation.[14] In the last volume of the *History,* a henchman of Clark's claimed to have found quotations to show that the author "had a profound contempt for the Farmer's Alliance, the Populists, greenbackers, bi-metalists, trades unionists, small office seekers, Italians, Poles, Hungarians, pensioners, strikers, armies of unemployeed."

Late in Feburary, Hearst began to devote front pages to abuse of the Governor, denouncing him as a Tory, a Judas, "a perfect jackrabbit of politics." Wilson had firmly rejected suggestions from the journalist's agents that, like other candidates, the Governor should write a letter welcoming Hearst back into the party. "God knows," he said, "I want the Democratic presidential nomination and I am going to do everything legitimately to get it, but if I am to grovel at Hearst's feet, I will never have it." When Wilson publicly commended the appointment of his Princeton classmate, Chancellor Pitney of New Jersey, to the United States Supreme Court, he subjected himself to criticism from labor organizations against which the conservative judge had made decisions; but when Hearst tried to exploit this situation and attacked Wilson's views on labor, the executive committee of the New Jersey Federation of Labor circulated an endorsement of their governor.

Among one group of voters, however, the attacks of the Hearst press did irreparable damage. Passages from the *History* were quoted to make foreign-born voters fear that, if he became president, Wilson would act to restrict immigration. The foreign-language press took alarm and openly denounced the candidate. Though he wooed Polish

13 A statement written by Tertius Van Dyke, son and biographer of Henry Van Dyke, to Edith Gittings Reid, dated Jan. 21, 1949, which was shown to the writer by Mrs. Reid, effectively disposes of the likelihood that such a letter existed. There was, however, a damaging letter from Cleveland to Prentiss Bailey, editor of the Ithaca *Observer*. See p. 115.

14 When a new edition of Wilson's *History* was published, Mrs. Wilson wrote to Harvey to express the hope that the "limelight" of publicity would make the new edition sell enormously, explaining that the appeals to aid this and that were already legion and it was very inconvenient for a public man to be penniless. *Harper's* sent agents into New Jersey towns after Wilson's public appearances and promoted the sale of the *History*. See James Kerney, *The Political Education of Woodrow Wilson*, p. 126.

and Italian editors contritely and even swallowed his professional pride
to the extent of asking his publishers if he might revise certain passages, and though he established the fact that he had protested against
the restriction of immigration in 1906, Wilson lost the confidence of
many foreign-born voters.

Wilson's letters to intimates give glimpses of the pain that human
perversity caused this man who wished above everything to love and
be loved, to win and hold the confidence of the American congregation.
To Edith Gittings Reid, for example, he wrote: ". . . the world grows
sometimes to seem so brutal, so naked of beauty, so devoid of chivalrous
sentiment and all sense of fair play, that one's own spirit hardens and
is in danger of losing its fineness. I fight on, in the spirit of Kipling's
'If,' but that is oftentimes a very arid air." As he felt his candidacy
growing in strength he thought himself the more put upon by men who
were determined to destroy his character by fair means or foul. He told
his daughters that there were some people who could not be trusted.
His moods oscillated between neurotic suspicion and childlike faith,
and sometimes his family noticed an ominous twitching in his right
eye.

Wilson had been annoyed, in 1911, by persistent rumors that the
Princeton trustees would reveal the inside story of his controversies, and
he had suggested to his friends on the board that they might join with
him in meeting the situation publicly; but he was advised that probably
nothing would be done openly that might involve the university in
political controversy and enhance Wilson's position as a prophet of
democracy. Privately, however, his enemies worked with his political
opponents to undermine him. On February 9, President Taft wrote
to West that Wilson was "getting what his shifty dishonest nature
deserves." [15]

Occasionally Wilson responded directly and hotly to the abuse of
adversaries. Sometimes he steadied his nerves by quoting from Kipling:
"If you can wait and not be tired by waiting, or being lied about, don't
deal in lies." Often he forced himself to reply to attacks obliquely, by
dwelling on the debasing effect of mudthrowing upon the personnel of
government. "Misrepresentation," he complained to sympathetic Mayor
Gaynor of New York, "is the penalty which men in public life must
expect in the course of their effort to render service . . . These things

[15] West Papers (Princeton University Library). The Wilsons suspected that "the fine
Italian hand" of Dean West reached President Nicholas Murray Butler, of Columbia, whose
influence in Republican councils was great. E.A.W. to Nancy Toy, Sept. 23, 1912.

should be borne with fortitude, if not indifference, in order that our duty may be rendered without regard to our personal feeling."

The embattled candidate perhaps found his greatest comfort in the words of Peter Finley Dunne, whose column he liked to read to his family in extravagant brogue. "I don't know," said Mr. Dooley, "what'll happen to th' professor next. If I was him I wudden't walk on th' sidewalk; I'd always be home before sunset, I'd be careful what I et an' dhrank, an' if I saw a friend fr'm Princeton comin' tow'ds me with a pleasant smile on his face an' givin' me th' high sign iv our secret s'ciety, I'd run."

CHAPTER XIII

CHOICE OF THE DEMOCRACY

AT PHILADELPHIA, ON FEBRUARY 2, 1912, Wilson spoke to hundreds of periodical publishers on the same platform with Senator Robert M. LaFollette of Wisconsin. The audience was largely one of Republican reactionaries, and remarkably sensitive to public opinion. They saw revolutionary omens in the political skies, in this most critical year of American politics since 1860. Large strikes had charged the air with electricity of high potential. Socialist Eugene Debs had a vociferous following. At last it seemed clear that the voices of revolt were loud and articulate enough to influence political action.

LaFollette, a powerful orator, went to Philadelphia commanding Wilson's respect as "a very high minded champion of progressive ideas." Bitterly insurgent, he had for years been fighting special privilege and corruption, had made himself the very soul of grass-roots progressivism in the Republican party. But to prove that he was of presidential stature, he would have to capture the intellectual liberals of the East. And that he failed to do. Weakened by an attack of ptomaine poisoning, his nerve shaken by the deflation of his presidential boom by what he regarded as a betrayal by Roosevelt, he was in no condition to match oratory with Woodrow Wilson at the gathering of sophisticated publishers. Usually a temperate man, on this occasion he drank a stimulant to fortify his weakened vitality, and the effect was tragic. He spoke twice too long, became lost in repetition, ranted against newspapermen.

Wilson's briefer talk was urbane and charming even in its criticism of his hosts the publishers: "I used to be afraid that they would not publish what I offered them, but now I am afraid they will"—deftly discriminating in its definitions and prescriptions: "Progressivism means not getting caught standing still when everything else is moving . . . we are not steering by forms of government, we are steering by principles of government." In contrast, LaFollette's uncouth, humorless denunciation seemed as grim as a Puritan sermon. From the back of the hall men shouted "Sit down!" The audience melted away, LaFollette's star faded, and a few days later Theodore Roosevelt, with protestations of self-sacrifice, whooped, "My hat is in the ring!"

If the election of a Democratic president had already seemed a probability, it now appeared to be almost a certainty. But in spite of the rift in the Republican party Wilson continued his appeals to the voters. Late in February he went into progressive strongholds; and at Des Moines, addressing insurgent Republicans as well as Democrats, he inveighed against monopoly and special interests, called the United States Senate "a seat of privilege," and explained that the only difference between himself and the followers of LaFollette was over the tariff. "You speak of the tariff with a certain air of piety and I don't," he said. Closing his winter campaigning at Brooklyn, he asserted that the people were to be "absolutely trusted" in choosing their leaders and that those chosen would be responsible for the working out of a *modus vivendi*, before the "seething millions" of America turned upon themselves and the social melting pot grew "hotter and hotter." In general, however, in the speeches delivered in the East during the winter, the candidate held himself to inoffensive generalities and by sheer eloquence commanded the respect of his audiences.

In planning the campaign for the votes of the delegates, McCombs decided not to compete in states in which native sons were candidates. By a hands-off policy he hoped to win goodwill that would result in second-choice support for his man. Therefore, no fight was made for Wilson when Missouri, the first of the states to instruct its delegates to Baltimore, held its primary election on February 11. The vote of the machines of Kansas City and St. Louis ran heavily toward Congressman Clark, a strict party man. Distinguished and pleasing in manner, he did not have the magnetism of the nation's great progressive personalities. His progressivism lacked intellectual base and moral compulsion, but had proved to be a winning card; and agrarians felt that they knew him better than Wilson.

In the Midwestern primaries that followed shortly after that of Missouri, Wilson was entered by his managers and had the better of the voting. The tide turned, however, in April. In Illinois the Hearst press, the local progressive leaders, and a swarm of able speakers joined forces to draw out a 3-to-1 vote for Clark. His prospects grew even brighter when Bryan's Nebraska delegation was instructed in favor of the Missourian; and several other states fell in line.

Wilson, now on the defensive, took off his cloak of academic diffidence and got into the fight with both fists. The campaign was becoming a game to be won, if win he could by fair means. In a little pocket notebook he wrote a list of all the states, the number of their delegates to the convention, and the names of the Democratic leaders with whom McCombs hoped to do business. Most of those sought out were progressives; but in at least two states conservatives were wooed, and in Illinois Boss Roger Sullivan was regarded as the best hope.

McCombs was frankly spurring his candidate to efforts that would pay off in votes. "Now I must rush out again in search of delegates . . ." Wilson wrote on April 1, "shy birds more difficult to find in genuine species than the snark itself!" Sometimes his zeal was more fervent than wise, from the point of view of hardened politicians. Going to Illinois and making a score of speeches in two days, for example, he failed to redeem a cause already lost and thus drew national attention to a defeat that was inevitable in that state. But he had the pleasure of speaking his mind about Hearst—"a character assassin." And he sowed grass-roots sentiment that was to blossom at the nominating convention.

Again, in mid-April, the Governor took the warpath in an effort to stem a flood of conservatism on which Southern Democrats were drifting toward Congressman Underwood of Alabama. Actually this candidate had been born of a Unionist family in Kentucky, had gone south as a commercial lawyer, and had become substantial, respected—and limited—by the sort of milieu that had repelled Wilson at Atlanta. Hoping that his own more genuine Southern background would appeal to the people of that section, Wilson made a four-day tour of Georgia, taking along his wife and W. G. McAdoo, both descendants of old Georgia families. The Wilsons were received warmly by friends and relatives and visited the manse at Savannah where they had been married; and the journals welcomed "Tommie" as a native son. But conservative state organizations raised the bogies of Bryanism, Oregonism, and mob rule, endorsed Underwood's distinguished record in Congress, and presented him as the "safe and sane candidate." Underwood won the primaries in Georgia, Florida, Mississippi, and Virginia. Wilson succeeded in winning only a working majority of the delegates from South Carolina and a fourth of those from Tennessee.

By the middle of May, McCombs was thrown into gloom. The candidate was even less effective in attracting funds to his campaign chest than he had been in gathering millions for Princeton. The Wilson headquarters was almost bankrupt, and all but a few loyal henchmen had fallen away. At the end of the month Colonel House doubted their man could win. Working on Bryan's sympathies in April, at breakfast in a New York hotel, he was ably seconded by Mrs. Bryan; but the Great Commoner had gone no further than declaring that either Clark or Wilson was acceptable, and House suspected that the Nebraskan still hoped to capture the nomination for himself. In May the Colonel was urging Wilson to declare that he would accept only a single term in the Presidency, hoping thus to mollify competitors who would not want to wait eight years to replace him. A few weeks later he tried to make common cause with the Bryans by writing Mrs. Bryan that the purpose of the interests opposing Wilson was to prevent the nomination of either Wilson or Bryan.

To remain in the running for the Presidency, the Governor had to continue to command the support of New Jersey. In the winter the Republican legislature had passed a bill that could embarrass the Governor whether he signed it or vetoed it. This measure required railroads to abolish grade crossings at a rate that to some men seemed confiscatory. It posed a delicate decision for Wilson: Tumulty was urging him to sign the measure, as evidence of his faithfulness to progressive ideals, while McAdoo was advising him that this legislation was unfair to the railroads and had been drawn for the purpose of putting the Governor in a political trap. Wilson challenged the good faith of the legislators by vetoing the bill and commenting that, if they really believed in the measure, the lawmakers could pass it over his veto. They did not do so.

When the Smith-Nugent forces, aided by a smart young lieutenant named Frank Hague, tried to send uninstructed, anti-Wilson delegates to Baltimore, the Governor appealed directly to the voters of New Jersey through a statement in the press. Speaking out against what was being done "very quietly and very secretly" by Smith, "who knows no other way of acting in politics," he did not mince words. "Do you wish to slip back into the slough of old despair and disgrace?" he asked the citizens.

The response was heartening. The forces of James Smith and James Nugent—now known as "the Jim-Jims"—elected only four delegates, all from Essex County, out of the twenty-eight who were to represent New Jersey at Baltimore. On the same day, May 28, Texas definitely committed its forty delegates to Wilson; and very soon Utah, the Dakotas, North Carolina, and Minnesota were in line.

But by all mathematical reckoning the Governor's chances of nomination were still slim. A vote of two-thirds of the delegates was needed; and Wilson fell just short of controlling a vetoing bloc of one-third.

Yet House's hope had revived. On June 7 he communicated his optimism to Wilson, counseling cautious inactivity on the part of the candidate. Plans for organizing the supporting delegates were "already under way," the Colonel wrote. Taking House's advice, of which he confessed that he stood in need, Wilson resigned himself to silence.

A week later, having moved with his family to Sea Girt for the summer, he wrote to Mary Allen Peck: "The day is gray and drizzly; the sea makes a dismal voice across the bleak camp ground in front of us; we have had to light a fire in the huge fireplace to keep our spirits (and our temperature) up; but here we are a home group with that within us that can defy the depressing influences of the weather. What we now look forward to with not a little dread are the possibilities of the next fortnight in politics. I was saying at breakfast this morning, 'Two weeks from to-day we shall either have this sweet Sunday calm again, or an army of reporters camped on the lawn and an all-day reception.' 'Which would you rather have?' Nell asked. 'Need you ask?' I exclaimed; and that is the way I feel . . . I am well (I do not count a teasing sick headache!) and underneath, deep down, my soul is quiet."

Amidst his duties at Trenton and Sea Girt, the candidate kept an eye open toward the Republican convention at Chicago. There, in mid-June, Theodore Roosevelt commanded at the same time the fealty of genuine progressives, the support of certain leaders of finance and industry, and the votes of what at first seemed to be a majority of the delegates—only to have his men denied seats or won away by bosses of the party who had resolved to renominate President Taft. Wilson let it be known to his friends that, if the Democrats named a candidate as conservative as Taft, they might expect Woodrow Wilson to bolt, as Roosevelt was threatening to do.

Meanwhile the impresarios of the Democracy were indefatigable in discussion of tactics for their convention; and sometimes the Governor joined his managers in talk of plans for high-pressuring recalcitrant delegates and for packing the galleries with strong-lunged undergraduates. The nomination was to be made at Baltimore, a city preferred by the Wilson managers because popular sentiment in the region favored their candidate and might be expected to influence a close contest. Toward the end of the month a Wilson headquarters was set up in the Emerson Hotel, whence a private wire ran to the candidate's room at Sea Girt. Zealous Wilson delegates from Texas and Pennsylvania planned a relentless campaign to win individual "converts" from other delegations. All was ready for the great trial of strength.

McCombs, who had been working without respite all through the spring, had gone into conference with House for several days in June. The manager's nerves were so worn that the Colonel doubted his ability to carry the fight through the convention; and House had coached the worried man, realizing that McCombs was inexperienced in such matters.[1]

On June 25 the Colonel sailed for Europe, explaining to Wilson that he was physically unequal to taking part in the convention, and assuring the Governor that he had done his best to prepare both McCombs and the Texans to anticipate every contingency. "It leaves an empty feeling in my heart . . ." Wilson replied, "but it would be selfish to ask you to stay."

Meanwhile, out at Chicago, where the surge of progressive sentiment was undermining the solidarity of the Republican party, another devoted Wilson man had executed a self-imposed mission. William G. McAdoo, convinced that Bryan held the key to victory at Baltimore, had determined to woo the Great Commoner. Going to the Republican convention, where Bryan was accredited as a reporter, he had found his man in shirt sleeves in a crowded hotel corridor and tried to make him see that Wilson was the only genuine progressive in the Democratic race. But Bryan gave his pat answer: as a member of the Nebraska delegation he was bound to vote as he was instructed—for Clark. The Nebraskan was curious to know the intentions of Tammany. He asked McAdoo, who was a member of the New York delegation, and was told that Boss Charles Murphy was planning to switch New York's vote from Harmon to Clark as soon as such a move would give the nomination to Clark.

"Humph!" Bryan exclaimed; ". . . after I have complied with my instructions, in good faith, I shall feel free to take such course in the convention as my conscience shall dictate. Moreover if, during the course of the convention, anything should develop to convince me that Clark cannot or ought not to be nominated, I shall support Governor Wilson."[2] McAdoo went straight to Baltimore, well satisfied, though some in the inner councils of the party suspected that no candidate would

---

[1] *House Papers,* I, 63, and House-McCombs correspondence in the House Collection. When McCombs claimed 800 delegates for Wilson, for example, House commended the exaggeration but warned against specifying the states from which they would come, since that would make it easy to refute the claim. Leaders of the Texas delegation had been present at the House-McCombs conference, and tactics had been worked out for organized proselyting by their men among delegates who had been instructed to vote for other candidates. It was hoped that thus they might block a two-thirds vote for Clark.

[2] William G. McAdoo, *Crowded Years,* pp. 135–36.

completely satisfy the Great Commoner except William Jennings Bryan, that he hoped to survive after his rivals had killed one another off.

Utterly devoted to the progressive cause, and anticipating that the standpatters in his own party would use the same tactics that had been successful in the Republican convention, Bryan began to set backfires against the Clark-Tammany threat. When the committee on arrangements proposed to give the temporary chairmanship of the convention to Alton B. Parker, the favorite of the New York delegation, the Great Commoner protested that it would be suicidal to have a reactionary for chairman. Moreover, Bryan telegraphed to Wilson, Clark, and several favorite sons to challenge them to support his protest against Parker. Thus, even before the convention met, Wilson was asked to choose between progressive principles and the votes of Tammany.

The Governor called his family around him and listened to their advice, his manner whimsically questioning. The voice that he trusted as loyal above all others said firmly: "There must be no hedging." Smiling, he agreed. Once he had said of his Ellen: "Neither the powers above nor below can shake her when a principle is involved." Sitting on the edge of a bed, he jotted on a pad this reply to Bryan: "You are quite right . . . The Baltimore convention is to be a convention of progressives—of men who are progressive in principle and by conviction. It must, if it is not to be put in a wrong light before the country, express its convictions in its organization and in its choice of the men who are to speak for it . . . No one will doubt where my sympathies lie . . ."

Wilson was the only candidate who dared to respond to Bryan's challenge so forthrightly. Tumulty and McAdoo were delighted when they learned what he had done; but McCombs, who had advised Wilson to straddle and hedge like the other candidates, was frantic. "The Governor can't afford to have a row," he wailed. But McAdoo, who a year before had urged that Wilson must scotch the accusation that he was "dangerous," now sensed the political magic that lay in a fight on high principles. And so he responded: "The Governor can't afford to have anything but a row. The bigger the row the better for us."

The first session of the nominating convention assembled on the afternoon of June 25. In Baltimore's armory, gay with flags and packed to the rafters, the name of Parker was proposed as temporary chairman. Immediately Bryan was on his feet. Wearing a dowdy sack suit, with low collar and black bow tie, his thin mouth set grimly and his black brows frowning beneath a pointed, bald dome, he held up his right hand for quiet. And then through his thick jowls his voice boomed to the corners of the hall. "The Democratic party is true to the people," he shouted. "You cannot frighten it with your Ryans nor buy it with your Belmonts." The sentence brought delegates to their feet, waving and yelling.

A few moments later Bryan was nominated for the temporary chairmanship, and a Texan took the opportunity to trumpet the issue plainly to the convention: ". . . the fight is on and Bryan is on one side and Wall Street is on the other." The Wilson delegates voted for Bryan; but when Clark's men cast 228 of their votes against them, Parker was chosen, 579 to 508.[3]

When a majority of the committee on rules tried to force each state delegation to vote as a unit—a measure that Wilson already had condemned as a violation of the principle of direct primaries—Mayor Newton D. Baker of Cleveland and other pro-Wilson delegates fought the move on the floor of the convention. In the course of the struggle that followed, an Ohioan happened to mention the name of the Governor of New Jersey, and instantly the bands and flag wavers that had been prepared by McCombs's "chief of enthusiasm" went into action. The hall was in pandemonium for a half hour. The unit-voting rule was beaten and nineteen Ohio delegates who had been instructed for Wilson by the voters of their district were allowed to vote for him.

Bryan relentlessly pressed his crusade by forcing through a motion that put the convention on record as "opposed to the nomination of any candidate for President who is the representative of or under obligation to J. Pierpont Morgan, Thomas F. Ryan, August Belmont, or any other member of the privilege-hunting and favor-seeking class." Wilson's eyes sparkled when news of this move by Bryan reached him. "The old lion is at his best," the Governor said to his family.

Bryan's anti-Wall Street resolution was approved by a vote of more than 4 to 1; and finally, on the night of June 27, the formal nominations began. The naming of Clark by James Reed of Missouri set off a demonstration that lasted for an hour and five minutes. It was after three o'clock in the morning when Judge Wescott, chairman of the New Jersey delegation, rose and presented his candidate. The judge had come to adore Wilson as the first man in history to identify statesmanship with Christianity. Quoting from the speech at Pittsburgh in

[3] Parker was not made permanent chairman. The progressives combined to elect Ollie M. James, a friend of Bryan and a supporter of Clark, and a man who, in the view of the Wilson managers, would have been more troublesome at large on the floor of the convention than in the presiding chair.

which Wilson had bared his soul and denounced the Philistines of Princeton and the nation, Wescott went on to say: "He has been in political life less than two years. He has had no organization of the usual sort; only a practical ideal, the re-establishment of equal opportunity. The logic of events points to him . . . Every crisis evolves its master. Time and circumstance have evolved the immortal Governor of New Jersey." Wilson's cohorts outdid the demonstration for Clark by ten minutes—parading, flaunting banners, yelling, whistling, and tooting horns in a jamboree that expressed the college spirit of many of the participants.

Daylight was creeping in at the end of the hall when blind Senator Gore of Oklahoma rose to second the nomination. The first ballot was not taken until seven o'clock. It gave Clark 440½ votes and Wilson 324.

The changes on the next eight ballots were so slight that, when Tumulty reported the results to the Governor, Wilson said that he was reminded of two men who were walking and stopped three times to ask the distance to their destination and each time got the same answer: "Well," exclaimed one of them at last, "thank God, we're holding our own."

On the tenth ballot, however, came the break that had been feared by the Wilson men. Boss Murphy of Tammany shifted the ninety votes of New York to Clark. The partisans of the Missourian celebrated for more than an hour, hoping to stampede the convention. Clark now had 556 votes, a majority of the total. For sixty-eight years every Democratic candidate who had reached that point had gone on to win two-thirds of the votes and the nomination. Clark, in the speaker's office at Washington, prepared a telegram of acceptance.

McCombs's nerve broke completely after the all-night session that culminated in the tenth ballot. The next morning he telephoned to Sea Girt, just as Wilson was coming down to breakfast, to suggest that the delegates pledged to him be released. But just as he was about to give this advice McAdoo thrust him aside and seized the phone and said: "McCombs is going to tell you to withdraw. No one else believes you should." [4]

Though Wilson did not withdraw, he did not expect the nomination now. He was both disappointed and relieved. He anticipated the prospect of a trip to the English Lakes with his wife. His sense of humor

---

[4] Louis Brownlow, who was present, to the writer, and in a lecture at the University of Chicago, March 2, 1956.

came to his rescue too. Finding an advertisement of coffins in his mail, he quipped: "This company is certainly prompt in its service." All through the balloting he had remained serene—playing golf, reading aloud with his wife, walking along the shore, taking automobile rides with friends, telling stories to reporters who worked in a tent on the lawn.

All was not lost, however. The Wilson men had expected Tammany to shift to Clark still earlier in the balloting and had been prepared to stand firm against an attempted stampede. When the results of three ballots following the tenth showed little change, it was apparent that the Clark men had played their best card to no avail. When they departed so far from progressive gospel as to add Murphy and Tammany to their company, it was too much for the Democracy of the West to stomach. Bryan and other Nebraskans were in a mood to revolt against their instructions.

As the thirteenth ballot was being taken, Wilson sensed the trend of feeling and took the offensive, giving McCombs a message for delivery to Bryan. In it the Governor criticized the effort of the New York delegation to control the convention, declaring it "the imperative duty of each candidate . . . to see to it that his own independence" was "beyond question." "I can see no other way to do this," he said, "than to declare that he will not accept a nomination if it cannot be secured without the aid of that delegation. For myself, I have no hesitation in making that declaration. The freedom of the party and its candidate and the security of the government against private control constitute the supreme consideration."

When Bryan received this manifesto of Wilson's independence, he was already preparing to transfer his vote from Clark to Wilson. Finally, the opportunity came to explain his position on the floor of the convention. On the fourteenth ballot Senator Hitchcock of Nebraska, following a policy that McCombs had urged, demanded that his state's delegation be polled publicly. Since Clark had shown himself willing to accept the nomination from the hands of Murphy, Bryan explained that he felt bound by the spirit of his instructions to withhold his vote from Clark so long as New York supported him. Making himself heard through an uproar of yells, catcalls, and hisses, Bryan cast his vote for Wilson with the proviso that it would be withdrawn if New York should give its allegiance to that candidate.

The polling of the Nebraska men had only a slight effect on the totals; but Bryan's shift, topping a ground swell of popular opinion that was being expressed in the liberal press and in the polling of state delegations loosed a moral force that was titanic. A torrent of telegrams assured the Great Commoner that the people were with him. "Wait till you hear from the folks back home," the Wilson slogan advised.

Clark men now were on the defensive, raging at Bryan as "a money-grabbing, selfish, office-seeking, favor-hunting, publicity-loving marplot" who was deliberately throwing the convention into a deadlock so that he himself might be nominated. By this accusation any aspirations that Bryan may have had were effectively blocked.[5]

Meanwhile Bryan's move was embarrassing McCombs in his efforts to persuade the New York men that Clark could not win and that they should vote for Wilson. McCombs went so far as to ask the Governor whether he might assure conservatives that, if Wilson was elected, Byran would not be made secretary of state. Early in the campaign, however, Wilson had laid down the law: there was to be no commitment that would bind him in administering the government, no bargaining for votes. Politely, he said "no" to McCombs; and, to allay rumors that trading in public offices was being done in his name, he asserted to the Baltimore *Sun* that "not a single vote can be or will be obtained by means of a promise."

At Sea Girt the Governor still maintained his air of insouciance. While his daughters sat up late, eager for news, the candidate retired early and slept soundly, sometimes for as much as twelve hours. At meals, talk of politics was forbidden and the paterfamilias entertained his ladies on lighter subjects. All through the day newsmen ran in and out without knocking; and Tumulty paced up and down, watch in hand, eyes popping at each tidbit of news, denouncing all opponents as "damned crooks." The Governor amused himself by reading in his

---

[5] Actually, the Great Commoner had confirmed the impossibility that Clark could be nominated, but without committing himself irrevocably to Wilson. He openly suggested that the progressives might well compromise on another candidate; and he said to scouts of Roger Sullivan of Illinois that, if the convention should feel that it must nominate him, the party leaders would find it easier to deal with him than with Wilson. Though he told his wife that he would accept his fourth nomination only in the event of a hopeless deadlock and if he could unite the party, the stage was undeniably set, whether by accident or design, for a display of any pro-Bryan sentiment that might have been latent among the delegates.

Though Bryan's wife and brother have denied that the Great Commoner wanted the nomination for himself and Josephus Daniels believed that if that was his desire he would have played his cards differently, Carter Glass, John W. Davis, and other party men thought that Bryan intended to prolong the contest and eventually receive the nomination. In his autobiography, Cordell Hull wrote: "It was not generally known, but the truth is that Bryan felt that he was entitled to the nomination. I learned that very definitely later." *See* Wayne C. Williams, *William Jennings Bryan*, p. 331; Josephus Daniels, *The Wilson Era: Years of Peace*, pp. 64–65; and John W. Davis MS, Oral History Project, p. 117, Columbia University.

secretary's face the nature of each report from Baltimore and teased him by humming the Clark campaign song.

Gradually the delegates at the convention fell away from Clark and the work done by Wilson's managers in lining up second choices bore fruit. By the end of the day on which Bryan announced his shift, Wilson had gained more than eighty votes. Last-ditch efforts were made by the bosses, during the lull in balloting that was enforced by the Sabbath, to tempt some of the ablest of the Wilson supporters to desert. But something of their leader's Covenanting spirit seemed to bind his men; and this loyalty was strengthened by Sunday headlines of the pro-Wilson press. To the *World,* the nomination of Wilson was "a matter of Democratic life and death."

The first important break in the ranks of the boss-dominated states came when the votes of Indiana's favorite son, Thomas R. Marshall, were delivered to Wilson. One by one, men who worshiped success deserted their candidates and scurried under the winning colors, as McCombs hinted at the political perdition awaiting obstructing minorities; but not until the thirtieth ballot, when Iowa transferred fourteen of her votes, did Wilson's total exceed that of Clark. At that moment a band struck up "Glory, Glory, Hallelujah!" and Wilson men joined in a chant of triumph. When the newsmen at Sea Girt, with eyes sparkling, hunted out the candidate and shouted "You've passed him, governor!" he responded to their request for "a statement" by remarking casually: "You might say that Governor Wilson received the news that Champ Clark had dropped to second place in a riot of silence."

Then the crescendo stopped, and Wilson lost a vote. His managers were fearful that Bryan again would be the standard-bearer. Determined to prevent a debacle, they accentuated their wooing of Roger Sullivan, whom they had helped to seat his Illinois delegates against Hearst's opposition and who had promised to aid Wilson's cause whenever his nomination became likely. On the forty-third ballot, Sullivan delivered the fifty-eight votes of his state.

However, even when Virginia at last endorsed her native son, Wilson's nomination was still blocked by hundreds of delegates who were loyal to Clark and Underwood; and there were rumors that Sullivan was prepared to swing Illinois back to Clark if Wilson could not soon command the necessary two-thirds of the votes. Finally, fervent pleading by Congressman Burleson resulted in the release of the Underwood delegates, many of whom already had been committed to Wilson as their second choice as a result of effective canvassing by the Texans.

On the forty-sixth ballot Wilson was given a nominating vote of 990. The action was made unanimous and, at 3:30 on the afternoon of July 2, Woodrow Wilson was declared the Democratic nominee for the Presidency of the United States.

Hearing the news, Tumulty rushed to the porch at Sea Girt and waved wildly toward a clump of trees. He had a brass band hidden there; and now it emerged, playing "Hail, the Conquering Hero Comes!" Slyly, the Governor asked what instructions had been given to the musicians in case of defeat. "I can't effervesce in the face of responsibility," he said to his family in explanation of his calmness; but, for the first time in his life, Woodrow Wilson let himself go to the extent of commissioning an aide to buy a box of cigars. The nomination seemed to him a sort of political miracle.

The vice-presidential nomination went to Governor Thomas R. Marshall of Indiana, who was a protégé of Tom Taggart, the first of the state bosses to desert Clark for Wilson. Thinking Marshall an agreeable fellow but a man of small caliber, Wilson would have preferred Underwood. When the Alabaman refused, however, the presidential candidate let the managers have their way.

The party platform, which in this convention was of far less importance than the nominee, bore the imprint of Byran. Neglected by the convention until the last moment, it was read perfunctorily by a hoarse clerk and adopted without discussion.[6]

Through all the muddy performance at Baltimore, Woodrow Wilson had managed to keep his exacting conscience clear. His position was the same as it had been after the nomination in New Jersey. He was the nominee because the people wanted him; because the people wanted him, the bosses thought that he could salvage their derelict hulk of a party. He rejoiced in writing to his nephew, George Howe, "The nomination has been won in such a way as to leave me absolutely free of private obligations." Only as Princeton served the nation had he thought its existence justified; only as the Democratic party served the United States could Woodrow Wilson act as its sponsor.

[6] The platform promised to transmute the progressive sentiment of the country into law, to prosecute trusts and regulate business. It proposed constitutional amendments providing for an income tax and the direct election of senators. To please the American Federation of Labor, jury trials were advocated in cases of criminal contempt of court and labor organizations were declared to be not properly subject to antitrust laws. The establishment of a central banking system of the sort proposed by Republican Senator Aldrich was opposed. Moreover, the party's platform committed their presidential candidate to the principle of a single term of office, a pledge with which Wilson differed.

CHAPTER XIV

WINNING THE PRESIDENCY

THE SPOTLIGHT THAT FELL on Woodrow Wilson at Sea Girt, in July of 1912, was garish, relentless, and worldly. He squirmed in rebellion as political impresarios, news reporters, brass bands, photographers, and autograph hunters swarmed over the lawn, up on the porch, and even into the house. Outside of his bedroom the Governor had no privacy. Some ten thousand letters came in—more than half from people who said that they had *prayed* for the nomination of Wilson. He was awed by the trust of the masses and frightened by the pathetic faith of individuals in the omnipotence of their ruler.

Soon he was protesting: ". . . the more these new things crowd upon me the more I seem to be dependent for peace and joy upon those I love. The more public my life becomes the more I seem driven in upon my own inner life and all its intimate companionships." Most of all he rested on the devotion of Ellen Wilson, who was absolutely sure that all this great faith in him would never be disappointed. But he still demanded the refreshment that came in letters from Bermuda, messages trifling and humorous that he could share with his family. "The life I am leading now can't keep up," he wrote to Mary Allen Peck ". . . Not a moment am I left free to do what I would. I thought last night that I should go crazy with the strain and confusion of it." Coming out dripping from a hot room in which he had been sealed up to make phonograph records for the coming campaign, he exclaimed: "If any man ever tries to get me to run for president again, I'll break his neck!" [1]

Democrats from many states descended on Sea Girt to see the new chief. On the Fourth of July thirty-five members of the National Committee, some of them still sulking over the nomination of an amateur, came to listen and went away enthusiastic. The loyalty of Tammany and of Underwood and his followers was pledged. McCombs was welcomed with thanks for a hard job well done; but this man, who for months had simmered between the fire of Wilson's righteousness and the caldrons of the party bosses, was in no physical condition to

[1] Robert W. Woolley to the writer.

235

manage a presidential campaign. Many Democrats disliked him and preferred to work under McAdoo. More and more, however, Wilson was showing loyalty of strong fiber. Once he became accustomed to work with a man he hesitated to change for any but the most compelling reasons. And in this case his inclination was supported by expediency, for advisers warned him that to cast aside his campaign manager would be to stir up new charges of ingratitude. Therefore Wilson decided that McCombs should be made chairman of the National Committee, insisting at the same time that McAdoo be vice-chairman.

Soon, however, the feud between the two men became so bitter that Wilson felt that he must go to New York to restore order. Finally, on August 12, McCombs was prostrated with neurasthenia and taken to the Adirondacks and McAdoo became the acting director of the campaign. "It's hard on you, my dear fellow, but you're handling it magnificently," Wilson said to his new manager, with a hand on his shoulder; and McAdoo's energy for selfless service was quickened. From this point on, McCombs was a liability and, moreover, one that had to be carried indulgently and cheerfully.[2] As much as possible, however, Wilson held himself aloof from the details of organization, fearful of making a *faux pas* that might damage the favorable position that he held in the presidential race. More and more, during the autumn campaign, he came to depend on House. "Your advice is as necessary as it is acceptable," he wrote to the Colonel in September. "Here's hoping soon to have you at my elbow."

[2] "Never fear," Wilson wrote to House on September 11, "I shall not be so foolish as to accept McCombs's resignation." From the Adirondacks, McCombs went to Boston to confer with House and won the sympathy of the colonel by talk of perfidy on the part of McAdoo. McCombs asked House to see Wilson in his behalf. (*See* House Diary, Oct. 6, 1921, Yale University Library.) On Wilson's advice, the "wisdom" of which House confessed that he "afterward learned," the colonel investigated the row and found that his sympathy for McCombs was not justified, that "McAdoo was scarcely to blame at all." But Wilson was very careful to avoid criticizing McCombs even to such a close friend as Cleveland Dodge, writing, "He is really very unwell, poor heroic chap." The break with Harvey had taught Wilson that he must avoid even the appearance of ingratitude. But to his young cousin, Fitz William Woodrow, Wilson said apropos McCombs: "Don't ever get so ambitious that you forget you're playing on a team." F. W. Woodrow to the writer, April 12, 1948.

Though McCombs returned to campaign headquarters, his malady continued to express itself in unreasonable irritation, alcoholism, secretiveness, and insane jealousy of McAdoo, who had been receiving newspaper publicity. McAdoo wanted "to fire the whole headquarters crowd," and McCombs would have dismissed McAdoo had Wilson permitted it. The fact that McAdoo had raised less money than McCombs elevated the former in Wilson's esteem, for the Governor suspected, despite emphatic denials, that McCombs had made unethical promises to contributors. "McCombs is in conference most of the time with old-style politicians," House recorded in his diary late in October. "The whole character of the callers has changed since he took charge, and for the worse."

To compose his acceptance speech in tranquillity, Wilson confessed playfully, he ran away early in July from the buzz and glare of Sea Girt, put himself "in retreat" at the home of a friend, and then escaped by sea for six days on Dodge's yacht, carrying under his arm a copy of the party platform and an editorial from the *World* entitled "Planks to be Broken." For relaxation, he could not hear enough of recordings of the Scottish songs of Harry Lauder; and on his return to dry land he entertained reporters with this limerick:

> "I wish that my room had a floor;
> I don't care so much for a door;
> But this walking around
> Without touching the ground
> Is getting to be a damned bore."

When he came back to Sea Girt the candidate thought and prayed over the new responsibility before him. The address of acceptance that he had written was no hodgepodge of "expert" advice or "ghosted" phrasing, but a clear, straightforward exposition of the political philosophy of Woodrow Wilson himself. He was doing his best to belie the picture of a successful presidential candidate that his own yeasty pen had drawn some thirty years before, in *Congressional Government.*[3]

On notification day, August 7, great crowds gave to Sea Girt an air of fiesta. Standing on the porch, responding to the speech of notification, the prophet held out his hand for silence. He conceived that he spoke to "an awakened nation, impatient of partisan make-believe." The country, he believed, stood "confronted with an occasion for constructive statesmanship such as has not arisen since the great days in which her government was set up. Plainly, it is a new age. The tonic of such a time is very exhilarating. It requires self-restraint not to attempt too much, and yet it would be cowardly to attempt too little. The path of duty soberly and bravely trod is the way to service and distinction . . ."

It was a challenge to the restless spirit of a people still growing, as well as to intellects that had matured in wisdom. The voice that already had mastered great congregations in New Jersey was now appealing for the confidence of a people more heterogeneous. The prophetic art that he had cultivated so long and so well, generalities that healed wounds made by the barbs of factional argument, phrases that lifted thought

---

[3] ". . . he should wear a clean and irreproachable insignificance," young Wilson had written, ". . . the shoals of candidacy can be passed only by a light boat which carries little freight and can be turned readily about to suit the intricacies of the passage." *Congressional Government,* pp. 42–43.

above the spite of politics and arrayed it in the robes of statesmanship
—these touched his oratory with the sanction of divinity. Though he
thought the occasion too solemn for extemporaneous speech, he occasionally turned from his script and spoke familiarly. "I feel that I could
be a great deal more interesting," he said, "if I didn't have to read this
speech."

Running quickly over those provisions of the Democratic platform
that he approved, Wilson directed attention to the character and ideals
of the man who must be chosen to effect proposed reforms rather than
to analysis of the reforms themselves. Then, so that his people might
know him through and through, he set forth the ideals of representative
government that were dear to him.

At the end of his address he appealed to all classes and interests to
respect the common good. "We represent the desire to set up an unen-
tangled government," he asserted, "a government that cannot be used
for private purposes, either in the field of business or in the field of
politics . . . It is a great conception, but I am free to serve it, as you
also are. I could not have accepted a nomination which left me bound
to any man or group of men. No man can be just who is not free . . .
Should I be entrusted with the great office of President, I would seek
counsel wherever it could be had upon free terms."

Wilson gave evidence that he was thinking deeply and constructively
on the problems that the progressives of both parties were agitating.
He placed his greatest emphasis on the *bête noire* that he had fought
persistently for thirty years. "Trade is reciprocal," he said; "we cannot
sell unless we also buy." He left no doubt that he would seek to lower
tariffs. He proclaimed: "The tariff was once a bulwark; now it is a
dam." And then, parenthetically, "you can spell the word either way."

With the attitude of one trying to understand and not to blame, he
admitted that "up to a certain point (and only up to a certain point)
great combinations effect great economies in administration, and increase efficiency by simplifying and perfecting organization," that "the
organization of business upon a great scale of cooperation is, up to a
certain point, itself normal and inevitable." But his instinct for equality
of opportunity was too strong to permit him to let the case for trusts
rest on its economic justifications. "Big business is not dangerous because
it is big," he went on, "but because its bigness is an unwholesome
inflation created by privileges and exemptions which it ought not to
enjoy." He prophesied a restoration of "the laws of competition and of
unhampered opportunity, under which men of every sort are set free

and encouraged to enrich the nation," and asserted that the general terms of the federal antitrust law had apparently proved ineffectual.

Moreover, laws must be devised, he said, to prevent associations of capitalists in great financial centers that gave rise to suspicion of a "'money trust,' a concentration of the control of credit which may at any time become infinitely dangerous to free enterprise." Admitting that he did not know enough about banking to be dogmatic, he gave notice that "no mere bankers' plan" for reform would do.

There were other major issues that were challenging the government to act in the common interest. ". . . we have not yet found the rule of right in adjusting the interest of labour and capital," he reminded his people. No law that safeguards "the working people of America—the backbone of the Nation—can properly be regarded as class legislation or as anything but as a measure taken in the interest of the whole people . . ."

In dealing with the issues of the day [4] the prophet was not yet prepared to say that he had found a solution. He was now merely attempting to educate the people in his philosophy of reasoned adjustments of law in the public interest. Standpatters were reassured by the moderateness of his position. Here was a man who was aware of social evils and was temporate in his conception of remedies. In asserting that prices had climbed faster than wages, he had struck a note that rang sweetly in the ears of a people who were awakening to their needs as "consumers." Editors hailed the honesty, ability, and sanity of the speaker. The speech of acceptance became the keynote of Wilson's campaign. He ingeniously presented the same arguments again and again, freshly organized and phrased.

Wilson's tone was the more reassuring to thoughtful Americans in contrast with Bull Moose trumpeting. "After the earthquake a still small voice," the New York *Evening Post* commented. Just the day before the acceptance speech at Sea Girt, Theodore Roosevelt was nominated at Chicago by a convention of progressives who had rallied to that leader to form a third party. It was a constituency of diverse interests and opinions, drawn together by devotion to one of the most compelling

---

[4] As trustees for the Filipinos, Wilson asserted, "America was to set up the rule of justice and of right" in the Philippine Islands. He advocated a parcel post service, and provision for the health of the people. In conservation of the nation's resources, he said that "use and development must go hand in hand. The policy we adopt must be progressive, not negative, merely, as if we did not know what to do. With regard to the development of greater and more numerous waterways and the building up of a merchant marine, we must follow great constructive lines and not fall back upon the cheap device of bounties and subsidies . . . Such expenditures are no largess on the part of the Government; they are national investments."

personalities in American history. Social workers, random reformers, suffragettes, politicians with grievances, and an associate of J. P. Morgan —they were all there to cheer "Teddy." Their hero felt, he said, like a bull moose; and in accepting the nomination of the new party, he bellowed like one. His "Confession of Faith" struck his hearers like an evangelical challenge. It was a two-fisted, straight-from-the-shoulder appeal for a square deal for all the people, from a magnetic personality who in eight years in the Presidency had talked loudly about the curbing of trusts and had achieved little except conservation of certain natural resources.

Two of the great leaders in the early marches of the Western progressives already had fallen in step behind Wilson. At Baltimore, William Jennings Byran had surrendered the party standard to him. Though Senator LaFollette had remained nominally in the Progressive party after the split at Chicago, he thought Roosevelt's desire for a third term egotistical, his record as president opportunistic and unduly cooperative with undesirable corporate monopolies; and privately he expressed the hope that Wilson would "make no mistakes that would result in Roosevelt's election." Moreover, other Republican progressives were swinging toward the Democratic candidate, seeing the issue of the campaign as "Wall Street vs. Wilson."

The die-hard followers of Roosevelt, however, gave voice to the same criticisms of Wilson that George L. Record had raised at first in New Jersey. The educator might be a true progressive, they admitted; but was he not in reality just respectable window-dressing for a shop that was incorrigibly boss-ridden? Pleading fervently for paternalistic laws that would regulate trusts and set fair wages and working hours for women and children, Roosevelt declaimed fanatically about "establishing righteousness," cursed the Democrats, damned their platform as "vicious" and a model of "dangerous insincerity and bad faith," and nominated their candidate for the "Ananias Club." His staff had analyzed Wilson's record and speeches minutely, and hoped that the Democratic candidate, whom they recognized as their strongest foe, would be goaded into intemperate retorts.

Wilson, for his part, remarked that anyone arguing with the Bull Moose must be prepared to "adjourn his manners" and contradict categorical statements. He had protested against Roosevelt's "insane temper of egotism"; but later he exclaimed, "Yet what a glorious egotist he is!" There was a thrill for Wilson in the prospect of battling such a manly adversary. It made the game worth playing.

However much the Princeton scholar might disdain the intellect of his adversary, Wilson did not underestimate the physical and emotional force that he would have to overcome through appeals to reason. He counted President Taft out of the running. "The people will have none of him," Wilson thought. But of Roosevelt he wrote, late in August: ". . . just what will happen, as between Roosevelt and me, with party lines utterly confused and broken, is all guesswork. It depends upon what people are thinking and purposing whose opinions do not get into the newspapers—and I am by no means confident. He appeals to their imagination; I do not. He is a real, vivid person, whom they have seen and shouted themselves hoarse over and voted for, millions strong; I am a vague, conjectural personality, more made up of opinions and academic prepossessions than of human traits and red corpuscles. We shall see what will happen!"

Actually, Roosevelt's tricks of oratory were wearing thin. He fought by the law of the African jungle in which he loved to hunt, and often evoked sympathy for the object of his attack. The common touch that he had once exercised so masterfully had grown unpleasantly prickly with vituperation and braggadocio. "He has promised too often the millennium," Wilson observed. Moreover, Roosevelt's record as president had exposed him to accusations of opportune action at the expense of devotion to principle. He had definitely aligned himself with imperialists and advocates of a big navy, and thus forfeited the confidence of idealistic workers for world peace. But perhaps most damaging of all, he was challenging the American tradition that so far had forbidden more than eight years in the Presidency for any man.

In contrast, Wilson had made few enemies among progressives and his leadership in New Jersey had endeared him to Americans who put more faith in achievement than in words. More than forty thousand Republicans joined the Wilson Progressive Republican League and idealistic college men turned to the Democratic candidate in droves. Moreover, the chief financial support of the campaign came from new blood. Wilson stood strictly on his policy of accepting no contributions from men whose names had become politically bankrupt. At his direction, his financial managers were the first in an American presidential campaign to control expenditures under a budget. Wilson encouraged them to make "dollar drives" for "the people's candidate" and, enlisting the support of newspapers and banks in organizing such appeals, they took in almost a third of a total income of $1,110,952 in sums under $100. On the other hand, more than a third was contributed by forty wealthy givers—men from whom Wilson felt that gifts could be accepted without incurring embarrassing obligations. Enterprising men of proved intellect, drawn to an inspiring leader, were supplanting hacks, bosses, and demagogues in the inner councils of the party.[5]

Slipping away from Sea Girt occasionally in the late summer—but not always eluding his "keepers," as he called the newsmen—the Governor would spend a weekend in covert in New York, reveling in a gay show at the Hippodrome or in Isadora Duncan's dancing, and then sleeping around the clock at his club. He had come to find relaxation, too, in sources as diverse as detective stories and a translation of Chinese philosophy. To his lady friends he would quote respectfully from an Oriental sage. In spite of his resources for diversion, however, Wilson could not forget his aging arteries. He was a confirmed valetudinarian and still felt that the strain of the Presidency would take his life.

The candidate consented to deliver three speeches in New Jersey in August, but they were more polished and pleasant than moving. His thought floundered for a while in the gulf between his faith in local government and his recognition of the need for a strong executive, between his expressed fear that "government regulation will enslave us" and the rational conclusion that only by regulation could the power of monopoly be curbed. He was fearful that he might seem to be dividing the nation into "classes" and to be appealing to one against another. This was one thing, he said, that he prayed God he might never do.

Some critics found it hard to distinguish between the progressivism of Roosevelt and that of Wilson.[6] The Democratic candidate had criti-

---

[5] In New Jersey, Sugar Jim Smith tried to run again for the United States Senate and Wilson scourged him out of politics. William Hughes was nominated by a vote of almost two to one.

In New York, Wilson publicly called for a progressive candidate for governor and used his influence against the nomination of Dix by Tammany; but House, who was equally anti-Tammany but who had learned by experience "to work with the best material at hand," persuaded Wilson to compromise and to let a "bossless convention" nominate another Tammany brave.

[6] The appeal of Roosevelt, the New Yorker, was largely to urban voters and industrial workers. Having wandered far from his earlier conviction that individuals must work out their own destiny, Roosevelt seemed now to be leaning toward the sort of state socialism that had been introduced in Germany. The committee on resolutions of the Progressive party had approved a platform plank that would put teeth in the Sherman Antitrust Law. But George W. Perkins, Morgan partner and financial godfather of the party—a man who had lost the confidence of the people when Charles Evans Hughes had charged him with questionable business practices—had vetoed the antitrust proposal. And giving the dubious excuse that he feared the Sherman Law might be weakened, Roosevelt had concurred. He seemed willing to accept trusts, under safeguards to be imposed by government; and his supporters argued that there was no danger in having the people's affairs administered by a government that they themselves controlled. See George E. Mowry, *Theodore Roosevelt and the Progressive Movement*, pp. 270–71, and Richard Hofstadter, *The Age of Reform*, pp. 222–48.

cized Roosevelt's administration for its "passion for regulative legislation"; and in his speech of acceptance he had promised to restore "the laws of competition and of unhampered opportunity." But he was not well enough versed in the intricacies of trust regulation to combat his rival convincingly. A virile, disinterested intellect was needed to crystallize the virtuous impulses and tentative thoughts that were being generated by the prophet's will to serve.

In the fall of 1912 the counsel that Wilson needed was found in the mind of Louis Dembitz Brandeis. This brilliant lawyer belonged to a Hebrew family that for four generations had known the bitterness of war, revolution, and oppression. In his practice of corporation law, and in preparing lectures on business law for college students, Brandeis's sensitive mind perceived differences between legal justice and moral law. The strike of steelworkers at Homestead, the pitched battle of organized laborers with a private army of organized capital, set him thinking beyond the letter of the common law and in terms of the common welfare. He resolved to allow himself the luxury of helping to solve public problems, without compensation.

Brandeis thought of himself as a conservative, a conservator of the Constitution by the exercise of eternal vigilance against socialism, on the one hand, and unproductive, inefficient private monopoly of economic power, at the other extreme. He pleaded for the regulation of competition voluntarily, as far as possible, through cooperation within each industry; but by law when necessary in order to preserve equality of opportunity. In pursuit of these ideals he had subjected himself to the stern discipline that was required to walk the precarious tightrope of individual enterprise over the widening economic chasm. Nevertheless, when he pleaded in the public interest he was accused of inconsistency with arguments that he had previously put forth in behalf of private clients. Like Woodrow Wilson, he became a center of violent controversy. In Boston he was hated alike by the Irish bosses of the Democratic party and by reactionary bankers and lawyers.

Brandeis was wooed by Roosevelt's party, but thought of T.R. as a trumpeter of progressive impulses who had outlived his usefulness and of Wilson as "a man of substance" who could effectively put theory into action. A week after the Baltimore convention, Brandeis strongly endorsed Wilson. Early in August the two exchanged letters, and late in the month the lawyer was summoned to Sea Girt. The men talked for hours, mainly on the problem of curbing monoplies. "It seems to me," Brandeis wrote afterward, "that he has the qualities for an ideal

President—strong, simple, and truthful, able, open-minded, eager to learn and deliberate." And Wilson saw in the people's attorney a soul that shared his aspirations and a scintillating intellect.

In talks with Brandeis and in reading articles that the lawyer had written, Wilson found the technical advice that he needed on the problem of monopoly. On the issue that was foremost in the minds of sincere progressives, he could now attack the program of Roosevelt.

Beginning on Labor Day, the prophet spoke with new assurance, explaining the difference between the "New Freedom," as the Wilsonian program came to be called, and the "New Nationalism" of Roosevelt. Addressing ten thousand laborers at Buffalo, Wilson bitterly attacked Roosevelt's policy of retaining a protective tariff and legalizing monopolies under government supervision. The great monopolies were likened by Wilson to "so many cars of juggernauts" and he did not "look forward with pleasure to the time when the juggernauts are licensed and driven by commissioners of the United States." Regulation of trusts by "a self-appointed divinity" or a "board of experts," he asserted, gave to the "wage slaves" no choice but that of involuntary servitude. "If you want a great struggle for liberty that will cost you blood," Wilson told the workers, "adopt the Roosevelt regulation programme, put yourself at the disposal of a Providence resident at Washington, and then see what will come of it . . ." He appealed to the common sense that he believed to reside in every responsible adult.

To seek specific ways of regulating competition without bringing government monopoly, Wilson went again to Brandeis. He was given a large dossier of papers on which he drew freely; and the advice of the counselor was given a bitter-sweet flavoring that made it no less palatable to Wilson. "I have no doubt," Brandeis wrote, "that your definite declaration on the lines indicated in this letter will make some enemies, as well as friends, but I assume that you have considered that matter adequately." Both the record and the philosophy of this legal genius were congenial, and he thanked Brandeis cordially.

In September the candidate set out on the first of two swings through the West. He was given an old, wooden private car that was attached to a slow train, and its frequent stopping made him talk from the rear platform more often than he wished. But in all his speeches on this trip he managed to set forth his ideas in ways so varied that even his traveling companions were not bored. Nine newsmen traveled with him, and clamored for advance drafts of his speeches; but after devoting two days to dictating addresses, he exclaimed: "By thunder, I've made my last speech to a stenographer!" He liked to talk, he said, right out of his mind as it was working at the time. Even when scripts were prepared, he did not follow them but used a few notes instead; and so, to protect him against misquotation, a recorder was employed to set down every word as he spoke it. He was grimly amused when told that his views on national politics, which seemed to him of more than passing importance, could compete with stories on the World Series only by prior reservation of newspaper space. He chatted with reporters who accompanied him, joked with them about their fortunes at poker, and amused them with anecdotes from his notebook collections. He was always solicitous for their comfort. Once, after a day of speechmaking, he said, "I'm going to recuperate by having some fun with with you boys"; and he sat up and swapped stories until nearly two o'clock. They marveled at his coolness under fire, his perspective. "It seems as if I can see myself and the campaign from a distance," he once remarked.

In South Dakota he gave voice to Brandeis's contention that Roosevelt's proposal to legalize trusts had originated in the minds of the president of the United States Steel Corporation and George W. Perkins. Conceding that "for all I know" it might be an honest proposal, Wilson argued that the effect of government sanction of this monopoly would be "to save the United States Steel Corporation from the necessity of doing its business better than its competitors." It was not mere bigness to which he was objecting—he knew that many voters worshiped bigness—but monopoly, which Americans hated because it crushed such competition as helped to maintain economic efficiency and industrial freedom. Yet he still distrusted federal regulation of trusts. "The history of liberty is the history of the limitation of governmental power," he said on September 15 to the New York Press Club. And Roosevelt took this vivid assertion out of context and declared that to limit the power of the people's government was in effect to deny the citizens the right to check monopoly. Nevertheless, Wilson persisted in his argument, conferring with Brandeis again at the end of September and declaring to a New England audience: "I don't know enough to take care of the people of the United States."

In the speeches in the West, Wilson was slow to make contact with the mind of Main Street. When he made an obvious effort to lower the tone of his remarks, the effect was not happy; "let Roosevelt tell it to the Marines," he suggested awkwardly in one descent into the vernacular. His exalted concept of the office for which he was now a candidate made the gulf between him and his audiences wider than it had been in the New Jersey electioneering. His ingenuity was taxed to find ways of winning votes without offense to his concept of the dignity of the Presidency.

At Scranton, Pennsylvania, on August 23, he spoke in a hall with bad acoustics to an audience already wearied by other speakers. Appealing to the underdog—"the man who is knocking and fighting at the closed doors of opportunity" —he identified his personal revolt with the cause of all who were fighting monopoly. "I do feel proud of this," he said; "that no law, no rule of blood, no privilege of money, picked me out to be a candidate even . . . it is a fine system where some remote, severe, academic schoolmaster may become President of the United States." Then he went on to declare that, whether elected or not, he would find some way to keep on fighting. His audience cheered wildly.

Toward the end of September he went to New England, where the labor question had been dramatized by a violent strike at Lawrence. There he fitted his talks carefully to the biases of his audiences, assuring the people of the insurance center of Hartford that "the ancient traditions of a people are its ballast," telling the factory workers of Fall River that "we ought to hold a brief for the legal right of labor to organize," making a slashing attack at Bridgeport on "the money trust," but mollifying Boston investors by assuring them that he was not "fighting the trusts" but was "trying to put them upon an equality with everybody else." He was trying to reassure all of his congregation, to let every soul know that its prayer was heard by a leader who was both sympathetic and just. He waved gaily and threw out campaign buttons to crowds that gathered to catch a glimpse of him. Addressing admirers perched on boxcars in a railroad yard at Willimantic, he saluted them as "fellow-citizens and gentlemen in the pit, and ladies and gentlemen in the boxes," his literary mind not asking, apparently, how many of the boxcar sitters knew what "the pit" was.

Though he could not accept all the invitations to speak that came to him from local Democratic leaders, the oratorical artist in him was made supremely happy by the frequency of his bookings. In a flush of satisfaction over the feeling that he was winning because the people understood him, he gained seven and one-half pounds in two months. But the pace was grueling. Twice he narrowly escaped serious injury: once when a freight car sideswiped his Pullman, broke the windows and tore away the brass rail on the rear platform; again, when a rut in the road threw him against the top of the automobile in which he was riding and stitches had to be taken in his scalp. Outdoor speeches were always an ordeal for him, and after an attempt to make a huge audience hear without an amplifier, he complained that his voice "went wheezy and had no volume or resonance in it."

At times the whisperings of malevolent foes made him sick at heart. In December of 1911, New York newspapers had reported that Mary Allen Peck entered a libel for divorce against her husband, from whom she had been long estranged; and in 1912 she won her suit and reverted to the name of her first husband, Hulbert. The tongues of gossip had wagged damagingly, perverting facts that none of the principals tried to conceal from their true friends. To acquaintances in Bermuda the lady had often read letters from her dear friend at Princeton, and sometimes she lent them; and Wilson read her replies to the circle of family and friends in the house on Cleveland Lane. Shocked by the publicity given to her suit for divorce and by the malice of rumormongers, Mary Allen Hulbert told him that she raged inwardly, and sometimes laughed—it seemed so absurd. When an undertone of grief crept into her gay letters, Wilson responded with chivalrous loyalty, told her how much it meant to have a true friend, urged her to release her spirit by confiding in him without restraint, comforted her with the reminder that the divorce proceedings could reveal nothing to be ashamed of. Again, recklessly projecting his own ideals into the character of another, he created a beautiful figment of virtue set free. Her inner resources were unparalleled, he assured her, and she would emerge from her ordeal finer than ever. He confessed that his pastoral pride was touched by his success in drawing out the sweetness of her nature.

Political foes gleefully misunderstood. In April of 1912, Wilson's valise was stolen at Chicago; and apparently suspecting an attempt to find incriminating letters, he said very gravely to his family circle: "No letter of mine, nothing I have ever written, could hurt my reputation if published." But scurrilous minds, and politicians who pandered to such, continued to whisper; and the aspersions were the more insidious because they were confined to conversational sewers. Theodore Roosevelt himself had written similar letters to "Dear Maria"—Mrs. Bellamy Storer; but he delivered the unkindest slur of all against his Democratic rival. "It wouldn't work," he squeaked. "You can't cast a man as Romeo who looks and acts so much like an apothecary's clerk."

Toward the end of September the rumor reached Wilson that a scandal was being fabricated against him. When some of his political associates questioned him, he solemnly assured McAdoo that he had never written a word to any woman that he would not read to his wife. House understood, and explained: "We Southerners like to write mush notes." When the canard ran to the effect that Thomas Peck had insinuated certain things to a certain judge, Wilson suspected the integrity of the magistrate and of another who was in a position to give evidence, criticized a judge whom he thought ungallant to his friend, wanted to break the neck of one of her persecutors.[7]

Sometimes it seemed hardly worth while to fight on in a world so sordid. Halfway through the campaign, Wilson protested to Mary Peck —now Mary Hulbert—that "there would be no bearing its tremendous burdens if there were not the element of large duty and serviceableness in it. There *are* great issues, the greatest imaginable, issues of life and death, as it seems to me, so far as the sound political life of the country is concerned; and I therefore keep heart and strength." The blood of his pioneering ancestors was still stirring in the migrating mind. Like a frontiersman, he would clear away the dead timber in the political wilderness, would plow and harrow and plant seed that season and climate demanded, would tend good old roots and try to make them blossom more gloriously.

Millions of hearts were touched by the message of the prophet as he campaigned through the West in October. At the baseball park at Indianapolis the throng was so large that all could not hear; and when a cry of "louder" arose, a man near the platform yelled: "Never mind, Woody old boy. If they can't hear, we'll tell them about it tomorrow." [8] The candidate's eyes glistened as he swept the crowd toward him. "To my mind," he said, "it is a choice between Tweedledum and Tweedledee to choose between the leader of one branch of the Republican party and the leader of the other branch of the Republican party." Asserting that Roosevelt was not a genuine progressive, he asked his hearers whether they could see "any breach anywhere in the Democratic ranks."

The *Star* reported that the speech at Indianapolis was Wilson's "first real campaign punch," and afterward the candidate said to a newsman: "Did you hear? They called me 'Woody'!" He seemed to the journalist

---

[7] The unpleasantness of the Peck divorce is suggested by an item in the gossip column of *Town Topics* of June 24, 1909: "Pittsfield, Mass., is now devouring with great glee the contents of the little notes which Thomas D. Peck has been sending out to tradespeople carrying information that he has made Mrs. Peck a liberal allowance and that hereafter she will pay all bills which she may contract . . ."

It seemed to Mary Peck that the very walls of her home reeked with suspicion, jealousy, and melancholy. Mary Allen Hulbert to R. S. Baker, July 28, 1928.

[8] John W. Davidson, Jr., *A Crossroads of Freedom*, p. 318.

a jolly fellow who embraced throngs with the same thrill that comes in a first dance with a beautiful girl.

In Nebraska the candidate's throat was filled with dust and in ten talks his voice was worn to a hoarse whisper; but Byran was ably supplementing his efforts, averaging ten speeches a day for seven weeks, imploring his loyal Nebraskans to do twice as much for Wilson as they ever did for Byran and telling newsmen that Wilson was an expert campaigner and knew how to adapt himself to crowds. Resting on the Sabbath, as was his custom, the candidate stayed at Bryan's home at Lincoln; and the prophets went together to a Presbyterian service, the Great Commoner serving communion. A journalist begged him to pose for a picture with Bryan, shaking hands. The Nebraskan held out his, willingly; but Wilson said, "No, I'll not pose. It's too artificial."

At Denver, where they had not forgotten his great speech on the English Bible, Wilson paraded the streets between thousands of enthusiasts.[9] At St. Louis he encountered bagpipers, bands, tooting horns, and torches flaming in a procession four miles long. Men rioted to force their way into the packed Coliseum. At Chicago scores of thousands stood outdoors in a cold rain to cheer the candidate: offices were closed, streets festooned with streamers. In these cities, and at Cleveland, Wilson responded as well as his failing voice would permit. Stopping at Springfield, Illinois, he asserted that Roosevelt was "a very erratic comet now sweeping across the horizon," that the Democratic party was now more faithful than its opponent to the principles of Abraham Lincoln. Fatiguing as it was to throat and nerves, the Western trip helped the prophet to share the idealism of his people. His spirits were lifted, his resolution strengthened. Having spoken more than thirty times in ten days, he rested at home in mid-October.

While Wilson's fervor had deepened, Roosevelt's tactics were becoming more and more hysterical. The Bull Moose was using all his talent for showmanship. Climbing into the cab of a railroad engine, he ran it down the track, much to the discomfort of the passengers. When wounded in the chest by a fanatic at Milwaukee, he persisted in filling a speaking engagement at the risk of death. Wilson sent a message of personal sympathy. Colonel House, who liked to say that "the best politics is to do the right thing," went against the opinion of the campaign committee in urging their candidate to make the chivalrous

---

[9] In this visit to Denver, Wilson became specific in naming conditions that in his view led to monopoly and should be controlled by law: viz., collusion in fixing high prices, pre-emption of raw material, espionage, cutthroat competition, restrictive contracts.

gesture of canceling his speaking engagements until Roosevelt recovered; and Wilson saw the political effectiveness of such a move as
well as its fairness. "Teddy will have apoplexy when he hears of this,"
he chuckled. He did, however, fill engagements already made, directing
his fire against Taft and the conservatives rather than against the
wounded leader of the Progressives. When Roosevelt, resuming his
campaign, advocated antitrust laws so definite that judgments would
not be exercised by any man or men, Wilson did not make capital of
this shift toward his own position.

In Delaware the Democratic prophet paid tribute to La Follette, who
was now wholeheartedly behind Wilson, and at Pittsburgh he harked
back again to the American Dream, maintaining that it had been kept
alive by the Democrats through a period of repression by monopolies.
"The Democratic party," he asserted, "has stood steadfast in a deeprooted faith . . . a faith as old as human liberty. It is . . . the only
faith that has ever made the intolerable burden of life possible to bear,
namely, the faith that every man ought to have the interest of every
other man at his heart. The faith that would set up a government in
the world where the average man, the plain man, the common man,
the ignorant man, the unaccomplished man, the poor man had a voice
equal to the voice of anybody else in the settlement of the common
affairs, an ideal never before realized in the history of the world."

The shooting of Roosevelt was a reminder that every presidential
candidate lived under the shadow of violent death. After an anonymous
Italian had threatened to "shoot Wilson the same as Roosevelt was shot,"
Ellen Wilson did not sleep well until her husband was placed by
Colonel House under the guard of Captain Bill McDonald of the Texas
Rangers—a crack shot who was said to be able to hit a mosquito's eye
at fifty paces. During the closing weeks of the campaign this guardian
dogged the steps of the candidate, kept his eyes open, his mouth shut,
and his finger on the trigger of his "artillery." When dense crowds
hemmed in the candidate, Captain Bill lowered his shoulders and
plowed a way through.

Even a bodyguard, however, could not protect Wilson from the
heckling of special pleaders and fanatics who revived many canards
that had proved effective among certain groups of voters. But Wilson
had learned to laugh at the charges. "If all these fabrications could be
brought together," he wrote to McAdoo on October 23, "they would
leave a very flat taste in the mouth, for they would entirely neutralize
one another and prove that I was nothing and everything. I am a normal

man, following my own natural course of thought, playing no favorites, and trying to treat every creed and class with impartiality and respect." Through the campaign he had held himself accountable to history. Someday, he told one audience, a quiet jury would sit in a room, surrounded by books and documents, and judge him. "I think of the anticipated verdict of another generation," he said, "and I know that the only measure and standard by which a man can rise or fall is the standard of absolute integrity; that he can deceive nobody but himself and his own generation for a little space."

He had revealed himself to the people as he was—compassionate pastor, philosopher, historian, and orator, a man of intellect who could be depended on to act in the national interest. On October 26 he published a recapitulation of his campaign arguments: The nation must be free in order to be strong; and monopolies, protective tariffs, and political graft were the greatest obstacles to freedom. "Bosses cannot exist without business alliances," he said. "With them politics is hardly distinguishable from business."

By the last week of the campaign it seemed obvious that Wilson would be the winner. Gambling odds were 5 to 1 in his favor, and his final public addresses were saluted with all the ardor that crowds can bestow on a man crowned with success and riding to power. On October 31 the campaign came to its climax in New York City. The night before, the Bull Moosers had given Roosevelt an ovation that lasted forty-five minutes. To outdo them, the Democracy yelled and whistled for more than an hour. Even Bryan at the height of his power had evoked no outburst like this. After sixteen lean years, the wolves of the party smelled red meat. Overwhelmed and bewildered, gazing at Ellen Wilson as if to restore his equilibrium, the candidate forgot what he had planned to say, gave a rambling summary of the issues, and confidently put the case in the hands of "the jury." The Progressives had been inspired personally by their leader. "Follow, follow," they had sung, "we will follow Roosevelt; anywhere he leads we will follow him." But the enthusiasm of the Democrats, Wilson told his New York audience, thrilled him because it was a demonstration for a cause and not for a man. "What the Democratic party proposes to do," he told the people, "is to go into power and do the things that the Republican party has been talking about doing for sixteen years." He issued a national appeal for support for the Democratic candidates for the Congress; and the last few days of the campaign found him pleading before the voters of New Jersey for the party ticket. Then he retreated to the sequestered house on Cleveland Lane, to sleep soundly and await the verdict of the nation.

At ten o'clock on election day, November 5, the Democratic candidate walked down familiar Princeton streets to the polls in the firehouse. Refusing a preferred place in the line of voters, he cast his ballot. In the afternoon McAdoo and Josephus Daniels, for whom the Governor had developed "a real affection," joined the family, and the men took a long walk to the historic sites of the town. In a university building Wilson showed them the framed diploma of James Madison, the only Princeton man ever elected to the Presidency.

After supper the family circle gathered for a reading from Browning. As favorable returns came in, Wilson's face turned grave. At ten o'clock a message came to Ellen Wilson. Placing her hand lightly on the shoulder of her husband, she said: "My dear, I want to be the first to congratulate you." He took her hand and they stood in silence, but her serene face seemed to say: "I believed he could and he has." A half hour later McCombs confirmed the news and reported that the election of a Democratic Congress seemed assured also.

The covenant was now sealed; and Woodrow Wilson accepted the mandate of the people as solemnly as he had regarded his profession of faith, in adolescence, in the humble chapel of the Columbia Theological Seminary. But now there was no time for meditation. The college bell was pealing. More than a thousand students, waving flags and torches, were cheering in his yard, singing "Old Nassau." He went to the front door, stood on an old, broken rocking chair that his friends held firm. The light of a red flare fell on his face. When the boys saw him, they whooped jubilantly. The jaunty front that he had put on in the campaign wilted now. Tears filled his eyes, and for a few minutes he was silent. Then, with such emotion as he had felt when he bade farewell to his university congregation, he said: "Gentlemen, I am sincerely glad to see you . . . There is so much to reconstruct, and reconstruction must be undertaken so justly and by slow process of common counsel, that a generation or two must work out the result to be achieved . . . I summon you for the rest of your lives to work to set this government forward by processes of justice, equity, and fairness. I myself have no feeling of triumph tonight. I have a feeling of solemn responsibility."

As they swarmed up to him, Wilson shook hands with each briskly, thanked them "for caring so much." To his best friends, regardless of rank, he said heartily, "Go on inside." [10] Intimates went to the dining

[10] Mrs. George McLean Harper and F. C. MacDonald, who were present, to the writer.

room to enjoy Ellen Wilson's hospitality, and soon the house was seething with people and buzzing with talk. The President-elect escaped to bed as quickly as he could; and on the morrow, which President Hibben had declared a university holiday, Wilson went out to watch football practice.

When the final tally was made, it showed Wilson commanding 435 electoral votes, against 88 for Roosevelt and 8 for Taft. His popular vote was only a plurality and was less than that of Byran in the election of 1908. Like Jefferson and Lincoln, Woodrow Wilson had profited by a split in the opposing party. The victory was not of the Democracy, but rather a triumph of the spirit of the times and of a man's sincere sharing of that spirit. The validity of Edmund Burke's philosophy of representative government was being proved on the American scene. The needs of the people were to be served by reasoned change in the laws. There would not be another revolution now, or another civil war.

CHAPTER XV

TIME TO THINK

THE VERY DAY after the election, full consciousness of the weight of his mantle fell upon the prophet. Still as intellect-conscious as when he had first boasted to his father that he had a mind, Wilson felt that the issues of the campaign had been vague and nothing of importance had been settled. The prophecy of Henry Adams had been fulfilled: the progressives had voted for "anybody sooner than Taft"; the conservatives had "let in anybody sooner than Theodore." This political shindy had not satisfied a man who aspired to debate great issues in parliamentary dignity.

To his family he remarked: "One is considered queer in America if one requires time for concentrated thought." And yet he said boldly to the people: ". . . the time has come now to do a lot of thinking." Wilson now considered himself free to let his mind work at its natural pace and depth, at whatever cost in popularity.

However, some fifteen thousand messages came in and challenged his desire to meditate. Many of them were more concerned with preferment of the writers than with congratulation of the recipient. McCombs brought a list of Democrats "entitled to immediate and generous consideration" and reminded Wilson that party men wished to have their say about appointments. But the President-elect replied icily: "I must have a chance to think."

To cut himself loose from such stifling concerns, Wilson escaped to Bermuda. There—in a cottage [1] "free to the wind, open to the sun"— he relaxed and played with those dearest to him. He was getting "many kinks" out of his head, he wrote to McCombs. He wore old clothes, did the family marketing by bicycle, and brought food home in a basket hung on the handlebars. Sometimes the Wilsons would picnic on a beach, and he would display the treasures of scenery that he had discovered in previous visits. Then coming home for tea they would criticize canvases that Ellen Wilson had painted; and at supper, sitting

[1] With his wife and two younger daughters Wilson occupied the home of Mary Allen Hulbert, who was in New York. Margaret Wilson stayed at New York to continue her singing lessons.

by candlelight on a porch above lapping waters, they tried to see into the future. Wilson had just been plagued by neuritis and was often attacked by sickening headaches; and for several days after reaching Bermuda he suffered from indigestion. His wife watched over him anxiously, controlled his diet, stood behind his chair and massaged the back of his neck. In spite of the flushes of good health that had always come to him when he had dropped administrative cares and vacationed out of doors or indulged in the give-and-take of electioneering, Wilson had not been able to escape the invalidism that had been fixed on him six years before.

Even in the island haven his privacy was invaded. The Bermudians let him alone; but the soldierly governor general, who lived in a guarded palace and ruled some twenty thousand souls with Old World pomp, bowed to the civilian leader of a hundred million Americans by rapping at the kitchen door of his cottage. However, Wilson was so annoyed by curious tourists that he decided to forsake his bicycle for a carriage and to follow the local custom of "hanging out the basket" to signify that he was not at home and callers might leave their cards.

Trailed by news hawks who sought world-shaking import in every move, he indulged an impulse to tease them.[2] "Gentleman," the President-elect said to them one day, "you have interrupted me in the preparation of an important state paper." And then, as they apologized and backed away, he grinned and explained that he was drawing up a "domestic formula" for Mrs. Wilson to follow in entertaining the governor general at tea. At other times he would greet journalists with a look that led the unwary to hope for great revelations but was interpreted by veterans to mean that he had just made a discovery of colossal unimportance. Once he confided that by looking sideways at the waves on the South Shore, he and his daughters had tested and proved the theory that if one looks at a thing with head on one side, or upside down, the result is a compressed and comprehensive view of the beauties of the object. Ellen Wilson entertained journalists so delightfully that they were diverted from their quest. But let a reporter overstep a line of decorum that Wilson defined, and his wrath would rise quickly.

2 At least once during the election campaign Wilson had delighted in deflating importunate and self-important newsmen. He took joy in his ability to manipulate words so that he could lead reporters to delude themselves. Colonel House called it "grazing the truth." Once two young cubs who had naïvely fallen into a trap set for them tried to rebuke Wilson by giving him a cold shoulder, and he had laughed uproariously and said to them, "Oh, come off your perch." See C. W. Thompson, *Presidents I've Known*, pp. 297–303. It was the feeling of this correspondent that Wilson had no desire to be mean or tricky, but was playing a game with words, as he had played in boyhood with his father.

One day, as he was courteously asking cameramen not to photograph the ladies of his family, a cad aimed his lens at Jessie Wilson. The cheeks of the outraged father flamed, he clenched his fists and started toward the man; and then, remembering himself, he shouted: "You're no gentlemen! I want to give you the worst thrashing you've ever had in your life; and what's more, I'm perfectly able to do it!" However, the intrusions that fame had brought upon him did not break the spell of the island. It was still, to him, a fairyland where make-believe was real, a place in which it was almost impossible to do anything but play, where one could lie abed in the afternoon and savor Kipling's *Rewards and Fairies.* Only by closing the blinds and turning on the electric lights, he said, could he recall the United States and its business.

After a few days of rest the President-elect devoted himself to answering messages from those whom he esteemed. He assured his classmate Hiram Woods that he wished him never in any circumstances to drop the old epithets of intimacy. Replying to Dean Fine's congratulations, he wrote of "the old days in Princeton, days of strain and pain . . . days when men were bound together by something more than ordinary affection," a feeling that "seemed to have iron put into it by the influences of strong conviction." He wrote affectionately to his nephew, George Howe, and invited him to visit at the White House. The President-elect yearned to be the same "Tommie" Wilson, the same Uncle Woodrow, unaffected by pride of position.

In the clear calm of life on Bermuda, Woodrow and Ellen Wilson meditated upon what would face them in Washington. He contemplated "plunging into the maelstrom" with many grave thoughts. "But having sought the opportunity, I must face it and meet it with the best that is in me," he wrote to George Howe.

In his island retreat the President-elect read a novel entitled *Philip Dru, Administrator,*[3] which Colonel House had written and given to him just before he left New York. Hoping to give wide circulation to his ideas for progressive federal legislation, the Colonel, in a vague and experimental way, had tried to express them through a fictional hero who forcibly seized the government of his state and became a beneficent dictator. In that position he established a league of nations that was based on Anglo-Saxon solidarity. Moreover, he destroyed trusts by abolishing protective tariffs and worked out a progressive income tax and a banking system that presaged the Federal Reserve. Believing that

[3] House's book, published in 1912, was dictated hurriedly, lacked literary merit, and did not circulate widely. House intimated that his hero was "all that he himself would like to be but was not." *See* Alexander L. and Juliette L. George, *W. W. and Colonel House,* p. 131.

"labor is no longer to be classed as an inert commodity to be bought and sold by the law of supply and demand," House's hero worked out a plan for social security.

Returning from Bermuda with idealistic fervor refreshed, Wilson gloried in using the prestige of a president-elect to strike out for what he conceived to be the interest of the people of New Jersey. During the Governor's absence, Tumulty had had to fight—figuratively and literally —to prevent the election of a Nugent-Hague man as speaker of the Assembly. Wilson returned in time, however, to oppose State Controller Edwards for the office of state treasurer. But he could not overcome the opposition of the bosses to proposals for revising the constitution of the state and transferring the power of drawing juries from the sheriffs to a governor's commission.[4]

Wilson's last months as governor, like his closing years as president of Princeton, were marked by impetuousness as the aspirations of his spirit broke through the restraint of administrative responsibility. He seemed determined to assert that he was a free individual, that his pledge of emancipation from control by all pressure groups was not just political talk. Speaking briefly at Trenton, he told the party men that only progressives would be chosen by him to guard the interests of the people. Goaded by assertions of Roosevelt's managers that New Jersey was the mother of trusts and that the Governor had failed to alter the laws, Wilson had the chancellor draw up remedial legislation and espoused it in his annual message, on January 14, Seven bills[5] were drafted to curb price fixing and other acts of collusion in restraint of trade. Applying Wilson's doctrine that "guilt is personal," this legislation provided for the fine and imprisonment of guilty directors of corporations. The measures were forced through the legislature by the Governor in February. The "Seven Sisters Acts" gave warning of what might soon be expected on a national scale if offending trusts did not put their houses in order of their own free will. Sincere progressives could not forget that, in two years under Woodrow Wilson, New Jersey had made greater strides toward good government than under any other governor.

---

[4] Wilson left the White House in the spring of 1913 to take the stump in New Jersey in behalf of these reforms. Finally, the legislature passed a compromise measure for jury reform that was declared unconstitutional by the courts.

[5] George Record, who had drafted the earlier reform bills and was not consulted about the "Seven Sisters Acts," felt that they were "stupid laws." Record to R. S. Baker, April 6, 1926. The effect of the laws, which followed interpretations of the antitrust laws by the United States Supreme Court, was to make corporations seek refuge in Delaware. The legislature began to amend them in 1915 and repealed them in 1920.

Now that he was no longer dependent on newsmen for favorable interpretation to the voters, the President-elect made less effort to conceal his scorn and irritation at their tactics. Nothing vexed Wilson more than self-appointed oracles who ventured to speak for him, unless it was opponents who strove to embarrass him by quoting his past words against his present beliefs. When a reporter pestered him for news of his choices for the Cabinet, he exploded with "Damn it, man, can't you take me as you find me?" and in the next breath he begged pardon for "blowing up."

In Bermuda he remarked, offhand, that it would be better if the inauguration could be held later than March 4 and was amazed when this personal whim was cabled to New York. Good copy became scarce, as the door closed on Wilson's policy of "pitiless publicity"; and in the absence of fact, reporters indulged in speculations that angered the Governor. In the last days at Trenton, there descended a cold front that presaged chilly press conferences in the White House.

Colonel House's apartment in New York was one of the few havens in which Wilson felt secure enough to express himself freely. A year after he met the Colonel, Wilson had had enough doubts about his friend to ask Captain Bill McDonald whether House had always been successful in his Texas campaigns and what sort of men he had chosen. But now Wilson knew that he could trust both the information and the judgment of the "Little Wizard" in New York. House could see so much more than other men and report it so much better, always getting the right point! The hand of the Colonel was constantly on the shaping of the President's Cabinet.

More than once the Wilsons ran up to New York for a night with the Houses and went to the theater with them. The President-elect was embarrassed by the applause of the audience. The colonel prompted him to bow; and after complying he spoke to his host, whose father was English born and who had gone to school in England, of the sense of fair play that prevented theatergoers at London from staring at royalty. Returning to House's rooms, the men would munch sandwiches and chat as Southern gentlemen.

The Colonel was impressed by his friend's essential gallantry. The talk drifted to the subject of war; and Wilson, though he thought it economically "ruinous," asserted that there was no more glorious way to die than in battle. "White lies" were discussed: Wilson thought them justified when the honor of a woman was concerned and also when the welfare of a people was at stake. But when House dissented mildly and suggested silence as a better means of defending secrets of public policy, Wilson agreed. Princeton affairs were reviewed without bitterness, and the President-elect expressed a yearning for ten million dollars to buy the university and make it what he thought it should be. On another evening he spoke to House of a college friend who harrowed him by complaints of huge responsibility and almost certain failure. As for himself, he confessed, he would lose his reason if ever he gave way to his apprehensions. House reassured him, saying that he would find strength in serving his fellow men without regard to self-interest. This had never been done by any other American leader, the Colonel suggested. "No," Wilson replied, "not since Jefferson." This fellow Virginian, the idol of Grandfather James Wilson, had grown in the esteem of the President-elect, who now wrote of Hamilton exactly what he had said of Jefferson years before: he was "a great man but not in my judgment a great American."

Woodrow Wilson could be depended on to pattern his policies on those of no other President. It seemed to him that the thought of a leader, like democracy itself, must be "a stage of development" if it was to be politically valid. He had once explained that, like all great men of affairs, Thomas Jefferson "took leave to be inconsistent and do what circumstances required, approaching the perfection of theory by the tedious indirections of imperfect practice." Only a few basic principles of government were rigidly fixed: as to the details of their application to social and industrial conditions in the year 1913, Wilson's mind was still open to advice from those who sincerely shared his fundamental purposes.

The President-elect of the nation had serious business afoot. He must be "Prime Minister," he thought, "as much concerned with the guidance of legislation as with the just and orderly execution of the law." When young Franklin D. Roosevelt came to Trenton to call and when Wilson began to summon congressmen to confer on federal legislation for the special session of Congress that he promised to convoke in April, it became evident that the national government was soon to feel the full force of the reforming will that had not spent itself at Princeton or in New Jersey. He found the national politicians self-centered and given to laboring the obvious, was as impatient with them as with badgering newsmen.

In Woodrow Wilson the protests of Greenbackers and Populists, of agrarians and laborers, had a spokesman who was solicitous for their economic freedom. Impulses that had agitated American society for decades were now mellowed, rationalized, and blessed in the person of the new President. Was his mind sufficiently free from the formalism of the Old South and the bonds of scholasticism to inject the moving blood of immigrants and frontiersmen into the hardening veins of a government that was leaning toward plutocracy and a statism that threatened the freedom of individuals? Would his own aging arteries bear the strain? Was he now completely master of his impetuous right-eousness, his pride, his high temper?

Woodrow Wilson knew his failings as well as his responsibilities, in the winter of 1913. Twenty years before, in writing of Abraham Lincoln, he had conceived the burden of the Presidency as "too great to harden and perfect any sinew but that which was already tough and firmly knit." Characteristically, as he now faced up to the great challenge himself, Wilson found strength in ideas that in the eyes of little men of the hour were illusory but in the longer view of the prophets of man-kind were eternal. In 1911 he said: "I have found more true politics in the poets of the English-speaking race than I have ever found in all the formal treatises on political science."

On the morning of March 3 came the hour for leaving Princeton. The trustees of the university had extended formal congratulations but they had planned no farewell for the prophet whom they declined to follow.

His people, however, let the President know how they felt. The boys added a verse to their faculty song:

> Here's to Woodrow Wilson who
> Cleaned up Taft and Teddy, too.
> So once in a hundred years we nip
> The Pres-i-dential championship.

And one night a crowd of three thousand villagers paraded to the house on Cleveland Lane, led by the president of the bank and the president of the Woodrow Wilson Club of Princeton. Bearing a loving cup to their hero, they clamored for a speech; and Wilson responded earnestly, as a citizen to his neighbors.

The man who sometimes had held himself aloof in pulpits of execu-tive responsibility became again the youth who had reveled in singing glees, in ball games, burlesque shows, Coney Island, and Dwight Moody evangelism. He spoke tenderly of neighborliness and community fel-lowship. "If there is one thing a man loves better than another," he said, "it is being known by his fellow-citizens."

It would be a "very poor President," Wilson asserted, who lost consciousness of his home ties. He had always believed, he said, "that the real rootages of patriotism were local, that they resided in one's consciousness of an intimate touch with persons who were watching him with a knowledge of his character.

"You have got to know people in order to love them. You have got to feel as they do in order to have sympathy with them. And any man would be a very poor public servant who did not regard himself as a part of the public. No man can imagine how other people are thinking. He can know only by what is going on in his own head, and if that head is not connected by every thread of suggestion with the heads of people about him, he cannot think as they think.

"The real trials of life are the connections you break . . . I have never been inside the White House, and I shall feel very strange when I get inside of it. I shall think of this little house behind me and remember how much more familiar it is to me than that is likely to be . . . One cannot be neighbors to the whole United States. I shall miss my neighbors."

He would miss his college boys, too, and they did not forget him. Hiring a special train to Washington, they crowded into the coaches, cheering and shouting. They took the Wilson luggage to the station, and many tagged along with a band as the Wilsons, rebelling against the cavalcade of autos awaiting them at their door, walked the half mile to the train, past the home on Library Place that they had built twenty-one years before, and within view of Witherspoon Hall, where "Tommie" Wilson had discovered his mental powers. Stepping confidently, the President-elect swung his cane and doffed his tall hat and his Ellen smiled serenely. Old friends stopped them to say goodbye; and to one of them, a Presbyterian minister, the President-elect replied: "Had you not better pray for me?" Entering a parlor car at the end of the train that had been reserved for his party, Wilson heard the Princeton locomotive cheer—sharp, solid, and clear—and waving from the back platform, he joined in singing "Old Nassau" as the train gathered speed.

The singing was choked in some throats, and the Wilsons looked very wistful as the towers of the university sank into the horizon. The break with Princeton was complete; never again did Wilson spend a night in the village that had been his home for twenty-two years.

CHAPTER XVI

At Home in the White House

DURING WILSON'S FIRST HOURS in Washington, Princeton associations were perpetuated. On the evening of his arrival a cheering mob of undergraduates escorted him to the Willard Hotel, where eight hundred alumni honored him at dinner and heard him say: "As I stand here upon the eve of attempting a great task, I rejoice that there are so many men in the United States who know me and understand me and to whom I do not have to explain everything . . . I thank God that it is so, and thank you profoundly for this evidence of it." The next day Princeton colleagues came to lunch at the White House, and in the evening he shared his exalted hopes for his country with the old boys of the Class of '79.

He had asked that he be allowed to take office without any extravagance that might overtax his physique or his pocketbook. As it was, he had to borrow a large sum—for the first time in his life—in order to finance the move to Washington and to outfit himself and his family. Ellen Wilson bought suitable jewels and dresses for her daughters, and a handsome gown for herself—not because she cared for clothes, she explained, but to do justice to Woodrow's inauguration. Her husband insisted on giving her a diamond pendant that became known, *en famille*, as "the crown jewel." But he decided that—for the first time since the inauguration of Princeton's other American president, James Madison—there would be no inaugural ball. He disliked making himself and his family the center of social and commercial aggrandizement. It was bad enough that his wife had come home from a shopping expedition complaining that she had felt, under the gaze of vulgar eyes, like an animal in a zoo. The ladies of the family wished to carry themselves with the easy grace that had marked them in the South as "quality," and though their man found it difficult to take himself seriously as a political figurehead, and danced around his Ellen in the privacy of their hotel room chanting "we're going to the White House today," [1] nevertheless, he assumed in public the dignity that he thought befitting the

---

[1] Alice Wilson McElroy to the writer, April 30, 1950.

Presidency. This citizen who had been accustomed to dress casually and to polish his own shoes and who had never owned a vehicle grander than a bicycle was unchanged beneath his tall hat and immaculate clothes when he stepped into the two-horse victoria that was to take him to his new home.

Inside the White House he was greeted by retiring President Taft. Together they faced a battery of cameras on the south porch, toeing a line that was made by face powder from the vanity box of a woman photographer. It was suggested that a view be taken that required the men to look away from the cameras; but Wilson remarked that they would much prefer to look toward the lady. Anxious faces broke into smiles, and the incoming President was off on the right foot in his first ordeal of publicity in the White House.

From the south porch the men went to a four-horse landau, and soon trumpets sounded and they were moving toward the Capitol. The air was balmy with promise of spring, buds were bursting, and the sky was overcast as they passed through the swampy lowlands and the motley stores and residences that bordered Pennsylvania Avenue. For the moment Wilson was diverted by the traditional pageantry of the day. The elite Essex Troop from his own New Jersey preceded him, and crowds kept cheers in the air until the procession reached the Capitol.

When the party appeared on the steps above the rostrum, tens of thousands of expectant faces turned upward and roared a welcome. William Howard Taft, ruddy and jovial, moved ponderously to his seat, while Woodrow Wilson, spare and alert and very solemn, showed signs of strain as he came face to face with the responsibility that he feared and the opportunity that he coveted. In front of the stand a large area had been kept vacant by cordons of cadets and midshipmen. Perceiving this, and seeing seas of eager faces beyond the pale, the President-elect motioned to a guard and said: "Let the people come forward!" Thus, in a phrase that became a watchword, Wilson's pastoral instinct asserted itself.

And come forward the crowds did, so that they might the better hear this prophet accept the charge that was administered by Chief Justice White. Wilson had asked that his wife's little Bible be used for this occasion, as it had been when he took his oath as governor of New Jersey; and when it was opened at random for the touch of his lips, it happened that a ray of sunlight broke through the overcast and fell upon the words of the 119th Psalm:

And take not the word of truth utterly out of my mouth; for I have hoped in thy judgments.

So shall I keep thy law continually for ever and ever.

And I will walk at liberty: for I seek thy precepts.

I will speak of thy testimonies also before kings, and will not be ashamed.

When the twenty-eighth President of the United States stepped forward to deliver his inaugural address, the anticipation of his people reached a climax. Would he talk to them now in the vein of his pre-election speeches? Would he follow through and redeem his pledges? Only two people knew. He had composed his message in the recesses of the Princeton library, and had shared its text with his dearest confidants. One of these, Edward M. House, who disliked crowds and remained quietly in his club that morning, had read the address and characterized it as "*off the beaten track* and full of spirituality." The other intimate was present, however. During the ceremony she slipped inconspicuously from her place on the rostrum and, going to a spot directly beneath, gazed up with maidenly rapture at the noticeable man whom she had served and guided for thirty years. For this was a great day of fulfillment for Ellen Axson Wilson, as for her brilliant husband. He had confessed to her, the very last thing before they were swept apart by the people, that without her he never would be where he was.

His voice was strong and clear, but not oratorical, as he explained the real significance of the most portentous time of change that the United States had experienced since the Civil War. The occasion, his scholarly perspective revealed to him, meant much more than the mere triumph of a political faction.

"The success of a party," he asserted, "means little except when the nation is using that party for a large and definite purpose. No one can mistake the purpose for which the nation now seeks to use the Democratic party . . ." Americans had a new insight into their national life and found it great in material wealth, in moral force, and in its system of government. But evil had come with the good, corroding fine gold. "With riches has come inexcusable waste. We have squandered a great part of what we might have used . . . We have been proud of our industrial achievements, but we have not hitherto stopped thoughtfully enough to count the human cost . . .

"We have come now to the sober second thought," the prophet went on. "The scales of heedlessness have fallen from our eyes. We have made up our minds to square every process of our national life again with the standards we so proudly set up at the beginning and have always carried at our hearts. Our work is a work of restoration."

And then, after enumerating some of the measures that he proposed to take, he came to a climax of challenge:

The nation has been deeply stirred. . . . The feelings with which we face this new age of right and opportunity sweep across our heartstrings like some air out of God's own presence, where justice and mercy are reconciled and the judge and the brother are one. . . .

This is not a day of triumph; it is a day of dedication. Here muster, not the forces of party, but the forces of humanity. Men's hearts wait upon us; men's lives hang in the balance; men's hopes call upon us to say what we will do. Who shall live up to the great trust? Who dares fail to try? I summon all honest men, all patriotic, all forward-looking men, to my side. God helping me, I will not fail them, if they will but counsel and sustain me!

It was one of the briefest inaugural addresses in the history of the nation, and one of the most moving.

The ceremony concluded, the incoming servants of the Democracy swarmed to the White House. When the President reached the mansion he found more than a hundred there—family, friends, and members of his Cabinet with their wives. The guests were all very polite, very deferential to the great man of the hour, and his face flushed with embarrassment when they kowtowed to him and called him "Mr. President." He was impatient, though, to go out front, where bands would be playing and men parading.

A little after three o'clock Wilson laid his plate aside and took his place on the reviewing stand as commander in chief of the armed forces, looking every inch the part. Again, as at the Capitol, he took thought for the people milling about below him. Noticing a lame woman who moved with difficulty through the pressing throng, he leaned over anxiously, intent upon helping her; and when someone went to her side his face brightened in a smile. In the exhilaration of cheers, music, and sunshine on glittering uniforms, Woodrow Wilson was happy and radiant, as on the holidays at Princeton when he used to say to his daughter: "Now let's find a band, Nellie." His family marked a change —a greater buoyancy in his walk, a gleam in his changeable gray-blue eyes. There was a chiseled keenness in the strong, deep-lined face that he had described as "that of a horse." God had made him ugly, a friend said, "but Woodrow has made himself handsome."

When it was over, he was reminded that he was no longer free to celebrate at will; for the police and secret service men closed around him and escorted him back into the White House. Once there, he thanked the Inaugural Committee and went quickly to join his family. But they could not yet be alone. Dozens of relatives had come to celebrate the investiture of the Wilsons. The clan were in high spirits as they ran hither and yon, exploring every cranny of the old mansion, exclaiming at their discoveries, impressing on the staff, with free-and-easy ways and drawling speech, the fact that, for the first time in forty years, the President was Southern bred.

Woodrow Wilson entered the jamboree with tolerant good humor, and joined with his kin in singing "Now Thank We All Our God." Finally, going to his room toward midnight, he rang for his trunk. Not knowing which bell to push, he tried several; and soon a doorkeeper appeared and found him prepared to sleep in underwear. The missing trunk was not delivered until one in the morning; and so at the end of his first arduous day in the capital, the President of the United States crept into the big carved bed of Abraham Lincoln without benefit of nightclothes.

The next morning he surprised a maid in the hall with a cheery "Good morning!" At breakfast he was in rare form, relating little incidents of the day before that had struck his funny bone, amusing the relatives and guests. He had his usual fare—two raw eggs in grape juice, and porridge and coffee. Exactly at nine he left for his office to prepare for the first meeting with his Cabinet.

The composition of the Cabinet was a secret that Wilson had shared only with his family and Colonel House. Immediately after election he had begun to worry about selecting men. He had found himself face to face with the constitutional question that he had analyzed in writing of Cleveland's administration twenty years before. Should the President take the Constitution literally, choose "a purely administrative cabinet," and himself dictate policy to it? Or should the party be held responsible for the character and motives of the men that it supplies to guide the President? The tendency had been in the direction of the latter system until Cleveland had included several independent citizens in his second Cabinet.

In 1893, Wilson himself had inclined toward party responsibility, feeling that efficiency in administration could not be attained unless the Cabinet served to link the President with his men in Congress. Yet when the problem became his own in the winter of 1913 he was moved, by academic impulses that had become ingrained, to appoint the ablest servants of his purposes regardless of party influences; and he let it be known that those who applied for jobs were least likely to be appointed. He told House that he wanted *practical* idealists of constructive ability —men who were honest, brave, efficient, and imaginative. However, much as he desired an official family that would be able and devoted to his higher purposes, he could not ignore political considerations.[2]

Even before the election House had begun to look for good men for Cabinet posts, so that he would be ready with counsel if consulted; and candidates for office, sensing this and flattered by the skill with which he played up to their egos, had made House a target of their pleas for recognition. Democratic politicians had sat so long in the seats of minority and opposition that their inexperience in leadership was equaled only by their long-starved appetite for perquisites. After the triumph at the polls the pressures increased, and the Colonel served as a buffer against them. He tactfully fended off men of influence who wished to hold office or to give advice. His experience told him that such men could be venomous if their urge for recognition was not gratified; and as he entertained them and mollified their fears, he learned much from one about another.

As early as September of 1912 the Colonel thought that he had convinced Wilson that it would be best to take William Jennings Bryan into the Cabinet, rather than risk the embarrassment that might result if the orator should turn his great influence against the Administration. The Colonel urged in November that his friend invite Bryan into conference and consider offering him the portfolio of State; but Wilson was reluctant to make direct contact, for fear that Bryan would insist on discussing appointments and other matters on which they could not agree. He was aware that the Great Commoner might try to sweep into office the great train of henchmen who had followed him without reward through twenty years of famine. Though he respected the sincerity of Bryan's emotions and was convinced by a flood of messages that it would be political suicide to exclude him from the Cabinet, Wilson asked House three or four times whether the Colonel persisted in recommending that this politician be made secretary of state. Receiving an affirmative answer each time, he offered Bryan the portfolio on December 21. The Great Commoner feared that his unwillingness to have liquor at his table might be embarrassing; but getting Wilson's

2 Of the candidates for the Cabinet chosen tentatively by Wilson and House in November, the Colonel noted that five had voted for Taft and some had not voted the Democratic ticket for sixteen years. He spoke to Ellen Wilson about this and she replied: "But you would not keep them out of the Cabinet on that account?" No, the Colonel trimmed, but he would not include too many who were not rock-ribbed Democrats. He foresaw that, twenty years in the future, "no one would know how the different departments of the government had been run and . . . the President's fame would rest entirely upon the big constructive measures he was able to get through Congress; and in order to get them through he had to be on more or less good terms with that body." It seemed to House that this was one of the most important things to be considered and that Wilson's future reputation would rest almost wholly upon it.

assurance that he could suit himself in this matter, he tentatively consented to serve.

Distressed by a tendency of journalists to picture Bryan as an arbiter of policy and appointments, Wilson had several earnest talks with House in January. Inviting the Colonel to dinner at the Princeton Inn, the Wilsons questioned him on many matters of policy and etiquette that were plaguing them. On this occasion House was asked to choose for himself any of the Cabinet seats except that to be filled by Bryan. The Texan, however, did not wish to tie himself down to a responsibility that might overtax his strength. He still coveted the role of a "free lance" with a roving commission to serve. The day after their talk at Princeton he wrote to his friend: "As an ex-officio member . . . I can do my share of work and get a little of the reflected glory." [3]

In the disinterested spirit that he insisted on displaying, the colonel continued to act as conciliator and intermediary. In dealing with the rivalry of McAdoo and McCombs for the Treasury portfolio, however, House's talent was severely taxed. For some time Wilson had looked with favor upon William G. McAdoo, hero of the Baltimore Convention. Unlike his rival, William F. McCombs, who had asserted that if his erratic services as campaign manager were not rewarded with the Treasury post he would accept nothing,[4] McAdoo had put forward no impor-

---

[3] *House Papers,* I, 100–101; and House Diary, Jan. 8, 1913. Charles Seymour has suggested that House must have been influenced, at least subconsciously, by another consideration that had been impressed upon him by his experience in serving the governors of Texas. "He believed," Seymour wrote, "that in essential matters he and Wilson would agree in principle, but they might conceivably disagree as to method. If he were in an official position such disagreement would compel his resignation, unless he were to be placed in the unpleasant position of carrying out a line of action which he disapproved. So long as he remained in a private capacity, he could give what advice he chose; and if the President did not follow it, House could shrug his shoulders and turn his attention to other matters in which Wilson might accept his guidance. 'Had I gone into the Cabinet,' House once said, 'I could not have lasted eight weeks.' Outside of the Cabinet he lasted for eight years."

When House finally assumed official responsibility as an associate of Wilson at the Paris Peace Conference, the position actually did prove to be an "unpleasant" one for the colonel. (*See* Vol. II of this work.)

[4] McCombs complained that the President was ungratefully trying to banish him "to St. Helena." The neurotic invalid was with the President-elect for an hour late in December, and when he went Wilson felt weak and ill, as if he had been sucked by a vampire.

Colonel House tried to finesse by advising McCombs not to resign from the chairmanship of the National Committee, and trusting to his contrary nature to impel him to do the opposite. McCombs persisted in holding on, however, and threatened to do what he could to obstruct the administration if he was not treated better. Though Wilson refused to compromise by offering a Cabinet post to the man with a private understanding that it would be declined, he finally gave McCombs a public statement that both saved the man's face and protected Wilson himself against charges of ingratitude.

On May 2, House arranged a meeting between McCombs and McAdoo at the Vanderbilt Hotel and the latter reported afterward to the Colonel that the two "Macs" had "buried the hatchet" under six drinks. Told of this, Wilson exclaimed: "What children!"

tunate claim to recompense for his loyalty. In fact he sometimes gave the impression that, like House, he would prefer to be independent. On February 1, despite strenuous efforts by his rivals to block his appointment, he was called to the room of the President-elect at the University Club in New York and asked whether he would do Wilson the honor of serving as secretary of the Treasury. Flattered by the offer and the courteous way in which it was tendered, McAdoo expressed appreciation; but doubting his fitness for the position, he protested that he was neither banker nor financier. It was being gossiped about that he was too much the promoter to cope with technical problems of finance and that, on the other hand, his close associations with New York bankers might brand him as an agent of Wall Street.

Wilson reassured him, however. "I don't want a banker or a financier," he declared. "The Treasury is not a bank. Its activities are varied and extensive. What I need is a man of all-round ability who has had wide business experience. I know you have the necessary qualifications . . . We must enact a new tariff bill and a new currency or banking measure to fulfill our platform pledges. The Treasury will have to play an important part in this legislation." Denying that he was trying merely to pay off a political obligation to McAdoo, the President-elect went on: "The responsibilities of the Presidency are great and I cannot perform them alone. If I can't have the assistance of those in whom I have confidence, what am I to do?" [5]

Having squared himself with his chief's principles, the man of enterprise who had once himself been bankrupt agreed to undertake the arduous task of financing the "New Freedom." McAdoo's political acumen won the respect of Colonel House and immediately showed itself in a magazine article interpreting the capacities and the manly compassion that he saw in his chief: "The Kind of Man Woodrow Wilson is," he entitled it.

When the President went into the Cabinet room on the morning after inauguration, he found Bryan on his right and McAdoo on his left. Beyond them sat three men who had served him well at Baltimore and

---

Bitterly disappointed because the President-elect had appointed only one of the thirteen men recommended by him for high offices, McCombs felt that his talents had been exploited by a sort of hypnotic power in Wilson, who had then treated him "like a red-headed stepchild." McCombs went to Paris in the summer of 1913, suffered an appendectomy, got married, and, appalled by the high cost of embassy life, decided once and for all in August to refuse the ambassadorship at Paris which Wilson had offered. But he remained chairman of the Democratic National Committee until 1916. Until his death, in 1921, he bitterly reviled Woodrow Wilson.

[5] W. G. McAdoo, *op. cit.*, p. 178.

were to stand by until his work as president was over: Josephus Daniels, Albert S. Burleson, and William B. Wilson. Daniels, the genial North Carolina editor who had been a disciple of Bryan and a member of the party's National Committee for sixteen years, had been considered for the office of postmaster general; but when House suggested that that office required a more aggressive man and one better known in Congress, Wilson offered Daniels the Navy.[6]

Congressman Burleson of Texas was appointed postmaster general. Wilson had wanted "one thorough-going politician" in his Cabinet—someone who had the confidence and esteem of legislators; but his first thought had been to keep Burleson in Congress, where he had sat in seven Houses of Representatives, and to use his influence there among the party men. But Burleson had worked for Wilson at Baltimore, and when the Colonel argued that to ignore the man would suggest ingratitude, Wilson and Burleson came to an understanding. The practical politician said: "I will be loyal to your administration and sympathetic with your policies. When I reach the point where I cannot give you my undivided loyalty, I will tender my resignation. When I talk to you, I will always tell you my candid views." And to this the idealist replied: "Burleson, that is just the kind of man I want."

William B. Wilson, unrelated and personally unknown to the President-elect, had been made secretary of labor after his sponsor, Senator Hughes of New Jersey, had declined the post. This Wilson had come from Scotland at the age of eight, had begun work a year later in Pennsylvania coal mines, had helped to organize the United Mine Workers of America, and had served as its secretary-treasurer for eight years. W. B. Wilson had once been imprisoned for defying an injunc-

---

[6] The appointment of Daniels was strongly urged upon Tumulty and Wilson by Thomas J. Pence of Raleigh, who had worked with Daniels on campaign publicity. Many Democrats felt that Daniels lacked executive ability and was ignorant of the Navy's problems.

Wishing to choose an assistant secretary of the navy from upper New York State, Wilson asked Herbert Bayard Swope of the *World* for suggestions and was told that Frank I. Cobb favored young Franklin D. Roosevelt. Secretary Daniels, who had been attracted by Roosevelt's enthusiasm for Wilson as a spectator at Baltimore and by his fight for liberal causes in the New York Senate, recommended the New Yorker to Wilson, who said, "Capital!" Daniels told the President that it had been suggested to him that every Roosevelt wanted to direct everything and that this one would try to become secretary of the navy. When Daniels asserted that any man who feared supplanting by his assistant thereby confessed that he didn't think himself big enough for his job, Wilson concurred. Roosevelt accepted the office on March 9 and told Daniels that McAdoo had asked if he would like to go into the Treasury but the Navy post would please him most since he loved ships and had studied naval affairs. Herbert Bayard Swope's review of Frank Freidel's *Roosevelt* in the *New York Times Book Review*, Nov. 9, 1952; Letter, Swope to A. M. Schlesinger, Jr., Dec. 6, 1954, in the possession of the latter; *F.D.R.: His Personal Letters*, 1928–45, p. 1121; Daniels, *The Wilson Era: Years of Peace*, p. 124; Daniels Diary (Library of Congress), March 6, 1913.

tion, but had a reputation for integrity, fairness, and devotion to the cause of industrial peace. Elected to the House of Representatives, he had played a part in developing the Bureau of Mines and had helped to draft the bill creating a separate Department of Labor; and it seemed fitting that he should become its first secretary.[7] Moreover, President Samuel Gompers of the American Federation of Labor had gone to Trenton to urge this appointment.

In addition to these stanch henchmen—Daniels, Burleson, and W. B. Wilson—there was another who was destined to serve the President-elect to the very end. David F. Houston was of all the Cabinet the closest to his chief in intellectual capacity, experience, and philosophy. He had attended South Carolina College when Uncle James Woodrow taught there and had seen Woodrow Wilson for a few moments in the revered professor's house. Houston had studied history and economics at the Harvard Graduate School, specializing in government and finance, and had served on the faculty and as president at the University of Texas. He had observed local politics keenly and had conceived a deep respect and admiration for Edward M. House; and when he had dined with Wilson and discussed the tariff, he had found the Governor to be "the straightest thinking man in public life." Believing himself better fitted for the portfolio of Agriculture than for the Treasury, which House once suggested to him, Houston was recommended to Wilson by both House and Walter Hines Page. He agreed to take the secretaryship of Agriculture with the understanding that he might retire at the end of two years, but became so devoted to his work and his chief that he remained in the Cabinet for eight.

House felt that he had found a liberal candidate for the Department of Justice in the person of James C. McReynolds. This man—a Democrat whom Theodore Roosevelt had made assistant attorney general—had acquired a reputation for radicalism as a result of his insistence on invoking criminal provisions of the antitrust law against tobacco and coal operators. In the view of McReynolds, who was actually the most conservative and consistent of legalists, his duty was to enforce the law, whatever its purport; and he had dramatized his prosecution of corporate interests by resigning when Taft's attorney general had made a settlement that seemed to nullify his efforts. The Colonel arranged a casual meeting between Wilson and McReynolds in mid-February, and

[7] The secretaryship of Commerce and Labor—an office established by an act of 1903—had not pleased either management or labor. An act creating separate departments of Commerce and Labor was signed by Taft barely in time for Wilson to appoint secretaries before Inauguration Day.

the President-elect was so well impressed that he appointed the man.

The Interior Department had worried the incoming President, for the problems of conservation were charged with political dynamite. During Taft's administration the national resources had been handled in a way that led to allegations of corruption and privilege; and progressives were wondering whether Wilson could find a man who would be able to resist private interests and state politicians that wished to exploit government lands. Here again Colonel House led Wilson to a promising candidate. Franklin K. Lane, born on Prince Edward Island, educated in California, and seasoned in many a battle for progressive principles, had been appointed by Theodore Roosevelt to the Interstate Commerce Commission. Now chairman of that body, he told House that he was content to remain in his position. The more Lane protested his unfitness for the Cabinet, however, the greater had been the inclination of Wilson and House to find a place for him. They were impressed by a thoughtful letter that he wrote to recommend a fellow Californian for the Interior portfolio, and he had a reputation as a speaker of charm. Asked by the President to sound out the candidate, House had brought his persuasive powers to bear and had secured Lane's consent to serve in any capacity that Wilson thought best—even the Interior Department, which he considered the most prickly of Cabinet seats. They planned to give him the War portfolio at first; but when Newton D. Baker refused to leave his reform commitments as mayor of Cleveland to join the Cabinet [8] and when party leaders vetoed Walter Hines Page as secretary of the interior, Wilson turned to Lane and appointed him at the last moment.

This left the War portfolio vacant. Various names were discussed; and Hugh C. Wallace, who later became ambassador to France, was given an invitation and declined. Finally Tumulty, who had been urging that at least one New Jersey man should sit in the Cabinet, looked through the Lawyers' Directory and ran across the name of Lindley M. Garrison,

---

[8] Wilson grieved over Baker's decision. This former student (at the Johns Hopkins) had worked effectively in the progressive movement in Ohio and had supported Wilson energetically at Baltimore, but had felt obliged to stay at Cleveland and try to carry out certain reforms that he had promised before his election. Declining Wilson's offer, he said that he considered the misgovernment of large cities the greatest disgrace to American citizenship. After Baker had gone out of the room, House—according to his Diary—"braced the Governor up again and told him not to mind Baker's refusal and that we could arrange without him." In March of 1916, Baker became secretary of war.

Party leaders had objected to Page because, as a Southerner, he was unacceptable in a post that controlled the distribution of Civil War pensions and, as an associate in a publishing business that operated an open shop, he might be a target of labor.

vice-chancellor of the state's highest court, whom he remembered as a judge of high repute. Thereupon Wilson invited Garrison to his office, sized him up quickly, and persuaded him that he owed it to his country to give up his secure position and risk the hazards of Cabinet life.

Likewise the secretaryship of Commerce, which had just been separated from that of Labor, had not been filled until the last moment. Wilson had intended to appoint Louis D. Brandeis, who had more support from progressives than any other candidate for the Cabinet. But a rumor of this possibility had created a panic of protest among businessmen, some of whom had supported Wilson; and five days before the inauguration opposition had grown so strong that the President had to cast about for another man.[9] It was finally settled on February 28 that the Commerce Department would be administered by William C. Redfield of New York, a manufacturing executive and a congressman whom Wilson had at first intended to make postmaster general. The President-elect was impressed by a tariff speech by Redfield that had been sent to him by Villard.

The casualness of Wilson's efforts in completing the choice of a Cabinet had been in contrast with the enthusiasm that he had shown for this responsibility just after the election. The Democratic party was destitute of seasoned officials and there were deficiencies in the group brought together. The South, represented by five of the ten men, was given unwarranted recognition, especially in view of the fact that much of Wilson's strength had come from the West. Moreover, most of the Cabinet were devoid of experience in the matters they were to deal with, and many of them were deplorably weak in political prestige. They

[9] After the election Wilson had been urged to make Brandeis attorney general and had given much thought to this possibility, but House dissuaded him from putting this controversial figure in the Department of Justice. When it was objected that Brandeis was a Jew, Wilson retorted: "And a fine one!" On Jan. 3, 1913, the President-elect wrote to his friend Tedcastle regarding Brandeis: "Of course I know how some of the best men in Boston hate him, but I think I know the reason for that feeling, and I want to get outside that circle." On Jan. 27, 1913, he wrote to Bryan, who favored having a Jew in the Cabinet but apparently distrusted Brandeis: "I think that Brandeis has been very grossly aspersed but of course I am looking into the matter very carefully and shall do nothing to bring the administration into question in any way."

Assured by the journalist Norman Hapgood, who had led him to Brandeis, that the charges against the man's integrity were groundless or distorted, Wilson made it plain that he would listen to objections based on political expediency but that, if more allegations were made against Brandeis's character, he would appoint the man forthwith. McCombs, Governor Foss of Massachusetts, and others induced Redfield to say that he would not serve in the Commerce Department under Brandeis; and then, on Feb. 27, they gave to Wilson a long list of opponents, including many congressmen. When financiers of the stature of Henry L. Higginson and Cleveland Dodge joined in the protest and House added a word of caution, Wilson yielded in order to preserve party harmony.

were, as Wilson himself had put in writing of Cleveland's advisers, "without Washington credentials." Only Bryan had a large and compact following in the party, though Burleson had influence in the House, W. B. Wilson had prestige among labor organizations, and McAdoo had made rapid progress toward political leadership. Obviously it would require heroic efforts for the Administration, which had come into office on a minority vote of the American people, to generate power to enact the legislation to which its leader was committed.

When the President greeted the gentlemen of the Cabinet on the morning of March 5, he looked very trim and fit. Taking the chair at the head of the long table, he talked with an assurance that was in contrast with the nervousness of Redfield, who incessantly brushed back his reddish whiskers with finger and thumb, and with the ebullience of Daniels, who had entered the room exclaiming: "Isn't it great? Isn't it wonderful?" Burleson, who affected sideburns and the dress and manner of an uncouth politician and went about with a black umbrella hung on his arm, sat with a priestly dignity that led Wilson to call him "The Cardinal." Lane was bald, plump, and sociable. The others were decorously expectant. W. B. Wilson, the self-made man, seemed shy in this imposing company; and Garrison the jurist was ill at ease in his sudden plunge into a strange environment.

After a brief pause Wilson said, quite simply: "Gentlemen, I thought we had better come together and talk about getting started on our way." Then he and Bryan told a few stories.

When the Cabinet came together again the next day, they underwent an ordeal by photography. Finally the President, wearying under the steady fire, said that they had had enough; and after the photographers left he told of a spiritual convert who vowed to control himself, but, presiding at a religious meeting in which a controversy reached a climax in the throwing of eggs at himself, finally drew his revolver and shouted: "This damn Job business is going to last just two seconds longer!"

There were three meetings of the Cabinet during that first week; and the secretaries who had not known their chief intimately saw clearly now that the caricature of the cold and bookish Wilson was based on myths. He proved to them that he was not what Bryan once had pictured him to be: an incorrigible schoolmaster under whom no self-respecting man could serve and who would leave nothing of the Democratic party when he was through with it. He conducted the sessions like the experienced moderator that he was. First he presented matters on which he wanted "common counsel"; and after getting the opinions of the men, he then called on them one by one, in rotation, to present questions from their respective departments that required general consideration. There were sometimes sharp differences of opinion; and after listening well, Wilson would try to arrive at the sense of the meeting and to state it succinctly. He did not force through policies that did not commend themselves to the understanding of the body; and he drew upon his fund of stories to shut off discussions that grew fatuous or dangerously controversial. His courtesy kept the spirit constructive and friendly.

Moreover, he soon made it clear that they must have no secrets from each other. When Bryan whispered something to him and the others were obviously embarrassed, he said to them: "Mr. Bryan was just telling me," and then repeated the remarks. He feared that it might be inferred that the secretary of state and he had secrets from their colleagues. "I do this in the beginning," he explained, "because I recall the severe criticism in Gideon Welles's *Diary* because, as he said, Secretary Seward would upon occasion lead Lincoln into a corner and they would talk in an undertone for minutes while the other members of the Cabinet sat as if they had no part in the important matters that Seward was communicating in the President's ear. There will be no secrets between this President and the secretary of state and our colleagues at the Cabinet table." [10]

The qualities of leadership that had charmed men of the Princeton faculty and the New Jersey legislature were captivating the little band of public servants at Washington. They believed in one another and in their chief and were exhilarated by a feeling that they were achieving great things. They soon found their leader willing to delegate to them the management of their departments, ready with counsel when they sought it, and reluctant to interfere except when questions of foreign policy or Congressional leadership were at stake.

In the meetings of the Cabinet the President made quick estimates of

[10] Daniels, *The Wilson Era: Years of Peace,* pp. 140–41. After only a week in service Franklin K. Lane wrote to Walter Hines Page: "The President is the most charming man imaginable to work with . . . There has been a particularly active set of liars engaged in giving the country the impression that Woodrow Wilson was what we call out West 'a cold nose.' He is the most sympathetic, cordial, and considerate presiding officer that can be imagined. And he sees so clearly. He has no fog in his brain. As you perhaps know, I didn't want to go into the Cabinet, but I am delighted that I was given the opportunity and accepted it, because of the personal relationship; and I think all the Cabinet feel the way I do." Lane, *Letters,* p. 133. More than a year later Lane testified to House that at no time had the President hurt the feelings of any member of his Cabinet. House Diary, April 29, 1914. Houston thought Wilson "amazingly considerate . . . even more amazingly patient and tolerant." David F. Houston, *Eight Years with Wilson's Cabinet,* I, 88–89. On the other hand, Vice-President Marshall, invited by Wilson to attend Cabinet meetings, came to only one and felt that he would not be listened to. D. C. Roper, *Fifty Years of Public Life,* p. 287.

his men. On Saturday the 8th he talked them over with the Colonel,
whom he invited to the White House to chat with him at nine in the
morning. Dressed in a sack suit of gray, wearing a gray tie, Wilson
chatted with his confidant for more than an hour and described the
behavior of each of the secretaries at their first meeting. Houston had
had a good deal to say and Burleson had been so garrulous that, if
he kept it up, he would have to be suppressed. Redfield had shown the
best mind for analysis, but Lane could analyze and at the same time
use a lively imagination. McReynolds had talked seldom, but always
to the point. Bryan had been the most surprising of the group. He had
shown a restraint and a reasonableness that had endeared him to his
chief, who soon was referring to his secretary of state *en famille* as "my
elder son." [11]

Wilson gave himself conscientiously to the routine duties of an incoming president. He showed appreciation of traditional etiquette. On the
afternoon of his first day in office he received 1,123 guests: the entire
Democratic National Committee, legislators with constituents, officials,
editors, and ambassadors. One of these, Lord Bryce, he met with genuine delight as an esteemed fellow scholar. He made contact, too, with
the office staff that was taken over from Taft's regime and that now
was to be directed by Joseph Tumulty.

For a time he had doubted that Tumulty, who was only thirty-three,
could fill a position as exacting as that at the White House; and he
was not unimpressed by hundreds of letters warning him against the
dangers implicit in his secretary's Catholicism. But much as he liked
Tumulty and appreciated his devotion,[12] he felt that a collectorship
of revenue would be a more appropriate position for him than secretary
to the President, and Wilson had hoped to persuade someone of the
caliber of Newton D. Baker to serve him at Washington. House and
McAdoo, however, had felt that Tumulty's "political instinct" would
be an essential asset. Bryan had spoken in favor of including a Catholic

[11] Marjorie Brown King to the writer. When he became secretary of state, Bryan retired
from the active staff of the *Commoner*. With Wilson's consent, he arranged to supplement his
salary by lecturing to Chautauqua audiences. However, when leaving for one of his speaking
trips the secretary of State notified the President that he was subject to recall to Washington
at any moment. "It would be as unfair to me as to yourself," Bryan wrote, "to allow a
pecuniary consideration to have a feather's weight if the public good is at stake."

[12] Wilson had named Tumulty clerk of the Supreme Court of New Jersey in the spring
of 1912, though he had continued to serve the Governor as secretary without salary. When
forming the Cabinet, Wilson and House looked for an eligible Catholic of Cabinet timbre and
found none available. House Diary, July 7, 1914. House recalled later that, since his own experience had been confined to gubernatorial secretaries, he had accepted Tumulty at McAdoo's
estimate. House Diary, May 24, 1916.

in the official family; journalists to whom Tumulty had endeared himself by joining in their pranks now stood by their jolly accomplice; and when Ellen Wilson added her endorsement of the young man to whom she had become a second mother, Wilson's conscientious doubts had been overcome. Casually, one day in February, he had asked his secretary if he would like to continue in his position, and the young man had gone out and exploded to a friendly reporter: "Charlie, I've got it!"

The presence of Tumulty brought practical jokes and merriment into the office in the West Wing of the White House. Moreover, it brought assurance that the routine of public business would go on much as it had in the governorship, and it gave Woodrow Wilson the comfort that he always derived from familiar associations.

Tumulty sat in the next room of the West Wing, free to enter the President's office at any time, and strove to stem the torrent of callers and correspondents. He digested incoming letters for his chief, and amused Wilson by deftly culling grains of sense from verbose documents from Very Important People.[13] Every day Tumulty gave editorials to his chief, who read only a few of the friendly papers. The youthful secretary was a political weather vane and helped in the process that Wilson was wont to refer to, mystically, as "sitting quietly and listening with the inner ear." The President attributed to him an extraordinary appreciation of how a thing would "get over the footlights" and thought him his most valuable audience. Many of Wilson's speeches and state papers went to Tumulty for criticism that proved effective. Moreover, the President's secretary took initiative and showed genius in carrying out his chief's promise of "pitiless publicity" for affairs of state.

Soon after taking office Wilson institutionalized press relations by establishing regular conferences. All his life he had been devoted to the ideal of a free press. He hoped that press conferences might give his people the reassurance that the British derived from question periods in Parliament. Facing about a hundred correspondents at the White House, he replied extemporaneously with the understanding that he would not be quoted directly. He was sometimes stricken with self-consciousness when he remembered that the whole nation was listening

[13] The President, wishing to avoid waste of time and to guard himself against being influenced by personalities, preferred succinct memoranda to oral reports. He indicated approval by an initialed "Okeh." Franklin D. Roosevelt once said that he learned a trick from Woodrow Wilson, who had told him: "If you want your memorandum read, put it on one page." Louis Brownlow, *The President and the Presidency*, p. 62.

for his words. At times his social instincts got the better of his reserve and he volunteered confidential remarks without making it clear that they were "off the record"; and when these were printed he felt that the reporters had been unappreciative of his frankness. His feelings hurt, he would turn cold and seem intellectually arrogant.

Sometimes he lectured the newsmen on his philosophy of journalism and invited criticism. Suggesting in his first conference on March 15 that the men "go into partnership" with him, he appealed to them to bring in a "precious freight of opinion" from the nation and then join him in making "true gold" to send out from Washington. He could share the objective view of able journalists toward the Presidency, but sometimes found it hard to understand when newsmen criticized him in good faith. He lacked time and energy to cultivate the friendship of individual journalists, except for a few who had won his confidence and respect. Indeed, he had learned at Trenton that by granting personal interviews to certain newsmen he might sow jealousy in the hearts of others.

During the first months in the Presidency, Wilson maintained spasmodic contact with the Washington correspondents. Six weeks after inauguration he enjoyed the traditional dinner of the Gridiron Club, where, he said, he received his "first public discipline as President, responsible to all who look on." Describing the occasion to Mary Hulbert, he wrote: "It was very amusing and very instructive, in a way, and I was treated with singular sympathy and consideration, as if they really liked and admired me, and were a wee bit in awe of me! Fancy! Can you imagine it? I was a good deal moved, and very much stimulated." Unfortunately he disappointed the journalists by failing to rise to their gibes with repartee, in the manner of Taft and Roosevelt.

Though Wilson at first held news conferences twice a week, he came to regard them as ordeals and was glad to avoid them whenever he could plead overwork or a critical need for national security. Tumulty supplemented the formal conferences with blarney and merriment—sometimes at the President's expense—and handled the journalists with a warmth that won affection for himself and loyalty to administration policies. He often worked discreetly to persuade his chief to send personal words of appreciation to deserving newsmen.[14]

---

[14] The press conferences were given up in the summer of 1915.

For an analysis of Tumulty's work and methods, *see* Blum, *Tumulty*, pp. 62 ff. The secretary made few mistakes in public relations, but his dealings with members of the Cabinet and others close to his chief were marred by self-assertion and jealousy. House kept the President alert to his secretary's fits of temperament; but the President continued to be fond of the young man in spite of his shortcomings.

The President could depend as surely on Tumulty's jovial, friendly propagation of the Word among the public oracles as upon House's handling of more sophisticated personages. He came to lean on others, also, in lesser matters. The clerical staff, which found itself handling a far greater volume of correspondence than during Taft's regime, soon came to respect not only the tidiness of the new chief's flat-top desk but the orderliness of his mind and the sureness and consistency of his rulings. It seemed as if they could see the shutter of memory open and close in his brain, as he recalled details of a case that was still open or disregarded them in a case in which he was satisfied that he had been all around the clock and reached a reasoned conclusion. They were to find him meticulously punctual, never willing to dodge a difficult assignment by working on an easier one, and masterful in handling the stream of callers who had appointments each morning. Still regarding Kipling's "If" as a model of conduct, he seemed determined "to fill the unforgiving minute with sixty seconds worth of distance run."

In the choosing of minor officials, Wilson soon found that he could not delegate authority without abnegating principles that were dear. Along the road to the Presidency he himself had incurred few political debts, and he dared to hope that he could choose men with the same freedom that he had enjoyed at Princeton and in New Jersey. He wished to refuse to bargain with campaign contributors or with members of Congress. He had taken so conscientious a view of his appointive power that he was oppressed by it. Sometimes, when the dictate of duty crossed personal inclination, he protected his own feelings by a brusqueness that seemed callous to those who did not understand the torment that he suffered. He confessed that he was often torn between the sacred duties of friendship and those of office, that sometimes it seemed as if he must choose between losing a friend and betraying his public trust.

His conscience had told him, at first, that he should pass upon the fitness of every appointee, even the thousands of postmasters; but after his election, so many supplicating letters had come to him that by March 5 he was ready to announce publicly that minor appointments would be made only through the heads of executive departments. "Gentlemen," he said to the Cabinet, "I shall have to ask you to sift the applicants for me and to make your recommendations. I think I owe this to the people." Nevertheless, he recorded in a notebook the major offices to be filled, kept an "eligible list" of about sixty names, set down the principal federal posts, with their salaries, and then figured up how much money each state would receive through offices held by its sons.[15]

Wilson insisted that his men observe certain basic principles that he had set forth in *Constitutional Government*. When Burleson said in Cabinet meeting that he would not present the name of anyone who had fought the President's candidacy, Wilson took issue with him quickly. He thrilled public servants like Houston by saying, straight from the shoulder: "It makes no difference whether a man stood for me or not. All I want is a man who is fit for the place, a man who stands for clean government and progressive policies."

At first the President stood resolutely against the use of patronage to build political power for congressmen. Facing Burleson one day over a pile of documents having to do with appointments, he had it out with his postmaster general. "Now, Burleson," he began, "I want to say to you that my administration is going to be a progressive administration. I am not going to advise with reactionary or standpat senators or representatives in making these appointments. I am going to appoint forward-looking men and I am going to satisfy myself that they are honest and capable."

Foreseeing ruin for the administration if the prophet persisted in this course, Burleson decided to be faithful to his pledge of entire frankness. Fixing his cold gray eyes on Wilson, firming his chin, and orating as if he were addressing an audience, he said that he proposed to appoint honest and capable men,[16] but that he must consult the legislators from the localities concerned. When the President bristled at this and alluded to his fights with reactionary Democrats in New Jersey, the postmaster general argued that they must avoid the sort of rows that Cleveland had had with Congress if they were to swing the party to a progressive program. "They are mostly good men," said this ex-congressman of his former colleagues. "If they are turned down, they will hate you and will not vote for anything you want. It is human nature. On the other hand, if you work with them, and they recommend unsuitable men for the offices, I will keep on asking for other suggestions, until I get

---

[15] Houston, *op. cit.,* I, 41. Joseph Wilson, a political reporter in Tennessee, had, at his brother's suggestion, kept a file on the politicians of that state. Wilson had this file at the White House and used it. "If I had such a record for every one of the states," he said to Louis Brownlow, "my political position would be impregnable." Brownlow Lecture at the University of Chicago, Feb. 21, 1956.

[16] Actually, Burleson was an advocate of the merit system and did much to extend its application to postmasterships. However, he went along with the dominant conservative machine in several Southern states, to the sorrow of progressives whom Wilson would have liked to favor.

good ones. In the end we shall secure as able men as we would in any other way, and we will keep the leaders of the party with us."

Wilson promised to ponder the matter, and a week later sent for the postmaster general to resume their discussion. Taking up a specific case—an appointment recommended by a Tennessee congressman—he told Burleson of hot protests against the candidate. Leaning back and throwing up his arms he said: "Burleson, I can't appoint a man like that!"

But the practical politician persisted. He reviewed all the factors in the case under consideration, all the typical ins and outs of small-town politics and the power of deeprooted party tradition. It was difficult to withstand Burleson's bull-like determination—"you have got to give him what he wants or 'kill him,'" a colleague wrote of him. When the postmaster general finished, the President consented to make the appointment. Wilson's sympathy for the better type of politician grew, and soon he was telling his Cabinet: "Poor Burleson has the hardest sledding of all." Yet the President always kept his eye open for rare men—"genuine progressives" who were free from "privileged interests." Seeking a comptroller of the currency a few months after inauguration, he wrote to his friend Thomas D. Jones: "What I want is a man of rising reputation and career and yet not a man who would use the place as a stepping stone to something better in a business way. Men who have made use of the place have invariably commended themselves, in one way or another, to the bankers with whom they were dealing." Wilson had the satisfaction of bringing to Washington a few Princeton colleagues and former students for whose integrity he could vouch.

To get experts for a Commission on Industrial Relations, Wilson went to Brandeis; and he had not been in the White House for a month before he asked House to take general charge of the whole matter of major political appointments. Nevertheless, Wilson himself never could escape worry over appointments. "The matter of patronage," he confessed to a friend six months after inauguration, "is a thorny path which daily makes me wish I had never been born."

Wilson was not willing at first that patronage should be a Democratic monopoly. Republican legislators were asked whether they objected to candidates proposed for appointment in their districts. "I feel it my constitutional duty . . . to make independent inquiries wherever possible . . ." the President wrote to a Democratic congressman two months after inauguration, "but I shall hope in every possible instance to comply with the recommendations and wishes of my colleagues in the House." Soon he was using his obligations to the Congress as a counterweight against Bryan's importunities in behalf of incompetent friends.

Though Wilson soon accepted the fact that a President cannot make all appointments conform to his own desires, he continued to insist that he must not favor his family in any way. It was arranged by Tumulty that a young Woodrow cousin should have a clerkship in the office of Attorney General McReynolds; but when told of it the President laid down the law: relatives could not accept jobs from men whom he had appointed, though he had no objection to their taking positions from officials who had been chosen by Taft.[17] When his own, and only, brother was recommended for office, it pained him to have to write thus:

April 22, 1913

My dear, dear brother:

I never in my life had anything quite so hard to do as this that I must do about the Nashville Post Office. Knowing as I do that a better man could not possibly be found for the place, and sure though I am that it would meet with the general approval of the citizens of Nashville, I yet feel that it would be a very serious mistake both for you and for me if I were to appoint you to the Postmastership there. I cannot tell you how I have worried about this or how much I have had to struggle against affection and temptation, but I am clear in the conviction that in the long run, if not now, you will agree with me that I am deciding rightly.

I can't write any more just now, because I feel too deeply.

With deepest love, I remain

Your affectionate brother,
WOODROW WILSON

Five days before the inauguration he confessed to House that he had almost lost the serene faith in friendship that had sustained him so often. Sooner or later self-interest seemed to crop out in even the best of comrades. He became especially distrustful of new friends, and of gifts that flooded in from many states. He refused to accept a keg of whisky from Andrew Carnegie, but feared to give offense to the philanthropist by sending it back. Finally, after a horned toad had arrived

---

[17] This rule was applied also in the case of another cousin, who had been offered second choice of McAdoo's appointments. When asked for advice, Wilson said that it was McAdoo's business, but he would prefer that the offer be declined. It was. Fitz William Woodrow to the writer, and James Woodrow to the writer, June 14, 1949.

from Texas, he remarked that he didn't want so much as a potato given
to him, and large gifts were returned.

But hard as his conscience was set against family and personal friends
in matters of public business, the President delighted in indulging
them once he had left the executive offices in the West Wing and
gone "home" to the White House. He liked to gather around him those
on whose disinterestedness he knew that he could depend. All those
welcomed into the inner circle were relatives or loyal friends, so that
Wilson, who seldom talked shop at meals, could sit with them afterward
and open his mind with confidence that he would not be betrayed.

All was so jolly and novel during the first week in the new home that
it was hard for the Wilsons to understand what Taft meant when he
said to the President-elect on Inauguration Day: "I'm glad to be going
—this is the loneliest place in the world." Woodrow Wilson loved the
swift pace of family life about him. He insisted that his wife and
daughters preserve the candor and integrity of their own personalities,
follow their own inclinations, and engage in no social activities with
ulterior political motives. He wanted no weaving spiders in his household. Margaret's devotion to singing and Jessie's work for good causes
gave him joy; and he shared in the ecstasy of Nellie as she lost her shyness in the bustle of the new life and gave play to frivolous girlish
impulses. The normality of their doings helped him to escape unhealthful moods. His new office demanded dignity, but he could not put it
on without being conscious of acting and, therefore, a little ashamed of
himself. He liked to think of himself as standing next to the chair of
State, not sitting on it. "The old kink is still in me," he explained to
Mary Allen Hulbert. "Everything is persistently *impersonal*. I am administering a great office—no doubt the greatest in the world—but I
do not seem to be identified with it . . . This impersonality of my life
is a very odd thing . . . but at least prevents me from becoming a
fool and thinking myself *it*!"

He kept his spirit young and humble by playing tag and rooster
fighting with daughter Nellie in the White House corridors. Sometimes
he would spend an evening at billiards. Adhering to the habits of earlier
years, he punctually followed a daily schedule. Rising early, he sharpened his razor on a heavy leather strop and fancied that he could predict
the weather by the sound. He retired at a discreet hour, as he had all
his life; and when owls hooting in the magnolias awakened him, he
would go to the window and hoot back, and then at breakfast boast
that he had "hooted the hooters away." He refused to join the fashion-

able Chevy Chase Club, for fear that he might be buttonholed by lobbyists, and he best found relaxation at vaudeville shows, where he could himself become one of "the people" to whom he was devoting himself. He discouraged the playing of the national anthem and the rising of the audience when he entered. He often laughed aloud at slapstick antics and endeared himself to the actors as a sympathetic, uncritical patron, a man who went to the theater for fun and wanted no tragedies or problem plays. Sometimes he would send Tumulty to scout a show in advance; and once, taking Mrs. Wilson and the secretary of War to a performance that Tumulty had approved, he said afterward that he should have taken Secretary Daniels because it was a "naval display."

Even in the White House, Wilson could persist in practicing the manners of a gentleman in his own home. Servants who had seen Theodore Roosevelt set the pace in going through doorways with a cheerleader's flourish were impressed by the insistence of Wilson that others precede him. He had a sixth sense for the feelings of guests who had to rise from their chairs when the President did, and he quickly made them forget the elegance of their surroundings. His family continued to marvel at his deft use of humor to break social strains and at his attentiveness to his own kin even when entertaining distinguished guests at table.

Under her new responsibilities Ellen Wilson was unchanged. "Ike" Hoover, the head usher, admired her genius in "coseying up" the big mansion. Familiar rugs and furniture were transported from Princeton, with the piano and favorite books. Moreover, she soon saved enough from annual appropriations so that she could redecorate some of the rooms and divide attic spaces into small guest chambers. Soon the family regarded the White House as "home," and visiting relatives remarked that Ellen's homes, no matter where they were, always had the same feeling.

The President loved to operate the little electric elevator in the White House, with its panels of mirrors, and his favorite apartments were the dining room and the Blue Room. Next to the Oval Room, where the immediate family spent their evenings, was his own study. In this sanctum he could be alone with his choicest books and with the old, familiar typewriter and its noisy clack—"it and I have gone through many thoughts together, and many emotions," he had written on it a month before taking office. His desk here, unlike the official one in the West Wing, was always piled high with documents.

Though he plunged like a bridegroom into the events of Inauguration Day, his strength was overtaxed in that first week by the ordeal of speeches and handshakings, family reunions and Cabinet meetings, problems of personnel and of etiquette. He still had the knack of relaxing in a nap whenever there were idle moments, but no opportunity came during the first exciting days in the White House. He had been giving himself constantly, and by the end of the week he was exhausted and his digestion failed him.

Fortunately there was a physician at hand. Annie Howe, the President's sister, had fallen on the stairs in the White House on Inauguration Day and gashed her forehead, and Dr. Cary Grayson had been called to attend her. This young medical officer of the Navy had served Taft, and in introducing him to Wilson the ex-President said: "Here is an excellent fellow that I hope you will get to know. I regret to say that he is a Democrat and a Virginian, but that's a matter that can't be helped."

On Sunday morning, March 9, Dr. Grayson attended the President and began his study of a case that was to absorb him for eight years. He found that Wilson was accustomed to taking a good deal of medicine and to have his stomach pumped out now and then, that he suffered occasional twinges from his old enemy, neuritis. Grayson learned, too, that the sight of one eye was still defective as a result of the attack of arteriosclerosis suffered in 1906, and that Dr. S. Weir Mitchell of Philadelphia doubted that the President could stand the strain of his new duties. Here was a mortal with symptoms of chronic invalidism, undertaking the arduous life of an office that, Wilson himself once said, requires "the constitution of an athlete, the patience of a mother, the endurance of the early Christian." [18]

On March 25, Wilson told his Cabinet that he would have to limit his indulgence in social affairs. Remarking that social life seemed to be the serious business of the greater part of Washington, he explained:

[18] Ruth Cranston, *The Story of W.W.*, p. 114. Grayson treated Wilson's neuritis by baking and massage, and doing away with medicines, put him on a diet of orange juice and raw eggs. Downing the first egg, the President said: "I feel as if I were swallowing a newborn babe." Dr. Grayson probably was less inclined than modern physicians would have been to associate the President's occasional digestive upsets with the progress of arteriosclerosis. On March 9 he ordered his patient to stay in bed, but Wilson protested that he would set a bad example to his people if he did not go to church, and he went. Dr. Taylor, his minister at the Central Congregational Church, recollects that Wilson appreciated "the quietness and great courtesy of the congregation." Dr. Taylor also records that the President inquired about pew rents and regular sittings and discussed gifts to current expense and benevolence, that Wilson stayed after one Sunday service for a business meeting, and that he sent flowers every Saturday, never on Sunday. James H. Taylor, *W.W., in Church.*

"While I am not ill, my health is not exceptionally good, and I have signed a protocol of peace with my doctor. I must be good."

On his first Sunday in the White House, Woodrow Wilson was serene in the knowledge that the launching of his administration had been auspicious. He did not, however, let his spirits run with the lavish optimism that had been his undoing at Princeton. He knew now that there were men who could not be trusted and enemies awaiting a chance to strike. "Remember," he cautioned Nellie one day when she exulted over his success, "the pack is always waiting near at hand to tear one to pieces. Popularity is the most evanescent thing in the world, and the most unimportant."

CHAPTER XVII

REVOLUTION IN A DEMOCRACY

ONCE HE HAD MADE himself and his kin at home in the White House and had put himself on friendly terms with his official family, Woodrow Wilson lost little time in undertaking to satisfy the expectations that had shone from the faces of the multitude at the inaugural ceremony. The Presidency, of which he had written so perceptively, was now his own office, to be made consequential or paltry in the history of his age. All depended on his will and the scope of his powers. The president had it "in his choice," Wilson had written in 1907, to be the political leader of the nation: "Let him once win the admiration and confidence of the country, and no other single force can withstand him, no combination of forces will easily overthrow him. His office is anything he has the sagacity and force to make it."

To achieve the leadership that he had described, Wilson could be expected to deny his mind the "literary" indulgence of regarding principles as "unities." [1] As a political leader, his ear "must ring with the voices of the people" and he must check his prophetic impulses and "serve the slow-paced daily need." To keep aloft in the gusty air of spiritual controversy, from which he had fallen disastrously at Princeton, he would now have to convince a national constituency that every venture was conceived for the common interest and without regard to his own welfare. If his office was to have prestige and power, Woodrow Wilson would have to keep himself personally humble.

The President-elect was singularly free from affiliation with any selfish interest. He could justly claim—though he was too modest to do so—that his own livelihood had come from honest intellectual toil and a touch of native genius. He liked to feel that those who had financed and promoted his election had done it not for him, personally, or for material reward, but rather out of devotion to ideals that they shared with him.

[1] Wilson had written in "Leaders of Men" in 1890: "Principles, as statesmen conceive them, are threads to the labyrinth of circumstances. . . . Throw the conceiving mind, habituated to contemplating wholes, into the arena of politics, and it seems to itself to be standing upon shifting sands, where no sure foothold and no upright posture are possible." Motter (ed.), *Leaders of Men*, p. 46.

Wilson came to the White House with faith that he was predestined to give effective expression to the progressive impulses that had been agitating American society with growing insistence for twenty years. He believed that the discontent of masses of citizens must be met by constructive law lest it erupt in violence. Theodore Roosevelt had dramatized the cause of equal opportunity for the plain people, and Taft had dallied with it; but it devolved on Wilson to put trained and sympathetic minds to work upon social maladjustments that had accompanied the growth of economic colossi. Obviously the ever-shifting line between the "necessary" and the "optional" functions of government—the line that he had defined a quarter century before in *The State*—would have to be plotted and drawn anew, under the breadth and majesty of the Constitution.

While resting in Bermuda after the election and reading *Philip Dru, Administrator*—the novel in which House set forth his philosophy and program of reform—Wilson had written a preface for a book that was to bring together significant sayings from his campaign speeches.[2] In this work, entitled *The New Freedom*, he wished "to express the new spirit of our politics and to set forth, in large terms which may stick in the imagination, what it is that must be done if we are to restore our politics to their full spiritual vigor again." In the view of this prophet, the natural foe to freedom was an irresponsible governing group who might use political power to serve selfish ends. Whether it was a military autocracy, a proletarian bureaucracy, or a plutocracy, the outcome would be the same. There would be tyranny and not freedom. With all the fierce tenacity of his blood, Woodrow Wilson was clinging to his overpowering purpose—the preservation of the liberty of the individual. Lecturing on constitutional law in 1907, he had said, "Liberty fixed in unalterable law would be no liberty at all. Government is a part of life, and, with life, it must change, alike in its objects and its practices; only this principle must remain unaltered—this principle of liberty, that there must be the freest right and opportunity of adjustment." This dynamic purpose was to be the gyroscopic stabilizer of his ship of state.

Coming back from his island meditations full of crusading vigor and with the direction of his thinking set, Wilson had determined to keep alive the sense of accountability that he had preached during the cam-

---

[2] *The New Freedom* was first published in monthly installments in *World's Work*, January–July, 1913. This book was too much clouded by the dust of political battle to be taken seriously by students of the government. Many dismissed it as "a maze of words" and regretted that there were few specifications for translating the words into deeds.

paign. Having won the election, he was free to speak his heart and conscience without fear that any man would accuse him of soliciting votes; and his tongue was loosed by the exposure in a Congressional investigation of methods by which bankers controlled vast industrial enterprises.[3] Unprepared as he was to present any reasoned, consistent plan for economic reform, he had given way to his feelings in tirades that shook the confidence of businessmen who were committed to special interests.

At a dinner of the Southern Society of New York, whose leaders had promoted his candidacy, the prophet had loosed the indignation that had been festering in him ever since his frustration at Princeton. His tense, resonant voice had asserted, as the hall became quiet and people sat forward in their chairs: "Business cannot be disturbed unless the minds of those who conduct it are disturbed." To Wilson a panic—like hell—was merely "a state of mind," because, he said, "when a panic occurs there is just as much wealth in the country the day after the panic as the day before." Sometimes, he explained, "panics are said to occur because certain gentlemen want to create the impression that the wrong thing is going to be done." To any man living who dared to precipitate a panic in that way, Wilson promised "a gibbet . . . as high as Haman's." And then he had added: "But that is only figuratively speaking. What I will do will be to direct the attention of the people to him, and I think that they will cut him to the quick."

In the view of progressives, here was a new sort of political leader —a man who dared to say the same thing after election day that he had said in the campaign. Four other addresses of similar tone had followed. Two were delivered at Staunton, Virginia, at a celebration of the prophet's fifty-sixth birthday. He slept in the old manse, in the room in which he was born; and speaking in the church in which his father had served a Presbyterian congregation, he warned businessmen that "they must render a service or get nothing," that in the future "the men who serve will be the men who profit." After quips that were reminiscent of his father's humor, he grew grim with reminders that the Presidency was "an office in which a man must put on his war paint," that there were "men who will have to be mastered in order that they shall be made the instruments of justice and mercy."[4]

---

[3] See p. 301.

[4] Josephus Daniels, in *The Wilson Era: Years of Peace* (pp. 521–23), has pointed out that these words were directed particularly against the Democratic machine in Virginia and Senator Martin, its boss. A friend of Thomas F. Ryan, Martin had regretted Wilson's nomination at Baltimore and had had a ferocious argument with Wilson when both were guests at the home of President Alderman of the University of Virginia.

To the minds of financiers whose thinking grew out of experience rather than theorizing, such talk was frightening. Consternation seized Wall Street and stock averages slid off 10 per cent.

At that juncture Colonel House, who immediately after the election had persuaded Wilson to say a few words to soothe the nerves of financiers, had stepped into the breach. Wilson could not have had a better advocate than the polite, well-groomed Texan who had a reputation for integrity in handling other people's money. Attending a dinner in New York at which five billions of capital were represented, House used all his conversational art to convince the diners that Woodrow Wilson would sign no demagogic laws and was not a despoiler of legitimate investment, but rather a leader intent on establishing conditions under which men of good character could do business with decency and security. The financial uncertainty of the day was caused by their own fears, he said boldly, and not by the President-elect. Three months before, when votes were sought, House had advised McCombs how to make political capital out of the opposition of these very financiers; but now that the election was over, the Colonel counseled conciliation.

Wilson himself had realized that he should coax as well as threaten in order to enlist businessmen in the progressive cause. Having driven his mind "all the way around the clock," he had become specific and had presented four points of policy that reflected advice received from Brandeis and House. Admitting his own inexperience in commerce, Wilson said at Chicago, in January of 1913: "I must take counsel with the men who do understand business, and I dare not take counsel with them unless they intend the same things that I intend . . . There is no bright prospect otherwise."

In the offices that he had filled before coming to the Presidency, Wilson had achieved initial success by concentrating upon just a few reforms that were both urgent and practical. "It will not do," the college professor had said fifteen years earlier, "to incarnate too many ideas at a time if you are to be universally understood and numerously followed." To give effect to his program the President would have first to agree with the Congress upon a few vital measures and then to per-

---

In an article entitled "Freemen Need No Guardians," Wilson alleged that "the masters of the government of the United States are the combined capitalists and manufacturers of the United States," that "the government of the United States at present is a foster-child of the special interests. It is not allowed to have a will of its own. It is told at every move, 'Don't do that: you will interfere with our prosperity.' And when we ask, 'Where is our prosperity lodged?' a certain group of gentlemen say, 'With us.' "

suade committeemen to accept the provisions that competent experts wished to write into law. Fortunately, the way had been smoothed, in the House of Representatives, by a wave of progressive bills that had been put through by a Democratic majority only to meet doom in the Senate or on the desk of President Taft.

In his inaugural address Wilson had itemized the matters that most obviously called for legislative action.

A tariff which cuts us off from our proper part in the commerce of the world, violates the just principles of taxation, and makes the Government a facile instrument in the hands of private interests; a banking and currency system based upon the necessity of the Government to sell its bonds fifty years ago and perfectly adapted to concentrating cash and restricting credits; an industrial system which, take it on all sides, financial as well as administrative, holds capital in leading strings, restricts the liberties and limits the opportunities of labor, and exploits without renewing or conserving the natural resources of the country; a body of agricultural activities never yet given the efficiency of great business undertakings or served as it should be through the instrumentality of science taken directly to the farm, or afforded the facilities of credit best suited to its practical needs; watercourses undeveloped, waste places unreclaimed, forests untended, fast disappearing without plan or prospect of renewal, unregarded waste heaps at every mine.

Not only must the economy of these things be studied, he said, but means must be perfected by which government might serve humanity by safeguarding the health and the civic rights of the citizens. And all these matters must be considered, he insisted, without forgetting "the old-fashioned, never-to-be-neglected, fundamental safeguarding of property and of individual right." This was "the high enterprise of the new day" to which he dedicated his administration. "We shall restore, not destroy," he promised. ". . . Justice and only justice, shall always be our motto."

A few days after the inauguration, White House spokesmen announced that the new President would help to construct important legislation.[5] Ten days later they added that he would go frequently to the Capitol to confer with party leaders. And less than a month after he had taken office Wilson read to his Cabinet a message for the legislators that called for action on the tariff. He would begin with this issue, he explained, because the party was united on it.

5 Some of Wilson's advisers felt that reform legislation should be deferred. However, when Houston raised objections to immediate action, House explained that bills could be passed most expeditiously before all the patronage was distributed.

When a Cabinet member recommended caution in lowering tariff rates, in view of uncertainty in business, Wilson replied that others had given that advice and that he was reminded of a cartoon of himself in a Western newspaper. He explained: "It pictures a great beast of a man standing over me saying: 'What do you mean by meaning what you said?' I must say now what I said before election."

Thirty years before, as a lawyer at Atlanta, Wilson had spoken before congressmen against protection; and in the long interval since, neither study nor experience had altered his view that the only justification for duties on imports was the need for revenue. He had denounced the Payne-Aldrich Law of the Taft regime as "merely a method of granting favours." He proposed no change so sharp or sudden that it might dislocate the economy, but wished to withdraw protection "steadily and upon a fixed programme upon which every man of business can base his definite forecasts and systematic plans." Reduction of duties had been a dominant issue in his campaign for the Presidency.

Once in office, however, Wilson knew that it would not be easy to redeem his pledge of tariff reform, in spite of the fact that many citizens attributed a sharp increase in the cost of living during the preceding decade to the high duties of Republican regimes. Cleveland's ship of state had foundered twice on the reef of tariff protection, and Taft had failed to effect the changes that his party's progressive faction had demanded. Consequently, Wilson resolved to dramatize the issue with a direct challenge to the legislators by his strongest weapon—the spoken word. He decided that he would speak before a special session of the Congress on April 8. It would be a long step toward the ideal of parliamentary responsibility that he had championed since youth.

When he told his Cabinet that he was thinking of taking this direct way of establishing a ministerial relation with the Congress, the men had qualms. To avoid offending the legislators, they decided to go to hear their chief individually instead of in a body; and Bryan, fearing that Speaker Champ Clark would be angered, decided to stay away. No president since the elder Adams had been so bold as to appear on the legislative rostrum. Jefferson had rejected the procedure as too reminiscent of addresses from the throne. Succeeding chief executives had transmitted their ideas by scripts that had grown voluminous. Droned by a clerk, they had lost point and bored those whom they were intended to exhort. And now, when an orator-president threatened to break tradition of more than a hundred years' standing and revert to a still earlier custom, there were fiery speeches from Democratic senators to whom the doctrine of "separation of powers" was sacred. Jealous of executive encroachment on their vested rights, senators were so obstructive that Vice-President Marshall, presiding over the Senate and fearing that formal action might result in a rebuff, declared the question to be one of high privilege for which unanimous consent was not necessary.

There was no doubt of the success of the President's bold venture in so far as it arrested unprecedented attention on the part of the legislators and the voters of the nation. Spick-and-span in a Prince Albert coat, Wilson left a Cabinet meeting to go to the hill soon after noon on April 8. He found the corridors of the Capitol thronged with men and women clamoring for admission. The members of Congress and hundreds of spectators had crowded into the House chamber, and when the President entered all rose to applaud. Yet there was embarrassment in the air, nervousness among the legislators, and sullen looks here and there. Wilson himself was a trifle pale and tense as he walked briskly to his place, for he was aware that the ice on which he trod was thin. After his old rival, Speaker Champ Clark, had mumbled an introduction, the invader from the Wihte House stood quiet for just a moment with a trace of a smile on his lips, quaking inwardly. Then he launched into a disarming introduction that he had drafted with meticulous fondling of words.

He was glad, he said, to have this opportunity to verify the impression that the President was "a human being trying to cooperate with other human beings in a common service" and not "a mere department of the Government hailing Congress from some isolated island of jealous power, sending messages, not speaking naturally with his own voice." After this pleasant experience, he assured the legislators, he would feel quite normal in dealing with them.

The latent opposition thawed as he went on to win the confidence of his audience. Explaining that he had called Congress into extraordinary session so that the duty laid upon the majority party at the election might be performed and so that businessmen might not have to be kept too long in suspense as to fiscal changes to come, he said: "Only new principles of action will save us from a final hard crystallization of monopoly and a complete loss of the influences that quicken enterprise and keep independent energy alive. It is plain what those principles must be. We must abolish everything that bears even the semblance of privilege or of any kind of artificial advantage, and put our businessmen and producers under the stimulation of a constant necessity to be efficient, economical, and enterprising, masters of competitive supre-

macy, better workers and merchants than any in the world. Aside from
the duties laid upon articles which we do not, and probably can not,
produce, therefore, and the duties laid upon luxuries and merely for
the sake of the revenues they yield, the object of the tariff duties henceforth laid must be effective competition, the whetting of American
wits by contest with the wits of the rest of the world." They must not
move "with reckless haste," and should seek "a more free and wholesome development, not revolution or upset or confusion."

In ten minutes he had covered his subject and was through. After
a moment of silence the applause overwhelmed him. Delighted by the
success of his bold stroke of statesmanship, he laughed gaily when Ellen
Wilson told him, during their ride home, that it was the sort of thing
that Roosevelt would have enjoyed doing, had he thought of it. "Yes,"
he responded, "I think I put one over on Teddy."

The day after his address to the Congress, enheartened by editorial
approval of his venture, Wilson took the novel step of going to the
President's room at the Capitol and conferring with a committee of
the Senate. In 1897 he had written that Cleveland was disliked by
Congress because he was an "outsider." By cultivating close relations
with legislators he hoped to avoid similar embarrassment. He asked for
an album of photographs of the members of Congress and spent hours
in studying their faces. He set apart three hours each week to welcome
calls from them, and when he was unable to receive unannounced
visitors from the Hill, Tumulty did his best to assuage their disappointment. Freshman congressmen found him a sympathetic listener, for he
made them feel that he, like themselves, had much to learn about a
new job.

Woodrow Wilson's appearances in the Capitol in defiance of tradition were a symbol to his people of his creed. By taking initiative he
put upon private lobbies the burden of proving that their proposals
were in the public interest, and he discouraged logrolling among the
legislators. Moreover, he had ready for the congressmen a definite
schedule of revised tariffs that was the result of long study and that was
based on Democratic bills that Taft had vetoed. For months past Wilson
had conferred and corresponded with Chairman Oscar W. Underwood
of the Ways and Means Committee, an opponent for the nomination
at Baltimore who had now become a willing collaborator; and the
party's caucus had decided to gather into an omnibus bill the various
proposals of reform with which Democrats and Republican insurgents
had been inconclusively waging guerrilla warfare in 1911 and 1912.

Wilson had taken a hand in the setting of rates on sugar and wool that were lower than the party men dared to propose. Early in April he engaged in what he regarded as "a death grapple" with the sugar lobbyists and gave them an ultimatum: if they did not accept a drastic reduction in the duty on raw sugar for a trial period of three years,[6] he would insist on free sugar immediately.

When it became apparent that the reductions in tariffs would leave the government impoverished, it was decided to take advantage of the Income Tax Amendment, which had just been ratified by the states. Welcoming the opportunity to shift some of the burden of taxation from the poor to the rich, though with no intention of using the new tax to distribute wealth, Congressman Cordell Hull drafted a provision that the President studied with keen interest. Wilson explained that he wished to exempt everyone receiving less than $3,000 a year from making a report. He would burden as few as possible with "the obligations involved in the administration of what will at best be an unpopular law."[7]

The tariff bill that Underwood's committee reported favorably to the House on April 22 provoked debate that at times became acrimonious. The President and his lieutenants, however, stood solidly together. When opponents insinuated in the press that Underwood's prestige was being enhanced and might eclipse Wilson's, the President commented: "If Mr. Underwood or anybody else can displace me by the work they do in the service of the country, they are fully entitled to do so, and I have no jealousy in the matter. But I do not believe, for my own part, that there is any such thought or purpose." Under skillful leadership the tariff bill, with the income-tax provision, passed the House on May 8 with a majority of 281 to 139.

The outcome was not surprising, for more than a third of the 290 Democratic members of the new Congress had been elected for the first time under Woodrow Wilson's banner and therefore looked naturally to the President for direction. Furthermore, the old war horses, once they were assured that Wilson and Burleson would consult them on matters of patronage and would not supplant them with progressives in the committee chairmanships, were willing to cooperate

---

[6] Wilson set the trial period at three years in the hope that sugar would be on the free list before the end of his term of office. Daniels Diary, April 4, 1913.

[7] W.W. to Underwood, April 16, 1913. A corporation excise tax had been included in the Payne-Aldrich tariff to get revenue, and Hull persuaded the House to extend this to individuals. *See* Cordell Hull, *The Memoirs of Cordell Hull*, I, 70 ff. A "graduated income tax" was one of the measures advocated by Colonel House's fictitious administrator, Philip Dru.

with the leader who had brought the Democrats back to power. Realizing that the party's welfare depended on the success of the Administration, the legislators were eager to help their chief make good. Moreover, there was a disposition to act promptly, since the party, which had been voted into office by a minority of the ballots cast, could count on ascendancy only until the next Congressional election, a mere year and a half away.

The history of tariff legislation, however, gave warning that the Underwood Bill would not go through the Senate without controversy and change. Though Nelson Aldrich was gone from the Republican ranks, stalwarts were left who were competent to make the most of all the devices of obstruction. Moreover, the Democratic majority in the Senate was too small to be conclusive without unanimity, and it was certain that senators from states that raised sugar and wool would be under intense pressure from constituents who would be hurt by the new rates.

While the tariff bill was in the House, Wilson had worked—often at the instance of Congressional leaders—to bolster the morale of key men by conference or letter. He failed, however, to assure harmonious party action by immediately effecting a caucus of Democratic senators; and as soon as the Underwood Bill was put before the Senate, the air reeked with the sort of propaganda that the President had hoped to circumvent. When it was reported in the press that he sought a compromise, he said to newsmen: "When you get a chance just say that I am not the kind that considers compromises when I once take my position." Politicians and lawyers who were retained to represent business interests that would suffer under the proposed rates besieged the Capitol and asked to be heard before the Finance Committee. However, when the Administration argued that the issues already had been made clear through endless discussion, the Democrats stood together to defeat the obstructionists on the floor of the Senate by five votes.

This rebuff merely intensified the activity of interests that in the past had virtually dictated the rates that were to apply to their several products. Their pestiferous agents infested hotels, clubs, and even private homes. It seemed to Wilson that "a brick couldn't be thrown without hitting one of them." Senators were wooed by threats and entreaties, by editorials, pamphlets, and resolutions, and by a mass of personal messages. The President was alarmed; for if he failed in this venture he could expect to achieve little in other directions. When congressmen urged him to issue a blast that would put the lobbyists immediately on the defensive, he gave a bold statement to the press without consulting his Cabinet. Published on May 26, it read: "Washington has seldom seen so numerous, so industrious, or so insidious a lobby . . . It is of serious interest to the country that the people at large should have no lobby and be voiceless in these matters, while great bodies of astute men seek to create an artificial opinion and to overcome the interests of the public for their private profit . . . Only public opinion can check and destroy it." Thus did the prophet turn his well-known spotlight of "pitiless publicity" upon the "invisible government" at Washington.

This aggressive stroke in the public interest provoked resentment. Was there improper lobbying, the *New York Times* asked editorially, or were protected producers simply taking legitimate steps to present their cases to the Congress? Republican legislators complained that the President was aspersing their integrity, and they retaliated by insinuating that Wilson used questionable means to control the voting of his Democrats. Determined to make the President prove his imputation that senators were improperly influenced by "insidious" lobbies, the opposition proposed that a committee of five be appointed to investigate the matter. This move worked to Wilson's advantage, however, when Senator LaFollette made a suggestion that turned the investigation into a series of hearings in which, for the first time in American history, his colleagues had to bare their private economic interests to public scrutiny. Democrats who felt responsible to high-tariff constituencies could not withstand this ordeal by publicity, especially when it was supplemented by personal pressure from the White House.

The President hesitated to invite interviews, and explained his reluctance to Senator Hitchcock thus: "I shrink more than I think many persons realize from seeming to try to press my own views upon men who have an equal reponsibility with myself." Ellen Wilson, however, persuaded him to invite influential legislators to dinner; and after ironing out wrinkles in the tariff program with them, the President said to Grayson: "You see what a wise wife I have!" Realizing that on so vital an issue he must be aggressive, he received many delegations of senators and conferred with them often in his room at the Capitol. His argument followed the pattern used with the New Jersey legislators. "Here are the facts; here are the principles; here are our obligations as Democrats." What were they going to do about it? If they failed to share his feeling of the inevitability of a certain course of action, his smiles gave way to grim challenge. If they did not agree with him, they would still have to follow, for the responsibility had been put upon him by the people. If they wished to debate the matter with him before the people, that was their privilege. But to most legislators it was not a privilege to be lightly exercised. To a group of seven legislators from west of the Mississippi, who warned that the proposed bill so offended sugar producers that, if enacted, it would prevent their re-election, the President replied that if the party were to repudiate its tariff pledge it would not matter whether or not it had any senators from the West because it would "be kicked out of office by the American people."

Wilson had a special telephone put in so that he might keep in touch with the Capitol constantly; and from the piles of commendatory messages that came to him from the people he forwarded to wavering senators those from members of their own constituencies. Sparks from his waving torch had set off rockets at the grass roots that were scorching the representatives of the people. Even hostile newspapers were marveling at the consistency of the philosophy of the new President and at his "matchless political strategy."

Finally, on June 20, Wilson succeeded in bringing together a caucus of Democratic senators—the first, remarked the *New York Times*, that anyone could remember. At the end of a fortnight of hot discussion, free sugar and free wool were approved and it was understood that the bill would be a party undertaking that all Democrats were committed to support.

When the measure was formally laid before the Senate on July 11 by Simmons of North Carolina, whom Wilson had been persuaded not to punish for voting for the Republican tariff bill in 1909, it was clear that the President was winning the battle on which he had staked his program. The Republicans prolonged debate; and the President failed to convince the Louisiana senators that, having dutifully spoken in caucus of their constituents' objection to free sugar, they were bound by party loyalty to abide by the decision of the majority.[8] Yet after an attack by radicals of both parties on the proposed income-tax schedules forced a compromise that raised both the exemption and the rates for the higher brackets, the tariff bill was passed. It went through on September 9 by a vote of 44 to 37. A few days later the President had a gay letter from Walter Hines Page, who had gone to London as ambassador: "I have been telling Bagehot's successor in the editorship

[8] On July 15, Wilson wrote to Senator Thornton of Louisiana thus: "No party can ever for any length of time control the Government or serve the people which cannot command the allegiance of its own minority. I feel that there are times, after every argument has been given full consideration and men of equal public conscience have conferred together, when those who are overruled should accept the principle of party government . . ."

of the *Economist* that the passing of commercial supremacy to the United States will be dated in the economic histories from the tariff act of 1913."

After conferees from the Senate and the House had ironed out differences, the final measure, known as the Underwood-Simmons Bill, went to the White House for signature. Fifty loyal Democrats were at the executive offices on October 3 to celebrate the triumph. They clapped as their hero approached the desk where the act lay, ready for his signature, and he responded with deep feeling: "I have had the accomplishment of something like this at heart since I was a boy," he said, and then—appropriately enough in view of the loyal influence that Cabinet officers had wielded among the party's legislators—"I know men standing around me can say the same thing."

The act had been put through after what some men regarded as the most significant tariff battle in American history. It established the principle that the income tax was to supplement import duties as a major source of federal revenue, and one whose relative incidence on citizens of varying wealth could be precisely adjusted. Moreover, the new law effected a reduction in duties that to reactionaries seemed revolutionary.[9] The Underwood-Simmons Act had been honestly drafted, and as it underwent changes in the Senate the President had kept a vigilant eye on its wording and on at least one occasion had detected a "joker." He had made sure that this law would not, like the Payne-Aldrich Tariff Law, harbor devices that concealed exhorbitant rates from the eye of the casual reader.

By bold, aggressive tactics the new President had come through his first major offensive against reactionary forces and had established mastery of his party's legislators. The man of promise had become a man of achievement.

[9] In the new act the average *ad valorem* rate of the Payne-Aldrich tariff of 1909 had been brought down from over 40 per cent to about 25. In addition to putting raw wool and other staples on the free list, the new measure removed or reduced duties on goods that America supplied in great quantity to the world market, such as agricultural machinery and other manufactures. Altogether, tariffs were lowered on more than 900 items.

CHAPTER XVIII

Banking and Currency Reform

Exhilarating as wilson's triumph was, he did not gloat long over it, for there was still more difficult business afoot. In the same breath with which he congratulated his associates upon the passage of the tariff act, the President said: "There is every reason to believe that currency reform will be carried through with equal energy, directness, and loyalty to the general interest." This was the second step that he had proposed —to set the business of the country free.

Woodrow Wilson had come into the Presidency less expert in the technique of banking than in that of tariff making, but his grounding in the philosophy of credit was both broad and deep. At the Johns Hopkins he had read almost every treatise on the monetary history and experience of the United States and had mastered Bagehot's *Lombard Street*. His interest in the subject had quickened as a result of the Panic of 1893 and popular agitation for free silver, and in 1897 he had asserted that nothing but currency reform could touch the cause of discontent. He had ascribed the Panic of 1907, which had obstructed his quadrangle plan, in part to the nation's banking practice. Standing under a giant rubber tree in a Bermuda street, he had said to a friend: "I would reform the banking laws; they are a disgrace to our great country." [1]

The Panic of 1907 had stimulated bankers, under the leadership of Republican Senator Aldrich, to try to substitute a centralized banking system for the inelastic and unscientific credit structure that had collapsed three times since the Civil War. A National Monetary Commission studied the banking systems of the world and reported to Congress, in 1911 and 1912, a plan that was drawn up largely by Paul M. Warburg of Kuhn, Loeb & Company and endorsed by the American Bankers' Association. A great central institution was proposed, with fifteen regional branches that were to be controlled by member banks.

This proposal, and a Republican act of 1908 that had increased the reserve of currency, did not satisfy progressives, who dreaded the "money power" with which the name of Aldrich—a protectionist—was

[1] Mrs. Borden Harriman to the writer, Feb. 22, 1951.

indelibly associated. They feared a revival of the national bank that Andrew Jackson had destroyed. Wilson, however, saw both the economic advantages of the sort of scheme that Aldrich proposed and the danger of its exploitation by selfish interests. His essential problem was to give to the nation the technical safeguards against panic that the Republicans had worked out and, at the same time, to reassure his progressive Democratic colleagues by providing a controlling personnel in whose altruism the public would have confidence. This was by far the greatest challenge to his leadership that Woodrow Wilson had yet faced. Clearly envisioning the evil to be overcome and the goal to be attained, he knew that only by a concert of trained and selfless minds could a sound path be plotted.

Between election and inauguration, Wilson felt the full force of a new explosion of antitrust sentiment. During that period Congressman Pujo's Committee on Banking and Currency, which had been instructed by the House of Representatives to investigate the extent and significance of money monopolies, held spectacular hearings to which famous private bankers were summoned. There was an airing of the legal devices by which a few financiers, keeping clear of the Sherman Antitrust Act, were able to exert control over vast industrial empires. J. Pierpont Morgan, who had participated in drastic action to check the Panic of 1907, was forced to testify; and he and his associates, unskilled in public relations and unable to make clear the respects in which their interests coincided with those of the nation, left an impression of callousness to the common welfare. The Pujo Committee handed in a report of its investigation just four days before Wilson took office, the press played it up sensationally, and progressives looked the more eagerly to the new Administration for quick and decisive relief.

Fortunately, the Congressional probe of the trusts had a more constructive aspect than that which was luridly publicized. While one subcommittee was making sensational disclosures, another, directed by Representative Carter Glass and advised by an expert, H. Parker Willis, had taken in hand the report of the National Monetary Commission and was formulating a substitute for the Aldrich plan. Two days after the election Glass had written to Wilson, whom he had met and come to admire during the campaign, to report that a tentative bill had been drafted and that he wished advice from the President-elect, since the matter would require stern executive leadership in the next Congress. Impressed by the earnestness of this letter, Wilson replied: "The question of the revision of the currency is one of such capital importance that I wish to devote the utmost serious and immediate attention to it." Making good his intention, the President had studied the matter during his vacation in Bermuda. He invited reports from Professor Royal Meeker of Princeton, with whom he had discussed the possibility of giving flexibility to the gold content of the dollar; moreover, he had letters of advice from House, who as a banker and cotton planter in Texas had learned to distrust money monopolies and an inelastic currency.[2]

At first Wilson agreed with Bryan in distrusting the centralized nature of the Aldrich plan, and shared Glass's inclination toward a system of disconnected regional banks; and when House questioned the wisdom of this, the President referred him to the plank in the party's platform opposing "the so-called Aldrich plan or the establishment of a central bank."[3] The President was eager for more knowledge, more time to reflect, as he approached this massive legislative problem, which he described to House as "the most fundamental question of all."

Returning to Princeton from Bermuda in December, the President-elect had been ready to act. Though bitterly cold weather and Christmas festivities combined to put him to bed, he propped himself up with pillows and received Glass and Willis on December 26. Icicles hung outside the frosted windows as discussion began upon the most momentous economic legislation of twentieth-century America. Balancing his spectacles on his thumb, Wilson listened to the proposal of his advisers. Soon his eyes brightened and he said that they were "on the right track." He showed willingness to oppose banking interests on a principle that seemed economically sound; and then he made several suggestions. One of his proposals was to be a bone of contention for months to come. He recommended that supervision of the new system be entrusted, not to a board of bankers, as the Aldrich plan had contemplated, nor to the comptroller of the currency, as Glass proposed, but rather to an altruistic Federal Reserve Board that would stand at Washington as a "capstone" of the structure. He wished this body to exercise only supervisory powers and not the commercial functions

[2] On March 21, 1913, Meeker sent to Wilson a list of five questions that had been sent to twenty-four leading economists, with a summary of their replies.

[3] Baker has suggested (IV, 142 n.) that House's effort to justify a centralized system without dishonoring the platform may have resulted from the Colonel's being misled by the Democratic Textbook for 1912, which printed the plank in question so that it read, erroneously: "the so-called Aldrich plan *for* the establishment of a central bank." This would have permitted House to argue in good faith that the platform did not forbid any central bank, but simply one of the type proposed by Aldrich.

that had led to disaster in the past. He was for "plenty of centralization," he said, "but not too much."[4]

Glass had been impressed by the President-elect's insistence upon action and by his deference to expert advice. Red-haired and wiry, the Virginian had a peppery temperament that expressed itself forcefully in his newspaper and in the House of Representatives, where he had served ten years. Like Wilson, he had revolted against a state political machine; and when House came to offer him state patronage in return for his support for sound banking legislation, the Virginian's sense of propriety had been outraged. Glass had been bombarded by thousands of messages from citizens in all walks of life demanding reform legislation. Like Wilson, he had kept an open mind and listened to disinterested, scholarly advice. Though at first Glass looked askance at the President-elect's suggestion of a "capstone" board of control, he and Willis, after committee hearings at which bankers and businessmen advocated a system highly centralized and privately controlled, had drafted a bill that embodied Wilson's idea and had taken it to him at Trenton on January 30. The President-elect covenanted to support Glass when he learned that reactionaries were opposing the choice of the Virginian as chairman of the Currency Committee in the new House of Representatives. He told House and McAdoo that suggestions on banking legislation should be put before Glass.

On March 28, reading to his Cabinet the special message on the tariff that he was to give to the Congress in person, Wilson alluded to the reform of the banking and currency laws as a matter that "should press close upon the heels of the tariff changes, if not accompany them." He explained that he wanted action on currency legislation during the current session of Congress despite the desire of some Democratic legislators to concentrate on tariff reform for the present. Wilson felt that the prospect of salutary currency legislation would reassure those who feared that after tariff reductions there would not be enough money to do the increasing business of the nation.[5]

The details of the currency bill were so well guarded that serious controversy within the party had been avoided until the inauguration was over. However, the essence of the plan leaked into circulation and through news stories it reached the Cabinet members and also Robert

---

[4] Carter Glass, *An Adventure in Constructive Finance,* pp. 81–82; H. P. Willis, *The Federal Reserve System,* pp. 141 ff.

[5] Daniels Diary, Mar. 28, 1913. The party was committed to this course, Wilson reminded his men, even though the Administration might sign its own death warrant at the polls; in any event, it would be realized someday that they were serving the real interests of the people.

L. Owen, a friend of Bryan's who was chairman of the Senate Finance Committee. The senator wondered why he had not been consulted. Himself president of a bank in Oklahoma, Owen was drafting a currency bill that differed from Glass's measure in two important particulars: it would put control of the new system firmly in the hands of a board of public officials appointed by the President rather than a body in which bankers would be represented; and currency issues were to be the responsibility of the government rather than of the reserve banks.

When Bryan told the President that he shared the views of Senator Owen, Wilson was distressed. He saw the approach of the inevitable crisis that he had dreaded. The time was coming to deal with the agrarians. Although Wilson already had told Glass of his sympathy with progressive demands for control of the banking system by a board on which public appointees would predominate, but he had not reached a conclusion regarding responsibility for the issue of currency. Colonel House, influenced by the views of financiers with whom he maintained contact—especially Paul Warburg, Aldrich's collaborator—had been warning the President against any concession to unsound sentiment. On the other hand, Wilson had to satisfy the agrarian progressives in order to hold his party together.

The thinking of the plainsmen was so foggy, in the view of the economists who were advising Glass, that it seemed best to solicit their political support by wooing Bryan himself. The conversion of the Great Commoner to a measure that was based essentially on spadework sponsored by Senator Aldrich, a Republican conservative, called for masterful leadership.

House set the stage for agreement by preliminary talks with both Bryan and Wilson; and on May 19 the President had it out with the colleague whose political support he needed in order to put Owen and the Senate behind a sound currency act. The President had been assiduous, since his inauguration, in reciprocating the goodwill that Bryan had shown. When he read the Glass Bill to the Great Commoner, therefore, Bryan responded in good spirit, offering to resign if his views embarrassed his chief and agreeing not to make his objections public. However, his criticisms of the draft were definite and apparently ineradicable. He was not willing to give private bankers control of the issue of currency. Moreover, he suggested that banking reform should not be brought up in Congress until the tariff bill had been passed and signed.

Having assured Bryan that he would be given another chance to review the bill, Wilson then asked Tumulty to try his hand at mollifying the veteran crusader by expressing the President's high regard for him. Accordingly, Tumulty called at the home of the secretary of state; and there, beaming with boyish pride, Bryan showed the emissary a picture that Wilson had autographed for him and spoke with deep feeling of his admiration for the President. Tumulty was able to allay Bryan's suspicions that Wall Street men were influencing the drafting of the measure; and when he returned to the White House he took with him the text of the Democratic platform and called to the President's attention certain passages on currency reform that Bryan had read to him. "I am convinced that there is a great deal in what Mr. Bryan says," Wilson commented noncommittally, and he permitted Tumulty to place Bryan's views before Glass and to suggest that the latter confer with McAdoo and Senator Owen in an effort to reach an understanding. Obviously it would take more pleading, and perhaps some concessions, to make the banking bill palatable to the secretary of state and his following in Congress.

Fortunately, the President had a secretary of the treasury who was both dynamic and tactful. Wilson discussed currency reform with McAdoo shortly after the inauguration, and the men found themselves in agreement on the vital points. McAdoo kept in touch with both conservative and progressive sentiment, and bankers gave him technical advice in conferences that he arranged at New York. It seemed to Wilson that his secretary of the treasury might aid in the education of their colleague, Bryan, and he asked McAdoo to undertake this.

Wooing the goodwill of the secretary of state without losing patience at his ignorance of fiscal realities, McAdoo appealed to Bryan's sense of responsibility as a member of the government. He made the Great Commoner see that, if the United States was to be responsible for the issue of currency under the Federal Reserve plan, as Bryan and Senator Owen wished, the notes must be secured by solid assets such as those of the member banks. Thus in the end the Great Commoner, softened by the blandishments of Wilson, House, and Tumulty, succumbed to McAdoo's patient accommodation of argument to Bryan's power of comprehension.

Meanwhile Colonel House was assiduous in catalyzing the meeting of minds. He dined with Owen and eased him back into sound channels when the senator broke loose with Bryanesque ideas; and he suggested that the currency measure be called "the Glass-Owen bill," hoping thus to flatter the senator and induce him to work harmoniously with Congressman Glass. Dining with prominent bankers whom he respected, the Colonel assured them of the soundness of the Administration's intentions. When they showed eagerness to participate in writing the new banking legislation, he reminded them gently that progressives were insisting that the President take no advice from financiers who had large private interests. Through the Colonel, Wilson could keep in touch with the thinking of financiers with whom he could not talk directly without forfeiting the confidence of agrarian progressives. But when House wanted to work with McAdoo and Glass to "whip into shape" a conservative measure that could be handed to Senator Owen, Wilson did not respond. House was a dear fellow and invaluable as an intelligence agent; but sometimes the friendly Colonel seemed to give his heart too freely to the last great man with whom he had dined and chatted, whether it was conservative Paul Warburg or trust-busting Samuel Untermyer. Wilson did not think it wise to prescribe to the Senate any bill prepared by House, McAdoo, and Glass. Desiring to avoid the appearance of dictating legislation, he preferred that Senator Owen, like Congressman Glass, should take the initiative and come to him for counsel.

Making himself available at all times to his lieutenants and putting his persuasive eloquence and the prestige of his office at their disposal, Wilson shrank from direct contact with strong prejudices, whether of the right or the left. As the ideas of bankers, economists, and politicians funneled in upon him, he tried to understand the reasoning of all but was aware of the bias of each.

In the last analysis, if his vision was to amount to more than a fancy, he must depend on the staff of his ship of state, who would float or sink together on the sea of history. He had to do business with Glass and Owen, who were the initiators of action in Congress, and with McAdoo, who was responsible for the credit of the government. But before sitting down with these men to make a final bill that would fully reconcile the Glass version with a draft that Owen sent to the White House late in May, Wilson turned once more to Louis D. Brandeis.

Denied a seat in the Cabinet, the "people's lawyer" lunched often with other liberal attorneys and publicists at the Willard Hotel in an informal group that called itself "the doughtnut Cabinet." Brandeis had been called to the White House to give advice at least twice since the inauguration, and he conceived that his role was to promote a harmonious council of progressives within the Administration. The attorney had perceived, in his studies of insurance and railroad corporations, how control had been concentrated in the hands of a few financiers who sometimes used their positions to increase their own economic power rather than to serve the public. After conferring with Wilson on June 11, he wrote on the 14th to the President thus:

> The power to issue currency should be vested exclusively in government officials, even when the currency is issued against commercial paper. The American people will not be content to have the discretion necessarily involved vested in a Board composed wholly or in part of bankers, for their judgment may be biased by private interest or affiliation. The function of the bankers should be limited strictly to that of an advisory council. . . . Nothing would go so far in establishing confidence among businessmen as the assurance that the government will control the currency issues . . ."[6]

With this support from Brandeis, the President was convinced that he had been right in suggesting to Glass, months before, that the new banking system should be supervised by an altruistic public board rather than by representatives of member banks. Moreover, he was inclined now to reject House's final advice against government guarantee of currency and to support Bryan and Owen in this matter provided that the notes be based on the assets of the reserve banks. He was impressed also by Brandeis's proposal of an advisory board of bankers, thinking that this would help to ensure cooperative participation by those who would be responsible for the technical operation of the new system.

On June 18, Wilson called McAdoo, Glass, and Owen to the White House and told them that the Federal Reserve Board would be made up of Treasury officials and men appointed by the President, and that the currency would be guaranteed by the government, though issued by the member banks against commercial assets and a gold reserve. On the next day the text of the measure was published officially.

Glass rebelled against control of the reserve system by a government board, for he dreaded the possibility of political interference with sound banking. Wilson and McAdoo insisted, however, upon regulation in the public interest; and when McAdoo's fertile mind put forward a suggestion that appealed to Glass as a compromise, the congressman agreed to a "capstone" board of seven men, of whom two or three would be ex officio.[7]

6 Alpheus Thomas Mason, *Brandeis,* pp. 398–99.

7 Later it was decided that five of the seven-man board would be appointed by the President. Though Glass acted upon his chief's decision in the matter of government control, he was not convinced. Afterward he wrote a letter reiterating his views, and later he brought a

Having won Glass's reluctant acquiescence in this matter, the President had less difficulty in persuading the congressman to accept government guarantee of currency. At first, however, Glass enumerated the many kinds of security already provided for the notes to be issued and argued that an additional safeguard would be mere pretense.

"Exactly so, Glass," Wilson replied with a twitching of his left eye that bespoke his earnestness. "Every word you say is true: the government liability *is* a mere thought. And so, if we can hold to the substance of the thing and give the other fellow the shadow, why not do it, if thereby we can save the bill?"

While yielding to agrarian sentiment for government control of currency issue, Wilson would retain the solid substance of bank assets behind the notes. To make sure that his position was understood by Glass's committee, who had been consulted very little during the drafting of the bill and who had not organized until early June, he invited the members to the White House on June 20. It seemed to Glass that "the intimate touch of a tactician" was needed, and this the President tried to supply. One of the men asked rudely why they were there, since the text of the bill already had been settled. Taking offense at this imputation of dictatorship, Wilson was tempted to invite the questioner to leave the room; instead, he went on to answer queries courteously, parry objections with gentle reasoning, and command the respect of these politicians for himself, for Glass, and for their cause.

Finally, on June 26, Glass and Owen submitted identical bills to the House and the Senate, embodying Wilson's final decision. It was understood that, having chosen the ground with care, the Administration would stand and fight upon it no matter how hot the Washington summer or how heavy the fire of the enemy. When Wilson told Bryan of the compromise decisions, the Great Commoner assured him that the legislation would be acceptable to progressives and that he would release a statement to that effect.

The President himself brought the currency battle into the public

---

delegation of bankers to the White House to help him convince the President that he was wrong. Though two of the financiers assailed Wilson forthrightly and bitterly, the President listened so courteously that Glass was shamed and began to wish that he had not brought the men. When they were through, Wilson turned toward two caustic attackers and asked mildly: "Will one of you gentlemen tell me in what civilized country of the earth there are important government boards of control on which private interests are represented?" Getting no answer, he went on: "Which of you gentlemen thinks the railroads should select members of the Interstate Commerce Commission?" Carter Glass, *An Adventure in Constructive Finance,* p. 116. Thus the bankers were silenced and Glass was convinced. It was an interview that Wilson took a grim pleasure in recounting on occasions when the primacy of the public interest was challenged.

arena and fired the first shot at one o'clock on June 23, a few hours after Bryan had made known his endorsement of the program. The tariff bill had been passed by the House but was still in the Senate when Wilson went before the Congress for a second time to accelerate the momentum that he had gained by his unprecedented leadership. Cautious advisers had suggested that, if the wounds made in the tariff fight were irritated during the hot weather, it might be fatal to party harmony; but the President was so consumed by his cause that he could not free his mind of it for an hour. "Everybody must be seen," he confided to Mary Hulbert the day before going to the Capitol. "Every right means must be used to direct the thought and purpose of those who, outside of Washington, are to criticize it and form public opinion about it. It is not like the tariff, about which opinion has been definitely forming long years through. To form a single plan and a single intention about it seems at times a task so various and so elusive that it is hard to keep one's heart from failing." But he assured himself that his heart was not in the habit of failing.

He presented his banking program to a joint session of the Congress in a talk that was over in ten minutes. The principles were clear: there must be a currency "readily, elastically responsive to sound credit," a mobilization of reserves for legitimate uses, a ban upon concentration of resources for speculative purposes, and controls vested in the government, "so that the banks may be the instruments, not the masters, of business and of individual enterprise and initiative." Thus once more Woodrow Wilson singled out a great cause and dramatized it as a crusade for virtue in which he would march shoulder to shoulder with loyal comrades of the faith.

Having demanded that the Congress sit through the summer and legislate on the tariff and the currency, he could not himself escape from Washington. In the spring he had discussed vacation plans with his family, and falling in love with pictures of Harlakenden, an estate at Cornish in the hills of New Hampshire, they had rented it. Wilson hoped at least to escort his family to Harlakenden or to spend the Fourth of July there. The slow progreess of legislation, however, made him put off their departure for days. Finally Mrs. Wilson and the girls were persuaded to start out. The President could go with them only as far as the railroad station. When he left, his wife wept and lay in her berth and refused food. But once settled in the hill colony of artists and men of letters she took up her painting and lived from mail to mail, craving news of her husband. And as for him, it set his apprehensive mind at ease to read newspaper accounts of his Ellen's tea parties and to think of his dear ones amidst artists and literary folk. Such an idyllic environment was "just where they belonged," he thought.

July 2 was set as the date for announcement of the betrothal of his second daughter to Francis B. Sayre, whom the President had received, at first, with his usual stiffness toward suitors of his daughters, but whom he had come to regard as "almost good enough for Jessie." Wilson could not attend the engagement party because of an invitation to speak at Gettysburg on the Fourth, and he wrote on June 29 to break the bad news to his Ellen:

My darling sweetheart,

I can hardly keep back the tears as I write this morning. It is a bitter, bitter thing that I cannot come to my dear ones; but the duty is clear, and that ought to suffice. I cannot choose as an individual what I shall do; I must choose always as a President, ready to guard at every turn and in every way possible the success of what I have to do for the people. Apparently the little things count quite as much as the big in this strange business of leading opinion and securing action; and I must not kick against the pricks . . . The President is a superior kind of slave, and must content himself with the reflection that the *kind* is superior!

Explaining that he had declined the invitation to speak at Gettysburg with others of the same sort, but that Congressman Palmer had heard talk in Congress that had made the occasion seem of great importance, he went on:

It is no ordinary celebration. It is the half-century celebration of the turning battle of the war. Both blue and gray are to be there. It is to celebrate the end of all strife between the sections. Fifty years ago, almost, also on the Fourth of July, Mr. Lincoln was there (in the midst of business of the most serious and pressing kind, and at great personal cost and sacrifice to himself). If the President should refuse to go this time and should, instead, merely take a vacation for his own refreshment and pleasure, it would be hotly resented by a very large part of the public. It would be suggested that he is a Southerner and out of sympathy with the occasion. In short, it would be more than a passing mistake; it would amount to a serious blunder. And so I surrendered—the more readily because all this would have been so serious a misapprehension of my own real attitude. Nothing, while I am President, must be suffered to make an impression which will subtract by one iota the force I need to do the work assigned me. I can do this without any real risk to my health, and shall lose, not what I need but only what I want (ah, how much!).

My glimpse of Harlakenden is only postponed, my sweet one, and I shall study to get a little pleasure and frequent refreshment here . . . I shall thrive, *if only I surrender my will to the inevitable.*[8]

How shall I tell you what my heart is full of? It is literally full to over-flowing with yearning love for you, my incomparable darling, and for the sweet little daughters whom I love with so deep a passion, and admire as much as I love! I dare not pour it out today. I am too lonely. I must think quietly and not with rebellion. The big house is still: I must copy its stately peace, and try to be worthy of the trust of those whom I try to serve and who make [*sic*] happy by their wonderful love!

Your own

Woodrow [9]

The address at Gettysburg was the only one that Wilson delivered during the summer, and he made several short trips to Harlakenden; but even when there he was bound to the White House by wire and his conscience was haunted by responsibility. However, among the creative spirits at Cornish he could confide his ambitions for America to sympathetic ears. He told a poet that he wanted to encourage a renaissance of his people that would express itself socially and artistically as well as politically, but that first he must construct solid economic piers for society.

Washington was unusually sultry that summer. The White House lawn yellowed under the sun and the President found little coolness in a marquee that had been set up on it. Nevertheless, he had spirit enough to write, and enjoyed keeping bachelor quarters with Dr. Grayson and Tumulty—"lovely fellows, both of them, and good company all the while," he thought them. Tactful and entertaining, the physician became the President's comrade day in and day out and cared for him with a solicitude that seemed to him motherly. Wilson had shrunk from personal relations with the men at Washington with whom he did business, dreading intimacies that might stir jealousies or expose him to pressures for unmerited favors. But Grayson's comradeship seemed legitimate, for no one could criticize a president for having his doctor constantly at his side. With the physician as opponent, and always using the same caddy, he played golf several afternoons each week because it took him outdoors and because it helped him "to keep alive and spend and be spent." After four or five holes he found that he

---

[8] This theme recurs in a letter written on the same day to Mary Hulbert in which Wilson said: "The most I can hope is, that by the end of the session I shall have learned not to tug at my chain and lacerate—my feelings! It's fine discipline, but it comes late in life! I learn hard. I am not so pliable as I once was."

[9] Unpublished letter, given to the writer by Eleanor W. McAdoo.

could forget the office and concentrate on the little ball. Then his game would improve, his spirits rise, and he would jest, swing his arms, and sometimes hum a merry tune. At the clubhouse he would permit no special attention, and he refused invitations to play through those ahead of him who had equal standing on the course. "My right eye is like a horse's," he explained to fellow golfers one day. "I can see straight out with it but not sideways. As a result I cannot take a full swing because my nose gets in the way and cuts off my view of the ball." [10] His score for eighteen holes usually exceeded a hundred.

He continued to draw refreshment from gallant correspondence. In refined, intelligent womanhood he could find some of the spiritual values that he missed in the public men with whom he had to do business. A lovely lady remained in his view a soul to be exalted and cared for. He maintained his friendship with Mary Allen Hulbert and wrote to her regularly on Sunday afternoons, confiding the thoughts that came to him as he moved like a ghost through the echoing rooms and corridors of the White House during the summer. He found being President a solitary business, for he seemed to be the only one whose duty it was to look out for the welfare of the whole country, to study the pattern of affairs as a whole, and to live "all the while in his thoughts with the people of the whole country." With his household devoid of women, he found it hard not to fall in love with actresses in the stock company whose performances he attended twice a week. "Fortunately," he wrote, "I have a special gift for relaxation and for being amused. But even then it is lonely, very lonely." He confessed roguishly that he had "a private eye out for all the fun available and for every escape not regarded as scandalous—especially seeking to see all that is amusing in the frailties of fellow politicians."

Of his life on summer Sabbaths—the days on which he experienced a "delightful renewal" of his normal thoughts and feelings—he wrote: "I do not get out of bed on Sundays until about ten o'clock, just in time to get a little breakfast and get to church; and after my letters are written in the afternoon the doctor and I go off for a little drive in the motor—unless, as this afternoon, a thunder storm comes up out of mere exasperation that there should have been so sultry a day. It seems to come up after such a day exactly as if in a bad humor, to drive the maddening airs away, chasing them with its great angry breath and

[10] David Lawrence, *The True Story of W.W.*, p. 129. House sometimes accompanied the golfers around the course, though he did not play. He wrote in his diary on April 14, 1914: "It was evident to me that Grayson was not playing as well as he could, though I do not think that the President noticed it."

growling the while like a wild beast in the chase." He attended what he described as "a dear old-fashioned church such as I used to go to when I was a boy, amidst a congregation of simple and genuine people to whom it is a matter of utter indifference whether there is a season or not . . ." Feeling stale and dull one Sunday, he went to this unpretentious church in a white linen suit and created what he described as a "mild sensation." But, he went on blithely, "that of course is what every public man wishes to do, at church or anywhere else, and it did not in the least interfere with my own state of mind during the service." Actually, he explained, the people of the church were too genuine and self-respecting to violate the privacy of the Wilsons or to make capital of them; but the secret service men were a constant trial. "What fun it will be some day to escape from arrest!" he wrote.

Sometimes official life brought compensations, as when the lord provost of Glasgow, a cultivated and gifted Scot, turned an official call into a delightful conversation. When his wife and daughter surprised him pleasantly by running down from Cornish late in August, he wrote to Mary Hulbert: "It is beyond measure refreshing to see them and unbosom myself to them." But it made him uneasy to have them remain in the "debilitating atmosphere" of the city.

All through the torrid summer a legislative battle over the currency bill raged. Even before June 23, when the President had put his program before the Congress, a spate of billingsgate rose from Western Democrats in the House who saw an opportunity to make political capital by flaying "Wall Street." Congressman Henry of Texas, chairman of the Committee on Rules, organized a campaign of heckling, proposed a handout of unsecured currency to subsidize agriculture, commerce, and industry; and to give strength to his insurrection against Glass's leadership he tried to conjure with the name of Bryan. He even went so far as to arraign the President as a political martinet.

The radical agrarians, with some support from Brandeis and Untermyer, mustered enough power to demand an amendment prohibiting interlocking among bank directorates; and when after futile efforts to dissuade them Wilson conceded this, they introduced provisions for the discounting of short-term agricultural paper. The Eastern press scoffed at what it called "cotton currency" and "corn-tassel currency"; but Bryan thought the proposal reasonable and urged Wilson not to oppose it, and the congressmen of the South and West forced an amendment through the committee. Though Wilson had tried all his resources of flattery, courtesy, and reason, he was not able to overcome impulses rooted in decades of polemics.

Finally when Glass, buffeted by the agrarians beyond endurance, came to his chief and offered to resign, Wilson was moved to profanity. "Damn it!" he said to his hard-pressed lieutenant, "don't resign, old fellow. Outvote them!"

The loyal Democrats on the committee did just that, and no vital provision of the bill was amended. To be sure, the dissenters carried their opposition into the party caucus that met on August 11; but the ground was cut from under them when Glass read decisive words that Bryan had written to him:

> You are authorized to speak for me and say that I appreciate so profoundly the service rendered by the President to the people in the stand he has taken on the fundamental principles involved in currency reform, that I am with him in all the details. If my opinion has influence with anyone called upon to act on this measure, I am willing to assume full responsibility for what I do when I advise him to stand by the President and assist in securing the passage of the bill at the earliest possible moment . . .

At hearing this the caucus submerged the obstructionists under cheers of derision and it was voted to support the Glass Bill with the amendment for agricultural credit and a few lesser changes. The measure finally was approved on September 18 by the House, 287 to 85.

The major battle, however, was still to come. Bankers saw behind government regulation the bugaboo of political influence and feared that the business mechanism they understood so well would be thrown out of adjustment. Some chattered of "confiscation"; and while one warned of "alarming inflationary features," another predicted "disastrous constriction of commercial credits." Thus the bill that had been carefully calculated to stabilize business was assailed as a disturber of stability.

Even enlightened bankers who had interviewed Wilson and Glass still protested the regulative provisions on which the President and Bryan insisted. Propaganda was organized, and journals devoted columns to attacks on the Glass Bill. A conference of bankers at Chicago issued a manifesto that seemed to Wilson and his friends to be an attempt to intimidate other financiers and threaten the government; and the President responded by telling newsmen that he wanted no suggestions from hostile interests. Certain editors took the view of protesting bankers and pictured Wilson as a master bending Congress to his indomitable will. "That is, of course, silly . . ." Wilson wrote in protest to Mary Hulbert. "I do not know how to wield a big stick, but I do know how to put my mind at the service of others for the accomplishment of a common purpose. They are using me; I am not driving them . . . And what a pleasure it is, what a deep human pleasure, to work with strong men, who do their own thinking and know how to put things in shape! Why a man should wish to be the whole show and surround himself with weak men, I cannot imagine! How dull it would be! . . . That is not power. Power consists in one's capacity to link his will with the purpose of others, to lead by reason and a gift for cooperation. It is a multiple of combined brains."

He wrote this in the flush of the victory won in the House of Representatives three days before. However, a week later he had to face the fact that certain Democratic senators were not disposed to work with him in the smooth way that he idealized. There were suggestions in hostile journals, also, that delay and reconsideration were desirable. Wilson, however, saw in these ideas a familiar device of obstructionism; and he feared that, while senators procrastinated, uneasiness among bankers might provoke a financial crisis.[11] He thought he detected a conspiracy "to poison the public mind against the currency bill." He therefore called the party's senatorial steering committee to the White House and discouraged adjournment for more than three days at any one time. Doubting that he could deal with the upper house in the ideal role of a statesman among peers, he was willing to use the lash if it became necessary. "Why *should* public men, Senators of the United States, have to be led and stimulated to what all the country knows to be their duty!" he complained to Mary Hulbert. "To whom are they listening? Certainly not to the voice of the people, when they quibble and twist and hesitate. They have strangely blunted perceptions, and exaggerate themselves in the most extraordinary degree. Therefore it *is* a struggle and must be accepted as such. A man of my temperament and my limitations will certainly wear himself out in it; but that is small matter; the danger is that he may lose his patience and suffer the weakness of exasperation. It is against these that I have constantly to guard myself."

11 On October 11, Wilson wrote to his friend Senator Williams: "Things are going on in the banking world which are evidently based upon a desire to make the members of the two houses uneasy in the presence of the bankers' power, and it is possible that with expanding business and contracting credits a panic may be brought on while we wait. There is absolutely no excuse for the fall in the market value of the two-per-cents. It is being brought about by those who misunderstand or misrepresent, or have not read the bill."

His imagination delighted in exalting his correspondent in Bermuda as *Democracy personified*. He would resort to her, he wrote, as the high priestess of Democracy; and he asked how the picture looked to her from her island shrine. "It is more important to me to know how it looks outside of Washington than how it looks inside," he explained. "The men who think *in Washington* only cannot think for the country. It is a place of illusions. The disease is that men think of themselves and not of their tasks of service, and are more concerned with what will happen to them than what will happen to the country. I am not complaining or scolding or holding myself superior; I am only analyzing, as a man will on Sunday, when the work pauses and he looks before and after. My eye is no better than theirs; it is only fresher, and was a thoughtful spectator of these very things before it got on the inside and tried to see straight there."

In August he wrote to Edith Reid: "Hard as it is to nurse Congress along and stand ready to play a part of guidance in anything that turns up, great or small, it is all part of something infinitely great and worth while, and I am content to labor at it to the finish . . . So far things go very well, and my leadership is most loyally and graciously accepted, even by men of whom I did not expect it. I hope that this is in part because they perceive that I am pursuing no private and selfish purposes of my own. How could a man do that with such responsibilities resting upon him! It is no credit to be sobered and moralized by a task like this . . ."

Woodrow Wilson did not allow himself to forget that he was "nursing" Congress and not driving it. It hurt him to read reports that he had characterized dissenting senators of his party as "rebels and no Democrats," and he protested in a letter to the Washington *Post*: "Of course I never said any such thing. It is contrary both to my thought and character, and I must ask that you give a very prominent place in your issue of tomorrow to this denial."

Confident that, under his leadership, political motives could not corrupt the Federal Reserve System, Wilson felt that the New York bankers were "too much in the atmosphere of the thing" to see the situation whole. Roland Morris, one of his Princeton boys, reported to him that many financiers were embittered; but the President was not moved to reconsider the currency bill. Fixing his eyes intently on the man, he said: "Morris, I have seen those men. They came down here with a long brief. The essence of their case was that nothing whatever should be done. They asserted that the time was inopportune. I told them that so far as their principal contention was concerned the case was decided. It was *res adjudicata*. Something was going to be done. I told them I would be glad to have them suggest changes or criticisms to help me in making a better law. They went home and afterwards sent down a long brief which I considered carefully. I found that in its essence it was only a repetition of their former contention, really an argument to do nothing. What is the use of my seeing them again? I will not see them again. You can tell them exactly the reason why I will not see them again."

The bankers intensified their protests in the autumn. Paul Warburg wrote House that he was mortified by the "suicidal stubbornness" with which sound suggestions had been swept aside. Early in October the acting president of the American Bankers' Association denounced the Federal Reserve plan as "an invasion of the liberty of the citizens" and "unjust and un-American," and on the 23rd President Vanderlip of the National City Bank of New York proposed an alternate plan. But Wilson said promptly and emphatically that he would not have the national banking system dictated by any bankers.

McAdoo noted that the President's jaw was setting hard on the currency issue and feared the effect of his schoolmastering habits. Banking reform had become a cause so sacred to Wilson that he was prepared to build fires under the senators by direct appeals to the people. He had not forgotten what he had said in an academic lecture: the president had "no means of compelling Congress except through public opinion." Wilson's nerves were fraying badly. Difficulties with Mexico were irritating him and he suffered a week of illness that he laughed off as "a little spell of indigestion . . . due, undoubtedly, to my being worn out and unable to run both my stomach and the government."

Nevertheless, he managed to get off a note to his "precious sister," Annie Howe. "What a delight it was to get your letter," he wrote. "I am going to steal time enough to answer it on my own typewriter, as in the old days. I have to *steal* it . . . It is as if the office swallowed up the individual life, whether you would or not, and used every nerve in you, leaving you only the time you were in bed, in the deep oblivion of utter fatigue . . . There have been times, of course, when I have felt terribly fagged, and almost down and out, but I have come out of them at once all fit again. I am beginning to think that I am rather a tough customer, after all, physically, if not otherwise!"

The prophet's confidence in his cause was justified by the returns from local elections in November. Moreover, it was clear that many bankers, especially those outside New York, preferred the Glass-Owen bill to an extension of the status quo, in spite of their distrust of government supervision; and on October 24 the national Chamber of Commerce approved the measure, 306 to 17. Finally, the President felt that he was strong enough to compel party unity by summoning a caucus of Democratic senators. He defended this action against a vigorous protest from Hitchcock of Nebraska. Explaining that he harbored "no jealousy of differences of opinion," he wrote thus to the senator on November 11: "In all these matters I feel that successful action depends upon the yielding of individual views in order that we may get a measure which will meet the well-known principles of the party and enable us, by *common* counsel, to arrive at what I may call a corporate result—corporate in the sense of being the result of a comparison of views among colleagues who are equally obliged to agree upon a measure which will afford the country relief."

Though unable to control all the party men, the caucus voted unanimously to forgo holidays unless the currency bill was passed before Christmas. On November 22 the measure was reported out of committee. Debate followed party lines for the most part; but Hitchcock introduced an alternate draft that commanded Republican support. The Administration's version of the bill was attacked vehemently by Elihu Root, who saw in it "financial heresy" that would put the nation "in pawn." It would induce dreams of prosperity, he alleged, but actually would bring inflation and a vanishing gold supply. Using the political jargon with which Republicans had fought populist demagoguery for decades, Root held the floor for three hours and was answered by Democratic spokesmen with argument equally vigorous and unscientific. Amendments were beaten off; and finally the opponents, unable to vote down the Administration bloc, tried to delay decision by proposing to the exhausted Senate that it recess until after the holidays. Wilson, however, stood by the verdict of the caucus and let it be known that he would sanction no respite. The bill was brought to a vote on December 19 and passed, 54 to 34, with every Democrat present in favor, and also six Senators of other parties.

The differences between the acts of the two Houses were reconciled speedily; and on December 22, at five in the morning, the conference committee reached agreement. When the Senate delayed a few hours before accepting the final version, Wilson, who had been kept in bed for days by a bronchial cold and a relapse, lost patience for a moment and spoke of the Upper House as a lot of old women, one of them so feminine that it was immodest of him to wear trousers. But on the 23rd the Federal Reserve Act was on the President's desk for signature.

This law, over which Congress had labored for nine months, set up a central structure that would serve the nation's bankers by pooling reserves to meet the danger of credit stringency, providing an elastic currency, and supplying a national clearing system. Moreover, it gave the federal government adequate banking facilities; and by provisions for changes in rates, open-market operations, and examination of banks, it made it possible for a public board to prevent the sort of panic that had been disastrous more than once.

But in extending federal control over the nation's banks, the Federal Reserve Act had a significance still more far-reaching. The momentum that began with tariff and income-tax legislation was developing a force that was to carry the responsibility of civil servants into still other fields that previously had been left to private enterprise.

Wilson's pioneering spirit quickened at contemplation of what had been wrought on the legislative frontier. "There have been currents and countercurrents," he said on the day of signing the Glass-Owen Act, "but the stream has moved forward." In securing effective action on the tariff and on banking and currency, the prophet had realized the two visions of reform that had most allured him through the years when he had been only an outside influence in politics.

It was a radiant group that gathered at the executive offices to watch the signing of one of the most significant pieces of legislation of the twentieth century. Woodrow Wilson came in smiling, started to sit down at his desk, then hesitated and looked around the circle of friends for Carter Glass, who was standing at the end of the room. As the taciturn Virginian came forward, the President shook his hand warmly and invited him to stand with Senator Owen beside his desk. Sitting down, he signed the Federal Reserve Act with four gold pens, remarking, "I'm drawing on the gold reserve." Then he told his comrades of his appreciation of their steadfastness, and in letters to McAdoo, Owen, and Glass he repeated his praise of their efforts. But these lieutenants knew that the enactment of the law was due most of all to the guidance of their chief.

Wilson realized that too much trust must not be placed in the letter of any law, that the success of this one depended largely on the character and ability of the seven men who would sit on the Federal Reserve Board. While Tumulty was importuning the Chief to make appointments immediately, McAdoo was cautioning him to act deliberately.

Asked to take a hand in the matter, House gave to the President, on the day before the act was signed, some names that he had brought together on twenty-four hours' notice.

Wilson, however, wished time to meditate on appointments so vital. He had no sympathy for McAdoo's feeling that a board should be chosen that could be counted on to work in harmony with the secretary of the treasury. "McAdoo thinks we are forming a social club," he complained to House,[12] agreeing with his friend that they must not risk offending the secretary of the treasury by letting him know the extent of their discussions of his department. The President wanted board members who were removed as far as possible from politics and obviously beyond the influence of either Treasury or White House; and it was not until August of 1914 that he found five appointees who were satisfactory to himself and to the Congress.[13]

The President nominated Thomas D. Jones, who with his brother had defended Wilson's position at Princeton. This close friend, however, was a director of the International Harvester Company, then under indictment as an illegal combination. When senators from agrarian states feared to approve Jones, the President tried to defend his friend by explaining, in a public letter to the Senate Banking Committee, that Jones had become a director of the harvester company with a view to reforming its practices. When the candidate came before the senators, however, he bluntly asserted his approval of his corporation's acts. Wilson gave up and wrote to his friend thus: "I cannot say when I have had a disappointment which cut me more keenly than this . . . I am facing this outcome of the matter with the keenest personal sorrow." This defeat, in July of 1914, was the first that Wilson suffered in Congress.

It was a strenuous year, all in all, that Woodrow Wilson put behind

[12] Later McAdoo reported to Wilson that the members of the Federal Reserve Board were disgruntled because the State Department's expert in protocol ruled that the social precedence of the new body among the government commissions must be determined by the date of its creation. "I can do nothing about it, I am not a social arbiter," was the President's disdainful reply. And then, when McAdoo pressed him for a decision, he said with a broad smile: "Well, they might come right after the fire department." W. G. McAdoo, *op. cit.,* pp. 287–88.

[13] After dinner on Jan. 21, 1914, the Colonel commented that the success of the Federal Reserve System would depend largely on the character of the men who administered it; and Wilson replied: "My dear friend, do not frighten me any more than I am now." Remarking that the judgment of men was with him largely a matter of instinct, the President reacted decisively against a candidate who had been promoting his own name. He had not wanted a banker as treasurer of New Jersey or as secretary of the treasury, and he did not wish the new board to be controlled by bankers. Nor did he want to appoint as many as three members from the Treasury staff. House Diary, April 28, 1914. "I wonder if you have been able to get on the track of any really big, available, suitable businessman for the Federal Reserve Board," Wilson wrote to House on Feb. 16, 1914.

him when he signed the Federal Reserve Act and prepared for a Christmas holiday. But it was one of his great years, comparable to periods of spectacular success at Princeton and at Trenton and to the lofty summit of achievement on which he was to stand at Paris early in 1919. Like an architect who builds for an epoch rather than for a day, he had laid for twentieth-century America, in the tariff and banking acts, two piers strong enough to bear the stresses of an economy of freedom and opportunity.

Political opponents as well as loyal partisans applauded the achievement of the new President. Even the Republican New York *Tribune* praised him: "President Wilson has brought his party out of the wilderness of Bryanism. It has been a great exhibition of leadership." Progressive journals were appreciative; and William Howard Taft wrote generously in the *Saturday Evening Post*: "Never before, in its recent history certainly, has the Democratic party exercised such self-control. It is due to the circumstances and to Mr. Wilson's masterful personality and attitude . . ." And the New York *World* wrote of "a year of achievement for which there have been few, if any, parallels in American history."

Such opinions did not make Wilson complacent, but served rather to stimulate his pioneering impulses. When he signed the Federal Reserve Act he proclaimed that it was but "the first in a series of constructive measures." As at Princeton and Trenton, where his first years in office had been his most successful, there was to be no change in the direction of his enterprise, and confidence in himself and his cause was to tip the balance dangerously against his inclination to meditate.

CHAPTER XIX

Clarifying the Antitrust Laws

At times, during his first months in the Presidency, it had seemed to Woodrow Wilson that the American people whom he loved would kill him. Illness put him to bed for a few days in December and convinced him that he must have rest. His family had returned from New Hampshire in October. In November, however, daughter Jessie was married, and the loss cut deeply. After the ceremony Ellen Wilson was heard to say to a friend: "I know; it was a wedding, not a funeral, but you must forgive us—this is the first break in the family."

When Wilson was ill, in December, Colonel House went to his bedside and told him jokes and discouraged discussion of public affairs that might be exhausting; and afterward he recorded complacently in his diary that the President had been offended because he stayed overnight with McAdoo instead of at the White House. After a vacation trip to Europe,[1] House had returned in the autumn to his role as the President's confidant. He had found that he could aid the Administration by frequent visits with Cabinet members; and he cultivated rapport particularly with Bryan, McAdoo, and Houston, for these officials were the ones whom the President heeded most frequently in general matters. When the genial Colonel came smiling into the departmental offices, passing on words of praise that the President had spoken to him in private or dropping a hint of suggestion, the secretaries were as attentive as if they were facing the Chief himself. House was able to sound out the Cabinet members on their opinions of each other as well as of the President. Both Wilson and his men confided to him things that they would not say to one another, and without betraying confidences the Colonel prevented or alleviated frictions. Moreover, he kept informed about local situations that the President had no time to follow.[2]

[1] Explaining that he was going abroad to conserve his strength so that he might serve the President the better, House had written in May: "My faith in you is as great as my love for you—more than that I cannot say." He could not go to Washington in the summer, he explained in a letter written on Aug. 6 to Dr. Grayson, because he had suffered a heat stroke some years before and had been forced to avoid hot weather as he would the plague.

[2] The Administration had not been in office two months before *Collier's* had printed an

Realizing the value of these voluntary services, one day when House persuaded him to break an agreement with a senator that might violate the Constitution, Wilson told the Colonel to "scold" him frankly whenever he contemplated doing anything that might be wrong. Declaring that "he did not know how he could carry on without this friend," he thanked him again and again, addressed him in letters as "my dear friend," signed himself "affectionally yours," told him that, with one or two exceptions, he was the most efficient man he had ever known. The Colonel helped to solve the problem that Cleveland had once described to Wilson as one of the President's hardest: how to get the truth unwarped by flattery or self-interest. Wilson knew that this friend would not press matters of business upon him when he was too worn to discuss them; and House seemed always ready to respond with cheer for despondent moods, caution for moods of elation and overconfidence.

On the night before the signing of the currency act the Colonel stayed at the White House and was charmed by the unpretentious living of the first family. The adviser had noted that the President listened to advice from others when it was tactfully given, but that it was seldom invited; and the Colonel sympathized with Cabinet members who regretted that :'eir business was discussed by the President with House more often than with themselves. Hoping to encourage his friend to keep his mind open, the Colonel congratulated him on never having reached "the 'know-it-all' attitude"; and he kept his tongue in his cheek when Wilson replied that his long university training had helped him to derive new and helpful ideas from conferences.[3]

---

article on "The President's Silent Partner." Wilson read the article, and his love for the Colonel was not diminished. But House wrote to his brother-in-law: "I do not know how much of this kind of thing W.W. can stand. The last edition of *Harper's Weekly* spoke of me as 'Assistant President House.' I think it is time for me to go to Europe or take to the woods." House to Mezes, April 24, 1913, *House Papers*, I, 150.

"The President has been so generous and kind to me in all my relations with him," the Colonel wrote in his diary on June 12, "that I cannot feel anything excepting the closest comradeship for him, and I express myself to him in a way that I seldom do to any other friend in the world."

[3] House Diary, Dec. 22, 1913. Four months later House was recording the same opinions, fortified by testimony from members of the Cabinet. When Wilson referred to Hamilton as "easily the ablest" of the fathers of the nation, the Colonel suggested that Washington's ability to use Hamilton was a measure of the greatness of the first President. "I told him," House wrote, "that all the really big men I had known had taken advice from others, while the little men refused to take it . . . He agreed to this. At another time in our conversation, he remarked that he always sought advice. I almost laughed at this statement." House Diary, April 15, 1914, in *House Papers*, I, 126.

Wilson's increasing reluctance to take his Cabinet into his confidence resulted in part from leaks of information that Wilson and other officials attributed to Secretary Lane's inclination to chat with newsmen and foreign diplomats after Cabinet meetings. W.W. to Redfield, Feb. 11, 1923, Redfield Papers.

While they were talking, Ellen Wilson came in and laid the family's financial problems before the Colonel, whom she trusted implicitly. The President remarked that he had not been able to supplement his salary by writing, because what he wanted to write would have little market.[4] Since inauguration they had paid their debts, given $5,000 to relatives, and saved about $2,000 a month. House offered to make a list of securities that a president could properly buy; and urging his friend to concentrate his thought on ways of leaving an impress of usefulness on the history of his times, he agreed with Mrs. Wilson that they would correspond on financial problems without bothering her husband.

It was nearly midnight when finally they left the study. Speaking of his satisfaction in talking without having to calculate either the substance or the effect of his words, Wilson accompanied his guest to his chamber and with affectionate solicitude all but tucked him in bed. This gentle, compassionate counselor who never oversold himself or his ideas had so won the confidence of the President's family that Helen Bones said one day to Mrs. House: "When Cousin Woodrow and the Colonel are together the family feels the country is safe, and nothing can happen." And at the same time the Colonel was recording in his diary: "There is not a piece of legislation he has advocated, a policy, or an important appointment that he has not discussed with me frankly, fully and frequently." No one but Jack Hibben ever had made himself so valuable to the Wilsons as friend and adviser. "What I like about Colonel House," the President said one day to a journalist, "is that he holds things at arm's length—objectively. He seems to be able to penetrate a proposition and get to its essence quickly." Sometimes he referred to the Colonel as his "eyes and ears." [5]

On the evening of December 23—the day of the signing of the Federal Reserve Act—the Wilsons set out by train for Pass Christian, a sleepy village on the coast of Mississippi, where they settled into the meandering life of the Old South. "This proves to be just the place we wanted," Wilson wrote to House from his retreat on December 27. "I have, myself, a greater sense of relief than I have had in many a long day." Living in a house built before the Civil War, they enjoyed the Negro servants and the gentle neighbors.

It was particularly comforting at this time for Wilson to live in a

[4] A year later Wilson told his family that someone wanted to serialize his *History of the American People* in the daily papers. Asked by a daughter whether there was "any money in it," he replied: "Oh yes—but that's the reason why I don't want to do it while I am the President."

[5] Lawrence, *op. cit.*, pp. 68, 71.

normal Southern community, for at Washington he had been under extreme pressure from progressive Negroes and their Yankee partisans. The Wilsons respected good colored folk but had little sympathy with aggressive ones. At Princeton they had been unwilling to force the issue of a Negro's right of admission to the university. It seemed to the President that segregation of the races kept embarrassing problems from arising and he did not comply with repeated pleas from champions of Negro rights whose support he had sought in the election campaign.[6] Urged to appoint a national commission to study problems of race relations, Wilson had explained in the summer of 1913 that such a move would rouse resentment among Southerners in Congress and thus put his vital legislative program in jeopardy.

Wilson condoned segregation of races in government bureaus as a policy "distinctly to the advantage of the colored people themselves" and one that made them the more safe in their possession of office and the less likely to be discriminated against. He was moved by the sentiment that had possessed Ellen Wilson when, stepping by mistake into a Jim Crow railway car, she had sensed a feeling on the part of its colored occupants that their rights had been violated by her intrusion. In reply to protests against segregation that came from Villard, the grandson of Garrison the abolitionist, the President wrote: "I hope and, I may say, I believe that by the slow pressure of argument and persuasion the situation may be changed and a great many things done eventually which now seem impossible. But they cannot be done, either now or at any future time, if a bitter agitation is inaugurated and carried to its natural ends. I appeal to you most earnestly to aid in holding things at a just and cool equipoise until I can discover whether it is possible to work out anything or not."

He had fended off protests from Southern legislators against the advancement of able Negroes in federal services. Moreover, he had no sympathy with extremists in his party who discharged and demoted colored workers without justification; and after the protests of Northern reformers were echoed by many progressive leaders, at least one federal department, the Treasury, began quietly to modify the policy of segregation. Though he had grown up in the South, he had never absorbed its extreme views. He spoke of himself as "a recent immigrant."

6 In the 1912 campaign Wilson went no further than to promise "justice executed with liberality and good feeling" and "absolute fair dealing," and to make it clear that he would appoint no man to office because he was colored and also that he would appoint colored men on their merits. These generalities had convinced many champions of the Negroes that he was more to be trusted than his opponents.

The President had been equally patient and moderate in dealing with another social movement of which he had been made embarrassingly aware during his first winter in office. The day before his inauguration militant suffragettes had taken part in a parade in the capital. Before Wilson's departure for Pass Christian, lobbyists for woman suffrage had invaded the executive offices and presented their cause forcefully; and when the President's annual message to Congress had failed to mention the issue, they accused him of "dodging." The spokesman for a delegation of a hundred agitating women asked him point-blank: "Have we anyone to present our case to Congress?" He tried to turn the query by saying, with a laugh, that he had found the suffragists well able to speak for themselves; but when they pinned him down, the muscles of his face twitched for an instant and he gave them a blunt "no."

Under pressure from his daughters, Wilson had to some degree overcome the aversion to emancipated womanhood that had been bred in him and strengthened by his experience as a teacher at Bryn Mawr; but he was not yet convinced that suffrage was one of those compelling causes of which he had written in *Leaders of Men*—a "permanent purpose of the public mind of which a statesman must take account to keep himself in office," rather than a mere "breeze of the day" to which a demagogue might trim his sails. However, when he was reminded by a militant woman that she had been led to believe before his election that he would support the movement, and was accused of having "gunned for votes," his sensitive conscience was pierced and his face flushed. He explained that he had spoken then as an individual, but must now represent a party whose platform had not endorsed suffrage and whose Southern members were opposed to it. He was, he said, "tied to a conviction" that suffrage qualifications should be controlled by the states.

Actually, the force of public opinion was not yet strong enough to overcome the personal feelings of Woodrow and Ellen Wilson. Moreover, the President's understanding of feminine psychology cautioned him against giving the ballot to women. It seemed to him that they thought too directly to be enfranchised *en bloc*. They might refuse to recognize obstacles and to circumvent them wisely. "A woman will not do that," he said to a friend. "If she cannot do directly and immediately what seems to her logical, she won't play."[7] Once, asked for his

---

[7] Lawrence, *op. cit.*, p. 136. To Oliver P. Newman, Wilson said "We cannot enfranchise the women all at once. It would be very dangerous. Woman's mind is too logical . . . In politics, in governmental affairs, and in life you cannot go in a straight and logical line."

views on woman suffrage, he told of a deacon who escorted two ladies down a slippery hill and, when they began to lose traction, clung to a post and shouted as they gathered speed: "It grieves me sadly, ladies, but I can accompany you no further."

Wilson the man of thought realized that the issues of race equality and woman suffrage involved slow changes in the social mores of his people. He knew that he could not act upon them with constructive decisiveness, as in the case of economic maladies that obviously demanded remedy. In taking this view he disappointed ardent reformers.

The most baffling issue before Wilson, however, as he enjoyed Southern life at Pass Christian at the end of 1913, was the problem of trust regulation. He pondered much on the question and worked on a statement for the Congress. This was a matter that touched sensitive property rights and involved many frictional crossings of political and economic views. There was little unanimity of opinion as to what should be done—only vague sentiment that action should be taken to end abuses of economic and financial power. It was more difficult to bring practical politicians into agreement on antitrust laws than it had been to get assent to specific reforms of the tariff and the banking system. There were differences of opinion in the Cabinet, and Wilson's powers were taxed as he tried to keep his men functioning as a team in spite of them.[8]

Of all the Cabinet members, McReynolds had perhaps the most perplexing task, for it devolved upon him to prosecute corporations for breaches of law in a field where there were vague statutes and little precedent. The attorney general was determined to apply Wilson's policy of preserving conditions favorable to competition, and he intended to prosecute suits already pending in the courts against certain

---

At times Wilson's patience with importunate women gave way. Once, receiving a letter from a suffrage state warning that the women of the state would vote against him unless he did thus and so, the President replied that he thanked them and sincerely hoped that they would.

"Suffrage for women," Wilson said to Nancy Toy, "will make absolutely no change in politics—it is the home that will be disastrously affected. Somebody has to make the home, and who is going to do it if the women don't?" Toy Diary, Jan. 6, 1915. Wilson later gave vital support to the suffrage amendment.

[8] A month after inauguration the President had directed Burleson's thinking toward the possibility of government ownership of telegraph lines; but when the postmaster general proposed taking over private property at the value of the physical plant and operating it at a profit to the Post Office Department, Wilson thought that the time was not ripe for such a radical move and Burleson, who had to dispel rumors by issuing a public denial, felt that he had been made a "goat." House Diary, Dec. 22, and 23, 1913. Talking with Burleson on Oct. 30, House had considered the proposal for government ownership "a doubtful expedient" and had spoken of the wide ownership of the stock of the American Telephone and Telegraph Company.

large corporations. In this purpose he was supported not only by the President but by House, who was disturbed particularly by the restraint upon fair competition that was imposed by interlocking directorates. However, when Henry Clay Frick of the United States Steel Corporation, which had been reproved by the Pujo Committee, went to the Colonel confidentially and asked him to arrange a settlement of the government's suit out of court, both House and Wilson thought it politic to refer the matter to McReynolds, with no recommendation except that this corporation should enjoy exactly the same consideration as any other and should be allowed to propose a settlement.[9]

Brought face to face with the vast problem of government regulation of big business, Wilson and House were glad to evade responsibility for specific action. The President was perplexed because he owned nine shares of preferred stock of the United States Steel Corporation. He feared that if he sold them he might seem to be trying to escape the consequences of the government's suit, and if he held on he might be criticized if the outcome of the litigation favored the corporation.[10]

Woodrow Wilson had not been in office many weeks before he had become embarrassingly aware of the intertwining of problems of labor interest with those of trust regulation. For some years the American Federation of Labor had been struggling to have certain of its tactics, particularly the secondary boycott, exempted from prosecution under the Sherman Antitrust Law; and to further this purpose Democratic legislators had attached to the Sundry Civil Appropriation bill of 1913 a rider that prohibited the use of any of the appropriated funds for the prosecution of labor unions. Though Taft had vetoed this provision and had denounced it as "class legislation of the most vicious sort," Wilson had intimated soon after his inauguration that he would not oppose the measure if the Congress sent it to him. Samuel Gompers had put his arguments before Wilson in a long letter, and the President

[9] Left free to use his own judgment, McReynolds complained that the President seldom discussed policies with him. House Diary, Mar. 29 and May 7, 1914. The attorney general thought that the settlement proposed by the steel men would not restore fair competition in the industry and therefore he refused to accept it. *Ibid.,* Mar. 22, 24, 26, Sept. 30, 1913. House and Houston thought that certain interests were hoping to break down the attorney general and thus attack Wilson. Houston to Page, June 30, 1913, and House to Page, July 27, 1913. Page Papers (Houghton Library, Harvard University).

[10] House suggested that Wilson solve his dilemma by selling the stock and appointing a special counsel to handle the suit for the government, and the President made a note of the suggestion in shorthand. The Colonel had his own perplexities. Only three weeks after the inauguration he wrote in his diary: "It is a difficult task to steer oneself steadily in the uncertain seas where politics and finance meet. Hereafter, I shall refuse to have anything to do with the financial end of it, and confine myself to advising the Administration."

had replied cordially to this labor leader who had supported him in the election campaign. He was impressed by the insistence of Gompers that unions of workingmen were based on certain human considerations that forbade their classification with combinations of dealers in commodities.

When the appropriation bill reached Wilson's desk with the rider included, however, conservatives in his Cabinet and outside pressed him to reject it. It was an embarrassing dilemma, for he was unwilling to jeopardize the operations of the government by blocking the appropriation of funds in general. Finally, on June 23, he carried through his intention of signing the measure, but at the same time he announced that he would have vetoed the rider if it had come to him separately, that he considered it merely an emphatic expression of Congressional opinion, and that the Justice Department would find resources to prosecute any group that broke the antitrust law.[11]

Though the flurry of agitation over the labor rider on the Sundry Civil bill had impressed upon Wilson the sensitivity of the unions to any legislation governing corporations, it was but a passing diversion in the long search for legal remedies against abuses of economic power. For years Woodrow Wilson had been observing the problem, and in speeches and essays he had traced its general outline. He had not been blind to the commendable efficiency of large units in some industries; but where monopolies were inevitable or desirable, he insisted, with Brandeis, that they should be owned, not merely regulated, by the state. Private monopoly was anathema.[12] "A trust," Wilson wrote in *The New Freedom,* "does not bring efficiency to the aid of business; *it buys efficiency out of business.* I am for big business, and I am against the trusts." Wilson's Republican predecessors had been concerned chiefly with the

11 Wilson gave warmer approval to another labor measure that had been vetoed by Taft— a bill to regulate conditions of maritime labor that had been originated by President Andrew Furuseth of the Seamen's Union and sponsored in Congress by Senator LaFollette and by William B. Wilson, now secretary of labor. The State Department opposed action on this measure, which would unilaterally abrogate treaties with other maritime powers providing for the arrest of foreign seamen who deserted while their ships were in American ports. But the President finally signed the Seamen's Bill on March 4, 1915, after eloquent pleading by Furuseth had won over Secretary Bryan and LaFollette had promised that the State Department would be given time to adjust international agreements.

12 After inauguration Wilson had stood on the plank of his party's platform: "A private monopoly is indefensible and intolerable. We therefore favor the vigorous enforcement of the criminal as well as the civil law against trusts and trust officials, and demand the enactment of such additional legislation as may be necessary to make it impossible for a private monopoly to exist in the United States." Moreover, he affirmed the party's demand for "the prevention of holding companies, of interlocking directorates, of stock-watering, of discrimination in price, and the control by any one corporation of so large a proportion of any industry as to make it a menace to competitive conditions."

immediate manifestations of economic maladies. By the Sherman Act and the creation of an Interstate Commerce Commission an effort had been made to protect small business from the power of firms that had grown large and monopolistic. But, eager to preserve the efficiencies resulting from large operating units, they had given little thought to nurturing the inventive and organizing genius that had made corporations great and that might guide new and still more efficient businesses to greatness.

Wilson had perceived that, if America was to continue to grow in strength, there must be freedom for the working of a process of natural selection that would eliminate inefficient enterprises and allow more worthy ones to prosper: for example, smart inventors and manufacturers, making a start perhaps in private cellars and attics, must have access to capital that would make them financially able to distribute their improved goods and processes. It was not enough merely to protect the financially weak from unscrupulous practices by those who had grown strong: all individuals and corporations must be guaranteed freedom to compete on equal terms in contributing to the nation's wealth and comfort. Otherwise, Wilson feared, enterprise might wither, and American industry might fall under the curse of the prophet Habbakuk: "Behold, it is laid over with gold and silver, and there is no breath at all in the midst of it."

During the 1912 campaign, when he had sought advice from Brandeis in order to combat Roosevelt's New Nationalism, Wilson had received proposals for clarifying the almost defunct Sherman Antitrust Act of 1890, facilitating its enforcement in the courts, and creating a fact-finding body to aid in making the provisions effective. After taking office the President had summoned Representative Stanley, chairman of a legislative committee that had probed the United States Steel Corporation, and listened intently for two hours while the congressman talked of disclosures of corporate wrongdoing. At the same time Wilson maintained contact with the "doughnut Cabinet." Moreover, the President studied magazine articles by Brandeis that were published in a book entitled *Other People's Money* and kept in touch with investigations by the Justice and Commerce Departments that attempted to determine whether certain corporations were violating the antitrust law and to what extent they controlled their industries.

Finally, in December of 1913, when passage of the Federal Reserve bill was certain, Wilson talked seriously with his Cabinet of pressing for new legislation that would supplement the inconclusive Sherman

Act. Attorney General McReynolds and others, however, thought the old law sufficient if it were enforced properly, and they feared that Congress would specifically exempt labor and farm organizations from a new act, and thus again put the President in the awkward position in which the Sundry Civil bill had placed him. It seemed to Houston that industrial activity had been chilled by the tariff and currency measures, that if the Administration made haste slowly it might reach its goal more surely.[13] Bryan, however, was urging that the party carry out its pledge to fight monopoly and Brandeis was advising that "the fearless course is the wise one."

As opinion in the Cabinet divided on the issue of monopoly, Wilson showed his stature as a leader of men. "I wonder that he does not explode sometimes," wrote Secretary Houston, his colleague of academic training, "when he has to listen to a lot of ill-considered, confused, and irrelevant advice. How refreshing his clear, concise, and well-expressed views!"

Sitting down before his typewriter at idyllic Pass Christian, his mind filled with the counsel of Cabinet colleagues, legislators,[14] and experts,

[13] In November the Cabinet had been reluctant to press the criminal action against officials of the New Haven Railroad that House's friend, Thomas Gregory, had been retained to direct. Brandeis had studied the situation thoroughly and had become convinced that the railroad, which had passed a dividend in December of 1913 for the first time in forty years, suffered both from excessive size and from monopolistic practices; and in 1914, he prodded both the Interstate Commerce Commission and the Justice Department to act.

Despite protests from the presidents of Yale and Harvard, Wilson bore down upon the officials of the railroad in July of 1914, when industrial depression was turning sentiment against progressive measures and peace in Europe hung in the balance. He studied reports of proceedings by the Justice Department and asserted, in a letter carefully drafted, that the directors of the railroad had failed, upon slight pretext, "to carry out an agreement deliberately and solemnly entered into and which was manifestly in the common interest." [The agreement referred to was made by officials of the railroad and the Justice Department on Jan. 10, 1914.] Wilson directed that a proceeding in equity be filed seeking dissolution of "the unlawful monopoly of transportation facilities in New England now sought to be maintained by the New York, New Haven, and Hartford Railroad Company; and that the criminal aspects of the case be laid before the grand jury." W.W. to the attorney general, July 9, 1914. When the Justice Department carried out the President's order, the railroad officials accepted the government's terms. See Mason, Brandeis, pp. 199–213.

[14] Beginning in November, Wilson had sought the views of party leaders in Congress; and when he went to Pass Christian, he had their recommendations as well as an elaborate report from Joseph E. Davies, whom he had appointed commissioner of corporations in the Commerce Department. (Unable to offer William F. McCombs any post that he would accept, Wilson had explained to Davies, who had been in charge of the Western headquarters in the election campaign, that he must appoint some campaign manager to something as a defense against charges of ingratitude to those who had served him. Davies to the writer, March 7, 1951.)

The Bureau of Corporations, created in 1903 in the new Department of Commerce and Labor, had, with President Roosevelt's support, investigated corporate practices and issued shocking reports. After talking with Davies, House commended to Wilson a proposal made by this adviser for an industrial commission that would build up a body of rule and procedure for relations between government and industry that would be similar to the work done in the field of transportation by the Interstate Commerce Commission. "It would largely take the

Wilson was ready to frame a program for legislation on the third of the economic ills that he had enumerated in his inaugural address: "an industrial system which, take it on all sides, financial as well as administrative, holds capital in leading strings, restricts the liberties and limits the opportunities of labor, and exploits without renewing or conserving the natural resources of the country."

At this juncture news came from New York that was given sensational play in the press. J. Pierpont Morgan and other financial magnates announced that, deferring to a change in public sentiment, they were withdrawing from the directorates of many corporations in which they held interests. "It may be," Morgan conceded, "that we shall be in a better position to serve such properties and their security holders if we are not directors." Though at first acclaimed as a "surrender of the Money Trust," the move was suspected by some observers to be mere "gallery play," and the *New York Times* pointed out that the withdrawals were so arranged as to leave the bankers with one member on most of the boards with which they had been affiliated.

Wilson was pleased by this symptom of the hold of his New Freedom on public opinion. Yet he was not convinced, and telegraphed to ask Tumulty and House for their interpretations of the news story. His secretary replied that the resignations were "an act of good faith on the part of 'big business' "; and the Colonel characterized the move, somewhat naïvely, as "an indication that big business is preparing to surrender unconditionally" and advised his friend to congratulate the country on the spirit that leading citizens were displaying. House was tiptoeing more cautiously than ever around the pitfalls that beset an advocate of antitrust legislation. He wished his friends to understand that he was "not unfriendly" to big business but dreaded the political uproar that would ensue if he were quoted publicly as "friendly" to the interests.

The President's mind ran parallel to House's thinking in the message that he was preparing for the Congress. To be sure, he persisted in dramatizing the situation as a fight in which "the masters of business

---

wind out of T.R.'s sails," the Colonel wrote, "and would not run counter to your views upon this subject . . ." Wilson replied that he had already given careful attention to the report of Davies. House to W.W., Dec. 31, 1913, and W.W. to House, Jan. 3, 1914.

Davies's proposal was contrary to the legalistic view of the attorney general. Noting that there was friction between these men, Wilson spoke of it to Davies one day, saying: "You don't like McReynolds and he doesn't like you. More causes have been lost through personal friction than for any other reason." Davies was moved to attempt to make peace. Joseph E. Davies to the writer.

on the great scale" had "begun to yield their preference and purpose, perhaps their judgment also, in honorable surrender." Going on, however, he became more generous and conciliatory. Government and business, he wrote, were ready "to meet each other halfway in a common effort to square business methods with both public opinion and the law." He aspired to be the spokesman of "the best informed men of the business world." Though the message lacked oratorical flourish, it closed with a typical challenge: "Until these things are done, conscientious business men the country over will be unsatisfied."

Sitting in the driver's seat when he returned to Washington in January of 1914, the President decided to deliver his message promptly in order to obtain laws that would facilitate an alliance between legitimate business and the public interest. There were final conferences in which the document drafted at Pass Christian was read and the support of legislative leaders was pledged. Then, according to Wilson himself, he gave his text the "doctoring" that he was accustomed to administer after using all the brains that he had and all that he could "borrow." On January 20 he made his fifth appearance within a year before a joint session of the Congress and read the message. It gave notice that he would like to "prevent such interlockings of the *personnel* of directorates of great corporations . . . as in effect result in making those who borrow and those who lend practically one and the same, those who sell and those who buy but the same persons trading with one another under different names and in different combinations, and those who affect to compete in fact partners and masters of the whole field of particular kinds of business." The President then went on to apply this principle to the specific case of the railroads, where the evils of interlocking directorates had seemed especially flagrant. The Interstate Commerce Commission, he said, should be given power to regulate the financing of railroads, as a step toward the separation of the business of production from that of transportation.

To meet these objectives, three bills that were based on the disclosures of the Congressional investigation of the steel industry were combined in an omnibus measure known as the Clayton bill. Studying the text and keeping in touch with Congressional leaders, Wilson guided the legislation through both houses of the Congress. "I think it is wise that we take only one step at a time," he cautioned Underwood.

The new antitrust bill contained a provision on farm and labor organizations that was so significant that he later referred to it as a "primer of human liberty." It declared:

The labor of a human being is not a commodity or article of commerce. Nothing contained in the anti-trust laws shall be construed to forbid the existence and operation of labor, agricultural, or horticultural organizations, instituted for the purposes of mutual help and not having capital stock or conducted for profit, or to forbid or restrain individual members of such organizations from lawfully carrying out the legitimate objects thereof, nor shall such organizations or the members thereof be held or construed to be illegal combinations or conspiracies in restraint of trade under the anti-trust laws.

This pronouncement fell short of demands made upon the President and the Congressional committees by labor leaders who wished to exempt their unions entirely from the scope of the new law. Despite a threat from union spokesmen that they would join the Republicans in defeating the entire antitrust program, Wilson refused to concede more than an amendment providing for jury trials in cases of criminal contempt and limiting the issue of injunctions. He approved the clause permitting labor and farm organizations to pursue "legitimate objectives" with immunity from prosecution, but at the same time he declared that under these provisions labor was not authorized to make war by methods already condemned by the courts. Thus he adhered to the compromise position that he had taken in dealing with the embarrassing Sundry Civil bill. As a result, Samuel Gompers of the American Federation of Labor, who had never ceased to insist that the principle of labor's immunity from antitrust action be written into substantive law, acclaimed the provisions of the Clayton Act as labor's "Magna Charta," while, on the other hand, the counsel of the American Anti-Boycott Association was satisfied and noted that actually the new bill made few changes in existing laws regarding the use of injunctions and contempt proceedings.

The Clayton Act was passed by Congress and signed by the President on October 15, 1914. Personal guilt clauses were omitted; and though the law prohibited price discrimination and certain practices that tended to create monopoly, it seemed to at least one progressive senator that it lacked teeth "to masticate milk toast."

Before the Clayton Act was ready for the President's signature, another bill was passed that set up machinery to facilitate application of the principles of the measure without involved processes of law. This supplementary antitrust legislation, which proved to be more constructive and far-reaching than the Clayton Act, was written in response to a proposal in Wilson's message to Congress in January of 1914. During the first months of the year the sag in industrial activity that had appeared in 1913 had grown worse and had been aggravated by a constriction of credit in Europe, where war clouds were hovering. The volume of business dropped, failures abounded, and opportunities for employment shrank. Accordingly, the Administration came to be moved less by the punitive zeal with which Wilson had denounced monopolies in his preinauguration speeches and more by a desire to help businessmen of good faith to operate their monopolies in the public interest. Realizing that businessmen lived in fear of being jailed for violation of a law against "restraint of trade" that they could not understand, Wilson said to the Congress: "Nothing hampers business like uncertainty. Nothing daunts or discourages it like the necessity to take chances, to run the risk of falling under the condemnation of the law before it can make sure just what the law is." One remedy was to make very plain, by statute, exactly what practices were forbidden and what the penalties were; but the President felt that businessmen would not be satisfied merely to have the menace of legal action made clear.

Enterprising Americans who believed, like Wilson, in common counsel, had faith that there was a better, more constructive remedy. The President sensed this and recommended to Congress that such citizens be given "the definite guidance and information which can be supplied by an administrative body, an interstate trade commission." Wilson once had dreaded that such a commission might become a tool of monopolies, and he made it clear now that the proposed commission would not be expected "to make terms with monopoly or in any sort to assume control of business, as if the Government made itself responsible." It would serve rather as an instrument of information and publicity and a clearinghouse for facts, and as an instrumentality for doing justice to business where the processes of the courts or the natural forces of correction outside the courts were inadequate.

To create a federal trade commission, a bill was drawn by congressmen that supplanted Davies's Bureau of Corporations by a body with five members. For months the President listened to the arguments of progressive and conservative spokesmen as to the powers to be entrusted to the new commission. Southern agrarians and disciples of Bryan wished to provide for strict regulation of stock exchanges, a confiscatory tax on the largest corporations, and complete destruction of those interlocking relationships that allowed businessmen to act on both sides of a transaction. On the other hand, the national Chamber of Commerce, embracing the ideal of "self-regulation" by business, wanted only friendly advice from a federal commission.

Finally, in an effort to achieve legislation that would be both effective and practical, Wilson went again to Brandeis for counsel. And on this occasion, as before, the tribune of the people had a solution ready. Brandeis, who wished to elevate "business" to the level of a profession in which all would have equal access to essential knowledge and all would practice uniform methods of accounting, had drafted a bill for a commission that would have plenary authority to issue cease and desist orders against monopolists, but not to punish offenders.

Calling Brandeis to the White House on June 10, Wilson told him that his bill, which already had been introduced in Congress, would be the foundation of the Administration's antitrust program; and three days later the measure appeared as an amendment of the Federal Trade Commission bill when it was reported out of committee in the Senate. Despite ardent efforts by Wilson and his advisers to overcome the opposition of conservative Democrats, provisions were added that would protect corporations against cease and desist orders by guaranteeing review in the courts. With this safeguard, the bill was passed, and signed on September 26, 1914.[15]

Thus the second of the remedies that the President had sought in his January message to Congress was enacted.[16] During 1914, Woodrow Wilson had veered far from the emphasis on personal guilt that had marked the impractical "Seven Sisters" acts of New Jersey, and toward acceptance of responsibility by the government in accordance with progressive policies. The Presbyterian moralist had yielded to the compelling logic of Brandeis, the social scientist who blamed current evils on the nature of the economic system. Wilson's concept of the "necessary functions" of the federal government had broadened.

In 1914, however, with foreign problems claiming an increasing quota of his time, Wilson found it impossible to satisfy all the champions

[15] The appointment of suitable men to the new body presented problems no less difficult than those faced in choosing the Federal Reserve Board. Joseph E. Davies was the logical choice for the chairmanship. House's diary records that on Nov. 5, 1914, he and the President went to Wilson's study after dinner and agreed on the commission's personnel "within the hour." Appointments were not made, however, until Feb. 22, 1915. George Rublee—an appointee who had the confidence of Brandeis—was prevented from serving when Senator Gallinger, minority leader, blocked his appointment on personal grounds. Brandeis felt that Wilson's appointments to this body were unfortunate and that its administration was "stupid."

Although in the autumn of 1913, before the recession of business and the outbreak of war in Europe, the President had advocated "real dissolution" of offensive trusts, and though he had to give the commission restraining powers, he later hoped and expected that it would not be necessary to use them extensively. He thought of the body as a counselor and friend of business rather than a policeman.

[16] The third specific recommendation of the address on trust regulation, advocating control by the Interstate Commerce Commission of the issue of new securities by the railroads, was the subject of a bill drawn by Brandeis and Representative Rayburn, which passed the House but became the first casualty of the New Freedom program after war broke out in Europe.

of sundry reforms. Speaking to the National Press Club at a house-warming in their new quarters, he cried out on March 20: "God knows there are enough things in this world that need to be corrected." Before the journalists he talked as a writer among his fellows. Protesting against the popular impression that he was a "thinking machine" that turned "like a cold searchlight" on national problems, he confessed that actually, inside, he sometimes felt like "a fire from a far from extinct volcano." He gave vent to his sentimental affinity for crowds. "A crowd picked up off the street is just a jolly lot," he said,"—a job lot of real human beings, pulsating with life, with all kinds of passions and desires." It refreshed him to mingle with them, in his imagination, or to "get a rattling good detective story, get after some imaginary offender, and chase him all over"; in such "blessed intervals" he could forget that he was a monumental robot that had to shake hands of all sorts, even those belonging to "that class that devotes itself to 'expense regardless of pleasure.'" He confessed that he had thought often of buying an assortment of beards, rouge, and coloring. "If I could disguise myself and not get caught," he said, "I would go out, be a free American citizen once more and have a jolly time." [17]

In the same talk to the journalists Wilson gave voice to his sense of humility in the face of the expectations of the voters who had charged him to administer a part of their government: "When I think of the number of men who are looking to me as the representative of a party, with the hope for all varieties of salvage from the things they are struggling in the midst of, it makes me tremble. It makes me tremble not only with a sense of my inadequacy and weakness, but as if I were shaken by the very things that are shaking them and, if I seem circumspect, it is because I am so diligently trying not to make any colossal blunders. If you just calculate the number of blunders a fellow can make in twenty-four hours if he is not careful and if he does not listen more than he talks, you would see something of the feeling that I have." Two months later, under pressure that seemed to him "unconscionable," Wilson told a journalist that he felt like displaying in his office a sign that was once put up on the organ loft of a country church to defend the organist: "Don't shoot; he is doing his damnedest."

However, during the first months in office the President had not been so busy that he ignored heads of evil that had been sprouting from the

[17] One day Wilson actually made good his escape from the Presidency. Stuffing an old felt hat inside his coat, he eluded the secret service men and walked out the door of the White House, forbidding the doorkeeper to give him away. They found him later in a five-and-ten-cent store, buying penny candy for a gang of dirty-faced children.

hydra at which he had struck during his governorship in New Jersey. Going back to his own state to stimulate the passage of his jury-reform bill in a special session of the legislature that was called by Acting Governor Fielder, Wilson had flayed the bosses as of old. "There was a time," the President said at Newark, "when only two things would move those who defied the sovereignty of the people: fire and fodder. I am going to put the fire beneath them. Fodder has gone out of fashion." Though this foray gave heart to Jersey progressives and contributed to the election of Fielder as governor, it led doubters to ask whether the President had not diverted too much energy from his own job.

Wilson could count now on the continuing hatred of the New Jersey bosses as well as upon that of Tammany, which he defied by two successive appointments of collectors of the port who were outside the New York wigwam. Moreover, Senator O'Gorman of New York was hurt because he was not consulted and also because the President had not thanked him personally for support in the election or for a laudatory magazine article. Democratic senators of the old regime were complaining of the entertainment offered at the White House: one grievance, O'Gorman told Colonel House, was that at a conference with the President no drink but water was offered, and nothing to smoke. Sometimes, too, Wilson spoke unkindly to his intimates about legislators with whom he disagreed, and his critical attitude was magnified by political adversaries who felt, like Senator Lodge, that the President had won the plaudits of superficial people by exercising despotic power over Congress to a degree hitherto unknown.

Moreover, during his first year in office Wilson had made enemies among special interests that could be expected to denounce his efforts for the common good. Strong individuals who had made the most of the equality of opportunity in the United States were wondering whether private enterprise would be allowed sufficient reward to make it worth while. There were irresponsible whisperings of socialism, confiscation of wealth, and dictatorial trespass on legislative functions. Merchants and industrialists resented the tax placed on large incomes, and Washington storekeepers had not forgotten the loss incurred because of the President's insistence on a simple inauguration. The Administration was in disfavor with men whose advice had not been asked about the tariff and currency acts, as well as with some who had been consulted and not heeded. In a speech delivered at the Republican Convention of New York State on August 18, 1914, Senator Root recapitulated the complaints of Eastern businessmen, asserting that the new tariff had dampened industry without lowering the cost of living, the Federal Reserve Act had frightened venture capital, the income tax had discriminated against the East, and the Federal Trade Commission was merely one more dangerous step toward bureaucracy. Moreover, Root made the sort of allegation that had transformed the academic dispute at Princeton into class warfare: he declared that Wilson's policy was based on jealousy and ill-will toward successful businessmen.

Sensing the antipathy of conservatives, realizing that he was being blamed for a recession of commerce in the spring of 1914, Wilson made a speech in June that was intended to allay uneasiness. Insisting that signs of a revival of trade were more evident each day, he spoke of the criticism of business methods that had been rising for ten years. After ten years of apprehensive guessing, he asserted, businessmen now had a definite program of constructive correction. He promised that the anti-trust laws would give opportunity for "rest, recuperation, and successful adjustment."

It was not only the materialists who had to be mollified, however. Ardent reformers likewise were disgruntled and had lost heart because Wilson's achievement had fallen short of their dreams. To be sure, he had insisted to his party men upon "the absolute necessity of a carefully considered and wisely balanced budget." [18] But he had disappointed militant suffragists, importunate champions of the Negro, the promoters of many other causes. Though at first giving support to proposals for conservation of natural resources, he had to conclude early in 1914 that they were beyond a possibility of legislative approval, save for an act that safeguarded valuable Alaskan resources. In May of 1913, fearful of "artificial disturbances," perhaps a strike of capital, he had suggested that Congress authorize a program of public works to stimulate business and afford employment; but nothing had come of this. The President had assented, under pressure from agrarians, to the inclusion in the Federal Reserve Act of a provision for agricultural credit and had approved a proposal of the Rural Credits Commission for a system of land banks that would be privately controlled, under federal

---

[18] Letter, W.W. to Tillman, read aloud at a Democratic caucus on Mar. 15, 1913. The letter predicted: "This business of building up the expenses of our Nation, piece by piece, will certainly lead us to error and perhaps embarrassment." In April of 1913, Brandeis and others conferred with Wilson on economy and efficiency in government and Brandeis urged, as a first step toward getting more value for expenditures, that a budget be adopted and administered by a legislative or legislative-executive committee. See Mason, Brandeis, p. 397. The budget bill constructed during Wilson's administration was not passed until 1921. (See volume II.)

charter. In his first annual message to Congress, in December of 1913, he commended the report of the commission to the attention of the legislators; but when, in the spring of 1914, a bill was introduced that would require the government to finance and operate the new land banks, Wilson shrank from the prospect of subsidy.[19]

Perceiving that misapprehension of his purposes was shaking the confidence on which commerce depended, Wilson welcomed delegations of bankers and businessmen to the White House and received such leaders as J. P. Morgan and Henry Ford. Moreover, he approved an announcement by McReynolds inviting corporations that had doubted the legality of their structure to go to the Justice Department for friendly advice.

Often in facing the struggles between capital and labor he drew on his inmost resources in order to keep his mind open and fearless. When coal operators and miners in Colorado came to a break over the issue of the "closed shop" and state authorities failed to prevent bloodshed, the President reluctantly supplied federal troops to suppress violence and at the same time he tried to persuade the operators to accept the mediation of the Department of Labor. He worked to set up an intermediary that would command the respect of each faction, until finally state agencies came to his aid and the ugly strike was settled, in March of 1916. His faith in the lawfulness of responsible labor leaders won respect; and when William B. Wilson was accused of partiality, the President went to the defense of his secretary of labor, declaring that he had "never known a more careful or judicial mind."

It was only in cleaving to purposes that he ascribed to God that Woodrow Wilson could find stability in the maelstrom of pressures that whirled about him in the year 1914. Though he was happy and comfortable in the White House, that residence was not the haven that his own house at Princeton had been. He no longer felt at home anywhere, and this was unsettling. The President might have taken deep comfort, however, had his ever-restless soul been willing to stake its immortality on the service that he had already given to his people. For under his leadership most of the great measures that House had planned for his

---

[19] "I have a very deep conviction," the President wrote to a caucus of House Democrats, "that it is unwise and unjustifiable to extend the credit of the Government to a single class of the community." This conviction, he went on, was clear and permanent and had come to him as if "out of fire." W.W. to Glass, May 12, 1914.

Angered by Wilson's letter, the agrarians declined the sort of banking bill that was offered and there was no legislation until 1916, when the President changed his position under different political conditions. (*See* Volume II.)

fictional Philip Dru and that Wilson had espoused had become law or were on the way to enactment. In parrying the pressures of self-interested lobbies—bankers, industrialists, farmers, laborers—Wilson had fought valiantly for the exalted concept of public interest that he had set forth when he had written in *The New Freedom* of "a time when the systematic life of this country will be sustained, or at least supplemented, at every point by governmental activity." Within the short space of nineteen months his administration had gone far toward writing into statute the grass-roots tide of protest that had carried him into the Presidency. The stirrings of unrest that had agitated both political parties had at last been codified under the Constitution by a leader who was sentient, inspiring, and masterful.

Theodore Roosevelt had found no adequate force within the Republican party that would follow him to Armageddon; but Wilson had marshaled the support of Democrats who in many cases had more enthusiasm for political success than for the ideals that their leader pursued. Ruling elders of the party whose eyes centered on the next election had proved to be receptive to his doctrine of national salvation and more constant in their support than the independents and the progressives. With their aid he had fulfilled a large part of the charge that he conceived that his Presbyterian God had laid upon them.

However, Wilson the historian shrank from attempting to evaluate the legislation that had been enacted during his first two years as president. Addressing the Sixty-third Congress, on December 8, 1914, he ventured to predict that that body would long be remembered for its constructive labors. "But no doubt," he added, "we stand too near the work that has been done and are ourselves too much part of it to play the part of historians toward it."

CHAPTER XX

Moral Frontiers Abroad

Although the president concentrated in 1913 on domestic reforms that had long challenged him, the affairs of the State Department pressed upon him with a force that he could not ignore.

The country that Woodrow Wilson undertook to lead occupied a peculiar place among the nations of the world. The American vision of manifest destiny shone brightly in the minds of its citizens. The genius of inventive pioneers, exploiting the riches of a pristine land, had amassed fabulous wealth. An ideology of enterprise had grown up and was now burgeoning beyond the boundaries of the United States.

The outward thrust, having little of the force of economic necessity behind it, had not followed the grim course of imperialism that had been made familiar in the nineteenth century by overcrowded nations of Europe.

Nevertheless, venturesome missionaries and traders had caused problems in diplomacy. In penetrating areas of political vacuum they had become entangled not only with rivals from European powers but with native caciques and the local prejudices on which they thrived. Soon the United States found itself assuming responsibility for political development in the Philippines, the Caribbean region, and elsewhere. During Taft's administration, American financiers had made efforts to deal with weak foreign economies by the methods that had led to monopolies in domestic industry. Critical issues of diplomacy had arisen that made the American people listen anxiously for a statement of foreign policy from their new leader. An editorial in the *New York Times* observed that current foreign problems were of a gravity unknown since 1865.

Woodrow Wilson had said nothing about external affairs in his inaugural address, and very little during the campaign. One could not be certain, as in the case of domestic legislation, what his direction would be. Before leaving Princeton for the capital he said to a colleague: "It would be the irony of fate if my administration had to deal chiefly with foreign affairs." Until he went to Bermuda in December of 1912 he did not fully comprehend the specific foreign problems facing the nation, nor had he evolved a policy for meeting them.

If during the past decade they had read Wilson's words on foreign affairs, however, his people could feel assured that he had sensed the world-wide political currents of his age and appreciated the opportunities and responsibilities of his office. As early as 1900, Wilson had perceived the major trends of the times. He had been aware then that the enterprise of Americans abroad had given great potential to the foreign policy of their government.[1] He accepted the end of isolation as not only the inevitable result of a "wholesome and natural impulse" to trade and profit but as an opportunity and a challenge to America to champion pure democracy in a world that had reacted against its eccentric manifestations in France and in South America. It seemed to Wilson that the end of isolation had been hastened by the closing of the American frontier, which had fixed in individuals a habit "of acting under an odd mixture of selfish and altruistic motives." Himself a grandson of immigrants, he sensed the restlessness of men who were beginning to feel crowded, even in America, by the forces that their ancestors had fled when they left Europe. At the turn of the century Woodrow Wilson had extended to the whole world his prophecy of "a time of change."

With this affirmation of the mission of the United States in the twentieth century, however, had gone a warning. Wilson declared that the ideals of democracy could not be realized fully at home if Americans allowed them to be discredited among the peoples who had yet to see liberty under just laws. The preservation of her own democracy, as well as the responsibility for weaker brethren, compelled the United States to break out of her traditional isolation.

Wilson had shown little confidence in the effectiveness of "international law," in which he had given a course at Princeton, and compared it with those social laws that a man does not break for fear of ruining his career. He had placed more faith in the combining of great powers

[1] The United States, Wilson prophesied in his *History of the American People*, was ready to become a creditor nation, and "might command the economic fortunes of the world." Writing a preface in 1900 for a new edition of *Congressional Government*, he had observed that after the Spanish-American War the Chief Executive had "greatly increased power and opportunity for constructive statesmanship"; and he suggested that the President might "substitute statesmanship for government by mass meeting." Pointing out that the Chief Executive could initiate negotiations with foreign powers and complete them without disclosing the steps of his dealings and asserting that the President, after heeding expert counsel, should exert a will and definite choice of his own, Wilson had foreseen that the President of the United States "must always, henceforth, be one of the great powers of the world."

Even before President McKinley announced that isolation was no longer possible or desirable, Wilson had declared that George Washington, in warning against foreign entanglements, merely had bidden his people to set their own house in order and wait until they were big enough to stand competition of foreign countries and go abroad in the world.

in understandings based on popular feeling; and he had been groping his way toward a political order such as mankind had not seen—a world in which democracy would prevail under an imperial guarantee.

Nations and their leaders, Wilson believed, were subject to the political morality that was natural in individual men. When a leader made a decision for a whole people he did so "at the risk of the integrity of his own soul." Legal rights, particularly in a field so ill-charted as that of international law, were secondary to ethics and the dictates of dedicated consciences. To a friend whom he met at Edinburgh in 1908 Wilson had remarked that nations were beginning to feel their way toward the consciousness that they were under the same moral order as individuals. "They have not got far yet," he remarked, "and very few would think it practical, but I suppose we will come to it some day."

To Wilson, as to Burke, a nation was "a moral essence." The moralizing of this American had a proselyting force that was lacking in the philosophy of his British hero. America came into the world in 1776, Wilson once said, with "a spirit and a mission" that was inherited from the Bill of Rights; and she had grown as if by predestination. As apostles of liberty and self-government, Americans had special responsibilities. Repeatedly proclaiming a sense of duty that was extralegal, the prophet had declared: "I will not cry 'peace' so long as there is sin and wrong in the world. . . . America was born to exemplify that devotion to the elements of righteousness which are derived from the revelations of Holy Scripture." Mere national patriotism, he had told his Princeton boys, was a narrow and provincial feeling. It was America's destiny to show other nations "a fortunate way to happiness," to "go to the ends of the earth carrying conscience and the principles that make for good conduct."

Wilson's intellect told him that every people should be free to work out their own political system; and at Princeton he had told a colleague that the Russian peasants enjoyed relative freedom, provided that they knew nothing better. But at the same time the evangelistic impulses in his blood told him that those who lacked the qualities needed to achieve political stability should be tutored by the more mature nations. They were not to be free to escape this schooling, which was to be administered by persuasion if possible, by force if necessary. He observed that before the American Revolution even the Ango-Saxons had had to learn to govern themselves in a peace-group that was ruled absolutely by a king; and Wilson felt that duty had compelled the United States to resort to the crude expedient of force against Filipino rebels who could be "moralized" only in that way. But the bond of conscience also required America to desist from exploitation and to allow the people of the Philippines to govern themselves as soon as they could be made ready.

Second only to his concern for international morality, during his academic years, had been Wilson's confidence in the political equilibrium of Anglo-Saxon peoples. He had not lost the kin-feeling for England that had taken root in him during his boyhood years in the South and had been nourished by travel in Britain, by youthful worship of British statesmen, and by studies at the Johns Hopkins into the origin of democracy among the German tribes and its transmission through Anglo-Saxons.[2]

In the years of his presidency at Princeton, Wilson had come to place less dependence on British precedent; and as his own spirit was hurt by frustration his religious zeal surged into his pronouncements on foreign affairs. In 1907, before the battle for the college quadrangles had been lost, he seemed to accept economic imperialism: "concessions obtained by financiers," he had written, "must be safeguarded by ministers of state, even if the sovereignty of unwilling nations be outraged in the process." By the spring of 1910, however, a few days after his prophetic fire had been released at Pittsburgh, Wilson was talking about a "day of reckoning" in international competition for trade. Henceforth there was to be "a new ideal of endeavour"—the public interest of "a world drawn together into one community." In the autumn of 1910, Wilson had asserted that the manifest destiny of America was not to rule the world by physical force or to accumulate a "mere mass of wealth," but to "do the thinking of the world." [3] The United States seemed to Wilson the ideal leader as she was swinging out of her isolation and joining the family of nations.

[2] Criticizing Cleveland's lack of diplomacy in the dispute with England over the Venezuela boundary, Wilson had written: ". . . only our kinsmen overseas would have yielded anything or sought peace by concession, after such words had been spoken." "Mr. Cleveland as President," March, 1897. In presenting John Hay for an honorary degree at Princeton in 1900 he had referred to that statesman as one who had "confirmed our happy alliance of sentiment and purpose with Great Britain." *Princeton University Bulletin,* XII (1900), 12. In 1901 he had conceived of the establishing of better government in the Far East as a joint responsibility of America and England, who could "moderate" the impact of Western standards on the Far East "in the interests of liberty." "Democracy and Efficiency," *Atlantic Monthly,* March, 1901.

[3] In December of 1911, Wilson's outreaching spirit was applied to an immediate issue: he spoke warmly in favor of reciprocity with Canada and regretted that the United States had neglected opportunities for trade with neighbors both to the north and to the south. By 1912, Wilson had lost his earlier hope that the Far East might provide a new field of expansion for the United States.

Thus had Wilson's thought run, spasmodically and often superficially, upon the affairs of the nations and the role of the United States in the contemporary world. Once the supreme responsibility had been fixed upon him, however, the President-elect determined to fail neither in understanding of specific foreign problems nor in judicious decision. In Bermuda, Woodrow and Ellen Wilson had applied their long-standing habit of joint study to the details of current issues. They pored over letters and reports on their country's relations with Mexico. Far Eastern affairs claimed much of their thought. They asked well-informed men for light on the Philippine situation and the character of the Filipinos. The President-elect gave consideration, too, to China and Japan, assuring Sun Yat-sen of his strong sympathy. Russia's treatment of the Jews, of which Wilson had made political capital in a New York speech in 1911,[4] was still a sore subject; the treaty that since 1832 had governed the relations of the United States with Russia was to expire in a few weeks, and Wilson asked for advice from the American envoy at Moscow so that he might thoroughly understand the matter.

The incoming President could ill afford to leave the appointment of diplomatic representatives to the whim of his secretary of state. Before inauguration he had thought it necessary to warn Bryan against appointing foreign-born citizens to posts in their native lands, as a sop to hyphenated Democrats. However, he had shared the secretary's concern for the encouragement of missionary enterprise in China and Japan; for his own Grandfather Woodrow had been a missionary and at one time his daughter Margaret aspired to be one. He had tried, without avail, to send to Peking first Charles W. Eliot of Harvard and then John R. Mott of the Y.M.C.A., whom he thought of as "a robust Christian." He had been usuccessful, too, in efforts to send Eliot to London and Henry B. Fine of Princeton to Berlin.[5]

<hr />

[4] On Dec. 6, 1911, Wilson spoke in Carnegie Hall at a meeting protesting discrimination against American Jews by the Russian government. "The plain fact of the matter is," he said, "that for some fifty years we have observed the obligations of our treaty with Russia and she has not. That can go on no longer. So soon as Russia understands that it can go on no longer . . . the air will clear." The Congress and President Taft were impressed by the lobbying that resulted from the Carnegie Hall meeting, and the treaty with Russia was abrogated.

[5] The President-elect told House that he had offered Eliot the ministry at Peking in "such a complimentary way" that Eliot had intimated that he would accept if Mrs. Eliot assented. The offer eventually was refused, however, and also a later tender of the London embassy. When House told Bryan of the intention to send Eliot to China, the evangelistic secretary of state objected that Eliot as a Unitarian did not believe in the divinity of Christ and would be the worst possible representative in China, where a new civilization was being built upon the Christian movement! House Diary, Jan. 31, 1913.

In inviting Fine to go to Berlin, Wilson offered a subsidy that was to be provided by Cleveland Dodge. Ellen Wilson reinforced her husband's plea by writing to Fine's sister: "We have

Before the inauguration Wilson had been reluctant to discuss diplomatic appointments with his secretary of state, for he had foreseen that he could not in good conscience accept all the "deserving Democrats" whom the Great Commoner wished to reward and he did not know in what spirit his veto would be received; but once they were in office and had established cordial personal relations, Wilson and Bryan conferred and corresponded at great length. The President kept a record of their decisions in his own hand. In a loose-leaf notebook he jotted responsibilities that he denoted as "immediate" (for example: "learn law and decide on policy regarding consular service"). He drew up long lists of positions to be filled, and the names of leading candidates and their sponsors. As in the case of domestic appointments, he recorded political considerations, such as the state in which each candidate lived and the proportion of patronage it already enjoyed. During his first six months in office, more than half the chiefs of missions were replaced by men approved by the President. Though insisting that consular promotions be governed by rule, Wilson wished to choose personally the ambassadors who were to represent him in dealings with other heads of state.[6]

It was difficult, he found, to select men who could afford the expense of diplomatic life and who were at the same time free from corporate interests. Asked what was causing delay in making appointments, he replied: "Lack of good men." Having failed to draft Eliot and Richard Olney to fill the vacant ambassadorship at London, he turned to his magnetic friend, Walter Hines Page. Another man of letters, Thomas Nelson Page of Virginia, was sent to Rome. The ambassador to France

---

no complicated relations with Germany . . . It would be a splendid 'vindication,' like the Presidency for Woodrow—and just think how furious it will make West and the others!" Letter, Ellen Wilson to May Margaret Fine, Mar. 18, 1913. Fine, however, wished to devote himself to teaching and to purge the air at Princeton of the poison lingering from the Wilson-West feud. Moreover, he feared that in an official position at Berlin he might not see eye to eye with Wilson and might have to resign. Philena Fine Locke to the writer, Oct. 15, 1955. Refusal by his steadfast Princeton colleague made Wilson "feel blue." ("I do not know any man I would more like to honor than Harry," he wrote to Dodge on March 30.) He had better success, however, in persuading Professor Edward Capps to serve at Athens and in inducing Professor Henry Van Dyke to go to The Hague.

[6] On Sept. 17, 1913, Wilson explained his policy regarding foreign service appointments thus, in a letter to President Charles W. Eliot: "We are following the merit system in the consular service more strictly even than either of the preceding administrations and shall continue to do so . . . In the matter of the diplomatic service . . . we find that those who have been occupying the legations and embassies have been habituated to a point of view which is very different, indeed, from the point of view of the present administration. They have had the material interests of individuals in the United States very much more in mind than the moral and public considerations which it seems to us ought to control. They have been so bred in a different school that we have found, in several instances, that it was difficult for them to comprehend our point of view and purpose."

was William B. Sharp, an Ohio manufacturer who had contributed liberally to party coffers; and Henry Morgenthau, another financial supporter, was sent to Turkey. The Russian embassy, which House had thought of as a safe repository for Bryan, was not filled for months, then given to a wealthy Californian who lacked qualifications for the post. Mayor Brand Whitlock of Toledo was chosen for Belgium, after Newton D. Baker wrote tactfully to Tumulty to praise the Administration and to express his reluctance to commend Whitlock to the President directly for fear of seeming to press his personal judgment too far. This was the sort of approach that Wilson seldom resisted; but he reacted against the importunities of friends of James W. Gerard of New York. He had appointed several men from that city already; and, although Gerard had contributed lavishly to the Democratic campaign fund, he had supported Champ Clark for the nomination. Finally, however, after this Tammany man had persuaded House and Senator Hughes of New Jersey to promote his name, Wilson reluctantly appointed Gerard to the foreign post that was to prove most critical of all—the ambassadorship at Berlin.

The President was disappointed because he had had to give so many of the foreign posts to inexperienced men of wealth who coveted them. He did not instruct each of the ambassadors, but left personal contacts largely to House, whom he had consulted repeatedly in choosing them. In the case of Page, he merely asked the Colonel to ascertain whether the editor would accept the post at London, and Page, calling at the White House for parting instructions, was disappointed because Wilson had nothing to say except that he wanted to have a friend at London on whose judgment he could rely. Seeing a prospect of indulging an ambition to play a part in international politics, House was assiduous in winning the confidence of the appointees. He reminded Page to pay his respects to Bryan, and accompanied him to the State Department, anxious that these officials comprehend each other. He put himself on intimate terms, also, with Gerard. In his outreaching mind there was taking shape a grand vision, a design for an understanding among the United States, Britain, and Germany that would clarify the Monroe Doctrine and would give Germany opportunity to develop trade outlets of which Britain would not be intolerant. Gerard was sent to Berlin by way of London, with a note to Page suggesting that a time might come when the American ambassadors to Britain and Germany should work together.

Well aware of Bryan's shortcomings, Wilson took the precaution of placing a distinguished jurist, John Bassett Moore, in the State Department as counselor, with power to sign documents for the secretary. Furthermore, the President soon applied his own mind to foreign affairs. Calling the Senate Foreign Relations Committee to the White House in the spring of 1913, he spent an evening in giving them a panoramic view of the specific problems facing the nation. He proposed that the several issues be dealt with under a policy that required understanding, patience, and scrupulous respect for obligations.

The time that Wilson devoted to the current problems of the State Department in the spring of 1913, after essential appointments were made, was claimed largely by controversies in the Far East and in Latin America. It was to these areas that the President most often turned the globe that he sometimes fingered in a corner of his study.

Before he had been in the White House for a week, New York bankers called on the secretary of state to ask whether they would be expected to participate in a six-nation consortium that was negotiating a loan to the Chinese government. Four New York banking houses had joined the international group in 1911 at the suggestion of Taft's administration, which wished to assure maintenance of an "open door" to all legitimate foreign interests in China. Though superficially a kindly provision of credit for a people going through political revolution, the proposed loan called for international supervision of the salt tax. The American minister at Peking, reporting opposition by Chinese patriots, was apprehensive of awkward entanglements and of wounds to China's pride and violations of her sovereignty in case the terms of the agreement could not be met in the future.

Bryan, whose impulse to help in the rebirth of the Chinese nation was at least as strong as that of his Republican predecessors, learned from New York financiers the terms on which they would be willing to go on with their negotiations. First, they desired for themselves a monopoly of America's share in the loan; secondly, the present combination expected to have the privilege of handling future loans; and thirdly, the national groups participating looked to their respective governments to use whatever measures might be needed, even a display of force, to make China carry out the terms of the contract. The secretary of state was urged to accept these conditions by men in his department who had served Taft and who argued for the sort of self-interested intervention that had come to be known as "dollar diplomacy."

When the secretary of state brought the matter before the Cabinet, Wilson was already convinced that the United States could help China in some better way. Nevertheless, he wished to hear the counsel of his Cabinet. On March 18 there was a long discussion of the matter. Bryan objected pointedly to the consortium, remarking that it gave a monopoly of American interest to four banking houses in New York and that, moreover, it granted a financial monopoly in China to an international group that would be free to violate that nation's sovereignty and to involve the United States government in a joint debt-collecting action that might be repugnant to American principles. McAdoo remarked that American bankers should not be asked to subscribe to the loan or to take a hand in managing China's economy. In the view of Lane it was as absurd to try to apportion China's debt as it would be to divide her territory: to him it seemed better for individual Americans to invest in China at their own risk, or even for the government to underwrite Chinese bonds rather than to license private bankers to take part in a scheme that had dangerous international ramifications. Essential to any settlement, Lane perceived, was preservation of China's self-respect. But Redfield reminded his colleagues of the realities of the financial market. Other nations, he warned, might make the loan if Americans did not, and then the United States might lose out in commercial competition.

As each man spoke from his own point of view or that of his department, it was evident that all were moved by a sentiment that was strong among the people. Every voice echoed the popular fallacy of the day: namely, that the millions of China, victimized by various manifestations of Asiatic despotism, were groping toward a Christian democracy patterned upon the Republic of the United States, and that it was the manifest duty of good Americans to aid them.

After listening patiently, the President told the men of his own conviction that better instruments to aid China could be found than the proposed loan. He read to them a statement of policy that he had drafted, naming certain nations and criticizing them severely. The text seemed amateurish to the Cabinet and they urged that he tone it down. Remarking that he seemed to be "a member of an anti-acid society," Wilson made changes; but in the afternoon he released the document, and it was still outspoken enough to arrest attention. Asserting that participation in the consortium would be "obnoxious to the principles upon which the government of our people rests," he promised that his administration would use all fair means to promote the trade of its citizens with China, but always through the Open Door—"the only door we care to enter." He pointed out that the conditions of the proposed loan seemed "to touch very nearly the administrative independence of China itself." [9]

The next day the New York financiers withdrew from the consortium, and they refused a request from Bryan that they extend the loan already made. Irresponsible journals, dramatizing the message from the White House, headlined their stories with such phrases as "a knockout for Wall Street."

Wilson promptly learned, however, that his sudden intrusion into affairs of state made enemies among diplomats both at home and abroad. Huntington Wilson, an assistant secretary of state who had urged dollar diplomacy on Bryan and had commended the Chinese loan to the President as an indispensable instrument of American policy, read the statement from the White House and reacted violently.[10] He sent off a letter of resignation by bearer to the White House; and the next day Woodrow Wilson, after consulting House, dictated a frigid acceptance and advised Bryan, who was out of town, that his assistant had been separated from the Department of State.

Moreover, the President's independent statement aroused suspicion among the governments of other nations whose bankers were participating in the loan to China and whom the American government had failed to apprise of its intentions through the usual diplomatic channels. Count Von Bernstorff, German ambassador, cited the act as an illustration of the fact that "the only consistency of the diplomacy of the United States lies in its surprises." Sophisticated chancelleries in Europe found it difficult to ascribe Wilson's profession to a pure missionary urge to help China; the German undersecretary for foreign affairs, for example, suspected with some reason that the New York bankers would

---

[9] *Papers Relating to the Foreign Relations of the United States* (hereinafter referred to as *F.R.*), *1913*, pp. 170–71. Wilson said to the Cabinet: "If we had entered into the loan with other powers we would have got nothing but mere influence in China and lost the proud position which America secured when Secretary Hay stood for the Open Door in China after the Boxer uprising." Wilson is reported to have declared, further, that the position of the United States would be stronger if she stood aloof and said to Russia: "What are your designs in Manchuria?" And to Japan, England, Germany, or any other nation: "What are your designs?" Wilson was assured by Mr. Rea, Sun Yat-sen's financial representative, that China could get private loans from American capital; and Secretary Redfield reported that an American manufacturer had just sent six modern engines to China.

[10] When Huntington Wilson gave his views to the President, the latter's face froze and the assistant secretary left with an impression of agile intelligence and overweening arrogance, and with his own views on the consortium hardened by opposition that he thought doctrinaire. H. Wilson, *Memoirs of an ex-Diplomat*, p. 249. In the view of loyal Democrats, however, Huntington Wilson, by rebuking a new president when he himself already had been notified that he was to remain in the State Department only a few weeks, "made an exhibition of himself."

be glad to be released from the consortium, and it was alleged that Wilson was yielding to their inclination in a way calculated to win Chinese friendship. Furthermore, the Japanese ambassador, eager to learn the "full mind" of the President, went to the White House to protest that Japan had been asked by the Taft administration to join in the loan.

At the next meeting of his Cabinet, Wilson acknowledged that in his preoccupation with American public opinion he had erred in giving his statement to the press before conveying it to the diplomats. "It seems," he said with a laugh, "that the United States has invited Japan to dinner and then absented itself when dinner was served, and Japan does not understand it." Though his precipitancy had offended conservatives and legalists and had added to the number of his personal enemies, his swift stroke for obvious fair play, following full and free discussion in the Cabinet, had bound his official family and many altruistic citizens more closely to him. Leaving the meeting at which the issue was discussed, Bryan exclaimed warmly: "I love his audacity and his courage." Moreover, the President had impressed upon emancipated Chinese minds the sincerity of American friendship—an impression that he deepened on May 2 by acting, against the advice of State Department experts and independently of other powers, to recognize the government of Yüan Shih-kai.[11]

Wilson was less fortunate during the first months of his presidency, however, in resolving a crisis that affected another Far Eastern nation and involved also a problem in American constitutional law. A critical issue had been raised when Democratic politicians in California tried to satisfy the prejudice of their voters against permitting Japanese colonists to own land in their state.[12]

[11] Though members of the Cabinet expressed doubt that the Chinese Republic was stable enough to merit recognition, and Bryan reported that there had been an assassination that might have had a political motive, it seemed clear to Wilson that the people had elected representatives to a parliament. Therefore, he decided upon recognition. He did not wish to make this action contingent upon that of any other nation, but directed Bryan to tell foreign ambassadors of his intention and express the hope that their governments might do likewise. Only Brazil and Mexico responded as the President hoped. When Bryan reported that the Russian envoy intimated that, since his government intended to follow United States policy in Mexico, the United States should reciprocate in China, Wilson and his advisers did not accept this proposal because conditions in Mexico and China seemed to them dissimilar.

Early in April Bryan had a talk with the Chinese minister, at the risk of giving offense by seeming to patronize. The secretary of state urged that the Chinese officials and their people be impressed with the importance of conducting themselves in such a way as to win the respect of other nations.

[12] The question of Japanese immigration was not a new one. It had annoyed Theodore Roosevelt, who had spoke softly through a diplomatic gentlemen's agreement and, at the same time, in order to serve notice that immigration was essentially a domestic concern, had shaken a "big stick" in Japan's face by sending battleships across the Pacific.

On the day after the inauguration, Ambassador Chinda called on the new President to seek his help in allaying resentment in Japan against the affront that the Californians proposed, and thus Wilson was forced immediately to deal with the matter. The President was not unsympathetic toward the feelings of his fellow citizens on the Pacific coast. During his election campaign he had confessed to James D. Phelan, a party leader in San Francisco, that he favored the exclusion of unassimilable foreigners; and in April of 1913 he reassured the same man of his understanding of California's problem and of his hope that any legislation passed might be "so modulated and managed" that it would give as little offense as possible to the pride of Japan. He suggested a compromise formula to Governor Hiram Johnson. When news came of a huge mass meeting in Tokyo that advocated dispatch of Japan's powerful fleet to California and when missionaries denounced the proposed legislation, Wilson and Bryan addressed a cautioning message to Johnson. The President was by no means sure that the federal government had legal power to override the constitutional rights of a state in such a matter, for it was a point never determined by the courts. Nevertheless, on April 22 he went so far as to appeal publicly to the California legislature to act in a conciliatory way rather than make invidious discriminations that would "draw in question the treaty obligations of the United States." [13] And on the same day the Cabinet discussed the matter and Bryan was asked to go to Sacramento to try to moderate the jingoism of the politicians. Wilson thought that the voice of the Great Commoner, speaking for the nation's security, would be heeded by the Western radicals.

The legislators on the Pacific coast, however, did not yield to persuasion. Though the California Assembly passed a bill that set a ban on landownership in tactful terms and included an assurance that the measure was in accord with the provisions of the nation's treaty with Japan, the state's Senate insisted on defining the interdict as one against persons not "eligible to citizenship" [14]—a phrase that provoked Japanese resentment. And despite Bryan's attempt to persuade the governor to veto it, the Alien Land Bill became California law on May 19.

13 Telegram, W.W. to H. Johnson et al., April 22, 1913. Japan contended that the California measure would violate an American-Japanese treaty of 1911. Wilson suggested to the Californians on April 22 that the measure might violate the treaty. His papers preceding this date did not raise the question of legality. See Harley Notter, The Origins of the Foreign Policy of W.W., p. 236 and footnote. Counselor Moore of the State Department gave an opinion that the law could be set aside by federal courts.

14 On May 13, Bryan told the Cabinet that the Californians refused to apply the ban to all foreigners "eligible to citizenship" for fear of discouraging French and German investors in California.

For a few days war clouds hovered over Washington. Ambassador Chinda delivered a protest in which the California law was called obnoxious, discriminatory, unfair, unfriendly, and in violation of a treaty.

Though Wilson deplored the decision of the Californians to put politics above statesmanship, he thought the Japanese statement unfair. It seemed to him that all treaty rights were safeguarded in the text of the California law and, moreover, that Japan was as free as the United States to air her grievances in a court of law. Agreeing that Japan's protest should be held in confidence, in order to avoid public excitement, the President authorized Bryan to tell Chinda informally that the language used was objectionable. Characteristically, he charged his secretary of state to heed the manner and expression of the Japanese spokesman in order better to appraise the intent of his nation.

At last, in the middle of May, the behavior of Chinda and activities of Wilson's own Joint Army-Navy Board brought the President to realize fully that the threat of war was serious. Admiral Fiske and General Leonard Wood, comrade-in-arms of Theodore Roosevelt, won the Joint Board and the assistant secretary of the navy, Franklin D. Roosevelt, to a policy of preparedness in the Pacific. The board decided that naval vessels should be ordered at once to reinforce Manila, Honolulu, and the Panama Canal. Stating that war was "not only possible, but even probable," the Joint Board warned against leaving the United States as unprepared as China and Russia had been when Japan attacked them suddenly.

When Wilson learned of this through press reports he was amazed that his subordinates should have acted on so vital a matter without consulting their commander in chief, and, worse yet, that they should have allowed their decision to leak out to newsmen. It seemed to him, and to Secretary of the Navy Daniels, that an effort was being made to force his hand. He feared that irresponsible news reports might lead the Japanese people to think that the United States expected war.

When he brought the matter before his Cabinet on May 16, Secretary of War Garrison intimated that that body's views on military affairs were not particularly valuable, especially when compared with those of the Joint Board. At this Bryan flared up and with flushing face bellowed that army and navy officers could not be trusted to decide what should be done in time of peace, that the problem was not how to wage war but how to keep out of war, that if ships were moved about in the Pacific it would be an incitement to hostilities. The debate was so heated, and the matter so critical, that at the end of the meeting Wilson asked the secretaries of war and the navy to come to the White House for further discussion. Sitting in the garden that afternoon, the three men talked for a long time. Garrison insisted on approval of the action of the Joint Board. He pleaded that the United States was well within her rights in moving her own ships as she pleased, and he stressed the responsibility of the Administration for national defense.

Wilson, though realizing that he would be criticized for unpreparedness if war came, decided to take the risk of ordering that the vessels remain where they were. He saw strong logic in the argument of the secretary of the navy that any movement of armed force that was not large enough to make victory certain might be provocative, and hence worse than inactivity. "We must not have war except in an honorable way," he said to Daniels, "and I fear the Joint Board made a mistake." [15]

On the same day on which the indiscretion of the Joint Board was discussed, the Cabinet considered a reply to Chinda that the President had drafted. Afterward Wilson rewrote it, in conference with Bryan; and on May 20, upon the signing of the Alien Land Act in California, the secretary of state gave it to the Japanese envoy. The note took issue with many of the arguments advanced in Japan's protest; but Bryan softened the effect by assuring Chinda orally that the federal government would do its best to prevent financial damage to Japanese in California and to induce Congress to compensate them for any losses incurred—also that the Administration would use its good offices to advance court hearings of Japanese citizens who had grievances. These oral assurances, Bryan told Chinda, were to be forwarded to Tokyo only if the Japanese government found itself seriously embar-

[15] Daniels Diary, May 16, 1916. Admiral Fiske was disappointed when he learned of the decision. Undeterred, however, he came to Daniels the next morning and asked that Wilson be requested to approve a recommendation by the Joint Board that naval vessels on the coast of California be sent at once to Hawaii. The President was "greatly put out," Daniels recorded in his diary, when he heard of this and of newspaper stories about differences between his views and those of his military advisers. It seemed to Wilson that the board had no right to discuss such a matter after the Cabinet had given its decision. "I wish you would say to them," Wilson declared, "that if this should occur again, there will be no General or Joint Boards. They will be abolished." Thereupon Daniels, about to leave the city, sent word to Fiske that the board should meet no more until he could talk to the admiral. Wilson ordered the board not to meet again without his permission, which he did not give until Oct. 16, 1915, when Daniels suggested that the body prepare to give advice on preparedness for the possibility of war in Europe. Daniels Diary, May 16, 17, 1913.

Another rebuke to indiscreet officers was delivered when Wilson demanded that a reprimand be given to members of the Military Order of the Carabao who had served in the Philippines. At a dinner on Dec. 11, 1914, at which Cabinet members were present, these men had ridiculed the Administration's Philippine policy and Bryan's addiction to grape juice. They had sung a song with the refrain: "Damn, damn, damn the insurrectos." If their officers did not hold their loyalty above all "silly effervescences of childish wit," Wilson wrote to Secretaries Daniels and Garrison on Dec. 22, 1913, what about their profession did they hold sacred?

rassed by jingoes. After this talk Bryan was able to say, at a garden party at the White House: "There will be no war. I have seen the Japanese Ambassador, and I am letting the old man down easy."

Unlike the problem of the Chinese loan, the issue with Japan was too incendiary to permit Wilson to use his favorite strategy of pitiless publicity. Instead, by taking decisive executive action, he had caused a relaxation of jingoistic tension. Negotiations for a mutual treaty on landownership went on for months through diplomatic channels, but Wilson and Bryan were unable to find an opportunity for getting favorable action from Congress. And so the wound to Japanese pride, which aggravated the hurt inflicted when Wilson had spoken out on the Chinese loan without consulting Japanese diplomats, was allowed to remain open and to fester.

In the spring of 1913, then, in crises involving China and Japan, Woodrow Wilson learned much about the realities of diplomacy. The sensitivity of national feelings and the need for constant vigilance had been brought home to him as it had never been by his academic studies.

Even more worrisome than the Far Eastern problems, however, were issues that arose from regions to the south. There was chronic conflict in Latin America between economic and political forces. At one of its first sessions, Wilson's Cabinet discussed policy in the Caribbean area. Their Republican predecessors had kept a strong hand upon native governments in that region and their policy had stemmed from enlightened self-interest and a desire to improve the living conditions of the inhabitants rather than from motives of political evangelism. At the same time, the Democratic minority in Congress had resisted economic and military pressures upon Latin America; and when the new Administration took office, native politicians hoped for a softening of policy on the part of the "Colossus of the North."

During his first days in the White House, Woodrow Wilson undertook to come to grips with the Latin-American situation that he had inherited. Fearing that irresponsible caciques, possibly with support from foreign interests, might take advantage of the change at Washington and instigate revolutions, the President decided to let it be known at once that the United States would recognize no government that was set up to line the pockets of either native dictators or foreign exploiters. On March 11, therefore, indicating to his Cabinet that he would take a personal hand in dealing with major international problems, he read a text that he himself had drafted. Secretary Bryan smiled approvingly; but other members of the Cabinet feared that the statement proposed by the President might seem superfluous and amateurish, and that such nations as Argentina and Chile would be insulted if they were included among countries in need of admonition. Finally, after a few changes, it was decided to release the statement through the press the next day.

Asking cooperation among the peoples of the Americas and their leaders, Wilson's plea set forth the fundamentals of Anglo-Saxon democracy and gave notice that the United States would "lend its influence of every kind" to the realization of his democratic ideals. "We can have no sympathy," he warned, "with those who seek to seize the power of government to advance their own personal interests or ambitions."

While denouncing leaders who violated private rights and constitutional processes, Wilson at the same time disclaimed selfish motives on the part of his own people. "The United States has nothing to seek in Central and South America," he asserted, "except the lasting interests of the peoples of the two continents, the security of governments intended for the people and for no special group or interest, and the development of personal and trade relationships . . . which shall redound to the profit and advantage of both and interfere with the rights and liberties of neither."

In this message appeared a tendency that presaged a major theme of Wilsonian foreign policy: distinction between peoples and their governments. Moreover, the President alluded to an abiding truth: there could be no lasting or stable peace among such governments as existed in certain Latin-American countries, for "mutual respect" was "the indispensable foundation of friendship between states, as between individuals." Wilson's first pronouncement on foreign policy projected into the politics of the hemisphere, and by implication into world affairs, the intellectual and moral criteria of his earlier years; and it was made clear to neighboring peoples that henceforth their governments would be judged by the United States not for their subservience to special interests but for their responsiveness to the common good.

CHAPTER XXI

PHILISTINES IN MEXICO

THOUGH THE PRESIDENT's first paper on foreign affairs was couched in general terms, it pronounced a curse upon a conspirator who had violently seized control of Mexico. This adventurer, General Victoriano Huerta, had revolted against his chief, President Madero, who in 1911 had promised to liberate his people from the semifeudal system under which Mexico had been ruled by old Porfirio Diaz for a generation.

Madero was besieged in Mexico City on February 9, 1913, by troops commanded by Felix Diaz, a nephew of the former ruler; and after resigning and accepting Huerta's promise of safe-conduct out of the country, Madero was shot dead on the 23rd while being taken from prison to a penitentiary by an armed escort. Huerta's junta claimed that the prisoner was attempting to escape, and Henry Lane Wilson, the ambassador of the United States at Mexico City, voiced the satisfaction of the foreign colony in the restoration of order after days of violence. Many Americans, however, were not satisfied by the official explanation of Madero's death, which seemed to them merely a Latin euphemism for murder. It was taken for granted that Huerta was, to say the least, not ignorant of the plot; and there were allegations that the ambassador could have saved Madero's life.

The shooting of Madero filled Woodrow Wilson with indignation so deep that it seemed impossible for him to deal with the usurper. Among the White House family, Huerta's name could not be mentioned without a grimace and a scorching adjective, and Mrs. Wilson equated the rascal with all that was vile. "I will not recognize a government of butchers," the President said to a friend. Fearing that similar brutality might appear in other Latin-American countries, he proclaimed through the press on March 11: "We can have no sympathy with those who seek to seize the power of government to advance their own personal interest or ambition."

Alarming reports of violence came from American consuls in Mexico, and news that a follower of Madero—Venustiano Carranza of Coahuila Province—had proclaimed himself provisional president. All this made Wilson dubious of Huerta's assertion that he had pacified the country and would arrange constitutional elections. He distrusted reports favorable to the new government that came from Ambassador Wilson, who was actively nurturing the new regime, asserting its stability, and condoning its methods as traditional in Mexico and conducive to the sort of order that Porfirio Diaz had maintained.

It became clear that this new President of the United States was going to ignore the long-established policy under which his nation had given *de facto* recognition to new governments without too close scrutiny of the means by which they gained power. American mining and banking interests that hoped for restoration of the stable conditions of the Diaz regime brought pressure upon Wilson. Thinking him unrealistic and self-righteous, they approached him through House, who forwarded their proposals to the President with the comment that the situation had reached a point at which it seemed desirable that the United States take a hand. One interest advocated forcible intervention by the United States. Another complained that British citizens had been given an advantage through provisional recognition of Huerta by London, and urged that Washington recognize the dictator after exacting suitable constitutional guarantees both from him and from Carranza. A third proposal came from a New York banker who was anxious about redemption of a loan that was coming due in June. This man warned that, without recognition, payment would be difficult and as a result the regime at Mexico City might collapse financially and the United States might have to intervene.

Responding to these propositions, and to a statement from Counselor Moore of the State Department pleading for *de facto* recognition and warning against the assumption that the United States had a right to pass judgment on the legitimacy of another nation's government, Wilson at first was inclined to follow the advice of the businessmen, and the more so because one of them was vouched for by his dear friend Cleveland Dodge. But after hours of study and meditation with Ellen Wilson and with his Cabinet, he said: "I have to pause and remind myself that I am President of the United States and not of a small group of Americans with vested interests in Mexico." Great principles of constitutional government were at stake, and it was essential that they be regarded as primary.

Convinced that Huerta, once recognized, could not be controlled except by force, Wilson felt that he should go no further than to agree to leave Henry Lane Wilson in the embassy at Mexico City and to announce publicly that the United States would deal through him with the new regime "on the basis of its existence." Only time would tell whether

Huerta would make good on a promise that he had made to arrange an election. The President felt that he could afford to wait for any step that might advance the Mexican people toward the democratic order that he envisioned for them; for without constitutional government in Mexico and improvement of the lot of its masses, he despaired of enduring peace in North America.

Feeling a need of information more reliable than that coming from Ambassador Wilson, the President took a step that was to become characteristic of his diplomacy. On April 19, with Bryan's acquiescence, Wilson addressed a confidential letter to William Bayard Hale, his campaign biographer. "I am writing to ask," he said, "if you would be willing to undertake a tour of the Central and South American states, ostensibly on your own hook, in order that officially and through the eyes of an independent observer we might find out just what is going on down there." Hale, who had little background for an understanding of Mexican affairs, accepted the mission and soon was reporting that only a constitutional election could avert a crisis that would require forcible intervention by the United States.

That eventuality was regarded with dread by Wilson, the historian who had set down the Mexican War of 1848 as an inexcusable aggression on the part of a nation that had shown itself "disposed to snatch everything" from a weak neighbor; and moreover, armed interference in Mexico appealed no more to Wilson's common sense than to his historical judgment. "When two drunks are in a brawl across the street," he said to Stockton Axson one day, "law-abiding citizens don't cross over and mix in." Though he discussed the possibility of war realistically with House, it seemed to the President impossible to reach the individual culprits who were at the root of the trouble by attempting to fight the whole country of Mexico.

The Cabinet, too, feared military involvement; and on May 23 members spoke in favor of recognizing Huerta, arguing that the chief cause of the crisis was rivalry of British and American mining interests, that Europeans would support any dictator who preserved order, and that the United States would have to recognize him eventually.[1] Finally,

---

[1] In the Cabinet discussion of May 23, Houston warned that by accepting the usurper the United States would restore his credit; and Daniels declared that any deal with a foreign power that deprived the Mexican people of their mineral resources would be "immoral." When Secretary of War Garrison read an editorial that supported his insistence on recognition of Huerta as the only alternative to intervention, the President broke into the discussion. "That reminds me," he said, "of a statement made by Carlyle, who said that every man regarded an editorial in a newspaper as very wise and able if it voiced the opinion which he himself held." Daniels Diary and Daniels, *The Wilson Era: Years of Peace*, pp. 181–82; Houston, *op. cit.*, I, 69.

it was agreed that Bryan should ask the English and French ambassadors whether their governments were sponsoring loans to Mexico, and should warn that a credit guaranteed by a pledge of customs duties could not be enforced.

Meanwhile interested citizens of the United States grew impatient at their government's policy of watchful waiting. Accustomed to act aggressively, and eager above all to get political stability, the businessmen brought forward another proposal on May 26. This time they did not urge recognition, but rather a fair election, to be achieved by the mediation of the United States between Huerta's provisional government and Carranza's Constitutionalists.

These investors were representative of a group of citizens whom the President was irritating by tariff and currency reforms, and he had no desire to provoke other controversies with them. Finally the Administration broke its silence with a declaration that, if Huerta would assure a free election soon, refrain from being a candidate himself, and guarantee "absolute amnesty," the United States would try to reconcile the contending factions under one government. After a conference with Bryan and with Garrison, who had prepared the Army for intervention, this statement of policy was sent confidentially on June 14 to Ambassador Wilson.

That diplomat, however, was more active in pressing the State Department for recognition than in urging constitutional guarantees upon Huerta. He saw that the sending of an unofficial agent to an unrecognized government caused confusion among Mexicans, as well as resentment; and he understood how deeply Mexican pride was hurt by any hint of patronizing.

But the President trusted Hale's conscience and the objectivity of his view. He was impressed by his envoy's report that the ambassador was damning the Administration at Washington as "a pack of vicious fools"; and when he learned that Huerta had been invited to dine at the embassy, he was so shocked that he suggested to Bryan that Henry Lane Wilson be recalled. This was done in July, "for consultation." After an interview at the White House in which the Wilsons utterly failed to sympathize with each other's purposes, the ambassador's resignation was accepted and the embassy at Mexico City came under the direction of Secretary Nelson O'Shaughnessy, whom Hale had commended as a "perfectly honest man."

The aversion that Wilson had at first felt toward Huerta crystallized in hard, implacable denunciation. He was ready to feud with a usurper whose hand was strengthened by loans from other nations and by the assignment to Mexico City of an English envoy who was thought to be anti-American and sympathetic to oil interests that were vital to the British Navy.[2] The dictator was able to turn Wilson's innocent offenses to national pride to his own advantage and to command the support of Mexican jingoes by defying the "Colossus of the North." The unscrupulous mestizo was a tough antagonist. He was said to be able to clear his brain by heavy drinking, and Indian blood gave him a tenacity that matched that of the Scot in the White House. On August 2 he announced that he would neither resign nor permit foreigners to interfere in a matter involving his honor and that of his nation. And the next day Wilson accepted the challenge, writing to Mary Hulbert that he must consider "how that murderous Castro is to be choked off and kept in cold storage."

At this point the influence of the dean of Wilson's personal agents was felt. Colonel House, who had gone to Europe in May, talked frankly about Mexico with Sir Edward Grey, British foreign secretary. The Texan found in this unassuming philosopher a friend in whom he took delight. When he lunched at Sir Edward's home on July 3, the foreign secretary asked about the President's intentions toward Mexico. The Colonel replied, with more assurance than was justified by Wilson's inmost inclinations, that it was immaterial which Mexican faction held power, as long as order was maintained. This was the traditional English attitude and therefore pleasing to Sir Edward,[3] who responded, a month later, by instructing his minister at Mexico City to say to Huerta informally that refusal to receive an envoy from the United States would be a grave mistake and would put Mexico in the wrong. France also urged conciliation; and Germany, whose views were utterly materialistic, grudgingly cooperated.

At this juncture the President sent a second special envoy to Mexico

[2] Sir Lionel Carden, whose recall from a previous post in Cuba had been sought, unsuccessfully, by Secretary of State Knox. Wilson was led by undocumented reports to believe that Garden was the tool of Lord Cowdray and British oil interests. See p. 367 n. and Link, *W.W., The New Freedom,* p. 371 ff.

[3] A few days after the Colonel left England, Sir Edward Grey told Ambassador Page that House was a man whom he was glad to know and whom he hoped to see whenever the Texan visited London. Here was a fellow more practical than the ebullient Page, who provoked laughter from Sir Edward by advocacy of an "idealistic" intervention in Mexico that would "shoot men into self-government." Burton J. Hendrick, *The Life and Letters of Walter Hines Page,* I, 188. Hereinafter this work is referred to as *Page Letters.*

Page generously wrote to House about Sir Edward's remarks; and when House showed Page's letter to McAdoo, the latter insisted upon taking it to the President so that Wilson would fully appreciate the value of the Colonel's services. As soon as House returned to the United States, he asked McAdoo to tell the President of his talk with Britain's foreign secretary. House Diary, July 20, 1913.

City. John Lind of Minnesota, a political friend of Bryan who was without experience in diplomacy or in Mexican culture, was commissioned as "advisor to the American Embassy," and bidden to reassert the altruistic and paternalistic motives of the United States and to offer to mediate on terms that would end Huerta's dictatorship and bring peace.

Huerta's government scornfully rejected the suggestion of mediation that Lind brought. On August 16, in a letter filled with innuendo and sarcasm, the Mexicans asserted that they could not consider "for one moment" the conditions that Wilson had sent to them, and accused the Americans of trying to bribe them by offering a loan.

Lind was handicapped not only by the coolness of O'Shaughnessy and the foreign colony at Mexico City but by a feeling on the part of Mexicans that there was a serious division of opinion within the United States that might be exploited profitably. When the President's agent reported this to Washington and suggested that a strong statement of policy to Congress might be helpful, Wilson acted to uphold the hand of his envoy. The prophet in the White House was now in the sort of position in which he took delight. He was challenged to compete with a strong but wicked Philistine in a contest for public confidence, and he responded with a righteous thrill. In one of his Sunday letters to Mary Hulbert he referred to himself as a "President trying to handle an impossible President of Mexico," and two weeks later, in August, he wrote: "Our friend Huerta is a diverting brute! . . . He is seldom sober and always impossible, and yet what an indomitable fighter for his own hand!"

Wilson's ardor for moral triumph was heightened by the fact that Republican senators had been nourishing Mexican hopes for a division of opinion at Washington. Protests were being received from constituents, and there was a demand for a Congressional inquiry. On July 19, for example, Senator Albert B. Fall, who was sympathetic to the Doheny oil interests in Mexico, introduced a resolution calling on his government to give full protection to its citizens abroad and to their property. Among the prominent Republicans in the Senate only Elihu Root, whose experience as secretary of state had given him a deep comprehension of the forces at work in Mexico, gave general approval to Wilson's policy. Seizing upon this support from a political opponent, the President wrote to Root to express his "deep gratification." Furthermore, he conferred with the Foreign Relations Committee of the Senate and told them frankly what he was trying to do.

Dispatches from his personal agents in Mexico came so voluminously in August that Wilson found it difficult to settle upon a text for the message to Congress that Lind had suggested. But, finally, on the 27th he was ready to address the legislators. He asserted that all the Americas were waiting upon the development of Mexico, where the benefits of peace could be enjoyed only through "genuine freedom" and "a just and ordered government founded upon law." Present circumstances did not "promise even the foundations of such a peace"; and therefore he had volunteered the good offices of the United States through John Lind. His overture had been rejected by the authorities at Mexico City because they could not comprehend the altruistic spirit behind the offer, and also because they did not believe that the President spoke for the people of the United States. It would be futile for his government to thrust its services upon the Mexicans, Wilson declared. "So long as the misunderstanding continues we can only await the time of their awakening to a realization of the actual facts . . . We can afford to exercise the self-restraint of a really great nation which realizes its own strength and scorns to misuse it."

He urged that all Americans should be asked to leave the country immediately and Mexican authorities should be held strictly accountable for the safety of any who chose to remain. Furthermore, using authority granted to him by Congress, he would forbid the export of war materials to any part of Mexico. In conclusion, he asserted that all the world expected the United States to act in this crisis in her "immemorial relation" of "nearest friend and intimate adviser" to Mexico.

To newsmen he put it more bluntly: "If the Mexicans want to raise hell, let them raise hell. . . . It is their own government, it is their own hell . . . unless you let them have it out, they won't have a government that will stay put."

For six weeks after Wilson's declaration before the Congress the Mexican horizon was comparatively tranquil. In the month of October, however, another storm broke. By the 7th it became clear that Huerta had no intention of arranging the constitutional election that Wilson understood to have been promised. On October 10 the dictator dissolved the Chamber and imprisoned a hundred and twelve deputies; and the United States was begged by the families of the proscribed men to save them from death. A farcical election was held on the 26th; but after it Huerta declared that, since so few had voted, his hand-picked Chamber would be seated and he would remain provisional president.

Wilson's moral sense was shocked again, the more so because he had allowed himself to believe undocumented reports that Huerta had promised not to be a candidate in the election. He bade O'Shaughnessy accuse the provincial government of "an act of bad faith toward the United States." Huerta not only had violated constitutional guarantees, the President said, but he had destroyed all possibility of a free and fair election.[4]

At the same time the President was indignant at Sir Lionel Carden, who, by formally presenting his diplomatic credentials to Huerta the very day after the imprisonment of the Mexican deputies, seemed to give the sanction of London to the dictatorship. Thinking that the British people would overthrow their government if they knew of an alliance of English oil interests with Huerta, Wilson tapped out on his typewriter one of the most incendiary notes that the machine ever produced. Accusing European powers of upholding Huerta and thwarting the efforts of the United States to establish constitutional government in Mexico, he asked the State Department to draft a circular note "as strong and direct as the courtesies and proprieties of pacific diplomacy permit." Bryan then worked with him on a message that reproached non-American nations for allowing their citizens to support Huerta in return for economic concessions. In his angry mood of frustration the prophet was ready to extend the Monroe Doctrine to preclude financial intervention by Europeans in the Americas. On October 27 his indignation stirred him to proclaim [5] "A New Latin-American Policy" and to inveigh against "concessions" in Latin America to foreign capitalists. He was willing to take strong measures even at the risk of provoking a coalition of European powers against the United States.

However, the impetuous President was dissuaded from folly by diplomats at home and abroad. Though he paid little heed to the advice of career men in the State Department, whom he thought wrapped up in legalisms and corrupted by experience in dollar diplomacy, he heeded John Bassett Moore, the scholarly jurist whom he had made counselor of the department as a steadying influence upon William Jennings Bryan. When Bryan requested Moore to polish the sharp note that he and Wilson had drafted and asked that a clause invoking the Monroe

---

[4] Huerta informed the diplomatic corps on Oct. 23 that if he were elected, his election would be null and void, for it was prohibited by the constitution and he had given his word not to be a candidate. His secret instructions to election officials on Oct. 22, however, spoke in a contrary vein. Notter, *op. cit.,* p. 265. On Nov. 8 the dictator notified the foreign powers that he would remain in office until he had pacified Mexico. On the same day the President gave notice that his fight to depose Huerta would go on.

[5] In an address at Mobile, Ala., before the Southern Commercial Congress. (*See* pp. 80–81.)

Doctrine be added, the counselor volunteered a professional opinion that made the President's position untenable.[6]

Like Wilson, Sir Edward Grey was disturbed by the sudden turn for the worse in Mexican affairs. With civil strife still unchecked, it seemed vital to come to an understanding that would preserve American goodwill and at the same time assure protection of British interests. The situation was "very grim," he told Page. To relieve the tension, the English diplomat sent abroad his engaging secretary, Sir William Tyrrell, as a temporary substitute for Sir Cecil Spring Rice, who had succeeded Lord Bryce as British ambassador at Washington and was ill at his summer home in New Hampshire.

When Sir William arrived at the capital, early in November, public feeling had been somewhat soothed by inspired press reports from London that there was no intention to thwart American policy in Mexico. Tyrrell called on the American secretary of state and found him unbelievably *gauche*. Haranguing the English visitor on the wickedness of the Empire, Bryan charged that British oilmen in Mexico were the "paymasters" of their nation's Cabinet. Fortunately the envoy from London had a sense of humor that enabled him to turn the insult aside lightly.

House, responding to a plea from Page[7] that Sir William Tyrrell

[6] Moore to W.W., Oct. 28, 1913. The United States, Moore pointed out, had never presumed to regulate European recognition of Latin-American nations or foreign investment in the Western Hemisphere. It was Moore's view that any such interference would be resented by other American peoples just as much as it would have been objected to by the United States in the days when they had needed capital. Moreover, the counselor reminded his chief that foreign loans had served, in all the Americas, to develop industrial and financial strength and, thus, political stability and independence. Such a note as the President proposed would anger Europeans and defeat his purposes; and it seemed particularly unwise to irritate Britain at the moment in view of other issues that were under discussion with that government.

Bryan, fearing that European loans to Latin America would lead to violations of the Monroe Doctrine, proposed that the United States government make nonprofit loans; but Wilson feared that this would "strike the whole country . . . as a novel and radical proposal." Wilson to Bryan, Mar. 20, 1914.

[7] Page—a sensitive, charming gentleman who was galled by the restrictions of official intercourse—had maintained friendly contact with Sir Edward and had reported faithfully to the State Department despite chilly silences from that organization. He found that he could reach Wilson most surely and sympathetically through House. In frank epistles that he often marked "good to burn" the ambassador confided his troubles to the Colonel.

In response to Page's laments, House wrote comforting replies, explaining the handicaps under which the State Department had been placed by inexperience and by Congressional restrictions on funds, assuring the ambassador that Wilson had enjoyed his remarks about Bryan and his artistic descriptions of life at London. When House was about to burn one of Page's letters, after reading it to the President, Wilson asked him to wait until he was sure that he had its content well in mind and then repeated the text almost verbatim before the Colonel dropped it in the grate. House Diary, Dec. 12, 1913. Though amused, he took his Ambassador's complaints to heart and replied: "We must certainly manage to keep our foreign representatives properly informed. The real trouble is to conduct genuinely confidential corre-

should "get the President's ideas about Mexico, good and firm and hard," took it upon himself to prepare the minds of both the President and the British visitor for an intimate talk. He persuaded Ellen Wilson to go to the theater with Tyrrell, though her husband could not join them. The President was unnerved by his quandary. As he lay awake he prayed that it would not be necessary to use force.[8]

With the President's authorization, the Colonel lunched with Tyrrell the next day and prepared the envoy's mind for an interview with Wilson at the White House. Nevertheless, the men were a trifle embarrassed when they confronted each other, the prophet wearing a gray sack suit and the Old World diplomat, an impeccable cutaway. Soon, however, each was speaking with confidence in the understanding of the other. The President outlined his policy toward Mexico; and Tyrrell agreed that Huerta by his highhanded action had forfeited British recognition. The visitor denied, however, that British commercial interests had formed the alliance with Huerta that the President suspected but could not prove. Moreover, he asserted that Carden was not antagonistic to the United States but was merely doing his duty.[9] It seemed

spondence except through private letters, but surely the thing can be changed and it will be if I can manage it." *Page Letters,* I, 212, 222.

In October, when the Mexican situation became critical, Page reported that he had explained the President's position to Grey, who had shown appreciation and increasing respect for Wilson's ideas, but seemed to be under financial pressure that was irksome." Page to secretary of State, Oct. 21, 1913.

[8] W.W. to Mary A. Hulbert, Nov. 2, 1913. In his extremity during these days Wilson talked for more than an hour with Chairman Bacon of the Senate Foreign Relations Committee, hoping to find help in this senator's long experience. He was vexed because there had been a leak of a dispatch sent by Bryan to Mexico City, stating that the United States would insist on forcing Huerta's abdication. When newspapers published this message, it became impossible for the dictator to resign without appearing to surrender to foreigners. This was a bad jolt, coming just at a time when Huerta seemed responsive to a final effort by Wilson's agents to persuade him to retire. House Diary, Nov. 5, 1913.

[9] House Diary, Nov. 13, 1913.

Ambassador Page was not able to adduce proof of his suspicions of Carden, and the President could not help him. On Jan. 6, 1914, Wilson wrote to Page: "I do not think you realize how hard we worked to get from either Lind or O'Shaughnessy definite items of speech or conduct which we could furnish you. It simply was not obtainable. Everything that we got was at second or third hand. That he was working against us was too plain for denial, and yet he seems to have done it in a very astute way which nobody could take direct hold of . . ." *Page Letters,* I, 221.

"Whatever British interests were doing in Mexico was entirely unknown to me," Grey wrote later in his autobiography. Since the British government could not interfere in Mexico without violating the Monroe Doctrine and the United States had thus far declined to assume responsibility, it seemed to the foreign secretary only fair that British interests should make any terms possible with whoever at Mexico City had power to protect or destroy them. Sir Edward Grey, *Twenty-five Years, 1892–1916,* p. 100.

Page asserted, in a letter of Mar. 19, 1914, to Wilson, that the British oilmen were "not dishonest, by their standard," but that their standard "permitted their taking the earth, if nobody got in the way."

to Sir William that rumors of British involvement with Huerta's cause had sprung from mischievous attempts to stimulate intervention.

The statesmen reached an understanding, not only on the Mexican issue but also about the revision of discriminatory Panama Canal tolls and the larger question of curbing armaments and the power of finance over world politics. Sir William was pleased by the President's sympathetic reception and afterward told House, with whom he arranged to perpetuate their informal contact, that never before had he talked so frankly about matters of such import. "If some of the veteran diplomats could have heard us," he confided, "they would have fallen in a faint." The Wilson-Tyrrell conversation and talks between Page and Grey brought about a change of sentiment at London.[10]

On the second day of the new year, while Wilson was vacationing at Pass Christian, he went far out into the Gulf to confer with John Lind aboard a cruiser that had brought that envoy from Mexico. Lind confirmed disturbing rumors that had reached the President earlier. Returning ashore to his family, Wilson told them that Huerta, made desperate by threats to his life and by lack of funds and a paralysis of government in central Mexico, was ready to declare war against the United States in a rash effort to unite all Mexicans under his leadership. He was said to await only the arrival of two shiploads of munitions from Germany.

It was difficult, Wilson explained, to piece out the truth from reports that came to him from men who had various points of view. He said that he was growing crosseyed, watching so many people in so many directions at the same time. "I listen carefully to what everyone says," he remarked, "and then piece together the parts that fit. Parts of truth

---

[10] Sir Lionel Carden, setting a precedent for European diplomats in Mexico, advised Huerta to abdicate. Furthermore, Sir Edward Grey gave the President a free hand to remove the dictator and pacify the country as best he might. Wilson was jubilant over the change in London's attitude, and congratulated Page on the way in which he was "pounding elementary doctrine" into the British statesmen.

One of Page's confidential letters (undated and marked "good to burn") informed House that he had notified the State Department of a rumor of Sir Lionel's impending transfer, that the message had leaked out, to Page's humiliation, that the Foreign Office had had to deny the report, and that the same sort of thing had happened twice before. Page to House, Jan. 8, 1914. Page blamed the State Department for the leak, but some of the Cabinet members suspected that Secretary Lane was responsible. The matter was discussed in Cabinet meeting on Dec. 19, and thereafter Wilson gave his official family even less insight into his thoughts on foreign policy and kept copies of important letters in a personal file, under lock.

Meanwhile, Ambassador Spring Rice had been complaining to his good friend, Sir Edward Grey, about Wilson's intransigence. Though the President was "extremely friendly," the envoy reported that it was quite out of the question to change his Mexican policy by talking to him. "There is nothing to do with this hardened saint," Spring Rice wrote on Feb. 7, 1914. And as for the secretary of state, talking with Mr. Bryan was "like writing on ice." Stephen Gwynn (ed.), *Letters and Friendships of Sir Cecil Spring Rice*, II, 202.

always match." He seemed to be putting his trust in infinite patience and absolute firmness; but his family noted that he was deeply troubled. Armed conflict with Mexico was to him a horrible prospect, and he turned more avidly than ever to comic relief. He communed at this time with no serious poets—only with humorists; and he tried, rather feebly, to rally his spirits with laughter over the dictum of Mr. Dooley's Hennessy: "Sure, with Mexico so contagious, we'll be takin' it soon whether we want it or not."

Wilson reluctantly reached the conclusion that force must be used to dislodge Huerta, but he hoped that it would not have to be the force of the United States. He continued to withstand European pleas for military action and to resist demands for armed intervention that were put forth by panicky Americans in Mexico and were taken up in the United States by certain Republicans and by jingoistic journals.

The President's mind had been turning toward Carranza as the best instrument for forcing Huerta from power and uniting the country. The name of the Northern faction—"the Constitutionalists"—charmed him. Wilson soon found, however, that Carranza's native pride was as sensitive as Huerta's when it came to accepting American advice on political matters. But Carranza did desire to be allowed to import arms, for he had been paying more for munitions than Huerta, who controlled seaports through which they could be brought from Europe.

Should the United States abandon its neutrality to the extent of permitting Carranza to get weapons that were denied to Huerta? On the evening of January 21, Colonel House found his friend "terribly worried" over the problem. Wilson said that the Constitutionalists, like Huerta's junta, were not beyond suspicion of receiving funds from oil interests—in this case American; but he felt that he could truthfully defend himself against any charge that he was favoring any such influence. Though Wilson foresaw that even if Huerta was eliminated the Constitutionalists still would make war on his successor, he concluded finally that Carranza's faction held out the only hope for avoiding intervention and yet doing away with feudal conditions that lingered in Mexico.

When Carranza sent an envoy to Washington to discuss the matter, the President called upon another special agent to help him to keep negotiations confidential. Evening after evening he received William Phillips [11] in his study and mulled over reports of conversations that

[11] Phillips, a young Republican who had been an assistant secretary of state under Roosevelt and who was commended to Wilson by Page, was asked to leave his post as secretary of the Harvard Corporation and go to Washington for a secret assignment, with the understanding that if he was successful he would become third assistant secretary of state.

Phillips had held during the day with Carranza's envoy, who brought assurance of the interest of his faction in land reform. After the President had puzzled for a while and thought out his course, he would go to his typewriter and tap out instructions for the next day, brief and to the point. He instructed Phillips to keep Bryan informed, but wanted the State Department to assume no part in the dealings. Because of leaks, he did not trust the ordinary channels of diplomacy; nor did he hazard discussion of his intentions with his Cabinet. He was taking the responsibility entirely on his own shoulders, where his conscience told him that it belonged in a matter affecting the peace of the continent, perhaps that of the world.

Finally, on February 3, after getting the general assent of the Senate Foreign Relations Committee, the President revoked the embargo on arms shipments. Though this act did not openly discriminate between the Mexican factions, its practical effect was to notify the world that Wilson put his trust in Carranza's leadership.

Huerta raged against outside interference, rallied conservative patriots to his support, and seemed to be entrenching his regime more strongly than ever. Early in March, after a British citizen had been killed by Constitutionalist forces under General Villa and Sir Edward Grey's policy was challenged in Parliament, Wilson was importuned to appoint a commission of distinguished jurists to deal with the Mexican problem —a proposal toward which both Huerta and Carranza seemed favorably disposed. But he had been "around the clock" and had shut his mind against any compromise with the political immorality that Huerta represented. He had publicly arrogated to the United States the duty of ousting the dictator, and it was unthinkable that he should default upon this responsibility. Huerta must go. But he still hoped to avoid the forcible intervention with which Lind had threatened Huerta if the usurper remained in office after an election.

In the spring, however, a chain of events forced the President's hand. Troops of the Mexican factions came face to face at Tampico with warships of the United States that were standing by to protect foreign oil installations. A paymaster and sailors from the USS *Dolphin* landed a whaleboat without permission in an area that was under martial law and were arrested by a Mexican colonel. They were promptly released and the Huertista commanding officer made a personal apology to Admiral Mayo. But the admiral, unsatisfied, sent an ultimatum that demanded a formal apology, punishment of the offending colonel, and the firing of a twenty-one-gun salute to the American flag. Huerta immediately responded with an expression of regret and assurance that the offending colonel would be punished if found guilty; but he asked at the same time that Mayo's ultimatum be withdrawn.

Thus the thing happened that Wilson had been dreading for months and had been praying to avert. The 14th of April was a harrowing day. The Cabinet discussed the crisis and were almost united in determination to follow up the ultimatum, when the time limit expired without Mexican action. The President was distressed by the admiral's boldness, but he had been convinced by other apparent insults [12] to his country that failure to support the ultimatum would enhearten Huerta and weaken the position of the United States. Later in the day he sent a sharp message to notify Huerta that he expected "prompt acceptance" of Mayo's terms. Suffering under moral responsibility that he had assumed, he besought his colleagues to ask God for peace if they believed in the efficacy of prayer. But he also took steps to keep his powder dry. He dispatched more warships to Tampico, though the Navy warned that such a concentration of power might lead to war. It was a "psychological moment" for a display of force, he said afterward, for the Constitutionalists seemed at last to have an open road to Mexico City.

In the crisis the President felt impelled to consult the Congress. On the 15th, therefore, he informed legislative committeemen of the steps already taken and agreed with them that, though he had power to order occupation of a foreign port to protect American lives and property without Congressional action, it would be best to ask for authorization.

When the President returned to Washington on April 20 from a weekend at White Sulphur Springs, where his wife was ill, it seemed clear that Huerta, though making concessions that satisfied Secretaries Bryan and Daniels, would not yield unconditionally to the American demand.[13] Meeting in the morning with his Cabinet, some of whom had been up half the night planning for a blockade and possible warfare, Wilson outlined an address that he proposed to deliver before the Congress that day.

Early in the afternoon he read his message to members of the Con-

[12] Two incidents that Wilson seized upon to buttress his position and that now seem insignificant are related in Baker, IV, 317, and in *P.P.*, III, 100. In one case the Mexican authorities were exonerated after an investigation by Admiral Fletcher. *F. R., 1914*, p. 465.

[13] It amused Huerta that Mayo's exaction should be made upon a government whose existence had not been recognized, and he sardonically agreed to give the requested salute if the Yankees would return it volley for volley. This proposal was viewed at Washington as a trick to get recognition and hence was rejected, though Mayo was willing to return a Mexican salute in the manner prescribed by naval custom.

gressional committees. It had been released to the press, and it was too late to change it; but at the conference Senator Lodge took exception to many aspects of it. The statement seemed to him weak and unsatisfactory—in reality a declaration of war against an individual. When Lodge told the President that under international law he could not, without a war blockade, carry out his intention of intercepting a cargo of German arms destined for Huerta, Wilson explained that he would seize the weapons at the customhouse at Veracruz after they were landed. The President had not given up hope of a solution that would be both peaceful and effective.

At three o'clock Wilson entered the Capitol to read his message as he had drafted it. There was an air of martial expectancy in the chamber. The galleries applauded, in violation of the rules, and the "rebel yell" of Civil War days arose from Democratic benches. The Cabinet sat in chairs flanking their chief, Bryan looking white and worn and fingering his chin nervously.

In the address Wilson detailed the several incidents of the past few days that had made him feel that the United States had been singled out for insult. "The manifest danger of such a situation," he warned, "was that such offenses might grow from bad to worse until something happened of so gross and intolerable a sort as to lead directly and inevitably to armed conflict." He was forced to sustain Admiral Mayo, he explained, in order to make Huerta understand that there must be no more incidents. War with the people of Mexico was not in question, he asserted emphatically. He was now trying to do, in dealing with a nation, what he had advocated doing in regulating corporations—fix the guilt on an individual and punish him. "If armed conflict should unhappily come . . ." he declared, "we should be fighting only General Huerta and those who adhere to him and give him their support, and our object would be only to restore to the people of the distracted Republic the opportunity to set up again their own laws and their own government." With no thought of selfish aggrandizement, he asked authority to use the armed forces of his nation not against the people of Mexico but "in such ways and to such an extent as may be necessary to obtain from General Huerta and his adherents the fullest recognition of the rights and dignity of the United States."

His audience found it difficult to comprehend this untraditional venture in diplomacy, and to many the incidents cited seemed trivial and inconclusive. The Congress could scarcely refuse to support the Administration in a matter in which national prestige had been made an issue; and yet it was not until two days later, after Wilson had made a trip to the Capitol to urge haste upon the Democratic leaders, that the Senate finally passed a resolution justifying the President in using the armed forces of the nation.

Wilson was thrown into a black mood by the attitude of the Senate. During the evening after his address he told his family that the reaction had not been very favorable; and then, with grim sadness, he said: "People seem to want war with Mexico, but they shan't have it if I can prevent it." [14] His military and naval chiefs conferred with him to perfect plans for sending Marines ashore at Veracruz when the German arms arrived; and Woodrow Wilson went to bed more conscious than ever of the threat of war.

At about three in the morning he was awakened by the telephone. It was Bryan calling, to transmit a report that one of the expected shiploads of munitions was destined to reach Veracruz in seven hours. Daniels was on the wire also, and joined the secretary of state in recommending that the Navy be ordered to intervene. The President felt that he must act immediately, under his own powers and without the advice of Congress, else Huerta would get guns that might be turned on Americans. When Daniels recommended that warships at Veracruz be directed to seize the customhouse, Wilson assented, while Tumulty, listening in on the conversation, marked the cruel irony of a situation that forced three lovers of peace to sanction an act of war.

The President expected no serious opposition to this illegal act of force. When news came that heroic Mexican naval cadets had given their lives in opposing the landing and that American bluejackets had been sniped at and nineteen had been killed, Wilson suffered as if a son of his own had been lost. He looked ill, his skin pale as parchment, as he faced newsmen to answer their queries. All day he was abnormally quiet and went methodically about his business, and finally he said to Tumulty: "I cannot get it off my heart. It had to be done. It was right. Nothing else was possible, but I cannot forget that it was I who had to order those young men to their deaths."

For four days the President was in a quandary and his spirit vacillated from stubborn optimism to dread that Huerta, cornered and at bay, would "stake everything on a dramatic exit." The dictator sent all available troops toward Veracruz, and American consulates were

[14] Asked by newsmen whether it was possible to deal with a *de facto* regime by using the Navy without declaring war, Wilson replied: "Why, certainly. It has been done many times." He cited the naval action at Greytown, Nicaragua (in 1854) as an example. Swem notes, Princeton University Library.

attacked and their officials imprisoned. Moreover, Carranza's tone became so menacing that the American embargo on arms was reimposed and more troops were sent to the border. Furthermore, there were diplomatic complications with Germany.[15] But worst of all the results of the futile landing at Veracruz, jingoism in the United States threatened to get out of control: the debate in the Senate had shown that the opposition wanted full-scale intervention on grounds that would stigmatize the United States in the eyes of the world as an imperialistic nation and would fan the antagonism that was now flaming in Latin America. Faced by all these consequences of his canny effort to intercept the German shipment by seizing the customhouse at Veracruz, Wilson realized that the path to war was very slippery indeed. He paced the south grounds of the White House, hour after hour, up and down, up and down, deep in speculation. "We have been in a blind alley so long," he wrote to a Princeton trustee who had befriended him, "that I am longing for an exit."

In his extremity, the prophet's God did not forsake him. On April 25, as Wilson was acting to check army plans for further operations in Mexico, Providence came to his rescue through the agency of three diplomats from South America. The envoys of Argentina, Brazil, and Chile offered their services as mediators. Wilson and House had discussed such a solution three months before, and the President seized upon it now on the very day of its proposal.

Immediately the air was cleared, not only at Washington but all through the hemisphere. By consenting to mediation the President gave proof of the just intent that he had been proclaiming. Moreover Huerta, as eager as Wilson to escape from the dilemma without loss of countenance, accepted the plan of the ABC powers; and on May 20 the commission went into session at Niagara Falls. Woodrow Wilson now had a judicious body before which to plead his cause, and during May and June he made the most of the unfolding opportunity for leadership of opinion by addressing a series of notes to the mediators. No solution would be acceptable to the United States, he warned, unless it provided for "the elimination of General Huerta" and "the immediate setting up in Mexico of a single provisional government acceptable to all parties." Moreover, the new government must satisfy "the just claims of the people of Mexico to life, liberty, and independent self-support."

---

[15] The State Department was forced to concede that the Navy had no right to order the arms-bearing German vessel to remain at Vera Cruz, with its cargo still aboard, and toward the end of May the ship unloaded its munitions at Puerto Mexico, a port through which arms passed to Huerta all through the spring.

At the same time the prophet exerted leadership through the press. On April 27, only a few hours after Huerta's acceptance of mediation, Wilson told Samuel G. Blythe, a journalist, that the mere removal of the dictator would not suffice. Sitting back in his desk chair with eyes half closed, the President put the current plight of Mexico in historical perspective while his auditor, accustomed to the muddied, platitudinous speech of politicians, listened with awe to the flow of language and was charmed by both words and gestures. Now and then the scholar lightened his phrasing with slang. ("We must hump ourselves," he said.) As he talked, his fingers laced and interlaced, not moving far or violently but conjuring up the image of a musician who accompanies his voice with the piano. Once they closed into a fist that banged the desk and set a paper knife rattling against a tray. As the prophet grew tense, cords stood out on his neck, his eyes narrowed, his lips parted, and he said: "My ideal is an orderly and righteous government in Mexico; but my passion is for the submerged eighty-five per cent of the people of that Republic who are now struggling toward liberty."

The President explained that revolutions in that nation had grown out of the passion of peasants for a fair share of the land. It was his conviction that landless people always furnished the inflammable material for revolt. The prospect of policing Mexico, and then retiring when order was restored, did not appeal to him. He saw that revolution would follow revolution until the Mexican people themselves solved fundamental political problems. "They say the Mexicans are not fitted for self-government," he said, moving his long white fingers in a gesture of contempt. "To this I reply that, when properly directed, there is no people not fitted for self-government." Minister and schoolmaster that he was, he proposed to help Mexicans to compose their differences, start them on the road to prosperity, and leave them to work out their own destiny; but at the same time he would watch them narrowly and insist that they accept help when they needed it. They would be "free" only so far as they showed themselves deserving of freedom.

Always the motive of the United States must be that of a good neighbor—not only human but humane. Though Mexico, like any self-respecting nation, would be expeced to compensate individual foreigners who suffered damages, the United States must demand no indemnities in terms of territory or money, in the manner of the nineteenth-century empires. Moreover, Wilson promised with stern visage: "There shall be no individual exploitation of Mexico if I can stop it." Thus the prophet drew from circumstances that he could not immediately control, a vision of a standard of conduct for Americans of the twentieth century who would find themselves exercising political responsibilities abroad. Putting his creed into a few eloquent words at the public funeral of the nineteen dead heroes of Veracruz, he said that Americans should be proud to die in a "war of service" but not in a "war of aggression." [16]

By the summer of 1914, Woodrow Wilson had learned something of the nature of the forces of opinion, at home and abroad, that he must reckon with if war was to be avoided. He could justly feel that, whatever mistakes he might have committed out of an excess of righteous zeal, he had held his nation in the main stream of political idealism of his age. He had definitely renounced the processes of nineteenth-century imperialism and had eliminated a despot whom it might have been to the material advantage of the United States to use. Furthermore, he had achieved these things without full-scale war.

[16] When Tumulty remarked that the President would be an easy mark for a bullet or a bomb if he rode with the cortege from the Battery to the New York City Hall, Wilson rose from his chair and said: "I am going to New York and am going to ride in that procession. . . . When the people of the United States elected a President, they had the right to expect that they had chosen a man and not a coward." Tumulty told Mrs. Wilson of threats of violence and begged her to dissuade him from going, but she smiled and said: "A soldier's wife has no right to interfere with his duty." She sensed that by exposing himself her husband hoped to atone in some measure for the deaths for which he felt responsible, and remembered that he had said on another occasion: "I am immortal until my time comes." Content with the protection of a cloak of righteousness, Wilson did not give way to the qualms of Mayor Mitchel, who had been shot at recently and urged the President not to expose himself by parading, or to the precaution of House, who, quick and accurate on the draw, carried a six-shooter when he accompanied his friend.

CHAPTER XXII

A Foreign Policy Takes Shape

As WOODROW WILSON dealt with the diplomatic crises that arose during his first year in office he did not lose sight of a fixed star on which the aspiration of idealists was beginning to center. Save for its brief hostilities with Spain, the United States had been at peace for almost a hundred years with the other great powers of the world: its people had grown physically strong, economically wealthy, and strategically secure against the fears and menaces that were rife on other continents. Out of their fortuitous isolation had grown a conviction that peace was normal and virtuous, war unnecessary and wicked. Failing properly to relate their political felicity to the geographic and economic conditions that made it possible, some Americans felt that they could dispense the blessings of peace to the world, along with democracy and Christianity.

During Wilson's academic years, his nation's desire to propagate peace had worked toward two goals: arbitration and disarmament. Unfortunately, proposals for curtailing the armed forces of the nations had not progressed beyond pious talk. Though the standing armies of the democracies were small, the empires of Central and Eastern Europe commanded vast forces; and moreover, the huge navies of Western Europe were being challenged by the growing fleets of Germany, Japan, and the United States.

Arbitration of disputes, however, was a process long familiar to the people of the United States, where a Supreme Court had acted for more than a century as arbiter of interstate differences. The American nation had applauded Theodore Roosevelt when he had mediated to end the Russo-Japanese War; and Americans had participated willingly in setting up a panel of judges at The Hague to serve nations that wished to submit their differences to law instead of a trial of arms. There was, however, no cosmic force to compel the submission of disputes to this judicial body, nor was there power to enforce its decisions. If peoples were sufficiently scared they would still demand the protection of armament; and if they became mad enough they would fight. In the Old World imperial ambitions and ancient grudges had created national psychoses that were unresponsive to ecumenical considerations.

As a university president Wilson had shown interest in conciliation among peoples through international agreements. In his inaugural address at Princeton, in 1902, he pointed proudly to the fact that his own country's greatest victories had been those of peace and humanity. He never escaped the grip that the horrors of the Reconstruction had fixed upon him in his adolescent years in old Columbia. Though not a pacifist, he joined the American Peace Society in 1908. His intellect told him that modern war was a brutal and clumsy way of getting at justice. Sometimes it struck him as silly. Riding from Princeton to take part in a celebration at the Bordentown Military Academy, he quoted this jingle to a young lady in his party:

> War is rude and impolite
> And quite upsets a nation.
> It causes weeks and months of strife
> And years of conversation.[1]

Wilson gave consideration to both disarmament and arbitration as means to peace. Though he said little or nothing in public about disarmament, he talked with Sir William Tyrrell of the necessity of curbing armaments and the power of financiers in politics. "It is the greatest fight we all have on today," he said, "and every good citizen should enlist." Moreover, he had spoken and written in favor of arbitration and, as we have seen, he accepted it eagerly in the crisis with Mexico.

Immediate problems had crowded upon the President so importunately after his inauguration at Washington, and he was so intent on his program of domestic reform, that the matter of world peace received little of his time. He was always conscious that it could not be bought, decreed, or even legislated if its roots did not lie deep in public opinion. He was sympathetic, however, to all sincere efforts to stimulate a love for peace and a will to maintain it; and when his associates took initiative in that direction, he gave his encouragement and blessing.

William Jennings Bryan had been obsessed since 1905 by a passion for a guarantee of the world's peace by international treaties. Before agreeing to serve as secretary of state he had secured Wilson's approval of such a program, and the two Presbyterians directed their energies toward the development of a kind of pact that promised to be more effective than those already in force.

The new type of treaty was designed to prevent friction between

---

[1] B. M. Green (Princeton, 1907) to Lewis, Lewis Papers (Princeton University Library).

nations, and not merely to compel arbitration of disputes that already had reached a dangerous temperature. Moreover, unlike the conventional treaties of arbitration,[2] it applied to all controversies that were not adjusted through diplomacy. Wilson and Bryan had not been in office two months before they were exchanging notes regarding drafts of the new instruments. After the secretary of state had discussed the matter with the Senate's Foreign Relations Committee and had found the members cooperative, it was put before the foreign diplomats at Washington. The plan, as outlined by Bryan and Counselor Moore, called for investigation of disputes by an international commission composed of two representatives of each of the interested parties, and a fifth commissioner whom they might select. Because the treaties provided that the signers would not resort to war until a year had been allowed for investigation and report, the measures came to be known as "cooling-off treaties."

Explaining the purpose of these pacts to his Cabinet, Wilson said that he was reminded of Major Bingham's school at Asheville, where the headmaster called in boys who had been fighting and said: "Any boy may fight another boy if he feels he has a grievance, but before doing so he must come to me and state his grievance and the fight must be supervised under the Queensberry rules." The result, the President explained, was that there was no fighting. When it was suggested that other countries might not be willing to submit to supervision of disputes, Wilson explained: "Let them say so. It will put them to their trumps to give a reason for not talking over the matter."[3]

Promoted by Bryan in a stirring speech on May 9, the "Treaties for the Advancement of the General Peace" were concluded with twenty-one nations, including several major powers, and they took effect during 1913 and 1914. Proud of the achievement, Wilson boasted to Congress in his first annual address that "so far the United States has stood at the front of such negotiations."

During the early months of his administration, while the Bryan treaties were being negotiated and specific threats to peace were being warded off, Wilson came to see that he should assert his leadership constructively in world affairs. In dealing with the crises in relations with China, Japan, and Mexico, the President had learned that the Christian goodwill that his secretary of state exuded was not adequate

---

[2] Elihu Root's treaties of limited arbitration were renewed with some twenty-four nations in 1914.

[3] Daniels Diary, April 8, 1913. Wilson's brother attended the Bingham school.

to maintain peace. Nor was he content merely to rest upon traditional pillars of American diplomacy, such as the Monroe Doctrine in the Americas and the Open Door policy in the Far East. The opening of the Panama Canal gave to the President of the United States a responsibility unknown to James Monroe—that of protecting one of the main trade arteries of the world—and the nation's Caribbean policy had to take account of this fact.

In the autumn of 1913, after Huerta had repudiated his promise to hold a constitutional election, Wilson's sense of responsibility for political order led him to prescribe Presbyterian morality for the salvation of all mankind. The occasion was a meeting of the Southern Congress at Mobile, Alabama, where delegates from Latin America convened with their North American friends. Just before going to the Gulf city Wilson took part in the dedication of Congress Hall at Philadelphia and exhorted his audience to "look abroad at the horizon" and take into their lungs "the great air of freedom which has blown through this country and stolen across the seas and blessed people everywhere." Going on to Mobile by train with Josephus Daniels, he thought aloud about what he would say and asked for criticism. He intended at first to talk on rural credits. On the morning of his appearance, breakfasting at Mobile's Battle House on broiled squab and blanket pompano à la Daniels, he still had written no text for his speech.[4]

When he faced the Southern businessmen, who had been confused by his policy toward Mexico and who sought a restoration of business-as-usual, the prophet spoke out from his heart and asked for a "spiritual union" between the continents of the Western Hemisphere. "Interest does not tie nations together," he proclaimed. "It sometimes separates them. But sympathy and understanding does unite them . . ." Charging that states in Latin America had been exploited by foreign capital, he warned his fellow citizens: "We must show ourselves friends by comprehending their interest whether it squares with our own interest or not."

Then the prophet went on to set forth a still larger concept—"the development of constitutional liberty in the world." As a professor he had written of liberty as a principle to be won by self-discipline; but when he himself had suffered under the restraints that economic forces exert upon liberty he had become less interested in personal austerity and more concerned with the control of restraining influences everywhere. Now he said:

[4] Daniels, *The Wilson Era: Years of Peace*, p. 183; and Leon F. Sensabaugh, "Some Aspects of the Mobile Meeting of the Southern Commercial Congress," *Alabama Review*, July, 1953.

Human rights, national integrity, and opportunity as against material interests—that, ladies and gentlemen, is the issue which we now have to face. I want to take this occasion to say that the United States will never again seek one additional foot of territory by conquest. She will devote herself to showing that she knows how to make honorable and fruitful use of the territory she has, and she must regard it as one of the duties of friendship to see that from no quarter are material interests made superior to human liberty and national opportunity.

Conceiving of the diplomatic questions of the day as "shot through with the principles of life," he concluded with a burst of prophecy:

I am fain to believe that in spite of all the things that we wish to correct, the nineteenth century that now lies behind us has brought us a long stage toward the time when, slowly ascending the tedious climb that leads to the final uplands, we shall get our ultimate view of the duties of mankind. We have breasted a considerable part of that climb and shall presently—it may be in a generation or two—come out upon these great heights where there shines unobstructed the light of the justice of God.[5]

In glorifying the concepts of righteousness that had taken shape on campuses and in churches of the United States, Wilson met resistance from men who worshiped other gods in other ways. He encountered Philistines both at home and abroad. At Berlin his gospel was dismissed as "colossal arrogance." Having predicted that the modern age was to be ruled by morality, Wilson was inevitably faced by the question: "Whose morality?" The concern that he showed for good government in other nations of the hemisphere was pastoral; but if implemented by men of less exalted spirit, it could easily become imperialistic.

This possibility was raised in 1913 by events in other Latin-American countries than Mexico. Wilson was being embarrassed by fellow citizens who were promoting their own fortunes in ways that often brought economic benefits to the natives but at the same time curtailed their political liberty. The President had a private report from a consul in Honduras, for instance, that told of the exertion of political pressure

[5] Speaking at Mobile immediately after his chief, Secretary Daniels commended the vision that had been revealed. Here, he said, was "another Monroe," blazing the way for American solidarity and equal sovereignty of all countries, great and small.

A few weeks after the speech at Mobile, Wilson said to Congress in his first annual message: "There is only one possible standard by which to determine controversies between the United States and other nations, and that is compounded of these two elements: Our own honor and our obligations to the peace of the world. A test so compounded ought easily be made to govern both the establishment of new treaty obligations and the interpretation of those already assumed." In the long run, he insisted, a nation was made formidable not by force of arms but rather by a sense of righteousness that appealed to all humanity, and an unselfish passion to extend to others the blessings of its own society.

in that country by a Yankee corporation that wanted economic concessions; and he acted to curb what he regarded as illicit use of material
power.[6]

Moreover, there were other awkward situations to the southward of
which Wilson had little firsthand knowledge and which he could not
investigate thoroughly. Yankees with interests in Nicaragua were urging
ratification of a treaty that would yield an option on a canal route and
would assure them of financial power in that country and give them a
right to intervene in its politics in order to enforce their standards of
civic order. Bryan himself refused to withdraw the Marines and expose
the country to chaos and, finding no escape from the inevitability of
dollar diplomacy, approved the financial arrangement of New York
bankers. "We cannot escape the responsibilities of our position," he
wrote to Wilson on June 12, 1914.[7]

Furthermore, in the Dominican Republic, where insurrection and
Yankee intervention had become chronic, a "deserving Democrat"
whom Bryan had appointed minister proved to be a partisan of a
financial interest and supported a native cacique against widespread
popular opposition; and a henchman of William F. McCombs showed
incompetence as a receiver of customs duties. Wilson tried to enforce
his ideals by sending commissioners to watch an election in December
of 1913. Moreover, he dispatched a financial expert, who gave Washington such a discouraging report that the President lamented to Bryan:
"What a perplexing question of duty Santo Domingo offers us"; and
a week later: "I am ashamed of myself that I have not been able to
think out a satisfactory solution."

Finally he appointed a commission and instructed it to attempt to
disband guerrilla forces and reconstruct political authority by super-
vising an election. Balloting was arranged and minorities were sternly

---

[6] The secret message from Honduras, sent by Consul General David J. D. Myers and
delivered to Wilson at Pass Christian by a young friend, Benjamin King, reported that an
American corporation had engineered a revolution that had overthrown a Honduran President
who had refused to grant certain concessions. Moreover, it was alleged that when the new
president also declined to do the company's bidding, the Yankees had decided to bring the
people to terms by refusing to buy their products. Few exports had moved for six months and as
a result conditions were very serious. When he learned of this, Wilson assured King that the
offending corporation would hear from him. Within a month after delivering his message to
the President, King had a letter from Myers stating that exports were flowing freely again
and that all was well. Letters, King to writer, Dec. 10, 1948, and Jan., 1955.

[7] "The proposed Nicaraguan treaty has my entire approval," Wilson wrote to Bryan on
June 19, 1913. By the end of 1915 Nicaragua was regarded in the State Department as a
"sphere of influence." On Aug. 5, 1914, the Bryan-Chamorro Treaty was signed, making
Nicaragua a protectorate of the United States; and on Feb. 18, 1916, the United States Senate,
fearful of German designs on Central America, approved it.

warned that they must abide by the outcome. Subsequently, however, it became necessary to send another special investigator [8] and to reappoint Taft's minister to supplant Bryan's appointee. Eventually, when fighting began in 1916, the Administration had to conclude that the only way to ensure peace was by exerting military control.

Moreover, when a revolution broke out in Haiti, early in 1914, American bankers proposed a plan for seizing the customhouses in that land, constructing a naval base, and taking as much responsibility for the government as seemed practical—a proposal not unacceptable to Bryan, who was alarmed by reports of German intrigues against the new Haitian regime. Though Wilson confessed to a "sneaking sympathy" for Haitian officials who resigned in protest, he talked with his Cabinet about applying commission rule, feeling it to be "necessary for Haiti's salvation." A year later a bloody revolt made it necessary to send bluejackets, and Haiti became a protectorate.

Thus in several instances Wilson's administration was pressed by interested individuals and by civic disorders to take political responsibility in regions to the south. It became embarrassing for the prophet to stand as the champion of liberty. This altruist who once had asserted that "free men need no trustees" was now in danger of incurring the onus of trusteeship. But in the cause of constitutional government he was as ready to bear the reproaches of jingoistic politicians in Latin America as he was to prevent ruthless exploitation of their peoples by foreign interests. As long as his conscience told him that he was acting unselfishly he could approve the use of force in Latin America.

However, the loftiness of his principles was poor consolation to proud Latins who resented Yankee meddling and the protectorates that resulted. The conclusion of the Bryan-Chamorro Treaty, for example, angered Nicaragua's neighbors, and they accused the United States of "flagrant" violation of international law and arraigned Nicaragua before the Central American Court of Justice.

To overcome the distrust and resentment of Latin Americans, an assertion of positive policy for the hemisphere was needed in the year 1914. Moreover, a bold move toward international reconciliation would contrast favorably with the ungloving of mailed fists in Europe. An idealistic project to preserve peace in the Americas was suggested to the President from several sources; and in the summer the possibilities of

---

[8] When this investigator, James D. Phelan, gave publicity to the shortcomings of the appointees sponsored by Bryan and Tumulty, Wilson was mortified and was disappointed in his secretary. Blum, *Tumulty*, pp. 113–15.

concerted action had been impressed upon him when the ABC powers had rescued him from his impasse with Huerta by proposing mediation.

Wilson responded with enthusiasm, therefore, when Colonel House urged upon him, on December 6, a Pan-American pact that would serve as a model for the European nations when they finished the war in which they were then deadlocked. Sensing a feeling among Latin Americans that the Monroe Doctrine was a one-sided understanding that the United States had imposed by *force majeur,* the Colonel envisaged an arrangement of mutual responsibility and mutual benefit. He hoped that, instead of merely resigning themselves to what they regarded as an offensive protectorate under the United States, the Latin peoples might come to give enthusiastic allegiance to a partnership and a pooling of interests. This ideal had been in the air since the time of Bolívar.

The wording of the pact that House envisaged was of little concern to the Colonel, provided that it was undertaken in a sincere spirit. Realizing that the President's creative impulse could be gratified by verbal expression, he asked his friend to draft a statement of their purposes. Thus encouraged, Wilson took a pencil and wrote words that were to have epochal significance in the history of the world:

1st. Mutual guarantees of political independence under republican form of government and mutual guarantees of territorial integrity.

2nd. Mutual agreement that the Government of each of the contracting parties acquire complete control within its jurisdiction of the manufacture and sale of munitions of war.

The President asked whether House had anything else in mind, and the Colonel replied that the two clauses seemed sufficient, taken in conjunction with the Bryan treaties of arbitration. Typing what he had written, Wilson gave the slip of paper to House to show to the ambassadors of Argentina, Brazil, and Chile, through whom it was planned to open negotiations. The President told House that in talking with the envoys he could be most emphatic in stating that the United States would not tolerate aggression upon other republics.

The Colonel began immediately to ingratiate himself with the ambassadors, and he returned to the President within a week bearing pledges of support from the emissaries of Argentina and Brazil. Wilson congratulated him, but wondered whether they might not be moving too fast for the Committee on Foreign Relations to follow. They decided to take up the matter with the senators immediately after Christmas, and the Colonel advised his friend to avoid making any appointments that might antagonize legislators whose support for the pact might be needed.

At the end of the year House still had no response from Chile, whose diplomats were embarrassed by a boundary dispute pending with Peru. Wilson continued to discuss the project with House; and he ascertained in a talk with Chairman Stone that the Committee on Foreign Relations would interpose no obstacles. He was anxious that news of the proposed pact should not leak out through unfriendly politicians, and accepted the suggestion of Argentina's envoy that terms should be agreed on in secret by the four initiating powers before the smaller republics were consulted.

Finally a reply came from Chile that, though ambiguous, was "favorable in principle." Reporting this to Wilson, House wrote on January 21: "Everything now seems in shape for you to go ahead. I believe the country will receive this policy with enthusiasm and it will make your Administration notable, even had you done but little else . . ."

A few days later House sailed for Europe, and in his absence neither Wilson nor Bryan took initiative to overcome Chile's aloofness. However, after the Colonel's return in June of 1915 the President talked more than once with him about reviving their plan for a Pan-American pact. The President typed out a new draft that set down four propositions;[9] and in an address to the Pan-American Scientific Congress on January 6, 1916, Wilson publicly announced the gist of his proposals. The nations of America had been uncertain, he confessed, as to what the United States would do with her power. "That doubt must be removed," he declared. "And latterly there has been a very frank interchange of views between the authorities in Washington and those who represented the other States of this hemisphere, an interchange . . . charming and hopeful." Detailing his four proposals, he then went on to invoke divine blessing on them:

They are going to lead the way to something that America has prayed for for many a generation. For they are based, in the first place, so far as the stronger states are concerned, upon the handsome principle of self-restraint

[9] Retaining as its first article the guarantee of "territorial integrity" and "political independence," the new proposal would commit the contracting parties (2) to try to reach amicable settlement of pending boundary disputes, either by direct negotiation or by arbitration; (3) to submit all unsettled questions to investigation by a permanent commission for one year, and then, if still undecided, to arbitration, "provided the question in dispute does not affect the honor, independence, or vital interests of the nations concerned or the interests of third parties"; and (4) to prevent forcible intervention and to embargo the shipment of arms in case of insurrections. For the text of the four articles, see *House Papers*, I, 233–34. Limitation of the private manufacture of arms, which had been included in Wilson's first draft, was now considered impractical because of the need that the United States government felt for a reliable supply of arms in case of involvement in the European war.

and respect for the rights of everybody. They are based upon the principles of absolute political equality among the States, equality of right, not equality of indulgence. They are based, in short, upon the solid eternal foundations of justice and humanity. No man can turn away from these things without turning away from the hope of the world . . .

Chile, however, remained unconvinced of the disinterestedness of the United States despite efforts by Colonel House at London to convert the Chilean ambassador there and to invoke the sanction of British opinion. Nevertheless, the President's enthusiasm for the project grew as he apotheosized it, and he was willing even to proceed independently of Chile; but without that nation's cooperation Argentina and Brazil were reluctant to go ahead. The atmosphere was clouded by the dispatch of a punitive expedition from the United States into Mexico, and the prospect of an American pact for peace faded. In the excitement of the 1916 election it was forgotten. When the United States found itself involved in war in 1917, the ideal that Wilson had failed to make effective in the Western Hemisphere was buried, only to be disinterred in 1918 and applied to the whole world.[10]

The proposal of a peace pact for the Americas aggravated the perplexity into which Latin-American diplomats were thrown by apparent contradictions between the protestations and the deeds of the "Colossus of the North." Intervention by force at Veracruz and in Nicaragua, Haiti, and the Dominican Republic, even though not without benefit to some of the inhabitants, comported little with Wilson's policy of watchful waiting and mediation and his concept of a Pan-American pact against aggression to be drawn up among equals. Latin Americans were at a loss to interpret the policy of a president who talked of liberty and constitutional processes while his fellow citizens wielded economic and military power.[11]

[10] In the spring of 1916, Wilson and House discussed the Pan-American pact several times and assigned to Ambassador Fletcher (who had served in Chile and was appointed to Mexico) the task of getting Chile's cooperation. When Wilson learned that Chile was demanding recognition of certain boundary claims as the price of consent, he refused to sanction any concession at the expense of weaker nations. Chile, for her part, suspected that the United States was interested chiefly in securing a share of Chilean minerals and in circumventing Japanese infiltration. It was House's hope that Britain might become a party to the envisioned pact in behalf of her American possessions, and the Colonel undertook to effect a change of phraseology that would make it possible for a monarchy to join an association of American "Republics." House Diary, May 13, 1916, and other entries. But British opinion, overruling Grey's desire to cooperate, feared to offend Japan by reassuring Chile, encouraging Canadian participation, or joining the pact in behalf of British Guiana and Honduras. *House Papers,* I, 222–31.

[11] The duality was nothing new in the history of the foreign relations of the United States. Wilson himself had perceived it in his professorial years. In 1901, writing on "Democracy and Efficiency," he had alluded to a "double temper" of the American people that had manifested

Realizing that the enterprising spirit of his people was natural, ineradicable, and precious if directed into virtuous channels, Wilson persisted in trying to guide it toward the accumulation of moral rather than material capital. He dared to undertake what only a great leader of men can achieve—to give to eternal political ideals a luster that would make them outshine, in the eyes of his people, the glitter of canals, roads, armaments, and financial profits.

The prophet's determination to make his nation stand before the world as the champion of international honor and justice led him, in the year 1914, to act decisively on two issues that grew out of the opening of the Panama Canal. These were questions that the President saw in black and white and he was willing to battle with advocates of dollar diplomacy to get a moral settlement.

In 1904, Wilson had questioned the justice of the coup by which Theodore Roosevelt had wrested the Panama Canal Zone from Colombia on terms unsatisfactory to that nation. To a student he had said: "Probably you have been taught that international law has no penal code. If it had, this would be described as petty larceny." [12] When the Colombian minister opened this old sore, the President was sympathetic. Declining to arbitrate the matter, the Administration undertook direct negotiations and showed a sincere desire to work out reasonable terms. Finally, in the spring of 1914, an agreement was reached by the diplomats. It provided that Colombia would have free use of the canal and an indemnity of $25,000,000—more than Wilson had offered at first and half of what Colombia had demanded. Further, the United States was to express "sincere regret that anything should have occurred to interrupt or to mar the relations of cordial friendship that had so long subsisted between the two nations."

When the compromise was submitted to the Senate on June 16, 1914, it drew the fire of Theodore Roosevelt, who looked upon it as a condemnation of his own work. He publicly damned the indemnity as "belated blackmail" and asserted that the Wilson administration had forfeited all right to the respect of the people of the United States.

The President, noting that the proposed agreement with Colombia was acclaimed more warmly by Latin Americans than by the people of the United States, explained publicly that ratification of the pact

---

itself in the days of Thomas Jefferson. "We have become confirmed," he had written, ". . . in the habit of acting under an odd mixture of selfish and altruistic motives." In 1911 he said: "We have a great ardour for gain, but we have a deep passion for the rights of man."

[12] Letter, Hugh MacNair Kahler to the writer, Nov. 10, 1955.

would give prestige to his country throughout Spanish America. "This nation can afford to be just," he declared; "even more, it can afford to be generous in the settling of disputes, especially when by its generosity it can increase the friendliness of the many millions in Central and South America with whom our relations become daily more intimate." But Wilson did not get the support in the Congress that he had hoped to enlist; and the Republican following of Roosevelt blocked ratification by the Senate.[13] However, all through his presidency his sponsorship of a compromise settlement of Colombia's claims commanded goodwill from the peoples to the south.

The other Panama Canal issue that challenged Wilson's sense of honor was that of tolls. In the Panama Act of August, 1912, the coast-to-coast ships of the United States had been exempted from canal charges. However, the British Foreign Office argued, quite correctly, that this measure violated the Hay-Pauncefote Treaty, which had been concluded between Britain and the United States in 1901. London proposed that the matter be submitted to arbitration, and just after the inauguration Ambassador Bryce pressed Bryan for immediate action.

President Taft and Secretary of State Knox had been willing to have the tolls issue studied, perhaps even arbitrated, by a commission. Furthermore, Wilson heard arguments for repeal from Elihu Root and from Joseph H. Choate, who had had a part in negotiating the Hay-Pauncefote Treaty. Before he entered the Presidency, Wilson had made up his mind that canal tolls should be paid by American ships as well as by those of other countries. He did not mention his decision in his inaugural address and did not reveal it to British statesmen. On April 15, 1913, however, he told his Cabinet that he was inclined to favor rescinding the exemption provision immediately. The nation's treaty of arbitration with Britain was to expire in June, he said, and it was doubtful that London would be willing to renew it until there was an adjustment of the tolls question.[14]

[13] When Wilson pressed the matter again in 1917, as a security measure in time of war, he was rebuffed. His statesmanlike long-range view was not accepted until the month after he left the White House, when Colombia was granted the indemnity but not the word of regret.

[14] To hasten action on renewal of the Root arbitration treaty of 1908, which Wilson thought "of the most vital importance" (W.W. to Bryan, June 13, 1913), Wilson talked personally with senators who feared that the pact might be an instrument for forcing the United States to yield on the matter of canal tolls. On July 3, 1913, Page and House explained to Grey why there was delay in repealing the objectionable tolls law. As a result the British statesman, perceiving that any semblance of pressure on his part would make it more difficult for Wilson to persuade the Congress to act, attempted to soothe the indignation of his own people. His patience was rewarded when, in November of 1913, the President explained to Sir William Tyrrell that he proposed to settle the controversy in conformity with the British view, which he considered the right one.

However, there was opposition from Anglophobes in the Senate, and Wilson wished to avoid unnecessary tiffs with party men while the tariff and currency bills were before them. Therefore, it was not until the very end of 1913, when the Federal Reserve Act had been signed and the new session of Congress began, that the tolls problem was formally introduced by Chairman Adamson of the House's Committee on Interstate and Foreign Commerce, with whom Wilson had discussed suspending the tolls exemption for a two-year period. Urged by Page to act before the British Parliament convened, the President decided to invite the Senate Committee on Foreign Relations to the White House. On January 26, in a three-hour conference that reviewed critical foreign issues, Wilson said that free use of the canal by American coastwise vessels was clearly a violation of the Hay-Pauncefote Treaty and should be stopped either by repealing the exemption clause of the Panama Act or by suspending its operation. A few days later Wilson wrote a letter for publication in which he denounced the tolls exemption not only as a breach of treaty but as an unfair benefit to a monopoly.

Finally, on March 5, 1914, he stated his position formally in a five-minute speech before the Congress. He did this without consulting his Cabinet, with whom the tolls issue had not been discussed for almost a year, and he based his case on world opinion rather than upon legalistic interpretations. He said: "I ask this of you in support of the foreign policy of the administration. I shall not know how to deal with other matters of even greater delicacy and nearer consequence if you do not grant it to me in ungrudging measure." [15]

The position that Wilson took warmed the hearts of Britain's noblest statesmen. Page was ecstatic, and in his ebullience he followed too closely the parting advice that the President had given him—"go, and be yourself." Making a public speech that reflected the remarks Wilson had made at Mobile, the ambassador said that Americans would "prefer" that European powers acquire no more territory on their continent.

Unluckily, Page's generous words were misinterpreted by the Anglophobe press in the United States to mean that the United States would not forbid European aggression in the Western Hemisphere. Malevolent fury stirred in Irish-Americans and German-Americans. Learning of

---

[15] On March 26, 1914, Wilson interpreted this cryptic sentence to newsmen as a reference to the reputation for good faith that would be needed in entering into new treaties. Giving credence to this motive as a partial explanation, Notter comments: "There would be no justification, however, for concluding that Wilson had not in mind also at this time the justice—and possibly the necessity—of giving support to the British argument against the toll clause in exchange for their support of his Mexican policy." Notter, *op. cit.,* pp. 286–87. When this interpretation was made by Republicans, Wilson called it a prevarication.

this, the ambassador quickly apologized to Wilson and offered to resign if he could thus gain a single vote for the cause in Congress; but the President, acknowledging that his friend had erred in touching even lightly upon a subject so explosive, loyally assured Page of his confidence and admiration. Contemptuous of those who were making trouble, Wilson wrote to his conscience-stricken ambassador: "We shall try to cool the excited persons on this side of the water, and I think nothing further will come of it." [16]

Page's indiscreet speech forced Wilson to fight all the harder to counteract the jingoism of hyphenated Americans and certain legislators who depended on their votes. On March 26, in a vigorous news interview, full of hard sense and homely anecdote, the President denied that the British government had been "exercising pressure" upon him; and to Democrats who thought themselves bound by the party platform he pointed out that actually there was in it two contradictory planks: one favoring free use of the canal; and another denouncing subsidies. Free tolls were in his view a subsidy. He welcomed support from Republican senators—the intellectual vigor of Root and the quiet voice of McCumber—and he took pains to acknowledge Lodge's "generous comprehension," first by letter and later by a telephone call. [17]

Wilson's heart was now thoroughly committed to battle and he put his weight behind a bill providing for outright repeal. He told Tumulty, who warned him of the reaction of Irish voters, that if Congress failed to support his position he would resign from office and go to the people and ask whether the United States was to stand before the world as a nation that violated its contracts as a matter of convenience and expedi-

---

[16] W.W. to Page, April 2, 1914. Page was writing to House that his expenses at London exceeded his means and that unless help was provided he must resign before the end of 1914. Page to House, undated, and *ibid.*, Jan. 30, 1914, House Collection. By summer the ambassador's distress became so acute that Wilson wrote his friend Cleveland Dodge that Page, who had "furnished him more light on difficult matters" than all other informants and advisers put together, needed an annual grant of $25,000 from a source that would not put him under obligations. Dodge agreed to provide the whole sum himself and to tell no one but his wife, and he thanked his friend for this "new mark of . . . confidence."

"Friendship such as yours," Wilson responded, "coming by fresh proof to me here in the midst of business at every turn of which it is necessary, in common caution, to scrutinize motives and reckon with what may be covertly involved, is like God's pure air to a man stifled and breathing hard to keep his lungs going." W.W. to Dodge, July 12, and 19, 1914; Dodge to W.W., July 13, 1914.

[17] Garraty, *Henry Cabot Lodge*, pp. 299–300. *Page Letters*, I, 257. As the battle of tolls repeal reached its height, Wilson was deprived of the services of Counselor John Bassett Moore of the State Department who, tired of working with Bryan appointees whom he thought incompetent (House Diary, Jan. 26, 1914), resigned on Mar. 4, 1914. He was succeeded on March 27 by Robert Lansing, a New York lawyer who was recommended by Elihu Root. House's Diary (Nov. 7, 1914) records that Wilson spoke of Lansing as more satisfactory than Moore.

ency. Bryan, who had been unconvinced until he felt the force of the President's appeal to righteousness, now supported him with an editorial in the *Commoner*; Burleson sat at the telephone and kept the wire to the Capitol hot with exhortations to legislators who looked to him for patronage; and Tumulty worked upon younger congressmen who were most responsive to the President's leadership. Despite the fiery opposition of Champ Clark and Underwood and the Irish-Americans, the House voted for repeal by a margin of 247 to 162. The Senate finally ended several weeks of oratorical fireworks by appoving the measure 50 to 35; and Wilson signed it on June 15, 1914.

With the tolls issue settled and Huerta shorn of power, Wilson was rid of two immediate problems that had been disturbing the relations of the United States with European powers. Sir Edward Grey, his patience vindicated, proclaimed in Parliament that Wilson's motive all along had been not an impulse to drive a bargain with Britain but rather a conviction that governments must never flinch from interpreting treaty rights in a strictly fair spirit. On March 11, London had approved the extension of the Anglo-American arbitration treaty of 1908; and on September 15 the two nations signed a Bryan pact.

The repeal of tolls exemption, however, was not so popular a triumph in the United States as those of the New Freedom had been. In bringing about repeal, the President had repudiated a plank in the party platform and had had to explain that a pre-election promise regarding foreign affairs is no more than "half a promise," and subject to foreign elements beyond control.

Wilson himself felt that the risk he had run in incurring the hostility of equivocating politicians was justified by the majesty of moral triumph. "If everything else in connection with this administration is forgotten," he said one day *en famille,* "the action in regard to Panama will be remembered because it is a long step forward in putting the relationships of nations and the dealings of one nation with another on a par with the dealings of honorable men, one with another."

By the summer of 1914, by force of necessity and the President's sense of personal accountability, foreign relations had replaced domestic reforms as the center of the President's interest. Wilson had come through the ordeal of foreign crises with his fundamental political faith unshaken. Holding his direction steadfastly toward morality and moderation, he had clung to his belief that the popular opinion of his hemisphere would respond to the ideals that he honored and that he had set forth publicly. Though he knew now, better than ever before, the strength of native pride and suspicion, he still imagined that among Latin-American peoples there existed a latent sense of political responsibility akin to that of his own people. Through conferences that would appeal to their common humanity, he saw hope of reaching solutions of hemispheric problems that would have effective sanction.

Woodrow Wilson's native faith had vaulted to embrace a hemisphere as nimbly as it had risen to take in a university, a state, and then a nation. Would its evangelistic power, feeding upon communion with congregations of increasing size, be strong enough to sanctify a new order in an entire world that, in the summer of 1914, seemed to be falling rapidly into political bankruptcy?

CHAPTER XXIII

In the Valley of the Shadow

As THE PROPHET reached out to embrace the peoples of the Western Hemisphere and make them a family of nations, the breaking up of his own idyllic household was piercing his heart.

Woodrow Wilson always had enjoyed sanctuary in a sympathetic home. His affection for his dear ones was childlike, his concern for their welfare almost motherly. He expected obedience from them, but exacted it courteously: one day when a daughter wished to go riding in the park with friends whom he thought undesirable, he asked, "M'dear, can't you find a better way to occupy your time?" [1] Often the Wilsons planned their engagements so that the clan could be together, alone, on birthdays and other special occasions; and once the President canceled a weekend trip on the *Mayflower* in order to give moral support to daughter Margaret, who would otherwise have to stay alone at the White House and prepare for a speaking engagement about which she was nervous. His second daughter, Jessie, had been married less than five months when his secretary of the Treasury came to him to ask the hand of his youngest, his spirited, lovable Nellie; and after this conversation McAdoo wrote confidentially to House: "Miss Eleanor and I are engaged! 'The Governor' has consented and I am supremely happy." [2]

It was difficult for Woodrow Wilson to accept the departure of his little playmate—the girl for whom he had toiled on an American History so that she might have a pony. "I shall be poor without her," he wrote to Mary Hulbert, "she and I have been such ideal chums! It's hard, very hard, not to be selfish and rebel,—or repine! But her happiness is of much more importance than mine,—I mean to me." At the wedding, as he walked down the corridor to the Blue Room, prepared to give her away, he was relieved by a chance to chuckle to himself when

---

[1] Mrs. Katharine Woodrow Kirkland to the writer.

[2] McAdoo to House, Mar. 3, 1914, House Collection. According to Edith Galt Wilson, Woodrow Wilson was opposed to the betrothal because of the difference in ages. E. B. Wilson to R. S. Baker, Jan. 4, 1926. This marriage posed problems of decorum. Foreseeing that the President might be embarrassed by the presence of a relative in his Cabinet, McAdoo offered to resign; but Wilson assured him that, since he had been appointed solely on grounds of merit, he must not think of leaving. The President was careful to preserve impartiality in Cabinet meetings and fairness in all other relations. House Diary, April 15, 28, 29, 1914.

the train of her wedding dress overturned and she whispered desperately to tell an attendant to right it; but when the wedding party went out to the porch to see the bride off, the President had no spirit for the occasion. He remained inside; and Colonel House, who stayed with him, jotted in his diary that night: "I think he loves her better than any member of his household."

At the same time Wilson was worried about the health of one whom he had loved longer than Nellie; and furthermore, one on whom he depended more implicitly than on any other living soul. It was the wisdom of Ellen Wilson that had made the White House the home that he needed. She cultivated family piety of the Roman sort, a devotion that was to her something in the blood that drew relatives together whether they found each other queer or not.

The responsibilities of her role sometimes had seemed more than she could bear. On Inauguration Day her courage had failed for a moment, and rebelling against the noise and confusion of notoriety, she had covered her face with her hands and wept. She had played her part pluckily, however. Delegating responsibility wisely, she made even the large functions beautiful and unpretentious.

Many times she visited back alleys in which Negroes lived in squalor, often taking congressmen with her. She talked to the people, helping them with food and money, and gently insisted that legislative action be taken. Finding no rest rooms in public buildings, she had them installed for the workers. Day after day she came home worn and pale, changed her dress, and went to the Red Room to receive guests with her sweet, calm smile. Energetic philanthropists perceived her sensitivity and exploited it for their favorite causes with tales of woe. "I wonder how anyone who reaches middle age can bear it," she said one day to a cousin, "if she cannot feel, on looking back, that whatever mistakes she may have made she has on the whole lived for others and not for herself."

Amidst all her duties, domestic and civic, she never failed her husband. Though never interfering in an embarrassing way, she proved herself one of his soundest advisers on matters of public policy; and because her devotion was unquestionable, her motives pure, and her wisdom proven, he listened to her counsel as to that of no man. Questions that perplexed him sorely, like relations with Mexico, she studied with him. She tempered his moral fervor with sweet reason and fostered his understanding with House, Tumulty, and the Cabinet. She even protected his ears from petty gossip that might arouse prejudice against men who were valuable to him.

Early in 1914, as the weakness of disease stole over her, Ellen Wilson had less heart than ever for political strife, and she joined Tumulty in an effort to persuade the President not to risk a split in the party by insisting on repeal of the Panama tolls exemption. But she still encouraged her husband in carrying on the badinage with other ladies from which he derived refreshment. Though for his sake she invited Mary Hulbert to visit the White House, she did not enjoy the artful nonsense of this guest; and she delegated to Helen Bones—who thought her Cousin Woodrow something of a goose to be so easily titillated—the duty of protecting the President from malicious gossip by chaperoning his rides with his playmate.[3]

On the first day of March Ellen Wilson fell on the floor of her bedroom, aggravating a kidney ailment that had bothered her for a long time. The shock and soreness kept her in bed for more than two weeks. By sheer will she gathered her forces, and at Eleanor's wedding on May 7 she seemed her old self; but soon nervous indigestion was plaguing her constantly and it seemed impossible to get enough food or rest. She insisted that she must diet but the President spent hours at her bedside, coaxing: "Please do eat just a little of this. You will soon get well, darling, if you'll try hard to eat something. Now please take this bite, dear."

Lying on her sofa, very white, she refused to let callers talk about her condition. She spoke with tender pride of her husband, who was still her "noticeable man," in need of her ministration, and only incidentally President of the United States. One day she wrote indignant notes, which were never sent, to senators who were attacking his policies. The White House gardens were a joy to her, particularly one that she had planned herself. On fair afternoons she sat among her flowers and watched them bloom while her strength faded. "It will be so lovely, Charley," she said one day to the gardener who was carrying out her plans, "but I'll never live to see it finished."[4]

Late in May Dr. Grayson was alarmed by her symptoms and called specialists. The case was one of Bright's disease and it was hopeless. There were rallies, but they were temporary. Gradually her husband came to realize the truth, though his physician, who had learned that there were indications of a hardening of the President's arteries, strove to protect him from the ravages of worry.

Snatching moments from his engagements to take tea with the family

[3] Several letters, Helen W. Bones to the writer; also R. W. Woolley's account of conversations with Stockton Axson; Elizabeth Jaffray's book, *Secrets of the White House*, p. 35, and her articles in *Cosmopolitan*, January and February, 1927.

[4] Charles Hemlock and Margaret Norris, "Flowers for First Ladies," the *Saturday Evening Post*, Nov. 28, 1931. And Helen Bones to Margaret Callaway Axson, June 25, 1914, letter in possession of the latter.

circle, Wilson kept his eyes upon his Ellen's face, and before leaving the room he would hold her close for a moment. Relatives who had never heard an irate word pass between them were impressed more than ever by the blend of love and respect in his voice when he spoke her name; and they felt that no man and wife could be more truly one. His walk was no longer buoyant, and deep lines furrowed his gaunt face. Anxiety hung heavy upon him, and he said that he felt like a man suffering from malaria.

As the summer's heat mounted, Ellen Wilson would not seek coolness and quiet at Harlakenden, for separation from her Woodrow appalled her more than hot weather. She urged him to escape to the golf course, but he would not. Instead he sat very quiet outside her room, trying to put his mind on public business, but now and then giving up and tiptoeing over to lean against her door to listen. Sometimes he would get up in the night to comfort her and would sit by her bed and do his work until early morning.

Toward the end of the month Dr. Grayson moved into a room next to hers, where he could be on duty day and night. When he told Wilson that his daughters should be close at hand, the President at last accepted the truth. In the wilting heat the White House seemed drained of life. "Cousin" Lucy Smith, whom Ellen Wilson had asked to come with her sister Mary to cheer Woodrow, was stricken with appendicitis and rushed to a hospital. Little Helen Bones, the President's playfellow since Eleanor had left the household, was ill, delirious with fever. Wilson was unresponsive to efforts of others to console him. "I carry lead at my heart all the time," he wrote to Mary Hulbert on August 2. "I am held in Washington by the most serious duties any President has had to perform since Lincoln."

During the months of Ellen Wilson's decline, the confidential messages that dropped upon the President's desk had revealed a menace of war abroad. For a year Page's letters had told of Europe's diplomatic dilemma. "There's no future in Europe's vision—no long look ahead . . . ." the ambassador reported. "The Great Powers are—mere threats to one another, content to check, one the other! There can come no help to the progress of the world from this sort of action: no step forward." Page had dared to dream that the President himself might go abroad and stand beside the King of England and let the world take a good look at them. "Nothing else would give such a friendly turn to the whole world as the President's coming here," Page had written to House on August 25, 1913. "The old Earth would sit up and rub its eyes and take notice to whom it belongs. This visit might prevent an

English-German war and an American-Japanese war, by this mere show of friendliness. It would be one of the greatest occasions of our time. Even at my little speeches, they 'whoop it up'! What would they do over the President's!"

Wilson had been tempted by the appeal and appreciated the reasons for it; but he had felt that he must decline. "The case against the President's leaving the country," he wrote, "particularly now that he is expected to exercise a constant leadership in all parts of the business of the government, is very strong and I am afraid overwhelming. It might be the beginning of a practice of visiting foreign countries which would lead Presidents rather far afield." [5]

Early in 1914, Wilson's popularity in England had risen, and the ambassador reported that his stock was "at a high premium." Thinking it more than ever desirable that the President's moral influence be exerted to keep peace in Europe, House developed a grand plan. Since the main obstacles to international reconciliation seemed to lie in Berlin, the persuasive Colonel proposed to beard the Junkers in their den and make them see the folly of their opposition to arbitration and disarmament. The Colonel perceived that a reconciliation of the naval interests of Britain and Germany might impair the power of the United States on the high seas; but he was willing to run this risk in the interest of peace, for he felt that the outbreak of a European war would end the long period of isolation in which the extraordinary prosperity of the United States had been incubated. Moreover, taking up a constructive suggestion that Page had made and that would put the principles of Wilson's Mobile speech in play, House aspired to commit the rulers of England and Germany to an understanding on other matters that threatened the world's peace.[6]

On December 12, 1913, the Colonel had found Wilson ready to

[5] *Page Letters,* I, 271, 275–76. The President's decision may well have been based, at least in part, on a fear of seeming to commit the United States to alliance with Britain.

[6] He was especially eager to set up international machinery for developing backward lands in the interest of their inhabitants.

The Colonel discussed this far-reaching and ultimately fruitful proposal with Sir Edward Grey and others on June 24. They approved the plan in general, but said that it must be initiated by the President, because of the Monroe Doctrine.

After further discussions with British diplomats, House reported to Wilson on July 4: "It was the general consensus of opinion that a great deal of friction in the future would be obviated if some such understanding could be brought about in this direction, and that it would do as much as any one thing to insure international amity." *House Papers,* I, 266. Moreover, Sir Edward Grey was deeply interested in the idea and pledged his government's cooperation. Further discussions at London were planned, but the outbreak of war caused the shelving of the proposal. However, House and Wilson did not forget it. The Colonel discussed it in a talk with Wilson on Aug. 30, 1914; and the principles of the development of countries under a trusteeship blossomed forth in the mandatory system of the League of Nations. It seemed to the Colonel that had such a plan been in force, with the powers meeting at regular intervals, World War I probably would not have occurred.

facilitate disarmament by seeking legislation that would permit him to cut his nation's battleship budget if the Europeans should agree on a naval holiday. And so House set out to learn all that he could about German psychology and the character of the Kaiser. In May of 1914, with Page's encouragement and with an informal note of credence from Wilson, he went to Berlin. Before the end of the month he reported to the President that jingoism had "run stark mad," that unless someone acting for the American President could intervene effectively, there would be "an awful cataclysm." Soon afterward House wrote that he had been granted a private conversation with Wilhelm II, that he had let it be known that the President of the United States had courage as resolute and a will as inflexible as Bismarck himself, and that it was arranged that the Colonel was to keep the Kaiser informed after the Foreign Office at London was sounded.[7]

Wilson joyfully welcomed the reports of his enterprising diplomatic spokesman. "Your letter gives me a thrill of deep pleasure," he responded on June 16. "You have, I hope and believe, begun a great thing and I rejoice with all my heart. You are doing it, too, in just the right way with your characteristic tact and quietness and I wish you Godspeed in what follows. I could not have done the thing nearly so well." It was "a great source of strength and relief" to have an understanding friend to interpret his purposes to European statesmen.[8] In replying to House the President rarely commented on specific policies and procedures: he was content, as in his relations with others to whom he had given his whole heart, to bless any arrangement that satisfied their common will to serve. House's aggressive venture stirred the frontier spirit in Wilson, and he hoped that his friend was finding it exhilarating.

While the diplomats of Europe dallied and the Kaiser raced in his yacht at Kiel, a fateful spark was struck in the Balkans. On June 28 the heir apparent to the throne of Austria-Hungary was murdered at Sarajevo, and the German government, believing that Russia would not intervene forcibly, sanctioned any punitive measures against Serbia that Vienna might decide upon. When House wrote to the Kaiser on July 7 to report that the British government desired to reach an understanding

---

[7] *House Papers*, I, 249; and House to Wilson, June 3 and 11, 1914. Wilhelm II concurred in the view that an agent of the American President might act more effectively to avert war than a European, and he seemed pleased that House was undertaking the task; but, being obsessed by distrust of Japan and Russia, he demanded a navy large enough for defense against the combined fleets of France and Russia. Moreover, he objected to treaties of arbitration for the reason that he conceived Germany's defense to rest upon a degree of preparedness for war that would bring a quick victory.

[8] W.W. to House, June 16 and 22, 1914, House Collection. The Colonel's ego was so flattered by the President's "thrill of deep pleasure" that he quoted part of the letter of June 16 to his son-in-law, Gordon Auchincloss.

that would lay the foundation of permanent peace and security,[9] it was too late to get a response. Wilhelm II had gone on a Scandinavian cruise, and the ignited fuse was burning rapidly toward the heap of fears and hates that had been piled up for a decade by powers that had been combining and arming for war.

At the end of July new problems piled suddenly upon the United States government. Ocean liners were held in ports and tens of thousands of travelers were clamoring for funds and for transatlantic passage. Domestic business, already shaken by prolonged strikes and by uncertainties aroused by the New Freedom, was further dislocated by dread of an armed conflict that, some thought, might put an end to modern civilization in Europe. When Austria-Hungary declared war on Serbia, on July 28, financial markets became panicky. On July 31 the New York Stock Exchange was closed. What the European governments had been preparing for they were now to have—war on a vaster scale than the world had ever experienced. Wilson was amazed that in the twentieth century mankind could be so stupid. Learning of Austria's declaration of war, he said to his family at luncheon: "Incredible—it's incredible."

Preoccupied as he had been by antimonopoly legislation and by Latin-American affairs, the President had given no deep thought to the European problems of which House had written informally. He had expressed fear [10] that the spark in the Balkans would set off a general explosion, but his envoys in Europe, save House, were writing that there was no great danger. He was as surprised by the outbreak of hostilities, and almost as grieved, as he had been by the Mexican resistance that had cost the lives of his boys at Veracruz. What was to happen? his daughters asked him. Would the whole world be involved?

He stared as if dazed, covered his eyes, and replied: "I can think of

[9] Actually, though Grey was sympathetic to House's ideas, British politicians feared that diplomatic talks with Germany might disturb the nation's defensive *entente* with France and Russia. Moreover, party feelings were strong in England, the Cabinet was preoccupied with a crisis in Ireland, and suffragettes were threatening to dynamite the Houses of Parliament.

[10] To Louis Brownlow on July 1, 1914. Brownlow lecture at University of Chicago, Mar. 2, 1956.

On July 3, Colonel House had written to inform Wilson that Sir Edward Grey wished him to convey the ideas of the British government to the Kaiser and to try to arrange a meeting at Kiel, "so there may be no go-between or misunderstanding." The Colonel's letter concluded: "So you see things are moving in the right direction as rapidly as we could hope." Though Sir Edward Grey sent word to House on July 20 that the Austro-Serbian crisis was giving him grave concern, the Colonel, sailing for Boston the next day, did not communicate Sir Edward's feelings to the President until July 31, after House had landed in the United States and war between Austria-Hungary and Serbia had begun; and even in his letter of that date the Colonel suggested that a general conflict might be averted as a result of the improvement in British-German relations that he fancied he had brought about. Wilson was without warning of immediate disaster from his trusted agent until he was informed by a House letter of Aug. 1 that Germany, realizing that her best chance of victory lay in striking fast and hard, might take precipitate action in what she conceived to be self-defense. See *House Papers*, I, 271–81.

nothing—nothing, when my dear one is suffering. Don't tell your mother anything about it." Ellen Wilson never knew of the blotting out of the vision of human concord that she had shared with her husband.

In the first week of August declarations of war were exchanged and German forces violated the Belgian border, striking quickly for victory, as House had warned they would. Ellen Wilson sank rapidly, and on the 6th Dr. E. P. Davis, one of "Tommie" Wilson's Princeton classmates, had to tell the family that the end was only hours away.

After luncheon the President went upstairs with his daughters. He sat on the edge of the bed, clasping his Ellen's hand, looking beseechingly at Dr. Grayson for a sign of encouragement. A murmur came from the serene face on the pillow as the physician bent over it: "Promise me that you will take good care of my husband." Then the breathing grew fainter. The daughters, kneeling, saw on their mother's face a smile that they thought divine. Downstairs the chimes of a clock struck softly, five times. The President asked: "Is it all over?" The doctor nodded, and Woodrow Wilson's head fell forward. "When you die, I shall die," he had once written to her.[11] Walking to a window and looking out, he cried: "Oh, my God, what am I to do?"

Mostly he kept his grief in his Scottish innerliness, not daring to give it any escape for fear that it would burst all controls. They heard him say, as he pulled himself together, "I must not give way." He sat in a chair for endless hours, day and night, in lonely vigil beside a sofa on which the lifeless figure lay, its shoulders draped by a white silk shawl that he himself had thrown over them. Fighting valiantly for self-mastery, he came in to the services in the East Room only when the guests had been seated. The family did not feel that their emotions could endure funeral music, and there was no sound but the rustling of palm leaves near the open windows, and the voice of the minister: "Let not your heart be troubled: Ye believe in God, believe also in me." Afterward the President sent for his pastor and, head bowed and shaking with grief, thanked him. Later in the day, driving to the station to take a train for Rome, Georgia, he went quietly through the less-frequented streets.

At the destination, while several cousins of Ellen Wilson placed the casket in the hearse, the President stood very erect and fixed his eyes upon it as if seeking to penetrate it. He remained there beside it, alone, until the time came to go to the service at Rome's Presbyterian church, where he first had been attracted by the radiance of Miss Ellie Lou.

[11] Letter of W.W. to E.A.W. read to the writer by Eleanor Wilson McAdoo.

After the pastor spoke briefly and two of her favorite hymns were sung, the mourners were driven in carriages to the Axson lot in the cemetery on Myrtle Hill.

Beneath a great oak overlooking the Etowah River, Woodrow Wilson stood over the grave. Tombs of Confederate soldiers were round about —reminders of the scourge that was threatening again, after a half century, to afflict the United States. A canopy protected the gathering from rain that was beginning to fall; but soon there was a rush of wind and the flowers were scattered. The President stood unmoved by anything but the emotional storm within. For several minutes after the casket had been lowered he remained beside the grave and his eyes glistened. He assured himself that the separation was, after all, only temporary, for their love was immortal. He told Colonel Brown—the cousin who had charge of the funeral arrangements—that he wished to have space made for his own burial by the side of his beloved, and it was arranged to broaden the terrace.[12]

To mark her grave he ordered a stone of rare Italian marble, on which a woman's profile was to be carved by Ellen Wilson's favorite sculptor. He insisted that the little monument should be simple and fitting, in harmony with the headstones of her relatives. To the inscription he gave as much care as he had bestowed on that for the grave of the other immortal soul to whom he acknowledged eternal gratitude —his father. Finally he chose lines of William Wordsworth:

> A traveller between life and death;
> The reason firm, the temperate will,
> Endurance, foresight, strength, and skill;
> A perfect woman, nobly planned,
> To warn, to comfort, and command
> And yet a spirit still, and bright
> With something of angelic light.

He went back to Washington more lonely than he had ever been. He must face not only his own anxious people, but a whole war-ridden world, alone. The only human being who knew him perfectly, the only one who could rest him, was gone. The personality that had given him

[12] Mrs. Hallie Alexander Rounseville and Wade Hoyt, who was a pallbearer, to the writer. The writer was told by Mrs. Rounseville, who was president of the Ellen Axson Wilson Memorial Circle of Rome ladies who undertook to beautify and care for the grave, that Mrs. Wilson's tomb was made waterproof so that the body could be moved in case the President was not buried at Rome. A clipping dated Aug. 12, 1914, from a newspaper that cannot be identified, reports that the grave was completely covered by concrete and steel. Clipping in possession of Margaret Callaway (Mrs. B. Palmer) Axson.

courage to enter public life was no longer present to sustain him. No gentle hand met his groping one. No longer, before falling asleep and after awakening, would he have a partner to whom he could safely confess everything and from whom he could get oracular advice.

Dr. Grayson and the ladies of his family looked out for his bodily and mental health. Daughter Margaret became head of the household and Helen Bones came out of her delirious fever to hear McAdoo say: "You must care for him now." This little cousin worked with devotion and understanding to alleviate the loss, seeking to rally the President with levity, mixing a mild toddy for him now and again, and occasionally teasing him to sip port after eating foods that the doctor prescribed. The Smiths stayed on at the White House, too, and within the little circle of adoring ladies who vied with each other to please the great man, Wilson bravely kept up his custom of good talk and readings of poetry. He indulged his relatives in many ways. He took some of them through the White House from top to bottom. Though he often had paced the main corridors alone, hands behind back, this was his first complete tour of his dwelling.

But among the friends and relatives there was no guardian angel for his soul, no one who could say "Oh, Woodrow, you don't mean that!" Sometimes he stole away to the Corcoran Art Gallery to look at pictures of which Ellen Wilson had been fond. He carried out her commitments to charities, insisting that a fund sponsored by her for the education of mountain youth should be administered in a nonsectarian spirit. When instances of injustice or misfortune to individuals came to the President's notice, in the months of mourning, he seemed to respond as she would have wished. Even in death his Ellen was an angel of charity and conciliation. Old friends who had been estranged were moved by her passing to write to him in genuine sympathy. And he replied warmly.[13]

Finally, on August 17, he summoned courage to reply to a letter of sympathy received from House: "My dear, dear Friend: . . . I have acknowledged many letters of condolence but I am writing today for the first time to those whose friendship is dearest to me because there is something deeper in that and it is harder to get one's self-possession in doing it. I do not know of any letter which touched me more deeply

[13] One of those who sent a letter of condolence was "Marse Henry" Watterson. Another was Jennie Hibben, who wrote from St. Moritz: "All the years of sad estrangement grow dim and we remember only the days when we were young and happy . . . Jack and Beth join me . . . Ever yours." To this Wilson replied on Sept. 18: "I sincerely and warmly thank you . . . In these days when the darkness has settled about me thoughts of those old days at Princeton 'when we were young and happy' flash in upon me with peculiar brightness, despite the sadness that inevitably follows them." Scloon Papers (Princeton University Library).

than yours did . . . May God show me the way! Affectionately yours."

In his bereavement Wilson grasped and relished every recollection that his memory could supply, as well as those offered by friends and relatives. Yet, shaken as he was, he was finding in himself, in the summer of 1914, a toughness that surprised him. When the heat in Washington reached 100 degrees in the shade, Grayson tried to make him board the *Mayflower* and cruise to Beverly to visit House. But he would not hear of it. Wilson still thought that the Presidency would kill him; but somehow the catastrophe did not come off. He went at his work grimly, hoping to find release from his grief there. Though he refused to grant nonessential interviews, he insisted on seeing full copies of the reports from his diplomats abroad. He found little light upon the causes and significance of the war in the dispatches that came daily from chancelleries beset by panicky American tourists; but he plodded through them and through the mass of messages and articles that piled up on his desk, in the hope of broadening his understanding of his responsibility.

During the first week of August, while his dear one lay prostrate, Woodrow Wilson had met the impact of world war as his own conscience dictated. His first impulse had been to minister to his own country. Controlling his own feelings superbly, he had left his wife's chamber on August 3 to address newsmen in another room of the White House. Warning them against rousing public hysteria, assuring them that the government was meeting the emergency in finance and trade, he said: "I want to have the pride of feeling that America, if nobody else, has her self-possession and stands ready with calmness of thought and steadiness of purpose to help the rest of the world. And we can do it and reap a great permanent glory out of doing it, provided we all cooperate to see that nobody loses his head."

Formal proclamations of neutrality were issued, but this conventional step did not satisfy the President's desire to lead his people in serving mankind. If his nation was to work effectively for peace, he foresaw, mere legality of action would not be enough. He must cultivate a national attitude that by its justness would win the respect of all belligerents. He was glad, therefore, to meet the wishes of Bryan, and at the same time carry out the will of the Senate, by sending an offer of mediation to the rulers of the belligerent powers. After a long session with his Cabinet on August 4—the day of Germany's violation of Belgium's "territorial integrity"—Wilson had gone to his wife's bedside and composed this message:

As official head of one of the powers signatory to The Hague Convention, I feel it to be my privilege and my duty under article three of that Convention to say to you in a spirit of most earnest friendship that I should welcome an opportunity to act in the interest of European peace, either now or at any other time that might be thought more suitable, as an occasion to serve you and all concerned in a way that would afford me lasting cause for gratitude and happiness.[14]

Unfortunately, the offer of mediation did no immediate good except to establish the intent of the United States, for each warring government replied with a justification of its position. The President's desk was bombarded by partisan views of war guilt and by pleas for American participation in the fighting. Wilson was sickened by the contentious frenzy of hyphenated Americans and of self-appointed dispensers of "justice." In his determination to preserve neutrality in thought and action he shied even from a suggestion made by House and Olney. These men thought that the press should be allowed to state, "on high authority," what the Colonel and Page had done to reconcile England and Germany; but the President sensed that such a revelation might place the United States government in the position of an accuser of Germany.

Wilson's scholarly training demanded that he keep his mind open to hard fact and wait as long as necessary to understand exactly how the war originated; and the very superficiality of his knowledge of the causes of conflict made it the easier for him to take a detached point of view. Reading an article by Professor Albert Bushnell Hart, whose criticism had helped him to produce his own best work in history, he was struck by the iniquity of the whole diplomatic web that had caught the statesmen of Europe in its meshes and held them from reaching a peaceful solution.[15] Between Germany and Russia he saw little choice. If the Central Allies won, German militarism would be supreme; if the Entente won, czarist tyranny would dominate the Continent. He had written appreciatively of Bismarck and had studied German law and

14 Wilson's offer was dispatched in spite of a cable sent by Page the day before, advising that it was the ambassador's "very definite opinion," and that of the British Foreign Office, that there was "not the slightest chance of any result if our good offices be offered at any continental capital." *F. R. Suppl., 1914*, p. 37.

15 Acknowledging Hart's article, Wilson wrote on Aug. 4 to Charles R. Crane, who sent it: "The more I read about the conflict across the seas, the more open it seems to me to utter condemnation."

More than two years later Wilson's mind was still open in regard to responsibility for the war. But on June 14, 1917, after the United States became a belligerent, he said: "The war was begun by the military masters of Germany, who proved to be also the masters of Austria-Hungary." For Wilson's subsequent views of war guilt, *see* Notter, *op. cit.*, pp. 316–17, footnotes.

politics; but as a devotee of the Virginia Bill of Rights he rejected the Hegelian concept that citizens find fufillment only as members of the state and that the ruler is responsible for the people but not to them. On the other hand, he regretted that the fortunes of Great Britain, most liberal of the European powers, should be allied with those of Russia, a most absolute monarchy.

Woodrow Wilson loved the British people, indeed was bound to them by blood and breeding. The war had been going on scarcely a month when Sir Cecil Spring Rice—Britain's ambassador and himself a writer of verse—drew tears from him by alluding to the sonnets written by Wordsworth at the time of the Napoleonic Wars. After the President remarked that he had these verses in his mind all the time, Spring Rice replied: "You and Grey are fed on the same food and I think you understand." Through the ambassador, Wilson sent his warmest greeting to Sir Edward. He said to Spring Rice, "Everything that I love most in the world is at stake," and he confessed a fear that he would be forced to take such measures of defense as would be "fatal to our form of Government and American ideals." He spoke of the long trial of the Civil War, and said with deep emotion that he was sure that Britain would show its powers of endurance for a high cause. Realizing that a dispute with Britain would be a calamity, he promised to do all that he could to maintain absolute neutrality.

Nevertheless, guarding his official conscience fiercely against his personal feelings for England's countryside, her poets and parliamentarians, Wilson held himself now to the ideal that he once ascribed to General Lee: "conscious self-subordination to principles which lay outside of his personal life." When war's first shock to public opinion was followed by an epidemic of apprehension and jingoism, he drew desperately on the resources that his wife had left within him. On the long trip back to Washington from her grave, as the train sped through country that had been bloodied in Wilson's youth by battles and their grisly aftermath, the President remained for an entire day alone on the observation platform. "I want to think," he explained to Dr. Grayson. He searched the depths of his soul for thoughts and feelings that would be shared by his people.

Unable longer to consult Ellen Wilson, he sought the comfort of baring his mind to her brother and her sister. "I must depend upon you very much more than I ever did before now," he wrote to Stockton Axson on September 14, 1914, begging him to make a long visit to the White House. He felt the need of a comrade with whom to share his thoughts, especially a man who could join him in communion with the immortal spirit that had departed. Sitting on the White House porch with his brother-in-law in the summer dusk, he said: "I cannot help thinking that perhaps she was taken so that she might be spared the spectacle of some awful calamity." He spoke with pleasure of a personal letter that Sir Edward Grey had found time to dispatch to him despite the crisis. This statesman, he said, had lost his wife but had an interest in birds and in fly-fishing—a deliverance he did not know. When he talked of "release" and return to private life, Axson reminded him of his great scholarly design—the *Philosophy of Politics* that he had envisioned in his academic years; but he had only this to say: "I thought of it once as a great book; I can put all I know now into a very small one." Later in the autumn, walking in the White House garden with the young sister-in-law whose idol he had always been, he said in the saddest tone that she had ever heard: "If I hadn't gone into politics, she would probably be alive now. The strain of it killed her."

Realizing that his own welfare lay in fixing his thoughts on his public duty—"I believe that this is good 'doctor' sense," he wrote House— Wilson thought long and deeply about the plight of mankind. One day, communing with Axson, he gave voice to ideas so startling that his brother-in-law recorded the conversation. "It is perfectly obvious," he said, "that this war will vitally change the relationship of nations. Four things will be essential to the re-establishment in the world after peace is made." The first condition—one that Wilson already had set forth in public—required that no nation should ever be permitted to acquire an inch of land by conquest. Other propositions, which seem to have grown out of his experience in Latin-American affairs, were that the rights of large and small nations must be recognized as equal, and that war munitions must be made under public control rather than by citizens who might manipulate their manufacture for profit. Most significant of the prophecies revealed to Axson, however, was the fourth and last: "There must be an association of the nations, all bound together for the protection of the integrity of each, so that any one nation breaking from this bond will bring upon herself war; that is to say, punishment, automatically." [16]

[16] Wilson was perhaps influenced by a letter from Charles W. Eliot, dated Aug. 14, 1914, that he showed to the Cabinet. The educator suggested that the United States enter into an alliance to rebuke and punish offending nations. A policing power, Eliot thought, might ultimately supplant the balancing of alliances as a guarantee of peace; and in the creation of an international force the peoples of Europe might form a federal relationship and the cost of armament might be cut.

Wilson's faith in the principles underlying Bryan's treaties of arbitration was strengthened by the sudden outburst of war in Europe. On Aug. 13, 1914, Wilson wrote thus to Senator

It had taken the shock of bloodshed in Europe, coming at a time when his emotions had been set free by worship of Ellen Wilson's sacrificial spirit, to drive him to put into his own political creed a tenet that his fellow countrymen were still far from accepting. He had been merely plodding along early in the summer, his senses almost deadened by the discipline that he imposed as he grieved for his sick wife. But in August his thought vaulted beyond the day's task and reached out for practical ways of applying the ideals of service that he had been preaching. There was a spiritual impulse behind his thinking, now. It might be strong enough to hold him in the direction that he felt to be right, no matter if it led to persecution and even to martyrdom. He had found his great Cause, as he had in every pastoral charge of his career. It was to be not "Princeton in the nation's service," now, but the United States at the service of all mankind.

But he was face to face with a war; and his people, as horrified as he, and even terrified, needed assurance and guidance. He did not fail them. On August 19, in a proclamation to the Congress, he revealed a vision that could hold them steady: "We must be impartial in thought as well as in action, must put a curb upon our sentiments as well as upon every transaction that might be construed as a preference of one party to the struggle before another. My thought is of America. I am speaking, I feel sure, the earnest wish and purpose of every thoughtful American that this great country of ours, which is, of course, the first in our thoughts and in our hearts, should show herself in this time of peculiar trial a Nation fit beyond others to exhibit the fine poise of undisturbed judgment, the dignity of self-control, the efficiency of dispassionate action; a Nation that neither sits in judgment upon others nor is disturbed in her own counsels and which keeps herself fit and free to do what is honest and disinterested and truly serviceable for the peace of the world."

In this appeal the President met his people on the level of their immediate thinking. Everyone was asking how the European war would affect life in the United States. The answer that he gave was neither profound nor soothing, but it was challenging. He told his fellow countrymen that everything depended on their own behavior. Thus, characteristically, he sought for his people not the security of the ostrich but the more valid protection that he had often found in a cloak of aggressive righteousness.

William J. Stone, whose Committee on Foreign Relations were then considering twenty of the "cooling-off" treaties: "Action on our part would make the deepest possible impression upon the world and I covet and pray for it on that account."

CHAPTER XXIV

CARRYING ON ALONE

THE AMERICAN people were as astonished as their President by the outbreak of fighting in Europe. Hating no other nation, innocent of any thought of making war, and defended from attack by the Atlantic Ocean, they could not understand such lusts and fears as those that possessed the Old World.

Once hostilities had begun, however, and the quilt of innocence that had covered the minds of Americans was torn apart, prejudices surged up that had lain more or less dormant. Old bias against imperial Britain, fanned by citizens of Irish and German blood, began to glow again. The Hohenzollerns, who by commercial and naval aggressiveness had made themselves hobgoblins in the American Dream, now took on the menace of ogres.

The press of the nation gave vent immediately to emotional pressures that had been building up. Editors reflected feelings of affection for France, sympathy for the gallant underdogs—Belgium and Serbia —distrust of colossal Russia, and resentment toward a Kaiser who was reported once to have said to his troops: "Be terrible as Attila's Huns."

Contemplating the eddying of opinion in the first dark days of August, Wilson was swayed neither by journalists nor by politicians. Six months before war broke out, the President had given warning, in a press conference, that newspapers could do "a vast deal of damage" by printing speculations on foreign affairs. He was confident that he intuitively understood the temper of the American people better than editors and publishers who had criticized his New Freedom and scorned his Mexican policy of watchful waiting.

Financial magnates looked to the White House for reassurance; and Wilson was not displeased to feel that he could be of service to men who had thought him an impractical college president. When the impact of the war made the custodians of private capital shrink into their shells, he felt that he must safeguard his program of reform. The Clayton Bill was not yet enacted, and the President was by no means sure how this and the income tax and the Federal Reserve Act would work out in practice. These measures were not thoroughly set, he said to Daniels one day. "Big Business will be in the saddle. More than that—Free Speech and the other rights will be endangered. War is autocratic."

The most critical emergency at the war's beginning was met immediately by steps taken by McAdoo after consultation with the President. Early in September Wilson replied to a fearsome letter from J. P. Morgan. Telling the banker that some features of pending anti-trust measures might be changed, Wilson replied: "I am sincerely sorry that you should be so blue about the situation. I believe that being blue is just the wrong thing, if you will permit me to say so."

While Morgan's letter was under consideration, Wilson heard a plea from six railroad presidents for support of their credit in the emergency brought about by the war. They had already petitioned the Interstate Commerce Commission for increases in rates, and they hoped that the President would say a good word for them. Meeting their request to the extent of writing a public letter to one of them, he showed broad sympathy and understanding.[1]

One of the calamities brought by war—the plight of the cotton planters who were prevented from disposing immediately of one of the largest crops in history—struck home with peculiar force to a statesman bred in the South. Rejecting price-fixing proposals as "unwise and dangerous," he promised that the government would give all the help possible "within the limits of economic law and safe finance." Before the end of October the British government was persuaded to rule that cotton was not contraband subject to seizure on the high seas. Moreover, McAdoo—"dear Mac" was bearing the brunt of the economic emergency so conscientiously that his nerves were worn bare and Wilson was "quite anxious about him"—cooperated with House and private bankers to raise a fund to help farmers to hold their crops until the demand stimulated by war conditions could make itself felt.[2]

[1] When it was suggested to him by Henry L. Higginson that he make recommendations to the Interstate Commerce Commission, Wilson drew back. How far was it proper for him to go, he wondered, in putting his personal convictions before the commissioners? "They are as jealous of executive suggestion as the Supreme Court would be," he reminded the Boston banker, "and I dare say with justification." He sent Higginson's letter, nevertheless, to Commissioner Winthrop M. Daniels, for he knew that this old Princeton colleague would understand. He hoped that Higginson's views, which he himself thought "in the main true," might impress the commissioners.

The commissioners asserted their independence by rejecting the plea and then, reconsidering the matter several weeks later on their own initiative, authorizing an increase in rates.

[2] Though Wilson had disliked subsidies that might make citizens less self-reliant, he concluded, after discussing the matter with House and getting a legal ruling from the attorney

Toward the end of 1914, when the twelve regional Federal Reserve Systems were opened, a measure of confidence came back and on December 12 the New York Stock Exchange was reopened. Early in 1915 the nation's banks returned about three-fourths of the currency that McAdoo had distributed in August as an emergency measure.

However, another crisis precipitated by the war—that in shipping—was a matter so entangled with the legal filaments of neutrality policy that it became a subject of bitter controversy and long legislative debate.

On July 31, even before it was certain that the European conflict would involve Britain, Wilson postponed his usual Cabinet meeting, called in two leaders of the Senate and two of the House and said to them: "Our bountiful crops are ready to harvest. Unless they can be carried to the foreign markets they will waste in the warehouses, if they do not rot in the fields." He asked for legislation that would provide ships to carry American commerce "to all ports of the world." A bill was introduced that made foreign-built vessels eligible for purchase and immediate registry under the American flag. The Congress passed the measure immediately, and on August 18 the President signed it.[3]

---

general, that the cotton pool stood in a class by itself and would not set a dangerous precedent. Before raising the cotton pool from private sources, McAdoo, building upon a Treasury-financed scheme that he had used to rescue cotton planters from a minor depression in the autumn of 1913, had acted in August, 1914, to issue emergency currency and to deposit government funds in Southern banks for loans to cotton and tobacco planters.

In the autmun of 1913 Wilson had congratulated the Treasury officials on their bold, prompt action, and he wrote in the New York Commercial, on Sept. 29: "The country has seen . . . McAdoo handle the money situation more successfully and with greater skill than the bankers have ever done . . . In the past secretaries of the Treasury have not put out Treasury funds before the harm was done, and then they devoted the money to checking panics in Wall Street, while the business of the country came to a standstill . . . Deep down in the mind of the public rests the suspicion that the banks have not been wise in the past and that government control in the open is something not to be feared."

In the autumn of 1914 Wilson confessed that the cotton crisis gave him "the greatest concern." Though the emergency fund was never applied effectively, a rise in the price of cotton somewhat alleviated the distress of the producers. On Aug. 20, 1915, the British government revised their ruling and declared cotton to be contraband. See Vol. II.

[3] Diplomats of the Allies protested against the Ship Registry Act. Their governments feared that Germany might receive, in payment for ships that were of no use in her war effort, credits that would buy essential munitions. Moreover, there was suspicion that contraband cargoes might be shipped to German ports in the interned German vessels, under the safe-conduct of the American flag.

The solicitor of the State Department, however, maintained that the transfer of ships to a neutral flag was legal even after the commencement of hostilities, if made in good faith; and Wilson, accepting this, wrote to Senator Saulsbury on Aug. 15 to explain that "the whole question comes down to the proof of bona fides in the transaction." The United States, he admitted, could not object to the seizure at sea of any ships that were not acquired in good faith. "I think," he wrote, "the whole thing can be divested of its risks by a wise and prudent administration of the law." On the legality of the Ship Registry Act, see Link, W.W. and the Progressive Era, p. 150.

Though Congress promptly followed up passage of the Ship Registry Act by approving a measure providing government funds for insuring merchant vessels, it was still obvious to Wilson, at the beginning of September, that private capital was too timid to make adequate plans for supplying the tonnage that was demanded by the nation's foreign trade. The nation as a whole could take the financial risk better than private owners, he thought.

Secretary McAdoo was concerned, too. Convinced that a few shippers were enjoying "an orgy of profiteering" while government-subsidized insurance relieved them of risk, he resolved to provide more vessels and lower rates. Conceiving a plan for a government-owned merchant marine, he drafted legislation providing for both the building and the buying of ships; and taking it to the President, he remarked that thus they could serve trade with Latin America that would not be exposed to the risks of war.

Wilson perceived immediately that the measure would be denounced by reactionaries as "socialistic" and took a day to meditate before giving his answer. Was the operation of shipping a "necessary function" that the government must perform in an emergency? This was not a revolutionary idea, for Roosevelt's administration had purchased the Panama steamship line and the government still operated it. The need for action on a larger scale now seemed dire, private enterprise hopelessly inadequate, and his son-in-law's vision compelling. The President handed the drafted bill back to the secretary of the treasury and said, smiling:

"We'll certainly have to fight for it, won't we?"

"We certainly shall," McAdoo replied.

"Well, then, let's fight."

Wilson called legislators to the White House on the day after he had signed the inadequate Ship Registry Act, and on August 24 McAdoo's new measure was presented in the House.

An immediate blast of protest came from businessmen and Republican politicians. Wilson was irritated again by lobbyists who infested Washington, but he announced through newsmen that if private capital would provide the facilities needed by exporters, which so far they had shown no intention of doing, the government might not carry out its shipping program. Otherwise, he said, much as he disliked to have

---

The qualms of shipowners were not diminished by a warning from Counselor Lansing of the State Department that every purchaser of a German vessel would have to satisfy the British government of his *bona fides* and that it was "too much to hope" that the belligerents would respect such transactions.

his administration enter into this business, he not only intended to press the legislation forward, but expected it to be enacted within two or three weeks. Journalists reported that the well-known jaw was setting hard.

By the end of September, however, the opposition had become so strenuous and persistent, and the Republicans were using it so tellingly, that Wilson's advisers wanted him to postpone legislation until the November election was over. There was resentment in the Cabinet because so important a measure had not been discussed there. Houston was opposed to it; and Secretary of Commerce Redfield, who bore the brunt of protests from shipping interests, complained that he could not understand its purpose. There was a feeling that the President already had asked so much of the legislators that their patience was at the breaking point. On September 29, therefore, when Wilson conferred with McAdoo, Tumulty, Burleson, and House, it was decided to let the legislators adjourn as soon as possible. And so the Sixty-third Congress, that had met continuously for more than a year and a half at Wilson's insistence and had enacted most of the reforms of the New Freedom, came to an end on October 24, two days after passing a bill voting higher taxes to meet a deficiency that was caused chiefly by shrinking import duties.[4]

With the fight for the shipping bill suspended, and the Clayton and Trade Commission Acts passed, the President was comparatively free to give attention to the forthcoming election, in which, under the Seventeenth Amendment, senators would have to face direct primaries and popular election.

The President was always under pressure, from one adviser or another, to make public statements in support of certain candidates and causes. This was particularly true in the months before elections. During October of 1914 he attended to the needs of his Congressional adherents. The President took a more indulgent attitude toward the bosses and wheel-horses of the party than he had shown earlier in his political career. "My head is with the progressives in the Democratic party," he told Tumulty, "but my heart, because of the way they stood by me, is with the so-called Old Guard in the Senate." The secretary—making the most of the days when the Governor seemed to be in an

---

[4] Appealing for additional revenue from internal taxation, Wilson said to Congress on Oct. 4: ". . . we ought not to borrow. We ought to resort to taxation, however we may regret putting additional burdens on our people . . . The country is able to pay any just and reasonable taxes without distress. . . . The people . . . know and understand, and they will be intolerant only of those who dodge responsibility or are not frank with them."

"Irish" mood—persuaded his chief to endorse two New Jersey congressmen whose tenure was in jeopardy and to appoint a lieutenant of despised James Nugent to the bench of the District of Columbia. Even the Tammany candidates in New York State received Wilson's blessing as a concession to the need for party harmony. The President was disturbed by conflict between two slates in the Democratic primary in that state—one supported by McAdoo, Mayor Mitchel, and Collector Dudley Field Malone, the other by Tammany and Tumulty. The rivalry was an irritating incident in a running feud that was developing between the President's secretary and his son-in-law, each of whom wished to command "the Governor's" entire confidence in political matters. Wilson did his best to requite the fealty of each of these lieutenants without giving offense to the other.[5]

On October 20 the President sent to Congressman Underwood a public letter that made it clear that if he seemed too indulgent toward some machine men, it was only because of his gratitude for past support in Congress and his hope of committing the party to liberal measures in the future. To strengthen the bond with progressive sentiment that had proved decisive in 1912, he expressed pride in reforms already put through and looked to the horizon of the future, beyond the emergency brought by war. He said that he was still contemplating strokes "to set business free."[6] In speeches before the American Bar Association and the Pittsburgh Y.M.C.A. he made appeals to the moral forces of the nation.

Woodrow Wilson seemed to be bringing to a focus, in the autumn of 1914, all of his talents for leadership. It was almost as if his whole life had become a testimonial to virtues of Ellen Wilson that he had always esteemed but never felt so poignantly. He had become truly a pastor to those near him. When jealousy between Tumulty and McAdoo became flagrant, he was constrained to remind his agitated secretary, in fatherly reproof, of "the green-eyed monster." He had grown fond of his son-in-law, with whom he shared a passion for detective stories, and he depended much on "dear Mac's" executive

[5] McAdoo, by his persistent interest in political appointments, seemed to show personal ambition. Colonel House took it upon himself to remonstrate with McAdoo, advising him that the surest path to the Presidency lay in doing his own job superlatively well, and not in interferences that would be interpreted as an attempt to build a machine for himself.

McAdoo took this advice "in an admirable spirit," the Colonel recorded, and was showing himself to be "one of the greatest Secretaries of the Treasury." House Diary, July 8 and Sept. 30, 1914.

[6] On Sept. 7, 1914, Wilson told Ray Stannard Baker that he had nearly reached the end of his economic program, but still hoped to develop a policy of "conservation for use." Baker, *American Chronicle*, p. 277.

genius. Yet it gave him indigestion when McAdoo talked business at meals. He told House that he would rather die than risk hurting the feelings of Nellie's husband; and so the tactful Colonel agreed to tell McAdoo that Dr. Grayson had asked him—House—to refrain from talking shop with the President at the table.[7]

The President encouraged his Cabinet to take part in the campaign. As he mended rifts and forged strong ties with political comrades, he rejoiced in a feeling that he was approved of and trusted by the party and the country.[8] But the satisfaction was only "for the moment," he told himself. There was still the old haunting dread of a turn in the tide, a premonition that someday he might find himself driven by conscience to do something that would make him intensely unpopular. He professed little interest in his own tenure in an office that had brought him "no personal blessing, but only irreparable loss and desperate suffering." He confessed to House that if he could feel that he was not obligated to stand for re-election in 1916 a great load would be lifted from him. He feared that the people would expect him to continue his pace of reform, and that it would be impossible.

As the President's prestige grew and both conservatives and progressives of his party fell in line behind him, the Republicans failed to mend the rift that had opened in 1912. Their leaders had endorsed Wilson's proclamation of neutrality at the outbreak of war; but now Root and Lodge and other regulars, with no aid from Taft, attacked the new tariff law and asserted that even in the war emergency there would be no need for increased taxes if only the President would practice the economy that he preached. At the same time Roosevelt aired intemperate views in print and on the platform, and thus dug a political grave for himself and his party.

On November 3 the President went with his people to the polls. His home town was still Princeton, where he had rented a room in a lodging house in order to keep his name on the rolls. A few old friends stood on the platform to greet him when he left the train,

---

[7] House Diary, Sept. 26, 1914. The same disinclination to risk any misunderstanding that might cause ill-feeling within the clan and hurt his daughter was apparent several weeks later, when Wilson urged House to discuss the prickly question of New York State politics with McAdoo. The Colonel thought it the President's duty to go to the bottom of this matter himself. House Diary, Nov. 6, 1914. On Jan. 3, 1915, Wilson asked Nancy Toy, a visitor at the White House, whether she thought that McAdoo could be elected to the Presidency if nominated.

[8] W.W. to Mary Hulbert, Sept. 20, 1914. Wilson's view was corroborated in the *New York Times* on Oct. 12: "Mr. Cleveland never, even in his first administration, had the grasp of it [the party] that Mr. Wilson has. The resemblances come down to the fact that his will is as iron as Cleveland's, though the iron hand is hidden in a velvet glove that Cleveland never wore. The fundamental difference is in the measure of success."

dressed as in the old days in a gray suit of rough texture, but wearing a black tie and a band of black on his sleeve. While they chatted, President Hibben suddenly appeared, a little breathless, and explained that he had been told by a student that the President of the United States was asking for him. Wilson thought that poor Jack Hibben was the victim of a cruel hoax. But he did not relent, and looking straight at the eager figure, he said only one word: "No." His manner was courteous, but his inflection of the single syllable seemed to ask why this man should imagine that the President of the United States might ask for such as he.[9]

Early returns suggested to Wilson that the electorate in the East, like the Princeton community, had surrendered to reactionary forces. When reports came in from the West, however, the President was enheartened. He got "solid satisfaction," he confessed, out of gains in the fields where he himself had once pioneered alone.

When the popular vote was checked, it was clear that the Democrats had suffered the slump that usually strikes the party in office at midterm. Though the voting power in the Senate did not change, the majority in the House was reduced from seventy-three to twenty-five. Progressives had drifted back into the Republican fold in large numbers.

The President was disconsolate because the nation as a whole showed so little appreciation of his labors. He wondered whether it was worth while to drive Congress as hard as he had driven it. House tried to comfort his friend by reminding him that he had not suffered defeat, himself; but for the present Wilson found the best solace for his ego in the vale of self-oblivion in which he had taken refuge since his bereavement. "My individual life has gone utterly to pieces," he wrote to Mary Hulbert five days after the election. "I do not care a fig for anything that affects me." The satisfaction that comes from service could not make him whole. There was no companionship in consorting with the policies of a state or the fortunes of a nation!

[9] Margaret Axson Elliott, *My Aunt Louisa and W.W.*, p. 268. Still unable to face up to his failure at Princeton, Wilson attended his thirty-fifth reunion in June of 1914, but refused an inviation to lead the Pee-rade with Hibben. In explanation of his attitude he wrote on May 21 to Robert Bridges: "I want everybody to forget for the day that I am anything except a member of the class of '79." After it was over, he admitted to Cleveland Dodge that being present cost him a good deal of pain. Returning to Washington, Wilson told Tumulty on June 23 that it should be made clear that he had not been forced out of the presidency at Princeton. "They would not have dared try it," he wrote, "but they were very glad to get rid of me because they were desperately fighting my attempt to change the social organization of the university." House noted that in their intimate talks they often drifted to the subject of Princeton, and on such occasions Wilson showed "how deeply the iron entered his soul."

He kept on functioning, he confessed, by holding himself to a daily routine. "On Sunday," he explained to Mary Hulbert, "all faculties seek rest and are in a sort of coma and I am no good. . . . I seem to be tough against all sorts of strain and all sorts of deep suffering. I have a vast deal to be thankful for, and I shall, I hope, never yield to the weakness of being sorry for myself." He did not impose the pall of an official period of mourning. He made his associates feel that they should carry on as usual, and even the concerts on the White House grounds went on.

When he sought refuge and relaxation in his automobile, and drove over routes that he named and numbered to suit his fancy, Helen Bones sat silent by his side as he dozed or put together the pieces of a puzzle of statecraft. When Grayson fell sick and was given a vacation to recuperate, she accompanied her cousin Woodrow around the golf course. "A perfect companion," he thought her, "because glad to think of me and what is best for me and not anxious to talk and to have her own way, bless her heart for the unselfishness! But I hate to think how dull it must be for her, and I chide myself for accepting such sacrifices." His "darling Nell" managed to run in on her father every day; and on Thanksgiving he went to Williamstown to visit the Sayres, who were soon to present him with his first grandson. When they came to the White House for the advent, the President stood outside the door of their chamber, eavesdropping, and when he imagined he heard two new voices, he whispered excitedly "Twins!"

But for all his fondness for his girls, he made it clear that his obligations to the American people superseded his parental love. At table, once, his daughters told him of a state governor who pardoned a son. They asked him, in jest, whether he could pardon them if they were convicted of a crime, and he grew very serious and replied, solemnly: "God help me, I don't believe I could."

Tumulty found, to his sorrow, that White House automobiles enjoyed no immunity from the laws to which other citizens were subject; and Wilson, relishing his secretary's discomfiture, had a habit of asking his family at dinner: "Well, who's been pinched today?" [10]

[10] Louis Brownlow to the writer, March 14, 1951. Appointing Democrats to the District Commission to fix party responsibility, Wilson said that, though he did not expect publicly to intervene, he wanted the commissioners to consult him about matters that in their judgment required his advice. He asked them to boil down their propositions, present them fairly, and tell him frankly what they thought he should do. "If you will do that and try to keep it all on one page and send it to me in mid-morning, I will try to do my part before it is night. . . . If you don't let me know exactly what you think, but try to pass the buck to me entirely, you may never get an answer, and certainly you wouldn't deserve one." Only once did Com-

It was not so easy now for Wilson to command the gay weekend mood in which he had been wont to write to Mary Hulbert; yet he was loyal to this old friend, and when she wrote of the loss of her small fortune through the bad judgment of an overambitious son, he tried to suggest ways in which both mother and son might find profitable employment, and wrote letters to his friends in their behalf. She brought her complaints, real and imaginary, to the White House. She reaffirmed her confidence in her great friend's gentleness and nobility; and each of these congenial spirits drew strength from the understanding and faith of the other.

As he wrote less to his "high priestess of democracy," he renewed an old correspondence with charming Nancy Toy—daughter of a Virginia clergyman and wife of an aged professor of Romance languages at Harvard University. Visiting the White House in January of 1915, Mrs. Toy joined appreciatively in the family evenings and the talk of poets and historians, of religion and philosophy. Wilson enjoyed the independence of mind that he found in her letters and assured her that she did "a real service" in informing him of what was being said by the critical people about her at Cambridge. It was not only the privilege but the duty of a loyal friend to tell him that he had made mistakes, he insisted. Nancy Toy pleased him immensely by giving him a great horn spoon for Christmas. "I am Scots very deep down in me," he wrote in thanking her, "and porridge in a great horn spoon seems to me like a thing of (minor) religion."

But Wilson did not find in Nancy Toy the intimate comradeship that his Scottish soul still craved. This lady, for one thing, felt that she could live a life worth while without depending on a personal God. When she advanced this view, he took up the challenge, declaring: "*My* life would not be worth living if it were not for the driving power of religion, for *faith*, pure and simple. I have seen all my life the arguments against it without ever having been moved by them . . . never for a moment have I had one doubt about my religious beliefs. There are people who *believe* only so far as they *understand*— that seems to me presumptuous and sets their understanding as the standard of the universe . . . I am sorry for such people."

In the President's loneliness, Edward M. House perhaps gave more comfort than anyone else to his friend's uneasy spirit. He felt that he

<hr />

missioner Brownlow fail to get an answer before nightfall, and then Wilson apologized, two days later, that he had had to communicate with Paris. Brownlow MS, *A Passion for Anonymity*.

could "unload his mind" to House; and when his friend took some of his rash impulses too seriously, he was mildly amused. The Colonel tried to supply the serene wisdom that Wilson always had found in his Ellen, and to give the President, in digestible doses, the criticism that he expected from loyal friends. Going to Harlakenden late in August for a weekend visit, accompanied by his devoted son-in-law, Gordon Auchincloss, House was met at the door by the President and shown to the room that had been Mrs. Wilson's and that was next his own, with a common bathroom between. They were in a wing of the house and quite by themselves. Descending a little staircase, they went down to a study where they sat and talked of the affairs of the world —the disappointing past and the dim future.

Wilson confessed he was heartsick over the narrow margin by which they had failed to prevent disaster in Europe. He condemned the philosophy of the German leaders as essentially selfish and lacking in spirituality; and of the Kaiser's idea of building a military machine as a means of preserving peace, he said in scorn: "What a foolish thing it was to create a powder magazine and risk someone's dropping a spark into it!" If Germany won, the President predicted, his own ambition for better international ethics would be frustrated and the United States would become a military nation. At one time their thought leaped to the distant future, and they speculated on the distribution of power in centuries to come. Wilson suggested that eventually there might be but two great nations in the world: Russia and the United States. House, however, thought there would be three: China, dominating Asia; Russia, Europe and a part of Asia; and the United States, dominating the Western world and perhaps the English-speaking colonies.

As the friends sat on the terrace and watched the afternoon sun throw the shadow of Vermont hills upon the broad valley of the Connecticut, the President began to talk of Ellen Wilson as if she were still a living presence. He showed photographs of her and read poems that she had written. Tears came as he said that he felt like a machine run down and dreaded the next two and a half years.

With an effort he shook off his gloomy thoughts, however, and tried to give the Colonel a good time. He joked about his ancestry, saying that he belonged to two clans that had been the worst lot of freebooters in Scotland. In the evening they played pool—"equally badly," House thought. The next morning the President rose very early so that he could finish shaving before his guest would wish to use the bathroom, and the Colonel's heart was touched by this little courtesy on the part of one so great. House—irrespressible flatterer though he himself was—felt flattered at being taken into the family so intimately. In his diary he recorded his host's attentions, and noted that Dr. Grayson filled his ear with mischievous, petty gossip of the White House that had not been reported to the President.

The ruling elder continued to whisper in Wilson's ear when appointments were to be made. He continued to protest that his motives were pure friendship and a desire to serve. When McReynolds was elevated to the Supreme Court, House recommended as attorney general his loyal Texas friend, Thomas W. Gregory. Furthermore, he persuaded Gregory to accept the post if it were offered and advised his protégé how to conduct himself.[11] Gregory was well prepared to serve, therefore, when the President, feeling that this man might reinforce the liaison with congressmen that Burleson and McAdoo had been maintaining, appointed him.

The President's dependence on his Cabinet seemed to be increased by his bereavement. On January 29 he invited the group for the first time to meet in the White House instead of in the executive office.

Another change in the Cabinet seemed likely. McAdoo was offered the presidency of the Metropolitan Life Insurance Company; and having been told by Grayson that the President had a tendency toward arteriosclerosis that was being aggravated by continual mental strain, he had inferred that Wilson would not run for a second term. This seemed to clear his own path to the Presidency, and so he confessed his ambition to friendly Colonel House and asked whether he would damage his prospect if he accepted the offer of the insurance company.

The Colonel was in a dilemma. McAdoo had shown himself a man of intemperate feeling and he did not work smoothly with Tumulty, with the Cabinet, or with the Federal Reserve Board. House felt that it would be best for all concerned that he be allowed to resign; but he knew that the very idea of a change would distress Wilson, and when he conferred with the President on October 29 he found him upset because McAdoo had come to the White House and suggested resigning. Wilson recalled that it had been said that the business interests intended to break up his Cabinet either by forcing men out or

11 House Diary, Aug. 10 and 30, 1914. Gregory must never get into tenuous argument, the Colonel warned, but must state his position briefly and, above all, never repeat. When he found that their minds were in agreement, he must never waste the President's time by giving reasons for his opinion. Gregory was "very receptive," House noted. A letter from Gregory to House, Aug. 26, 1914, breathes devotion and gratitude. House Collection.

buying them out; and now he suspected that the latter course was being followed. When the Colonel argued that it was unlikely that McAdoo could ever become president if he remained in the Cabinet, Wilson replied that connection with an insurance company surely would destroy his son-in-law's chances. A day or two later House revealed that McAdoo, still carrying on the feud with Tumulty that had grown out of New York politics, was denouncing the President's secretary as too subservient to business interests. At this exposure of petty criticism by a member of his family in whom he had placed great trust, Wilson's face flushed and then turned gray. "Has McAdoo gone crazy?" he asked.

The President passed a wretched night after this discussion. The next evening House avoided controversial subjects, and they talked of philosophy and political theory. Wilson made merry with limericks, and they were off to bed early. When the President returned House's visit a week later, in New York, they walked down to Herald Square one evening, stopping here and there to listen to curbstone harangues. When they were recognized, they ducked into a hotel, went up in an elevator, came down on the other side of the building, and went out without detection. Wilson enjoyed the game of hide-and-seek hugely, said he would give anything if only he could get lost in a crowd, and was delighted when the Colonel suggested whiskers as a disguise. The President spoke again of his loneliness, and confessed that he had wished, as they walked, that someone would kill him. But though feeling unfit to do the work before him, he said that he had himself so well disciplined that he well knew that, unless someone did kill him, he would go on to the end, doing the best he could.

They talked little of public business during this visit, though they gave a few minutes to consideration of a plan for Belgian relief for which there was strong popular demand. But after drafting his annual message, the President asked the Colonel to come to the White House to go over it with him; and after its delivery he wrote: "Well, the broadside has been fired and I hope sincerely that it will have the desired effect in quieting those who are seriously in danger of making trouble for the country. You will see that I added one or two little passages after reading it to you." [12]

[12] The Colonel's few suggestions were mainly in regard to foreign affairs. One of the dangerous citizens, House felt, was Bryan. After talking with the secretary of state on Nov. 8, the Colonel wrote in his diary: "He did not believe there was the slightest danger to this country from foreign invasion, even if the Germans were successful. He thought *after war was declared* there would be plenty of time to make the preparations necessary. He talked as inno-

The next time they met, the President was disturbed because Congress had rejected some of his nominations. He sought advice as to future tactics. House was ready with the answer: keep sending in other names of high quality as fast as suggestions were rejected, for thus the people could be made to perceive the obstructive spirit of their legislators. Two weeks later Wilson was inclined to let it be known that, if the senators would not accept his leadership, he would not be a candidate for re-election; but the Colonel advised him not to do it.

Both as comrade and as adviser, then, through the trying autumn of 1914, the Colonel comforted the sorrowing widower. No one was more selflessly devoted to his interest; no one could keep him so well informed about the feelings of his official family. The Colonel seemed to know all and to understand all. On Christmas Day, Woodrow Wilson gave expression to the gratitude that had been surging up within him. He wished he could see brought into House's life, he wired, some happiness and blessing equal to those brought into his by the Colonel's wonderful friendship.

At the beginning of the New Year, Wilson bore his cross with less protest. In February—six months after Ellen Wilson's death—a social party was given in the White House. The Cabinet and their families were invited to see moving pictures and partake of refreshments. The President was friendly and amazingly frank with the few chosen guests; but the old buoyancy of talk and manner were missing and Nancy Toy wondered whether in his formality she saw evidence of—in John Hay's words about Roosevelt—"the kingly shadow falling upon him."

However, the program that Wilson presented to the Congress on December 8, 1914, was mild and reasonable, and his manner was neither dictatorial nor importunate. Prolonging the keynote of service to mankind that he had already sounded so long and so loud, he called for action by the Senate on the Alexander Bill safeguarding the welfare of American seamen, on a measure providing for the development of the national domain under conserving safeguards, and on another bill that would grant more self-government to the Philippines.

---

cently as my little grandchild, Jane Tucker. He spoke with great feeling, and I fear he may give trouble."

When Bryan suggested a national primary law, House told Wilson that in practice, in Texas, such a measure had limited political candidacy to very rich men. "I advised the President to let Bryan direct the primary bill and get tangled in it as a fly in molasses," House recorded. "I told him not to help out, but to encourage him to go on, and I opined that the measure would be killed by the fact that Bryan was its sponsor. He seemed to like this."

He wished to make provision, too, for the survey and charting of the nation's coasts. He was not yet ready, he said, to make definite recommendations in the important field of rural credit—a matter that had been cared for to some degree by the Federal Reserve Act; but on the subject of governmental economy he delivered a little homily worthy of Poor Richard. Beyond the development of the National Guard and the training of citizens in the use of arms and the rudiments of military life, he felt that the time had not yet come "to turn America into a military camp" in anticipation of conflict, as some of his more rabid opponents advocated.

As for the emergency shipping bill, which had passed neither house of Congress, Wilson was emphatic. He was reluctant to try to drive this legislation through immediately, but he had covenanted on the measure with McAdoo, and House had pointed out that if the government was to act at all, it should do so while the need was acute and the necessary votes could be commanded in the present Congress.

But financiers raised questions. If the government were to conduct such businesses as shipping, and operate at a deficit as they were accustomed to do in state monopolies, the sources of taxes with which to meet such deficits would be reduced and the nation's economy would spiral downward to bankruptcy. Moreover, opponents of the shipping bill alarmed peace-loving citizens by citing the risk of war that would result if German vessels were operated by the American government in waters patrolled by the Allies. Cannily tying the issue to the President's Mexican policy, which had resulted in unnecessary fighting at Veracruz, Lodge addressed the Senate with great force on January 6, and on the 7th there was a clear breach between Wilson and the Congress on a bill to limit immigration.[13] At last it seemed as if the Republicans were making headway against the administration and the great advantage that its leader derived from the critical nature of the times.

Picking up their gauntlet on January 8, 1915, Wilson fought back. He had lost none of his sensitiveness to unjust criticism; in fact the wear of bereavement upon his emotions made him slug furiously at his tormentors. Speaking at Indianapolis on Jackson Day, he became

[13] This measure, supported by organized labor and passed by the Congress, was vetoed by Wilson on Jan. 28. He felt that he lacked a popular mandate, and he did not wish to exclude political refugees or demand a literacy test of "those to whom the opportunities of elementary education have been denied, without regard to their character, their purposes, or their natural capacity." Doubtless Wilson recalled the damaging attacks of the foreign-language press, during 1912, on anti-immigration statements in his *History of the American People*. The veto stood until 1917, when a similar immigration measure was passed over a presidential veto.

incoherent and came close to Jackson's summit of intellectual arrogance.

This outburst delivered Wilson from the morose thoughts that had afflicted him in his isolation at the White House from the people whom he loved and wished to serve. "It was good to get my blood moving in a speech again," he confessed. His audience was roused to loud cheers, and applauded wildly when they sensed in one of his remarks a hint that he would stand for re-election in 1916. Many friendly critics, however, regretted the excesses to which he had allowed his tongue to run. Actually, after his blood had cooled, the President confessed to "a palpable lapse of taste . . . produced by the psychology of the stump." He admitted that there was no excuse for it.

"But there is a real fight on," he insisted to Nancy Toy; ". . . the influences that have so long dominated legislation and administration here are making their last and most desperate stand to regain control." Criticism, if it was fair, he regarded as "the necessary tonic and test of men in public life." But he conceived that he was fighting against a formidable covert lobby. He wrote: "I think you cannot know to what lengths men like Root and Lodge are going, who I once thought had consciences but now know have none. We must not suffer ourselves to forget or twist the truth as they do, or use their insincere and contemptible methods of fighting; but we must hit them and hit them straight in the face, and not mind if the blood comes. It is a blunt business, and lacks a certain kind of refinement, but so does all war; and this is a war to save the country from some of the worst influences that ever debauched it. Please do not read the speeches in which I use a bludgeon. I do not like to offend your taste; but I cannot fight rottenness with rose water."

Wilson was not surprised when adversaries in the Senate filibustered against the shipping bill for thirty-seven hours. He attributed their position less to a desire to avoid involvement in a European war than to a fear of government encroachment on private property. When seven Democratic senators joined the opposition and the filibuster continued, with a Republican talking for thirteen hours and cots set up in the cloakrooms so that the talkers might snatch rest, Wilson was incensed. The sense of fealty that had compelled him to support his party's legislators at the polls was outraged by the defection of the seven.

As usual, opposition that he thought selfish hardened Wilson's mind against the arguments of sincere doubters. Charles W. Eliot, who was alarmed by the possibility that the government would involve the nation in war by using the interned German ships on transatlantic routes, warned the President that he was in danger of antagonizing "the great mass of the business men of the country," disrupting the Democratic party, and making a Republican victory in 1916 probable. But in reply the President bespoke trust for his administration, which, he said, was "very keenly alive" to the difficulties that it might encounter.[14]

Hoping that if he could drive the shipping bill through the House the Senate might follow, the President cracked the party whip; on February 16 the bill was passed by a vote of 215 to 121; and the next day Wilson wrote to Congressman Adamson: "You certainly are a fine soldier and I am your sincere admirer."

Dr. Grayson noted the grimness of his chief, and wrote to House that he feared that "Thomas" (the doctor had fallen in with the Colonel's use of code names) was taking the controversy "too hard personally." For two years the President had oscillated between periods in which he drove Congress harder than it had ever been driven before and times when he hesitated to risk insulting the legislators by expounding what he conceived to be their duty. Now he gave the appearance of a martinet who wanted only results, and no excuses. House had gone to Europe, McAdoo underwent an operation, and there was no First Lady to encourage him to make converts by persuasion. After talking with one legislator for an hour, he felt that he had "made about as much impression on him as on his chair." It seemed to him that there were too many "freaks" among the Democrats on the Hill, too many radicals, too many who held to their own little pet ideas. If only he could be a "mere figurehead," like the King of England, and his party could be led by a member of Congress! As it was now, no one heard what he said to the legislators individually, while the whole nation knew what was said at the Capitol. He had been thinking of writing another book on the subject that he had treated in his first essays on government; he would call it "Statesmanship," and it would stress the personal element in politics.

As Wilson shrank from fighting the shipping battle with time-honored tactics of American politics, his Republican opponents continued their appeal to popular fears and suspicions. When the loyal

---

[14] Eliot questioned whether "can you not trust *me?*" is ever a satisfactory answer to the allegation that a man or party possesses "illegitimate and dangerous powers." *See* Baker, V, 130–32.

Democrats in the Senate refused to consider amendments to the bill and used patronage to control votes, Lodge portrayed Wilson as an overbearing egotist and dictator, and persuaded himself that he was justified in this instance in using the filibuster, though he considered it an unethical procedure. "I never expected to hate anyone in politics with the hatred I feel towards Wilson," the senator wrote to Theodore Roosevelt. "I was opposed to our good friend Grover Cleveland, but never in any such way as this." [15]

With the support of the Republican leadership and the acquiescence of dissenting Democrats, the filibustering in the Senate went on. Wilson stubbornly refrained from making a frank statement of his plans for the German ships; and when one that had been purchased by an American citizen—the *Dacia*—was seized by a French cruiser on February 27, the potential danger was dramatized before all the world. The Congress adjourned on March 4 without any action by the Senate on the shipping bill. Wilson and McAdoo, however, did not give up the battle: a modified form of the measure was introduced early in 1916 and, the shortage of shipping having become obviously critical, the new bill was passed. But the prices that the government had to pay for ships were more than three times those that had prevailed in 1915.

The stormy session of Congress, in the winter of 1915, revealed that the flaw in character that had led to Wilson's defeat at Princeton still remained, more dangerous than ever. Shrinking into personal isolation, indulging in dreams of the ideal government and giving way to intolerance of the hard realities of politics, he had lost touch with seven important Democratic senators. His fury at them was so great that he wrote out a damning indictment that, fortunately, he was persuaded not to release. His friends wondered whether he had indeed cured himself, as he boasted in a talk to the Presbytery of Potomac, of the "very risky habit of always saying exactly what he thought"—a trait that he said he had "in part inherited" from his father.[16]

[15] Garraty, *Lodge*, pp. 310–14. This biographer observes that Lodge's hatred of the President was the more dangerous because the senator honestly thought himself a scholarly and unprejudiced observer who, in the war crisis, was trying to forget politics.
[16] James T. Taylor, *Woodrow Wilson in Church*, p. 18.

CHAPTER XXV

A LONELY MAN FINDS A COMRADE

WOODROW WILSON had never in his life been so lonely as in the early months of 1915. He was bereft not only of his Ellen, but of Colonel House, the man who could best counsel him with the sympathy that Wilson found so agreeable in ladies. The Colonel was in Europe, "Miss Margaret" was more interested in concert singing than in the duties of a first lady, and moreover, she and Cousin Helen Bones were too young and inexperienced in public affairs to be comforting confidantes.

Fortunately the President had a masculine friend who, though not competent to share the burdens of state, could minister to him in body and spirit. During the mortal illness of Ellen Wilson, Cary T. Grayson had established himself as a "Dutch uncle" to all the family. Not long after Wilson's inauguration the President had asked this navy surgeon why he, like many others, had not applied for permanent assignment to the White House duty that he was tentatively performing; and Grayson had given an answer that had melted his chief's heart: "I do not think that it would be in good taste." The doctor's tact proved to be as infallible as his droll good humor; and soon Wilson had been moved to say to Secretary Daniels, while laying a hand upon Grayson's arm: "I wish this part of the Navy for my very own."

Noticing that Helen Bones was still grieving for Ellen Wilson and lacked feminine comradeship, the doctor introduced her to an energetic matron who could persuade her to take outdoor exercise. Thus it was that Edith Bolling Galt, who was some fifteen years younger than the President, came into his family. A descendant of Virginia plantation owners and professional men, Edith Bolling had been married to Norman Galt, a Washington jeweler. Before his death, in 1908, her husband had given positions in his store to several of her brothers; and the widow had arranged to have the business carried on and drew from it enough income to live comfortably in the Galt house on Twentieth Street.

To Edith Bolling Galt, Woodrow Wilson had been just another transient in the White House. Dipping into *The New Freedom* at the urging of a sister, she had asked how such things could possibly be accomplished and had put the book aside. She had watched Governor Wilson reviewing New Jersey troops—"a thin man on a horse," she remembered. After he became president she saw him in his box at the theater and, noting that he ducked behind his program several times to yawn, thought him bored. Apparently, too, she imagined he was boring, for when her sister urged her to share an appointment to call on him, she replied: "Not if I know it. I have lived in Washington seventeen years and never been inside the White House. Why should I bother a tired, busy man to shake hands with me? I would feel like an idiot going in there."

Enjoying the outdoors, she succeeded in the mission that her friend Cary Grayson imposed. Helen Bones took long walks with her in Rock Creek Park and, confiding in her, spoke affectionately of "Cousin Woodrow" and of the desperate loneliness of the man, of his unfailing sweetness toward his relatives, his grave fortitude and devotion to duty.

One day in March, at the suggestion of Grayson, Helen Bones asked her new friend to return to the White House for tea. Edith Galt protested that her boots were too muddy; but she was persuaded, and when they stepped out of the elevator they met two men coming in from the golf links. "I think you might invite us to tea," said Dr. Grayson, introducing Mrs. Galt to the President.

After the golfers had changed and the shoes of the ladies had been scraped, they had a jolly party before the fire in the Oval Room. The guest declined to stay to dinner; but a few days later, after an automobile ride during which the ladies chatted on the back seat while the President rode in front and rested, Mrs. Galt dined at the White House. Cousin Woodrow read to them, and after a certain passage said: "If I had written that when I was a boy my father would have made me rewrite it until I really said what I meant!"

He fell to talking then about Joseph Wilson, and when he learned that Edith Galt also had a revered father, his heart was warmed and he listened while she regaled him with the folklore of the Old South— the sufferings of The War, the gallantry of the gentry, the faithfulness of the Negroes. Her voice was soft and musical, her accent Southern. She was both vivid and lovely: in fact, such a lady as he regarded as a "find," one about whom he would have raved to his Ellen. He no longer awed her as the President of the United States, or bored her as a tired, busy man. He was now a friend with whom she shared enthusiasms for the fine qualities of life and its humors. They motored often together, and he confided the perplexities of his position to her with faith that she would not betray him. His mind seemed cleared and sharpened during tête-à-têtes in the White House car in the cool, fragrant April evenings. Soon, however, there were whisperings of dismay among the servants and men of the executive staff who had sweet memories of Ellen Axson Wilson and recalled that she had been dead less than a year. Grayson became alarmed, and began to wonder what the friendship that he had encouraged might portend for the nation. He wrote to House, when the Colonel returned from Europe in June, that there was much to tell him—something very confidential that was worrying him a lot. He wanted the Colonel's advice badly, he said.[1]

On April 28 Wilson wrote his first letter to Edith Galt. Two days later he sent a corsage of roses, and an invitation to dinner at the White House. On May 3 she dined with him, dressed fetchingly in white satin and creamy lace, with a deep square neck edged by green velvet. He asked to be left alone with her on the south portico. Turning his luminous eyes directly upon her, he spoke quietly of love.

Startled by the suddenness and simplicity of his declaration, she reminded him that he had been widowed less than a year. "I know you feel that," he replied; "but, little girl, in this place time is not measured by weeks, or months, or years, but by deep human experiences; and since her death I have lived a lifetime of loneliness and heartache. I was afraid, knowing you, I would shock you; but I would be less than a gentleman if I continued to make opportunities to see you without telling you what I have told my daughters and Helen: that I want you to be my wife. In the circumstances of the spotlight that is always on this house, and particularly on me as the Head of the government, whoever comes here is immediately observed and discussed; and do what I can to protect you from gossip, it will inevitably begin. If you care for me as I do for you, we will have to brave this; but as I cannot come to your house without increasing the gossip, you, in your graciousness, will have to come here. . . ."

The sincerity of his proposal and his obvious concern for her welfare moved her, and she thanked him. Edith Galt felt that she must be sure that she loved the man for himself, quite apart from the glamor that surrounded him as President of the United States. She must see

---

[1] Grayson to House, June 21, 1915. *See also* I. H. Hoover, *Forty-Two Years in the White House*, p. 64. Dr. Grayson had been dismayed by a gossipy story printed in *Town Topics* of Feb. 15, 1915, to the effect that rumor linked the President's name with those of Mary Hulbert and Mrs. Borden Harriman, who had just lost her husband. Such rumors, Grayson told House in a letter of Feb. 15, made him "feel like sending for Captain Bill [McDonald] and shooting."

him often in order to be convinced, she explained. She would go
about with him under proper chaperonage.

The President threw himself into the pursuit. Noting that his lady
fancied purple orchids, he bought the best in the city and, to escape
the notice of gossips, had them delivered by "Ike" Hoover's little boy.
He invited her often to dinner at the White House and took her riding
frequently. He asked her to accompany him to New York on the *Mayflower*. Drifting down the Potomac, they stood together at the rail and
looked down at waters turned to silver by the moon, and she drew
from him a confession of problems that were weighing on his soul.
Each time she saw him, he stirred an impulse in her to love him and
help him to bear his burdens; and Helen Bones pleaded his cause on
days when duty held him at his desk.

On June 24 he bared his soul to House. The Colonel was the only
person in the world with whom he could discuss everything, he said.
What would House think of his marrying again? . . . Did he believe
it would lessen the President's influence with the American people?
. . . And when did he think it could be done? He needed companionship, he explained, and his "dear dead wife" would be the first to approve if she could know, for she had talked to him about it.

It seemed to the Colonel, who had just felt the passions of Europe
at first hand, that as a symbol of national good will Woodrow Wilson
was at that moment the greatest asset of the world. Convinced that the
President's physical welfare would be served by marriage, he encouraged his friend; but he suggested that the wedding would be more
acceptable to the people of the country if it were postponed until the
following spring. Noting that Wilson was mentally fagged after they
had talked all morning about affairs abroad and politics at home, the
Colonel advised him to have a long vacation and offered to take upon
his own back any burdens that seemed too onerous.

Wilson went off to Harlakenden and spent seven weeks at the New
Hampshire estate, with only a brief visit to Washington. "I have not
had such a period of comparative rest and freedom for four years," he
wrote to McAdoo, who came to see him early in August. His daughters
all visited him, and Edith Galt was induced to make a long stay. They
motored together, and enjoyed the country folk whom they met along
the way.

They would come home to tea on the terrace, or, on inclement days,
in front of a fire in the cozy living room, whence they could look
through a picture window over the Connecticut valley and toward

Mount Ascutney. And in the evenings they walked hand in hand in the moonlight, or sat with the family to talk and read—sometimes books, sometimes official dispatches that the President explained to them, and sometimes Wilson's own *History of the American People*. Once, when they asked him questions about that work, he replied: "Do you youngsters realize that I have taught most of my life, and that right now I am in the midst of so much history in the making that I cannot turn my mind back to those times?" He was finding it harder to make history than to write it, he once said.

When she left Harlakenden, Edith Galt was sure that she loved him and overcame her reluctance to assume the position of consort. He told the McAdoos of his good fortune, and before the end of August they wrote generous letters to his lady, welcoming her into the family.

Immediately Edith Galt was taken into the President's confidence. Every emotion and whim was confessed to her. He sent to her the latest dispatches on foreign affairs, many of them having to do with the crisis that followed the sinking of the *Arabic;* and to the dispatches he pinned slips on which he penciled his frank opinions of diplomats. Some of these were caustic. Even House did not escape censure. When the Colonel wrote to outline several courses that might be followed in dealing with the *Arabic* affair, Wilson wrote: "You see he does not advise. He puts it up to me." The little notes were a curious mixture of business and romantic sentiment. Once he sent a favorable editorial from the Milwaukee *Journal* with the comment: "This is pretty handsome, isn't it?" It seemed as if he still felt as he had in his younger days, that no woman would pay heed to him unless convinced that he was a "noticeable man."

Inevitably the politicians grew anxious. The image in which the people liked to cast him was that of their President in the last era of acute crisis—Abraham Lincoln—a remote, lonely patriarch, worn by personal sorrow and bowed by the grief of mankind. What would the people think if they learned that he was courting like a college boy?

Told of the concern of the party men, Wilson asked McAdoo to discuss the matter with House and Lansing. Grayson, too, continued to fear the sequel of the events that he had started. Feeling that the President was using House's approval as an excuse for absorption in his lady, the doctor went to Beverly at the end of July to tell the Colonel of his chief's infatuation. Some of what was said to House was so disturbing that the Colonel did not care to confide it even to his secret diary. But he regretted the timing of the President's love affair.

On September 10 Grayson wrote to House, using code names for people mentioned. He wished to give the Colonel warning, he said, that Wilson was going to ask for advice on "an extremely delicate matter." The President, he went on, wanted House's opinion—from a political viewpoint—the effect on the country if the engagement was announced in the fall. Tumulty, whose opinion Wilson contemplated asking, had told the doctor that it would be a fatal mistake. The lady herself felt that it would be well to wait until the next presidential election was over; but her suitor protested that he needed her now. "If the people do not trust me," he said, "now is the time to find out."

At this juncture Wilson's friends meddled in a way that threw the President into a painful dilemma. Grayson whispered to McAdoo that the Chief had sent a large check to Mary Hulbert; and McAdoo, suspicious and wishing to ferret out the truth, invented a ruse that would, he hoped, make the President confess any wrong of which he might be guilty.[2] He often lunched alone with his father-in-law during the autumn; and one day he fabricated a tale about an anonymous letter mailed from Los Angeles, where Mrs. Hulbert now lived. This fictitious letter, McAdoo said, asserted that that lady was displaying improper notes from the President and tongues were wagging on the Pacific coast.

Having no sin to confess, Wilson's conscience was untroubled. But having confidence in McAdoo's word, and a comprehension of the depths to which political enemies could go, he did not entirely disbelieve the cruel story of the anonymous letter. He could not understand, though, how anyone who seemed as virtuous as his good friend Mary Hulbert could stoop so low. He was resolved to permit no blackmail. But he could not bring himself to expose Edith Galt's name to political scuttlebutt.

He called Grayson to his desk and began to write a note to release his beloved from her pledge. Setting his jaw and turning white to the lips, he took up a pen; but his hand shook and he could set down nothing. Finally he said to the doctor: "I cannot bring myself to write this; you go, Grayson, and tell her everything and say my only alternative is to release her from any promise."

The doctor performed his mission faithfully, and his manner conveyed to Edith Galt the intensity of his chief's suffering. She was hurt

---

2 Edith Wilson testifies in *My Memoir* (p. 78) that House confessed to her, years later, that he and McAdoo had planned the ruse regarding Mrs. Hulbert together. "When I asked McAdoo about it," Mrs. Wilson wrote, "he said that it was entirely 'the Colonel's idea.'" In his diary House attributes the idea to McAdoo and calls it "cruel."

at first; but she wrote bravely to her beloved. "I am not afraid of any gossip or threat, with your love as my shield," she assured him. "This is my pledge, dearest one, I will stand by you—not for duty, not for pity, not for honour—but for love—trusting, protecting, comprehending love."

The letter reached the President on a Sunday morning, after a sleepless night. He felt sure that it would end his dream of happiness and, not daring to break the seal, he put it in his pocket unopened. For days he was sunk in a morass of gloom. On September 18 he stayed in his chamber all morning. Grayson, unable to rally him and fearing for his health, offered to go to Edith Galt and ask her to come to his room. Wilson remonstrated, said that it would be unfair to her; but nevertheless the doctor undertook this act of friendship.

She responded instantly to the appeal, wondering why her letter had not cheered her lover. Taken to a darkened chamber on the second floor of the White House, she saw on the pillow a pallid face with deep-set, glowing eyes. He said no word, but held out a thin hand. She took it and found it icy cold. When she released it, Grayson had gone, Brooks the valet had gone, and they were alone in perfect understanding.

A few days later, on September 22, the Colonel came to the White House in response to word from Grayson that the "California situation" had become "embarrassing." No friend or associate of the lonely man had yet dared to risk incurring displeasure by giving the advice that they thought essential to his political welfare. He would confide only in House. When he and the Colonel were alone, he confessed that, though his relations with Mary Hulbert had been entirely platonic, he had been indiscreet in writing to her more emotionally than was prudent.[3] Learning that her son had lost money in the fruit business in California, he had sent a check for $7,500 to buy mortgages of doubtful value. ("I am so glad, from the bottom of my heart, to have been able to help a little," he wrote to Mrs. Hulbert on November 10, 1915, "though it was no more than any friend would have done and involved no sacrifice of any kind.") Now he was told that Mrs. Hulbert had

---

[3] The quotations that appear in this book from the letters to Mary Allen Hulbert have been chosen with the intention of presenting a truly representative sample of this lively correspondence. Wilson was too gallant ever to write to Mrs. Hulbert of the suspicions that McAdoo had aroused, and he wrote on Oct. 4 to tell this lady that he wanted her to be one of the first to know of the "blessing" that had come to him. This is the last letter in the collection of typed manuscripts in the Princeton University Library except for one of Nov. 10, 1915. In the collection at Princeton, seventeen of the series of 219 letters are missing. Ray Stannard Baker is probably the only biographer who has seen the originals, in the Wilson Collection in the Library of Congress.

allowed his letters to become known to unfriendly gossips. If anyone intended to blackmail him, he told House, he was ready to let every letter he ever wrote be published.

The Colonel, perceiving immediately that he could not tell his friend the whole truth without exposing offenses by Grayson and McAdoo that might never be forgiven, could merely give reassurance in general. Asked to decide when the betrothal should be announced, he was moved by the pathos of his friend's loneliness. It seemed to him that scandalous gossip should be checked by announcing the engagement. Moreover, when he met Edith Galt he found her truly charming and inspiriting. His ego was touched by her lively interest in him and her revelation that the President spoke of him as a man of "lucid mind . . . almost like a business clearing-house."

After giving thought to the problem for a few days, the Colonel pronounced the verdict that his friend wanted. "I do not believe there is anything to be gained by delaying the announcement of your engagement," he wrote to Wilson on October 1.

With this advice, the President felt that he and Edith Galt were free to proclaim their love to their friends and to the world. Stockton Axson, a house guest at the time, shared in the happiness of his brother-in-law, and Wilson wrote radiantly to others who had been close to his Ellen, singing the praises of Edith Galt.[4] The President typed an announcement of his engagement and, after showing it to Mrs. Galt, gave it to Tumulty. The secretary released it with a pledge of Wilson's support to woman suffrage in New Jersey, hoping thus to minimize the adverse reaction of feminine voters.

Woodrow Wilson could go and come with Edith Galt openly now. He entertained her family at the White House and began to introduce her to his friends. He was as eager to embrace his old cronies in his new happiness as he had once been to share Ellen Axson with Heath Dabney. He wrote to his Princeton classmate, "Cow" Woods: "I will have to have the old gang over here sometime to make sure that Mrs. Galt gets authentic information about my past. I hope when the time comes you will all be easy on me." The Class of '79 was invited to dinner at the White House and elected the new First Lady an honorary member.

He made it clear that everything was to be shared in this marriage, as in his first: family, friends, and the secrets of state. When he had no

[4] Wilson was so considerate of the feelings of the White House servants who had loved Ellen Wilson that he was relieved when one to whom he confided his secret answered: "I am both glad and sorry. I believe if Mrs. Wilson could know, she would approve."

time to visit his lady he would sometimes convey, by telephone or by messenger, an idea of the problems that preoccupied him. But all day on Sundays, after church, he was with her; and on other evenings he stayed late at night at her house and then walked home briskly in the crisp autumn air, taking the curbs with a dance step and whistling a popular tune. Then he would be up early in the morning ready for golf. Dour secret service guards grinned at his boyish antics. It astounded them that a mortal of fifty-eight could be so agile, as he walked through Rock Creek Park holding hands with his lady and leaping over obstacles. The servants saw a change in his disposition. He took more interest in the affairs of the household and in his own appearance, was more considerate and understanding.

It seemed to House, who was conferring already with party leaders about tactics for the presidential election that was to come, that the President was so engrossed by his fiancée that he was neglecting public business. He appeared to be "dodging trouble" and, in the flush of self-confidence that came from success in courting, to be making indiscreet remarks about members of the Cabinet, the Senate, and the press.[5]

The Colonel was somewhat reassured when the lovers visited him in New York near the end of November and the President read his draft of an annual message to Congress that showed a masterful grasp of the issues of the day. Nevertheless, House was so concerned about Edith Galt's lack of experience for the duties facing her that he ventured to warn against people who would try to influence her husband through her. The Colonel suggested that she follow his own method of filing the names and causes of special pleaders, and explained that when he took his notes out of the file several weeks later, the problems

[5] Wilson appears to have been no less dependent upon House's friendly counsel, and perhaps more so, after becoming acquainted with Edith Galt. When, at the end of August, the *New York Herald* printed a story about a "break between the comrades over the question of recognizing Carranza," Wilson angrily banned all representatives of that paper from the White House, pending an apology and disavowal, and demanded the discharge of the offending reporter. To reassure the Colonel, the President wrote on Aug. 31: "Of course you have known how to interpret the silly, malicious lies that the papers have recently been publishing about a disagreement between you and me, but I cannot deny myself the pleasure of sending you just a line of deep affection to tell you how they have distressed me." Moreover, to show the public that there was no breach, Wilson insisted that House take a front seat in the presidential box when they went to the theater together on Sept. 24, 1915.

A few weeks later House was wondering whether the President was not indiscreet in showing the Colonel's letters to Lansing. "While Lansing does not show the slightest trace of jealousy," House wrote in his diary on Nov. 28, "I am wondering how much of that kind of thing he will be able to stand." Early in 1916 the Colonel, learning from Polk that Lansing showed pique at House's activities, cautioned the President to be careful. Wilson, who in the summer of 1915 had shown consideration for the *amour propre* of the secretary of state, now replied, bluntly, that Lansing must understand that the President himself was conducting foreign affairs and would do it in the way he thought best.

usually had solved themselves without any worry to the President. She promised to do this, and the Colonel then advised her to think aloud with her husband at all times and to let him be her only confidant.

They fixed December 18 as their wedding day. Rather than undergo the publicity of a White House function, they invited their relatives and the Cabinet to Edith Galt's little home for the ceremony. They made a game of their getaway, sitting behind drawn shades while their limousine outsped pursuing newsmen, and boarding a special train at Alexandria. Early the next morning, when they awakened at Hot Springs, Virginia, the bridegroom put on a frock coat and gray morning trousers, thrust his hands in his pockets, and danced a jig while he whistled a popular tune. The mountains were cloaked with snow, and in the crisp air they explored back roads by automobile and on foot. Woodrow Wilson was "exceedingly, perfectly happy," he wrote to Margaret Elliott the day after Christmas. "Edith is a very wonderful person, really and truly." At the same time Helen Bones was writing to Cousin Harriet Woodrow Wells, who had been Wilson's first love: "Perhaps few who don't know Cousin Woodrow can guess how truly he still loves Cousin Ellen, though he also truly loves this other sweet wife of his."

Edith Galt Wilson offered resources that he needed to nourish his spirit. They breakfasted alone before an open fire, following the homely custom of keeping dishes warm by setting them on the hearth. Then she would go with him to the study and blot his signatures on the stacks of routine papers that awaited him. Soon he depended on her to code and decode secret messages and to help him clear "The Drawer" of red-tabbed, urgent documents, some of which he burned as soon as he had read them. She would linger sometimes for the delight of hearing his fluent, lucid dictation. Going off for a while to attend to her own duties, she would watch from her window for a signal that he was ready to go to the executive offices. Then she would join him and they would stroll together for a few moments outdoors —in Ellen Wilson's rose garden if the weather was fair. Reaching the office door, he would look at his watch, kiss her, and follow her with his eyes as she walked back to the house. When she turned and waved, he looked at his watch again, and if there was a minute left before eleven o'clock, he walked quickly to meet her in one more embrace.

Her humor and radiance stimulated his love of fun. She rode with him occasionally, and they went golfing together often. He told her stories in dialect, as he was accustomed to do when playing with his other comrades of the links, Dr. Grayson and Colonel Brown; and he drew her laughter with impersonations that spared no one, not even Grayson. In the evenings she read aloud with him, and played the piano and sang to him, or joined him in parlor games or in clownish revelry.

In public, however, they were a portrait of grace and dignity. The President's bride was a handsome foil for the "Tommie" Wilson who loved parades, the noticeable man who wore formal dress elegantly and looked every inch a statesman. Her social gifts relieved him of much of the strain that state functions imposed.

On January 7, dressed in a white gown with "angel sleeves," she made a dramatic debut as First Lady, greeting more than three thousand guests at a ball given in honor of the Wilsons at the Pan American Union. Responding to the beauty of massed orchids mirrored in a pool, the court uniforms of the diplomats, and the scarlet-coated Marine Band, Edith Wilson herself added an exotic touch—a large fan like those used in ceremonies in the Far East, fabricated of gray feathers mounted on a handle of mosaic. And the morning after this venture into society she was ready, spick and trim in traveling attire, to accompany her husband on an arduous speaking tour.

The wistful widower who had dragged himself through the preceding winter by burying his mind in routine was now a bridegroom fit to fight wildcats. Political life had become again the adventure that it had been when he first took high office in New Jersey. His daily work seemed to him "interesting and inspiring," full of "electrical thrills."